THE HANDBOOK OF
CULTURE AND PSYCHOLOGY

The Handbook of

CULTURE

— *&* —

PSYCHOLOGY

EDITED BY

David Matsumoto

OXFORD
UNIVERSITY PRESS

2001

OXFORD
UNIVERSITY PRESS

Oxford   New York

Athens   Auckland   Bangkok   Bogotá   Buenos Aires   Cape Town
Chennai   Dar es Salaam   Delhi   Florence   Hong Kong   Istanbul   Karachi
Kolkata   Kuala Lumpur   Madrid   Melbourne   Mexico City   Mumbai   Nairobi
Paris   São Paulo   Shanghai   Singapore   Taipei   Tokyo   Toronto   Warsaw

and associated companies in
Berlin   Ibadan

Copyright © 2001 by Oxford University Press

Published by Oxford University Press, Inc.
198 Madison Avenue, New York, New York 10016

Oxford is a registered trademark of Oxford University Press

Library of Congress Cataloging-in-Publication Data
The handbook of culture and psychology / edited by David Matsumoto.
p.   cm.
Includes bibliographical references and index.
ISBN 978-0-19-513181-9
1. Ethnopsychology.   2. Personality and culture.   I. Matsumoto, David Ricky.
GN502 .H362   2001
155.8—dc21   00-051655

Printed in the United States of America
on acid-free paper

For Mimi

Preface

The importance of culture in understanding all aspects of human behavior is no longer debated in contemporary psychology or in any other field of science that purports to study human behavior. Culture is an important antecedent to and consequence of behavior, and it aids in facilitating and restricting behavior. As such, culture is a topic of major relevance for students and professionals in all fields of complex human behavior, theoretically sophisticated psychologists and other social scientists, and social and behavioral scientists who have had the experience of living in or visiting other cultures or those contemplating doing so in the future.

In psychology alone, the potential of culture to bring about fundamental and profound revisions to psychological knowledge, theories, and principles is enormous. Over the past few decades, the findings of many cross-cultural studies have challenged in many ways traditional knowledge in mainstream psychology about psychological processes thought to be true; each time the challenge has called for reconsideration of psychological truth and a reconceptualization not only of theory construction, but also of the process of knowledge creation. In short, cross-cultural psychology raises serious and basic questions about the nature of science and scientific philosophy, and all of psychology currently is trying to deal with these questions.

Indeed, these are exciting times in the evolution of cross-cultural psychology as a field, discipline, and method of inquiry. The cross-cultural findings afford exciting new challenges to psychological truth, the continued efforts of students and researchers of culture in dealing with and overcoming these challenges, and the resulting new boundaries and state of knowledge about people and human functioning that ensues. It is also exciting because of the uncertainty of what the future holds not only for cross-cultural, but also mainstream, psychology as scientists and theorists deal with extremely complex issues in understanding human behavior across increasing diversity in thought, emotion, motivation, and all aspects of psychology.

This book conveys this excitement by capturing the evolution of cross-cultural psychology across the history of work in this field like a snapshot in time. This book is unique in being the only one of its kind that attempts to do so in this burgeoning, yet important, area of psychological inquiry. While other books on cross-cultural psychology exist, of course, this volume is the only one available that provides an account of the current state of cross-cultural psychology across a wide range of topics that are well representative at the highest scholarly level of the vast topic areas encompassed within the discipline. Several important and unique characteristics of this book ensure that it portrays the excitement and evolution of cross-cultural psychology described here, including the following:

- *Selection of topic areas.* All areas of study represented in the various chapters are those most relevant to cross-cultural work, most exemplary of the work in the entire field, and most representative of the evolution of cross-cultural method and knowledge. They span a wide range of topics and paint a comprehensive scholarly picture of the current state of cross-cultural psychology in the broadest strokes possible.
- *The authors.* The authors of this volume represent a selection of some of the leading authors in the field of cross-cultural psychology; all represent the most advanced thinking and research in their respective areas.
- *Excellent reviews of topic areas.* Each chapter presents state-of-the-art reviews of the theoretical and empirical literature in each of the topic areas selected; these reviews stand alone as important contributions.
- *Objective evaluation of the literature.* Yet, each chapter author goes well beyond just an encyclopedic-type review of the existing knowledge to objectively evaluate the literature, including limitations to current theory and knowledge.
- *A vision of the future.* All chapter authors also go well beyond mere reviews and evaluations of their fields theoretically and empirically in presenting their visions of the future in their respective areas. They provide frank discussions about what they believe is necessary to make their visions reality, and they outline work that promises to guide researchers for the next decade or two.

Across all chapters and content, two major themes emerge early and are used repeatedly to focus each section and chapter of the book. These are

- A vision of the future as continued evolution of cross-cultural psychology, particularly as it aids in the creation of a universal psychology that is applicable to all people of the world regardless of cultural background; and
- How to achieve this vision in terms of changes, revisions, and improvements necessary in method and/or concept that go far beyond the ways in which research in psychology currently is conducted.

In its own way, each chapter addresses these two themes. The way in which it does this is highlighted at the beginning of each chapter in an editor's note, which ties the chapter not only to the themes of the book, but also to the other chapters. In addition, the book is divided into four parts, each including chapters that are grouped around four major topic areas: foundations, basic psychological processes, personality, and social behavior. Chapter introductions are provided at the beginning of each part. An introductory chapter describing the major themes of the book, as espoused by the chapter authors, sets the stage for the entire volume, while a concluding epilogue reinforces that message and issues a challenge to all future students of culture as well.

In all, this book represents what can be considered the collective wisdom of the leading thinkers and researchers in the field of cross-cultural psychology with regard to its current and future state. It not only provides an encyclopedic reference in each topic area, but also goes well beyond such reviews in providing a vision of the future and calling for fundamental revisions in the nature and scope of how we do research. It captures the current zeitgeist of cross-cultural psychology at the highest scholarly level in a consistent manner and tone and challenges our thinking and "doing" of science. It is the only resource of its kind in the field of cross-cultural psychology.

This book is intended for serious students of culture and human behavior, including social scientists in a variety of fields and disciplines, as well as advanced graduate students in these respective fields. The writing level is fairly high, and the messages clearly are intended to be relevant for those with sufficient theoretical and methodological sophistication. Yet, the message of the book is also applicable to all psychologists—mainstream or cross-cultural—because all psychologists are cross-cultural in some way; the only difference is in whether they are aware of the cultures being studied, and whether this comparison is explicit or implicit in their work.

This book achieves its goals if future researchers and students of culture are encouraged to take up the difficult endeavors outlined here and discussed throughout, and if all students of psychology and culture—researchers, teachers, administrators, therapists, counselors, consultants, and others—gain a deeper sense of appreciation for the influence of culture in all aspects of our lives, and translate those influences into meaningful ways of being and living.

San Francisco, California   D. M.
July, 2000

Acknowledgments

As with all projects of this scope and magnitude, I am indebted to literally hundreds of people over such a long period of time. Whatever minimal words of thanks, appreciation, and recognition I can give them here does not represent well the effort and support they have provided me not only in my cross-cultural research over the years, but also in the production of this book.

First, I would like to thank each chapter author for agreeing to contribute a chapter to this volume. I know that producing the kinds of reviews and chapters printed here required much time, effort, and sacrifice. I am indebted particularly not only because of their exhaustive reviews of each area of cross-cultural psychology, but also because of the amount of thinking put into their chapters with regard to the vision of the future and the methods required to achieve that vision. Indeed, this handbook was edited much more vigorously than in my previous experience with other books, and all chapter authors engaged in at least one major revision of their chapter after review and comments by me; some even engaged in multiple revisions. Their hard work, dedication, sacrifice, and commitment to this project is evident in the high quality of their submissions and of the work as a whole. I, and the entire psychology community, thank them.

In my career, I have been fortunate to have the privilege of collaborating with many fine researchers in the conduct of cross-cultural studies, and I would like to recognize them briefly here. Paul Ekman was instrumental at the start of my career examining human facial expressions of emotions cross-culturally, and I consider him today still to be my mentor and good friend. In addition, I have conducted cross-cultural research with Shoko Araki, Caran Colvin, Dale Dinnel, Wallace Friesen, Bob Grissom, Karl Heider, Natalia Kouznetsova, Jeff LeRoux, Motomasa Murayama, Takeshi Nakajima, Maureen O'Sullivan, Klaus Scherer, Harald Wallbott, Masayuki Takeuchi, Susan Taylor, Hiroshi Yamada, and Susumu Yamaguchi. All of these wonderful colleagues have contributed greatly to the work described in the chapter on emotion and to my overall thinking of cross-cultural issues in general, and I am indebted to them.

I would also like to thank the hundreds of students that have been my research assistants over the years at my Culture and Emotion Research Laboratory at San Francisco State University and previously. Without their hard work and dedication, it would have been impossible to complete much of the research reported in my chapter. I also give my thanks and appreciation to the many visiting scholars, professors, and researchers who have come from all around the world to live and work with me in my laboratory. They have contributed immensely to my own thinking and understanding of culture and psychology.

At San Francisco State University, I have been extremely fortunate to have the support of the administration to pursue research and scholarship at the highest levels, and I would like to extend my gratitude to them. I thank former chairs of the Psychology Department Paul Eskildsen, Ken Monteiro, Lilly Berry, and Susan Taylor, and especially the current chair Caran Colvin. I also thank Deans Julian and Kassiola for supporting me and my laboratory in all of our scholarly endeavors, as well as university president Robert Corrigan. Without their help and support, this volume and my cross-cultural research program would not have been possible.

The editorial staff at Oxford University Press have demonstrated beyond a shadow of a doubt that they are simply the best high-level academic publisher in the world. I offer my thanks to former editor Philip Laughlin, who had the foresight to sign the book and to work with me in its initial planning stages. I also thank Catharine Carlin, who has supported the work in so many ways through the completion of the chapters, the final editing, and production.

I am blessed to have a family that is supportive of my work and career and who have taught me much about culture, psychology, and life. As I write this note, our daughter Sayaka will be entering her senior year in high school. Having a great academic and athletic career already in place, she really has blossomed into a source of joy and pride not only for my family, but also for so many in the communities of our lives. Also, during this project, our twin boys—Satoshi Robert and Masashi David—were born; they have brought new joy and fulfillment to our lives as well. We are blessed each day in watching the interaction between culture and psychology in them. Above all, I am most indebted and grateful to the one person who gives all of us her time, energy, commitment, sacrifice, and love, the one who keeps all of us going in our daily lives and who has brought nothing but goodness and kindness in her heart to touch the lives of our family and so many people around us. To my wife Mimi, I offer my most heartfelt thanks and appreciation for coming into our lives and making us better persons.

Contents

Contributors

John Adamopoulos
Grand Valley State University

Daniel R. Ames
University of California, Berkeley

Deborah L. Best
Wake Forest University

Michael Harris Bond
City University of Hong Kong

David W. Carraher
TERC

Harry W. Gardiner
University of Wisconsin at Lacrosse

Yoshihisa Kashima
University of Melbourne

Uichol Kim
Chung-Ang University

Eric D. Knowles
University of California, Berkeley

Jayne Lee
University of California, Davis

Kwok Leung
City University of Hong Kong

Walter J. Lonner
Western Washington University

David Matsumoto
San Francisco State University

Joan G. Miller
University of Michigan

R. C. Mishra
Banaras Hindu University

Kaiping Peng
University of California, Berkeley

Analúcia D. Schliemann
Tufts University

Peter B. Smith
University of Sussex

Walter G. Stephan
New Mexico State University

Stanley Sue
University of California, Davis

Junko Tanaka-Matsumi
Hofstra University

James T. Tedeschi
University at Albany, State University
  of New York

Harry C. Triandis
University of Illinois

Fons van de Vijver
Tilburg University

Colleen Ward
National University of Singapore

John F. Williams
Georgia State University

Susumu Yamaguchi
University of Tokyo

THE HANDBOOK OF
CULTURE AND PSYCHOLOGY

1

Introduction

DAVID MATSUMOTO

No topic is more compelling in contemporary psychology today than culture, and no other topic has the potential to revise in fundamental and profound ways almost everything we think we know about people. The study of culture in psychology has raised questions about the nature of knowledge and psychological truth derived from mainstream psychological research based primarily on American or western European participants. The study of culture in psychology, at the same time, has answered some fundamental questions about some psychological processes, especially their specificity of universality versus culture. Culture is to human behavior as operating systems are to software, often invisible and unnoticed, yet playing an extremely important role in development and operation.

This book captures the current zeitgeist of cross-cultural psychology and describes its evolution as a discipline. It highlights the history of cross-cultural psychology from its foundation through its earliest studies and pioneers. It reports state-of-the-art literature reviews of theoretical and empirical work across some of the most pressing and relevant topic areas studied cross-culturally. And, it provides ideas and visions of the future and how cross-cultural psychology can help transform mainstream psychological theories and research radically from their current state in a monocultural psychology of behavior fragments into a universal psychology of the whole.

At the same time, this book describes the unique characteristics of cross-cultural psychology as a specialized method of inquiry. It describes the nature of cross-cultural investigation and describes how and why cross-cultural methods are useful for contemporary psychology. It encompasses different approaches to understanding human behavior and argues for the complementary integration of all such approaches rather than the unique parceling and fragmentation of approach that is typical of current research method and theory. It seeks to find new methods, often pushing us beyond the limits of our comfort zone, to deal with really difficult issues in understanding the true complexity of human psychological processes.

In this brief chapter, I will introduce you to the concepts, issues, and arguments that you will encounter in this book. I have categorized the main messages provided by all of the authors around two central themes. The first involves understanding the evolution of cross-cultural psychology, recognizing not only where it has been and where it is now, but also, more importantly, where it wants to go. In this sense, this book provides a collective vision of where the field of cross-cultural psychology should go, and what it should be when it gets there. This vision sees the contribution of cross-cultural psychology to the development of truly universal theories of psychological processes as the ultimate goal.

The second theme involves each author's suggestions of how to achieve the goal of evolution embodied in the first vision. Of course, each author's specific suggestions differ across chapters because of differences in the needs and realities of each topic. Yet, on closer examination, there is a commonality of message across all chapters and topics. This commonality suggests the necessity of fundamental changes in the way we do research in the future if we are truly to achieve the goals of this vision. Here, I describe these two themes in more detail.

The Evolution of Cross-Cultural Psychology: Where Have We Been, Where Are We Now, and Where Do We Want to Go?

Cross-cultural psychology has evolved in an interesting and important way over the past few decades. Early cross-cultural work was concerned primarily with the documentation of cultural differences in a variety of psychological processes. This work, of course, was very interesting and important as it highlighted time and again the ways in which psychological theories and models generated on the basis of mainstream psychological research mainly in the United States may not be applicable to people of other cultures. Although the earliest cross-cultural work was often seen as an area reserved for people with esoteric interests in such matters as culture, over the years, the testing and documentation of cultural differences in a wide variety of psychological processes came to play an important role in the establishment of cross-cultural psychology as an area of serious psychological inquiry.

In the past decade or so, however, cross-cultural psychologists have become increasingly discontented with the mere documentation of cultural differences. Indeed, they have come to recognize the theoretical and empirical necessity of thinking about exactly what it is about cultures that produces those differences and why. In this vein, an increasing number of writers have argued for the replacement of the global, abstract concept of "culture" with specific, measurable psychological variables that

researchers hypothesize account for cultural differences when they occur. Called *context* variables by some, contemporary cross-cultural researchers now often include such variables in their designs and studies, actually testing the degree to which such variables contribute to cultural differences in the target variables of interest.

At the same time, cross-cultural psychologists have also become increasingly sensitive to the use of psychological dimensions of culture to explain cultural differences. These dimensions—such as individualism versus collectivism—represent another level of the evolution of cross-cultural psychology as a scientific endeavor not only concerned with the documentation of differences, but also concerned with the creation and testing of theories about culture that explain why those differences occur in the first place. To this end, the increased awareness and adoption of meaningful dimensions of cultural variability, such as those of Hofstede, Triandis, or others, and the development of measurement techniques for some of these dimensions have contributed in meaningful ways to the transformation of cross-cultural psychology.

Some authors (e.g., van de Vijver, chapter 5 of this volume) have referred to the evolution or transformation of cross-cultural psychology in terms of stages or epochs in the history of the field. Thus, the period of time when cross-cultural psychologists were concerned primarily with the mere documentation of differences can be referred to as the first stage of cross-cultural psychology. The transformation of theories and methods to attempt to explain cultural differences through mediating context variables can be referred to as the second stage of cross-cultural psychology. We are in this second stage of cross-cultural psychology as many cross-cultural studies are concerned with identifying the relevant, specific psychological variables that account for cultural differences.

If these two great periods of study in cross-cultural psychology can be described as the first two stages of its evolution, then what is in store for the third stage? The third stage of the evolution of cross-cultural psychology, the vision I referred to above and to which most, if not all, cross-cultural psychologists desire, is the creation of universal theories of psychological processes. That is, the ultimate goal of cross-cultural psychology today is not the creation of "interesting" cross-cultural models of behavior applicable to people of "disparate" or "different" cultures, while other psychological models and theories in mainstream psychology coexist. Rather, it is the creation of truly universal models of psychological processes and human behavior that can be applied to all people of all cultural backgrounds and can supplement and even supplant current mainstream theories and knowledge.

The ultimate goal of cross-cultural psychology, therefore, is for a comprehensive evaluation of the pancultural applicability of psychological theory and knowledge, for testing of the basic tenets of those theories and their hypotheses, and for the profound and fundamental revision of mainstream theories of basic human psychological processes. This evaluation, testing, and revision is indeed mandated not only by the dynamically changing demographic characteristics of the United States and other countries and the fluid environment in which we all live, which undoubtedly has contributed greatly to the impact and importance of the study of culture, but also by our understanding of scientific philosophy and by the moral obligations we accrue as a field because of our understanding of how knowledge in psychology is applied each and every day to intervene in people's lives. That is, if we are to be true to our field as a science, then we need to embrace the questions about the logic of our science that cross-cultural methods of inquiry afford us. And, if we are to allow our findings, theories, and methods to be used to intervene in people's lives, in counseling and therapy, in organizations, and in everyday life, then we as a field in toto must meet a higher standard in the applicability and generalizability of our findings and the duties we incur to achieve those standards.

Thus, we look forward to the day when we can present theories of morality, development, personality, cognition, emotion, motivation, social behavior, and all topics of psychology that are truly universal—that is, applicable to all people of all cultures. This anticipation recognizes the vast limitations to such theories when research findings are based on participants who primarily represent a single culture or a limited number of cultures. This requires, therefore, future research on these topics to involve participants who represent a wide range of disparate cultural backgrounds; the research should be conducted in culturally sensitive and appropriate ways and involve multiple methods of data collection and analysis. The transformation of cross-cultural psychology into its

third stage of evolution—achieving the vision, if you will—therefore requires not only theories, but also methods fundamentally distinct from the current ones.

How Do We Achieve This Vision? Methodological and Conceptual Revisions in the Future

Thus, cross-cultural psychology as a discipline and a method of inquiry is a work in progress, and this book captures that work in progress like a snapshot in time. In this book, you will find reviews of cross-cultural theories and research relevant to basic psychological processes, personality, and social behavior and to selected topics specific to each area. In addition, a few introductory chapters discuss major perspectives in the field as a whole, as well as methodological issues specific to cross-cultural inquiries. The descriptions and distillations of the theoretical models described in each chapter and the comprehensive and timely reviews in each area are indeed priceless and stand on their own merit as the most up-to-date statements regarding those respective areas today.

Yet, each of the authors in this book goes beyond the mere review of the relevant theoretical and empirical literature. Indeed, they provide us with their perspectives as to what future research and theory in their respective areas should look like. In this fashion, each of the authors in this book provides a rare and unique opportunity for all students of culture not only to become acquainted with the relevant knowledge and facts of previous theories and research, but also to understand how research and theory need to be transformed if we are to help the field evolve to the third stage of its development and ultimately to aid in the creation of universal theories of psychology.

Here, I have distilled what I believe are the major issues that the authors in this volume have identified as crucial to our further evolution of cross-cultural psychology. They are not mutually exclusive of each other. It is hoped that these extractions can serve as a guide to help read, interpret, and evaluate the messages offered by the authors.

1. *Understand culture better.* Most authors argue that our ability to create universal theories of psychological processes will depend, to some degree, on our ability to improve our understanding of culture

itself. While the identification and adoption of cultural dimensions of psychological variability, as mentioned above, have been useful to the field, there are a number of other areas in which further theoretical work on culture is necessary. This includes refining and redefining our understanding of context and examining its relationship with culture and the need to examine all aspects of cultural influences, from culture as an antecedent of behavior to culture as a result of behavior (thus, culture as an independent variable, as well as a dependent variable). We also need to further our understanding of the role of culture as either constraining or inventing behavior.

2. *Integrate multiple, seemingly disparate approaches to theory and method with regard to culture.* Most authors argue that the approaches and perspectives of various orientations in understanding the relationship between psychology and culture and studying it needs to be integrated for further evolution in the field to occur. These orientations include the approaches characterized by cross-cultural psychology, cultural psychology, indigenous psychology, and psychological anthropology. While each of these fields is associated with different theoretical approaches and different methods of inquiry, in the future they will be required to be integrated into a single, comprehensive effort.

3. *Adopt a holistic approach to understanding psychological processes and their investigation.* Contemporary academic psychology has fragmented human behavior for the purpose of research so much that it is often difficult to tell the forest from the trees. It is time now for psychologists, cross-cultural and mainstream alike, to begin to adopt a holistic approach to understanding psychology and human behavior, to understand linkages across different theoretical perspectives of the same process, and to integrate different psychological processes into a cohesive whole.

4. *Integrate cross-discipline variables.* The creation of universal theories of psychology requires that we take into account variables that psychologists typically have relegated to other disciplines and ignored in psychological research and theory. These variables include such issues as the effects of the environment, political structures, weather and climate, geography, and the like. Indeed, it is highly improbable that panculturally applicable theories of human behavior can be created to the exclusion of such factors. As many authors in this volume suggest, culture, society, biology, and psychology need to come together for such theories to be developed.

5. *Integrate nonmainstream theoretical perspectives.* American psychological theories and theories published in English-language journals and outlets continue to dominate the creation of psychological theory. Many other perspectives exist, yet are largely unknown or ignored by researchers because they are indigenous to specific cultures or published in non–English language outlets. Such ignorance may result because of arrogance, limited language abilities, or a host of other factors, but must be overcome in the future if we are to be able to incorporate a variety of theoretical perspectives in our work.

6. *Integrate different and disparate methods.* To generate universal theories of psychology in the future, research needs to proceed in fundamentally different ways. Future research needs to integrate different methods for qualitatively different knowledge to be produced. These improvements include the incorporation of both quantitative and qualitative methods into the study of psychological processes across cultures and the continued incorporation of context variables to tease out the reasons why cultural differences occur in the first place. Future research will need to look at examining a wider range of individuals, not just university students, across a wider range of cultures and across time in longitudinal or quasi-longitudinal approaches. Gone are the days when a questionnaire was translated and imposed on students from different cultures and called "a cross-cultural study."

These six themes, while simple in concept, require that future research be conducted in fundamentally different ways than the current mode. Heeding this advice from the authors of this volume will result in research that is drastically different from and inherently more difficult than what is customary. It will force us to think in ways we may not be ready or willing to think. All in all, these notions lead to qualitatively different ways of working—empirically and theoretically—from what typically is done now. Yet, if we are to create and test truly universal theories that allow for pan-cultural similarities, as well as culture-specific processes, this work should be done.

The Goals of This Book

This book, therefore, represents the collective wisdom of some well-known leaders and researchers in cross-cultural psychology. This wisdom encompasses, as I mentioned, not only visions for the continued evolvement of cross-cultural psychology, but also how it can get there. The goals of this book, therefore, are defined by the messages that each of the authors have brought to bear. They are

- To capture the current zeitgest of cross-cultural psychology in its evolution;

- To offer readers ideas about visions of the future—what future theories and research will need to look like if the field is to continue in its evolution from merely finding differences to documenting how and why culture produces those differences, and to the creation of universal psychological theories; that is, in its journey through the stages of evolution; and
- To offer readers ideas about how to conduct research in the future that will help in the achievement of that vision and to aid in the continuing evolution of cross-cultural psychology.

If, by reading this book, we can encourage future researchers to take up these difficult endeavors and encourage all students of psychology and culture—researchers, teachers, administrators, therapists, counselors, consultants, and others—to gain a deeper sense of appreciation for the influence of culture in all aspects of our lives and to translate those influences into meaningful ways of being and living, then this book would have achieved its goals.

Part I: Foundations

The first part of this book presents four chapters that provide what I consider a necessary foundation of knowledge for all students of culture and psychology. The information provided here serves as a basis by which all other chapters in the book can be read and understood as these works depict the theoretical or methodological underpinnings that form the basis of most cross-cultural work in the field.

In chapter 2, Adamopolous and Lonner begin with a history of the field and the approach of cross-cultural psychology. By comparing and contrasting two seemingly differing approaches to the study of culture—cross-cultural and cultural psychology—they analyze how culture can be viewed in relation to human behavior to synthesize past and present research and theory and to clarify future empirical and conceptual work, highlighting the crossroads at which cross-cultural psychology currently stands.

In chapter 3, Triandis describes the derivation and utility of the construct known as *individualism and collectivism* to account for cultural differences in a wide variety of behaviors. He also argues for the integration of various approaches and methodologies to allow cross-cultural psychology to help mainstream psychology evolve into a universal psychology.

In chapter 4, Kim provides an elegant description of and persuasive argument for the integration and greater acceptance of the indigenous psychologies approach. By pointing out limitations in the way in which science has traditionally been conducted in mainstream psychology, Kim suggests that indigenous psychologies—with its focus on context, epistemology, and phenomenology—offers an alternative approach to understanding the relationship between culture and psychology, especially as mutually constituted phenomena.

In chapter 5, van de Vijver provides an excellent overview of the unique aspects of cross-cultural research. He describes in depth issues related to bias and equivalence and presents researchers with useful guidelines for the conduct of sound studies. He also argues for the integration of methodologies from seemingly disparate approaches, including cross-cultural and cultural psychology, to provide researchers with the vehicle to help cross-cultural psychology continue to evolve into a universal psychology.

These chapters provide the conceptual and methodological framework by which the two themes of this book—the vision of the evolution of cross-cultural psychology to universal theories of behavior and how to achieve that vision—are reinforced and understood throughout the rest of the volume.

2

Culture and Psychology at a Crossroad

Historical Perspective and Theoretical Analysis

JOHN ADAMOPOULOS & WALTER J. LONNER

Cross-cultural psychology as a serious field of inquiry, a methodological approach, and a clearinghouse for understanding the great diversity within which we live today has come a long way from the days when cultural differences merely were observed and reported. Cultural similarities and differences have been reported from a number of different perspectives and empirical approaches and today proliferate the literature across all areas of psychology, with their different theoretical orientations and empirical approaches. Students new and old to the study of culture in psychology easily can find themselves lost in the "facts" of cross-cultural psychology; at this point in its history, the study of culture and psychology needs clarity to make meaningful and productive headway into the next two decades. This chapter provides that clarity and sets the stage for understanding the complexity of culture and of culture-psychology relationships presented in the remaining chapters of this book.

In this chapter, to demonstrate the current pivotal point in the history of the field, Adamopoulos and Lonner present an excellent description of the development of cross-cultural psychology and an analysis of its current challenges. In the first part of their chapter, the authors describe the history of the cross-cultural psychology movement, from its modest beginnings as a meeting of scholars interested in culture to its diverse organizations, publication outlets, and topics that characterize the field today. They correctly highlight the limitations in psychological knowledge from research conducted in monocultural and otherwise limited settings, especially in terms of their assumed generalizability for all people of all backgrounds. In their historical review, Adamopoulos and Lonner also point out the ways in which cross-cultural psychology can be viewed not necessarily as a separate "field" of study, but rather as a special method of inquiry. In short, cross-cultural psychology can be understood not only in terms of the contents of its inquiries, but also in terms of scientific philosophy—the logic underlying the nature of science and the production of knowledge. As such, cross-cultural psychology is as much about critical thinking as it is about culture per se.

In the second part of their chapter, Adamopoulos and Lonner present an insightful analysis of the differences and similarities among seemingly different approaches that have become noteworthy of late; they compare and contrast cross-cultural psychology with cultural psychology. This analysis is sorely needed in the field, and all students of culture should become familiar with the distinctions made in this part of the chapter. As the authors suggest, each approach has its strengths and weaknesses, advantages and disadvantages. While personal preference for one's underlying approach to culture undoubtedly will influence how one interprets each approach, one cannot help but think that there are more similarities in the two approaches than purported differences in the search for the nature of mind that incorporates and produces culture, as well as psychology.

In the final part of their chapter, Adamopoulos and Lonner present their ideas concerning a rapprochement between the issues raised by the cross-cultural and the cultural psychology approaches; this rapprochement is not based on an effort to correct the other's limitations, but instead celebrates the strengths of each perspective within the context of its own ontological premises and related methodological commitments. To this end, the authors summarize an analysis of assumptions about culture in psychological theory based on whether culture is viewed as antecedent or consequent to human behavior and as enabling or restricting behavior. This viewpoint is useful not only because it allows one to understand the different aspects of culture captured by either the cross-cultural or the cultural psychology movement, but also because it allows students of culture to stand back and see culture in its enormity, understanding that culture serves all these functions and more. To the extent that students of culture can appreciate the complexity of culture-psychology relations in these or any other dimension for that matter, such an appreciation leads to fundamentally different ways of understanding culture and thus profoundly different ways of studying it in the next decade or two. As future researchers address the larger issues about the basic nature of the relationship between culture and psychology—including defining culture and psychology and where one ends and the other picks up—the analysis presented by Adamopoulos and Lonner promises to influence strongly this agenda, identifying the crossroads at which cross-cultural psychology now stands.

In this chapter, we present overviews of two major components that have contributed to the general characteristics and current status of the discipline of psychology and culture. The first component is a historical overview that provides primarily a brief look at the origins of cross-cultural psychology and explains how it can be understood today on the basis of several background considerations and developments that have taken place during the past 35 years. The second component addresses several theoretical issues and criticisms of the two main branches of the discipline, cultural and cross-cultural psychology, while the third part deals with the role that culture plays in psychology, as well as with the role that we think it *should* play. Together, these constituent parts describe both the nature of cross-cultural psychology and briefly take into consideration other orientations in psychology and neighboring disciplines in which the phenomenon of culture plays a central and indispensable role in helping to explain human thought and behavior.

Cross-Cultural Psychology in Brief Historical Perspective

A comprehensive inquiry into the history and development of cross-cultural psychology should begin with three major chapters (Jahoda, 1980, 1990; Jahoda & Krewer, 1997; Klineberg, 1980), each of which traces the "beginnings" of psychological interest in cultures other than one's own. Additional historical perspectives and essentially pre-1980 cross-cultural psychology would be enriched by the six-volume *Handbook of Cross-Cultural Psychology* (Triandis et al., 1980) and the enormous number of references of the 51 chapters that comprise the volumes. Further insight into the origins of cross-cultural psychology is provided by four short pieces by Diaz-Guerrero, Jahoda, Price-Williams, and Triandis that appear in the published proceedings of the 1998 Silver Jubilee Congress of the International Association for Cross-Cultural Psychology (Lonner, Dinnel, Forgays, & Hayes, 1999). These four individuals are among a small number of scholars instrumental in starting the "modern" movement in cross-cultural psychology.

Among the main points made in these historical snapshots and analyses is that the elusive term *culture* and the phenomena it represents have been around for centuries, and that efforts to use culture to help explain diversity in human thought and behavior are not new. Another important strand of thoughtful reflection contained in these perspectives is that a definition of cross-cultural psychology with which everyone agrees has not been found and still remains somewhat slippery. This problem has even stimulated some concern that the term might appear too limited and constraining, therefore perhaps necessitating a change in what cross-cultural psychologists call themselves (Lonner, 1992). While definitional difficulties and allegiances likely will remain ongoing matters of debate and discussion, and while some critics will continue to question the importance or veracity of cross-cultural psychology, perhaps the most important thing to keep in mind is that "what cross-cultural psychology is called is not nearly important as what it does—to ensure the broadest range of psychological topics be explored within the broadest possible spectrum of ethnicity and culture and by diverse methodologies" (Segall, Lonner, & Berry, 1998, p. 1102).

It is worth repeating that a comprehensive review of the world's psychological literature during the past century will show that many psychologists have been interested in culture, ethnicity, or national origin as "determinants," or at least as intervening variables (Lonner & Adamopoulos, 1997), in explaining human thought and behavior. Indeed, even the so-called father of modern experimental psychology, Wilhelm Wundt, could be called a pioneer in this area because of his interest in *Volkerpsychologie* (Wundt, 1900–1920), as generously witnessed by the 10 volumes he published under that title. Perhaps the first pioneer in exploring possible relationships between culture and basic psychological processes was W. H. R. Rivers (1901), of Cambridge University, who led an expedition of both psychologists and anthropologists to gather seminal data in the South Pacific and the east coast of India.

Considering all of psychology's history, if one wanted to find journal articles that to some extent involved *culture* or other descriptors used to characterize people who share a common heritage or destiny (such as *ethnic group*), the task would be rather easy. Despite the preponderance of research that has focused on relatively healthy and wealthy white people from industrialized societies as "subjects" in psychological research, it is nearly certain that any psychological topic one can imagine has been involved somehow, and in varying degrees of sophistication, in studies that included individuals from diverse cultural and psycholinguistic groups. This is especially true in such areas as intelligence testing, the study of "national character" or "modal personality," various ways to understand abnormal behavior, and especially within the broad domain of social psychology, which claims a majority of cross-cultural research.

However, with only a few notable exceptions, during the first two thirds of this century, there was no pattern or coherent program of research to guide these excursions. Indeed, "sabbatical opportunism" and "jet-set research" prevailed for years. This usually meant that an inquisitive and energetic psychologist, typically from the United States or the United Kingdom or their territorial and political extensions, would travel to some exotic corner of the world during an academic leave that lasted a few weeks to several months and inter alia "test" some principle or examine some theory of interest. Returning to the comforts of home, he (occasionally she) characteristically would write a report and submit it to some accommodating, if not enthusiastically welcoming, journal and thus gain some notoriety in helping to expand psychology's vistas.

While such reports may have been interesting at the time, there were few sustained efforts to develop a strategy of systematic research. Perhaps just as important, there were few books on methodology or organizations of like-minded people or other sources of support for such efforts. Moreover, psychologists who engaged in cross-cultural efforts were viewed frequently as rather odd creatures who tended to eschew orthodox and routine academic pursuits while living and working in the periphery or "lunatic fringe" of the discipline. Years ago, the prevailing opinion among academic psychologists was that culture as a respectable thing to study belonged to anthropologists. (That opinion is still held by some—especially those who may believe that psychology is a "natural" science, and therefore that "laws" of behavior transcend culture, just as laws of learning are often believed to be robust phylogenetically.)

The picture of cross-cultural research as isolated and disconnected changed radically in the mid-to-late 1960s when several strands of relatively independent efforts took place and then converged. During that active period, the modern era of cross-cultural psychology began. The first noteworthy event was a meeting at the University of Nigeria in Ibadan during the Christmas and New Year period of 1965–1966. Attracting about 100 primarily social psychologists, the meeting was designed to serve as a forum in which various social psychological perspectives could be discussed with respect to their cultural generalizability and their theoretical underpinnings.[1]

Those in attendance also developed ways to collaborate in the future. For instance, they agreed to keep in touch with each other through the irregularly appearing *Cross-Cultural Social Psychology Newsletter*, with Harry Triandis serving as its first editor. (The direct descendant of the newsletter is the quarterly *Cross-Cultural Psychology Bulletin*; William K. Gabrenya currently serves as editor.) John W. Berry initiated a second activity that involved the development of a directory of cross-cultural researchers. Originally containing a little more than 100 entries and published in 1968 in the *International Journal of Psychology*, the intent of that directory was to encourage cooperation and collaboration in various kinds of psychological research across the world. The directory was updated in 1970 and 1973 and twice in the 1980s; its most recent updating was done in 1998. The third significant activity was the development in 1968 and 1969 and then the inaugural publication in 1970 of the quarterly *Journal of Cross-Cultural Psychology*, with Walter J. Lonner serving as its founding editor. In 1995, the *Journal of Cross-Cultural Psychology* began bimonthly publication; the year 2000 marks its 31st year as the premier journal in the field.

The three activities described above combined to form a catalyst in 1971–1972. At the initiative of the late John L. M. B. Dawson, the inaugural meeting of the International Association for Cross-Cultural Psychology (IACCP) was held in August 1972 at the University of Hong Kong, where Dawson was head of the Department of Psychology. That meeting brought together about 110 psychologists (and a handful of anthropologists and psychiatrists) who knew about each other's work, but with few exceptions, had not yet met each other. At that time,

IACCP became an association of scholars, with officers, a constitution, and all the other trappings of a full-fledged (albeit small) professional organization. Jerome Bruner was its first president, and Dawson served as its first secretary-general. Western Washington University in Bellingham holds the copyright to the *Journal of Cross-Cultural Psychology* but permits IACCP to call it one of its "official" publications.

This convergence of events marked the first time that cross-cultural psychology was institutionalized and became official and sanctioned by a group of like-minded people. It instantly became associated with the *Journal of Cross-Cultural Psychology*, the *Cross-Cultural Psychology Bulletin*, and the publication of the selected proceedings of the biennial congress of IACCP. IACCP congresses have been held in 13 different countries; a recent meeting was the Silver Jubilee Congress held in early August 1998 at Western Washington University. The overview of the proceedings of that congress can be consulted for further background information (Lonner et al., 1999). The site of the most recent congress (July 2000) was Pultusk, Poland.

The events described above serve as an overview of the way cross psychology has developed at the organizational level. For this volume, the more important part of this effort is how the enterprise can be understood at the scientific and conceptual levels. These levels involve an assortment of methodological and epistemological matters in an attempt to explicate the connection of culture to human behavior. Our attention now turns to those considerations.

The Raison d'Être of Cross-Cultural Psychology

One could argue that there are many reasons why cross-cultural psychology is important. Who would disagree, for instance, that learning about other cultures is of great benefit to the learner if for no other reason that such knowledge may prepare the individual for more effective intercultural interaction? Similarly, who would argue that the exploration and understanding of other cultures or ethnicities is one of the hallmarks of an educated person? Studying the world beyond one's borders (Cole, 1984) is important in its own right and provides insight into who we are, where we came from, and where we may be going. For cross-cultural psychologists, however, the main and simple reason for the origination and continuation of cross-cultural psychology has been to extend the range of variation of psychological functioning.

Modern psychology is largely a Western academic affair that has basked in the glow of scientifically respectable research characterized by the legacy of logical positivism. Berry, Poortinga, and Pandey (1997) have used the acronym WASP (Western academic scientific psychology) to describe this historical fact, not just for Western psychology, but also for psychology as practiced in the United States and Great Britain and their cultural and linguistic extensions. Jahoda (1970) put the situation in colorful perspective when he commented on psychology's constrained borders. He said that this narrowness reminds one

of Parson Thwackum in Tom Jones [Henry Fielding's humorous 1749 novel about a commoner being raised among the English nobility] who said, "When I mention religion, I mean the Christian religion; and not only the Christian religion, but the Protestant religion, and not only the Protestant religion but the Church of England." This might well be suitably transposed as "When I mention a psychological subject, I mean a subject from a western industrialized culture; and not only from a western industrialized culture, but an American; and not only an American, but a college student." No doubt this is unfair, reflecting as it does on the amount of work that has been done in the United States. Nonetheless, the excessive concentration on such an odd (as far as humanity at large is concerned) population makes one wonder about the range of application of the "laws" experimentally derived in this manner. (p. 2)

In short, the majority of what is known about the psychological functioning of human beings has come from a massive amount of research and theory that originated in the "highly psychologized" world, the "first world" of psychology (Moghaddam, 1987). Little is known psychologically about vast portions of the rest of the world.

The Standard Methodological Paradigm in Cross-Cultural Psychology

Extending the range of variation, as noted above, is often given as the main reason for the advent of cross-cultural psychology. This usually means going to cultures other than one's own to investigate the robustness or generalizability of psychological findings that many, in the absence of disconfirming or conflicting evidence, consider to be true and invariant. Because the majority of psychological research has been conducted in the highly industrialized Western world by Western psychologists, these efforts quite frequently involve going to non-Western and relatively unacculturated places. However, for more general purposes, the definition of cross-cultural psychology provided by Berry, Poortinga, Segall, and Dasen (1992) is useful and provisionally acceptable. They say that cross-cultural psychology is "the study of similarities and differences in individual functioning in various cultural and ethnic groups; of the relationships between psychological variables and sociocultural, ecological, and biological variables; and of changes in these variables" (p. 2).

In the same book, Berry et al. (1992) outlined what generally is accepted as the standard (but not the only) methodological protocol in cross-cultural psychology: the transfer, test, and discovery procedure. This involves (a) selecting some psychological principle, test, or model that has worked respectably well in the originating culture, (b) "testing" what has been selected in one or more other cultures (of course, this is synonymous with extending the range of variation) to see the extent to which it generalizes elsewhere, and (c) discovering factors or elements in other cultures that were not present in the originating culture in which the psychological concept was promulgated. This procedure has most of the elements that characterize "mainstream" psychology. What seems to be evident in the orthodox cross-cultural research plan is that "other cultures" are treated as independent variables (or quasi-independent variables because cultures cannot be "manipulated," which of course is the key element in the definition of a real independent variable), a reduction or assumption that bothers some people (see below). Thus, Mother Nature is viewed as a quintessential expert in experimental design. The different experimental conditions or independent variables she has created are called cultures or ethnic groups or are recognized somehow as "different" from the people from some other culture whose participation was central to the original body of information.

In this standard, orthodox model, cross-cultural psychology can be viewed not as a field or separate discipline, but as a special method of inquiry. With that special method comes a set of unique methodological circumstances or problems that require careful attention. For instance, the selection of samples must be done carefully, and various problems associated with equivalence must be addressed. Ethical matters also require attention. Of course, those who design and carry out everyday, mainstream psychological research must also be attentive to problems associated with sample selection and its implications, as well as the nature of the tasks or conditions presented to participants. So must they be concerned about ethics. In cross-cultural research, however, the situation is usually much more complicated, time consuming, and controversial. We do not have space in this chapter to present all the details associated with solid cross-cultural methodology. However, if cross-cultural psychology is, as some suggest (as discussed below), "nothing more" than an extension of the standard empiricist/positivist inquiry, then the only substantial difference between the quests of psychological orthodoxy and cross-cultural psychology to establish universals or regularities in human thought and behavior are those special factors that make this line of research rather challenging in the realm of methodology and logistics. Much has been written over the years about the methodological problems and difficulties endemic in cross-cultural psychology (Berry et al., 1997; Brislin, Lonner, & Thorndike, 1973; Lonner & Berry, 1986; Triandis et al., 1980; van de Vijver & Leung, 1997).

An overwhelming majority of cross-cultural psychological research conducted since the mid-1960s can be characterized as extending the range of variation from the known and highly studied cultures to the unknown or little studied cultures. Dusting off one of the first books dealing with cross-cultural methodology (Brislin et al., 1973), we are reminded that a large part of that book (which reflected the main research activities in the late 1960s and early 1970s) was devoted to an examination of this "extending" function. One chapter focused on methodologies and problems associated with the cross-cultural use of psychological tests designed to measure a wide range of human attributes. Almost without exception, the tests, inventories, and scales surveyed in that chapter were devised by psychologists in the Western world. Thus, for instance, there was a review and discussion of the results of using the California Psychological Inventory in other cultures. Extensive discussion of the measurement of intelligence in other cultures was almost mandatory, largely because so much attention had been given over the years to what constitutes intelligence in general, let alone in specific, cultural contexts. There were many efforts, essentially all failures, to find the Rosetta stone in human abilities under the name of a "culture-free" test.

As noted above, in the majority of psychometrically oriented research involving other cultures, the devices used were developed in the Western world. It was as if researchers were saying, "Let's see how well they do on our bag of tricks," which would imply that "tricks" constitute the standard against which the performance of other people should be evaluated. Not surprisingly, the same rationale exists today, but with increased awareness, caution, and sophistication. For instance, in the area of personality testing, there has been extensive use of the NEO Personality Inventory (NEO-PI-R), which purports to measure the "Big Five" factors that many believe to be, at least in part, culture-general characteristics. It is rather impressive that the Big Five factors of personality appear to be rather robust; however, existence of these basic elements in one culture does not preclude the existence of one or more other culture-specific factors that cannot be detected by an essentially "etic" device patterned after standard paper-and-pencil tests (a procedure or format that alone has origins in the Western world). Others have used the MMPI-2 (Minnesota Multiphasic Personality Inventory-2) and its several versions, which appear in many languages. It may be difficult to find a psychometric device that has not been extended to other groups for the primary purpose of determining the universality of the underlying psychological construct. A recent special issue of the *Journal of Cross-Cultural Psychology* contains a wealth of information about measuring personality cross-culturally and includes interdisciplinary perspectives (Church & Lonner, 1998).

Also, starting in the mid-1960s (or continuing from the late 1940s and 1950s in a burst of post–World War II enthusiasm for psychology and its promise to contribute to a better world) were several other paradigms that guided a substantial amount of cross-cultural work. An example is research on achievement motivation. Based on one of the psychological needs that Henry Murray believed all humans possess to some degree, various researchers, notably McClelland (1961), sought to chart the nature and roots of the achievement motive and to understand essential components of achieving societies. There were even efforts to motivate economic achievement in other societies through techniques designed to stimulate and release the achievement motive (McClelland & Winter, 1969).

Another example of a paradigm that received considerable attention cross-culturally was Witkin's theory of psychological differentiation. That theory was a natural for extension to other cultures. In brief, it featured the *differentiation hypothesis,* which stated that various psychosocial and biological conditions lead to different *cognitive styles.* The cognitive styles central to Witkin's ideas are field independence and field dependence, both of which have characteristic modes of thinking and behaving. (This distinction presaged contemporary research on individualism and collectivism.) Cognitive style research was a "hot" topic cross-culturally throughout the late 1960s and 1970s (Witkin & Berry, 1975). Many efforts, led largely by Berry, attempted to chart the nature and developmental trajectories of cognitive style as they were shaped by different "ecologies." Incidentally, Berry's *ecocultural model,* widely touted as a useful template to help guide research projects, got its start in cognitive style research (Berry et al., 1992). Unfortunately, with Witkin's death in 1979 came a rapid decline of cross-cultural research using his ideas. Interests shifted elsewhere as others entered the scene with their own perspectives.

A few other influential frameworks described by Brislin et al. (1973) should be mentioned because of their early and continued influence. One was the research of Triandis (1972) on subjective culture; this research examined the various ways in which human beings perceive the human-made part of the environment. (See Adamopoulos & Kashima, 1999, for historical perspectives and legacies of this extensive program of research.) Research on subjective culture used methodologies that were direct descendants of Charles Osgood's measurement of metaphorical meaning, which featured the semantic differential technique and was also used extensively to explore possible universals in affective meaning (Osgood, May, & Miron, 1975). Another was research on *modernism* and its effects on people in various stages of adjustment to other societies. Research in that area has evolved into studies of acculturation and adaptation to change and continues

to be one of the more popular and practical areas of research (Berry & Sam, 1997).

Also influential in the 1960s, with interest in it continuing today, was Piaget's theory of cognitive development. The transportation of Piaget's views to cultures other than his native Switzerland is certainly one of the largest extensions of psychological theory in the history of the behavioral sciences, perhaps surpassed only by Freud's views on human nature and Pavlov's contributions to the nature of learning. Piaget's theory, which posits stages and rates of cognitive development, literally begs for testing in other cultures. The same can be said of Kohlberg's theory of moral reasoning. An extension and elaboration of Piaget's earlier theorizing on the moral development of children, considerable cross-cultural research featuring its methods and hypotheses has contributed to the accumulation of research on the human dilemma of choosing right from wrong (Eckensberger & Zimba, 1997).

While cross-cultural research on achievement motivation and psychological differentiation largely has disappeared, research using Piaget's ideas is still common, as are studies on modernism (currently under the general heading *acculturation research*). The basic methodological rationale has changed little, however. Research designs and hypotheses may be more sophisticated and enlightened currently, but the same general orientation has remained. Thus, interest has drifted into other paradigms, such as cultural definitions of self (Markus & Kitayama, 1991), individualism-collectivism (Triandis, chapter 3 of this volume), basic human values (Schwartz, 1994), work-related values posited by Hofstede (1980), and sex-trait stereotypes (Best & Williams, chapter 11 of this volume; Williams, Satterwaite, & Saiz, 1998). In all these frameworks, the abiding question concerns the issue of generalizability. Considering these efforts collectively, hundreds of studies have extended the basic ideas and methods to other cultures and societies in an effort to find patterns and trends that make sense. In addition to these popular paradigms, seemingly countless other investigations also focused on distinctions between the common and the unique or between the universal and the relative.

The Search for Psychological Universals: A Valid Enterprise?

Many cross-cultural psychologists believe that a central goal of their efforts is to work toward a basic understanding of the psychological functioning of all human beings—that is, to establish a universal psychology. Antithetic to radical relativism, the quest for universals remains both an elusive and a valid goal for psychology and anthropology (Brown, 1991). Actually, in one sense cross-cultural psychology can be characterized as a method used to help us understand how and why cultural and ethnic factors serve to mask, mediate, or modify an otherwise common core of regularities in human thought and behavior.

In an effort to make these efforts systematic, Lonner (1980) suggested seven levels of psychological universals. The first two levels were concerned with *true universals* and *variform universals.* An example of a true universal is human aggression. That humans are and always have been aggressive is an undeniable fact supported by the historical record, especially when aggressive behavior can range from all-out war and genocide to the type of verbal sniping with intent to injure that occurs among mates, lovers, roommates, or politicians. In other words, the true universal of aggression flourishes worldwide, but in varied form.

We submit that the majority of research done in the name of any of the cultural orientations is at least a search for variform universals, although researchers may not identify their efforts as such. In this book, for instance, there are numerous chapters written by productive and insightful people whose purpose is to explain cultural variations in specific areas of behavior. The study of emotion, child development, moral development, social cognition, values, gender, and so on all share that characteristic. The rationale or guidelines they use in this effort often are called "theories" or "paradigms," which of course are quite variable, but the basic point is that strong assumptions or conjectures are made about the essence of the human mind and how its interaction with culture produces a wide range of behavior. This situation is reminiscent of the "onion skin" analogy of culture, often used to emphasize that it is difficult to understand the core of a culture. In this view, the essence of a culture (the true universal) can be understood only if layer upon layer is peeled off to expose increasingly deeper and/or culture-specific variations of "psychic unity."

Other universalistic aspirations discussed by Lonner (1980) were categorized as diachronic (e.g., things stay pretty much the same over time), ethologically oriented (phylogenetic continuity), systematic behavioral (laws of learning or memory), those linked with human language and with biology, and a category termed *cocktail party universals.* This list may consist of things that are untestable in the strictest sense of scientific canon, but nevertheless exist (such as the inability to prove that my level of joy or pain is exactly what you feel).

It admittedly is difficult to put all human behavior in tidy universal categories. Indeed, it may be somewhat futile—some would say pretentious—to think along pantheistic lines. However, we submit that all psychologists, mainstream or not, think in universalistic terms. Those who are not particularly concerned about the "whys" of behavior seem to assume universality. Lectures in introductory psychology classes never begin with, "Today, we shall talk about [pick any topic]. However, I shall warn you that what I will say is only valid for white American people in their 20s." But, those who align themselves with one or more of the cultural perspectives—whether cultural, cross-cultural, or psychological anthropology (see below)—in psychology seem to share an interest in explaining *why* people differ along human dimensions. The five-factor model of personality, various perspectives on morality and values, conceptions of self, perspectives and models of human abilities, and a host of other theoretical dimensions are essentially efforts to search for commonalities in human thought and behavior. But, these efforts include a ready willingness to try to explain variations. Cross-cultural psychology is not an effort to rewrite psychology; rather, its intent is to encourage and welcome a more expansive and inclusive discipline.

A Plurality of Cultural Orientations in Psychology

It is important to recognize that what we have called *orthodox* cross-cultural psychology, which consists of organizational and conceptual-methodological levels, is not the only psychological perspective in the quest to understand culture's role in shaping and maintaining human behavior. It is also important to understand that the transfer-test-discover model explained in Berry et al. (1992) is not the only way that cross-cultural psychologists conceptualize and implement their research. While cross-cultural psychology in its early days may have espoused a fairly standard methodological protocol, it has changed with the times. For instance, the masthead policy of cross-cultural psychology's flagship journal, the *Journal of Cross-Cultural Psychology*, in part specifies that it is interested in publishing "papers that focus on the interrelationship between culture and psychological processes," and that submitted manuscripts "may report results from either cross-cultural comparative research or results from other types of research concerning the ways in which culture (and related concepts such as ethnicity) affect the thinking and behavior of individuals as well as how individual thought and behavior define and reflect aspects of culture."

In short, cross-cultural psychology is interested in how the interface between culture and psychology should be understood through careful research. Currently, it is conceptually, philosophically, and methodologically pluralistic. Several other approaches within the broad field of psychology also focus on culture as an important and dynamic ingredient in both theory and application. In at least three other perspectives, the study of culture is a critical part of their identity and preferred research strategies. Table 2.1 gives an overview of this family of closely allied endeavors, which are discussed briefly below.

Cultural Psychology

The closest relative to cross-cultural psychology is cultural psychology. Here, we present some of the characteristics of this orientation. In the second part, we discuss and contrast the differences between the two in substantial depth. Because cultural psychology has no clear organizational and methodological structure, it is somewhat difficult to pinpoint where cross-cultural psychology ends and cultural psychology begins. Moreover, while cross-cultural psychology has an agenda with which most of its adherents agree (basically, to examine the cultural generalizability of psychological laws and theories using diverse methodologies), those who identify with cultural psychology do not seem to have a tidy definition of their enterprise or a program of specific goals that guides their efforts. However, it is unlikely that any of its adherents would be bothered by its lack of a clear methodological or goal-directed identity. It may be correct to say that cultural psychologists view themselves and their efforts as broadly ecumenical in both conceptualizing and conducting research or in writing essays or commentaries, which concerns the centrality of culture in understanding the psychology of human beings.

Above, we pointed out that cross-cultural psychology should be defined primarily by what it does and not by some facile definition. We accord cultural psychology the same courtesy by saying that it, too, should be identified by what it does and more precisely by how it views relationships between the individual and the individual's culture. Miller (1997) commented that the core perspective of cultural psychology is that culture and individual behavior are inseparable components of the same phenomenon. Miller notes that this perspective contrasts with the tendency, particularly in early work in cross-cultural psychology, for culture and psychology to be somewhat dichotomized and understood as discrete phenomena, with culture conceptualized and used as an independent variable that affects the dependent variable of individual behavior. Boesch (1991), leader of what has been called the Saarbruecken school of cultural psychology, is strongly critical of treating culture as an independent variable and also of applying a positivist or natural science template in efforts to understand people from other cultures. In an interesting article, Boesch (1996) wrote about what he called cross-cultural psychology's seven "flaws," which range from the conceptual and methodological to the philosophical. A special issue of the journal *Psychology and Culture* (September 1997) was devoted to Boesch's ideas and to reflections of others about his influence.

As noted, cultural psychology is not a unified field. Several of the more productive scholars in the various cultural orientations have distinctive views of the differences between cross-cultural psychology and cultural psychology. For instance, Cole (1996) has delineated the main characteristics of what he thinks constitute cultural psychology:

- It emphasizes mediated action in a context.
- It insists on the importance of the "genetic method" understood broadly to include historical, ontogenetic, and microgenetic levels of analysis.
- It seeks to ground its analysis in everyday life events.
- It assumes that mind emerges in the joint mediated activity of people. Mind, then, is in an important sense "co-constructed" and distributed.
- It assumes that individuals are active agents in their own development, but do not act in settings entirely of their own choosing.

Table 2.1   Characteristics Associated with Major Perspectives in the Area of Psychology and Culture

Perspective	Basic Orientation and Purpose	Aims and Goals	Methodological or Conceptual Problems	Major Outlet for Published Research
Cross-cultural psychology	To study similarities and differences in psychological functioning in various cultures and ethnic groups; to assess changes in such functioning	To develop a more inclusive and universal psychology; to compare, explicitly or implicitly, thought and behavior in different cultures	Problems associated with functional, conceptual, and psychometric equivalence and with different levels of analysis (cultures, communities, persons, behaviors)	*Journal of Cross-Cultural Psychology*: focuses on the relationship between culture and psychology from either cross-cultural comparative research or from other research on how culture affects the thinking and behavior of individuals and how individual thought and behavior define culture
Cultural psychology	To advance the understanding of the person in a historical and sociocultural context	To understand how mind and cultural define and constitute each other in specific contexts; to avoid direct contrasts across cultures, except at times implicitly	Absence of a common and widely accepted research orientation. Diffuse methodologies ranging from the qualitative/ethnographic to the quantitative	*Culture and Psychology*: addresses the centrality of culture in understanding human beings: their identity, social conduct, intra- and intersubjective experiences, emotions, and semiotic creativity; includes formulating new conceptualizations of culture in psychology
Psychological anthropology	To study the relationship between the individual and the social milieu and the psychological and social disciplines	To contribute to the description of universal principles without a priori assumption of the existence of psychological universals	Difficulty in using a common scientific language and epistemology acceptable to psychology	*Ethos*: deals with the interrelationship between the individual and the social milieu and between the psychological disciplines and the social disciplines
Indigenous psychology	The psychological study of individuals in a specific cultural context by scholars in that context and for the benefit of people in that context	To encourage the development of a psychology that may be, but is not necessarily, universal and that has meaning and application in a specific cultural or ethnic context	Difficulty in avoiding already existing psychological concepts, theories, and research and, therefore, difficulty in determining exactly what is indigenous	Various national journals

- It rejects cause-effect, stimulus-response, explanatory science in favor of a science that emphasizes the emergent nature of mind in activity and that acknowledges a central role for interpretation in its explanatory network.
- It draws on methodologies from the humanities, as well as from the social and biological sciences. (p. 104)

Psychological Anthropology

The discipline of anthropology is the core of the cultural sciences. Having been around for at least as long as psychology, anthropology is broadly the study of humankind, including human origins and variations. Cultural scholars in other fields will benefit directly and indirectly from the insights provided by a large number of gifted anthropologists. Like psychology, the field of anthropology is subdivided into fairly discrete branches. One of these branches is psychological anthropology, a title first proposed by Hsu (1972) to replace the earlier subdiscipline of culture and personality. One of its leading contemporary proponents defines psychological anthropology as "anthropological investigations that make use of psychological concepts and methods" (Bock, 1994, p. ix). Bock insists that an anthropology "that takes account of individuals must make use of ideas from neighboring disciplines" (p. ix), an idea with which cross-cultural psychologists, as well as cultural psychologists, would agree heartily. The field of psychological anthropology is clearly and intentionally a hybrid animal. A classic chapter written by psychologist Donald T. Campbell and anthropologist Raoul Naroll (1972) argues that anthropology and psychology are mutually relevant methodologically, and serves well as both a methodological and conceptual bridge between these two important fields.

Psychological anthropologists have made major contributions to anthropology and have guided cross-cultural efforts in psychology in important ways. The study of culture and dreams, culture and mental illness, cognitive anthropology, the development of children, innovations in field research such as systematic observation in naturalistic settings, and many other orientations have proven immensely instructive to cross-cultural psychologists. The well-known Six Cultures Project, spearheaded by Beatrice Whiting and her late husband John (Whiting & Whiting, 1975), was basically a wide-ranging child development examination carried out under the aegis of psychological anthropology. Even if we had the space to do so in this limited chapter, we would not want to attempt a critical evaluation of this branch of anthropology. We primarily want to point out that psychological anthropologists have much to offer scholars in neighboring fields, and that their efforts have informed numerous efforts in cross-cultural psychology.

While not explicitly an association devoted to psychological anthropology, the Society for Cross-Cultural Research, which has met only in the United States, attracts many who strongly identify with this anthropological subfield. Two journals, *Ethos* and *Cross-Cultural Research*, publish many articles by psychological anthropologists. Finally, while it may not be entirely appropriate to mention it in this context, the journal *Transcultural Psychiatry* (which began in 1956 as the *Transcultural Psychiatric Research Review*) publishes articles and reviews that are consistent with psychological anthropology. The last periodical is of primary interest to ethnopsychiatrists and others, including many cross-cultural and cultural psychologists in the mental health field, who are interested in understanding social and cultural determinants of psychopathology and psychosocial treatment of mental disorders and conditions. The only organizational structures with which it obviously is affiliated are the broad international psychiatric and clinical psychology communities.

Indigenous Psychologies

Cross-cultural psychologists espouse methodological pluralism and an openness to various efforts that hope to explain both similarities and differences in human thought and behavior. Yet, perhaps because of the methods and concepts it typically uses, this area of inquiry is questioned by some and even vilified by others, with some claiming that it is nothing more than Western conceptual and methodological hegemony pretentiously playing the game of scientific reductionism using unsuspecting psychological subjects as pawns. Harsh as that characterization may sound, one can read analyses of the cross-cultural psychological effort by individuals who represent either cultural psychology or even mainstream psychology and can emerge with the impression that cross-cultural psychology "doesn't get it" and is an enterprise beset with "perilous problems" in a complex world populated by "moving cultures" (Hermans & Kempen, 1998).

One such suspicious quarter is championed by individuals who represent what its adherents call *indigenous psychologies* or the *indigenization of psychology*. The goal of this approach, according to its proponents, is not to abandon science, objectivity, the experimental method, and a search for universals (characteristics that they claim define cross-cultural psychology), but to provide a more rigorous science that is grounded firmly in human understanding (Kim, 1995, 1999; Kim, Park, & Park, 2000). Interestingly espoused and encouraged by both "militant" indigenously oriented researchers and "card-carrying" cross-cultural psychologists (Adair, 1992; Kim & Berry, 1993), this movement, if it can be called that, seems to have much in common with cultural psychology.

Consider a current definition of the indigenous psychologies approach:

> Culture is not viewed as a variable, quasi-independent variable, or category (e.g. individualistic or collectivistic), or a mere sum of individual characteristics. Culture is an emergent property of individuals interacting with their natural and human environment. Culture is defined as a *rubric of patterned variables . . . [and a] process definition of culture* [is that it] *represents the collective utilization of natural and human resources to achieve desired outcomes.* (Kim et al., 2000, p. 67)

It is hard to believe that cultural psychologists would have difficulty with that definition; indeed, it is difficult to believe that any cross-cultural psychologist would not nod his or her head in at least grudging approval. Perhaps the only factor with which cultural psychologists may quarrel is that proponents of the indigenous approach freely use many aspects of mainstream psychology to search for meaningful within-culture patterns of thought and behavior. For instance, several researchers have used fairly standard survey and questionnaire techniques that are as common as breathing in Western psychology in efforts to understand the nature and structure of personality (itself a Western term) in other societies (e.g., Chung & Leung, 1998; Guanzon-Lapena, Church, Carlota, & Katigbak, 1998). Indeed, it has been argued (Kim & Berry, 1993) that the only way to enter the pasture of a truly universal psychology is through the gates of potentially multiple paths patrolled and described by indigenous

perspectives. Thus, the sum of indigenous psychologies (that is, all that survive Procrustean tests in other cultures conducted by, for, and from within those cultures) is that elusive and oft-cited goal of a universal psychology.

Practical Applications of the Various Approaches

We have shown that there are at least four perspectives in psychology that share the view that an understanding of how culture affects the thought and behavior of individuals is critically important. Other efforts should be mentioned in this context. These other efforts decidedly tend to be "applied." One of these areas is concerned heavily with effective living and working abroad. The masthead policy of the *International Journal of Intercultural Relations*, which began publication in 1977, specifies in part that the field with which it is involved is "dedicated to advancing knowledge and understanding of theory, practice, and research in intercultural relations." Landis and Wasilewski (1999) explain that, "Intercultural research tends to focus on the penetration by a member of one culture into another culture. It is therefore more dynamic than cross-cultural research" (p. 536). Research concerning such highly individual matters as adaptation to foreign travel, culture shock, managerial success in other societies, and effective cross-cultural communication is common. There is also a strong training component is this area (Cushner & Brislin, 1996; Landis & Bhagat, 1996). These efforts and their adherents have an organizational structure that is largely based in the United States and is led by the International Association for Intercultural Research.

Another applied area concerns multicultural counseling. Extensive and growing literature encompasses this area (e.g., Pedersen, Draguns, Lonner, & Trimble, 1996). Largely a North American enterprise, researchers and practitioners in this domain are concerned with the various issues and problems that emerge when cultural and ethnic differences between therapist and client interfere with good therapeutic effectiveness and progress.

This completes the brief historical tour of cross-cultural psychology, a consideration of its methods, and a survey of various orientations that give careful attention to culture as a powerful factor in somehow shaping human behavior. We now turn our attention to a more comprehensive discussion of how the several faces of cultural efforts interact with psychological theory. We focus our attention on the philosophical, theoretical, and methodological commitments that underlie the confrontation between the two fundamental perspectives in the area of psychology and culture: universalism (cross-cultural psychology) and relativism (cultural psychology and social constructionism).

Culture and
Psychological Theory

The Two Faces of Culture
and Psychology

In recent years, the conceptual confrontation between comparativism/universalism and relativism—or between cross-cultural psychology on one hand and cultural psychology and various social constructionist positions on the other—has intensified significantly (for detailed descriptions of this issue, see Lonner & Adamopoulos, 1997, and Miller, 1997). Cross-cultural psychologists, using the mantle of scientific orthodoxy, have been arguing for the reemergence of psychic unity as an important goal of social science research (e.g., Berry, 1997). In that vein, they have criticized mainstream psychology, which in its most benign state ignores culture and in its worst argues for an "acultural psychology" (e.g., Sell & Martin, 1983). The latter is essentially the argument that culture tends to hide fundamental truths about human nature that can only be uncovered in the artificial world of the scientific experiment. Psychic unity in such a context is to be discovered in the tightly controlled and rigid experimental designs (and minds, according to some critics) of Western (especially North American) psychology. Cross-cultural psychologists have rightly criticized this approach for the parochialism, ethnocentrism, and basic laziness that it reflects. It is clearly bad science, and the arguments for an acultural or monocultural psychology, like the one mentioned above, are often indefensible.

Instead, cross-cultural psychologists have proposed the adoption of classical scientific methodology to investigate human behavior comparatively. In that sense, the criticism by Shweder (1990) that cross-cultural psychology is yet another branch of scientific psychology is very much to the point. For example, Segall, Dasen, Berry, and Poortinga (1999), in their introduction to the ecocultural framework write: "*all* human behavior is shaped by experience [and] is a product of a complex interaction involving genetic and experiential factors, with both present and past experience weighted heavily in its ultimate determination" (p. 25).

Most positivist and empiricist (typically mainstream) psychologists would feel comfortable with this perspective. Consider, for instance, the following statements, which appeared in a relatively recent statement about the status of modern scientific psychology by Kimble (1989) and are basic tenets of a fairly traditional approach to scientific psychology: "Individual behavior is the joint product of more or less permanent underlying potentials and more or less temporary internal and external conditions" (p. 493); and "Behavior is determined by genetic endowment and environmental circumstances" (p. 491). While Kimble—widely known for his early work on learning (e.g., Kimble, 1961)—and cross-cultural psychology appear to make strange bedfellows, statements of a similar nature have been made by other theorists in 20th century psychology, including, for example, Lewin (1951), who like Segall et al. (1999), emphasized the role of present and past experience in the explanation of behavior. Considering these similarities between mainstream and cross-cultural psychology, it is not surprising that Shweder (1990), a vociferous advocate of cultural psychology, seemed to have such a strong reaction to the whole enterprise of cross-cultural psychology.

Even the language used by Kimble (1984, 1989) and by cross-cultural psychologists to describe the differences between the two cultures of psychology on the one hand and the differences between cultural and cross-cultural psychology on the other seems identical. In describing divergent perspectives in general psychology, Kimble (1989) writes:

> One group of psychologists sees the field in terms of scientific values and accepts the concepts of objectivism, elementism, and nomothetic lawfulness. The group opposed sees psychology in terms of humanistic values and accepts the concepts of intuitionism, holism, and idiographic lawfulness. (p. 491)

Poortinga and Pandey (1997) use very similar words to describe the cultural/cross-cultural psychology debate:

> The cultural orientations tend to be holistic and idiographic, emphasizing the necessity to make unique culture-characteristic pat-

terns of behavior accessible to scientific analysis and leaning toward various forms of phenomenology in methodology. The cross-cultural orientations are more molecular and nomothetic, emphasizing the need to extend existing psychological theories to encompass behavioral phenomena found in other cultures. (pp. xxii–xiv)

We may very well ask at this point if there is anything wrong with cross-cultural psychology taking a mainstream orientation. After all, a number of eminent cross-cultural psychologists have explicitly advocated just that kind of perspective (see, for example, Poortinga's 1990 presidential address to the International Association for Cross-Cultural Psychology).

One of the problems, of course, is that culture, by necessity, can be viewed only in a very limited fashion within this perspective. To the extent that culture is some sort of mental construct—and most psychologists tend to view it that way—then it can most comfortably (if not exclusively) be treated as an intervening variable (as Kimble's 1989 analysis correctly implies). This necessarily limits our conceptualizations of culture. It is not surprising that, in the majority of cross-cultural psychological theories Lonner and Adamopoulos (1997) reviewed, culture is treated as a moderator or, occasionally, a mediator variable—in other words, as an intervening variable. While many psychologists may be comfortable with such a view of culture, cross-cultural psychology as a distinct discipline has not confronted this issue explicitly. Also, we should note that an important sequela to this perspective—one that is implicit, but very obvious, in Kimble's (1989) analysis—is that it is often difficult to think of intervening variables as causes or explanations. As Lonner and Adamopoulos have pointed out, this results in the degradation of the status of culture and makes it much easier to ignore in theory construction.

It is exactly on this point that cultural psychology and, more broadly, relativist orientations take a strong position. They rightly point out that culture more often than not is delegated to a secondary role in theorizing because, after all, the clear goal of cross-cultural psychological research is to establish universals and to highlight the importance of psychic unity. Thus, traditional cross-cultural theory has been accused or described (a) as just being another branch of mainstream, logico-empirical psychology (Shweder, 1990) and (b) as distinguish-

ing conceptually between culture and the psychological world. Miller (1997) has succinctly summarized these two approaches:

> The dominant stance within cultural psychology is to view culture and psychology as mutually constitutive phenomena, i.e., as phenomena which make up each other or are integral to each other. In such a view, it is assumed that culture and individual behavior cannot be understood in isolation yet are also not reducible to each other. Such a stance contrasts with the tendency particularly in early work in cross-cultural psychology, for culture and psychology to be understood as discrete phenomena, with culture conceptualized as an independent variable that impacts on the dependent variable of individual behavior. (p. 88)

This fundamental orientation of cultural psychology, supported by the positions that social constructionism (e.g., Gergen, 1985; Misra & Gergen, 1993) advocates, has created a powerful "relativist" alliance that challenges the dominion of cross-cultural psychology in the area of psychology and culture. On their part, some cross-cultural psychologists feel very uncomfortable with the notion that culture and psychology are to be treated as mutually constitutive phenomena. Such an idea has a nice ring to it and may sound like an admirable goal, but it is difficult to make it concrete within a particular investigative context. We simply do not have either the theoretical or the methodological sophistication—always in the classical scientific tradition—to accomplish this type of integration or to describe exactly how the two classes of phenomena constitute each other. Therefore, it is not surprising that some cultural theorists (e.g., Shweder, 1996) have tried to persuade us of the value of qualitative methodologies and of the fundamental, ontological differences between the qualitative and quantitative traditions. According to this critique, the two traditions differ, among other things, on the questions of the possibility of perceiving and understanding reality and whether meaning can be a proper object of scientific explanation.

Extending this line of thinking, it is possible to argue that, since the study of culture is necessarily—at least for psychology—the study of meaning, it can never be accomplished exclusively within the empirical/quantitative tradition. Thus, the notion that formal psychological structures and principles generated by a nomothetic science on the one hand and cultural meanings on the other hand can be studied at the same time and in the same context as phenomena that constitute each other may be at best a chimaera.

The difficulty of dealing with culture and psychology as constitutive phenomena can be portrayed more easily within the context of specific investigations. Miller (1997) suggests, for instance, that the work of Markus and Kitayama (1991) on culture and self-construal is one that follows the comparative approach while being totally compatible with cultural psychology. However, as Lonner and Adamopoulos (1997) have pointed out, Markus and Kitayama very clearly, though implicitly, appear to take a moderator-variable approach to the study of culture and the self. In other words, they tend to treat culture as an intervening variable, which is perfectly compatible with the mainstream cross-cultural perspective. They state, for example, that independent and interdependent "self-schemata"—which are a "product" of culture (product is their word)—influence most psychological functions. This is classical psychological theorizing, and there is nothing necessarily wrong with it. What is unclear, however, is exactly how it is that culture and psychology are seen as constitutive phenomena in this case. Markus and Kitayama seem to distinguish between antecedents and consequences, and culture is placed squarely on the side of antecedents. The self-system is not defined in terms of culture, and culture is not essential in the formation of a self-schema (see Markus & Kitayama, 1991, note 3, for a number of other factors that may contribute to the definition of the self-schema). In the absence of such an essential role that culture must play in the definition of an important psychological phenomenon, it is difficult to see how culture and psychology can be thought to be mutually constitutive (for a complementary, though not identical, analysis of the assumptions behind this work, see Matsumoto, 1999).

The basic conclusion one can reach here is that the discomfort of traditionalists in cross-cultural psychology with the positions advocated by cultural psychologists is understandable and justifiable. Both sides make important arguments, but neither side's basic positions are immune to serious criticism. It really comes down to a matter of preference, attitude, and philosophical orientation. It is also important to keep in mind that, in the end, both perspectives and their variants make genuine contributions that enrich psychology at least in an incremental, if not holistic, fashion.

From an ideological perspective, it is difficult to see an end to this intellectual conflict because there does not seem to be a solution—or even a viable compromise—to the conceptual and methodological dilemmas that both sides face. In addition, the language that each side uses in identifying and describing its subject matter is often incompatible with the language of the other.

However, at the same time that this ideological division appears to be pulling the discipline apart, there is a manifest change in the attitudes of many researchers in the area. Recent statements by Triandis (1997) point to a softening of positions and the search for compromise. Miller's work (1994) self-consciously attempts to bridge the divide between cultural and cross-cultural psychology. Perhaps most telling of this attitude shift, Shweder's (1990) early rhetoric has changed substantially. For example, the title of one of his recent publications with Much, Mahapatra, and Park (1997) is "The 'Big Three' of Morality (Autonomy, Community, Divinity) and the 'Big Three' Explanations of Suffering." In it, the authors outline a scheme that attempts to capture all major moral systems in the world. However one chooses to interpret this scheme, the allusion to the universal personality system that is so popular at this time in personality psychology (e.g., McCrae & Costa, 1997; McCrae, Costa, del Pilar, Rolland, & Parker, 1998) is a powerful indicator of shifting attitudes. Even Gergen, working within the constraints of social constructionism, occasionally has adopted relatively conciliatory attitudes toward cross-cultural psychology by at least acknowledging some of its contributions (e.g., Misra & Gergen, 1993).

If it is, in fact, the case that such a shifting of attitudes is discernible on both sides, it should be instructive to explore the genesis of this change. As stated above, we cannot perceive a fundamental theoretical or methodological innovation or breakthrough from either side that has led to this point of softening attitudes. Rather, this change may be due to the realization, on both sides, that there are important, and at present insurmountable, problems with each perspective. Such a realization makes most theorists more humble and more accepting of different orientations—a bit less ethnocentric, so to speak.

Major Difficulties Facing Each Perspective

Cultural psychology and constructionist approaches in general display at least three major problematic features:

1. *The absence of a consistent and widely applied methodology.* Cultural psychology has had a rather ambivalent attitude regarding an appropriate methodology—from the quantitative to the ethnographic—because, as argued here, it deals necessarily with multiple conceptualizations of culture and with an ambiguous conception of the relationship between culture and psychology. Thus, psychologically trained researchers rely primarily on quantitative methodologies, while many other social scientists are advocating qualitative methods. Perhaps both are useful—and certainly both have strengths—but it is difficult to make a case against a competing orientation if one cannot stand firm on one's own methodological ground.
2. *Relativism reconsidered.* The relativism implicit in both cultural psychology and social constructionism makes very difficult the development of a language for the description of subjectively defined objects or states in any theoretical context. Yet, this is essential for the development of any theory that transcends even the most modest cultural boundaries. Recent statements in cultural psychology (Shweder, 1986) and in indigenous psychology (Sinha, 1997) make it clear that such theories (i.e., theories that are applicable cross-culturally) are desirable. The question is how to construct them and test them under the constraints of relativism.
3. *Mindful construction of the social world.* Social constructionism, with its insistence on describing psychological phenomena as sociocultural constructions, naturally has to face another set of very difficult problems, many of which have been acknowledged recently even by sympathizers (e.g., Burr, 1995). Put rather simplistically, here is the basic problem: If all social and psychological phenomena—including psychological

theories—are only to be seen as social constructions, there has to be a mind that constructs them. Therefore, the search for this mind (the core goal of classical psychological research) is fundamentally a sound, if very difficult, endeavor. There are, of course, many well-known corollaries to this fundamental problem for social constructionism, including the problem of evaluating the outcome of the deconstruction of social relations, public behavior, and the like in the face of multiple and equally plausible realities.

On the cross-cultural psychology side, there are also a number of conceptual difficulties. Since some of these are discussed extensively above and seven flaws were identified by Boesch (1996), only two important ideas are mentioned briefly here:

1. *The dangers of conceptual rigidity.* The strong commitment by cross-cultural psychologists to the logico-empirical approach has meant that culture has been viewed primarily as an intervening (usually a moderator) variable. Within this perspective, however, as Kimble's (1989) analysis implies, it is difficult to give culture the status of an explanation. Instead, culture is relegated to the status of a descriptor of a state of affairs. For example, extensive descriptions of individualism and collectivism have appeared in the cross-cultural literature over the past 10 years in terms of attributional patterns, social behavior, self-construal, emotions, and the like (e.g., Triandis, 1993, 1995). Many researchers, however, have taken such descriptions to imply that individualism and collectivism are the *causes* of these patterns. Regardless of what researchers may wish to be able to accomplish, this general practice must be condemned: Individualism and collectivism *are* these patterns—not the explanations of the patterns. This places serious limitations on the type of theoretical work cross-cultural psychologists can do and on the usefulness of the construct of culture.
2. *Methodological overconfidence.* Regardless of what most psychologists choose or want to believe, data-level comparisons in cross-cultural psychology are extraordinarily difficult. Even a perfunctory consideration of the Duhem-Quine

thesis on the weakness of individual hypothesis testing will reveal that, particularly in cross-cultural research, the transition from theoretical constructs to measures and then to empirical observations is fraught with problems. These problems, which usually involve the lack of equivalence of concepts and measures across cultures, allow scientists to remain loyal to their favorite theories in the face of contradictory evidence. Adamopoulos (1988) commented on this problem more than 10 years ago, but there has been little change yet in the practices of cross-cultural researchers. Even the discipline's most cherished methodologies—like the emic-etic approach articulated by Segall et al. (1999) and many others—is conceptually ambiguous enough to allow a great deal of misunderstanding and abuse. For example, the difference between an "imposed etic" and an "emic"—the importation of an exogenous instrument to measure (albeit with some modification) a construct in a different cultural context—is not at all clear, and it often causes a great deal of confusion among researchers.

Conclusion

The rapprochement between cultural and cross-cultural psychology will be successful to the extent that the two disciplines complement each other and cover each other's major weaknesses rather than attempt to supplant each other. In particular, cultural psychology can make up for the limitations in cultural description that seem to be an inherent problem in cross-cultural psychology, while cross-cultural psychology can offer a more consistent and reliable—but by no means infallible—methodological approach to the study of culture and human behavior. Thus, such a rapprochement should have as its goal not a corrective effort on the part of one perspective with regard to the other perspective's weaknesses, but rather the celebration of the strengths of each perspective within the context of its ontological premises and related methodological commitments (see also Triandis, 1997). Boesch (1996) expressed a similar view when he said that the relationship between cultural and cross-cultural psychology is not one of either-or because each is needed at appropriate places. Thus, a solid cross-cultural study first should be in-

formed or complemented by a cultural investigation.

We now turn our attention to the various roles that culture can and does play in psychological theory, with an emphasis on future developments in the discipline.

The Place of Culture in Psychological Theory

As we implied, these are heady times for psychologists interested in the concept of culture. In fact, as psychology slowly, and perhaps even painfully, rediscovers the concept of culture and incorporates it into its theoretical repertoire, one could argue that these are the best of times and the worst of times for the study of psychology and culture. The increased interest in the area by mainstream psychologists is matched easily by the fury of the debate between universalists and relativists, cross-cultural psychologists and cultural psychologists, nativists and empiricists, and so on.

The most cursory review of developments in the field over the past decade reveals substantial growth and the emergence of divergent orientations. For example, and in addition to major perspectives like the ecocultural framework (Berry et al., 1992) and individualism-collectivism (Triandis, 1995), there appeared new models, as well as extensions of earlier ones, that take a utilitarian or functionalist approach to culture (Adamopoulos, 1991, 1999; Malpass, 1990), new versions of the evolutionary approach (Buss, 1989), and a number of what might be described as "contextualist" approaches, which treat culture as a rich medium within which are embedded inextricably various psychological processes and structures (e.g., Miller, 1994).

As described above, in the majority of these approaches, culture, however else construed, is conceptualized primarily as an antecedent to individual behavior. This is most clearly the case within cross-cultural psychology, but is also often implied in perspectives identified with cultural psychology. Lonner and Adamopoulos (1997) reviewed many of the psychological approaches to culture by examining especially two characteristics of these approaches: the status or importance (primary or secondary) of the construct of culture within each perspective and the type of influence (direct or indirect) that culture is assumed to have on individual functioning. Four distinct perspectives emerged from this analysis: (a) culture construed as an independent variable (or set of variables) that exerts a direct influence on behavior; (b) culture construed as the general context within which individual behavior is embedded; (c) culture conceptualized as a mediator variable, accounting for the manifest relationships among other variables (e.g., personality traits) with behavior; and (d) culture conceptualized as a moderator variable that alters significantly the relationship between two other variables of interest (e.g., a particular practice and an individual performance variable).

It turns out that most, if not all, cross-cultural perspectives can be classified within this scheme. Such classification is not always easy because so many theories and models in the area do not make explicit assumptions about culture. Often, however, they have to make implicit assumptions. For example, by allowing culture to alter theoretical relationships among psychological variables and behavior, a theory clearly treats culture as a moderator. Such assumptions make possible the classification of the models within this framework (see the example of self-construal mentioned in the section on the two faces of culture and psychology above).

A significant implication of the analysis by Lonner and Adamopoulos (1997) is that most cross-cultural theories treat culture as an antecedent to behavior—often even as a direct cause of behavior. Culture appears as a consequence of human behavior (in the simplest case, as a dependent variable) only rarely in the cross-cultural literature. Yet, as with all other phenomena, if we are to understand culture, we should be able to go beyond mere description: We should be able to explain it and perhaps even predict it in some form. For example, instead of discussing only the historical record on individualism and collectivism, as Triandis (1995) has done so ably, cross-cultural psychologists should try to predict their emergence and future manifestations, perhaps in the form of cultural institutions, interpersonal relations, and meaning systems. Unfortunately, very little of that has been done to date (see Adamopoulos, 1999, for such an attempt). The basic argument presented here is that such lack of effort and knowledge is based not only on the complexity of the issue, but also on the focus of research efforts almost exclusively on culture as an antecedent to individual behavior. Yet, culture can and should also be understood as the result of human activity, not only as the determinant or

antecedent of human activity (see also Berry, 1999).

Culture as Construction

Any human construction, including culture, can serve at least one of two main functions: It can help or enable further activity, or it can hinder or restrict it. In his philosophical analysis of rule-based behavior, Shwayder (1965) emphasized the distinction between enabling and restrictive rules. Enabling rules permit human beings to invent new ways of accomplishing tasks (e.g., the rules of language), whereas restrictive rules specify more precisely the course of activity (e.g., the rules of a game). Adamopoulos (1994) has used this distinction in work on the structure of situations and the conceptualization of social environments.

There are major differences among the various social sciences in the manner in which they approach culture. For example, anthropology and sociology have emphasized the enabling aspects of culture by stressing the importance of adaptation. On the other hand, psychology, with its concern with individual freedom, has implicitly stressed the restrictive aspects of culture. This may be something of an overgeneralization, but it does not necessarily reflect a Western bias toward the importance of individual freedom. Why would Confucius (ca. 551–479 B.C.) decry the "anarchy" of his days and advocate that people return to the "old ways" and become more obedient toward their rulers if individual freedom was not an issue even at that time in China?

Despite this concern with individual freedom in psychology, it may at first appear rather surprising that the main theories of cross-cultural psychology have taken a more anthropological perspective and approached culture primarily as enabling invention. As Figure 2.1 indicates, both the ecocultural framework and the theories on individualism-collectivism approach culture as an antecedent to behavior—sometimes even as an independent variable, as in the case of the ecocultural framework—and as invention. For example, Segall et al. (1999) clearly refer to cultural adaptations to the ecology as "inventions" and treat them as determinants of individual behavior. On the other hand, perhaps this approach should not be surprising. It may reflect a conscious attempt by cross-cultural psychologists to bring into mainstream psychology an alternative perspective without disturbing the traditional interests in social psychology in the situational determi-

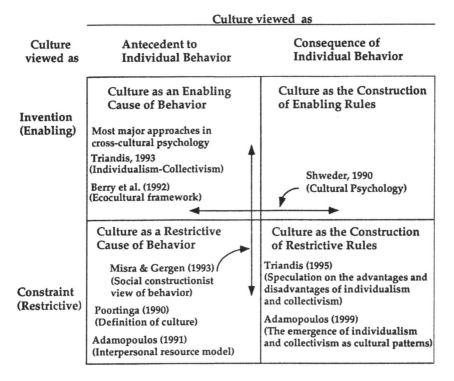

Figure 2.1   Assumptions about the Role of Culture in Psychological Theory

nants of behavior. Adamopoulos and Kashima (1999) have pointed to similar practices in early cross-cultural psychology as a means of gaining mainstream acceptance for culture-based theories, like Triandis's (1972) subjective culture framework.

As Figure 2.1 suggests, there have been few cases in cross-cultural psychology for which culture was viewed primarily as restrictive. Poortinga's (1990) definition of culture in terms of constraints that limit the behavioral repertoire of an individual is a good example. Adamopoulos (1991) has developed a model for the emergence of interpersonal structure that assumes that the differentiation of constraints on human interaction (e.g., the symbolic versus material nature of a resource being exchanged) over time leads to the emergence of specific meaning systems.

In general, social constructionist approaches have included a wider array of the features of culture outlined in Figure 2.1. Cultural psychology, at least as advocated by Shweder (1990), construes culture as both antecedent to and a consequence of individual activity. For example, Shweder tells us that "it is the aim of cultural psychology . . . to seek mind where

it is mindful, indissociably embedded in the meanings and resources that are its product, yet also make it up" (p. 13). Thus, while he does not talk about culture in terms of dependent and independent variables, he does admit to an interpenetration of individual and cultural processes in which each affects the construction of the other.

Misra and Gergen (1993), following a social constructionist approach, have concentrated on somewhat different features of culture. They have focused on its manifestation as an antecedent to behavior (broadly defined), but have emphasized both the enabling and restrictive aspects of the function of culture.

The bottom right cell in Figure 2.1, which is only sparsely inhabited currently, may become a focus of increased activity for cross-cultural psychologists. Approaches compatible with this particular classification would emphasize the construction of culture and view it as a human activity to be explained. At the same time, such approaches may be compatible with the classical focus of psychology on individual freedom and choice and may construe behavior as an attempt to break through the constraints of culture.

These ideas are not incongruous with current practice in cross-cultural and cultural psychology. Consider, for example, Triandis's (1995) work on the constraints that the orientations (syndromes) of individualism and collectivism generate for individual members of communities. Adamopoulos (1999) has extended his earlier work with interpersonal resources in a more recent model that traces the differentiation of social constraints to account for the emergence of individualism and collectivism as cultural patterns. Similarly, Miller's (1994) work on the construction of moral codes in different cultures points to the constraining role of the code of social responsibility on individual behavior in India. Finally, Jahoda's (n.d.) interesting reconceptualization of the study by Wassman and Dasen with the Yupno implies the significant role of culture in constraining collective representations of the world from which specific individuals try to break away. Along the same lines, the account by Berry et al. (1992) of individual differences in the use of the Yupno counting system also points to the ability of individuals to escape the constraints of collective representation.

There are many examples of the constraining or enabling role of culture. What is missing in much of current work is the exploration of the causes of individual activity that results in culturally constraining or enabling forms of social life. Early work on subjective culture by Triandis (1972) held the promise and potential for such an exploration. Subjective culture, defined as "a cultural group's characteristic way of perceiving its social environment" (p. 3), refers to the relationship between cultural variables and cognitive structures and thus easily can accommodate a constructionist view of culture. In fact, much of the research reported in Triandis (1972) can be conceptualized as a rich analysis of the connotative meaning of the collective constructions of societal groups (e.g., norms, roles and social relationships, and values). As suggested above, this work was used later as the foundation for more traditionalist research programs, for which cultural constructions like values and norms were viewed as determinants (antecedents) of individual decision making and social behavior (see, for example, Davidson, Jaccard, Triandis, Morales, & Diaz-Guerrero, 1976; Triandis, 1980). This shift in perspective might have been necessary for this work to become integrated into mainstream psychology (Adamopoulos & Kashima, 1999), but it clearly steered research away from the examination of culture as the outcome of human activity.

There have been other early research programs that have approached culture as the construction of enabling or restrictive rules. Among the most notable is the early work on reference groups by Sherif and Sherif (1964), in which norms, social behavior (e.g., conformity), and sociocultural variables frequently were presented as components of complex psychosocial systems (groups). However, as in most cases, the emphasis was mainly on individual behavior as a dependent variable. Furthermore, this rich research tradition did not become an exemplar for future work in the area.

Approaching culture as the consequence of individual activity, as Figure 2.1 implies, involves investigation of the processes through which groups of individuals structure their perceptions and expectations of the social environment. Some of the questions that should guide this alternative approach include the following:

- What individual and interpersonal activity results in the formation of cultural norms, values, and social relationships (among other rulelike constructs)?
- What motivates the formation of these constructs?
- What goals do individuals members of cultures pursue in constructing these rules?
- What resources are utilized in the construction of cultural rules?
- What particular characteristics of social interaction result in the formation of various cultural patterns?
- What societal goals are accomplished through the construction of restrictive rules?
- What do societies gain by constructing rules (norms, roles, values) that enable, rather than constrain, future human activity?
- What is the role of time in the process of cultural construction?

Investigating such questions holds the promise of developing cultural theories that are grounded more firmly in a context (e.g., ecology, resources). Furthermore, such theories are more likely to incorporate explicitly temporal elements in describing long-term and historical processes (e.g., norm formation), an attribute that is absent from most current theorizing in mainstream and cross-cultural psychology (Adamopoulos & Kashima, 1999). Finally, "culture-as-construction" approaches complement the more frequent "culture-as-antecedent" perspective in cross-cultural psychology and thus may allow more complete examination of the fundamental notion that culture and psychology constitute each other.

Notes

We are grateful to Christine O'Connor and David Bernstein for helpful comments on portions of this manuscript.

1. In 1968, there was a similar, but smaller, meeting at the East-West Center at the University of Hawaii, Manoa. Led by the late Kenneth Berrien, psychologists from both the United States and several Asian countries convened to discuss research in their respective countries for the purpose of possible collaboration.

References

Adair, J. G. (1992). Empirical studies of indigenization and development of the discipline in developing countries. In S. Iwawaki, Y. Kashima, & K. Leung (Eds.), *Innovations in cross-cultural psychology* (pp. 62–74). Lisse, The Netherlands: Swets & Zeitlinger.

Adamopoulos, J. (1988). Interpersonal behavior: Cross-cultural and historical perspectives. In M. H. Bond (Ed.), *The cross-cultural challenge to social psychology* (pp. 196–207). Newbury Park, CA: Sage.

Adamopoulos, J. (1991). The emergence of interpersonal behavior: Diachronic and cross-cultural processes in the evolution of intimacy. In S. Ting-Toomey & F. Korzenny (Eds.), *Cross-cultural interpersonal communication* (pp. 155–170). Newbury Park, CA: Sage.

Adamopoulos, J. (1994, May). *Culture-common features of context: Toward a general system for the classification of social situations.* Paper presented at the meeting of the Midwestern Psychological Association, Chicago.

Adamopoulos, J. (1999). The emergence of cultural patterns of interpersonal behavior. In J. Adamopoulos & Y. Kashima (Eds.), *Social psychology and cultural context* (pp. 63–76). Thousand Oaks, CA: Sage.

Adamopoulos, J., & Kashima, Y. (1999). Introduction: Subjective culture as a research tradition. In J. Adamopoulos & Y. Kashima (Eds.), *Social psychology and cultural context* (pp. 1–4). Thousand Oaks, CA: Sage.

Berry, J. W. (1997). Preface. In J. W. Berry, Y. H. Poortinga, & J. Pandey (Eds.), *Handbook of cross-cultural psychology: Vol. 1. Theory and method* (pp. x–xv). Boston: Allyn & Bacon.

Berry, J. W. (1999). On the unity of the field of culture and psychology. In J. Adamopoulos & Y. Kashima (Eds.), *Social psychology and cultural context* (pp. 7–15). Thousand Oaks, CA: Sage.

Berry, J. W., Poortinga, Y. H., & Pandey, J. (Eds.). (1997). *Handbook of cross-cultural psychology: Vol. 1. Theory and method.* Boston: Allyn & Bacon.

Berry, J. W., Poortinga, Y. H., Segall, M. H., & Dasen, P. R. (1992). *Cross-cultural psychology: Research and applications.* Cambridge: Cambridge University Press.

Berry, J. W., & Sam, D. (1997). Acculturation and adaptation. In J. W. Berry, M. H. Segall, & C. Kagitcibasi (Eds.), *Handbook of cross-cultural psychology: Vol. 3. Social behavior and applications* (2nd ed., pp. 291–326). Boston: Allyn & Bacon.

Bock, P. K. (Ed.). (1994). *Psychological anthropology.* Westport, CT: Praeger.

Boesch, E. E. (1991). *Symbolic action theory and cultural psychology.* Berlin: Springer-Verlag.

Boesch, E. E. (1996). The seven flaws of cross-cultural psychology: The story of a conversion. *Mind, Culture, and Activity, 1*(3), 2–10.

Brislin, R. W., Lonner, W. J., & Thorndike, R. M. (1973). *Cross-cultural research methods.* New York: Wiley.

Brown, D. E. (1991). *Human universals.* Philadelphia: Temple University Press.

Burr, V. (1995). *An introduction to social constructionism.* London: Routledge.

Buss, D. M. (1989). Sex differences in human mate preferences: Evolutionary hypotheses tested in 37 cultures. *Behavioral and Brain Sciences, 12*, 1–49.

Chung, F. M., & Leung, K. (1998). Indigenous personality measures: Chinese examples. *Journal of Cross-Cultural Psychology, 29*, 233–248.

Church, A. T., & Lonner, W. J. (Eds.). (1998). Personality and its measurement in cross-cultural perspective. *Journal of Cross-Cultural Psychology, 29.*

Cole, M. (1984). The world beyond our borders: What might our students need to know about it? *American Psychologist, 39*, 998–1005.

Cole, M. (1996). *Cultural psychology: A once and future discipline.* Cambridge: Belknap/Harvard.

Cushner, K., & Brislin, R. (1996). *Intercultural interactions: A practical guide* (2nd ed.). Thousand Oaks, CA: Sage.

Davidson, A. R., Jaccard, J., Triandis, H. C., Morales, M. L., & Diaz-Guerrero, R. (1976). Cross-cultural model testing: Toward a solution of the emic-etic dilemma. *International Journal of Psychology, 11*, 1–13.

Eckensberger, L. H., & Zimba, R. (1997). The development of moral judgment. In J. W. Berry, P. R. Dasen, & T. S. Saraswathi (Eds.), *Handbook of cross-cultural psychology: Vol. 2. Basic processes and human development.* Boston, MA: Allyn & Bacon.

Gergen, K. J. (1985). The social constructionist movement in modern psychology. *American Psychologist, 40,* 266–275.

Guanzon-Lapena, M., Church, A. T., Carlota, A. J., & Katigbak, M. S. (1998). Indigenous personality measures: Philippine examples. *Journal of Cross-Cultural Psychology, 29,* 249–270.

Hermans, H. J. M., & Kempen, H. J. G. (1998). Moving cultures: The perilous problems of cultural dichotomies in a globalizing society. *American Psychologist, 53,* 1111–1120.

Hofstede, G. (1980). *Culture's consequences: International differences in work-related values.* Beverly Hills, CA: Sage.

Hsu, F. L. K. (Ed.). (1972). *Psychological anthropology.* Cambridge, MA: Schenkman.

Jahoda, G. (n.d.). *The colour of a chameleon.* Unpublished manuscript.

Jahoda, G. (1970). A cross-cultural perspective in psychology. *Advancement of Science, 27,* 1–14.

Jahoda, G. (1980). Theoretical and systematic approaches in cross-cultural psychology. In H. C. Triandis & J. W. Berry (Eds.), *Handbook of cross-cultural psychology: Vol. 1. Perspectives* (pp. 69–142). Boston: Allyn & Bacon.

Jahoda, G. (1990). Our forgotten ancestors. In R. A. Dienstbier & J. J. Berman (Eds.), *Nebraska symposium on motivation: Vol. 37. Cultural perspectives* (pp. 1–40). Lincoln: University of Nebraska Press.

Jahoda, G., & Krewer, B. (1997). History of cross-cultural and cultural psychology. In J. W. Berry, Y. H. Poortinga, & J. Pandey (Eds.), *Handbook of cross-cultural psychology: Vol. 1. Theory and method* (pp. 1–42). Boston: Allyn & Bacon.

Kim, U. (1995). Psychology, science, and culture: Cross-cultural analysis of national psychologies in developing countries. *International Journal of Psychology, 30,* 663–679.

Kim, U. (1999). After the "crisis" in social psychology: The development of the transactional model of science. *Asian Journal of Social Psychology, 2,* 1–19.

Kim, U., & Berry, J. W. (1993). *Indigenous psychologies: Experience and research in cultural context.* Newbury Park, CA: Sage.

Kim, U., Park, Y.-S., & Park, D. (2000). The challenge of cross-cultural psychology: The role of indigenous psychologies. *Journal of Cross-Cultural Psychology, 31,* 63–75.

Kimble, G. A. (1961). *Hilgard and Marquis' conditioning and learning* (2nd ed.). New York: Appleton-Century-Crofts.

Kimble, G. A. (1984). Psychology's two cultures. *American Psychologist, 39,* 833–839.

Kimble, G. A. (1989). Psychology from the standpoint of a generalist. *American Psychologist, 44,* 491–499.

Klineberg, O. (1980). Historical perspectives: Cross-cultural psychology before 1960. In H. C. Triandis & W. W. Lambert (Eds.), *Handbook of cross-cultural psychology: Vol. 1. Perspectives* (pp. 31–68). Boston: Allyn & Bacon.

Landis, D., & Bhagat, R. (Eds.). (1996). *Handbook of intercultural training* (Vols. 1–3). Elmsford, NY: Pergamon.

Landis, D., & Wasilewski, J. H. (1999). Reflections on 22 years of the *International Journal of Intercultural Relations* and 23 years of other intercultural experience. *International Journal of Intercultural Relations, 23,* 535–574.

Lewin, K. (1951). *Field theory in social science.* New York: Harper & Row.

Lonner, W. J. (1980). The search for psychological universals. In H. C. Triandis & W. W. Lambert (Eds.), *Handbook of cross-cultural psychology: Vol. 1. Perspectives* (pp. 143–204). Boston: Allyn & Bacon.

Lonner, W. J. (1992). Does the association need a name change? *Cross-Cultural Psychology Bulletin, 26,* 1.

Lonner, W. J., & Adamopoulos, J. (1997). Culture as antecedent to behavior. In J. W. Berry, Y. H. Poortinga, & J. Pandey (Eds.), *Handbook of cross-cultural psychology: Vol. 1. Theory and method* (pp. 43–83). Boston: Allyn & Bacon.

Lonner, W. J., & Berry, J. W. (Eds.). (1986). *Field methods in cross-cultural research.* Thousand Oaks, CA: Sage.

Lonner, W. J., Dinnel, D. L., Forgays, D. K., & Hayes, S. A. (Eds.). (1999). *Merging past, present, and future in cross-cultural psychology: Selected papers from the 14th International Congress of the International Association of Cross-Cultural Psychology.* Lisse, The Netherlands: Swets & Zeitlinger.

Malpass, R. S. (1990). An excursion into utilitarian analysis. *Behavior Science Research, 24,* 1–15.

Markus, H. R., & Kitayama, S. (1991). Culture and the self. *Psychological Review, 98,* 224–253.

Matsumoto, D. (1999). Culture and self: An empirical assessment of Markus and Kitayama's theory of independent and interdependent self-construals. *Asian Journal of Social Psychology, 2,* 289–310.

McClelland, D. C. (1961). *The achieving society.* Princeton, NJ: Van Nostrand.

McClelland, D. C., & Winter, D. (1969). *Motivating economic achievement.* New York: Free Press.

McCrae, R. R., & Costa, P. T., Jr. (1997). More reasons to adopt the five-factor model. *American Psychologist, 44,* 451–452.

McCrae, R. R., Costa, P. T., del Pilar, G. H., Rolland, J.-P., & Parker, W. D. (1998). Cross-cultural assessment of the five-factor model: The Revised NEO Personality Inventory. *Journal of Cross-Cultural Psychology, 29,* 171–188.

Miller, J. G. (1994). Cultural diversity in the morality of caring: Individually oriented versus duty-based interpersonal moral codes. *Cross-Cultural Research, 28,* 3–39.

Miller, J. G. (1997). Theoretical issues in cultural psychology. In J. W. Berry, Y. H. Poortinga, & J. Pandey (Eds.), *Handbook of cross-cultural psychology: Vol. 1. Theory and method* (pp. 85–128). Boston: Allyn & Bacon.

Misra, G., & Gergen, K. J. (1993). On the place of culture in psychological science. *International Journal of Psychology, 28,* 225–243.

Moghaddam, F. (1987). Psychology in the three worlds: As reflected in the crisis in social psychology and the move toward indigenous Third World psychology. *American Psychologist, 42,* 912–920.

Osgood, C. E., May, W. H., & Miron, M. S. (1975). *Cross-cultural universals of affective meaning.* Urbana, IL: University of Illinois Press.

Pedersen, P. P., Draguns, J. G., Lonner, W. J., & Trimble, J. E. (Eds.). (1996). *Counseling across cultures* (4th ed.). Newbury Park, CA: Sage.

Poortinga, Y. H. (1990). Towards a conceptualization of culture for psychology. *Cross-Cultural Psychology Bulletin, 24*(3), 2–10.

Poortinga, Y. H., & Pandey, J. (1997). Introduction to volume 1. In J. W. Berry, Y. H. Poortinga, & J. Pandey (Eds.), *Handbook of cross-cultural psychology: Vol. 1. Theory and method* (pp. xxii–xxv). Boston: Allyn & Bacon.

Rivers, W. H. R. (1901). Introduction and vision. In A. C. Haddon (Ed.), *Reports of the Cambridge anthropological expedition to the Torres Straits: Vol. 2, Pt. 1.* Cambridge: Cambridge University Press.

Schwartz, S. H. (1994). Are there universal aspects in the structure and contents of human values? *Journal of Social Issues, 50*(4), 19–45.

Segall, M. H., Dasen, P. R., Berry, J. W., & Poortinga, Y. H. (1999). *Human behavior in global perspective: An introduction to cross-cultural psychology* (2nd ed.). Boston: Allyn & Bacon.

Segall, M. H., Lonner, W. J., & Berry, J. W. (1998). Cross-cultural psychology as a scholarly discipline: On the flowering of culture in behavioral research. *American Psychologist, 53,* 1101–1110.

Sell, J., & Martin, M. (1983). An acultural perspective on experimental social psychology. *Personality and Social Psychology Bulletin, 9,* 345–350.

Sherif, M., & Sherif, C. (1964). *Reference groups.* New York: Harper & Row.

Shwayder, D. S. (1965). *The stratification of behaviour.* London: Routledge & Kegan Paul.

Shweder, R. A. (1986). Divergent rationalities. In D. W. Fiske & R. A. Shweder (Eds.), *Metatheory in social science: Pluralisms and subjectivities* (pp. 163–196). Chicago: University of Chicago Press.

Shweder, R. A. (1990). Cultural psychology—What is it? In J. W. Stigler, R. A. Shweder, & G. Herdt (Eds.), *Cultural psychology: Essays on human cognitive development* (pp. 1–43). New York: Cambridge University Press.

Shweder, R. A. (1996). *Quanta* and *qualia*: What is the "object" of ethnographic method? In R. Jessor, A. Colby, & R. A. Shweder (Eds.), *Ethnography and human development: Context and meaning in social inquiry* (pp. 175–182). Chicago: University of Chicago Press.

Shweder, R. A., Much, N. C., Mahapatra, M., & Park, L. (1997). The "big three" of morality (autonomy, community, divinity) and the "big three" explanations of suffering. In A. M. Brandt & P. Rozin (Eds.), *Morality and health* (pp. 119–169). New York: Routledge.

Sinha, D. (1997). Indigenizing psychology. In J. W. Berry, Y. H. Poortinga, & J. Pandey (Eds.), *Handbook of cross-cultural psychology: Vol. 1. Theory and method* (pp. 129–169). Boston: Allyn & Bacon.

Triandis, H. C. (1972). *The analysis of subjective culture.* New York: Wiley.

Triandis, H. C. (1980). Values, attitudes and interpersonal behavior. In H. E. Howe & M. M. Page (Eds.), *Nebraska symposium on motivation, 1979* (pp. 195–260). Lincoln: University of Nebraska Press.

Triandis, H. C. (1993). Collectivism and individualism as cultural syndromes. *Cross-Cultural Research, 27,* 155–180.

Triandis, H. C. (1995). *Individualism and collectivism.* Boulder, CO: Westview Press.

Triandis, H. C. (1997, July). *Cross-cultural versus cultural psychology: A synthesis?* Paper presented at the Conference of the International Council of Psychologists, Padua, Italy.

Triandis, H. C., Lambert, W. W., Berry, J. W., Lonner, W. J., Brislin, R., Heron, A., & Draguns, J. (Eds.). (1980). *Handbook of cross-cultural psychology* (Vols. 1–6). Boston, MA: Allyn & Bacon.

Van de Vijver, F. J. R., & Leung, K. (1997). *Methods*

and data analysis for cross-cultural research. Thousand Oaks, CA: Sage.

Whiting, B. B., & Whiting, J. W. M. (1975). *Children of six cultures: A psycho-cultural analysis.* Cambridge, MA: Harvard University Press.

Williams, J. E., Satterwaite, R. C., & Saiz, J. L. (1998). *The importance of psychological traits: A cross-cultural study.* New York: Plenum.

Witkin, H. A., & Berry, J. W. (1975). Psychological research in cross-cultural perspective. *Journal of Cross-Cultural Psychology, 6,* 4–82.

Wundt, W. (1900–1920). *Volkerpsychologie* (Vols. 1–10). Leipzig: Englemann. *Elements of folk psychology.* London: Allen & Unwin, 1916.]

3

Individualism and Collectivism

Past, Present, and Future

HARRY C. TRIANDIS

No construct has had a greater impact on contemporary cross-cultural psychology than individualism and collectivism (IC). Students of culture have used it to understand, explain, and predict cultural similarities and differences across a wide variety of human behavior. Particularly in the last two decades, the IC construct has gained widespread attention as arguably the most important dimension of psychological culture to have emerged in the literature.

In this chapter, Triandis, widely acknowledged to be one of the founding fathers of the modern cross-cultural psychology movement and the leading proponent of the IC construct, gives us insight into the construct in terms of its utility as an explanatory concept. He provides a historical perspective on the development and treatment of the IC construct, including a personal account of how he became convinced of its power. He reviews some of the current state of research on these constructs and demonstrates the utility and applicability of IC to understand, explain, and predict cultural similarities and differences in a wide range of psychological functioning. This review is priceless and summarizes in a few short pages the wealth of information amassed in this area of culture and psychology over a few decades.

At the same time, another message that can be gleaned from this review is that perhaps the field has amassed enough "facts" about IC differences in human behavior. The continued accumulation of similar types of studies—essentially examining cross-national differences in behavior, with researchers making key assumptions about IC differences underlying the countries tested—may be less important for the field now. Indeed, what may be more important as we open the new century is a qualitative evolution in our understanding of IC and the methods that we use to test it and other cultural constructs.

In the second half of the chapter, Triandis helps us envision this evolution by presenting his ideas about the theoretical framework for thinking about the IC construct. By focusing on two cultural "syndromes"—complexity-simplicity and tightness-looseness—Triandis reviews the basic tenets of his theory about the determinants of IC. Recognizing that these ideas are yet to be tested formally, they provide future students and researchers of culture with an important platform with which to test the possible origins of IC as a cultural syndrome.

In discussing the measurement of the IC construct, Triandis compares and contrasts the methodological differences associated with the two approaches to studying culture, the cross-cultural approach and the cultural psychology approach. In sync with the overall message of Adamopolous and Lonner in chapter 2, Triandis argues that the methods of both need to be merged in future studies if IC, or any other cultural construct for that matter, is truly to contribute to the development of a universal psychology, which should be the ultimate goal of cross-cultural and mainstream psychologists alike. Methods in cultural psychology that focus on the development of culture within a culture across time—an essentially emic approach—need to be blended with the methods of cross-cultural psychology, with its focus on reliability, validity, and avoidance of researcher bias, which is inherently an etic approach. To the extent that such rapprochement, in the terms of Adamopolous and Lonner, is possible, they undoubtedly will contribute to the continued development and incorporation of cultural findings into mainstream psychological theories.

Triandis ends his chapter by issuing a challenge to all researchers—mainstream and cultural—in noting that psychologists often ignore culture because it is a complication that makes their work more time consuming and difficult. Given that humans may have an inherent tendency toward expending the least amount of effort possible in an endeavor, Triandis suggests that psychologists will need to reject the principle of least effort and its consequences if a universal psychology is to be created and developed. These challenges, not only in terms of methodology and scientific philosophy, but also in terms of possible human nature, need to be addressed if cross-cultural psychology, and the IC construct as well, will evolve in a qualitatively different fashion to achieve its goal of realizing a universal psychology, a message consistent with the rest of the book.

The constructs of individualism and collectivism have become very popular in cross-cultural psychology (see M. H. Bond & Smith, 1996; Smith & Bond, 1999) and are beginning to have a large impact on social psychology. For example, Smith and Bond made much use of the constructs in their social psychology text.

Collectivist cultures emphasize the interdependence of every human and some collectives (e.g., family, tribe, nation). Individualist cultures emphasize that people are independent of their groups. The key ideas of the constructs of individualism and collectivism, at least from my perspective, were presented in Triandis (1995). The constructs were defined by four attributes: the definition of the self as independent (in individualism) or interdependent (in collectivism), the primacy of personal or ingroup goals, the primary emphasis on attitudes or norms as the determinants of social behavior, and the importance of exchange or communal relationships (Mills & Clark, 1982).

In addition, each individualist or collectivist culture is likely to have unique aspects. For instance, Korean collectivism is not the same as the collectivism of the Israeli kibbutz. Triandis (1994) presented some 60 attributes that may distinguish different kinds of collectivism. For example, spirited argument within the in-group is seen as undesirable in many East Asian collectivist cultures, where harmony within the in-group is a strong value, but is perfectly acceptable in Mediterranean collectivist cultures.

One of the more important attributes that distinguishes different kinds of individualism and collectivism is the acceptance of a horizontal or vertical perspective. Horizontal cultures emphasize equality; vertical cultures emphasize hierarchy. Thus, horizontal individualism (HI) is characterized by emphasis on "all people are equal" but "each person is unique." Vertical individualism (VI) reflects both being distinct and "the best" in relation to others, as well as being different from others. College students in the United States are annoyed when an experimenter characterizes them as "average" (Weldon, 1984), suggesting that they see themselves as better than average. That is a vertical individualist tendency. Horizontal collectivism (HC) is characterized by merging the self into the in-group, but there is no suggestion that members of the in-group are different from each other in status. Vertical collectivism (VC), on the other hand, accepts hierarchy. In-group authorities have more status than ordinary members of the in-group. VC especially emphasizes the sacrifice of the individual for the preservation of the in-group.

The constructs are most important in understanding the way culture, as a system of shared meanings (Triandis, 1994; Triandis, Bontempo, Leung, & Hui, 1990), has an impact on perception and behavior.

This chapter begins with a personal account of why I became involved in the study of these constructs. Then, I cover some of the history of the use of the constructs.

Next, I review some of the current state of research on these constructs. I mention a theoretical framework for thinking about these constructs, which at this time is relatively speculative because the empirical support for it is meager. Nevertheless, I present it because it can provide a guide to future research on the constructs. Of course, such future research will depend on how we measure the constructs, so I review problems of the measurement of the constructs. At that point, I review problems of measurement. Next, I examine some major differences in the way researchers deal with the construct of culture in psychology. Especially important is the perspective of cultural psychology as opposed to cross-cultural psychology. I show that collectivism and individualism have some relevance for understanding why some psychologists prefer one methodology and others another methodology for the study of the relationship of culture and psychology.

Next, I discuss some promising future research that uses the collectivism and individualist constructs. Finally, I speculate about the future of the study of culture and psychology, paying some attention to the way individualism and collectivism will be implicated in such studies.

Personal Involvement with the Constructs

As a social psychologist, I have been very conscious of the fact that almost all the data of social psychology come from individualist cultures. Yet, the overwhelming majority of humans live in collectivist cultures. I grew up in Greece when it was a collectivist culture; thus, very often while I examined social psychology studies, I had the reaction that this "does not make sense in traditional Greece." Subsequent cross-cultural work has shown, for instance, that emphasis on cognitive consistency is a Western attribute, and people in Asia are not bothered very much by cognitive inconsistency (Fiske, Kitayama, Markus, & Nisbett, 1998). For example, an Indian friend says that he is a "veg-

etarian who eats meat." Americans find this category impossible; one can either be a vegetarian or not a vegetarian. But, my Indian friend says, "I am a vegetarian, but when others eat meat, I eat meat." Note the importance of the situation as a determinant of behavior and the tolerance of cognitive inconsistency in the case of collectivists.

Early in my career I felt that if cognitive dissonance theory does not make sense in some parts of Europe, it probably does not make sense in most parts of the world. Since I was dissatisfied with many of the findings of social psychology, I started studying other cultures. In the 1960s, I studied differences among Greece, India, Japan, and the United States (Triandis, 1972). There were many scattered findings that needed a theoretical framework for integration. When I reviewed the manuscript of Hofstede's (1980) book in 1978, I enthusiastically recommended its publication and saw the individualism-collectivism (IC) topic as the missing theoretical framework.

As I reviewed the literature about cultural differences even more broadly, it became apparent that IC had implications for understanding many empirical findings (Triandis, 1988, 1989, 1990, 1993, 1994, 1995, 1996). It was also central for training people to interact effectively with members of other cultures (Bhawuk, 1998; Triandis, Brislin, & Hui, 1988). As discussed below, it may even explain the behavior of psychologists who study the relationship of culture and psychology.

History of the Constructs

The constructs have been used by political philosophers for 300 years (see Triandis, 1995, chapter 2) and by social scientists for about a century. The French sociologist Durkheim (1893/1984) distinguished *mechanical solidarity* (similar to collectivism) from *organic solidarity* (similar to individualism). The first term referred to relationships that are based on common bonds and obligations; the latter term referred to relationships that are contractual. Similarly, the terms *Gemeinschaft* (community) and *Gesellschaft* (society) in German sociology or relational versus individualistic value orientation in anthropology have been used for some time. There is evidence that individualism emerged in England around the 12th century (see Triandis, 1995, chapter 2), although some have argued that it was already present among some of the ancient Greek philosophers (Skoyles, 1998).

Hofstede (1980) worked with the responses of IBM employees (117,000 protocols), covering a wide variety of occupations and demographic variables in 66 countries. He summed the responses of the subjects from each country to several value items and conducted a factor analysis of the mean responses to each of the value items based on a sample size of 40 (the number of countries with enough employees to provide stable means). He identified four factors in his study and called one of them Collectivism-Individualism. The other three factors, Power Distance, Masculinity-Femininity, and Uncertainty Avoidance, have received relatively little attention in the social science literature.

Note that Hofstede's work (1980) was done at the ecological or cultural level of analysis. That is, he summed the responses of N_i individuals in each culture to each of the n items of his survey and obtained as many means as items in each culture. Then, he factor analyzed the data across $k = 40$ cultures, that is, with 40 observations per variable. The results indicated that collectivism was the opposite of individualism. That conclusion is not obtained when we do analyses at the individual level. Here, we correlate the n by n variables based on N_i observations per variable in k different within-culture analyses. Another possibility is to do a pancultural factor analysis. In that case, the n times N_i observations per variable are used to obtain the k by k matrix of correlations, which is then factor analyzed. This solution has some technical problems, so Leung and Bond (1989) proposed a method, too complicated to discuss here, that does take care of some of these problems.

The within-culture analyses show that individualism and collectivism are not opposites. They must be conceived as multidimensional constructs. These analyses identified several psychological processes that are independent of each other and yet correspond to individualism and collectivism (Hui, 1988; Hui & Triandis, 1986; Triandis et al., 1986; Triandis, Bontempo, Villareal, Asai, & Lucca, 1988; Triandis, Leung, Villareal, & Clack, 1985). Specifically, individualism is often related to competition, self-reliance, emotional distance from in-groups, and hedonism; collectivism is often related to high family integrity (e.g., agreement with the statements "Children should not leave home until they get married" and "Parents should live

with their children until they die"), small distance from in-groups (e.g., feeling honored when an in-group member is honored), and high sociability and interdependence.

Later work has shown that self-reliance is also very high among some collectivists, but it has a different meaning: While individualists think of self-reliance as "being able to do my own thing," collectivists think of self-reliance as "not being a burden on my in-group." Thus, it is best not to include self-reliance in the constructs.

A basic difference across cultures in the relationship of individuals to in-groups was emphasized by Triandis, Bontempo, et al. (1988). Collectivists usually have one or two in-groups and are deeply (intimately) interrelated to them; individualists have very many in-groups, but their relationships to them are superficial, and they keep them only as long as "it pays to keep them," so they drop in-groups as soon as "better" in-groups are identified. For example, they work for one company, but if they get a better offer from the competitor of that company, they do not hesitate to join the competitor company. This aspect of the cultural construct has been verified in several investigations (for a review, see Earley & Gibson, 1998, p. 271).

Current State of Research on Constructs

Triandis (1972) found that traditional Greeks behave very differently toward their in-groups (people who are concerned with my welfare) and out-groups (strangers). Americans, on the other hand, do not behave so differently toward in-groups (people who are like me, especially in their attitudes and values) and their out-groups (strangers). This is probably a general pattern among collectivists and individualists. In fact, when collectivists meet another person, the first thought they are likely to have is, "What is my relationship with that person?" If the relationship permits classification in the in-group, they are likely to behave very positively—cooperating, supporting, going out of their way to help. If the other person is classified as an out-group member, they are likely to be indifferent or even hostile. Such sharp differentiation of in-group and out-group is not found among individualists. An example may help. I noticed that when I called the office of a relative or friend in traditional Greece, the secretary answered very harshly: "What do you want?" As soon as I established my relationship with her boss, she switched to being very polite. By contrast, American secretaries are polite no matter who calls.

Meta-analyses of studies that have used the Asch paradigm have shown that collectivism is related to conformity (R. Bond & Smith, 1996). Sacrifice for the in-group is also related to acceptance of instructions by in-group authorities and is correlated about .40 with right-wing authoritarianism (Triandis & Gelfand, 1998).

In addition, collectivist in-groups may be larger than individualist in-groups. For example, Sugimoto (1998) discusses when apologies are necessary in Japan and in the United States. The Japanese apologize about the actions of many more people. For example, when three Japanese terrorists massacred several passengers at Lod Airport in Israel, many Japanese youth visited the Israeli embassy to apologize for the incident, the president of the University of Kyoto bowed low to apologize for the fact that two of the terrorists had attended his university, the Japanese minister of education apologized for the shortcomings of the Japanese educational system, the foreign minister of Japan spoke of the dishonor to the nation, and the Japanese ambassador to Israel appeared on television and burst into tears at the end of his apology.

Individualist (e.g., American) in-groups are narrower. Americans might apologize for their own actions and the actions of a spouse, child, or pet, but rarely about the actions of unknown Americans. Of course, the U.S. government apologizes when a member of the U.S. military commits a crime, but the military are part of the government. The form of the apology is also different. Normally, American apologies are personal, while Japanese apologies are relational (e.g., "We have been friends for 20 years, and this terrible thing happened that is totally inexcusable").

Triandis (1995) argued that each society has its own type of predominant horizontal or vertical individualism or collectivism. For instance, Sweden has a horizontal individualist culture, U.S. corporate culture is vertical individualist, the culture of the Israeli kibbutz is horizontal collectivist, and an Indian village culture is vertical collectivist.

Taking into account the fact that results obtained at the cultural level of analysis are not always consistent with results obtained at the individual level of analysis, Triandis et al. (1985) introduced the terms *idiocentric* and *allocentric* for individual level analyses that correspond to individualism and collectivism at the cultural level, respectively.

Allocentric means a person who is paying attention to other people. An example may be useful. Triandis and Vassiliou (1972) asked Greek and American personnel directors to judge the files of a set of applicants for a position in an organization. The files manipulated systematically the letters of recommendation in the file, as well as objective attributes of the applicants. They found that Greek personnel directors paid more attention to the letters of recommendation than did American personnel directors. In short, they were more allocentric than the Americans. *Idiocentrics* pay principal attention to internal attributes, such as their own beliefs, emotions, and the like rather than to inputs from other people. Smith and Bond (1999) utilized this terminology in their text and also provided examples when results at the cultural level of analysis differed from results at the individual level of analysis.

The horizontal and vertical aspects of individualism and collectivism of Triandis (1995) do have relationships with Hofstede's work. The vertical aspect is related conceptually to Hofstede's (1980) power distance. Triandis (1994) has discussed tight-loose societies. That construct is related conceptually to Hofstede's uncertainty avoidance.

Triandis et al. (1986) replicated some of Hofstede's results related to individualism and collectivism with 15 samples from different parts of the world. Others, such as M. H. Bond (1988), working with the values of college students in 21 countries, have found factor-analytic results that were similar to those of Hofstede.

Triandis (1995) also suggested that HI, VI, HC, and VC should be conceived as "tools" that individuals utilize in different combinations, depending on the situation. So, an individual is likely to use all these tools, but across situations, the individual may behave predominantly like a horizontal or vertical idiocentric or allocentric.

The evidence that humans sample both collectivist and individualist cognitions can be seen in certain studies. For instance, Verma and Triandis (1998) found that people in an Indian sample selected HI responses 24% of the time, HC responses 28% of the time, VI responses 23% of the time, and VC responses 25% of the time, which contrasted with those in an Illinois sample, who sampled HI 38%, HC 26%, VI 23%, and VC responses 13% of the time. Clearly, the large differences were in

HI (Americans higher than the Indians) and VC (Indians higher than Americans). Since large samples were used in this study, even a 2% difference is reliable statistically, so that the above differences are extraordinarily reliable. In that study, which also presented data from Australia, Japan, Hong Kong, Korea, Greece, Germany, and the Netherlands, Germany had the most individualistic profile (HI = 43%, HC = 27%, VI = 20%, VC = 10%), while Hong Kong had the most collectivist profile (HI = 25%, HC = 36%, VI = 20%, VC = 19%). These percentages are important because they tell us that a culture should not be characterized as individualist or collectivist. That kind of characterization is simplistic. We need to examine the probabilities that different elements will be sampled. Certainly, Germany is more individualistic than Hong Kong, but even in Germany, people select collectivist cognitions 37% of the time, and in Hong Kong, they select individualist cognitions 45% of the time.

Situations are likely to shift these percentages. For example, when the in-group is under threat, most idiocentrics will activate allocentric cognitions. When the individual is alone, individualist cognitions are more likely. Trafimow, Triandis, and Goto (1991) found that instructing individuals to think for 2 minutes about what makes them the same as their family and friends results in responses that are more collectivist; instructing them to think for 2 minutes of what makes them different from their family and friends results in responses that are more individualist. Collectivist responses are those that reflect "social content" when people complete 20 sentences that begin with "I am . . ." For example, "I am an uncle" or "I am a member of the Communist Party" are collectivist responses. "I am kind" or "I am responsible" are not collectivist responses since they do not have obvious social or group (e.g., family) connotations. Illinois students of European background, randomly assigned to the "think common" and "think different" instructions mentioned above, completed the "I am . . ." sentences with 23% and 7% social content, respectively. Illinois students with Chinese names doing the same task provided 52% and 30% social responses, respectively, to the "I am . . ." task. In short, both the culture of the participants and the instructions were highly significant factors in determining the percentage of collectivist responses.

In social situations in which harmony, cooperation, and having fun are stressed, there is an emphasis on equality and hence on horizontal relationships. Inequality creates stresses, envy, and resentment. On the other hand, situations that stress competition, or that require subordination of the goals of most people to the goals of an authority, result in vertical relations. Limited resources are more likely to result in vertical than in horizontal relationships.

Differences between Idiocentrics and Allocentrics

A vast body of empirical research has developed that shows differences between idiocentrics and allocentrics. For example, the values of allocentrics emphasize tradition and conformity, while the values of idiocentrics emphasize hedonism, stimulation, and self-direction (Schwartz, 1990, 1992, 1994). At the cultural level of analysis, the values contrast conservatism (e.g., national security, family security) with autonomy (e.g., pleasure, creativity) (Schwartz, 1994).

Idiocentrics make internal attributions more often than allocentrics, who tend to make external attributions (Al-Zahrani & Kaplowitz, 1993; Morris & Peng, 1994; Na & Loftus, 1998; Newman, 1993). Allocentrics use the context (the situation) when they make attributions more than do idiocentrics (Miller, 1984).

This even appears in the way people from individualist and collectivist cultures view treaties and in how they negotiate. The Chinese, for instance, saw the treaty concerning Hong Kong's status that had been signed by Britain and China in 1897 in a historical context, and thus they did not see it as valid because it was imposed after Britain won the Opium War. Obviously, imposing opium on another country is immoral, so the treaty was not valid. The British saw the treaty's content only: A treaty is a treaty. Context has nothing to do with it.

Collectivists use action verbs (e.g., he offered to help) rather than state verbs (e.g., he is helpful). This is because they prefer to use context in their communications. Zwier (1997), in four studies, obtained support for this cultural difference. She found that the accounts of events given by Turkish and Dutch students showed this difference. She analyzed the contents of radio commentaries of Turkish and Dutch radio personalities and found the same difference. She asked Turkish and Dutch students to write a letter requesting a favor, and analyzed the content of letters. She examined the writing of Turkish/Dutch bilingual individuals when writing in the two languages and again found the same pattern.

Individualist cultures have languages that require the use of "I" and "you." (Kashima & Kashima, 1998). English is a good example. It would be difficult to write a letter in English without the use of these words; collectivist cultures have languages that do not require their use. Individualists are very positive about "me" and "we," while collectivists are sometimes ambivalent about "me," but very positive about "we" (Hetts, Sakuma, & Pelham, 1999).

Idiocentrics tend to have a very good opinion of themselves and to be self-enhancing, while allocentrics tend to be modest (Kitayama, Markus, Matsumoto, & Narasakkunkit, 1997). For example, when asked if they are "better than average" on some desirable trait, 80% to 90% of idiocentrics indicate that they are better than average, which is a mathematical impossibility. Idiocentrics select goals that fit their personal needs, while allocentrics pay more attention to the needs of others. Idiocentrics are more likely to display social loafing than allocentrics (Earley, 1989). Social loafing is the phenomenon that when n people work together, they do not produce n times as much output. Some people let others do the work and free ride. This is common among idiocentrics, but not among allocentrics working with in-group members. Idiocentrics also work better alone than with in-group members (Earley, 1993) and work best if they have a choice in what activities they will undertake (Iyengar & Lepper, 1999). On the other hand, allocentrics work well if they work with in-group members and also if their goals are set by respected members of their in-group. Idiocentrics are motivated by individual factors, while allocentrics are motivated by social factors (Yu & Yang, 1994). Pearson and Stephan (1998) reported that Brazilians were more collectivist than Americans and expressed more concern for the outcomes of others than did Americans, while Americans focused on their own outcomes. Brazilians, as expected from theory, made more of a distinction between in-group and out-group in their negotiations than did Americans. When making judgments about morality, allocentrics see more situations that require a person to help another person than do idiocentrics (Miller, 1994).

Harmony is an important value among many allocentrics. Thus, allocentrics expect social situations to be pleasant and to have few negative elements. Triandis, Marin, Lisansky, and Betancourt (1984) examined data from Hispanic and non-Hispanic sample groups and found that the Hispanics, relative to the non-Hispanics, anticipated higher probabilities of positive behaviors and lower probabilities of negative behaviors occurring in most social situations. They called this the *simpatia* cultural script. A person who wants to be "simpatico" (agreeable, pleasant, attractive, noncritical) would behave that way.

In social perception, allocentrics are most likely to perceive groups and their relationships; idiocentrics are most likely to perceive individuals. Thus, for example, during the Kosovo crisis, Russian and Serbian television focused on the bombing and had no images of the refugees. Conversely, Western television had much information about the refugees (individual stories, etc.) and relatively little about the confrontation of Serbia and NATO. In collectivist cultures, people insult others by insulting their in-group (e.g., "Your mother is a prostitute"), while in individualist cultures, they insult the person (e.g., "You are stupid") (Semin & Rubini, 1990).

Allocentrics in most cultures tend to be more sensitive to social rejection, lower in uniqueness, and higher in affiliation than idiocentrics. These data were collected in Japan, Korea, and the United States (Yamaguchi, Kuhlman, & Sugimori, 1995). Allocentrics are also more likely to feel embarrassed (Singelis & Sharkey, 1995). Research by Moskowitz, Suh, and Desaulniers (1994) suggests that idiocentrics are more dominant than allocentrics, and allocentrics are more agreeable than idiocentrics. Collectivists tend to change themselves to fit in rather than try to change the environment, while individualists try to change the environment rather than themselves (Diaz-Guerrero, 1979; Weisz, Rothbaum, & Blackburn, 1984). Collectivists usually establish intimate and long-term relationships (Verma, 1992). Individualists usually establish nonintimate and short-term relationships.

When resources are distributed, they may be distributed according to at least three principles: equality, need, or each person's contribution (equity). The general finding is that, when allocating in equal status situations, allocentrics who exchange with in-group members use equality and need more often than equity, but when they exchange with out-group members, they use equity. However, when the goal is to maximize productivity, even allocentrics working with in-groups use equity (Chen, 1995). Chen, Meindl, and Hui (1998) found that, in both the

United States and Hong Kong, when the goal was productivity or fairness, equity was used; when the goal was interdependence and solidarity, equality was used. In Hong Kong, the more allocentric the individual, the more equality was used; in the United States, there was no relationship between allocentrism and preference for equality.

On the other hand, idiocentrics use equity in most exchanges. Leung (1997) reviewed several empirical studies and concluded that, in general, in equal status situations, equality is preferred in collectivist cultures and equity in individualist cultures. Equality is associated with solidarity, harmony, and cohesion, so it fits the values of collectivists. On the other hand, equity is compatible with productivity, competition, and self-gain, so it fits the values of individualists.

Some collectivists even show a generosity rule when exchanging with in-group members. That is, they use equality even when their input or contribution is clearly higher than the contribution of other members. However, in the case of Chinese participants, the generosity rule applied only when the reward to be divided was fixed. When the reward was unlimited, there was a departure from the equality norm among both Chinese and U.S. participants (Hui, Triandis, & Yee, 1991).

Comparisons of individuals in Sweden and the United States showed that the Swedes followed the equality norm more than the need norm and least often followed the equity norm (Toernblum, Jonsson, & Foa, 1985). Chen, Chen, and Meindl (1998) extrapolated from these observations and suggested that, in individualist cultures, equity-based reward allocation will be correlated positively with cooperation in both short- and long-term work relationships, while in collectivist cultures, equity-based allocations will be correlated positively with cooperation in short-term relations, but equality-based systems will be related positively to cooperation in long-term work relations. These are very promising hypotheses that should be tested.

There is strong evidence that individualists prefer individual rewards and collectivists prefer group-based compensation practices (see Earley & Gibson, 1998, p. 284 for a review). In horizontal collectivist cultures, egalitarian rewards are best; in vertical individualist cultures, allocations based on proportional contributions (equity) are most effective.

Erez (1997) suggests that the principle of equality will be used more in horizontal cultures and equity more in vertical cultures. In the case of horizontal cultures, profit sharing, gain sharing, low salary differentials, and fringe benefits will be stressed. In the case of vertical individualist cultures, employees will receive individual incentives, and high salary differentials will be common. In horizontal collectivist cultures, equality of distribution of organizational rewards will be common. In the case of vertical collectivism, those at the top will be paid much better than those at the bottom, but group-based rewards may be used. In general, individual rewards are appreciated more by idiocentrics than by allocentrics, and group rewards, such as profit sharing, are appreciated more by allocentrics than by idiocentrics, but across many cultures rewarding *both* individual and group performance is optimal. This was also the recent experience of China (Wang, 1994).

Collectivists use indirect and face-saving communications more than individualists (Holtgraves, 1997; Hu, 1944). This means that E-mail will be less satisfying to collectivists since they will not have access to the context (gestures, eye contact, body placement, distance between bodies). Horizontal individualists will E-mail individuals more than groups, while vertical collectivists will E-mail groups more than individuals. Horizontal individualists will send their communications in any direction, while vertical collectivists will send mostly vertical communications.

Horizontal collectivists share information with in-group members, but do not communicate with out-group members. That is very undesirable from the point of view of organizations since key pieces of information are not available to some groups. Vertical collectivists limit the information they send to only some "important" people. Vertical collectivists can be abusive in their communications to low-status individuals and apparently can get away with such abuse (M. H. Bond, Wan, Leung, & Giacalone, 1985). Bad news is sent to the top less often by vertical collectivists than by horizontal collectivists.

Lin (1997) points out that ambiguity in communication can be very helpful in a vertical collectivist culture such as China, where clarity may result in sanctions. In short, one cannot point out to an official that he is wrong! One may do it very indirectly, but then there is the possibility of retaliation. The Chinese, he indicates, admire people who are frank, such as Judge Bao (p. 369), but do not emulate them.

In short, East Asian collectivists are expected to "read the other's mind" during communication, so that communication is quite indirect and depends on hints, gestures, level and tone of voice, body orientation, use of the eyes, and distance between the bodies. For example, in some collectivist cultures, serving tea and bananas means that the server disapproves of something that the other person is proposing. Since bananas are not served with tea when there is a good relationship, serving them with tea has a definite indirect meaning.

By contrast, many individualists say what is on their mind, even if the consequence is that the relationship is hurt. As a result, Chen et al. (1998) extrapolate that face-to-face communication will evoke higher levels of cooperation in collectivist cultures than in individualist cultures, while mediated partial communication (e.g., via electronic, paper means) will evoke higher levels of cooperation in individualist cultures than in collectivist cultures.

Leadership concepts are also quite different in collectivist and individualist cultures. Collectivists accept paternalism and emphasize the importance of the nurturance of the leader (House, Wright, & Aditya, 1997; Sinha, 1980, 1996). Individualists are often opposed to paternalism. Collectivists, at least in East Asia, tend to seek harmony and avoid conflict within the in-group. For example, Trubinsky, Ting-Toomey, and Lin (1991) compared Taiwanese and U.S. respondents and found that, in conflict situations, the former were more likely than the latter to use obliging, avoiding, integrating, and compromising styles of conflict resolution as opposed to a confrontational style.

Theoretical Perspectives

Triandis (1994) identified three kinds of cultural syndromes. A *cultural syndrome* is a shared pattern of beliefs, attitudes, self-definitions, norms, roles, and values organized around a theme. The first syndrome is *complexity-simplicity* and contrasts information societies with hunters and food gatherers. The second is *tightness-looseness*. Tight societies have many norms about social behavior, and people are punished severely when norms are disregarded. Loose societies have relatively few norms, and members of the society tolerate deviations from norms. *Individualism and collectivism* is the third cultural syndrome.

Triandis (1994) presented a theory about the determinants of individualism and collectivism: Collectivism is maximal in tight and simple cultures; individualism is maximal in complex and loose cultures. This theory has yet to be tested empirically, although measurements of tightness are in progress so that it can be tested in the near future.

It is possible to discover cultural syndromes. For example, if we present an element of subjective culture to groups of people who speak a particular language and ask them to make a judgment (e.g., Is this value important?), if they make this judgment as a group very quickly, say in less than 2 seconds, and if 90% of the groups that we study do the same, then we know that the judgment is shared widely, and thus it is an element of culture (Triandis et al., 1990). If many of these elements are organized around a theme, such as the importance of the individual (individualism) or the collective (collectivism), then we have identified a cultural syndrome.

The theory also states that complexity is associated with affluence and the size of settlements; tightness is associated with cultural homogeneity and activity interdependence. Looseness is found in societies that are at the intersection of many cultures (so that there are two or more normative systems present, and the individual has to tolerate deviations from any one normative system), or where population density is very low, so that what people do many miles away does not affect the in-group very much.

Prevalence of the Constructs

Individualism is found in affluent societies (Hofstede, 1980), especially if there are several normative systems (as happens at the intersection of many cultures or in some urban [Freeman, submitted], multicultural, cosmopolitan societies), in which case the individual has to decide whether to act according to one or another normative system. It is also high among the upper classes and professionals in any society (Freeman, submitted; Kohn, 1969; Marshall, 1997), among those who migrated (Gerganov, Dilova, Petkova, & Paspalanova, 1996) or were socially mobile, and among those who have been most exposed to mass media from the United States (McBride, 1998). Content analyses of soap operas made in the United States show that the major themes are individualist, and the focus is rarely on collectivist themes, such as doing one's duty. Among nonliterate societies, individualism is relatively high among hunters and gatherers, for whom conformity is not especially functional, while collectivism is common in agricultural societies, in which cooperation is highly functional. For instance, no individual can construct an irrigation system; harvesting requires the coordination of actions.

Marshall (1997) found that social class provided a stronger contrast than the difference between the cultures of Indonesia and New Zealand in determining the level of individualism of his samples.

Collectivism is found in minority groups in the United States (Gaines et al., 1997), in societies that are relatively homogeneous (so that ingroup norms can be accepted widely), where population density and job interdependence are high (because they require the development of and adherence to many rules of behavior), in agricultural societies, among older members of a society (Noricks et al., 1987), among those who are members of large families (because it is not possible for every member to do his or her own thing), and in groups that are quite religious (Triandis & Singelis, 1998).

Some critics have argued that individualism is just another word for "modernity." This view is incorrect. The essence of individualism is the definition of the self as independent from the group, the primacy of individual goals, the emphasis on attitudes rather than norms, and the computation of profits and losses as determinants of social behaviors. The essence of modernity (Sack, 1973) is activism, rejection of the white-collar syndrome, universalism, low integration with relatives, sense of personal trust and autonomy, rejection of the past, preference for urban life, and family modernism. While some of these elements overlap, there is much more difference than similarity between the two constructs. Furthermore, modernity means the use of computers, faxes, shopping centers, and the like. There are societies that are modern (Saudi Arabia), but collectivistic; there are societies that are individualistic (most hunting-and-gathering societies) and traditional.

Measurement of the Constructs

The measurement of the constructs has been extremely difficult and is still unsatisfactory. As Earley and Gibson (1998, pp. 296–297) state, the constructs are immensely rich, deep, subtle, and complex. Triandis, Chan, Bhawuk, Iwao, and Sinha (1995) discussed the problem of the bandwidth versus the fidelity of the measurement of constructs. If we measure a construct broadly, we have little fidelity (reliability). If we measure it narrowly, we have fidelity, but a narrow construct, such as patriotism, familism, or coworker loyalty. There are many theoretically interesting relationships that can be investigated best with broad constructs. On the other hand, there are phenomena that can be studied best with one of the narrow constructs. We should not hesitate to adapt our measurements to the needs of the particular research problem.

The measurement of tendencies toward individualism and collectivism has used a variety of methods (Hui, 1988; Matsumoto, Weissman, Preston, Brown, & Kupperbusch, 1997; Realo, Allik, & Vadi, 1997; Rhee, Uleman, & Lee, 1996; Singelis, 1994; Singelis, Triandis, Bhawuk, & Gelfand, 1995; Triandis, Chen, & Chan, 1998; Triandis & Gelfand, 1998; Wagner, 1995; Wagner & Moch, 1986; Yamaguchi, 1994). An examination of some of these methods (appendix in Triandis, 1995) shows that more than 20 methods have been used, and while the methods are correlated, they often defined separate factors in factor analyses (e.g., Triandis & Gelfand, 1998; Wagner, 1995).

In general, we should sample many methods and augment them with emic items from the cultures we are investigating. Then, we should do item analyses to drop items that do not perform well and finally test for both convergent and construct validity to determine which methods are best for the particular samples. Factor analyses also are useful and can detect both etic and emic factors. We can compare cultures only on the etic factors, but we can describe them using both emic and etic factors.

In analyzing data, we need to keep in mind that results obtained from cultural (ecological) and individual level analyses, as mentioned above, may be quite different. In addition, there are different perspectives in studying the relationship of culture and psychology.

The perspective of cultural psychology emphasizes the intensive investigation of a phenomenon in one culture in which emic items are used and ethnographic, qualitative methods are most useful. The perspective of cross-cultural psychology emphasizes the use of both etic and emic items and quantitative methods. The contrast is between description and understanding on one hand versus explanation and prediction of the other hand.

Cross-cultural psychology tends to be more "individualistic" than cultural psychology, which tends to be more "collectivist." The methods of cross-cultural psychology tend to be more decontextualized (e.g., questionnaires with little context, laboratory experiments) than the methods of cultural psychology. Cultural psychology uses ethnographic approaches, data collected in "real-life situations," and examines the context of many variables and their interactions. The studies of cultural psychology tend to be synthetic, holistic, and not deterministic, while those of cross-cultural psychology tend to be analytic and deterministic.

Developmental psychologists find cultural psychology most helpful because they work with children and their psychological development over time within one culture. They are interested in how the culture is internalized. Social and organizational psychologists, on the other hand, work with people who are already members of a culture. They look at their interactions. They describe and explain these interactions using observations, experiments, content analyses, responses to questionnaires, and personality inventories. They see culture "outside the person" rather than "inside the person," while cultural psychologists see the culture inside the person, and culture and psychology make each other up (Fiske et al., 1998).

We already saw that there are allocentrics and idiocentrics in all cultures, but there are more allocentrics in collectivist cultures. One speculation is that cultural psychology will be more compatible with the perspectives of researchers from collectivist cultures or the views of allocentrics from individualist cultures. Thus, even in distinguishing types of psychologists, we might find that the constructs we are discussing in this chapter may have some relevance.

The methods of cross-cultural psychology cannot be used when the research participants are not familiar with psychological methods. On the other hand, ethnographic methods do not have this limitation. Thus, in situations in which there is a large difference between the culture of the researcher and the culture of the research participants (a situation with much cultural distance), only the methods of cultural psychology can be used.

Cultural Distance

Theories that receive substantial support in the West will receive less and less support as the cultures under investigation are distant from Western cultures. That is, as the languages (e.g., Indo-European vs. phonetic), social structure (e.g., monogamy vs. polygamy), politics, religion, philosophic perspectives, economic conditions, and aesthetic preferences differ, support for the theories will diminish. Cultural syndromes are intervening variables that can help explain why the theories are not supported in other cultures.

Similarly, the methods that can be used to test hypotheses depend on the cultural distance between the culture of the researcher and the culture under study. If the distance is large, the methods of cross-cultural psychology are not likely to be understandable to the participants. Then, only ethnographic methods are possible.

Both perspectives are valuable. If one wants description and understanding, the methods of cultural psychology are excellent; if one wants prediction and explanation, one may try the methods of cross-cultural psychology. But, the latter methods are simply not usable when there is a large cultural distance between the culture of the investigator and the culture under study. Ideally, we should use both kinds of methods and look for consistencies in findings.

Relation of the Individualism/ Collectivism Constructs to Psychological Theories

As mentioned above, most theories in psychology were developed with regard to Western samples and have an individualistic bias. That means that they may or may not apply to collectivist cultures. We can use the cultural syndromes (Triandis, 1996) of collectivism, individualism, tightness, looseness, and vertical and horizontal relationships, among others, as "bridges" between the West and the rest. A theory that works well in the United States, which is an individualist, loose culture, may require substantial modification in a vertical, collectivist, tight culture.

Promising Research Areas

It is hoped that all psychology will become cultural. This is necessary if psychology will not be parochial and will become universal. At the same time, while some broad phenomena will be investigated by the methods of cultural psychology, very narrow phenomena might be submitted to laboratory investigations to determine causality in an unambiguous way. Thus, the first quarter of the 21st century may well be characterized by an examination of the aspects of psychology that are or are not valid in those parts of the world where they have not yet been studied. This is especially urgent in social psychology, but is relevant, to some extent, in all areas of psychology.

Many of the empirical findings presented in this chapter come from one study, done in two or three cultures, using a specific set of methods, at one point in time. Much needs to be done to replicate and check the generality of these studies across situations, cultures, and time periods and with different methods. It is especially important that data be collected in Africa since we expect most African cultures to be collectivist, but we are not sure that results obtained in East Asia will necessarily be replicated in Africa.

The theory that collectivism is maximal in simple and tight cultures and individualism is maximal in complex and loose cultures needs to be tested. Michele Gelfand has developed a team that is measuring tightness and looseness with multiple methods in several cultures. As soon as this work is completed, it will be possible to test the theory. We already have several methods for the measurement of individualism and collectivism. We can use income as a measure of complexity. Thus, once we have methods that measure tightness-looseness, we will be ready to test the theory.

More needs to be done in linking the cultural, indigenous, and cross-cultural methods. Cross-cultural methods can only be used when the research participants are familiar with psychological methods. This limits the samples that can be studied. Yet, cross-cultural methods can provide measures of reliability and validity and avoid researcher biases. Cultural and indigenous psychology do not have methods that reject poor findings or findings that reflect researcher biases. If the methods of cultural and indigenous psychology are "calibrated" in samples for which we can also use the methods of cross-cultural psychology and we obtain convergence in the findings, then the methods of cultural psychology can be used with greater confidence, and they can be used with samples that are exotic. Thus, the methods of cultural psychology can be used more widely, yet through convergence with the methods of cross-cultural psychology, they can acquire the status that they deserve, so that mainstream psychologists will pay attention to their results and incorporate the findings of cultural psychology in mainstream psychological theories.

Speculation

The statements of the preceding section are in part speculation, in part reflection on the need for a universal psychology. The challenge is to convince psychologists to undertake the work that is necessary for the development of a universal psychology. If the methods of cultural psychology are used more widely and in conjunction with the methods of cross-cultural psychology, as suggested in the preceding section, I expect that mainstream psychologists will pay much attention to the results of cultural psychology, and psychology will be on its way toward the development of a universal psychology.

However, I do have a concern. Humans are universally lazy. This is very clear from the universality of Zipf's (1949) law. Zipf determined that, in all languages he investigated (and he did look at a very large sample of languages), the shorter words are most frequent, and as a word becomes frequent, it becomes shorter (e.g., television becomes TV). The universality of this finding suggests that the principle of least effort is a cultural universal. For psychologists, least effort means to complete a study and then state: "What I found is an eternal verity, applicable universally." The principle of least effort, then, leads psychologists to ignore culture because culture is a complication that makes their work more time consuming and difficult. However, to develop the kind of universal psychology described above will require rejection of the principle of least effort and its consequences. Thus, the major question of this field may well be, Can cultural psychology develop if it is against human nature to develop it?

References

Al-Zahrani, S. S. A., & Kaplowitz, S. A. (1993). Attributional biases in individualistic and collectivist cultures: A comparison of Americans and Saudis. *Social Psychology Quarterly, 56*, 223–233.

Bhawuk, D. P. S. (1998). The role of culture theory in cross-cultural training. *Journal of Cross-Cultural Psychology, 29*, 630–655.

Bond, M. H. (1988). Finding universal dimensions of individual variation in multicultural studies of values: The Rokeach and Chinese Value

Surveys. *Journal of Personality and Social Psychology, 55,* 1009–1015.

Bond, M. H., & Smith, P. B. (1996). Cross-cultural social and organizational psychology. *Annual Review of Psychology, 47,* 205–235.

Bond, M. H., Wan, K.-C., Leung, K., & Giacalone, R. A. (1985). How are responses to a verbal insult related to cultural collectivism and power distance? *Journal of Cross-Cultural Psychology, 16,* 111–127.

Bond, R., and Smith, P. B. (1996). Culture and conformity: A meta-analysis of studies using Asch's (1952b, 1956) line judgment task. *Psychological Bulletin, 119,* 111–137.

Chen, C. C. (1995). New trends in reward allocation preferences: A Sino-U.S. comparison. *Academy of Management Journal, 38,* 408–428.

Chen, C. C., Chen, X-P., & Meindl, J. R. (1998). How can cooperation be fostered? The cultural effects of individualism-collectivism. *Academy of Management Review, 23,* 285–304.

Chen, C. C., Meindl, J. R., & Hui, C. H. (1998). Deciding on equity or parity: A test of situational, cultural, and individual factors. *Journal of Organizational Behavior, 19,* 115–129.

Diaz-Guerrero, R. (1979). The development of coping style. *Human Development, 22,* 320–331.

Durkheim, E. (1984). *The division of labor in society* (W. D. Halls, Trans.). London: Macmillan. (Original work published 1893)

Earley, P. C. (1989). Social loafing and collectivism: A comparison of the U.S. and the People's Republic of China. *Administration Science Quarterly, 34,* 565–581.

Earley, P. C. (1993). East meets West meets Middle East: Further explorations of collectivist and individualist work groups. *Academy of Management Journal, 36,* 319–348.

Earley, P. C., & Gibson, C. B. (1998). Taking stock in our progress on individualism and collectivism: 100 years of solidarity and community. *Journal of Management, 24,* 265–304.

Erez, M. (1997). A culture based model of work motivation. In P. C. Earley & M. Erez (Eds.), *New perspectives on international industrial and organizational psychology* (pp. 193–242). San Francisco: Lexington Press.

Fiske, A. P., Kitayama, S., Markus, H., & Nisbett, R. E. (1998). The cultural matrix of social psychology. In D. T. Gilbert, S. T. Fiske, & G. Lindzey (Eds.), *The handbook of social psychology* (4th ed., Vol. 2, pp. 915–981). Boston: McGraw-Hill.

Freeman, M. A. (submitted). *Demographic correlates of individualism and collectivism: A study of social values in Sri Lanka.* Manuscript submitted for publication.

Gaines, S. O., Jr., Marelich, W. D., Bledsoe, K. L., Steers, W. N., Henderson, M. C., Granrose, C. S., Barajas, L., Hicks, D., Lyde, M., Rios, D. I., Garcia, B. F., Farris, K. R., & Page, M. S. (1997). Links between race/ethnicity and cultural values as mediated by racial/ethnic identity and moderated by gender. *Journal of Personality and Social Psychology, 72,* 1460–1476.

Gerganov, E. N, Dilova, M. L., Petkova, K. G., & Paspalanova, E. P. (1996). Culture-specific approach to the study of individualism/collectivism. *European Journal of Social Psychology, 26,* 277–297.

Hetts, J. J., Sakuma, M., & Pelham, B. W. (1999). Two roads to positive regard: Implicit and explicit self-evaluation and culture. *Journal of Experimental Social Psychology, 35,* 512–559.

Hofstede, G. (1980). *Culture's consequences.* Beverly Hills, CA: Sage.

Holtgraves, T. (1997). Styles of language use: Individual and cultural variability in conversational indirectness. *Journal of Personality and Social Psychology, 73,* 624–637.

House, R. J., Wright, N. S., & Aditya, R. N. (1997). Cross-cultural research on organizational leadership: A critical analysis and a proposed theory. In P. C. Earley & M. Erez (Eds.), *New perspectives on international industrial and organizational psychology* (pp. 535–625). San Francisco, CA: Lexington Press.

Hu, H. C. (1944). The Chinese concepts of face. *American Anthropologist, 46,* 45–64.

Hui, C. H. (1988). Measurement of individualism-collectivism. *Journal of Research on Personality, 22,* 17–36.

Hui, C. H., & Triandis, H. C. (1986). Individualism-collectivism: A study of cross-cultural researchers. *Journal of Cross-Cultural Psychology, 20,* 296–309.

Hui, C. H., Triandis, H. C., & Yee, C. (1991). Cultural differences in reward allocation: Is collectivism the explanation? *British Journal of Social Psychology, 30,* 145–157.

Iyengar, S. S., & Lepper, M. R. (1999). Rethinking the value of choice: A cultural perspective on intrinsic motivation. *Journal of Personality and Social Psychology, 76,* 349–366.

Kashima, E. S., & Kashima, Y. (1998). Culture and language: The case of cultural dimensions and personal pronoun use. *Journal of Cross-Cultural Psychology, 29,* 461–486.

Kitayama, S., Markus, H. R., Matsumoto, H., and Norasakkunkit, V. (1997). Individual and collective processes in the construction of the self: Self-enhancement in the United States and self-criticism in Japan. *Journal of Personality and Social Psychology, 72,* 1245–1267.

Kohn, M. K. (1969). *Class and conformity.* Homewood, IL: Dorsey Press.

Leung, K. (1997). Negotiation and reward allocations across cultures. In P. C. Earley & M. Erez (Eds.), *New perspectives on international industrial and organizational psychology* (pp. 640–675). San Francisco, CA: Lexington Press.

Leung, K., & Bond, M. H. (1989). On the empirical identification of dimensions for cross-cultural comparison. *Journal of Cross-Cultural Psychology, 20,* 133–151.

Lin, Z. (1997). Ambiguity with a purpose. The shadow of power in communication. In P. C. Earley & M. Erez (Eds.), *New perspectives on international industrial and organizational psychology* (pp. 363–376). San Francisco: Lexington Press.

Marshall, R. (1997). Variances in levels of individualism across two cultures and three social classes. *Journal of Cross-Cultural Psychology, 28,* 490–495.

Matsumoto, D., Weissman, M. D., Preston, K., Brown, B. P., & Kupperbusch, C. (1997). Context-dependent measurement of individualism and collectivism on the individual level. The individualism-collectivism interpersonal assessment inventory. *Journal of Cross-Cultural Psychology, 28,* 743–767.

McBride, A. (1998). Television, individualism, and social capital. *Political Science and Politics, 31,* 542–555.

Miller, J. G. (1984). Culture and the development of everyday social explanation. *Journal of Personality and Social Psychology, 46,* 961–978.

Miller, J. G. (1994). Cultural diversity in the morality of caring: Individually-oriented versus duty-oriented interpersonal codes. *Cross-Cultural Research, 28,* 3–39.

Mills, J., & Clark, M. S. (1982). Exchange and communal relationships. In L. Wheeler (Ed.), *Review of personality and social psychology* (Vol. 3, pp. 121–144). Beverly Hills, CA: Sage.

Morris, M. W., & Peng, K. (1994). Culture and cause: American and Chinese attributions for social and physical events. *Journal of Personality and Social Psychology, 67,* 949–971.

Moskowitz, D. S., Suh, E. J., & Desaulniers, J. (1994). Situational influences on gender differences in agency and communion. *Journal of Personality and Social Psychology, 66,* 753–761.

Na, E., & Loftus, E. F. (1998). Attitudes toward law and prisoners, conservative authoritarianism, attribution, and internal-external control: Korean and American law students and undergraduates. *Journal of Cross-Cultural Psychology, 29,* 595–615.

Newman, L. S. (1993). How individuals interpret behavior: Idiocentrism and spontaneous trait inference. *Social Cognition, 11,* 243–269.

Noricks, J. S., Agler, L. H., Bartholomew, M., Howard-Smith, S., Martin, D., Pyles, S., & Shapiro, W. (1987). Age, abstract things and the American concept of person. *American Anthropologist, 89,* 667–675.

Pearson, V. M. S., & Stephan, W. G. (1998). Preferences for styles of negotiation: A comparison of Brazil and the U.S. *International Journal of Intercultural Relations, 22,* 67–83.

Realo, A., Allik, J., & Vadi, M. (1997). The hierarchical structure of collectivism. *Journal of Research on Personality, 31,* 93–116.

Rhee, E., Uleman, J. S., & Lee, H. K. (1996). Variations in collectivism and individualism by ingroup and culture: Confirmatory factor analyses. *Journal of Personality and Social Psychology, 71,* 1037–1054.

Sack, R. (1973). The impact of education in individual modernity in Tunisia. *International Journal of Comparative Sociology, 14,* 245–272.

Schwartz, S. H. (1990). Individualism-collectivism. Critique and proposed refinements. *Journal of Cross-Cultural Psychology, 21,* 139–157.

Schwartz, S. H. (1992). Universals in the content and structure of values: Theoretical advances and empirical tests in 20 countries. In M. Zanna (Ed.), *Advances in experimental social psychology* (Vol. 25, pp. 1–66). New York: Academic Press.

Schwartz, S. H. (1994). Beyond individualism and collectivism: New cultural dimensions of values. In U. Kim, H. C. Triandis, C. Kagitcibasi, S.-C. Choi, & G. Yoon (Eds.), *Individualism and collectivism: Theory, method, and applications* (pp. 85–122). Newbury Park, CA: Sage.

Semin, G. R., & Rubini, M. (1990). Unfolding the concept of person in verbal abuse. European Journal of Social Psychology, 20, 463-474.

Singelis, T. M., & Sharkey, W. F. (1995). Culture, self-construal, and embarrassability. *Journal of Cross-Cultural Psychology, 26,* 622–644.

Singelis, T. M., Triandis, H. C., Bhawuk, D. S., & Gelfand, M. (1995). Horizontal and vertical dimensions of individualism and collectivism: A theoretical and measurement refinement. *Cross-Cultural Research, 29,* 240–275.

Singelis, T. M. (1994). The measurement of independent and interdependent self-construals. *Personality and Social Psychology Bulletin, 20,* 580–591.

Sinha, J. B. P. (1980). *The nurturant task leader.* New Delhi: Concept.

Sinha, J. B. P. (1996). *The cultural context of leadership and power.* New Delhi: Sage.

Skoyles, J. R. (1998). Motor perception and anatomical realism in classical Greek art. *Medical Hypotheses, 51*, 69–70.

Smith, P. B., & Bond, M. H. (1999). *Social psychology across cultures.* Boston: Allyn & Bacon.

Sugimoto, N. (1998). Norms of apology in U.S. American and Japanese literature on manners and etiquette. *International Journal of Intercultural Relations, 22*, 251–276.

Toernblom, K. Y., Jonsson, D., & Foa, U. G. (1985). National resource class, and preferences among three allocation rules: Sweden versus USA. *International Journal of Intercultural Relations, 9*, 51–77.

Trafimow, D., Triandis, H. C., & Goto, S. (1991). Some tests of the distinction between the private and collective self. *Journal of Personality and Social Psychology, 60*, 649–655.

Triandis, H. C. (1972). *The analysis of subjective culture.* New York: Wiley.

Triandis, H. C. (1988). Collectivism versus individualism: A reconceptualization of a basic concept in cross-cultural social psychology. In G. K. Verma & C. Bagley (Eds.), *Cross-cultural studies of personality, attitudes and cognition* (pp. 60–95). London: Macmillan.

Triandis, H. C. (1989). The self and social behavior in differing cultural contexts. *Psychological Review, 96*, 506–520.

Triandis, H. C. (1990). Cross-cultural studies of individualism and collectivism. In J. Berman (Ed.), *Nebraska Symposium on Motivation, 1989* (pp. 41–133), Lincoln: University of Nebraska Press.

Triandis, H. C. (1993). Collectivism and individualism as cultural syndromes. *Cross-Cultural Research, 27*, 155–180.

Triandis, H. C. (1994). *Culture and social behavior.* New York: McGraw-Hill.

Triandis, H. C. (1995). *Individualism and collectivism.* Boulder, CO: Westview Press.

Triandis, H. C. (1996). The psychological measurement cultural syndromes. *American Psychologist, 51*, 407–415.

Triandis, H. C., Bontempo, R., Betancourt, H., Bond, M., Leung, K., Brenes, A., Georgas, J., Hui, C. H., Marin, G., Setiadi, B., Sinha, J. B. P., Verma, J., Spangenberg, J., Touzard, H., & de Montmollin, G. (1986). The measurement of etic aspects of individualism and collectivism across cultures. *Australian Journal of Psychology, 38*, 257–267.

Triandis, H. C., Bontempo, R., Leung, K., & Hui, H. C. (1990). A method for determining cultural, demographic, and personal constructs. *Journal of Cross-Cultural Psychology, 21*, 302–318.

Triandis, H. C., Bontempo, R., Villareal, M. J., Asai, M., & Lucca, N. (1988). Individualism and collectivism: Cross-cultural perspectives on self-ingroup relationships. *Journal of Personality and Social Psychology, 54*, 323–338.

Triandis, H. C., Brislin, R., & Hui, C. H. (1988). Cross-cultural training across the individualism-collectivism divide. *International Journal of Intercultural Relations, 12*, 269–289.

Triandis, H. C., Chan, D. K.-S., Bhawuk, D., Iwao, S., & Sinha, J. B. P. (1995). Multimethod probes of allocentrism and idiocentrism. *International Journal of Psychology, 30*, 461–480.

Triandis, H. C., Chen, X. P., & Chan, D. K.-S. (1998). Scenarios for the measurement of collectivism and individualism. *Journal of Cross-Cultural Psychology, 29*, 275–289.

Triandis, H. C., & Gelfand, M. (1998). Converging measurement of horizontal and vertical individualism and collectivism. *Journal of Personality and Social Psychology, 74*, 118–128.

Triandis, H. C., Leung, K., Villareal, M., & Clack, F. L. (1985). Allocentric versus idiocentric tendencies: Convergent and discriminant validation. *Journal of Research in Personality, 19*, 395–415.

Triandis, H. C., Marin, G., Lisansky, J., & Betancourt, H. (1984). *Simpatia* as a cultural script of Hispanics. *Journal of Personality and Social Psychology, 47*, 1363–1374.

Triandis, H. C., & Singelis, T. M. (1998). Training to recognize individual differences in collectivism and individualism within culture. *International Journal of Intercultural Relations, 22*, 35–48.

Triandis, H. C., & Vassiliou, V. A. (1972). Interpersonal influence and employee selection in two cultures. *Journal of Applied Psychology, 56*, 140–145.

Trubinsky, P., Ting-Toomey, S., & Lin, S. (1991). The influence of individualism-collectivism and self-monitoring on conflict styles. *International Journal of Intercultural Relations, 15*, 65–84.

Verma, J. (1992). Allocentrism and relational orientation. In S. Iwawaki, Y. Kashima, & K. Leung (Eds.), *Innovations in cross-cultural psychology* (pp. 152–163). Amsterdam/Lisse, The Netherlands: Swets & Zeitlinger.

Verma, J., & Triandis, H. C. (1999). The measurement of collectivism in India. In W. J. Lonner, D. L. Dinnel, D. K. Forgays, & S. A. Hayes (Eds.), *Merging past, present, and future in cross-cultural psychology.* Selected papers from the Fourteenth International Congress of the International Association for Cross-Cultural Psychology. Lisse, The Netherlands: Swets and Zeitlinger.

Verma, J., & Triandis, H. C. (1998, August). *The measurement of collectivism in India.* Paper presented at the meetings of the International

Association of Cross-Cultural Psychology, Bellingham, WA.

Wagner, J. A., III. (1995). Studies of individualism collectivism: Effects on cooperation in groups. *Academy of Management Journal, 38,* 152–170.

Wagner, J. A., III, & Moch, M. K. (1986). Individualism-collectivism: Concept and measurement. *Group and Organizational Studies, 11,* 280–304.

Wang, Z.-M. (1994). Culture, economic reform, and role of industrial and organizational psychology in China. In H. C. Triandis, M. Dunnette, and L. Hough (Eds.), *Handbook of industrial and organizational psychology* (2nd ed., pp. 689–726). Palo Alto, CA: Consulting Psychologists Press.

Weisz, J. R., Rothbaum, F. M., & Blackburn, T. C. (1984). Standing out and standing in: The psychology of control in America and Japan. *American Psychologist, 39,* 955–969.

Weldon, E. (1984). Deindividuation, interpersonal affect, and productivity in laboratory task groups. *Journal of Applied Social Psychology, 14,* 469–485.

Yamaguchi, S. (1994). Empirical evidence on collectivism among the Japanese. In U. Kim, H. C. Triandis, C. Kagitcibasi, S.-C. Choi, & G. Yoon (Eds.), *Individualism and collectivism: Theory, method, and applications* (pp. 175–188). Newbury Park, CA: Sage.

Yamaguchi, S., Kuhlman, D. M., & Sugimori, S. (1995). Personality correlates of allocentric tendencies in individualist and collectivist cultures. *Journal of Cross-Cultural Psychology, 26,* 658–672.

Yu, A.-B., & Yang, K.-S. (1994). The nature of achievement motivation in collectivist societies. In U. Kim, H. C. Triandis, C. Kagitcibasi, S.-C. Choi, & G. Yoon (Eds.), *Individualism and collectivism: Theory, method, and applications* (pp. 239–250). Newbury Park, CA: Sage.

Zipf, G. K. (1949). *Human behavior and the principle of least effort.* Cambridge, MA: Addison-Wesley.

Zwier, S. (1997). *Patterns of language use in individualistic and collectivist cultures.* Unpublished doctoral dissertation, Free University of Amsterdam, The Netherlands.

4

Culture, Science, and Indigenous Psychologies

An Integrated Analysis

UICHOL KIM

While cross-cultural psychological approaches to understanding human behavior generally have viewed culture as "affecting" behavior, this way of understanding the world and generating knowledge may be culture bound. As many authors in this volume point out, different perspectives exist to understand the relationship between culture and psychology, and while the cross-cultural perspective is certainly one of them, other perspectives need to be recognized and utilized if we are to gain a true appreciation of the relationship between culture and behavior.

In this chapter, Kim provides an elegant description and persuasive argument for the perspective encompassed by the notion of indigenous psychologies. He points out that the experimental approaches to psychology, rooted in a natural science tradition, may have its roots within western European and American belief systems developed at certain points in history. As such, they are rooted in particular worldview perspectives, cultural frameworks, and epistemologies that influence the way in which we think we want to understand behavior. As he points out, researchers thus may have focused too much attention on getting the "right answers," but have ignored the process by which to get them.

In contrast, Kim argues for the integration of an approach characterized by the term *indigenous psychologies.* In this framework, culture, language, philosophy, and science are products of collective human effort, and the relationship between an individual and a group needs to be viewed as a dynamic, interactive system of mutual influence. The indigenous psychologies approach emphasizes the understanding and utilization of three key aspects: context, epistemology, and phenomenology. That is, it focuses on the nature of the ecology within which individuals live and how they adapt culturally to those ecological conditions; it focuses on the intersections of religion, culture, and science and how they form different epistemological systems in different cultural environments and milieus. It also focuses on the different meaning systems, emotions, and ways of being that are rooted in different phenomenological systems associated with different cultural environments.

Kim suggests that current psychological knowledge, rooted in a western European or American way of being and understanding, in fact may represent the psychology of psychologists and not the psychology of the lay public. The indigenous psychologies approach represents a fundamental shift in scientific paradigm, from a positivistic conception of causality to a dynamic, transactional model of human functioning. It advocates lifting external impositions of academic dissections of the world into arbitrary packages (e.g., cognitions, emotions, and motivations) and instead advocates the experience of a phenomenon as an insider of a culture. Kim is forceful in suggesting that, while science is a product of collective human effort, we ought not become victims or slaves of scientific myths borne in a single cultural framework.

Virtually all authors in this volume recognize the importance of the alternative framework suggested by the indigenous psychologies approach and view not only its recognition, but also greater acceptance and integration into mainstream research endeavors and theoretical developments, as vital to a greater understanding of the relationship between culture and behavior. As such, this chapter serves as an important focal point for gaining a greater awareness of the focal underpinnings of the approach.

Wilhelm Wundt is considered to be the father of modern psychology (Boring, 1921/1950). In establishing psychology as an independent scientific discipline, he recognized two traditions in science: *Naturwissenschaften* (the natural sciences tradition) and *Geistewissenschaften* (the cultural sciences tradition; van Hoorn & Verhave, 1980). Although he was instrumental in establishing the experimental method in psychology, he recognized the limitation of the experimental method and emphasized the importance of *Volkerpsychologie* (translated as cultural psychology; Danziger, 1979). He observed that thinking is conditioned heavily by language and customs and regarded *Volkerpsychologie* to be a "more important branch of psychological science which was destined to eclipse experimental psychology" (Danziger, 1983, p. 307). In the later part of his life, he devoted his life to the examination of sociocultural influences in psychological processes by writing 10 volumes on *Volkerpsychologie* (1910–1920) (Wundt, 1916).

When psychology became established in North America, psychologists adopted a top-down approach in search of abstract, universal laws of human behavior, emulating natural sciences. Behaviorism emerged as the dominant paradigm and provided the paradigmatic direction, method, and substance. The subject matter of psychology became tailored to fit into the narrow definition of science that espoused positivism and operationalism (Koch & Leary, 1985). With the entrenchment of behaviorism as the dominant paradigm, influences from the cultural sciences tradition were eliminated (Danziger, 1983; Kim, 1999).

Within a short period, the diversity of methods, concepts, and theories that existed at the early stages of development became reduced to a narrow search for abstract behavioral laws.

Within this approach, culture is deemed a superficial contextual factor. It is considered unimportant since the underlying mechanism is assumed to be universal (Shweder, 1991). In the second camp, Darwinian theory is used to grade and rank cultures according to different stages of development or evolution (i.e., from traditional to modern, from primitive to civilized, and from backward to advanced). As a result, culture was ignored as a topic of investigation until recent times.

Scholars representing the cultural approach reject claims that current psychological theories are universal. They point out that many theories are ethnocentric, biased, and culture bound (Azuma, 1984; Berry, 1980; Shweder, 1991). Often, researchers use their own cultures implicitly as the standard by which other cultures are judged. They argue that each culture should be understood from its own frame of reference, including its own ecological, historical, philosophical, and religious context.

Echoing the criticisms of cultural psychologists, indigenous psychologies evolved around the world as a reaction to unjustified claims of universality (Kim & Berry, 1993: Sinha, 1997). Although existing psychological theories and concepts are assumed to be objective, value free, and universal, in reality they are deeply enmeshed with Euro-American values that champion rational, liberal, individualistic ideals (Azuma, 1984; Enriquez, 1993; Kim, 1995; Kim & Berry, 1993; Koch & Leary, 1985; Shweder, 1991). As such, they can be characterized as *imposed* or *pseudoetics* and not as true universals.

The indigenous psychologies approach represents an alternative scientific paradigm in which the subjective human qualities and emergent properties of culture are recognized as central elements (Kim, Park, & Park, 1999). In this chapter, two scientific traditions, representing the experimental psychology and the indigenous psychologies approach, are outlined. In the second section, analysis of culture is provided using the indigenous psychologies approach. In the final section, the content and context of cultural development and transformation are outlined in a comparison of Western culture with East Asian cultures.

Experimental Psychology and the Natural Sciences Tradition

During the Enlightenment period in western Europe, strict adherence to religious sources for understanding the natural and human world began to be challenged. Scientists discovered that the physical world could be explained in terms of mechanical laws, and they did not have to resort to intuitive, humanistic, or metaphysical explanations. Rather than relying on God for divine revelations, scholars realized that they could use their abilities to observe, analyze, rationalize, and experiment to test, challenge, and verify existing ideas. These abilities became powerful tools used to understand, explain, and manage the physical world. Thus, the scientific revolution in western Europe wrested the explanatory authority from religious sources to their own ability to analyze, rationalize, observe, and experiment and paved a way for discovering scientific laws that are universal and verifiable.

The physical sciences (e.g., astronomy, chemistry, physics) were first to develop. Newtonian physics provided a simple, elegant, and mechanical description and explanation of the physical world. Chemists discovered a list of basic elements and formulated the periodic table. These elements served as building blocks for understanding the structure and formation of complex objects.

The biological sciences were the next to develop. They began to provide physiological blueprints of living organisms, as chemists did with inanimate objects. Darwinian evolutionary theory provided a major breakthrough in supplying a theoretical framework for organizing and explaining diverse life forms. It also challenged previously held assumptions about the origin and nature of human beings. Human beings could no longer be considered the master of nature, but part of nature. These advancements in the physical and biological sciences paved the way for investigating the human world.

With the success of the natural sciences in illuminating the workings of the physical and the biological worlds, scholars began to turn their attention toward the human world. Both empiricists and rationalists argued that, similar to the physical world, there are objective causal laws operating in the social and psychological world. In 1748, Julien Offray de la Mettrie proposed that human beings are like machines (Leahey, 1987). Etienne Bonnot de Condillac in 1754 argued that all thought forms are mere transformations of basic sensations (Leahey, 1987). Thomas Brown in 1820 formulated the laws of association, which laid out the basic processes of how sensations are combined to produce complex ideas (Leahey, 1987). August Comte argued that all societies are governed by laws that could be discovered using scientific methods (Allport, 1968). John Stuart Mill urged the adoption and application of physical sciences methods to remedy the backward state of the human sciences, and he called this new science *social physics* (Lenzer, 1975).

Psychology, in its early period, was a hybrid of philosophy and the natural sciences. More than several thousand years of philosophical debate in the West of how people sense, perceive, remember, feel, behave, and interact now came under direct experimental scrutiny. Early breakthroughs in experimental psychology came with the process of translating mental processes into physical terms, measuring them, and conducting experiments. The most notable achievements were in psychophysics by E. H. Weber and G. Fechner, in reaction time by F. C. Donders, in sensory perception by H. von Helmholtz, and in human memory by H. Ebbinghaus (Leahey, 1987). Merz (1904/1965) declared, "The marvellous properties of higher creatures of the animal world which exhibit the phenomena of consciousness or of an inner experience . . . belong to the realm of natural science" (p. 468). Scholars were confident that the content of the human consciousness and of the social world could be quantified and investigated using the methods of the natural sciences.

Psychology was imported to North America by Wundt's students, who transplanted experimental psychology in various universities. The version of psychology that became transplanted and institutionalized in North America, however, stood in sharp contrast to that which Wundt advocated (Danziger, 1979). Wundt unequivocally stated that psychology must be regarded as a Geistewissenschaften and not as a Naturwissenschaften (van Hoorn & Verhave, 1980). The cultural sciences tradition, however, was ignored in North America (Danziger, 1979).

By emulating natural sciences, especially Newtonian physics, experimental psychologists hoped to discover universal laws of human behavior that transcend individual, social, cultural, temporal, and historical boundaries (Sampson, 1978). Elementary empirical facts, once discovered, could then serve as building blocks for understanding complex human behavior. Experimental psychology hoped to develop a "periodic table" of human behavior and laws that govern the formation of complex behavior.

Behaviorism provided a theoretical and methodological foundation for institutionalizing psychology as an independent, experimental science (Koch & Leary, 1985). First, behaviorists eliminated subjective aspects of psychology espoused by Wundt, such as introspection and consciousness. Since consciousness was deemed subjective, they chose behavior as the basic unit of analysis. Second, by eliminating consciousness and focusing on behavior, the differentiation between animals and human beings was eliminated. By affirming the continuation of species, human action, phenomenology, and social context were subsumed under the general study of behavior. Third, behaviorists assumed the existence of basic elementary behaviors that would serve as the foundation for understanding complex human behavior. By assuming the existence of elementary units and the continuation of species, experimentation in laboratories using animals became justified. Fourth, explanation of behavior was reduced to the physiological level, and psychological, social, and cultural level of analysis were eliminated. Finally, results of these laboratory studies would be generalized to human behavior, and they would become the basis for explaining complex behavior and social systems (Hebb, 1974).

In terms of causal explanation, experimental psychology has adopted the positivistic model of causality (see Figure 4.1). In this model, the goal of psychology is to discover the objective, abstract, and universal relationship between two observable entities, between an independent variable (Observable 1) and the dependent variable (Observable 2). Aspects that are not directly observable (such as human consciousness, agency, intentions, and goals) are considered "noise" and are eliminated from the research design. Psychological constructs (such as anxiety, motivation, or emotions) are inferred as intervening variables. Culture as a context variable was excluded from the research design. Classical conditioning, operant conditioning, and the information processing approach (e.g., Shepard, 1987) affirm the positivistic model of causality.

Cross-Cultural Psychology

Although the interest in cultural variations have fascinated many philosophers, traders, missionaries, and travelers, systematic documentation of cultural differences was not initiated until the mid-19th century. Psychological analysis of cross-cultural variation is a relatively recent endeavor (Klineberg, 1980). In cross-cultural research, the primary goal has been the testing of the universality of existing psychological theories (Berry, 1980).

Following the positivistic orientation, cross-cultural psychology has been defined by its comparative methodology rather than its content (Berry, 1980; Triandis et al., 1980). Cross-cultural research has been carried out in various area of psychology to test and verify the universality of psychological theories, such as in the areas of perception, cognition, development, personality, social, and clinical psychology (Triandis et al., 1980). Within this approach, three types of explanations have been advanced to account for observed cultural differences. In one camp, cultural differences are considered to be superficial contextual factors, and they are deemed unimportant since the underlying mechanism is considered to be universal (Shweder, 1991). In the second camp, Darwinian theory is used to grade and rank cultures according to different stages of development or evolution (i.e., from traditional to modern, from primitive to civilized, and from backward to advanced).

In the third camp, researchers became interested in examining the influence of cultures on behavior (Berry, 1980; Berry, Poortinga, Segall, Dasen, 1992; Segall, Dasen, Berry, & Poortinga, 1990). Consistent with the positivisitic model of causality, culture has been defined as a quasi-independent variable, and behavior is as the dependent variable (Berry, 1980). Since researchers cannot control culture like independent variables in a laboratory setting, it was considered to be a quasi-independent variable. For cross-cultural comparisons, a researcher typically selects cultures using the human relations area files (HRAF) or Hofstede's (1991) four

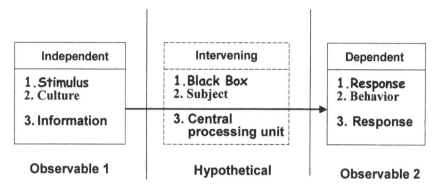

Figure 4.1   Positivistic Model of Causality

cultural dimensions (e.g., individualism-col-lectivism) and examines how cultures can be used to explain behavioral differences across cultures.

Shweder (1991) points out that cross-cul-tural psychology has occupied a marginal sta-tus and continues to do so since it adheres to the positivistic orientation:

> For one thing, cross-cultural psychology offers no substantial challenge to the core of Platonic principle of general psychology (the principle of psychic unity). Moreover, if you are a general psychologist cum Platonist (and a principled one at that) there is no theoretical benefit in learning more and more about the quagmire of appearances— the retarding effects of environment on the development of the central processing mech-anism, the "noise" introduced by translation or by differences in the understanding of the test situation or by cultural variations in the norms regulating the asking and answering of questions. Rather, if you are a general psy-chologist, you will want to transcend those appearances and reach for the imagined ab-stract forms and processes operating behind the extrinsic crutches and restraints and dis-tortions of this or that performance environ-ment. (pp. 85–86)

Second, there is also a logical flaw in selecting cultures using the HRAF or Hofstede's dimen-sions and then using culture as an explanatory construct. The HRAF and Hofstede's dimen-sions were created conceptually based on be-havioral and psychological data. Culture has not been measured directly. If psychological and behavioral indicators are used to define culture and then culture is used to explain them, researchers fall into a tautological trap.

Since cultures cannot be observed and mea-sured directly, psychologists cannot escape from the tautological trap within the positivis-tic framework. The basic problem in psychol-ogy and cross-cultural psychology is that the subject matter of the discipline has been subju-gated to misconceived ideas about science. We must recognize that the subject matter in psy-chology is different from that of chemistry, physics, and biology, and we must develop a science that is appropriate for psychology. A century of psychological research has been dis-appointing since we have limited our investiga-tion to the objective, third-person analysis (Cron-bach, 1975; Gibson, 1985; Koch & Leary, 1985). Even scholars from other disciplines (Boulding, 1980; Burke, 1985), physicists (d'Espagnet, 1979; Holten, 1988), and philosophers (Harré, 1999; Wallner, 1999) advocate a move away from the narrow conception of natural sciences. The indigenous psychologies approach advo-cated here represents a shift in scientific para-digm (Kim, 1999).

Transactional Model of Science

The central difference between natural and hu-man sciences is that, in the human sciences, we are both the object and the subject of investi-gation. The type of knowledge that can be ob-tained in the natural sciences is qualitatively different from the knowledge that we can obtain in the human world. According to Giovanni Battista Vico (in Berlin, 1976), in the physical world, we can obtain only objective, impartial, third-person knowledge. In the natural sciences (e.g., physics, botany, and entomology), for example, we can describe a table, a tree, and an ant; organize this information; and conduct experiments; but we cannot ascertain phenomenological knowledge (i.e., what it is like to be a table, a tree, or ant). In the human world, we can ascertain impartial, third-person knowledge, first-hand phenomenological knowledge ("who I am"), and second-person knowledge ("who you are"). In other words, unlike the physical world, we can know and feel what it is like to be a person, communicate this knowledge to others, and evaluate others as a third person. Language, nonverbal cues, and works of art (such as novels, paintings, movies, and music) are the media through which we communicate our inner phenomenology, intention, and goals. Although knowledge in the natural sciences is limited to objective, impartial, third-person knowledge, in psychology, first-, second-, and third-person knowledge can be obtained (Kim, 1999).

Second, in the natural world, we do not question the motives, intentions, and purpose of inanimate objects or animal behavior. Such an act would be considered irrational or an example of anthropomorphism or animism (Berlin, 1976). In the human world, these questions are central to understanding human action. We ask:

> Why do men act as they do . . . what mental states or events (e.g., feelings or volitions) are followed by what acts, but also why, why persons in this or that mental or emotional state are or are not likely to behave in a given fashion, what is, or what would be, rational or desirable or right for them to do, and how and why they decide between various courses of action. (Vico, in Berlin, 1976, p. 22)

In the case of the death of a person, we evaluate the act of the perpetrator in terms of his or her intention (i.e., whether it was premeditated or not) and agency (i.e., whether the person was insane, under the influence of alcohol, or responsible for his or her behavior). We impose different punishment based on how we evaluate his or her intention. The punishment for premeditated murder can be severe (such as life imprisonment or capital punishment); it can be moderate for involuntary manslaughter (5 to 10 years of imprisonment); and for self-defense, there may be no punishment. In the natural world, it is meaningless to classify ani-

mal behavior using these concepts, but in the human world, they are essential. Without these information institutions that uphold justice, ethics and law would not make any sense.

Third, we can distinguish experiential knowledge (phenomenological, episodic, and procedural knowledge) from analytical knowledge (e.g., semantic and declarative knowledge). Analytical knowledge represents information based on an objective, impartial, third-person analysis, often associated with academic and scientific understanding. Experiential knowledge represents subjective, first-person knowledge of the actor. For example, an adult, native speaker of English can freely express thoughts in English (i.e., procedural knowledge), but may not know the grammatical syntax or structure of the spoken words (i.e., semantic knowledge). In other words, the person knows how to produce the sentences, but lacks the analytical ability to describe how it was done. Conversely, a Korean may perform extremely well on an English grammar test, but may have difficulty conversing in English. This is because the

> description of the grammar of a word is of no use in everyday life; only rarely do we pick up the use of a word by having its use described to us; and although we are trained or encouraged to master the use of the word, we are not taught to describe it. (Ludwig Wittgenstein, in Budd, 1989, pp. 4–5)

Wittgenstein noted: "The meaning of a word is its use in the language" and not in the description of the word (in Budd, 1989, p. 21). In everyday life, a person may know how to perform certain actions, but may lack the analytical skills to describe how the actions are done. As Fuglesang (1984) points out:

> The farmer's knowledge is experiential. . . . He uses his knowledge like his hoe. He is in a sense not mentally aware of it. He is his knowledge. His knowledge is his self-image and his self-confidence as a community member. (p. 42)

Analytical knowledge, like grammar, is taught in school as a part of formal education, but it is different from practical knowledge. For example, a mother can raise a child efficaciously, but she may lack the analytical ability to describe how it was done. In contrast, a developmental psychologist can analyze and document successful mothering skills, but may lack the procedural skills in implementing this knowledge in raising his or her own children. The task of psychologists is to translate first-person experiential knowledge into analytical knowledge. This is done in various areas of our lives: in movies, by film critics; in cooking, by food critics; and in sports, by sports analyst or commentators. It is well recognized that, although a movie critic cannot produce movies and a sports commentator may not be able to play the game, they provide analytical information that helps us better appreciate the movie or the game.

In contrast to the reactive model of human functioning, a transaction model of causality that focuses on the generative and proactive aspects is provided as an alternative (see Figure 4.2). In this model, espoused by Bandura (1997), the unobservable human qualities (such as agency, intention, meaning, and goals) are the central concepts that link a situation on one hand with behavior on the other. Bandura investigated the generative capability known as self-efficacy to understand, predict, and manage behavior. He defines self-efficacy as "beliefs in one's capabilities to organize and execute the courses of action required to produce given attainments" (p. 3).

First, it is important to examine how an individual perceives and interprets a particular event or situation (Causal Linkage 1). This information can be obtained through self-report. The second step involves assessing individuals' performances based on their perception (Causal Linkage 2). In a study of management effectiveness with a group of graduate students of business, Bandura systematically elevated or reduced their levels of self-efficacy by providing them with preset feedback of how well they were performing compared to others. He found that the positive feedback increased their self-efficacy, and negative feedback decreased their self-efficacy (Causal Linkage 1). He found that participants with higher self-efficacy were more likely to use efficient analytical ability, were satisfied with their level of performance, and had higher performance ratings (Causal Linkage 2). The reverse was true for participants who were given negative feedback. Thus, individuals' performance can be elevated or depressed systematically by providing feedback information that increases or decreases their self-efficacy. The rise or fall in self-efficacy can be linked systematically to the subsequent rise or fall in their performance.

In another study that used both within-subject and between-subject design, Bandura, Reese, and Adams (1982) were systematically able to increase self-efficacy of people with phobias about snakes. He had them observe a model cope effectively with a snake. At this phase, the self-efficacy belief of participants in handling the snake was assessed through self-report. They found that watching a model cope effectively with the feared object increased the participants' self-efficacy (Causal Linkage 1). The second phase involved the subjects actually handling the snake. Those individuals with higher self-efficacy were more able to handle the snake in subsequent trials (Causal Linkage 2).

According to Bandura (1997), successful performance of a task can reverse the flow of causality. The successful performance can increase self-efficacy, which in turn can motivate individuals to modify their environment or to seek more challenging goals. An opposite pattern of results is found for failure experiences, which lowered self-efficacy, which in turn lowered the goal participants set for themselves.

Successful mastery experiences could lead to transformative changes in other aspects of a person's life. For example, mastery of the snake

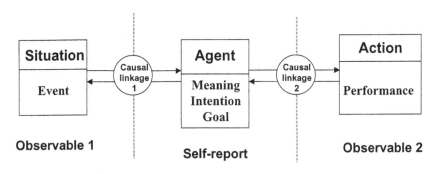

Figure 4.2   Transactional Model of Causality

phobia reduced social timidity, increased venturesomeness, boosted self-expressiveness, and increased desires to overcome other fears, such as fear of public speaking for some of the participants. These results could not be explained by stimulus generalizations or by the linear, additive model. The results could be explained in terms of a transformation of people's personal belief system—an emergent property not reducible to a single cause.

Another important aspect of the indigenous psychologies approach is the separation of different levels of analysis and understanding: physiological, psychological, and cultural. Although all actions must have a physiological or neurological basis, the reduction of behavioral explanations to the physiological level is a different explanation, rather than a causal explanation. For example, culture can be reduced to individual actions. All actions could be reduced to physiology and genetics. All genetics could be reduced further to four basic atoms (i.e., carbon, nitrogen, hydrogen, and oxygen), which in turn can be reduced to the three basic particles (i.e., electron, proton, and neutron). The important distinction between life and death, for example, cannot be defined through genetics since the genetic makeup of a person who has just died is the same as when he was alive. Harré and Gillet (1994) point out: "The brain, for any individual human being, is the repository of meaning in that it serves as the physical medium in which mental content is realized and plays a part in the discursive activities of individuals" (p. 81). Athletic, artistic, and scientific feats cannot be reduced to physiological, neurological, or genetics levels.

Finally, characteristics of collective entities such as groups, societies, and cultures are emergent properties that cannot be reduced to the mere sum of individual characteristics or their physiology. Although it has been assumed traditionally that our physiology affects our psychology in a simple, direct, and linear fashion, Francis, Soma, and Fernald (1993) have documented, in a study of African teleost fish, that the reverse is also true: Social status affects brain physiology and functioning. A similar pattern of results was found at the individual and group levels (Bandura, 1997) and in human history (Chorover, 1980). Culture, language, philosophy, and science are products of collective human effort. The relationship between an individual and a group needs to be viewed as a dynamic, interactive system of mutual influence.

Analysis of Culture

Culture is an emergent property of individuals and groups interacting with their natural and human environment. *Culture* is defined as a rubric of patterned variables. To use an analogy, painters use different colors to create their work of art. The different colors are like the variables that operate within a particular culture. These colors are used to create certain forms and patterns (such as a face, apple, or house). These forms are then combined to convey a particular ethos, providing an overall gestalt and coherence. The quality of a painting cannot be reduced to its constituent parts, such as wavelengths of light. Like a painting, culture is an emergent construct that provides meaning, coherence, and direction to its members. Like the different colors artists use, people use available natural and human resources to achieve their goals (such as solving subsistence and psychological needs). This is the process definition of culture: *Culture is the collective utilization of natural and human resources to achieve desired outcomes.*

From the perspective of an outsider looking in, culture is seen as affecting the way people think, feel, and behave (Berry et al., 1992; Segall et al., 1990). But, from an insider's perspective, culture is basic and natural. When children are born, although they have the potential to learn any language, they usually end up learning one language. To most adults, the particular language they speak is natural and basic, and other languages are incomprehensible, foreign, and alien. With the aid of their language, they organize their thoughts, communicate with others, and construct their social and physical world. To use an analogy, computers consist of hardware and software. Our physiology is like the hardware of a computer, and culture is like the software. Depending on the type of software downloaded, computers operate very differently. The difference between a computer and people is that human beings possess generative and creative capability that computers do not possess (Bandura, 1997; Harré, 1999; Kim, 1999).

Human physiology and genetics cannot explain human behavior and culture. Without culture, human beings would be reduced to basic instincts, and we would not be able to think, feel, or behave the way we do. Culture allows us to define who we are and what is meaningful, communicate with others, and manage our physical and social environments. It is through culture that we think, feel, behave, and interact with reality (Shweder, 1991). Because we think through culture, it is difficult to recognize our own culture. Culture provides a framework for perceiving what is meaningful, relevant, and salient. For a person born and raised in a particular culture, the person's culture is natural.

Differences in cultures exist because we have focused on and developed different aspects of our environment and attached different meanings and values to them. The difference, for example, between a weed and a vegetable is not determined by qualities inherent in a plant (i.e., whether it is edible). It has to do with our involvement with the plant (Shweder, 1991). What is considered to be a weed in one country (e.g., seaweed in France) is considered an important vegetable in another (e.g., Japan and Korea). What is considered a pest in Korea (e.g., snails) is considered a delicacy in France. Shweder notes that if a beautiful cabbage grew in a rose garden, we would treat it as a weed and pluck it out. The cabbage is treated as a weed since it was not our intention to grow a cabbage in a rose garden. Conversely, if a rose grew in a cabbage patch, it also would be treated as a weed. Thus, the distinction between a plant and a weed includes the ideas of edibility, meaningfulness, and intention.

To investigate a culture, the indigenous psychologies approach emphasizes the need to examine three key aspects: (a) context, (b) epistemology, and (c) phenomenology (see Figure 4.3). First, culture and psychology need to be understood in context, and the content of cultural variations must be examined. Cultural differences arise partly due to variations in ecology and human adaptation to it (Berry, 1976; Kim, 1994). Researchers have documented a systematic relationship among ecology, culture, socialization practices, and psychological functioning (Barry, Bacon, & Child, 1959; Berry, 1976; Berry et al., 1992; Kim, Triandis, Kagitcibasi, Choi, & Yoon, 1994). For example, although Canada and the United States are similar culturally and linguistically, Berry (1993) articulates the need to develop indigenous Canadian psychology based on its ecological conditions (such as people living in isolated areas, arctic and north temperate climates). Similarly, Georgas (1993) documents how ecology affected the development and transformation of Greek culture.

Ecology and Cultural Adaptation

Ecology refers to the total pattern of relationships between life forms and their environment and includes the natural environment that humans share with other living organisms. Climatic and natural conditions (such as temperature, humidity, water supply, soil conditions, and terrain) all affect the existence of various types of vegetation and life forms (Segall et al.,

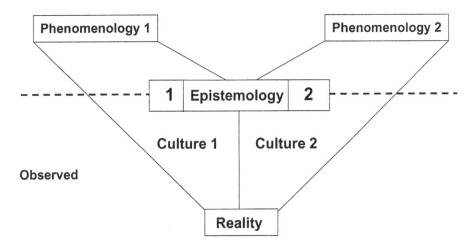

Figure 4.3   Knowledge and Culture

1990). Early in human history, collective units such as families, clans, and tribes developed strategies to cope with, and adapt to, their particular ecology. A critical element of survival rested on the availability of a food supply (Segall et al., 1990), which was determined largely by ecological conditions. Various collective responses appeared in reaction to the differing ecological pressures. For example, people living in mountainous areas, jungles, or deserts had a limited food supply. When it was depleted, they had to move to another region in search of a new food source. Hunting-and-gathering tribes subsisted by moving with or toward the food supply.

Some of these migratory tribes found land where the soil was rich, the water was abundant, and the terrain was flat. They used these favorable conditions to develop agriculture and animal husbandry. With increased agricultural efficiency and storage, people could depend on the food produced from the land and from animals that they raised for a steady supply of food. They no longer needed to migrate to find a new food source. The development of agriculture and animal husbandry is a form of collective human effort to manage and adapt to the environment.

Migratory tribes who lived in jungles, mountains, and deserts needed a specific set of skills to survive in their hostile environments. Barry, Bacon, and Child (1959) found that, in migratory tribes, socialization practices emphasized assertiveness, autonomy, achievement, and self-reliance. Adults in migratory communities tended to be individualistic, assertive, and venturesome, and they viewed these characteristics as being adaptive to their ecology. In the agricultural communities, socialization practices emphasized compliance, obedience, and responsibility. Adults in agricultural communities tended to be conscientious, compliant, and conservative. Berry (1976) found that ecological context has a significant effect on type of cultures that emerge, which in turn affect individual functioning, namely, cognitive style.

Ecology, however, does not explain the whole of culture. People living in similar desert conditions do not develop identical cultures. For example, in Europe, wheat became the staple crop, and it was grown in dry fields. In Asia, rice is the staple crop, and it is grown in wet fields. Cultures have also developed different epistemologies (e.g., religions, philosophies, and science) to understand, predict, and manage their environment. These organized bodies of knowledge provide meaning, direction, and coherence. Researchers have provided an extensive review of the systematic relationship between epistemologies (e.g., Buddhism, Confucianism, Communism, Hinduism, Islam, and liberalism) and how people conceive of themselves, interact with others, and manage natural and human resources (Boski, 1993; Hwang, 1998; Kim, 1994; Sinha, 1997).

Social and Cultural Change

Drastic alteration in the ecological context in western Europe began around the 18th century. From that time, human beings began to exert greater control over their environment, thereby significantly altering the ecological balance. Numerous factors contributed to the change: the rise of international trade and commerce, the rise of city-states, rapid developments in science and technology, greater agricultural efficiency, and industrialization. These changes resulted in a movement away from subsistence economies (largely determined by ecology) to market economies (created by human intervention).

For example, people did not have to migrate to find new food sources or till the soil to have dinner on the table. They did not have to store food for the winter. They did not have to sew to have clothing. They no longer needed their neighbors' help in putting up a barn. Instead, people worked for wages. Money earned could be used to buy necessary goods and services or deposited in a bank for future use. Money acted as an intermediary commodity that created the efficient movement of resources.

These changes drastically altered cultures and lifestyles in western Europe (Kim, 1994). With greater agricultural efficiency, many serfs and peasants were dislocated from their agricultural communities. They congregated in the newly formed cities in search of other forms of subsistence. Industrial factories paid wages for their labor. The new types of work demanded a different set of skills. People could no longer rely on the skills and knowledge that had been passed down for generations. The work involved acquiring new skills (such as working with machines) that could increase production and distribution.

Socialization practices in the industrial urban centers contrasted sharply with those of agricultural communities (Toennies, 1887/1963). In traditional agricultural communities, trust, cooperation, and conservatism were important aspects of daily life. In these communities, social intelligence was valued highly (Mundy-Castle, 1974). In the urban setting, however, technological intelligence began to play a prominent role (Mundy-Castle, 1974). In subsistence economies, the goal of socialization was survival and subsistence. In the newly formed urban communities, socialization emphasized the development of cognitive and linguistic skills that were necessary to acquire greater wealth and profit.

Industrial urban settings were full of unrelated strangers. The relationship a person had with an employer was contractual and not based on any long-standing relationship of trust and obligation. Workers provided services, and they received a wage for their labor. The wages that they received were fueled by the economic law of supply and demand. When demand for labor was low and supply was high, workers could be underpaid and exploited. In the 19th century, many industrialists exploited their employees in search of greater profit. In these settings, there was no one to protect the rights of these unrelated individuals.

Collective action began to appear to protest the working conditions and working relationships. A new form of collectives emerged in western Europe; it was defined by class (e.g., ruling class, merchant class, and working class) or by common interest (e.g., union). Members of the working class began to organize and lobby their interests through demonstrations and revolutions. These collective actions resulted in development of new political philosophies and institutions in the 20th century, such as democracy, fascism, and communism.

In western Europe, new collectives emerged with the separation from collective entities (such as family, community, clan, and religion). These new collectives were based on common interests, experiences, and goals. Cultures based on this type of realignment have been labeled *individualistic* (Hofstede, 1991). Cultures that maintain familial and communal relatedness have been labeled *collectivistic*. This distinction represents an outsider's analysis of cultural differences. These differences must be put in context in each culture by examining their corresponding epistemology and phenomenology.

Lomov, Budilova, Koltsova, and Medvedev (1993) point out that the research topics in Russia are influenced by epistemological beliefs, although secularization, individualism, and the separation of science and religion, which were prevalent in western Europe, were not in Russia. In Russia, the control of science and education was in the hands of the church. Theologians conducted research and lectured on psychological topics. The Russian brain research in the 19th century was stimulated by the belief that the soul resided in the brain. Similarly, Boski (1993) points out that humanistic values (a blend of Catholic and Marxist humanism) had a strong influence on psychological research in Poland.

Epistemology

In the Louvre museum in Paris, one can trace the development and transformation of Western cultures through the artwork. In most medieval paintings, Jesus, the Virgin Mary, or some other holy person occupies the center of the picture, and commoners are in the periphery (see Figure 4.4). These paintings represent the Judeo-Christian belief and value system at that time. God, as the Creator of the universe, represents the Truth, Light, Beauty, and Goodness and thus occupies the center. Human beings, who are the created, are in the periphery.

In medieval paintings, people's faces are not very expressive, except for to show reverence for Jesus and the Virgin Mary. A person's inner world or individuality was not considered to be important in medieval Christian cultures. To know the Truth, one had to seek the Will of God. The Truth was revealed only through Him or through His revelations, through priests, the bible, or nature. Even music was created especially for God. It was monotonic and directed toward heaven (e.g., Gregorian chants).

The Renaissance in western Europe represents a cultural revolution: a different way of perceiving and understanding the physical, human, and spiritual world. From the Renaissance, there was a shift in people's perception of reality. In the Louvre, one piece of artwork attracts enormous attention, and it is an example of this change of perception. Throughout the day, people queue in front of the painting of Mona Lisa (*La Giaconda*) hoping to take a picture of the painting. Why does this artwork attract so much attention even after 500 years? Mona Lisa was not a saint or gentry nor did she have extraordinary beauty (see Figure 4.5). She was a plain-looking commoner. There is, however, a striking difference between the painting of Mona Lisa and other medieval paintings. Compared to other traditional medieval paintings, the relationship between figure and ground

Figure 4.4
Piero della Francesca. *Madonna and Child with Angels, Saints, and Frederigo of Urbino.* Pinacoteca di Brera, Milan, Italy. Courtesy of Alinari / Art Resource, NY

is reversed: She is the center of attention, and the landscape is in the background. A commoner occupies the center of the painting, and she is the focus of the painting. Also, her expression shows inner emotions and individuality.

During the Renaissance, people began to discover the world around them and, more important, themselves; these discoveries were dormant during the medieval period. People discovered that individuals have the potential to discover the truth without the aid of religious leaders or the bible or through divine revelation. They realized that they had the capability to discover the Truth firsthand. Also, rather than viewing human beings as sinful and the world as a forsaken place, human beings were considered to be beautiful. In the medieval period, the human body was the symbol of lust and sin, and so it was kept covered. In contrast, the sculpture

David by Michelangelo is an example of the celebration of the beauty of the human body (see Figure 4.6).

Religion, Culture, and Science

René Descartes lived in a time during which many conflicting ideas, doctrines, and beliefs emerged, and new discoveries were being made. He was in turmoil due to these conflicting ideas. He decided to adopt a method of critical doubt in which he rejected all ideas, doctrines, and beliefs unless the truth was self-evident. He found he could doubt virtually everything: traditions, customs, beliefs, and even his own perception. There was, however, one thing he could not doubt—his own existence. His fundamental question was, "How do I know I exist?" He concluded that it is through rationality and rea-

Figure 4.5
Leonardo da Vinci (1452–
1519). *Mona Lisa (La
Giaconda).* c. 1503. Oil
on panel, 97 × 53 cm.
Louvre, Paris, France.
Courtesy of Giraudon /
Art Resource, NY

son that he could know this with certainty. Thus, Descartes concluded, "Cogito, ergo sum" (I think, therefore I am) (see Figure 4.7).

Descartes found that, through rationality and reason, he could understand not only himself, but also natural scientific laws and mathematical truths. This type of understanding was considered impossible in the medieval period because it was believed that only God could know and reveal the Truth. Furthermore, Descartes concluded that rationality is a special gift from God that allows us to know that God exists. People possess rationality, through which we can understand ourselves, God, and scientific and mathematical truths.

Rationality is what separates human beings from animals. Descartes separated our bodies from the mind. Our body, like that of other animals, is controlled by natural instincts. This was evidenced to Descartes by the reflex arc that he discovered through experimentation. Human beings, however, are different from animals because we possess rationality and reason. He was able to develop the Cartesian coordinate system, which allows us to describe our physical world mathematically.

The philosophy and discoveries of Descartes influenced the Judeo-Christian worldview. His ideas allowed the separation of science from religion. Science studied the physical world, and religion dealt with the spiritual world. His views created a duality of thought, dichotomization of the world between mind and body, good and bad, light and darkness, justice and deceit, heaven and earth. Life came to be viewed as a struggle between truth and light on one

Figure 4.6 Michelangelo Buonarroti. *David* (full, frontal view). Accademia, Florence, Italy. Courtesy of Alinari/Art Resource, NY

hand and evil and darkness on the other (see Figure 4.8).

Modern Western movies, television dramas, and novels reflect this basic struggle between good and evil and the triumph of the human spirit to overcome evil (e.g., the movies *Star Wars* and *Titanic*). Emotions, on the other hand, were considered unreliable as they were linked with the desires of the flesh, the body. Love was an emotion that could transcend rationality and reason since love was the embodiment of God.

The discovery of Descartes was a purely individualistic enterprise. He could determine Truth by himself instead of depending on some arbitrary body. According to Descartes, other people, authorities, and institutions cannot dictate what is right and or wrong. Only you can know what is true with absolute certainty. Western individualistic societies emphasize individual uniqueness and the pursuit of their unique identity, the Truth, and self-actualization.

Rationality became the pillar on which society was built and constructed. Liberal education provides the necessary training to discover one's rationality, with the belief that there is just one Truth. Only those individuals who are

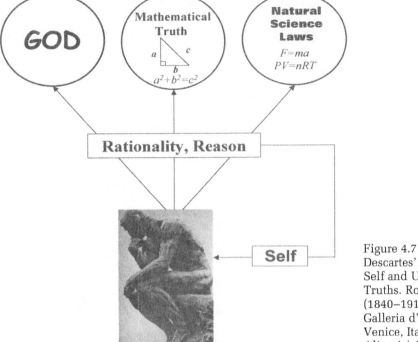

Figure 4.7
Descartes' Discovery of
Self and Undeniable
Truths. Rodin, Auguste
(1840–1917). *The Thinker.*
Galleria d'Arte Moderna,
Venice, Italy. Courtesy of
Alinari / Art Resource, NY

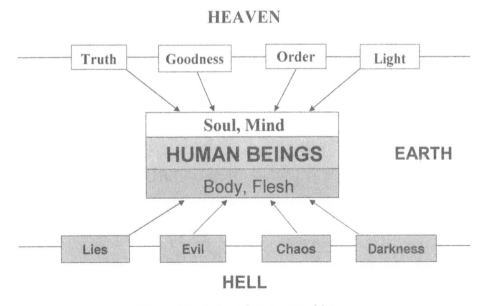

Figure 4.8   Judeo-Christian Worldview

considered rational are allowed to participate in societal decision making. For example, children, the mentally insane, and criminals are not given the basic right to vote. Through democratic discussion, people can arrive at this Truth (see Figure 4.9). Based on this belief, laws and social institutions are created.

In the West, the liberal tradition focuses on a rational individual's rights to choose, define, and search for self-fulfillment freely (Kim, 1994). The content of self-fulfillment depends on the goals that individuals freely choose. The nature of the goal can vary from one individual to another and can range from hedonistic fulfillment to self-actualization. This freedom of choice is guaranteed collectively by individual human rights. At the interpersonal level, individuals are considered to be discrete, autonomous, self-sufficient, and respectful of the rights of others.

From a societal point of view, individuals are considered to be abstract and universal entities. Their status and roles are not ascribed or predetermined, but defined by their personal achievements (i.e., by their educational, occupational, and economic achievements). They interact with others using mutually agreed upon principles (such as equality, equity, noninterference, and detachability) or through mutually established contracts. Individuals with similar goals are brought together into a group, and they remain with the group as long as it satisfies

their needs. Laws and regulations are institutionalized to protect individual rights; everyone is able to assert these rights through the legal system. The state is governed by elected officials, whose role it is to protect individual rights and the viability of public institutions. Individual rights are of prime importance, and the collective good and harmony are considered secondary.

Descartes grew up in France during the Age of Reason. If Descartes had been Chinese, Japanese, or Korean, how would he have answered the fundamental question of his existence? I believe he would have answered as follows: "I feel, therefore I am." In contrast to Western emphasis on rationality, Confucianism focuses on emotions, which provide a basis of harmonious familial and social relationships. In Asia, although Western science and technology have been adopted, traditional epistemological beliefs coexist with, and have not been replaced by, modern Western epistemologies (Kim, 1994; Sinha, 1997).

East Asian Perspective

In East Asia, individualism and rationality are viewed as being unstable, while relationships and emotional attachments are considered stable. This is not to say that individualism and

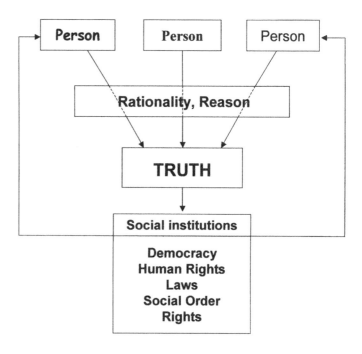

Figure 4.9
Individualistic Culture

rationality do not exist. They do exist, but they play a secondary role to relations and emotions. In other words, relationships and emotions are the focus, while individuals and rationality are relegated to the background. Relational emotions that bind and bond individuals together, not the private and narcissistic emotions, are emphasized.

In East Asian art, human beings are placed in the context of the natural and social environment. Individuality that creates interpersonal distance is not emphasized. In traditional landscape paintings, human beings are placed in the context of nature (see Figure 4.10). The expressions of individuals cannot be seen as in Western art. Human beings are considered to be part of nature in Confucianism, Buddhism, and Shamanistic epistemologies. In these philosophies, harmony is the most important value since it integrates human beings with nature, spirits, and other individuals.

Confucianism

Confucius (551–479 B.C.) saw the universe and all living things in it as a manifestation of a unifying force called the *Dao* (translated as the Truth, Unity, or the Way). Dao constitutes the very essence, basis, and unit of life that perpetuates order, goodness, and righteousness (Lew, 1977). Confucius, who was born in an agrarian society, expounded his moral and political philosophy to maintain, propagate, and reify natural order.

Dao manifests itself in the harmonious opposition of yin and yang and in humans through *te* (virtue). Virtue is a gift received from Heaven (Lew, 1977). It is through Virtue that a person is able to know the Heavenly Truth, and it is the "locus where Heaven and I meet" (Lew, 1977, p. 154). Virtue can be realized through self-cultivation. It provides the fundamental source of insight and strength to rule peacefully and harmoniously within oneself, one's family, one's nation, and the world.

There are two interrelated aspects of virtue: *ren* (Human-heartedness) and *yi* (Rightness). The basis of humanity and the individual is Human-heartedness. Human-heartedness is essentially relational. Confucius pointed out three related aspects of Human-heartedness. First, it "consists of loving others" (Confucius, 1979, Analects, XII, 22). Second, "the man of *ren* is one who, desiring to sustain himself, sustains others, and desiring to develop himself, develops others" (Analects, VI, 28). Third, one should not do to others "what you do not wish

Figure 4.10   Tao-chi, called Shih-t ao. Mountain landscape after Huang Kung-wang. Qing dynasty, reign of Kangxi, 1671. Ink, 86 × 41 cm. Musée Guimet, Paris, France. Courtesy of Giraudon/Art Resource, NY

done to yourself" (Analects, XII, 2). Mencius noted that without Human-heartedness, a person could not be considered a human being: "When you see a child drowning in a well, if you do not feel compassion, you are not human" (Mencius, II/A/6). Human-heartedness is an essential component of the self and relationships in Confucian cultures. Individuals are born with Human-heartedness and experience Human-heartedness through their parents. In Figure 4.11, the Confucian model of development is outlined as an alternative to the Western model.

The second concept, yi (Rightness), notes that an individual is born into a particular family with a particular ascribed status. Rightness articulates that individuals must perform and fulfill their duties as defined by their particular status and role. Confucius considered society to be ordered hierarchically, necessitating that people fulfill their duties: "Let the ruler be a ruler, the subject a subject, the father a father, the son a son" (Analects, XII, 11). Fulfilling one's given role as father, mother, elder brother, teacher, or ruler is considered a moral imperative.

Human-heartedness and Rightness are considered two sides of the same coin. For example, a virtuous father fulfills his duties because he loves his son, and he loves his son because he is the father. Through Human-heartedness and Rightness, individual family members are linked in Unity (Dao). The primary relationship is the parent-child relationship, as defined by xiao dao (Filial piety). Parents are the vehicles through which the Dao is transmitted and manifested in their children. Relationships between parents and children (and also between spouses and siblings) are not based on equality, but on Human-heartedness and Rightness. Parents demand love, reverence, obedience, and respect from children. Children expect love, wisdom, and benevolence from parents. The parent-child relationship involves more than just two individuals. Parents represent ancestors and the past, and children represent progeny and the future.

Confucius considered society to be ordered hierarchically and that each person has fen (portion or place) in life. Each fen has attached roles, and each person must fulfill these roles. Duties and obligations of each fen are prescribed by li (Propriety). Propriety articulates expectations and duties of each individual according to status and role. Social order and harmony are preserved when people observe their place in society and fulfill required obligations and duties.

The fourth concept is zhi (Knowledge). Knowledge allows us to understand the virtues of Human-heartedness and Rightness and to follow these virtues. It is the basis of the development of wisdom. The four concepts of Human-heartedness, Rightness, Propriety, and Knowl-

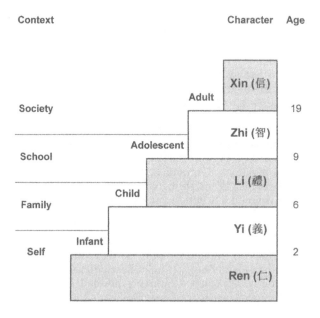

Figure 4.11
Confucian Developmental Stages

Ren = Human-heartedness   Yi = Rightness
Li = Propriety   Zhi = Knowledge
Xin = Trust

edge are the basis of Confucian morality. Like the two arms and two legs with which we are born, Human-heartedness, Rightness, Propriety, and Knowledge exist from birth, but we need to cultivate and develop them. Knowledge is refined further and extended in school. In school, teachers affirm morality as the basis for all thoughts, emotions, and behavior. Teachers are seen as extensions of the parents. They have a moral basis from which to provide children with education to develop Knowledge further. Finally, as children mature, they need to interact with a wider range of people, including strangers. As such, they need to develop *xin* (Trust).

Confucius distinguished two competing forces within the self: first-order desires (e.g., material and carnal desires) and second-order desires (i.e., virtues of Human-heartedness and Rightness). To be a virtuous person, one must overcome first-order desires and cultivate second-order desires. An inferior person is governed by egocentrism, selfishness, narcissism, and *li* (Profit). Confucius pointed out that a superior person cultivates the virtues of Human-heartedness and Rightness: "The superior man comprehends Rightness; and the small man comprehends Profit" (Analects, IV, 16). True freedom is obtained by overcoming first-order desires through self-cultivation. Self-cultivation, coupled with care and nourishment received from significant others, is considered the necessary and sufficient condition for development of a truly moral, virtuous, and free person.

Confucius considered all individuals to be linked to others in a web of interrelatedness. The fundamental principle for governing relationships among individuals, family, society, the world, and beyond is best articulated in his piece, "Righteousness in the Heart" (in a chapter called the "Great Learning" in *The Book of Rites*). Although he considered individual morality to be central, the individual is still situated in a web of interpersonal and social relationships. He states that

If there be righteousness in the heart, there will be beauty in character,
If there be beauty in character, there will be harmony in the home.
If there be harmony in the home, there will be order in the nation.
If there be order in the nation, there will be peace in the world.

Confucian morality places priority on substantive goals over individual self-interests. Each individual has roles and a position in the family. The behavior of each role and position is formalized in the Confucian code of behavior. Within a family, the father is considered the symbolic head. As such, he holds the authority to represent the family and to speak and act on behalf of the family, but not against the family. For example, property is the communal possession of a family. Although the father has the right to dispose of the property, the other family members also have rights to the property. In the selling or leasing of family property, Lee (1991) found that, in traditional China, family members other than the father or the eldest son (such as other sons, daughters, or even grandsons) also sign sales and lease contracts. An arbitrary decision by the father generally is considered uncustomary or an illegitimate act (Lee, 1991).

A father has the authority, duty, and responsibility of handling family property on behalf of the family and not for his own benefit. Thus, wisdom and benevolence are necessary to ensure that his decisions are not myopic or self-serving. He must consider the long-term implications of his decision for individual family members, the family's reputation, and the family's position, ancestors, and progeny. The role of other family members is to obey and respect his decisions. Rights and obligations in Confucianism are thus role attached, unequal, welfaristic, paternalistic, and situational (Lee, 1991)

Although Confucianism emphasizes emotions and relationships, Confucian cultures have also evolved in the modern era from the traditional agricultural communities to rapidly developing industrialized nations. Many people think that East Asian societies have simply Westernized, but the situation is much more complex. Although some aspects of Western cultures have been adopted, the more significant changes involve the transformation of Confucian cultures that now emphasize the future rather than the past (Kim, 1998) (see Table 4.1).

Limitations on Using Confucianism to Explain Behavior

It is tempting to use Confucian philosophy to explain the behavior of the East Asians. There are four reasons why Confucianism cannot be used in this way. First, Confucianism can be used as a descriptive model, but it should not be used as an explanatory model. Ideas articu-

Table 4.1   Transformation of Values

Rural	Urban
Agricultural	Industrial
Past oriented	Future oriented
Extended family	Nuclear family
Ancestor	Children
Status quo	Change
Conservatism	Progress
Harmony with nature	Control environment
Formalism	Pragmatism
Cooperation	Competition
Wisdom acquired through experience	Analytical skills acquired through formal education
Sex differentiation	Equality

lated by Confucianism must be translated into psychological concepts and then empirically verified. Empirical verification is the feature that distinguishes science from philosophy.

Second, there are blind spots and biases in all philosophical traditions. In Confucianism, the father-son relationship is considered primary and the prototype for all relationships. However, if we examine developmental research in East Asia, the father-son relationship turns out to be secondary, while the mother-child relationship is primary. In traditional East Asian societies, fathers participated in socialization of children after the age of 3 or 4, which is after mothers have socialized children with basic linguistic and social skills. Also, the emphasis on paternalism and sex-role differentiation may have been functional in traditional agrarian societies, but in modern society, it may create social and organizational problems (Kim, 1998). In families, schools, companies, and society, paternalism must be supported by maternalism to achieve balance and harmony (Kim, 1988).

Third, the lay public may not be fully aware of basic Confucian concepts such as Human-heartedness, Rightness, Propriety, Knowledge, and Trust. These are philosophical concepts that are learned through formal schooling, but they are not psychological concepts. It is necessary to translate these philosophical concepts into psychological constructs and relate them to everyday terminology. For example, in Korea, the concept of *chong* (defined as the "affection and attachment for a person, place or thing") may be the functional equivalent of Human-heartedness (Kim, 1998). In Japan, *amae* (sweet indulgence) may be its functional equivalent (Kim & Yamaguchi, 1995). Although *chong*

and *amae* have very different denotations, psychological analysis reveals a similar pattern of results, capturing the essence of Human-heartedness (Kim, 1998; Kim & Yamaguchi, 1995). Filial piety can be interpreted as an example of Rightness (Kim, 1998). Although researchers examined the functionality of filial piety (such as taking care of parents in their old age), all children must fulfill the duties of filial piety as a moral imperative. The East Asian concepts of loyalty and duty may also capture the essence of Rightness. Finally, the concept of "face" may be an example of Propriety (Choi, Kim, & Kim, 1997).

The final limitation of using a philosophical text is that, within a particular culture, there are competing philosophies and worldviews. For example, Buddhism outlines an alternative conception of self, relations, and society in East Asia. In addition, native religions (such as Shamanism in Korea, Shintoism in Japan, and Daoism in China) have influenced both Buddhism and Confucianism. These three epistemologies have mutually influenced each another and have been integrated and blended into a synthetic form (Kim, 1998).

Confucian philosophy can be used as a starting point for research, but not as the end point. Confucian ideas can be used to develop hypotheses, constructs, and theories about human development and relationships. Once these ideas are developed, researchers need to test and verify them empirically.

Although it is important to examine indigenous text as a source of information, researchers should not assume automatically that Chinese will follow the Confucian way, or that Hindu Dharma automatically will explain the behavior of Indians. Although these indigenous texts were developed within a particular culture, they could also be a form of imposition that represents the interests of a particular religious group (e.g., Brahman caste in India) or social class (e.g., the ruling elite in East Asia). To use these texts, researchers must translate them into psychological concepts or theories and then empirically verify whether they influence how people think, feel, and behave. Indigenous texts may be useful for developing an alternative descriptive framework, and they may serve as a useful source of knowledge, but they may not be able to explain within-culture variations.

Although we must be careful of cross-cultural impositions, we must also be wary of within-culture impositions. Molding lay knowledge into institutionalized psychological theories is an example of the external imposition. Heider (1958) suggested, "The ordinary person has a great and profound understanding of himself and of other people which, though unformulated or vaguely conceived, enables him to interact in more or less adaptive ways" (p. 2). Based on Heider's preliminary work, Julian Rotter developed his theory of locus of control, and Bernard Weiner developed his attribution theory. These theories, however, are far removed from people's conception about attribution and control; more important, they possess low internal and external validity (Bandura, 1997; Park & Kim, 1999). The main problem with these approaches is that they have eliminated the influence of context and agency, which are central to understanding people's conception of a control and belief system (Bandura, 1997; Park & Kim, 1999).

Kim, Park, and Park (2000) contend that current psychological theories represent psychologists' conceptions, interpretations, and explanations rather than an accurate representation of human psychology. In other words, the current psychological knowledge can be described as the psychology of psychologists and not the psychology of the lay public (Harre, 1999; Koch & Leary, 1985).

Phenomenology

As pointed out above, even native philosophy can be an external imposition. It is important to understand how the ideas contained in native philosophies are understood, used, and modified in everyday life. They need to become integrated with the phenomenological lives of individuals.

The greatest variation across cultures exists in the area of phenomenology. In a cross-cultural study of child development, Azuma (1988) provides a poignant example of a phenomenon as viewed from within and from without. In a collaborative study with Robert Hess, they studied the behavior of mothers in the United States and Japan in regulating and disciplining their children. When a child refused to eat vegetables, a Japanese mother responded, "All right, then, you don't have to eat it." The U.S. research group coded the Japanese mother's response as giving up after a mild attempt at persuasion. The Japanese research group, in contrast, insisted that the response was a strong threat. The U.S. research group initially could not understand and accept the Japanese interpretation since the mother explicitly allowed the child to do as he pleased. Azuma (1988) explained that the purpose of the mother's utterance was to elicit guilt from the child: "It made the child feel that mother was suffering, and implied a threat to terminate the close mother-child tie" (p. 4). Although mothers in the United States are encouraged to reason with the child and provide a rational explanation of their request, in East Asia, interpersonal distancing is used to socialize children (Azuma, 1986; Ho, 1986; Kim & Choi, 1994). A threat to terminate the close mother-child relationship could be viewed as one of the most severe forms of punishment (Azuma, 1988).

According to Azuma (1988), the U.S. researchers interpreted the concept of guilt very differently from the Japanese researchers. Consistent with Western psychoanalytic and psychological theories, the U.S. researchers viewed the concept of guilt negatively: Guilt was presumed to be based on irrational beliefs, unrealistic fear, or forbidden wishes. Extensive use of guilt is believed to cause later developmental problems in adolescence. In East Asia, it is considered appropriate that children feel guilty toward their parents for the devotion, indulgence, sacrifice, and affection that they receive from them (Kim & Choi, 1994). Through the feeling of indebtedness, children feel guilty since they are unable to return the love, affection, and care that their parents provided them. Guilt in East Asia is viewed as an important interpersonal emotion that promotes filial piety, achievement motivation, and relational closeness.

Finally, Azuma (1988) points out that the U.S. method of discipline (i.e., enforcing adults' rules for children: Eat your vegetables!) could be considered cruel in Japan. In East Asia, children should not be punished for refusing to comply with adults' rules that they do not understand. Rather than punishing the child or reasoning with the child, the mother should reveal her hurt feelings and disappointment to the child, especially since she is trying to do what is best for the child. In East Asia, a mother should use her close emotional and relational bonds to convince the child to behave appropriately (Azuma, 1986; Ho, 1986; Kim & Choi, 1994). Through the use of close relationship and interpersonal bond emotions, the indulgent child is transformed into a compliant child.

Finally, as outlined by Tobin, Wu, and Davidson (1987), the indigenous psychologies approach encourages the use of the multivocal approach. In this approach, participants and observers other than researchers are allowed to evaluate and interpret psychological phenomena. Tobin et al. (1987) found that the greatest variations across cultures appeared in the way people interpreted and evaluated people's behavior.

Conclusion

Traditionally, indigenous psychologies have been often viewed as anthropological studies of exotic people living in distant lands. The approach also has been identified as a political voice against the dominant groups and colonial powers (Kim, 1995; Kim & Berry, 1993). The indigenous psychologies approach, however, represents a fundamental shift in scientific paradigm, from a positivistic conception of causality to a dynamic, transactional model of human functioning.

The indigenous psychologies approach is different from indigenization as advocated by Sinha (1997). Indigenization involves modifying and adapting existing theories, concepts, and methods to better fit a different culture or integrating Western theories with indigenous philosophies, such as Hinduism and Confucianism (Sinha, 1997). While indigenization represents an extension of the existing approach, the indigenous psychologies approach represents an alternative scientific paradigm.

Rather than emulating the natural sciences, the indigenous psychologies approach recognizes that the subject matter of psychology is fundamentally different, complex, and dynamic. Epistemology, theories, concepts, and methods must correspond with the subject matter of investigation. The goal of the indigenous psychologies approach is not to abandon science, but to create a science that is grounded firmly in the descriptive understanding of human beings. The goal is to create a more rigorous, systematic, universal science that can be verified theoretically and empirically rather than naively assumed.

We must be cautious of external impositions that may distort our understanding of psychological phenomena. First, researchers in the field of psychology imposed the natural sciences model to study human beings. In the rush to become an independent and respected branch of science, early psychologists tailored the psychological science to fit the natural science paradigm (Kim, 1999). Although psychologists were able to achieve a modest degree of methodological sophistication, psychological understanding became distorted.

The second imposition is the assumption of the universality of psychological theories. With very little development, testing, and data, psychological theories are assumed to be universal. This assumption is particularly problematic since most theories are developed in the United States and tested mainly on university students. In other words, theories that were tested on less than 1% of the total population have been assumed to be universal. Enormous amounts of time and resources have been wasted testing the universality of these theories without seriously questioning their basic assumptions, conceptualization, methodology, and scientific foundations. As a result, when these theories are applied, within and especially outside the United States, results are extremely disappointing (Kim, 1995).

Third, expert or professional knowledge has been imposed on the lay public. In most cases, the predictive value of these theories is very low when compared to the natural sciences. Psychologists may have been premature in developing theories, concepts, and methods without properly understanding the phenomenon itself. Psychologists largely have failed to describe psychological phenomena from the inside, from the person experiencing it. Instead, psychologists have dissected the world into cognitions, motivations, attitudes, values, emotions, and behavior, whereas in real life, these elements are components of experience and not the unit of experience. Perhaps the assumed expertise of the psychologists is a fabrication rather than firmly based solid evidence since researchers have difficulties in predicting, explaining, and modifying human behavior.

The indigenous psychologies approach advocates lifting these external impositions and advocates the experience of a phenomenon as an insider. Researchers may have focused too much attention on getting the right answer and ignored the process by which to get it. Along the way, psychologists have discarded many central constructs, such as agency, consciousness, or intentions as the extraneous variable. However, this is the "stuff" that makes human beings human. Psychologists have been focused on finding the basic components of behavior, and we have not realized that behavior is an emergent property of cognition, emotions, intention, and agency.

Finally, the indigenous psychologies approach emphasizes practical validity. Our knowledge should provide insights into the human world and should have practical applications. Indigenous analysis should be both basic and applied. The knowledge and insight that we obtain from indigenous field research should be able to assist parents to raise their children more efficaciously, teachers to educate students more effectively, businesspeople to make more money, politicians to rule effectively, and scientists to make the world a better place to live (Kim et al., 1999). Although science can provide the most accurate understanding of the world, it can also blind and limit our understanding.

Research is a humbling experience in which ideas accepted with certainty can be refuted or refined after further investigation. Researchers all start with an idea, model, theory, or method to uncover yet another secret of life. A researcher's preconceptions can aid, as well as limit, scientific discovery. A number of external impositions described above have limited the development of psychology. Science, above all, is a product of collective human effort, but often we become a victim or slaves of scientific myths.

The indigenous psychologies approach advocates a linkage of humanities (which focus on human experience) with social sciences (which focus on analysis and verification). We have focused most of our attention on internal or external validity and not on practical validity (Kim et al., 2000). In other words, do our theories help to understand, predict, and manage human behavior? In a practical sense, perhaps the greatest psychologist may have been William Shakespeare. He was not an analyst like Freud or Piaget, and he did not conduct experiments like Skinner, but he was able to capture human drama on paper and on stage. His dramas have been performed over the past centuries in many cultures and are loved throughout the world. In a similar vein, the greatest therapist might have been Ludwig van Beethoven or Wolfgang Amadeus Mozart, whose music is able to soothe frazzled nerves and the frustrations of daily life. Walt Disney could be considered the most notable developmental psychologist. He was able to capture the hearts and minds of the young and the young at heart. We not may think of these people as psychologists, but they have captured and reproduced human psychology on stage, film, tapes, or paper for many centuries and across different nations. We need to learn from them and to translate their phenomenological knowledge into analytical forms.

References

Allport, G. (1968). Historical background of modern social psychology. In G. Lindzey & E. Aronson (Eds.), *Handbook of social psychology* (Vol. 1) (pp. 1–79). Reading, MA: Addison-Wesley.

Azuma, H. (1984). Psychology in a non-Western country. *International Journal of Psychology, 19*, 145–155.

Azuma, H. (1986). Why study child development in Japan? In H. Stevenson, H. Azuma, & K. Hakuta (Eds.), *Child development and education in Japan* (pp. 3–11). New York: W. H. Freeman.

Azuma, H. (1988, September). *Are Japanese really that different? The concept of development as a key for transformation.* Paper presented at the 24th International Congress of Psychology, Sydney, Australia.

Bandura, A. (1997). *Self-efficacy: The exercise of control.* New York: Freeman.

Bandura, A., Reese, L., & Adams, N. E. (1982). Microanalysis of action and fear arousal as a function of differential levels of perceived self-efficacy. *Journal of Personality and Social Psychology, 43*, 5–21.

Barry, H., Bacon, M. K., & Child, I. L. (1959). Relations of child training to subsistence economy. *American Anthropologist, 61*, 51–63.

Berlin, I. (1976). *Vico and herder: Two studies in the history of ideas.* New York: Viking.

Berry, J. W. (1976). *Human ecology and cognitive style: Comparative studies in cultural and psychological adaptation.* New York: Wiley.

Berry, J. W. (1980). Introduction to methodology. In H. C. Triandis & W. W. Lambert (Eds.), *Handbook of cross-cultural psychology: Methodology* (Vol. 2, pp. 1–29). Boston: Allyn & Bacon.

Berry, J. W. (1993). Psychology in and of Canada: One small step toward a universal psychology. In U. Kim & J. W. Berry (Eds.), *Indigenous psychologies: Research and experience in cultural context* (pp. 260–277). Newbury Park, CA: Sage.

Berry, J. W., Poortinga, Y. H., Segall, M. H., & Dasen, P. R. (1992). *Cross-cultural psychology: Research and applications.* Cambridge: Cambridge University Press.

Boring, E. G. (1950). *A history of experimental psychology.* Englewood Cliffs, NJ: Prentice Hall. (Original work published 1921)

Boski, P. (1993). Between West and East: Humanistic values and concerns in Polish psychology. In U. Kim & J. W. Berry (Eds.), *Indigenous psychologies: Research and experience in cultural context* (pp. 79–103). Newbury Park, CA: Sage.

Boulding, K. (1980). Science: Our common heritage. *Science, 207,* 831–826.

Budd, M. (1989). *Wittgenstein's Philosophy of Psychology.* London: Routledge.

Burke, J. (1985). *The day the universe changed.* Boston: Little, Brown & Co.

Choi, S. C., Kim, U., & Kim, D. I. (1997). Multifaceted analyses of chemyon ("social face"): An indigenous Korean perspective. In K. Leung, U. Kim, S. Yamaguchi, & Y. Kashima (Eds.), *Progress in Asian social psychologies.* Singapore: John Wiley & Sons.

Chorover, S. L. (1980). *From genesis to genocide: The meaning of human nature and the power of behavior control.* Cambridge: MIT Press.

Confucius. (1979). *The analects.* Harmondsworth, UK: Penguin Books.

Cronbach, L. J. (1975). The two disciplines of scientific psychology. *American Psychologist, 12,* 671–684.

Danziger, K. (1983). Origins and basic principles of Wundt's *Volkerpsychologie. British Journal of Social Psychology, 22,* 303–313.

d'Espagnet, B. (1979). The quantum theory and reality. *Scientific American, 241,* 158–181.

Enriquez, V. G. (1993). Developing a Filipino psychology. In U. Kim & J. W. Berry (Eds.), *Indigenous psychologies: Research and experience in cultural context* (pp. 152–169). Newbury Park, CA: Sage.

Francis, R. C., Soma, K., & Fernald, R. D. (1993). Social regulation of the brain-pituitary-gonadal axis. *Neurobiology, 90,* 7794–7798.

Fuglesang, A. (1984). The myth of people's ignorance. *Developmental Dialogue, 1–2,* 42–62.

Georgas, J. (1993). Ecological-social model of Greek psychology. In U. Kim & J. W. Berry (Eds.), *Indigenous psychologies: Research and experience in cultural context* (pp. 56–78). Newbury Park, CA: Sage.

Gibson, J. J. (1985). Conclusions from a century of research on sense perception. In S. Koch & D. E. Leary (Eds.), *A century of psychology as science* (pp. 224–230). New York: McGraw-Hill.

Harré, R. (1999). The rediscovery of the human mind: The discursive approach. *Asian Journal of Social Psychology, 2,* 43–63.

Harré, R., & Gillet, G. (1994). *The discursive mind.* Thousand Oaks, CA: Sage.

Hebb, D. O. (1974). What psychology is about. *American Psychologist, 29,* 71–79.

Heider, F. (1958). *The psychology of interpersonal relations.* New York: Wiley.

Hofstede, G. (1991). *Organizations and cultures: Software of the mind.* New York: McGraw-Hill.

Holten, G. (1988). *Thematic origins of scientific thought: From Kepler to Einstein* (Rev. ed.). Cambridge: Harvard University Press.

Hwang, K. K. (1998). Two moralities: reinterpreting the findings of empirical research in Taiwan. *Asian Journal of Social Psychology, 1,* 211–238.

Kim, U. (1994). Individualism and collectivism: Conceptual clarification and elaboration. In U. Kim, H. C. Triandis, C. Kagitcibasi, S. C. Choi, & G. Yoon, G. (Eds.), *Individualism and collectivism: Theory, method, and applications* (pp. 19–40). Thousand Oaks, CA: Sage.

Kim, U. (1995). Psychology, science, and culture: Cross-cultural analysis of national psychologies in developing countries. *International Journal of Psychology, 30,* 663–679.

Kim, U. (1998). Understanding Korean corporate culture: Analysis of transformative human resource management. *Strategic Human Resource Development Review, 2,* 68–101.

Kim, U. (1999). After the crisis in social psychology: Development of the transactional model of science. *Asian Journal of Social Psychology, 1,* 1–19.

Kim, U., & Berry, J. W. (1993). *Indigenous psychologies: Experience and research in cultural context.* Newbury Park, CA: Sage.

Kim, U., & Choi, S. C. (1994). Individualism, collectivism, and child development: A Korean perspective. In P. M. Greenfield & R. Cocking (Eds.), *Cognitive socialization of minority children: Continuities and discontinuities* (pp. 227–258). Hillsdale, NJ: Lawrence Erlbaum.

Kim, U., Park, Y. S., & Park, D. H. (1999). The Korean indigenous psychology approach: Theoretical considerations and empirical applications. *Applied Psychology: An International Review, 45,* 55–73.

Kim, U., Park, Y. S., & Park, D. H. (2000). The challenge of cross-cultural psychology: The role of indigenous psychologies. *Journal of Cross-Cultural Psychology, 31*(1), 63–75.

Kim, U., Triandis, H. C., Kagitcibasi, C., Choi, S. C., & Yoon, G. (Eds.). (1994). *Individualism and collectivism: Theory, method, and applications.* Thousand Oaks, CA: Sage.

Kim, U., & Yamaguchi, S. (1995). Conceptual and empirical analysis of *amae*: Exploration into Japanese psycho-social space. In *Proceedings of the Japanese Group Dynamics 1995 Conference.* Tokyo: Japanese Group Dynamics Association.

Klineberg, O. (1980). Historical perspectives: Cross-cultural psychology before 1960. In H. C. Triandis & W. W. Lambert (Eds.), *Handbook of cross-cultural psychology: Perspectives* (Vol. 1, pp. 31–68). Boston: Allyn and Bacon.

Koch, S., & Leary, D. E. (Eds.). (1985). *A century of psychology as science.* New York: McGraw-Hill.

Leahey, T. H. (1987). *A history of psychology: Main currents in psychological thought.* London: Prentice-Hall.

Lee, S. H. (1991). *Virtues and rights: Reconstruction of Confucianism as a rational communitarianism.* Unpublished doctoral dissertation, University of Hawaii, Honolulu.

Lenzer, G. (1975). *August Comte and positivism: The essential writings.* New York: Harper & Row.

Lew, S. K. (1977). Confucianism and Korean social structure. In C. S. Yu (Ed.), *Korean and Asian religious tradition* (pp. 151–172). Toronto: University of Toronto Press.

Lomov, B., Budilova, E. A., Koltsova, V. A., & Medvedev, A. M. (1993). Psychological thought within the system of Russian culture. In U. Kim & J. W. Berry (Eds.), *Indigenous psychologies: Research and experience in cultural context* (pp. 104–1117). Newbury Park, CA: Sage.

Merz, J. T. (1965). *A history of European thought in the 19th century.* Cambridge: Harvard University Press. (Original work published 1904)

Mundy-Castle, A. C. (1974). Social and technological intelligence in Western and non-Western cultures. *Universitas, 4,* 46–52.

Park, Y. S., & Kim, U. (1999). Conceptual and empirical analysis of attributional style: The relationship among six attributional style in Korea. *The Korean Journal of Educational Psychology, 137*(3), 119–165.

Sampson, E. E. (1978). Scientific paradigms and social values: Wanted—A scientific revolution. *Journal of Personality and Social Psychology, 36,* 1332–1343.

Segall, M. H., Dasen, P. R., Berry, J. W., & Poortinga, Y. H. (1990). *Human behavior in global perspective: An introduction to cross-cultural psychology.* New York: Pergamon.

Shepard, R. N. (1987). Toward a universal law of generalization for psychological sciences. *Science, 237,* 1317–1323.

Shweder, R. A. (1991). *Thinking through cultures—Expeditions in cultural psychology.* Cambridge: Harvard University Press.

Sinha, D. (1997). Indigenizing psychology. In J. W. Berry, Y. H. Poortinga, & J. Pandey (Eds.), *Handbook of cross-cultural psychology: Theory and method* (Vol. 1) (pp. 129–170). Boston: Allyn & Bacon.

Tobin, J., Wu., D. Y. H., & Davidson, D. H. (1989). *Preschool in three cultures: Japan, China, and the United States.* New Haven, CT: Yale University Press.

Toennies, F. (1963). *Community and society.* New York: Harper & Row. (Original work published 1887)

Triandis, H. C., Lambert, W. W., Berry, J. W., Lonner, W., Heron, A., Brislin, R. W., & Draguns, J. G. (1980). *Handbook of cross-cultural psychology* (Vols. 1–6). Boston: Allyn & Bacon.

van Hoorn, W., & Verhave, T. (1980). Wundt's changing conceptions of a general and theoretical psychology. In W. G. Bringmann & R. D. Tweeney (Eds.), *Wundt studies: A centennial collection.* Toronto: Hogrefe.

Wallner, F. (1999, August). *Constructive realism.* Paper presented at the Third International Conference of the Asian Association of Social Psychology, Taipei.

Wundt, W. (1916). *Elements of folk psychology: Outlines of a psychological history of the development of mankind* (E. L. Schaub, Trans.). London: George Allen & Unwin.

5

The Evolution of Cross-Cultural Research Methods

FONS VAN DE VIJVER

As cross-cultural psychology has evolved as a discipline, new developments have occurred not only in theory and concept, as discussed in all other chapters, but also in empirical methods. These changes reflect more than minor adjustments to traditional approaches to experimental psychology; indeed, these developments have brought about an evolution in technique and method in cross-cultural research that has resulted in fundamentally different and unique ways of conducting studies. Indeed, while cross-cultural methods continue to be influenced by mainstream methodologies, they are being adapted and modified continually to incorporate new technologies and methodological innovations specific to cross-cultural inquiry.

In this chapter, van de Vijver provides an excellent overview of those methodological issues unique to cross-cultural research. He describes the most characteristic distinguishing features of cross-cultural methods and discusses those methods in a historical perspective. His comparison and contrast with the traditional experimental approach in psychology is especially useful, and the reader will find an eloquent discussion of how the developers of cross-cultural methods first adopted mainstream experimental methods and then adapted them to fit the unique needs of cross-cultural study, adjusting its methods as findings from cross-cultural research drove psychological theories in fundamental ways.

In particular, van de Vijver's treatment of issues relating to bias and equivalence—acknowledged by many as the most pressing issues related to cross-cultural research methods—is excellent. He not only reviews a definition of these terms, but also discusses in particular detail the possible sources of bias in cross-cultural research, as well as how to deal with bias. His review of translation, methodological, and procedural issues relating to multilingual studies is also informative and fascinating.

The reader will find tables that are particularly useful; they summarize typical sources of bias and strategies for dealing with bias in cross-cultural research. These tables summarize more than adequately the expanded discussion of these same issues in the text and serve as a handy reference guide for all cross-cultural researchers, experienced and not. Also useful is the Appendix, which provides 22 guidelines for cross-cultural research; these guidelines were generated by the International Test Commission and provide a fairly comprehensive list of suggestions and advice that ensures the conduct of cross-cultural research of the highest quality.

Van de Vijver's main thrust is to examine how cross-cultural research methods have evolved ("adjusted" in his terminology), adapting methods of mainstream psychological experimentation to improve the suitability of extant methods in cross-cultural inquiry. As the basic goal of cross-cultural inquiry has evolved from merely documenting cross-cultural differences to examining what it is about cultures that produces those differences and why, it is only natural that the methods of inquiry to address this changing goal also evolve in nature. This suggests that methods of cross-cultural science, like the findings and knowledge produced by the field, are fluid and dynamic, ever changing over time, reacting to while producing cutting edge findings about the nature of cultural influences on behavior.

At the same time, van de Vijver suggests that these evolving methods of cross-cultural psychology need to be incorporated with methods of cultural psychology—with its focus on local surveys and in situ examinations of behavior—to evolve further into a yet newer methodology. This new methodology will be one with a truly cultural perspective and one that will be most able to help us produce a universal psychology, which is the goal of students of culture and psychology. In this sense, van de Vijver's overall message is exactly the same as that of other authors in this part of the book, and he provides us with the methodological clues as to how to achieve the goals of rapprochement and evolution. As the ultimate goal of cross-cultural psychology to aid in the creation of a universal psychology is a fundamentally different goal for research than has been previously held, it necessitates further evolution in method as well.

Research methods, a generic term for all aspects of study design and data analysis, have always been important in cross-cultural psychology. It has even been argued that cross-cultural psychology is primarily a method. This was probably an accurate statement in the early days of cross-cultural psychology; both the theoretical background and instruments in cross-cultural studies were borrowed from mainstream, Western psychology, and cross-cultural research elaborated on mainstream psychology by (and only by) examining different samples. Much of this research critically reflected on the often implicitly assumed universal validity of Western theories and instruments. In the course of history, however, the cross-cultural field began to develop its own array of empirical studies and theories, such as the theory about the influence of ecocultural style on psychological functioning (Berry, 1976) and models of cross-cultural differences and similarities in attitudes and values (e.g., Hofstede, 1980; Schwartz, 1992). Yet, throughout the history of cross-cultural studies, methodological aspects have retained a prominent place.

The present chapter sets out to address the following questions about cross-cultural research methods:

1. What are the distinguishing features of cross-cultural research methods?
2. What is the history of the field?
3. What is the current "state of the art"? What are current standards of good research practice in cross-cultural psychology?
4. What is the future of the field? What important developments can be expected to take place?

Distinguishing Features of Cross-Cultural Research Methods

Like all sciences, cross-cultural psychology is about making inferences. Input to these inferences usually comes from individuals from different cultural groups. In most studies, we are not particularly interested in the specific subjects. It is also uncommon to find studies in which the contents of items are the focus of interest. Rather, samples and instruments studied are mere carriers and are interesting only inasmuch as they provide access to inferences that transcend their boundaries. If properly composed, samples have a well-described, mathematical link to the population from which they are drawn. Particularly, in comparative survey research, much attention is paid to sampling schemes to ensure that the link between the sample and the population of interest can be fully exploited (Gabler & Haeder, in press; Kish, 1965). Analogously, items of an appropriately designed instrument can be considered to be samples of behaviors, attitudes, or other psychological characteristics from an underlying psychological universe (e.g., a trait, ability, or attitude), usually called the *domain of generalization*.

Inferential leaps from sample to population of interest and from test score to domain of generalization cannot always be taken for granted. Many problems of cross-cultural research can be seen as emanating from questionable inferential leaps. Two kinds of incorrect inferences are recurrent in cross-cultural research: They can be either incorrect or too broad. An example of an incorrect inference would be when two groups show differences in social desirability that are not taken into account in interpreting score differences on some measure, such as a personality or individualism-collectivism inventory. Cross-cultural differences in the latter may be overestimated or underestimated, depending on the direction of the influence of social desirability. Problems arising from overly broad generalizations abound in cross-cultural psychology. We are often inclined to generalize scores obtained from a small sample of university students to the population at large. The atypical nature of student samples is well documented (e.g., their narrow range of age and intelligence), but is infrequently taken into account (Smith & Bond, 1993).

The methodological problems of cross-cultural research are not unique and play in various branches of psychology that study intact groups, such as clinical, educational, and industrial, and organizational psychology. However, the problems are often more prominent in cross-cultural research because of the nature of culture (or ethnic group) as a variable of interest. From a methodological perspective, it is difficult to deal with culture as a variable.

Experimental studies are popular in psychology. The "mother" of all research designs is still the experiment in which subjects are allocated randomly to experimental treatments (Campbell & Stanley, 1966; Cook & Campbell, 1979; Poortinga & Malpass, 1986). Several variations on the general design can be found, such as the use of double-blind, placebo-controlled, and/or crossover conditions (Christensen, 1997). The major advantage of the design is its strict control of ambient variables. Experimental and control groups differ only in the experimental treatment and are matched on all other factors that are relevant to the experimental outcome. When a statistically significant difference is found between experimental and control groups, we feel confident in concluding that the experimental treatment had an impact on the dependent variable of interest.

Although developed for Western laboratory research, true experiments have a pancultural validity. An example of an experiment in a non-Western context is provided by Shrestha, West, Bleichrodt, van de Vijver, and Hautvast (in press), who were interested in the influence of iodine and iron deficiency on mental development. A group of primary school children in the Ntcheu district in Malawi, where goiter and iron deficiency are endemic, was split randomly into four treatment conditions: One treatment group received iodine supplementation, one received iron supplementation, one received a combination, and one received a placebo. The children were allocated randomly, and test administrators did not know to which treatment group any child belonged. For various cognitive tests, such as fluency and vocabulary, the scores of the iodine-supplemented group was on average one standard deviation above those of the placebo group; for iron, smaller, though still significant, effects were found. By adhering to the rigor of the experimental approach (e.g., a random assignment of subjects to experimental conditions, the presence of a placebo group, and the absence of any information among the testers about the supplementation the children received), the authors felt confident that observed supplementation effects were valid and not due to unintended artifacts, such as accidental differences in treatment groups.

Although the example may well demonstrate the global adequacy of true experiments in cross-cultural psychology, its limitation should be acknowledged: All four treatment groups came from the same culture; hence, the study was not culture comparative. The question can be asked whether such true experimental designs apply to cross-cultural comparisons. The answer is negative; an experimenter cannot assign subjects randomly to cultures. Like all intrinsic subject characteristics, membership of a culture cannot be manipulated experimentally.

The implications for a culture-comparative methodology are severe; it implies that cultural groups, unlike treatment groups in a true experiment, can and often will differ in many respects. Score differences in different cultural groups may in principle be engendered by all factors in which the samples differ, such as age, gender, educational level, experience with psychological tests, motivation, and interest in the study. If the focus of a cross-cultural study merely is documentation of cross-cultural differences, there may be no need to bother about confounding differences. If a producer of soft drinks who introduces an existing drink in a new country wants to know if the taste should be adjusted, there may be little concern with confounding differences. The producer may be less interested in comprehending the reason for the taste difference across countries than in specific and valid information about the optimal level of sweetening and other taste-related aspects in the new country. In cross-cultural psychology, our interest is often broader, and the observation of differences only marks the beginning of a search for their explanation.

Everyday explanations of cross-cultural differences are often based on a simple reasoning scheme: If Japanese and American women behave differently, this is due to their difference in cultural background. From a scientific perspective, this reasoning is not very revealing (Lonner & Adamopoulos, 1997; Poortinga & van de Vijver, 1987). Saying that a Japanese and an American woman behave in different ways because they belong to different cultures merely paraphrases these behavioral differences and the existence of cross-cultural differences; it dodges the question of the source of these differences. It is a bit like saying that my car does not work because it is broken. However natural the reasoning may sound, a car mechanic will not be able to help me until a more specific description of the problem can be given. Analogously, a good explanation does not refer to cultural background in toto, but explores more specific factors that may account for the difference.

In attempts to explain cross-cultural differences, we often need to choose among a host of available explanations. Theoretical and methodological considerations may govern the choice. As an example of the former, individualism-collectivism is often used to explain patterns of cross-cultural differences; observed score differences are then placed in a broader theoretical framework. A methodological rationale can be based on the explicit measurement of constructs that constitute rival explanations (e.g., social desirability).

The problematic methodological nature of culture as a variable in cross-cultural research has various ramifications that are explored in the next sections. Because culture is such a broad summary label, encompassing hosts of underlying differences, a central problem of cross-cultural research is the exact delineation of the source of cross-cultural differences; from a methodological perspective, an important aspect of doing cross-cultural research is dealing with alternative explanations.

History of Research Methods in Cross-Cultural Psychology

The methodological roots of cross-cultural research are more situated in psychology than in cultural anthropology, with its emphasis on the observation of in situ behavior (participatory observation), the use of informants as experts, and the reliance on qualitative methodology. The last are more frequently employed in cultural psychology (Cole, 1996; Greenfield, 1997a; Miller, 1997).

A major event in the methodology of psychology was the publication of Campbell and Stanley's (1966) *Experimental and Quasi-Experimental Designs for Research*. It epitomizes the thinking on methodology current in those days. The true experiment, described in the previous section, is seen as the "royal road" to establish valid, replicable knowledge in psychology. The monograph has become highly influential and has set the standard for psychology and for cross-cultural psychology. There is an emphasis on internal validity and on identifying and remedying threats of internal validity (e.g., carryover effects in pretest-posttest studies).

The adoption of prevailing psychological methods gave an impetus to the emergence of the field of cross-cultural research. One could rely on well-established means of researching, analyzing, and reporting data. Unfortunately, the reliance on psychological methods also had its problems. It has been repeatedly argued that, to some extent, the classical experimental framework was a Procrustean bed for branches of psychology that work with intact groups (i.e., groups without random assignment), such as cross-cultural, educational, clinical, and organizational research.

The experimental framework may work well when an experimenter wants to carry out an experiment in different cultures; however, the framework may be of limited value when dealing with culture as an experimental variable. A good example can be found in the classical Neyman-Pearson framework that forms the basis of current hypothesis testing practice. If we compare two means in a *t* test, we often choose an alpha level of .05 or .01. A low value is chosen to ensure that observed differences that show statistical significance are not due to random fluctuations, but reflect genuine differences in population means. Now, suppose that a battery of cognitive tests has been administered to urban Anglo American children and illiterate rural children from Bangladesh. Differences in cognitive test scores of these groups can be expected to be large because schooling has been found to show a pervasive influence on cognitive tests scores (e.g., Rogoff, 1981; van de Vijver, 1997). A test of the null hypothesis of no cultural differences is not a very meaningful approach to examine these groups. It could even be argued that the cultural distance of the cultures is so large that an observation of no significant differences for any test of the battery would be more informative than the finding of a significant difference. In general, a framework of null hypothesis testing of no cultural differences may be useful for comparing closely related cultural groups, such as Dutch-speaking and French-speaking Belgians, but the framework may be more a liability than an asset in comparing groups that are highly divergent culturally. The implicit focus in the Neyman-Pearson framework on avoiding Type I errors (rejecting the null hypothesis when it is true) constitutes a questionable base for hypothesis testing in cross-cultural psychology. In sum, the classical experimental paradigm needed to be adjusted to cater for the needs of cross-cultural researchers.

Many publications on cross-cultural research methods exemplify this new "adjustment perspective." The question of how we can apply or adapt methods from mainstream psychology to make them suitable for use in cross-cultural research runs like a thread through various publications on cross-cultural research methodology, such as Brislin, Lonner, and Thorndike's (1973) *Cross-Cultural Research Methods*; chapters on methodology in Triandis and Berry's (1980) first edition of the *Handbook of Cross-Cultural Psychology*; Lonner and Berry's (1986) *Field Methods in Cross-Cultural Research*; and van de Vijver and Leung's (1997a, 1997b) chapter and book.

In the last decades, considerable progress has been made in the "adjustment perspective." First, cross-culturalists can draw on work by others on the limited applicability of true experiments and the ubiquity of quasi-experimental designs in psychology. Cook and Campbell's (1979) *Quasi-Experimentation* is an extension of Campbell and Stanley's (1966) original work in a direction relevant to cross-cultural psychology. There is a discussion of causality in nonexperimental research and validity threats and enhancement in quasi-experimental research. Second, advancements in statistics have made it possible to analyze problems previously not tractable in cross-cultural research (see p. 90, this volume).

Current Standards in Cross-Cultural Research

Bias and Equivalence: Definitions and Classifications

Suppose that a depression inventory has been administered in two countries, and that the symptoms referred to in the inventory are both somatic (e.g., loss of appetite, sleeplessness) and psychological (e.g., sadness, lack of interest in other people). Furthermore, suppose that somatization of problems is commonly encountered in one of the cultures, and that psychological symptoms are not seen as part of depression. A cross-cultural comparison of mean scores on the inventory has low validity. Because of the different manifestations of depression in the cultures, the question of which group shows more depressive symptoms is not easy to answer; it is definitely not solved by carrying out a *t* test of the mean scores of the two cultural groups.

The two most essential concepts in cross-cultural methodology, bias and equivalence (Poortinga, 1989), can be illustrated on the basis of the example. *Bias* refers to the presence of nuisance factors that jeopardize the comparability of scores across cultural groups. If scores are biased, their psychological meaning is group dependent, and group differences in assessment outcome are to be accounted for, at least to some extent, by auxiliary psychological constructs or measurement artifacts.

The presence of bias has a bearing on the comparability of scores across cultures. The measurement implications of bias for comparability are addressed in the concept of *equivalence*. It refers to the comparability of test scores obtained in different cultural groups. Obviously, bias and equivalence are related. It may even be argued that they are mirror concepts: Bias is then synonymous to nonequivalence;

conversely, equivalence refers to the absence of bias. This practice is not followed here because, in the presentation of cross-cultural research methodology, it is instructive to disentangle sources of bias and their implications for score comparability.

Following van de Vijver and Leung (1997a, 1997b), three sources of bias in cross-cultural research are distinguished. The first is called *construct bias*; it occurs when the construct measured is not identical across groups or when behaviors that constitute the domain of interest from which items are sampled are not identical across cultures, as illustrated in the example of the depression study. An empirical example can be found in Ho's (1996) work on filial piety (psychological characteristics associated with being a good son or daughter). The Western conceptualization is more constricted than the Chinese, according to which children are supposed to assume the role of caretaker of their parents when the parents grow old and are in need of help from others. Construct bias precludes the cross-cultural measurement of a construct with the same measure. An inventory of filial piety based on the Chinese conceptualization will cover aspects unrelated to the concept among Western subjects, while a Western-based inventory will leave important Chinese aspects uncovered. Embretson (1983) coined the related term *construct underrepresentation* to refer to an insufficient sampling of all relevant domains in an instrument. There is an important difference between construct bias and Embretson's term; whereas construct underrepresentation is a problem of short instruments measuring broad concepts, which can usually be overcome by adding items from the same domain, construct bias can only be remedied by adding items from a new domain.

An important type of bias, called *method bias*, can result from sample incomparability, instrument characteristics, tester and interviewer effects, and the method (mode) of administration. In general, method bias is a label for all sources of bias that stem from aspects described in the method section of empirical papers. Examples are differential stimulus familiarity (in mental testing) and differential social desirability (in personality and survey research). In the depression example, method bias could be induced by, among other things, age, gender, self-disclosure, or social desirability to report mental health problems.

Finally, the last type of bias refers to anomalies at the item level; it is called *item bias* or *differential item functioning*. According to a definition that is widely used in psychology, an item is biased if persons with the same standing on the underlying construct (e.g., they are equally intelligent), but coming from different cultural groups, do not have the same average score on the item. The score on the construct is usually derived from the total test score. If a geography test administered to pupils in Poland and Japan contains the item, "What is the capital of Poland?" Polish pupils can be expected to show higher scores on the item than Japanese students, even when pupils with the same total test score are compared. The item is biased because it favors one cultural group across all test score levels. If, in our depression example, somatic symptoms would be shared by the cultural groups, while psychological problems are part of depression in only one culture, an item bias analysis may identify the items about psychological problems as biased. Of all bias types, item bias has been the most extensively studied; various psychometric techniques are available to identify item bias (e.g., Camilli & Shepard, 1994; Holland & Wainer, 1993).

Four different types of equivalence are proposed here (cf. van de Vijver & Leung, 1997a, 1997b). The first type is labeled *construct nonequivalence*. It amounts to comparing "apples and oranges" (e.g., the comparison of Chinese and Western filial piety, discussed above). Because there is no shared attribute, no comparison can be made. The second is called *structural* (or *functional*) *equivalence*. An instrument administered in different cultural groups shows structural equivalence if it measures the same construct in these groups. Structural equivalence has been examined for various cognitive tests (Jensen, 1980), Eysenck's Personality Questionnaire (Barrett, Petrides, Eysenck, & Eysenck, 1998), and the so-called five-factor model of personality (McCrae & Costa, 1997). Structural equivalence does not presuppose the use of identical instruments across cultures. A depression measure may be based on different indicators in different cultural groups and still show structural equivalence.

The third type of equivalence is called *measurement unit equivalence*. Instruments show this type of equivalence if their measurement scales have the same units of measurement and a different origin (such as the Celsius and Kelvin scales in temperature measurement). This type of equivalence assumes interval- or ratio-level scores (with the same measurement units in each culture). At first sight, it may seem unnecessary or even counterproductive to define a level of equivalence with the same measurement units but different origins. After all, if we apply the same interval-level scale in different groups, scores may be either fully comparable or fully incomparable (in the case of nonequivalence).

The need for the concept of measurement unit equivalence may become clear by looking at the impact of differential social desirability or stimulus familiarity on cross-cultural score differences in more detail. Suppose that the Raven test has been administered to literate and illiterate groups. It is not farfetched to assume that cross-cultural differences in stimulus familiarity will affect the scores. The literate subjects are expected to show higher scores and to have a larger stimulus familiarity. At least some of the observed score differences may have to be accounted for by differential stimulus familiarity, which will obscure real cross-cultural differences. When the relative contribution of both sources cannot be estimated, the interpretation of group comparisons of mean scores remains ambiguous. A correction for differential familiarity would be required to make the scores comparable. It may be noted that the basic idea of score corrections that are needed to make scores fully comparable is also applied in covariance analysis, in which score comparisons are made after the disturbing role of concomitant factors (bias in the context of the present chapter) is statistically controlled.

Only in the case of *scalar* (or *full-score*) *equivalence* direct comparisons can be made; it is the only type of equivalence that allows for statistical tests that compare means (such as *t* tests and analyses of variance). This type of equivalence assumes the same interval or ratio scales across groups, and that the role of bias can be neglected safely. Conclusions about which of the last two types of equivalence applies are often difficult to draw and can easily create controversy. For example, racial differences in intelligence test scores have been interpreted as due to valid differences (scalar equivalence) and as reflecting measurement artifacts (measurement unit equivalence).

Structural, measurement unit, and scalar equivalence are hierarchically ordered. The third presupposes the second, which presupposes the first. As a consequence, higher levels of equivalence are more difficult to establish. It is easier to demonstrate that an instrument measures the same construct in different cultural groups (structural equivalence) than to demonstrate numerical comparability across cultures (scalar equivalence). On the other hand, higher levels of equivalence allow for more precise comparisons of scores across cultures. Whereas only factor structures and nomological networks (Cronbach & Meehl, 1955) can be compared in the case of structural equivalence, measurement unit and full-score scalar equivalence allow for more fine-grained analyses of cross-cultural similarities and difference. It is only in the case of full score equivalence that mean scores can be compared across cultures in *t* tests and analyses of (co)variance.

Sources of Bias

Bias and equivalence are not inherent characteristics of an instrument, but arise in the application of an instrument in at least two cultural groups; they are characteristics of a cross-cultural comparison. Decisions on the level of equivalence and the presence or absence of bias should be empirically based. The plea for such a validation should not be interpreted as a reliance on blind empiricism and the impossibility of implementing preventive measures in a study to minimize bias and maximize equivalence. Quite on the contrary, not all instruments are equally susceptible to bias. For example, more structured test administrations are less prone to bias than open-ended questions. Analogously, comparisons of closely related group will be less susceptible to bias than comparisons of groups with widely different cultural backgrounds. To prevent bias, one will need to have insight into its potential sources. The overview in Table 5.1 is based on a classification by van de Vijver and Tanzer (1997; cf. van de Vijver & Poortinga, 1997). The overview can only be tentative because bias sources are numerous.

Construct Bias

Construct bias can occur if cultural definitions of a construct do not completely coincide across groups. Ho's (1996) work on filial piety was mentioned above. Another example comes from personality research. Yang and Bond (1990) presented American and indigenous Chinese person descriptors to a group of Taiwanese subjects. Factor analyses showed differences in the Chinese and American factors. Similarly, Cheung et al. (1996) found that the five-factor model of personality (McCrae & Costa, 1997) that is Western based does not cover all aspects

Table 5.1 Typical Sources for the Three Types of Bias in Cross-Cultural Assessment

Type of Bias	Source of Bias
Construct bias	Culture-specific definitions of the construct across cultures
	Differential appropriateness of the behaviors associated with the construct (e.g., skills do not belong to the repertoire of one of the cultural groups)
	Poor sampling of all relevant behaviors (e.g., short instruments)
	Incomplete coverage of all relevant aspects/facets of the construct (e.g., not all relevant domains are sampled)
Method bias	Differential familiarity with stimulus material
	Differential familiarity with response procedures
	Differential response styles (e.g., social desirability, extremity scoring, acquiescence)
	Incomparability of samples (e.g., caused by differences in education, motivation)
	Differences in environmental administration conditions, physical (e.g., recording devices) or social (e.g., class size)
	Ambiguous instructions for respondents and/or guidelines for administrators
	Differential expertise of administrators
	Tester/interviewer/observer effects (e.g., halo effects)
	Communication problems between respondent and tester/interviewer (including interpreter problems and taboo topics)
Item bias	Poor item translation and/or ambiguous items
	Nuisance factors (e.g., item may invoke additional traits or abilities)
	Cultural specifics (e.g., incidental differences in connotative meaning and/or appropriateness of the item content)

Source: After van de Vijver & Tanzer, 1997.

deemed relevant by Chinese to describe personality. In addition to the Western factors of extraversion, agreeableness, conscientiousness, neuroticism (emotional stability), and openness, two more Chinese factors were found: face and harmony.

Construct bias can also be caused by differential appropriateness of the behaviors associated with the construct in the different cultures. An example comes from research on intelligence. Western intelligence tests tend to focus on reasoning and logical thinking (such as the Raven's Progressive Matrices), while tests of acquired knowledge have typically been added in large batteries (such as Vocabulary scales of the Wechsler scales). When Western individuals are asked which characteristics they associate with an intelligent person, skilled reasoning and knowing much are frequently mentioned. In addition, social aspects of intelligence are mentioned. These last aspects are even more prominent in everyday conceptions of intelligence in non-Western groups. Kokwet mothers (Kenya) said that an intelligent child knows its place in the family and its expected behaviors, like proper ways of addressing other people. An intelligent child is obedient and does not create problems (Mundy-Castle, 1974, cited in Segall, Dasen, Berry, & Poortinga, 1990).

Studies in Zambia (Serpell, 1993) and Japan (Azuma & Kashiwagi, 1987) also show that descriptions of an intelligent person go beyond the school-oriented domain with which intelligence is commonly associated in the United States and Europe, and that social aspects may be deemed more relevant in non-Western countries. Kuo and Marsella (1977), who studied Machiavellianism in China and the United States, have reported another example. A comparison of factor analytic results clearly showed country differences in behavioral referents associated with the construct in both countries.

Finally, poor sampling of all the relevant behaviors indicative of the construct can give rise to construct bias. Triandis (1978) complained more than 20 years ago that our measures are often a poor sample of the comprehensive constructs that we want to measure. Embretson's (1983) notion of construct underrepresentation refers to the same problem of short tests that measure broad constructs. Pleas to discontinue this practice tend to fall on deaf ears. Poor sampling can also come from another source. Some empirical studies of item bias have reported such large proportions of items to be biased that their removal would lead to construct underrepresentation. Van Leest (1997a, 1997b) found more than half of the items of a

Dutch personality inventory to be biased in a comparison of native and migrant job applicants in the Netherlands. Similarly, in a cross-cultural Rasch analysis of the Cattell Culture Fair Intelligence Test between American and Nigerian students, Nenty and Dinero (1981) had to remove 24 of 46 items because these items either did not fit the Rasch model or showed cross-cultural bias.

Method Bias

Sample bias is more likely to threaten cross-cultural comparisons when the cultures examined differ in more respects; such a larger cultural distance will often increase the number of alternative explanations for cross-cultural differences to be considered. Recurrent rival explanations are cross-cultural differences in social desirability and stimulus familiarity (test-wiseness). The main problem with both social desirability and testwiseness is their relationship with a country's affluence, often made operational as the country's gross national product (per capita). Van Hemert, van de Vijver, Poortinga, and Georgas (in press) examined the relationship of Lie Scale scores (a scale of social desirability that is part of the Eysenck Personality Questionnaire) and the gross national product. They found a highly significant negative correlation of −.70. More affluent countries tend to show lower scores on social desirability. Similarly, Williams, Satterwhite, and Saiz (1998) asked students in 10 countries (Chile, China, Korea, Nigeria, Norway, Pakistan, Portugal, Singapore, Turkey, and the United States) to rate the favorability of 300 person-descriptive terms. Favorability is probably closely related to social desirability. A country average of the 300 items (which presumably reflects social desirability as the adjectives represent a broad sample of both favorable and unfavorable descriptors) correlated −.66 with affluence.

Subject recruitment procedures are another potential source of sample bias in cognitive tests. Thus, the motivation to display one's attitudes or abilities may depend on the amount of previous exposure to psychological tests, the freedom whether to participate, and other outcome-relevant characteristics.

Administration bias can be caused by differences in the environmental administration conditions, whether physical, technical, or social. For example, when interviews are held in the houses of respondents, physical conditions (e.g., ambient noise, presence of others) are difficult to control in cross-cultural studies. Examples of social environmental conditions are individual (vs. group) administration, amount of space between testees (in group testing), or class size (in educational settings). Other sources of administration bias are ambiguity in the test instructions and/or testing guidelines or a differential application of these instructions. To what extent the presence of the test administrator or interviewer impinges on the measurement outcome has been empirically studied; regrettably, various studies apply inadequate designs and do not cross (i.e., make all combinations of) the cultures of testers and testees. In cognitive testing, the presence of the tester is usually not very obtrusive (Jensen, 1980). In survey research, there is more evidence for interviewer effects (Singer & Presser, 1989). Deference to the interviewer has been reported; subjects were more likely to display positive attitudes to a particular cultural group when they were interviewed by someone from that group (e.g., Aquilino, 1994; Cotter, Cohen, & Coulter, 1982; Reese, Danielson, Shoemaker, Chang, & Hsu, 1986).

A final source of administration bias is communication problems between the respondent and the tester/interviewer. For example, interventions of interpreters may influence the measurement outcome. Communication problems are not restricted to working with translators. Language problems may be a potent source of bias when, as is not uncommon in cross-cultural studies, a test or interview is administered in the second or third language of interviewers or respondents. Illustrations for miscommunications between native and nonnative speakers can be found in Gass and Varonis (1991).

Instrument bias is a common source of bias in cognitive tests. An interesting example comes from Piswanger's (1975) application of the Viennese Matrices Test (Formann & Piswanger, 1979), a Raven-like figural inductive reasoning test, to Austrians and (Arabic-educated) Nigerian and Togolese high school students. The most striking findings were cross-cultural differences in the item difficulties related to identifying and applying rules in the horizontal direction (i.e., left to right). This was interpreted in terms of the different directions in writing Latin versus Arabic (the latter is written from right to left).

Item Bias

Item bias is commonly induced by poor item translation, ambiguities in the original item, low familiarity/appropriateness of the item content in certain cultures, and influence of cultural specifics, such as nuisance factors or connotations associated with the item wording. Poor item translation can be caused either by translation errors or by "genuine" linguistic idiosyncrasies. Even translations that are linguistically correct may still have low quality from a psychological point of view. A good example given by Hambleton (1994, p. 235), is the test item, "Where is a bird with webbed feet most likely to live?" which was part of a large international study of educational achievement. Compared to the overall pattern, the item turned out to be unexpectedly easy in Sweden. A back translation revealed why. The Swedish translation of the English "bird with webbed feet" was "bird with swimming feet," which provides a much stronger clue to the solution than the English original item.

Cultural specifics in content and/or connotation of the item are a frequently observed source of item bias. The following example given by Szalay (1981) may serve as an illustration of culture-specific connotations:

The English word corruption corresponds beyond a shadow of a doubt to the Korean word pupae, but this does not ensure that the cultural meanings of the two words are the same. Different cultural experiences produce different interpretations not shown in conventional dictionaries. A systematic comparison of the Korean and American meanings of corruption shows that for both groups it involves negative, bad, improper behavior. An important difference is that in the American interpretation corruption is rejected on moral grounds; it is wrong and it is a crime. For Koreans corruption is not morally wrong; it is only bad in the sense that it interferes with the proper function of the government and social institutions; and it is bad in its social consequences. (p. 141)

Item bias can also stem from idiomatic expressions or words that translate poorly, such as the well-known German term Zeitgeist, which has no one-to-one English translation, and the English word distress, which does not have an equivalent in many languages.

Dealing with Bias

There are various ways to deal with bias (cf. Poortinga & Van der Flier, 1988). A first option is to ignore bias. At first sight, it may seem paradoxical to mention this option as ignoring

bias cannot be considered as a real way of dealing with it. The reason to mention it here is its popularity. Many cross-cultural studies are reported in the literature in which there is no analysis of bias, and in which observed cross-cultural differences are interpreted at face value. From a methodological perspective, this "hit-and-run" approach is hardly defensible; it may indeed be one of the determinants of the slow theoretical progress in cross-cultural psychology. Second, bias can be seen as an indicator that an instrument is inadequate for cross-cultural comparison; once bias is observed, a researcher can decide to refrain from such comparisons. Such an approach is prudent, although highly restrictive. Bias may be unavoidable, particularly in the comparison of highly dissimilar cultural groups (e.g., differential testwiseness in comparing pupils from highly different educational systems). Third, bias can be seen as providing important clues about cross-cultural differences. In this approach, bias defines cultural specifics, whereas instruments (or parts thereof) that do not show bias point to universals.

A comparison of biased and unbiased aspects of an instrument yields important clues about cross-cultural differences. For instance, Tanaka-Matsumi and Marsella (1976) asked Japanese and American individuals to generate words associated with depression; the latter group referred more often to mood states, while the former gave more somatic responses. It is quite likely that a bias analysis would have demonstrated structural equivalence for a few somatic symptoms and a lack of structural equivalence for most other symptoms. The somatic responses defined the common aspects, while the mood states were more culture specific.

Fourth, an attempt can be made to reduce bias. A well-known method to reduce method bias is cultural decentering (Werner & Campbell, 1970) (see Table 5.2). Words and concepts that are specific to one particular language or culture are eliminated (e.g., Cortese & Smyth, 1979). The approach may work best by combining the linguistic and cultural expertise of researchers of all cultures under study. Another way of dealing with construct bias involves the convergence approach: Instruments are independently developed in different cultures (languages), and all instruments are then translated and administered to subjects in all these cultures (Campbell, 1986).

Table 5.2   Strategies for Identifying and Dealing with Bias in Cross-Cultural Assessment

Type of Bias	Strategies
Construct bias	Decentering (i.e., simultaneously developing the same instrument in several cultures)
	Convergence approach (i.e., independent within-culture development of instruments and subsequent cross-cultural administration of all instruments)
Construct bias and/or method bias	Use of informants with expertise in local culture and language
	Use bilingual subjects in the samples
	Use of local surveys (e.g., content analyses of free-response questions)
	Nonstandard instrument administration (e.g., "thinking aloud")
	Cross-cultural comparison of nomological networks (e.g., convergent/discriminant validity studies, monotrait-multimethod studies, connotation of key phrases)
Method bias	Extensive training of administrators (e.g., increasing cultural sensitivity)
	Detailed manual/protocol for administration, scoring, and interpretation
	Detailed instructions (e.g., with sufficient number of examples and/or exercises)
	Use of subject variables (e.g., educational background)
	Use of collateral information (e.g., test-taking behavior or test attitudes)
	Assessment of response styles
	Use of test-retest, training, and/or intervention studies
Item bias	Judgmental methods of item bias detection (e.g., linguistic and psychological analysis)
	Psychometric methods of item bias detection (e.g., Differential Item Functioning analysis)
	Error or distracter analysis

Source: After van de Vijver & Tanzer, 1997.

Some bias reduction techniques address a combination of construct and method bias. These often amount to working with nonstandard samples or methods of data collection. For example, local informants can be asked to judge the accuracy of an instrument, local surveys can be held, or instruments can be administered in a nonstandard way to examine whether the questions-as-responded-to are the questions-as-intended. The role of local informants is well illustrated in a study by Brandt and Boucher (1986), who were interested in the place of depression in emotion lexicons. These authors did not present a list of emotion terms, but gathered these terms from local informants (in Australia, Indonesia, Japan, Korea, Malaysia, Puerto Rico, Sri Lanka, and the United States). A distinct depression cluster was found only in Japan, Indonesia, Sri Lanka, and the United States. For the other languages, depression-type words were predominantly subsumed by sadness clusters.

That a nonstandard administration can be useful is illustrated in a study by Broer (1996). He wanted to administer the Viennese Matrices Test (Formann & Piswanger; 1979) to freshmen in Chile and Austria. In a pilot study, it was discovered that the Chileans took more time to respond. The manual specifies a total testing time of 25 minutes, which is sufficient for most subjects in Austria (where the test was developed) to complete the task. This time limit was lifted in the cross-cultural study to ensure that all subjects would have ample testing time. It was found that over 90% of the Austrians, but only 55% of the Chileans, completed the test in 25 minutes. The average test scores obtained with an unlimited testing time did not differ significantly. Interestingly, scores were also recorded after 25 minutes, and these showed significant differences by country. The cross-cultural differences obtained under standard instructions might have been significant, thereby incorrectly indicating that the groups differed in inductive reasoning skills.

In some studies, it may be possible to involve bilingual individuals. For example, Hocevar, El-Zahhar, and Gombos (1989) administered anxiety and arousability questionnaires to English-Hungarian bilingual individuals in both languages. Working with those who are bilingual is often attractive, although the limitations should be acknowledged. Bilingual individuals are usually not representative of the larger population because they are often better educated and have been in more contact with other languages and cultures.

Extensive training of testers and the standardization of test administrations, to be specified in a test manual, is an important tool in reducing method bias. When cultures are close to each other, such a standardization may go a long way to prevent the emergence of unwanted score differences.

When the cultural distance between the groups is large, extensive training and a detailed manual may not suffice, and additional steps need to be taken. Examples are the use of collateral test information (such as test-taking behavior or testing time in power tests) or the assessment of outcome-relevant characteristics in which cultures differ, such as the measurement of educational background in mental testing or the administration of a social desirability questionnaire in personality or attitude measurement. Poortinga and van de Vijver (1987) coined the term *context variables* for presumably outcome-relevant characteristics of persons, samples, and the test administration. By including context variables in a study, it becomes possible statistically to check its influence in a covariance or hierarchical regression analysis, even when the cultural distance of groups is so large that matching on these variables cannot be achieved or would yield samples that are highly atypical of the populations from which they have been drawn.

As an example, Poortinga (in Poortinga & van de Vijver, 1987) examined the habituation of the orienting reflex among illiterate Indian tribes and Dutch conscripts. The amplitude of the skin conductance response, the dependent variable, was significantly larger in the Indian group. He hypothesized that intergroup differences in arousal could account for these differences. Arousal was measured as spontaneous fluctuations in skin conductance response in a control condition. Cross-cultural differences in habituation of the orienting reflex disappeared after statistically controlling for these fluctuations in a hierarchical regression analysis.

Evidence on the presence of method bias can also be collected from applications of test-retest, training, and intervention studies. Thus, Nkaya, Huteau, and Bonnet (1994) administered Raven's Standard Matrices three times to sixth graders in France and Congo. Under untimed conditions, score improvements were similar for both groups, but under timed conditions, the Congolese pupils progressed more

from the second to the third session than did the French pupils. Ombrédane, Robaye, and Plumail (1956) have shown that, in some groups, repeated test administrations can also affect the relationship with external measures. The predictive validity of the Raven's test score was found to increase after repeated administration in a group of illiterate Congolese mine workers. It is likely that the results of both studies are due to learning processes that took place during the testing, such as better task comprehension and more acquaintance with the test and the testing procedure. In this line of reasoning, the validity of the first test administration is challenged by sources of method bias.

The last type of approach to deal with bias focuses on item-level anomalies. Item bias is usually assessed in either of two ways: judgmental (linguistic and/or psychological) and psychometric. An example of a linguistic procedure can be found in Grill and Bartel (1977). They examined the Grammatic Closure subtest of the Illinois Test of Psycholinguistic Abilities for bias against speakers of nonstandard English. Error responses by American Black and White children indicated that more than half of the errors were accounted for by responses that are appropriate in nonstandard English. In the last decades, dozens of statistical techniques have been developed, and existing procedures have been modified to identify item bias; examples are the Mantel-Haenszel procedure (Holland & Wainer, 1993), logistic regression (Rogers & Swaminathan, 1993), and item response theory (Hambleton & Swaminathan, 1985).

Empirical studies of psychometric procedures are numerous. Valencia, Rankin, and Livingston (1995) examined item bias of the Mental Processing Scales and the Achievement Scale of the Kaufman Assessment Battery for Children in a sample of Mexican and European American pupils. Using a partial correlation index (that controlled for age, sex, and ability), the authors found 17 of 120 items of the first scale and 58 of 92 items of the last scale to be biased. Obviously, it is questionable whether the remaining 34 items will constitute an appropriate instrument that still measures the same construct as the full scale. Ellis, Becker, and Kimmel (1993) studied the equivalence of an English-language version of the Trier Personality Inventory and the original German version. Among the 120 items tested, 11 items were found to be biased. A replication study with a new U.S. sample showed that 6 of the 11 biased items again were biased. This number is considerably higher than most studies of item bias would suggest.

In my view, some tentative conclusions can be drawn from the numerous item bias studies. The identification of sources of anomalies in cross-cultural research at the item level is of obvious relevance, both theoretical and practical, but its implementation has met with major difficulties. First, it is often difficult to comprehend why an item is biased. Second, results of different procedures for identifying bias often do not show the same results. Convergence of bias statistics has been studied from several perspectives. Some studies have addressed the convergence of findings across widely different statistical techniques. Low-to-moderate correlations between different methods have been repeatedly reported, particularly in older studies (e.g., Devine & Raju, 1982; Ironson & Subkoviak, 1979; Rudner, Getson, & Knight, 1980; Shepard, Camilli, & Averill, 1981). More recent studies report more agreement, probably because there is now more insight in what are statistically appropriate procedures (e.g., Huang, Church, & Katigbak, 1997; Raju, Drasgow, & Slinde, 1993; Rogers & Swaminathan, 1993). Also, the stability of item bias statistics tends to be poor, in both test-retest studies and cross-validations (e.g., Skaggs & Lissitz, 1992). Finally, a low correspondence of judgmental and statistical procedures has been found (Engelhard, Hansche, & Rutledge, 1990; Van Leest 1997a, 1997b). In sum, we hardly know what kind of items can be expected to be biased, or as L. Bond (1993) put it: "Theories about why items behave differently across groups can be described only as primitive" (p. 278). It is not surprising that item bias studies have not produced guidelines for cross-cultural research.

The focus on items as the sole source of bias has led to a remarkable and regrettable one-sidedness in current thinking on and treatment of bias. Empirical studies of bias tend to focus exclusively on item bias, implicitly and incorrectly assuming that once this type of bias is removed, all bias has been eliminated (e.g., Thissen, Steinberg, & Gerrard, 1986). This line of reasoning is based on a simplified view of bias sources in cross-cultural research and does not do justice to construct and method bias. Particularly, method bias tends to have a global influence on the separate items of an instrument. Differential stimulus familiarity will often influence all items of a test, thereby leading to different origins of the scale across groups.

Measurement unit equivalence is then the highest attainable level of equivalence. Analogously, if one addresses item bias, it will be impossible to demonstrate that a measure of filial piety, administered to subjects in the United States and China, shows construct bias. By ignoring sources of bias at the level of the instrument, sample, administration, and the underlying construct, it is difficult or even impossible to identify, among other things, cultural variations in everyday conceptualizations of a concept, differential social desirability, differences in administration conditions, and sample incomparability; in short, a focus on item bias is an impediment to overcoming the Western bias of many theories and instruments because it bypasses all global sources of bias.

Multilingual Studies

Cross-cultural research is often multilingual. There is a clear trend in the literature to integrate linguistic, psychological, and methodological considerations when producing instruments in multiple languages. It is widely accepted that the translation of psychological instruments involves more than rendering text into another language (Bracken & Barona, 1991; Brislin, 1986; Geisinger, 1994; Hambleton, 1994). Recently, a set of recommended practices has been formulated by a group of psychologists with experience in test translations; these recommendations are reproduced in the Appendix (see also Hambleton, 1994; van de Vijver & Hambleton, 1996). The integration of linguistic and cultural considerations, as well as the address bias and equivalence, are expressed clearly in these guidelines.

Two kinds of translation procedures can be envisaged, depending on whether a new instrument is developed for use in a multilingual context or whether an existing instrument is to be translated. The former is known as *simultaneous development* and the latter as *successive development*. Simultaneous development is less likely to run into problems of bias and lack of equivalence because there is much freedom in choosing stimulus material, thereby leaving ample opportunity to disregard presumably suspect stimulus material. The main reason to pay much attention to successive development is its frequent employment in cross-cultural research; simultaneous developments are exceptional.

In addition to issues like bias and equivalence that are common to all cross-cultural research, there are methodological aspects that are unique to multilingual studies. For example, a translation procedure has to be chosen. There are two procedures that are often combined in practice. The first utilizes a translation–back translation design; back translations are used to examine the adequacy of the forward translations (Werner & Campbell, 1970). A text is translated from a source into a target language, followed by an independent translation of the target language into the source language. Close similarity of the original and back-translated versions ascertains translation adequacy. The procedure has been applied widely, and it can identify various kinds of errors even when a researcher does not know the target language. A disadvantage of back translations is their emphasis on literal translations, thereby possibly neglecting other issues, such as readability and ease of comprehensibility of the source text and applicability of the item contents in the target culture. The last problems are more likely to be detected in the second procedure, the committee approach. A translation is made by a group of people; relevant areas of expertise are combined (such as cultural, linguistic, and psychological). The major strength of the committee approach is its scope for active cooperation between persons with different areas of translation-relevant domains of expertise.

The outcome of a translation process can take on one of three forms, depending on how much of the original is still retained in the translated version (van de Vijver & Leung, 1997a, 1997b). The first is *application* (or *adoption*). It amounts to a close (often fairly literal) translation of an instrument into a target language, implicitly assuming that no changes in the instrument are needed to avoid bias. These close translations are by far the most common type. The second option is *adaptation*. It amounts to the literal translation of a part of the items, changes in other items, and/or the creation of new items. Adaptations are needed when the application option would yield a biased instrument (e.g., the item contents may be inappropriate for the target culture). In current writings on multilingual research, the need to adjust instruments is so widely acknowledged that the term adaptation has been proposed as the generic term for translations. Finally, the adaptations of an instrument may be so comprehensive that, practically speaking, a new instrument is assembled. This third option is called *assembly*. In particular, when construct bias constitutes a real threat, a direct comparison, the assembly of a new instrument, is called for (cf. Cheung et al., 1996).

The level of equivalence that can be attained in multilingual research depends on the translation option chosen. Assembly, which amounts to the composition of an entirely new instrument, precludes measurement and full-score equivalence. This restriction is less serious than may be thought. When designing an instrument with the aim to maximize its ecological validity (an "emic" measure), analyses will focus on establishing the instrument's construct validity (i.e., Does the test measure what it is supposed to measure?) and structural equivalence by examining its nomological network.

The statistical analysis of adaptations may be more intricate. Strictly speaking, score comparisons in a *t* test and analysis of variance are not allowed because the items are not identical across cultures. Restricting the comparison to the set of items shared across all cultural groups is usually not attractive because it is at variance with the basic idea underlying test adaptations that the common items do not cover the target construct adequately. In the last decades, statistical techniques have been developed that can cater to partial dissimilarity of items without challenging metric equivalence. If there is a common set of items that measures the same latent trait in each cultural group, item response theory allows for the cross-cultural comparison of item and person parameters (such as item difficulties and personal ability levels), taking into account the partial dissimilarity of stimuli (e.g., Hambleton & Swaminathan, 1985; Hambleton, Swaminathan, & Rogers, 1991). Similarly, structural equation models allow for testing the equality of factor structures even when not all stimuli are identical across groups (Byrne, Shavelson, & Muthén, 1989).

The statistical treatment of applications is simple and straightforward. They are the only type of translation in which scalar equivalence can be easily maintained, and *t* tests and analyses of variance can be computed on total test scores. The opportunity to carry out score comparisons is undoubtedly one of the main reasons for the popularity of applications. It should be acknowledged, however, that this convenience has a high price: Applications require the absence of all types of bias. It is the researcher's task to address the bias by examining the equivalence across the languages studied and not, as often is done, to load this burden on editors, reviewers, or readers.

Future Developments

Procrustes, a robber in famous Greek legends, had an iron bed on which his victims had to lie. By hammering body parts or cutting off the legs of his victims he made them fit the bed's length. His victims always died in the process. According to some authors, mainly in cultural psychology, Western tests and methodology do essentially the same with cross-cultural differences. For instance, Greenfield (1997b) argues that ability tests are so context bound that attempts to transport them to other cultural contexts are futile and bound to fail. Similarly, according to Miller (1997), a comparative framework is unable to reveal the essence of cultural phenomena. I agree that there is a problem of misfit between the currently available and desired tests and methodological tools. Yet, it is an overstatement to argue that we should disregard existing cross-cultural research and start from scratch. Important reasons for attempting to retain and refine our comparative framework are as follows:

- Cross-cultural psychologists cannot close their eyes for the globalization of the economic market and the implications for their profession. There is an expanding market of test consumers who want to compare scores across cultural groups, such as in educational testing and selection in a multicultural group. Specialists in assessment and cross-cultural psychologists have a professional obligation (and an economic interest) to support this process with their knowledge.
- There is much evidence that the application of Western or adapted instruments can yield valuable insight into the universality and cultural specificity of psychological constructs (e.g., intelligence). Studies of the patterning of cross-cultural differences are part and parcel of the psychological enterprise, and it is difficult to see how we can advance when we shy away from all comparative test usage.
- The achievement of theoretical and empirical studies of bias and equivalence cannot be dismissed simply as misguided. We now are well able to identify various problems that arise in cross-cultural assessment, and in many cases, there are adequate remedies. It may be granted that not all methodological issues can be solved, but this does not mean the approach is meaningless. We go to see a doctor when

we have a physical problem, although we know that medicine cannot cure all ailments.

In my view, cross-cultural and cultural approaches are less antithetical than often assumed (Jahoda, 1982). If we are interested in a psychological construct, say friendliness in Libya and Japan, we could try to study the phenomenon "in situ" and we could attempt to apply a well-established Western instrument to Arabic subjects. Both approaches have their strengths and weaknesses, but it would be naive to argue that only one approach "works." Without a local survey and other means of collecting information that typically are associated more with a cultural approach, it would be difficult to find sources of cultural bias, while without a culture-comparative approach, it would be too difficult to find any patterning of cross-cultural differences in friendliness. Combining these approaches will advance our knowledge of the relation of culture and the psyche. The major methodological task ahead of us is the change from an "adjustment perspective," by which we adopted and adjusted prevailing methodologies, to a truly cultural perspective that transcends the borders of a specific cultural context.

To argue that all methodological problems in cross-cultural psychology have been solved would be a gross overstatement. Our methodology is still very much part of the experimental paradigm, although as argued, experimentation in cross-cultural research is not common, and the paradigm cannot deal in a fully adequate way with culture as an independent variable. More developments in the adjustment perspective are still needed. Whereas in the past methodological innovations were developed in other branches of psychology and then imported to cross-cultural psychology, it may well be that in the future cross-culturalists may assume a more proactive role. Due to the increasing popularity of cross-cultural studies, there is an ever-expanding database of empirical studies that can help to understand the size and patterning of cross-cultural differences. The number of studies that deal with cross-cultural and ethnic differences has risen steadily in the last decade (van de Vijver & Lonner, 1995). Meta-analyses are used increasingly in cross-cultural psychology as a means of identifying the patterning of cross-cultural differences (e.g., R. Bond & Smith, 1996; Georgas, van de Vijver, & Berry, in press). Better comprehension of cross-cultural differences will make us more aware of their nature and may facilitate the development a research methodology that is better suited for examining intact groups.

The aims of cross-cultural psychology have been described by Berry, Poortinga, Segall, and Dasen (1992) as (a) transporting Western theories, models, and methods to previously unexplored cultures; (b) testing their applicability in these cultural contexts; and (c) developing a truly universal psychology that transcends the cultural boundaries of present mainstream psychology. The aims show a temporal relationship; the second aim assumes the realization of the first, and the third assumes realization of the second.

Analogous triple aims can be used to summarize the history of methodology of cross-cultural research. In the initial stage, methodology was borrowed from mainstream psychology. In the early days, that framework served its purpose because cross-cultural psychologists did not have to reinvent the "methodological wheel." However, it was soon realized that methods and instruments developed with a Western laboratory as the frame of reference might not be optimal in field research involving non-Western subjects. In the second stage (and this is our current level of development), adjustments have been made to improve the suitability of extant methods. In a final stage, we may see developments in methodology and statistics that are really tailor-made for cross-cultural research. It is unlikely, and even undesirable, that cross-culturalists do this on their own. Rather, accumulated experiences may be combined from various branches of psychology in regard to work with intact groups so that the development of a new framework receives more momentum.

The development of an adjustment perspective is a long-term goal. Other developments are necessary before this distant perspective comes within reach. At least two developments may be relevant in cross-cultural research methodology in the near future. First, there will be statistical innovations with a bearing on cross-cultural issues. An example is the development of multilevel models in which individual and cultural differences are studied together (Bryk & Raudenbush, 1992; Muthén, 1994). The question can then be addressed as to whether individualism is the same concept at the individual and country levels. The second development will be the further dissemination of rules of proper cross-cultural research. The increased interest in cross-cultural research will lead to a higher level of knowledge of cross-cultural research methodology. It can be assumed safely that authors, editors, and reviewers of cross-cultural manuscripts will become more aware of issues of bias and equivalence, and that it will become more difficult to publish research reports that ignore these issues. There is a bright future ahead of us.

Appendix

On the initiative of the International Test Commission, a committee with members from various international psychological associations has formulated guidelines that specify recommended practices in test translations/adaptations. The 22 guidelines for carrying out multicultural studies are divided into four types: context guidelines (general principles of test translations), development guidelines (more specific recommendations on how to enhance equivalence), administration guidelines (to ensure comparability of administration across language versions), and documentation/score interpretations guidelines (which describe aspects of the manual that are specific to instruments that are or will be translated).

Context Guidelines

1. Effects of cultural differences, which are not relevant or important to the main purposes of the study, should be minimized to the extent possible.
2. The amount of overlap in the constructs in the populations of interest should be assessed.

Development Guidelines

3. Instrument developers and publishers should ensure that the translation/adaptation process takes full account of linguistic and cultural differences among the populations for whom the translated/adapted versions of the instrument are intended.
4. Instrument developers and publishers should provide evidence that the language use in the directions, rubrics, and items themselves, as well as in the handbook, are appropriate for all cultural and language populations for whom the instrument is intended.
5. Instrument developers and publishers should provide evidence that the choice

of testing techniques, item formats, test conventions, and procedures are familiar to all intended populations.

6. Instrument developers and publishers should provide evidence that item content and stimulus materials are familiar to all intended populations.

7. Instrument developers and publishers should implement systematic judgmental evidence, both linguistic and psychological, to improve the accuracy of the translation/adaptation process and compile evidence on the equivalence of all language versions.

8. Instrument developers and publishers should ensure that the data collection design permits the use of appropriate statistical techniques to establish item equivalence between the different language versions of the instrument.

9. Instrument developers and publishers should apply appropriate statistical techniques to (1) establish the equivalence of the different versions of the instrument and (2) identify problematic components or aspects of the instrument that may be inadequate to one or more of the intended populations.

10. Instrument developers and publishers should provide information on the evaluation of validity in all target populations for whom the translated/adapted versions are intended.

11. Instrument developers and publishers should provide statistical evidence of the equivalence of questions for all intended populations.

12. Nonequivalent questions between versions intended for different populations should not be used in preparing a common scale or in comparing these populations. However, they may be useful in enhancing content validity of scores reported for each population separately.

Administration Guidelines

13. Instrument developers and administrators should try to anticipate the types of problems that can be expected and take appropriate actions to remedy these problems through the preparation of appropriate materials and instructions.

14. Instrument administrators should be sensitive to a number of factors related to the stimulus materials, administra-

tion procedures, and response modes that can moderate the validity of the inferences drawn from the scores.

15. Those aspects of the environment that influence the administration of an instrument should be made as similar as possible across populations for whom the instrument is intended.

16. Instrument administration instructions should be in the source and target languages to minimize the influence of unwanted sources of variation across populations.

17. The instrument manual should specify all aspects of the instrument and its administration that require scrutiny in the application of the instrument in a new cultural context.

18. The administration should be unobtrusive and the administrator-examinee interaction should be minimized. Explicit rules that are described in the manual for the instrument should be followed.

Documentation/Score Interpretations Guidelines

19. When an instrument is translated or adapted for use in another population, documentation of the changes should be provided, along with evidence of the equivalence.

20. Score differences among samples of populations administered the instrument should NOT be taken at face value. The researcher has the responsibility to substantiate the differences with other empirical evidence (emphasis in original).

21. Comparisons across populations can only be made at the level of invariance that has been established for the scale on which scores are reported.

22. The instrument developer should provide specific information on the ways in which the sociocultural and ecological contexts of the populations might affect performance on the instrument, and should suggest procedures to account for these effects in the interpretation of results.

References

Aquilino, W. S. (1994). Interviewer mode effects in surveys of drug and alcohol use. *Public Opinion Quarterly, 58*, 210–240.

Azuma, H., & Kashiwagi, K. (1987). Descriptors for an intelligent person: A Japanese study. *Japanese Psychological Research, 29*, 17–26.

Barrett, P. T., Petrides, K. V., Eysenck, S. B. G., & Eysenck, H. J. (1998). The Eysenck Personality Questionnaire: An examination of the factorial similarity of P, E, N, and L across 34 countries. *Personality and Individual Differences, 25*, 805–819.

Berry, J. W. (1976). *Human ecology and cognitive style. Comparative studies in cultural and psychological adaptation.* Beverly Hills, CA: Sage.

Berry, J. W., Poortinga, Y. H., Segall, M. H., & Dasen, P. R. (1992). *Cross-cultural psychology: Research and applications.* Cambridge: Cambridge University Press.

Bond, L. (1993). Comments on the O'Neill and McPeek's paper. In P. W. Holland & H. Wainer (Eds.), *Differential item functioning* (pp. 277–279). Hillsdale, NJ: Erlbaum.

Bond, R., & Smith, P. B. (1996). Culture and conformity: A meta-analysis of studies using Asch's (1952b, 1956) line judgment task. *Psychological Bulletin, 119*, 111–137.

Bracken, B. A., & Barona, A. (1991). State of the art procedures for translating, validating and using psychoeducational tests in cross-cultural assessment. *School Psychology International, 12*, 119–132.

Brandt, M. E., & Boucher, J. D. (1986). Concepts of depression in emotion lexicons of eight cultures. *International Journal of Intercultural Relations, 10*, 321–346.

Brislin, R. W. (1986). The wording and translation of research instruments. In W. J. Lonner & J. W. Berry (Eds.), *Field methods in cross-cultural research* (pp. 137–164). Newbury Park, CA: Sage.

Brislin, R. W., Lonner, W. J., & Thorndike, R. (1973). *Cross-cultural research methods.* New York: Wiley.

Broer, M. (1996). *Rasch-homogene Leistungstests (3DW, WMT) im Kulturvergleich Chile-Österreich. Erstellung einer spanischen Version einer Testbatterie und deren interkulturelle Validierung in Chile* [Cross-cultural comparison of the Rasch-calibrated tests 3DW and WMT between Chile-Austria and the development of a Spanish version of the test battery]. Unpublished master's thesis, University of Vienna, Austria.

Bryk, A. S., & Raudenbush, S. W. (1992). *Hierarchical linear models: Applications and data analysis.* Newbury Park, CA: Sage.

Byrne, B. M., Shavelson, R. J., & Muthén, B. (1989). Testing for the equivalence of factor covariance and mean structures: The issue of partial measurement invariance. *Psychological Bulletin, 105*, 456–466.

Camilli, G., & Shepard, L. A. (1994). *Methods for identifying biased test items.* Thousand Oaks, CA: Sage.

Campbell, D. T. (1986). Science's social system of validity-enhancing collective belief change and the problems of the social sciences. In D. W. Fiske & R. A. Shweder (Eds.), *Metatheory in social science* (pp. 108–135). Chicago: University of Chicago Press.

Campbell, D. T., & Stanley, J. C. (1966). *Experimental and quasi-experimental designs for research.* Chicago: Rand McNally.

Cheung, F. M., Leung, K., Fan, R. M., Song, W. Z., Zhang, J. X., & Chang, J. P. (1996). Development of the Chinese Personality Assessment Inventory. *Journal of Cross-Cultural Psychology, 27*, 181–199.

Christensen, L. B. (1997). *Experimental methodology* (7th ed.). Boston: Allyn & Bacon.

Cole, M. (1996). *Cultural psychology. A once and future discipline.* Cambridge: Harvard University Press.

Cook, T. D., & Campbell, D. T. (1979). *Quasi-experimentation: Design and analysis issues for field settings.* Chicago: Rand McNally.

Cortese, M., & Smyth, P. (1979). A note on the translation to Spanish of a measure of acculturation. *Hispanic Journal of Behavioral Sciences, 1*, 65–68.

Cotter, P. R., Cohen, J., & Coulter, P. (1982). Race-of-interviewer effects in telephone interviews. *Public Opinion Quarterly, 46*, 278–284.

Cronbach, L. J., & Meehl, P. E. (1955). Construct validity in psychological tests. *Psychological Bulletin, 52*, 281–302.

Devine, P. J., & Raju, N. S. (1982). Extent of overlap among four item bias methods. *Educational and Psychological Measurement, 42*, 1049–1066.

Ellis, B. B., Becker, P., & Kimmel, H. D. (1993). An item response theory evaluation of an English version of the Trier Personality Inventory (TPI). *Journal of Cross-Cultural Psychology, 24*, 133–148.

Embretson, S. E. (1983). Construct validity: Construct representation versus nomothetic span. *Psychological Bulletin, 93*, 179–197.

Engelhard, G., Hansche, L., & Rutledge, K. E. (1990). Accuracy of bias review judges in identifying differential item functioning on teacher certification tests. *Applied Measurement in Education, 3*, 347–360.

Formann, A. K., & Piswanger, K. (1979). *Wiener Matrizen-Test. Ein Rasch-skalierter sprachfreier Intelligenztest* [The Viennese Matrices Test. A Rasch-calibrated non-verbal intelligence test]. Weinheim, Germany: Beltz Test.

Gabler, S., & Haeder, S. (in press). Sampling and estimation. In J. Harkness, D. Alwin, F. J. R. van de Vijver, & P. Ph. Mohler (Eds.), *Cross-cultural and multinational surveys: Research methods and practice with standardised instruments.*

Gass, S. M., & Varonis, E. M. (1991). Miscommunication in nonnative speaker discourse. In N. Coupland, H. Giles, & J. M. Wiemann (Eds.), *Miscommunication and problematic talk* (pp. 121–145). Newbury Park, CA: Sage.

Geisinger, K. F. (1994). Cross-cultural normative assessment: Translation and adaptation issues influencing the normative interpretation of assessment instruments. *Psychological Assessment, 6,* 304–312.

Georgas, J., van de Vijver, F. J. R., & Berry, J. W. (in press). *Ecosocial indicators and psychological variables in cross-cultural research.*

Greenfield, P. M. (1997a). Culture as process: Empirical methods for cultural psychology. In J. W. Berry, Y. H. Poortinga, & J. Pandey (Eds.), *Handbook of cross-cultural psychology* (2nd ed., Vol. 1, pp. 301–346). Boston: Allyn & Bacon.

Greenfield, P. M. (1997b). You can't take it with you: Why ability assessments don't cross cultures. *American Psychologist, 52,* 1115–1124.

Grill, J. J., & Bartel, N. R. (1977). Language bias in tests: ITPA grammatic closure. *Journal of Learning Disabilities, 10,* 229–235.

Hambleton, R. K. (1994). Guidelines for adapting educational and psychological tests: A progress report. *European Journal of Psychological Assessment, 10,* 229–244.

Hambleton, R. K., & Swaminathan H. (1985). *Item response theory: Principles and applications.* Dordrecht, The Netherlands: Kluwer.

Hambleton, R. K., Swaminathan, H., & Rogers, H. J. (1991). *Fundamentals of item response theory.* Newbury Park, CA: Sage.

Ho, D. Y. F. (1996). Filial piety and its psychological consequences. In M. H. Bond (Ed.), *Handbook of Chinese psychology* (pp. 155–165). Hong Kong: Oxford University Press.

Hocevar, D., El-Zahhar, N., & Gombos, A. (1989). Cross-cultural equivalence of anxiety measurements in English-Hungarian bilinguals. In R. Schwarzer, H. M. Van der Ploeg, & C. D. Spielberger (Eds.), *Advances in test anxiety research* (Vol. 6, pp. 223–231). Lisse, The Netherlands: Swets.

Hofstede, G. (1980). *Culture's consequences: International differences in work-related values.* Beverly Hills, CA: Sage.

Holland, P. W., & Wainer, H. (Eds.). (1993). *Differential item functioning.* Hillsdale, NJ: Erlbaum.

Huang, C. D., Church, A. T., & Katigbak, M. S. (1997). Identifying cultural differences in items and traits: Differential item functioning in the NEO Personality Inventory. *Journal of Cross-Cultural Psychology, 28,* 192–218.

Ironson, G. H., & Subkoviak, M. J. (1979). A comparison of several methods of assessing item bias. *Journal of Educational Measurement, 16,* 209–225.

Jahoda, G. (1982). *Psychology and anthropology: A psychological perspective.* London: Academic Press.

Jensen, A. R. (1980). *Bias in mental testing.* New York: Free Press.

Kish, L. (1965). *Survey sampling.* New York: Wiley.

Kuo, H. K., & Marsella, A. J. (1977). The meaning and measurement of Machiavellianism in Chinese and American college students. *Journal of Social Psychology, 101,* 165–173.

Lonner, W. J., & Adamopoulos J. (1997). Culture as antecedent to behavior. In J. W. Berry, Y. H. Poortinga, & J. Pandey (Eds.), *Handbook of cross-cultural psychology* (2nd ed., Vol. 1). Chicago: Allyn & Bacon.

Lonner, W. J., & Berry, J. W. (Eds.). (1986). *Field methods in cross-cultural research.* Newbury Park, CA: Sage.

McCrae, R. R., & Costa, P. T., (1997). Personality trait structure as a human universal. *American Psychologist, 52,* 509–516.

Miller, J. G. (1997). Theoretical issues in cultural psychology. In J. W. Berry, Y. H. Poortinga, & J. Pandey (Eds.), *Handbook of cross-cultural psychology* (2nd ed., Vol. 1, pp. 85–128). Boston: Allyn & Bacon.

Muthén, B. O. (1994). Multilevel covariance structure analysis. *Sociological Methods and Research, 22,* 376–398.

Nenty, H. J., & Dinero, T. E. (1981). A cross-cultural analysis of the fairness of the Cattell Culture Fair Intelligence Test using the Rasch model. *Applied Psychological Measurement, 5,* 355–368.

Nkaya, H. N., Huteau, M., & Bonnet, J. (1994). Retest effect on cognitive performance on the Raven-38 Matrices in France and in the Congo. *Perceptual and Motor Skills, 78,* 503–510.

Ombrédane, A., Robaye, F., & Plumail, H. (1956). Résultats d'une application répétée du matrix-couleuré une population de Noirs Congolais [Results of a repeated application of the colored matrices to a population of Black Congolese]. *Bulletin, Centre d'Etudes et Recherches Psychotechniques, 6,* 129–147.

Piswanger, K. (1975). *Interkulturelle Vergleiche mit dem Matrizentest von Formann* [Cross-cultural comparisons with Formann's Matrices Test]. Unpublished doctoral dissertation, University of Vienna, Austria.

Poortinga, Y. H. (1989). Equivalence of cross-cultural data: An overview of basic issues. *International Journal of Psychology, 24,* 737–756.

Poortinga, Y. H., & Malpass, R. S. (1986) Making inferences from cross-cultural data. In W. J. Lonner & J. W. Berry (Eds.), *Field methods in cross-cultural psychology* (pp. 17–46). Beverly Hills, CA: Sage.

Poortinga, Y. H., & Van der Flier, H. (1988). The meaning of item bias in ability tests. In S. H. Irvine & J. W. Berry (Eds.), *Human abilities in cultural context* (pp. 166–183). Cambridge: Cambridge University Press.

Poortinga, Y. H., & van de Vijver, F. J. R. (1987). Explaining cross-cultural differences: Bias analysis and beyond. *Journal of Cross-Cultural Psychology, 18,* 259–282.

Raju, N. S., Drasgow, F., & Slinde, J. A. (1993). An empirical comparison of the area methods, Lord's chi-square test, and the Mantel-Haenszel technique for assessing differential item functioning. *Educational and Psychological Measurement, 53,* 301–314.

Reese, S. D., Danielson, W. A., Shoemaker, P. J., Chang, T., & Hsu, H.-L. (1986). Ethnicity-of-interviewer effects among Mexican-Americans and Anglos. *Public Opinion Quarterly, 50,* 563–572.

Rogers, H. J., & Swaminathan, H. (1993). A comparison of logistic regression and Mantel-Haenszel procedures for detecting differential item functioning. *Applied Psychological Measurement, 17,* 105–116.

Rogoff, B. (1981). Schooling and the development of cognitive skills. In H. C. Triandis & A. Heron (Eds.), *Handbook of cross-cultural psychology* (Vol. 4, pp. 233–294). Boston: Allyn & Bacon.

Rudner, L. M., Getson, P. R., & Knight, D. L. (1980). A Monte Carlo comparison of seven biased item detection techniques. *Journal of Educational Measurement, 17,* 1–10.

Schwartz, S. H. (1992). Universals in the content and structure of values: Theoretical advances and empirical tests in 20 countries. In M. Zanna (Ed.), *Advances in experimental social psychology* (Vol. 25, pp. 1–65). Orlando, FL: Academic Press.

Segall, M. H., Dasen, P. R., Berry, J. W., & Poortinga, Y. H. (1990). *Human behavior in global perspective. An introduction to cross-cultural psychology.* New York: Pergamon Press.

Serpell, R. (1993). *The significance of schooling. Life-journeys in an African society.* Cambridge: Cambridge University Press.

Shepard, L., Camilli, G., & Averill, M. (1981). Comparison of six procedures for detecting test item bias using both internal and external ability criteria. *Journal of Educational Statistics, 6,* 317–375.

Shrestha, R. M., West, C. E., Bleichrodt, N., van de Vijver, F. J. R., & Hautvast, J. G. A. J. (in press). Effect of iodine and iron supplementation on mental performance in Malawian children.

Singer, E., & Presser, S. (1989). The interviewer. In E. Singer & S. Presser (Eds.), *Survey research methods* (pp. 245–246). Chicago: University of Chicago Press.

Skaggs, G., & Lissitz, R. W. (1992). The consistency of detecting item bias across different test administrations: Implications of another failure. *Journal of Educational Measurement, 29,* 227–242.

Smith, P. B., & Bond, M. H. (1993). *Social psychology across cultures.* Hemel Hempstead, UK: Harvester Wheatsheaf.

Szalay, L. B. (1981). Intercultural communication—a process model. *International Journal of Intercultural Relations, 5,* 133–146.

Tanaka-Matsumi, J., & Marsella, A. J. (1976). Cross-cultural variations in the phenomenological experience of depression: I. Word association studies. *Journal of Cross-Cultural Psychology, 7,* 379–396.

Thissen, D., Steinberg, L., & Gerrard, M. (1986). Beyond group-mean differences: The concept of item bias. *Psychological Bulletin, 99,* 118–128.

Triandis, H. C. (1978). Some universals of social behavior. *Personality and Social Psychology Bulletin, 4,* 1–16.

Triandis, H. C., & Berry, J. W. (Eds.). (1980). *Handbook of cross-cultural psychology. Methodology* (Vol. 2). Boston: Allyn & Bacon.

Valencia, R. R., Rankin, R. J., & Livingston, R. (1995). K-ABC content bias: Comparisons between Mexican American and White children. *Psychology in the Schools, 32,* 153–169.

van de Vijver, F. J. R. (1997). Meta-analysis of cross-cultural comparisons of cognitive test performance. *Journal of Cross-Cultural Psychology, 28,* 678–709.

van de Vijver, F. J. R., & Hambleton, R. K. (1996). Translating tests: Some practical guidelines. *European Psychologist, 1,* 89–99.

van de Vijver, F. J. R., & Leung, K. (1997a). Methods and data analysis of comparative research. In J. W. Berry, Y. H. Poortinga, & J. Pandey (Eds.), *Handbook of cross-cultural psychology* (2nd ed., Vol. 1, pp. 257–300). Boston: Allyn & Bacon.

van de Vijver, F. J. R., & Leung, K. (1997b). *Methods and data analysis for cross-cultural research.* Newbury Park, CA: Sage.

van de Vijver, F. J. R., & Lonner, W. (1995). A bibliometric analysis of the *Journal of Cross-Cul-*

tural Psychology. *Journal of Cross-Cultural Psychology, 26*, 591–602.

van de Vijver, F. J. R., & Poortinga, Y. H. (1997). Towards an integrated analysis of bias in cross-cultural assessment. *European Journal of Psychological Assessment, 13*, 29–37.

van de Vijver, F. J. R., & Tanzer, N. K. (1997). Bias and equivalence in cross-cultural assessment: An overview. *European Review of Applied Psychology, 47*, 263–280.

Van Hemert, D., van de Vijver, F. J. R., Poortinga, Y. H., & Georgas, J. Structure and score levels of the Eysenck Personality Questionnaire across individuals and countries. (under review)

Van Leest, P. F. (1997a). Bias and equivalence research in the Netherlands. *European Review of Applied Psychology, 47*, 319–329.

Van Leest, P. F. (1997b). *Persoonlijkheidsmeting bij allochtonen* [Assessment of personality for ethnic minorities]. Lisse, The Netherlands: Swets.

Werner, O., & Campbell, D. T. (1970). Translating, working through interpreters, and the problem of decentering. In R. Naroll & R. Cohen (Eds.), *A handbook of cultural anthropology* (pp. 398–419). New York: American Museum of Natural History.

Williams, J. E., Satterwhite, R. C., & Saiz, J. L. (1998). *The importance of psychological traits.* New York: Plenum Press.

Yang, K. S., & Bond, M. H. (1990). Exploring implicit personality theories with indigenous or imported constructs: The Chinese case. *Journal of Personality and Social Psychology, 58*, 1087–1095.

Part II: Culture and Basic Psychology Processes

This part of the book presents cross-cultural work concerned with several basic human psychological processes, including development, cognition, morality, emotion, and gender. These processes and issues play an important role in understanding all psychological aspects of human functioning and have been well studied cross-culturally for many years.

In chapter 6, Gardiner identifies four emerging themes in the contemporary literature on cross-cultural human development and discusses how an evolution in knowledge and method will aid in the ultimate creation of universal theories of human development.

In chapter 7, Mishra provides an up-to-date review of cross-cultural work in several areas of cognition, including categorization, learning and memory, schooling and literacy, spatial cognition, problem solving and verbal reasoning, and creativity. By discussing the complexity of understanding the influences of multiple factors on the process of cognitive development, Mishra argues for an integration of theory and method across disciplines to obtain a more unified understanding of cognition across cultures.

In chapter 8, Schliemann and Carraher describe cross-cultural work in the field of everyday cognition; they compare and contrast it with more traditional approaches of studying cognitive abilities. Using math abilities as a platform, they offer a number of suggestions for future work in the area, with each suggestion related to the central theme of integration of theory, method, concept, and discipline for continued evolution of the field.

Perhaps no other topic is more central to the meaning and definition of culture than morality; in chapter 9, Miller describes the limitations of current mainstream approaches with respect to the incorporation of culture and reviews in detail how current cross-cultural research informs this area of inquiry. She argues for the incorporation of culture in future integrative studies of morality along with self, personhood, harm, and other topics across cross-cultural and indigenous approaches.

In chapter 10, Matsumoto describes cross-cultural work in the area of human emotion, first presenting this work in historical context and then in relation to its contributions to mainstream psychology. He demonstrates how cross-cultural research on emotion judgments has evolved from merely documenting differences to explaining why those differences occur. In discussing future research areas, the importance of integration is once again stressed as valuable to the continued development of knowledge in this area.

In chapter 11, Best and Williams provide a complete overview of cross-cultural research in the area of gender; they include concepts on the individual adult level, relations between males and females, gender differences in behaviors, and theories that account for differences on both the individual and cultural level. They suggest that the refinement of research, through the incorporation of methods across disciplines and subfields and of theories that account for the complexity of the factors that contribute to gender in sociocultural context, is necessary for the development of adequate pancultural theories of gender in the future.

Each of these chapters describes in its unique way how each respective area contributes to the vision of the evolution of cross-cultural psychology to create universal theories of psychological processes and the path to achieve them. As described in the introduction, the methodological revisions necessary for each area to continue to evolve will require fundamental changes in the way we do research in the future.

6

Culture, Context, and Development

HARRY W. GARDINER

Issues concerning human development are of concern to all psychologists and for years have been a major focus of cross-cultural theorists and researchers in many disciplines. Indeed, aside from examinations of social behavior, questions about the etiology of cultural similarities and differences have plagued students of culture for decades. Fortunately, this has resulted in a rich and expansive cross-cultural literature on development in several fields, especially in anthropology, psychology, and sociology.

In this chapter, Gardiner presents an excellent overview of the field of cross-cultural human development. After defining terms, he presents a historical overview of the field and discusses its relationship to mainstream psychology. In observance of the enormity of this area of study in cross-cultural psychology, he cites many other useful resources for the reader to gain a greater understanding and appreciation of the work conducted to date. He reviews a number of theoretical perspectives and models and discusses the similarities and differences among anthropological, cross-cultural, and cultural psychological approaches.

Of particular importance is Gardiner's identification of emerging themes in the study of developmental issues across cultures. One of these themes, for example, is the emergence of the importance of contextual influences. As Gardiner argues forcefully, it is difficult to think of any contemporary theory or study in cross-cultural or mainstream psychology without dealing with the possible influence of context on behavior. While these ideas are not new, as Gardiner describes at the beginning of the chapter, they are more important now because of the increasing frequency with which they appear in contemporary literature.

Another important emerging theme is the application of work on cross-cultural human development to social policy issues. By citing numerous examples, particularly the Turkish Early Enrichment Project established by Cigdem Kagitcibasi, Gardiner deftly highlights how monocultural and monolithic research findings in traditional, mainstream psychology cannot address the developmental needs of many vastly diverse populations around the globe and how studies of cross-cultural human development are sorely needed to help create developmental programs to aid in the socialization and enculturation of these diverse populations.

A third emerging theme identified by Gardiner concerns cognitive development, most notably the emerging importance of the work by the Soviet psychologist Vygotsky. While definitely acknowledging the importance of the work of Piaget, whose writings for decades have had a profound influence on mainstream psychological theories of development, Vygotsky's work is important because of the different viewpoint it brings to development. In a similar vein, other alternative viewpoints of development that originate from other cultural frameworks will also be useful in the future.

In this light, the final theme identified by Gardiner—that of the indigenization of developmental psychology—is also particularly important. Gardiner suggests, and rightly so, that future knowledge about cross-cultural human development will be influenced profoundly by understanding development as it uniquely occurs in each specific and different cultural context. Of special interest are his ideas concerning the development of multicultural awareness and identity, in which an individual moves from cultural dependence to independence to multicultural interdependence. Given the increasing globalization and localization of the world, such ideas are bound to be radically important to future theories of human development.

Gardiner, like all other authors in this handbook, sees the creation of universal theories of human development as the next stage in the evolution of cross-cultural psychology. Like many authors, however, Gardiner also sees that considerable work is necessary to achieve that realization. Such work involves not only theoretical developments and the uncovering of knowledge, models, and ways of thinking that may not be well represented in mainstream developmental psychology, but also the adoption of new research designs and methods that go beyond our current practices. In particular, the evolution of method, including the use of triangulation approaches and the integration of qualitative with quantitative methods, will be particularly important to the continued evolution of knowledge about cross-cultural human development. In this fashion, Gardiner's message about the need for an integration of cross-cultural and cultural psychology, and their related methods and theories, is entirely consonant with the message delivered by all other authors in this handbook and is a necessary condition for the creation of future pancultural theories of human development.

If asked to select just one word to describe the present status of cross-cultural development and the direction it might be headed at the beginning of the new millennium, that word would be *contextualization* or the view that behavior cannot be studied meaningfully or fully understood independent of the (cultural) context in which it takes place.

Contextualization and recognition of the important role played by cultural influences in development are by no means recent phenomena. In part, their origins are firmly rooted in a wide array of early theoretical orientations and perspectives, including Mead's symbolic interactionism (1934), Lewin's field theory (1951), and Bronfenbrenner's ecological systems approach (1975, 1979, 1989), to mention just a few. What is striking is the frequency with which ideas associated with contextualization and development are appearing in contemporary literature and the increasingly large number of research studies and scholarly publications being devoted to the topic.

The goal of this chapter is to discuss the origins of cross-cultural development, consider its relationship to the wider field of psychology, evaluate its current status, and speculate its direction in the first decade or two of the 21st century. This is a major challenge, and not everyone will agree with the decisions to include or exclude specific theories, perspectives, research findings, or topics of interest. In this regard, we are in agreement with Berry, who said it well in his autobiography in Bond's 1997 book, *Working at the Interface of Cultures*:

> My view is that the ecological perspective is a continuing and evolving theme in thinking about the origins and functions of human diversity, and that a periodic attempt to synthesise and organise such thoughts into frameworks is a useful exercise. (pp. 139–140)

If the reader goes away knowing more about cross-cultural development than before reading this chapter and is stimulated to seek additional information, be critical of what is found, and engage in some integrative efforts, I will have accomplished one of my major goals.

What Is Cross-Cultural Development?

The fields of cross-cultural psychology and developmental psychology are remarkably diverse, and those who contribute to each bring with them a variety of viewpoints, including different definitions of the fields (H. W. Gardiner, Mutter, & Kosmitzki, 1998).

Let us begin by defining some of the principal terms and concepts that appear in this chapter. First, the framework includes the definition of cross-cultural psychology set forth by Berry, Poortinga, and Pandey (1997) in the recently revised *Handbook of Cross-Cultural Psychology*. They view it as "the systematic study of relationships between the cultural context of human development and the behaviors that become established in the repertoire of individuals growing up in a particular culture" (p. x). This definition clearly emphasizes the importance of the cultural context and focuses on cross-cultural psychology as a scientific endeavor, sharing with its sister disciplines the use of theories, scientific methodologies, statistical procedures, and data analysis.

Second, human development can be thought of as "changes in physical, psychological, and social behavior as experienced by individuals across the lifespan from conception to death" (H. W. Gardiner et al., 1998, p. 3).

Finally, cross-cultural human development refers to "cultural similarities and differences in developmental processes and their outcomes as expressed by behavior in individuals and groups" (H. W. Gardiner, 1999).

Culture and Development

Traditionally, in efforts to understand human behavior, developmental psychology was neither cross cultural nor interdisciplinary in its approach, while cross-cultural psychology failed to be developmental in its approach.

The anthropologist Theodore Schwartz (1981), writing nearly 20 years ago on the acquisition of culture, asserted that "anthropologists had ignored children in culture while developmental psychologists had ignored culture in children" (p. 4). Two years later, John Berry (1983), a pioneering Canadian cross-cultural psychologist and researcher, stated that the discipline of cross-cultural psychology was "so culture-bound and culture-blind . . . [that] . . . it should not be employed as it is" (p. 449).

However, in 1986, Gustav Jahoda, a well-known and respected European psychologist and early contributor to the developing discipline, while criticizing the field for being "too parochial in its orientation" (p. 418), also expressed optimism by pointing out that cross-cultural studies of human development had been increasing slowly but steadily. In the last two decades, the pace has accelerated dramatically, and current evidence suggests we may be approaching the age of development. In this chapter, an effort is made to show the progress, excitement, and promise of this increasingly important area of scientific interest and research.

As the field of cross-cultural psychology has evolved, research interests and concerns in the area of development have undergone a number of significant changes. Parke, Ornstein, Rieser, and Zahn-Waxler (1994) have succinctly summarized and discussed the changes in developmental focus over the past century. There were five major topics of interest 100 years ago: emotional development, biological bases of behavior, conscious and unconscious processes, cognitive development, and the role of self in development. During the 1950s and 1960s, the focus moved toward learning theory, experimental child psychology, operant analysis of children's behavior, infant sensory and perceptual development, and measurement of cognitive understanding among preverbal infants. Today, there is a revitalized interest in emotional development, children's cognitive abilities, biological bases of behavior, and social relationships. According to the authors, the "most unanticipated theme is the continuing discovery of the precocity of infants and young children—not only cognitively but also socially and emotionally" (p. 8).

Recently, Super and Harkness (1997), while discussing cultural structuring in child development, made the following important point:

An enduring theme in studies of child development across cultures has been the idea of the environment as a communicative medium. In this metaphorical contextualization, two systems—the individual and the contextual—interact, each sending "messages" that are assimilated into the other's respective internal organizations. Historically, cultural researchers, like early developmentalists, focused their attention on messages from the environment to the child; only more recently have cultural theorists, following trends in developmental psychology, recognized the agency of the individual and the bidirectionality of influence. (p. 8)

Relationship to the Field of Psychology

An understanding of developmental processes (within a single culture or among several cultures) is central to psychology's basic goals of describing, understanding, explaining, and predicting behavior. Looking at the titles of the other chapters in this handbook, one immediately notices the pivotal role development plays in helping us understand such diverse behaviors as emotion, moral development, abnormal psychology, social influence, and social cognition, as well as others.

In a recent article, Segall, Lonner, and Berry (1998) ask

Can it still be necessary, as we approach the millennium (as measured on the Western, Christian calendar), to advocate that all social scientists, psychologists especially, take culture seriously into account when attempting to understand human behavior? (p. 1101)

Unfortunately, even with the remarkable progress that has been made, including inclusion of increasing quantities of cultural material in introductory textbooks (Berk, 1998; Cole & Cole, 1996; Sternberg, 1995; Wade & Tavris, 1996), the answer is yes. However, as pointed out, the situation is vastly improved and only continues to get better.

Obviously, cross-cultural psychology and its subdiscipline of cross-cultural human development have long historical connections to general psychology. Although, as Klineberg (1980) pointed out nearly two decades ago, "There is no specific date that can be identified with the onset of interest in cross-cultural comparisons" (p. 34). Jahoda and Krewer (1997), in an essay on the history of cross-cultural and cultural psychology, suggest some of its origins may date to the 17th century since "the dominant perspective of enlightenment philosophy was highly compatible with cross-cultural psychology's model of man" (p. 11).

Segall et al. (1998) stress that, in the modern era (since the 1960s):

Research has focused on phenomena of fundamental importance in general psychology, with particular emphasis on abnormal psy-

chology, cognitive psychology . . . [and that] . . . topics in social psychology have been studied cross-culturally more than any other domain, followed by developmental psychology. (p. 1105)

There are clearly links to other social sciences as well, most notably anthropology and sociology, as noted above. While sharing some commonalties in concepts, methodologies, and approaches, research interests (e.g., family influences and socialization processes), the interface between psychology and anthropology has not always been a smooth one. The uneasiness in this relationship was recognized by C. M. Super (1981) nearly 20 years ago when, commenting on the deficiencies in comparative studies of infant development, he noted:

For the past few decades they . . . [anthropology and psychology] . . . seem to have withdrawn from the interface, especially with regard to infancy, to tend to their own theories. Very few of the studies reviewed here achieve, or even attempt, an integration of infant care and development, on the one hand, with functional and value characteristics of the larger culture, on the other. (p. 246–247)

He followed up by pointing out that, "Success in this direction requires both sound ethnographic knowledge of the culture as well as a quantitative baseline of information about infants daily lives" (p. 247). A similar plea was made more recently by Weisner (1997) when he asserted that ethnography is well suited for understanding human development and culture, especially in situations when families, and the communities in which they live, are trying to achieve their goals in "their cultural world."

In an effort to explore the relationship between psychology and anthropology, Jahoda (1982), a psychologist with close ties to anthropology and a deep appreciation and understanding of each discipline's history, wrote an interesting and entertaining volume, *Psychology and Anthropology: A Psychological Perspective.* On the back cover of the book, it states:

Anthropologists have always been concerned with psychology, even if unwittingly. . . . However, this interest has not been reciprocated by psychologists and psychology has, in many respects, remained narrowly culture-bound, largely ignoring the wider perspectives provided by anthropology.

One can hope, as Piker (1998) does, that cross-cultural psychology and psychological anthropology will once again become friendly partners and work toward the establishment of an empirically based understanding of human behavior within varying cultural contexts. Our goal should be to seek out and nurture relevant treads of common interest where they intersect between psychology and other disciplines. Such alliances can only enrich our understanding of human development and the critical role culture plays in it.

Understanding Culture and Development: Some Resources

During the last 20 years, most notably within the past 5 years, social scientists have become increasingly aware of the significant contributions that cross-cultural research findings can make to our understanding of human development. For example, two reviews of recently published developmental textbooks indicate that references to cross-cultural topics and findings have become more frequent, although there is still room for improvement (Best & Ruther, 1994; H. W. Gardiner, 1996).

To summarize and evaluate an entire discipline, or even an important subfield within it, is a major challenge. In a chapter with the broad title of development, the task is impossible and would require a volume at least the size of the present one. For this reason, the reference section at the close of this chapter is extensive and points readers to areas we either are unable to discuss adequately here or that others have covered so well that they should be consulted as original sources.

For those interested in a more comprehensive view of cross-cultural human development, or for those wishing to explore particular topics in greater depth, a number of specific suggestions are made. One might begin by looking at such classics as *Two Worlds of Childhood: U.S. and U.S.S.R.* (Bronfenbrenner, 1970) and a series of volumes, *Six Cultures* (Whiting, 1963; Whiting & Edwards, 1988; Whiting & Whiting, 1975).

For an extremely interesting and detailed look at 50 years of cross-cultural research on Japanese child rearing and socialization that places current findings in historical context and offers concrete suggestions for new research, there is a book by Shwalb and Shwalb (1996). The book consists of a collection of retrospectives by noted senior investigators, known for their groundbreaking studies on Japanese children; these are followed by reaction papers that present current findings by younger researchers. Much of the book's value lies in its discussion of the implications of the research for the study of development across cultures; it should be of interest to those concerned with Japanese culture, as well as with human development. Future researchers are encouraged to take a serious look at this work as a possible model worthy of replication and extension in a variety of different cultural settings.

In addition, there is the recently revised three-volume *Handbook of Cross-Cultural Psychology* (Berry et al., 1997), which contains several chapters relevant to the study of cross-cultural development, as well as the role of cross-cultural theory and methodology. Particular attention should be given to Volume 2, which is devoted to basic processes and human development. It includes an enormous amount of material on such topics as the cultural structuring of child development, socialization and identity strategies, human development in culture across the lifespan, perception, cognitive development, language acquisition and bilingualism, emotion, and moral development.

Other useful books include the *Handbook of Parenting* (Bornstein, 1995), *Human Behavior in Global Perspective* (Segall, Dasen, Berry, & Poortinga, 1999), *Family and Human Development across Cultures* (Kagitcibasi, 1996), and *Lives across Cultures: Cross-Cultural Human Development* (H. W. Gardiner, Mutter, & Kosmitzki, 1998). The last book, which emphasizes a contextual approach and a chronological-within-topics design, integrates basic developmental principles and research findings with concrete examples from scores of cultures to bring a cross-cultural dimension to the study of human development across the lifespan. It also contains an extensive bibliography (over 830 references) with recommendations for further reading.

A number of journals with an interest in cross-cultural and developmental psychology topics also are available, including the *Journal of Cross-Cultural Psychology, International Journal of Behavioral Development, International Journal of Psychology, Psychology and Developing Societies, Culture and Psychology,*

Cross-Cultural Psychology Bulletin, Cross-Cultural Research, and *World Psychology.*

Finally, the *Annual Review of Psychology* has published four reviews devoted to cross-cultural psychology (Brislin, 1983; Kagitcibasi & Berry, 1989; Segall, 1986; Triandis, Malpass, & Davidson, 1973), one on cultural psychology (Shweder & Sullivan, 1993), and one on personality development in the social context (Hartup & van Lieshout, 1995).

Theoretical Perspectives and Models

At the present time, one of the major debates surrounding efforts to link culture and psychology, including development, centers on those theorists and researchers using the "cultural psychology" approach and those who prefer the "cross-cultural psychology" approach. According to J. G. Miller (1997), "The dominant stance within cultural psychology is to view culture and psychology as mutually constitutive phenomena, i.e. as phenomena which make up each other or are integral to each other" (p. 88). Cross-cultural psychology, on the other hand, according to Segall et al. (1998),

> consists mostly of diverse forms of comparative research (often explicitly and always at least implicitly) in order to discern the influence of various cultural factors, many of them related to ethnicity, on those forms of development and behavior. In this comparative mode, culture is treated as comprising a set of independent or contextual variables affecting various aspects of individual behavior. Cross-cultural psychology typically seeks evidence of such effects. (p. 1102)

One of the foremost proponents of the cultural psychology approach to studying human development is Shweder. In an early review (Shweder & Sullivan, 1993), it was stated that

> An interdisciplinary subfield called "cultural psychology" has begun to emerge at the interface of anthropology, psychology, and linguistics. The aim of cultural psychology is to examine ethnic and cultural sources of psychological diversity in emotional and somatic (health) functioning, self organization, moral evaluation, social cognition, and human development. Its goal is to understand why so many apparently straightforward questions about human psychological

functioning . . . have not resulted in a consensus among qualified scientists, and why so many generalizations about the psychological functioning of one particular population (e.g. the contemporary secularized Western urban white middle class) have not traveled well across sociocultural, historical, and institutional fault lines. (pp. 497–498)

Anyone interested in this approach should read this review for an introduction to the concept, its historical development, its contexts, and several of its basic assumptions. Additional resources include writings by Cole (1996, 1998, 1999); Cole, Engestrom, and Vasquez (1997); D'Andrade and Strauss (1992); Goodnow, Miller, and Kessel (1995); Jahoda (1992); Jessor, Colby, and Shweder (1996); Shweder (1991); Stigler, Shweder, and Herdt (1990); and others.

Another important contributor to this viewpoint, Cole (1998), in his book *Cultural Psychology: A Once and Future Discipline,* offers both an introduction to cultural psychology and a carefully crafted synthesis of theory and empirical research that provides a stimulating and thought-provoking account of what cultural psychology is at the moment, what it has been in the past, and what it can be in the future. He admiringly achieves one of the major goals set forth in this volume: integration of cultural and historical ideas with the traditional findings and approaches of psychology. By doing so, he challenges readers to consider what they might contribute to the field. Finally, Cole et al. (1997), in another valuable book, assemble a collection of seminal articles that focus on the cultural and contextual foundations of human development. These include discussions of the nature of context, experiments as contexts, culture-historical theories of culture, and context and development and an analysis of classroom settings as contexts for development.

Another model, the contextual-developmental-functional approach, effectively illustrated in the work of Kagitcibasi (1996), attempts to link family socialization and family dynamics within varying sociocultural contexts to discover their functional (or causal) links with human development. This important work is discussed further below.

While it is not possible, within the limits of this chapter, to unravel all of the threads that weave their way through the cultural psychology and cross-cultural psychology debate, it is certainly an issue that will be with us in the next century, and one would do well to know as much as possible about it. Therefore, it is recommended that readers consult the various references mentioned above, as well as Saraswathi (1998), C. Super and Harkness (1997), and Valsiner and Lawrence (1997). The possibility that these divergent views may one day merge, or at least find a way to coexist, is found in a comment by Valsiner and Lawrence:

> The two disciplines converge in their interests in the contextualization of the person's life course. Each carries with it the potential for treating person-cultural contextual interactions as central units of analysis for understanding how lives change. (p. 83)

Kagitcibasi (1996) expresses a similar sentiment in her remark that

> I work from a cultural and cross-cultural perspective. A cultural approach is presupposed by contextualism, and a cross-cultural approach is required for the unambiguous interpretation of the observed cultural differences. (p. 2)

Emerging Themes

A review of the increasingly large (but not entirely well-organized) body of literature in cross-cultural human development points to the emergence of several important themes. While this is not an exhaustive and complete examination, it does underscore some intriguing and significant areas of research worthy of future attention and investigation.

Contextual Influences

As mentioned, studies of contextualization in development have increased dramatically in recent years and are likely to continue to do so in the next several years. For example, in a relatively brief, but noteworthy, commentary on parenting in different cultures, Stevenson-Hinde (1998), building on the work of Bornstein et al. (1998), proposed a framework applicable to all parenting studies. Her model acknowledges the importance of the cultural context and permits more precise measurement and better understanding of maternal and/or paternal practices and styles of parenting. Any researcher designing a study with a focus on cultural similarities and differences in parenting would do well to look at this framework.

Closely related, but (surprisingly) not cited by Stevenson-Hinde (1998), is an earlier attempt by Darling and Steinberg (1993) at creating an integrative model. Also focusing on parenting style as context, their model makes use of two traditional approaches to socialization (Baumrind, 1967, 1971; Maccoby & Martin, 1983), findings related to specific parenting practices and studies of global parent practices.

Finally, there is the recent work of Zevalkink (1997), which in the words of Stevenson-Hinde (1998), "provides a model for cross-cultural developmental research on parenting" (p. 699). Included in Zevalkink's approach is (a) a focus on how a specific aspect of parenting relates to a particular child behavior (e.g., maternal support and security of attachment), (b) careful selection of assessment methods, (c) evaluation of cultural contexts by a combination of methods (e.g., participant observation and ethnographic interviews), and (d) use of multiple samples within one culture to investigate socioeconomic differences, thereby helping to avoid the frequent assumption that a group selected by the researcher is "typical" of a specific culture. The model is unquestionably worthy of future study, as is the framework proposed by Stevenson-Hinde (1998).

Applications to Social Policy Issues

In his presidential address to the American Psychological Association, G. A. Miller (1969) urged members to "give psychology away." After a century of developmental research and decades of gathering information on cultural similarities and differences, I believe it is time to "give cross-cultural psychology away" by applying our findings to critical social policy issues.

A good beginning, aimed at integrating theory and practice, has been made by Kagitcibasi through her establishment of the Turkish Early Enrichment Project for mothers and children (1996). This pioneering effort, based on principles emerging from her nearly 20 years of research in both developmental and cross-cultural psychology, has positively transformed her country in ways that will be felt for decades to come. Critical of the dominant and widespread Western view of human development, Kagitcibasi points out that

> Diffusion of the Western model may be so pervasive as to promote the emergence of the human/family model of independence,

even though it is not necessitated by or even functional for the lifestyle in most specific contexts in the world. (p. 97)

Stressing the need for merging contextual theory with practical application, Kagitcibasi (1996) states that: "The weight of the evidence points to a contextual approach in early intervention, particularly in adverse socioeconomic conditions where there is less-than-adequate support for human development" (p. 184). She goes on to describe the successful application of cross-cultural developmental findings to such critical issues as mother training, early childhood intervention, and increased academic achievement. The author's success with Turkish mothers provides a most welcome and much needed model for those interested in the emerging trend toward contextualization in human development as well as the application of cross-cultural findings to issues of social policy.

Another study that focuses on the application of cross-cultural findings to a social issue, acculturative stress, is the work of Mishra, Sinha, and Berry (1996). The authors looked at three tribal groups in India (the Oraon, Birhar, and Asur) that differed in settlement and occupation patterns. Following extensive investigation of cultural lifestyles, patterns of socialization, cognitive behavior, and acculturation attitudes and experiences, they introduced strategies for reducing acculturative stress and providing better psychological adaptation.

Before bringing this section to a close, attention is directed to two chapters in the new edition of the *Handbook of Cross-Cultural Psychology* (Berry et al., 1997), which are highly applicable and provide a link among theory, research, and policy issues. Serpell and Hatano (1997), in a discussion of education, schooling, and literacy, effectively demonstrate how culture affects human behavior by integrating enculturation and socialization, educational and pedagogical processes, literacy and cognition, formal and informal schooling, and adaptation to cross-cultural contact. Their comprehensive historical and theoretical overviews provide a useful foundation for understanding the latest findings in these areas. In addition, it makes "an extremely important contribution to education, for it is almost certain that the citizens of the next generation will live in a world in which diverse cultures interact with ever greater intensity" (Serpell & Hatano, 1997, p. 371).

In the last chapter, Aptekar and Stocklin (1997) discuss the challenges of dealing with a worldwide issue, namely, "children in particu-

larly difficult circumstances," that is, "children traumatized by war, or natural and technological disasters, and those living and working without parents (street children)" (p. 379). The authors' attention to theoretical issues (cultural concerns in the definition of "difficult circumstances"), methodological issues (sampling), and researchers' personal challenges (emotional involvement) add significantly to our understanding of this very serious problem. They conclude that

> By bringing in all that is diverse among cultural variations in children's suffering, cross-cultural studies can contribute to defining what is universal about children's rights and, therefore, help to link the rights of children mentioned in the . . . [1989 Convention on the Rights of the Child by the United Nations] . . . to the reality of children's lives in diverse cultural situations. (p. 400)

One region of the world where psychologists have made the application of psychological principles to societal problems a priority is Africa. Durojaiye (1987, 1993), a pioneer in African cross-cultural psychology, has stated that, "There is a serious effort to make psychology an indigenous discipline useful to national development" (1987, pp. 34–45). A similar conclusion was reached by Mundy-Castle (1993) in his analysis of the psychological effects of rapid modernization among people living in African communities. The same is true of Nsamenang's (1992) studies of human development in the African context and his proposals for improving family life and child-rearing practices by making practical use of indigenous findings.

It is hoped, as we look to the future, there will be many more situations in which we can truly "give cross-cultural psychology away" by applying cultural findings to important real-world problems. In some parts of the world, particularly developing countries, the link among theory, research, and application is a major concern because, as Saraswathi (1998) points out, resources are scarce, and there is a strong emphasis on accountability, notably in terms of social relevance and problem-solving orientation.

Cognitive Development: Piaget versus Vygotsky

One of the most researched areas in development has been that of cognition, especially development in young children. For most of the last 40 years, cognitive studies in psychology and cross-cultural psychology have been dominated by the theories and ideas of the Swiss psychologist Jean Piaget (Dasen, 1972, 1975, 1977; Dasen & Jahoda, 1986; Piaget, 1954, 1972; Zigler & Gilman, 1998).

To Piaget, cognitive development is a dynamic process that results from an individual's ability to adapt thinking to the needs and demands of a changing environment. There is no question that Piaget's theory and the thousands of studies it has produced have made a significant contribution to our understanding of this important topic (for an extensive list of reviews of Piagetian research, see H. W. Gardiner, 1994). His delineation of the periods of sensorimotor, preoperations, concrete operations, and formal operations are a well-known part of our psychological terminology. As H. W. Gardiner et al. (1998) have pointed out,

> Whatever one's position is regarding Piaget's theory, it continues to have considerable influence on contemporary research and practice and has ... been applied to the study of cognitive development in large numbers of cultures throughout the world—with varying success. (p. 83)

For a review of the most common criticisms of Piaget's theory and reasons for defending his claims, see a 1996 article by Lourenco and Machado.

While Piaget viewed cognitive development as an individual accomplishment shaped, in part, by environmental factors, he devoted little attention to the social or cultural context. This became the focus of another, often overlooked, pioneer in cognitive development, the Soviet psychologist Lev Semyonovich Vygotsky.

Vygotsky's writings (1978, 1986), like those of Piaget, were inaccessible for many years to large numbers of monolingual psychologists because he wrote in his native language, and his output was limited due to his death at a relatively young age. Nevertheless, his view that cognitive development is the result of interactions between cultural and historical factors was an important contribution. He suggested the process involved three major components: the use of language, the role played by culture, and a child's zone of proximal development (ZPD) (Kozulin, 1990). The ZPD, or difference between what a child can achieve independently and what his or her potential level of cognitive development might be if given help

or guidance, emphasizes Vygotsky's view that social influences significantly contribute to children's development of cognitive abilities (Vygotsky, 1978).

Some argue that the zone of proximal development is not well defined and is incapable of being measured adequately (Paris & Cross, 1988), while others suggest parts of the theory have been lost or misunderstood in translation and, as a result, are incomplete (Nicolopoulou, 1993). Still, Vygotsky's theory represents an important contribution to cross-cultural development and is one that is receiving increased attention among many developmentalists (Rieber, 1998).

Indigenization of Developmental Psychology

Kim (1990) defines indigenous psychology as

> a psychological knowledge that is native, that is not transported from another region, and that is designed for its people. . . . It examines a phenomenon in a particular sociocultural context and examines how this context affects, shapes, and guides psychological description, explanation, and application. (p. 145)

In other words, its goal is to identify behavior as it is understood and experienced by people within their own unique cultural context (Bond, 1996). For more on this topic, see Kim and Berry's 1993 book, in which they discuss native psychologies in Russia, Mexico, India, Greece, Korea, and elsewhere. Rather than fragmenting psychology, these authors suggest such an approach actually may lead to the possibility of a universal psychology—a primary goal of cross-cultural and cultural psychology.

Sinha, writing in the *Handbook of Cross-Cultural Psychology* (1997), devotes considerable attention to indigenous psychology and the indigenization of developmental psychology in different regions of the world. As one example, he cites the work of Nsamenang (1992), who emphasizes the need for understanding developmental research in context and provides a framework for the contextualization of child rearing and human development in West Africa. For Nsamenang, the African life cycle, unlike the conventional Western stages (prenatal, infancy, childhood, etc.) consists of the *spiritual selfhood* (conception to naming of a child), *social selfhood* (naming to death), and *ancestral selfhood* (the period following biological death). As Sinha points out,

> Rather than the psychological tradition of hypothesis-testing using pre-structured instruments to measure planned samples of behavior, Nsamenang argues for an ethnographic approach that is open-ended, personally involved, and improvising. (p. 144)

In his review of Nsamenang's book, Serpell (1994) gives the unique approach high praise and says that its

> resonance with cultural preoccupations expressed by parents in many African societies, where social responsibility is valued above personal autonomy and intellectual alacrity, suggests that it will be well received in the emerging field of African psychology. (pp. 18–19)

The indigenous approach also plays a major role in China where developmental psychology receives a great deal of attention, especially in terms of family environment, children's social and personality development, and aging (Wang, 1993). Since the 1980s, the Chinese have carried out a number of truly large-scale research projects, including one by Liu (1982) in which more than 50 developmental psychologists from 12 cities investigated cognitive development among thousands of children 5–16 years old. In 1990, Zhu published findings from a 7-year series of cross-sectional and longitudinal studies of children and adolescents in which more than 200 psychologists from 50 institutions gathered systematic data from 23 provinces on such aspects of development as memory, perception, language, thinking, emotion, personality, mathematical ability, and moral sense. Because China is a large country with 56 national groups, psychological development of minority children has been given special attention. Zhang and Zuo (1990), in a comparison of problem-solving strategies among children from the Han majority group and several minority groups, found few differences. But, as Wang (1993) reports, "It was suggested that regional, social, and cultural factors play more important roles than nationality in children's cognitive and social developments" (p. 99).

Sinha (1997) reports that, although many Western theories, particularly those of Piaget and Kohlberg, have an influence, studies are increasingly taking on a distinctive Chinese character. For example, Kohlberg's model of moral development has been indigenized by including the notion of the "golden mean" (behaving in the way the majority of people do in society) and "good will" (the virtue of complying with nature). The Chinese model emphasizes *Ch'ing* (human affection or sentiment) more than *Li* (reason, or rationality), and the Confucian values of *jen* (love, human-heartedness, benevolence, and sympathy), filial piety, group solidarity, collectivism and humanity. (p. 146)

As for the role of culture, Wang (1993) reports that more studies are being conducted with an eye on the Chinese cultural context and has pointed out that "Chinese cultural traditions play important roles in current psychological research and applications, and in the interpretation of results" (p. 109).

According to Sinha (1997), developmental psychology in India adopted a cultural perspective and indigenization approach about 20 years ago. Especially popular among developmentalists are the "psychocultural analysis" technique of Whiting and Whiting (1975), the ecocultural framework of Berry (1976), the ecological systems approach of Bronfenbrenner (1989), and the developmental niche concept of Super and Harkness (1997).

In addition to the emerging research areas discussed in detail above, there are others worth noting (even briefly) for which culture and development are bound to intersect in the future. For example, as more intercultural marriages occur in the world, greater attention will be directed toward understanding child rearing in bicultural settings (Eldering, 1995), as well as the unique problems and adaptability strategies of bicultural children. The trend toward de-Westernization of psychology, particularly in the area of development, will continue at an accelerated pace, with increased attention given to studies that emphasize cultural traditions, values, and indigenous behaviors (Pandey, Sinha, & Bhawuk, 1996). Increasingly sophisticated studies of family structure across larger samples of cultures (Georgas et al., 1997) will result in the development of measurement devices that will more easily "cross cultures," thereby helping better explain variability between psychological variables and adding to the explanatory power of cross-cultural psychology.

As life expectancy increases in many parts of the world, more attention will be given to problems of ethnicity, aging, and mental health, and meeting these challenges should be made easier when placed within the context of the emerging frameworks proposed by Padgett (1995). Along these lines, we believe there will be more intergenerational comparisons of the longitudinal type conducted by Schneewind and Ruppert (1998) in their 20-year study of developmental, familial, and generational relationships among members of over 200 German families. According to Little (1999):

A particular strength of the work, which places it in the forefront of familial developmental psychology is the wealth of intrafamilial relationships that following parents and their offspring provides. . . . Another strength . . . is that it addresses and convincingly integrates vast topics of inquiry, from sociology to personality and all within the context of familial development. (p. 42)

Many of the developmental topics mentioned above are related in part to and influenced by aspects of one's cultural identity, defined as "an individual's awareness and appreciation of his or her heritage and values and the affective importance that he places on psychological membership in a particular group" (H. W. Gardiner et al., 1998, p. 266). In a series of research papers, H. Gardiner and Mutter (1992) and H. W. Gardiner and Mutter (1992, 1993, 1994) proposed a model for developing multicultural awareness and identity that is rooted firmly within the cultural context approach. They suggest that

An individual moves from cultural dependence, where an understanding and appreciation for one's own culture have been formed as part of his or her unique developmental niche, to cultural independence, where she steps outside the ecological setting of her culture to engage in new cross-cultural experiences, to multicultural interdependence, where she shares with her native culture new ways and experiences of viewing the world and by so doing influences the ecological settings that make up the native culture. (p. 270)

The model has recently been refined and expanded to include supporting data on identity formation among bicultural and monocultural German and American subjects (H. W. Gardiner et al., 1997). As the authors point out, much can be gained by extending this model to a wider array of cultural settings and developmental experiences including

(1) International students studying in a variety of cultural settings, (2) Native Americans, many of whom have traditionally grown up experiencing biculturalism as an integral part of their ecological system, (3) individuals engaged in cross-cultural marriage and childrearing, who need to combine and blend their diverse parental belief systems, ecological experiences, and understanding of cultures in order to raise children to have an appreciation for their bicultural identities, and (4) expatriates living and working in other countries. (H. W. Gardiner et al., 1998, p. 272)

Finally, there are those who would like to see the field move in totally new directions. For example, Hermans and Kempen (1998), in a very provocative article, point out that

The accelerating process of globalization and the increasing interconnections between cultures involve an unprecedented challenge to contemporary psychology. In apparent contrast to these trends, academic mainstream conceptions continue to work in a tradition of cultural dichotomies (e.g., individualistic vs. collectivistic, independent vs. interdependent), reflecting a classificatory approach to culture and self. (p. 1111)

They comment on three developments that challenge this approach, including the emergence of a heterogeneous global system, cultural connections leading to "hybridization," and increasing cultural complexity. They conclude that, "By elaborating on these challenges, a basic assumption of cross-cultural psychology is questioned: culture as geographically localized" (p. 1111).

A more controversial idea has been presented in Burman's (1994) call for "deconstructing developmental psychology." She argues that contemporary developmental psychology holds itself to very limiting, constraining, and indefensible positions regarding the universality of development and the significance of the individual, and there is too great an emphasis on individualism, which diverts attention from serious issues related to child-rearing practices. In a comprehensive review, Forrester (1999) suggests that developmentalists will probably ignore her ideas, which in his view, will be unfortunate because it "demonstrates how developmental psychology can become theoretically self-reflexive and much more sensitive to the social and cultural practices which constitute the discipline" (p. 308).

Thoughts on Future Directions

As we near the close of our discussion and look to the future, several critical and challenging questions emerge. What types of cross-cultural developmental studies should be conducted in the future? How similar or different should these be to current research? In what ways will these studies contribute to our understanding of human development and the ever-changing and increasingly complex world in which people will live? What implications will future research findings have for the construction of new developmental theories, and how will these new theories affect the design of even newer studies?

In the preceding section of this chapter, I made some preliminary suggestions that lead to a possible road map for future research. In addition to these ideas, I would like to draw attention to some other approaches that might assist in answering the questions just raised.

For example, researchers conducting developmental studies in the next millennium should seriously consider making greater use of triangulation design (use of multiple concepts and methods to study a single phenomenon). A good example is found in a recent cross-cultural study of child development in Jamaica (Dreher & Hayes, 1993). Specifically, this research consisted of an ethnographic study of marijuana use among rural Jamaican women and standardized clinical evaluations of the development and health status of their children. Commenting on the relevance of this approach for making cross-cultural comparisons and the contributions it can make to understanding complex behaviors, the authors state:

> Thus the methodological combination of ethnography and standardized instruments is not just a matter of coming at the same question from qualitative and quantitative perspectives. Rather, it is an essential feature of cross-cultural research . . . ethnography tells us what questions to ask and how to ask them. The open-ended inquiries commonly associated with ethnography, however, may sacrifice comparability when answers fall into different domains. Standardized instruments,

administered in as consistent a manner as possible, enhance comparability but are useful only when preliminary determination of the appropriate range and categories of responses are accompanied by ethnographic observations and interviews. (p. 227)

A study using a triangulation design will have several distinct advantages over those that do not and will allow for interaction between the qualitative and quantitative components, making modifications during the research process easier. As Fielding and Fielding (1986) point out, "Qualitative work can assist quantitative work in providing a theoretical framework, validating survey data, interpreting statistical relationships and deciphering puzzling responses" (p. 27). In addition, "selecting survey items to construct indices, and offering case study illustrations . . . can . . . [help] . . . identify individuals for qualitative study and to delineate representative and unrepresentative cases" (p. 27).

As we place greater emphasis on links between cultural contexts and individual behavior, as well as increase efforts to bridge the gap between theories and methods, researchers will continue to be confronted by a central question underlying cross-cultural developmental research: Which behaviors are indigenous or culture-specific and which are universal? The more carefully designed research we conduct, the closer we may one day come to answering this question. In the words of Kagitcibasi and Berry (1989):

> As cross-cultural psychologists pay more attention to the macro characteristics of the sociocultural context, ecology, or social structure and identify their linkages with micro (individual behavioral) variables, they will be in a better position to establish which characteristics are culture-specific, which show communality in several sociocultural contexts, and which are universal human phenomena. (p. 520)

Some insight and direction might come from looking into the recent past and a series of six articles published in a special section of a 1992 issue of *Developmental Psychology* and considered by Harkness (1992) to represent "the state of the art in cross-cultural research on child development" at the beginning of the 1990s. In evaluating this work, she states that:

> The articles document some of the diverse environments of child development, explore

questions of universality and cultural variation in mothers' and children's behavior, and attempt to delineate causal relationships among culture, parental behavior, and developmental outcomes. A common strength of the research is the collection of quantitative developmental data using familiar methods from Western-based research. However, most of the reports lack systematic information on relevant aspects of the cultural setting, making interpretation of results problematic. Further progress in the field will require integration of methods for the study of the child and the cultural context for development. (p. 622)

Although I am unable to provide definitive answers to the questions raised above (some of you may do that in the years ahead), I look forward to cross-cultural research efforts that focus on developmental comparisons (similarities and differences) within cultural contexts that attempt to combine, in part, the ethnographic approaches of the anthropologist, the psychological theories and methodologies of the psychologist, and the social policy concerns of the sociologist. In addition to highly creative and pioneering studies aimed at breaking new ground, I would like to see more attention given to clarifying, modifying, and extending existing knowledge and theories through careful (and well-designed) replication of previous findings. This is a frequently ignored (and often unappreciated) undertaking in which many findings may or may not be confirmed when viewed within sociocultural settings other than the ones in which they were conducted originally.

In these future efforts, we should consider how our findings can be "given away" in ways that will improve and enrich the lives of those who now live or will live in this increasingly complex, but continuously interdependent, world. Our shared contributions to improved cultural understanding can be a hallmark of the next millennium.

Epilogue

The first years of the new millennium will be witness to an exciting period of growth (and, perhaps controversy) in cross-cultural psychology as a discipline and human development as a significant part of it. As Smith (1995) has noted, "The past decade has seen substantial progress in the formulation of theories as to

where, when, and why cultural differences or convergences may occur" (p. 588). At the same time, Eysenck (1995), the well-known British psychologist, has taken the position that

> Psychology is split along a number of fault lines.... Such a science needs concepts, theories, and measuring instruments which are as universal as possible; otherwise our empirical findings will remain incapable of generalization beyond the narrow confines of a particular nation or state. Psychology cannot be American, or Japanese, or African; it must be universal. We can and must achieve greater unification through seeking greater cross-cultural coherence. (p. 26)

I agree with Cole and Cole (1996) when they state:

> We are gratified that the concern with cultural diversity has found a growing place in the study of child development, but we believe the urgency of understanding and appreciating the role of cultural diversity in human development is even greater today than ever before. (p. xxii)

It should be even more so in the years ahead.

In the end, as Segall et al. (1998), have noted, "When all psychology finally takes into account the effects of culture on human behavior (and vice versa), terms like cross-cultural and cultural psychology will become unnecessary" (p. 1101). At that point, *all* psychology will be truly cultural.

I believe the time has come to take this vast body of accumulating information and more effectively apply it in ways that will improve the lives of all people living together on this planet—and truly usher in the age of development.

The sentiment expressed in the closing lines of the 1998 book by H. W. Gardiner et al. on cross-cultural human development bear repeating here:

> Ahead of us lie tremendous challenges and opportunities. Speculating about where our cross-cultural journey will take us next is difficult. Wherever we go, it is certain to be an interesting and exciting adventure. Perhaps some of you will be the pioneer theorists and researchers who take us to the next point on this journey. (p. 274)

I, for one, eagerly look forward to that day.

References

Aptekar, L., & Stocklin, D. (1997). Children in particularly difficult circumstances. In J. W. Berry, P. R. Dasen, & T. S. Saraswathi (Eds.), *Handbook of cross-cultural psychology* (Vol. 2, 2nd ed., pp. 377–412). Boston: Allyn & Bacon.

Baumrind, D. (1967). Child care practices anteceding three patterns of preschool behavior. *Genetic Psychology Monographs, 75,* 43–88.

Baumrind, D. (1971). Current patterns of parental authority. *Developmental Psychology Monographs, 4*(1, Pt. 2 pp. 1–103).

Berk, L. E. (1998). *Development through the lifespan.* Boston: Allyn & Bacon.

Berry, J. W. (1976). *Human ecology and cognitive style: Comparative studies in cultural and psychological adaptation.* New York: Sage/Halsted.

Berry, J. W. (1983). The sociogenesis of social sciences: An analysis of the cultural relativity of social psychology. In B. Bain (Ed.), *The sociogenesis of language and human conduct* (pp. 449–454). New York: Plenum.

Berry, J. W., Dasen, P. R., & Saraswathi, T. S. (Eds.). (1997). *Handbook of cross-cultural psychology: Vol. 2. Basic processes and human development* (2nd ed.). Boston: Allyn & Bacon.

Berry, J. W., Poortinga, Y. H., & Pandey, J. (Eds.). (1997). *Handbook of cross-cultural psychology: Vol. 1. Theory and method (2nd ed.).* Needham Heights, MA: Allyn & Bacon.

Best, D. L., & Ruther, N. M. (1994). Cross-cultural themes in developmental psychology. *Journal of Cross-Cultural Psychology, 25,* 54–77.

Bond, M. H. (Ed.). (1996). *The handbook of Chinese psychology.* Hong Kong: Oxford University Press.

Bond, M. H. (Ed.). (1997). *Working at the interface of cultures: Eighteen lives in social science.* London: Routledge.

Bornstein, M. H. (Ed.). (1995). *Handbook of parenting.* Mahwah, NJ: Erlbaum.

Bornstein, M. H., Haynes, O. M., Azuma, H., Galperin, C., Maital, S., Ogino, M., Painter, K., Pascual, L., Pecheux, M. G., Rahn, C., Toda, S., Venuti, P., Vyt, A., & Wright, B. (1998). A cross-national study of self-evaluations and attributions in parenting: Argentina, Belgium, France, Israel, Italy, Japan, and the United States. *Developmental Psychology, 34,* 662–676.

Brislin, R. W. (1983). Cross-cultural research in psychology. *Annual Review of Psychology, 34,* 363–400.

Bronfenbrenner, U. (1970). *Two worlds of childhood: U.S. and U.S.S.R.* New York: Russell Sage Foundation.

Bronfenbrenner, U. (1975). Reality and research in the ecology of human development. *Proceedings of the American Philosophical Society, 119,* 439–469.

Bronfenbrenner, U. (1979). *The ecology of human development: Experiments by nature and design.* Cambridge, MA: Harvard University Press.

Bronfenbrenner, U. (1989). Ecological systems theory. In R. Vasta (Ed.), *Six theories of child development* (Vol. 6, pp. 187–250). Greenwich, CT: JAI Press.

Burman, E. (1994). *Deconstructing developmental psychology.* London: Routledge.

Cole, M. (1996). *Cultural psychology: A once and future discipline.* Cambridge: Harvard University Press.

Cole, M. (1998). *Cultural psychology: A once and future discipline.* Cambridge, MA: Belknap Press.

Cole, M. (1999). Culture in development. In M. Bornstein (Ed.), *Developmental psychology: An advanced textbook* (4th ed., pp. 73–123). Mahwah, NJ: Erlbaum.

Cole, M., & Cole, S. R. (1996). *The development of children* (3rd ed.). New York: Freeman.

Cole, M., Engestrom, Y., & Vasquez, O. (Eds.). (1997). *Mind, culture and activity: Seminal papers from the laboratory of comparative human development.* Cambridge: Cambridge University Press.

D'Andrade, R. G., & Strauss, C. (Eds.). (1992). *Human motives and cultural models.* Cambridge: Cambridge University Press.

Darling, N., & Steinberg, L. (1993). Parenting style as context: An integrative model. *Psychological Bulletin, 113,* 487–496.

Dasen, P. R. (1972). Cross-cultural Piagetian research: A summary. *Journal of Cross-Cultural Psychology, 7,* 75–85.

Dasen, P. R. (1975). Concrete operational development in three cultures. *Journal of Cross-Cultural Psychology, 6,* 156–172.

Dasen, P. R. (Ed.). (1977). *Piagetian psychology: Cross-cultural contributions.* New York: Gardner Press.

Dasen, P. R., & Jahoda, G. (1986). Cross-cultural human development [Special issue]. *International Journal of Behavioural Development, 9.*

Dreher, M. C., & Hayes, J. S. (1993). Triangulation in cross-cultural research in child development in Jamaica. *Western Journal of Nursing Research, 15*(2), 216–229.

Durojaiye, M. O. (1987). Black Africa. In A. R. Gilgen & C. K. Gilgen (Eds.), *International handbook of psychology* (pp. 24–36). New York: Greenwood Press.

Durojaiye, M. O. (1993). Indigenous psychology in Africa: The search for meaning. In U. Kim & J. W. Berry (Eds.), *Indigenous psychologies: Re-*

search and experience in cultural context (pp. 211–220). Newbury Park, CA: Sage.

Eldering, L. (1995). Child-rearing in bi-cultural settings: A culture-ecological approach. *Psychology and Developing Societies, 7*, 133–153.

Eysenck, H. J. (1995). Cross-cultural psychology and the unification of psychology. *World Psychology, 1*(4), 11–30.

Fielding, N. G., & Fielding, J. L. (1986). *Linking data qualitative research methods* (Vol. 4). Beverly Hills, CA: Sage.

Forrester, M. A. (1999). Recognizing the gauntlet: Anti-developmentalism in developmental psychology. *British Journal of Psychology, 90*, 305–311.

Forrester, M. A. (1999). Deconstructing developmental psychology (review). *British Journal of Psychology, 90*, 305–312.

Gardiner, H., & Mutter, J. D. (1992, July 14–18). *Developing multicultural awareness: A model for integrating learning and culture.* Paper presented at the 11th International Congress of the International Association for Cross-Cultural Psychology and the Association for Intercultural Research, Liege, Belgium.

Gardiner, H. W. (1994). Child development. In L. L. Adler & U. P. Gielen (Eds., August), *Cross-cultural topics in psychology* (pp. 61–72). New York: Praeger.

Gardiner, H. W. (1996, August). *Cross-cultural content in contemporary developmental textbooks.* Paper presented at the 13th Congress of the International Association for Cross-Cultural Psychology, Montreal, Canada.

Gardiner, H. W. (1999). *Future directions in cross-cultural human development.* Unpublished manuscript.

Gardiner, H. W., & Mutter, J. D. (1992, February). *Positive attitudes and cross-cultural experiences.* Paper presented at the 21st Annual Meeting of the Society for Cross-Cultural Research, Santa Fe, NM.

Gardiner, H. W., & Mutter, J. D. (1993, February). *An approach to integrating teaching and formal learning in a multicultural context.* Paper presented at 22nd Annual Meeting of the Society for Cross-Cultural Research, Washington, DC.

Gardiner, H. W., & Mutter, J. D. (1994, February). *Measuring multicultural awareness and identity: A model.* Paper presented at the 23rd Annual Meeting of the Society for Cross-Cultural Research, Santa Fe, NM.

Gardiner, H. W., Mutter, J. D., & Kosmitzki, C. (1997). *A model for understanding cultural identity.* Unpublished manuscript.

Gardiner, H. W., Mutter, J. D., & Kosmitzki, C. (1998). *Lives across cultures: Cross-cultural human development.* Boston: Allyn & Bacon.

Georgas, J., Christakopoulous, S., Poortinga, Y. H., Angleitner, A., Goodwin, R., & Charalambous, N. (1997). The relationship of family bonds to family structure and function across cultures. *Journal of Cross-Cultural Psychology, 28*, 303–320.

Goodnow, J. J., Miller, P. J., & Kessel, F. (1995). *Cultural practices as contexts for development.* San Francisco: Jossey-Bass.

Harkness, S. (1992). Cross-cultural research in child development: A sample of the state of the art. *Developmental Psychology, 28*(4), 622–625.

Hartup, W. W., & van Lieshout, C. F. M. (1995). Personality development in social context. *Annual Review of Psychology, 46*, 655–687.

Hermans, H. J. M., & Kempen, J. G. (1998). Moving cultures: The perilous problems of cultural dichotomies in a globalizing society. *American Psychologist, 53*, 1111–1120.

Jahoda, G. (1982). *Psychology and anthropology: A psychological perspective.* London: Academic Press.

Jahoda, G. (1986). A cross-cultural perspective on developmental psychology. *International Journal of Behavioral Development, 9*, 417–437.

Jahoda, G. (1992). *Crossroads between culture and mind: Continuities and change in theories of human nature.* London: Harvester Wheatsheaf.

Jahoda, G., & Krewer, B. (1997). History of cross-cultural and cultural psychology. In J. W. Berry, Y. H. Poortinga, & J. Pandey (Eds.), *Handbook of cross-cultural psychology: Theory and method* (Vol. 1, pp. 1–42). Boston: Allyn & Bacon.

Jessor, R., Colby, A., & Shweder, R. A. (1996). *Ethnography and human development: Context and meaning in social inquiry.* Chicago: University of Chicago Press.

Kagitcibasi, C. (1996). *Family and human development across cultures.* Mahwah, NJ: Erlbaum.

Kagitcibasi, C., & Berry, J. W. (1989). Cross-cultural psychology: Current research and trends. *Annual Review of Psychology, 40*, 493–531.

Kim, U. (1990). Indigenous psychology: Science and applications. In R. W. Brislin (Ed.), *Applied cross-cultural psychology.* Newbury Park, CA: Sage.

Kim, U., & Berry, J. W. (1993). (Eds.). *Indigenous psychologies: Research and experience in cultural context.* Newbury Park, CA: Sage.

Klineberg, O. (1980). Historical perspectives: Cross-cultural psychology before 1960. In H. C. Triandis & W. W. Lambert (Eds.), *Handbook of cross-cultural psychology* (Vol. 1, pp. 1–14). Boston: Allyn & Bacon.

Kozulin, A. (1990). *Vygotsky's psychology: A biography of ideas.* New York: Harvester Wheatsheaf.

Lewin, K. (1951). *Field theory in social science.* New York: Harper.

Little, T. D. (1999). Development across generations (and cultures?) [Book review]. *Contemporary Psychology, 44*(1), 42–44.

Liu, F. (1982). Developmental psychology in China [in Chinese]. *Acta Psychologica Sinica, 14*, 1–10.

Lourenco, O., & Machado, A. (1996). In defense of Piaget's theory: A reply to 10 common criticisms. *Psychological Review, 103*, 143–164.

Maccoby, E. E., & Martin, J. A. (1983). Socialization in the context of the family: Parent-child interaction. In P. H. Mussen (Series Ed.) & E. M. Hetherington (Vol. Ed.), *Handbook of child psychology: Vol. 4. Socialization, personality, and social development* (4th ed., pp. 1–101). New York: Wiley.

Mead, G. H. (1934). *Mind, self, and society.* Chicago: University of Chicago Press.

Miller, G. A. (1969). Psychology as a means of promoting human welfare. *American Psychologist, 24*, 1063–1075.

Miller, J. G. (1997). Theoretical issues in cultural psychology. In J. W. Berry, Y. H. Poortinga, & J. Pandey (Eds.), *Handbook of cross-cultural psychology: Theory and method* (Vol. 1, pp. 85–128). Boston: Allyn & Bacon.

Mishra, R. C., Sinha, D., & Berry, J. W. (1996). *Ecology, acculturation and psychological adaptation.* Thousand Oaks, CA: Sage.

Mundy-Castle, A. C. (1993). Human behaviour and national development: Conceptual and theoretical perspectives. *Ife Psychologia, 1*, 1–16.

Nicolopoulou, A. (1993). Play, cognitive development, and the social world: Piaget, Vygotsky, and beyond. *Human Development, 36*, 1–23.

Nsamenang, A. B. (1992). *Human development in cultural context: A third world perspective.* Newbury Park, CA: Sage.

Padgett, D. K. (Ed.). (1995). *Handbook on ethnicity, aging, and mental health.* Westport, CT: Greenwood Press.

Pandey, J., Sinha, D., & Bhawuk, D. P. S. (Eds.). (1996). *Asian contributions to cross-cultural psychology.* New Delhi: Sage.

Paris, S. G., & Cross, D. R. (1988). The zone of proximal development: Virtues and pitfalls of a metaphorical representation of children's learning. *Genetic Epistemologist, 26*, 27–37.

Parke, R. D., Ornstein, P. A., Rieser, J. J., & Zahn-Waxler, C. (Eds.). (1994). *A century of developmental psychology.* Washington, DC: American Psychological Association.

Piaget, J. (1954). *The construction of reality in the child.* New York: Basic Books.

Piaget, J. (1972). Intellectual evolution from adolescence to adulthood. *Human Development, 15*, 1–12.

Piker, S. (1998). Contributions of psychological anthropology. *Journal of Cross-Cultural Psychology, 29*, 9–31.

Rieber, R. W. (Ed.). (1998). *The collected works of L. S. Vygotsky: Vol. 4: Child psychology.* New York: Plenum.

Saraswathi, T. S. (1998). Many deities, one god: Towards convergence in cultural and cross-cultural psychology. *Culture and Psychology, 4*, 147–160.

Schneewind, K. A., & Ruppert, S. (1998). *Personality and family development: An intergenerational longitudinal comparison.* Mahwah, NJ: Erlbaum.

Schwartz, T. (1981) The acquisition of culture. *Ethos, 9*, 4–17.

Segall, M. H. (1986). Culture and behavior: Psychology in global perspective. *Annual Review of Psychology, 37*, 523–564.

Segall, M. H., Dasen, P. R., Berry, J. W., & Poortinga, Y. H. (1999). *Human behavior in global perspective* (2nd ed.). Boston: Allyn & Bacon.

Segall, M. H., Lonner, W. J., & Berry, J. W. (1998). Cross-cultural psychology as a scholarly discipline: On the flowering of culture in behavioral research. *American Psychologist, 53*, 1101–1110.

Serpell, R. (1994). An African ontogeny of selfhood (book review). *Cross-Cultural Psychology Bulletin, 28*, 17–20.

Serpell, R., & Hatano, G. (1997). Education, schooling, and literacy. In J. W. Berry, P. R. Dasen, & T. S. Saraswathi (Eds.), *Handbook of cross-cultural psychology* (2nd ed., Vol. 2, pp. 339–376). Boston: Allyn & Bacon.

Shwalb, D. W., & Shwalb, B. J. (Eds.). (1996). *Japanese childrearing: Two generations of scholarship.* New York: Guilford Press.

Shweder, R. A. (1991). *Thinking through cultures: Expeditions in cultural psychology.* Cambridge: Harvard University Press.

Shweder, R. A., & Sullivan, M. A. (1993). Cultural psychology: Who needs it? *Annual Review of Psychology, 44*, 497–523.

Sinha, D. (1997). Indigenizing psychology. In J. W. Berry, H. Poortinga, & J. Pandey (Eds.), *Handbook of cross-cultural psychology: Theory and method* (Vol. 1, pp. 129–169). Boston: Allyn & Bacon.

Smith, P. B. (1995). JCCP—Looking to the future. *Journal of Cross-Cultural Psychology, 26*, 588–590.

Sternberg, R. (1995). *In search of the human mind.* Fort Worth, TX: Harcourt-Brace.

Stevenson-Hinde, J. (1998). Parenting in different cultures: Time to focus. *Developmental Psychology, 34*, 698–700.

Stigler, J. W., Shweder, R. A., & Herdt, G. (Eds.). (1990). *Cultural psychology: Essays on compar-*

ative human development. Cambridge: Cambridge University Press.

Super, C. M. (1981). Behavioral development in infancy. In R. H. Munroe, R. L. Munroe, & B. B. Whiting (Eds.), *Handbook of cross-cultural development*. New York: Garland.

Super, C. M, & Harkness, S. (1997). The cultural structuring of child development. In J. W. Berry, P. R. Dasen, & T. S. Saraswathi (Eds.), *Handbook of cross-cultural psychology* (2nd ed., Vol. 2, pp. 1–39). Boston: Allyn & Bacon.

Triandis, H. C., Malpass, R., & Davidson, A. R. (1973). Psychology and culture. *Annual Review of Psychology, 24*, 355–378.

Valsiner, J., & Lawrence, J. (1997). Human development in culture across the life span. In J. W. Berry, P. R. Dasen, & T. S. Saraswathi (Eds.), *Handbook of cross-cultural psychology* (2nd ed., Vol. 2, pp. 69–106). Boston: Allyn & Bacon.

Vygotsky, L. S. (1978). *Mind in society: The development of higher psychological processes*. Cambridge: Harvard University Press.

Vygotsky, L. S. (1986). *Thought and language* (A. Kozulin, Trans./rev.). Cambridge: MIT Press. (Original work published 1934)

Wade, C., & Tavris, C. (1996). *Psychology*. New York: Harper Collins.

Wang, Z.-M. (1993). Psychology in China: A review dedicated to Li Chen. *Annual Review of Psychology, 44*, 87–116.

Weisner, T. S. (1997). The ecocultural project of human development: Why ethnography and its findings matter. *Ethos, 25*, 177–190.

Whiting, B. B. (1963). *Six cultures: Studies of child rearing*. Cambridge, MA: Harvard University Press.

Whiting, B. B., & Edwards, C. P. (1988). *Children of different worlds: The formation of social behavior*. Cambridge, MA: Harvard University Press.

Whiting, B. B., & Whiting, J. W. M. (1975). *Children of six cultures: A psycho-cultural analysis*. Cambridge: Harvard University Press.

Zevalkink, J. (1997). *Attachment in Indonesia: The mother-child relationship in context*. Doctoral dissertation, University of Nijmegen, Nijemgen, The Netherlands. (ISBN 90-9010829-7)

Zhang, Z., & Zuo, M. L. (1990). The development of children's strategy in problem-solving [in Chinese]. *Information on Psychological Sciences, 2*, 21–26.

Zhu, Z.-X. (Ed.). (1990). *Psychological development and education of Chinese children and adolescence* [in Chinese]. Beijing: Chinese Excellence Press.

Zigler, E., & Gilman, E. (1998). The legacy of Jean Piaget. In M. Wertheimer (Ed.), *Portraits of pioneers in psychology* (Vol. 3, pp. 145–149). Mahwah, NJ: Erlbaum.

7

Cognition across Cultures

R. C. MISHRA

One basic psychological process that has been well studied in mainstream and cross-cultural psychology is *cognition*, which is defined here as that group of processes by which individuals obtain and utilize knowledge of objects in their environment. The study of cognition and cognitive processes across cultures is especially informative because they inform us about how the environment and other sociocultural factors help to shape, mold, and transform the way we process, think, and act in the world.

In this chapter, Mishra provides an excellent overall review of cross-cultural studies on a variety of cognitive processes. He begins by distilling the main issues that have characterized research in this area for decades, as well as by describing the differences between the nativist and empiricist approaches to understanding cognitive development. Mishra's analysis of these issues, particularly concerning the rapprochement between contrasting viewpoints, and the realization that cognitive processes are universal to all, but that cultures shape the nature and direction of their development, is especially useful.

Mishra also delineates and describes four major theoretical approaches to understanding the relationship between cognition and culture. These include the viewpoint of general intelligence, genetic epistemology, specific skills, and cognitive styles. As Mishra suggests, these approaches are not necessarily associated with differences or disagreement in how they see the role of culture in cognition; rather, their differences lie in how they prefer to approach culture, cognition, and the relationship between the two. They also lead to different ways of conducting research.

The bulk of the remainder of the chapter provides a state-of-the-art review of cross-cultural research in various areas of cognition, including categorization, learning and memory, schooling and literacy, spatial cognition, problem solving and verbal reasoning, and creativity. Mishra skillfully describes research that has documented important cultural differences in each of these processes and that has begun to elucidate the nature of the reasons and bases underlying these differences. In particular, the complex interaction among cognition, environment, lifestyle, formal educational systems, and other factors suggests that understanding the influence of culture on cognitive development is not an easy task. As some cognitive processes develop as a result of long-term adaptation to environment and ecocultural settings, other cognitive processes develop in the course of adaptation to the new challenges of an ever-changing world. As such, disentangling the factors that contribute to this complexity is an undaunting task, and one that will require fundamentally different approaches to theory, as well as research, in the future. Indeed, Mishra argues for the adoption of alternative methods for designing studies to restructure our knowledge in this area and the integration of the approaches offered by studies of everyday cognition and cultural and indigenous psychologies. In the end, Mishra argues that different perspectives need to come together to present a more unified approach to understanding the relationship between culture and cognition in the future, a message that is consonant with the theme throughout this book.

This chapter attempts to examine the influence of culture on cognition. Cognition refers to those processes by which individuals obtain and utilize knowledge of objects in their environment. It includes processes like recognition, labeling, analysis, categorization, thinking, reasoning, and planning. The study of these processes has attracted not only psychologists and educators, but also child development personnel and policy planners. Consequently, a substantial body of knowledge has been accumulated through research on cognitive processes (see Altarriba, 1993; R. C. Mishra, 1997).

Main Issues

Cross-cultural studies of cognition seem to be concerned with three main questions raised by Berry and Dasen (1974). These relate to (a) qualitative differences in cognitive processes of different cultural groups, (b) quantitative differences in cognitive processes among different cultural groups, and (c) the characteristics of development of cognitive operations and their organization in different cultural groups. Cross-cultural psychology has an interesting history of research on these questions (see Jahoda & Krewer, 1997, and Segall, Dasen, Berry, & Poortinga, 1999, for a detailed discussion of historical developments).

In general, the research has rejected the notion of "superiority-inferiority" on the part of different cultural groups. It suggests that people in different cultures perceive and organize their worlds in many different ways. Cross-cultural psychologists try to understand and interpret differences in cognitive behavior of individuals or groups in terms of "culturally shaped experiences." No value, status, or hierarchy is assigned either to cognitive behaviors or to individuals and groups. This position stands in sharp contrast to the one held by psychologists who still attempt ranking of (racial/ethnic) groups according to cognitive ability.

Empiricist Approach

Research on cognitive development demonstrates the influence of nativists and empiricists. The nativists believe that all perceptual and cognitive phenomena are inborn, and these phenomena do not require any active construction by the organism. The empiricists, on the other hand, believe that organisms' response to various environmental stimuli is determined by experience and learning.

The empiricist theories have been central to cross-cultural studies of cognition; hence, these have been constructed in several ways. The theory of "transactional functionalism" (Brunswik, 1956) is most frequently utilized in cross-cultural studies of cognition. It places emphasis on the adaptive value of interactions and maintains that cognition helps individuals to cope with demands that their environments place on them. The approach has been used to explain the cognitive characteristics of several cultural groups (Berry, 1966, 1976; Berry et al., 1986; R. C. Mishra, Sinha, & Berry, 1996).

There have been attempts for rapprochement between these contrasting viewpoints. A widely shared view in cross-cultural psychology today is that cognitive processes are universal (shared by all populations). However, to understand the nature and direction of development of these processes, it is necessary to analyze the day-to-day situations in which these processes find expression in an individual's life. Studies suggest that different societies hold different meanings of cognitive competence (Berry, 1984; Berry & Bennett, 1991; Dasen, 1984; Serpell, 1989; Wober, 1974) and consider different behaviors as "valuable" for their members. We find evidence in many societies about the existence of cognitive goals that sharply differ from those valued in Western societies. Thus, for any valid assessment of cognitive processes, it is essential to understand (a) the ecological context of people, (b) the cognitive goals that are set for children in a given culture, and (c) the manner in which these are transmitted to children.

These analyses are also essential for the evaluation of an individual's progress with respect to cognitive development. The knowledge of a cognitive goal can tell us about the progress one has made in that direction. Research indicates that cultures do vary in placing value on certain cognitive behaviors. For example, in some societies, "holistic" problem solving based on "deliberation" is greatly valued, whereas in other societies, "analytic" problem solving based on "quick" individual decisions is valued. The individuals' cognitive development in these societies is likely to proceed in different directions.

All theoretical approaches that attempt to study cognitive development across cultures focus on these issues. The following section describes these approaches. Research guided by each theoretical position is also discussed briefly.

Theoretical Approaches

Four theoretical approaches have been adopted to understand the relationship between culture and cognition (Berry, Poortinga, Segall, & Dasen, 1992). These are the approaches of general intelligence, genetic epistemology, specific skills, and cognitive styles. These approaches differ from each other on three major issues: (a) conceptualization of ecocultural contexts, (b) organization of cognitive performances, and (c) the existence of central cognitive processors.

General Intelligence

The general intelligence approach is one of the earliest approaches to the study of cognition. It is based on the idea of a unitary cognitive competence, called *general ability*, which is reflected by positive correlation among performances on a number of cognitive tasks (e.g., verbal, spatial, numerical). A central cognitive processor, called the "g" factor (Spearman, 1927), is held responsible for varying levels of intelligence across individuals. Sociocultural background factors, such as economic pursuits and cultural and educational experiences, are believed to form a cluster. A large cluster represents an *enriched* environment, whereas a small cluster represents a *deprived* one. It is also believed that an individual who has an enriched sociocultural or experiential background will

have greater opportunity to develop the central processor and will exhibit greater intelligence (Carroll, 1983; Sternberg, 1985).

Cross-cultural studies of intelligence have demonstrated more specialized factors besides the g factor (Burg & Belmont, 1990; Irvine, 1979; Vernon, 1969). Vernon proposed a hierarchical model of intelligence. He called on Hebb's distinction between Intelligence A (genetic equipment) and Intelligence B (potentiality developed through interaction with cultural environment) and then introduced the notion of Intelligence C (performance on a particular test) as an important component. The distinction between Intelligence B and Intelligence C allows cross-cultural psychologists to examine the role of culture. Because Intelligence B is not properly assumed by the tests, Intelligence C does not represent the actual competence of an individual of a given culture. Several cultural factors (e.g., language, item content, and motivation) also contribute to individuals' performance on tests (Sternberg, 1994). Hence, it is extremely difficult to draw inference about an individual's intelligence simply based on test scores.

Some recent publications tend to claim a genetic basis for intelligence (Herrnstein & Murray, 1994; Rushton, 1995). Based on some superficial characteristics (e.g., skin color, hair texture) of populations, Rushton claims a genetic basis of individual, as well as group, differences in intelligence test scores. Such interpretations imply the notion of "deficit," whereas the cultural viewpoint emphasizes the notion of "difference." McShane and Berry (1988) have critically examined these notions. They argued that performance differences may be linked to a variety of factors, such as poverty, nutrition, health, or cultural disorganization. Irvine (1983) indicates that, in the Third World countries, these factors play an important role in determining performance on tests. Ceci (1994) has indicated that "years of schooling" alone account for significant variation in intelligence test scores in many studies. To make any valid inference about intelligence, therefore, control of these factors is essential.

Genetic Epistemology

The genetic epistemology approach deals with developmental processes that unfold in a chronological sequence. In this approach, it is held that performances are patterned on various cognitive tasks. According to Piaget's view, the cognitive development passes through four distinct stages (sensorimotor, preoperational, concrete operational, and formal operational). Although Piaget provided age ranges for these stages, he recognized that the exact age at which a particular child enters a specified stage could be significantly affected by the child's physical, cognitive, or cultural experiences (Piaget, 1974). The influence of cultural factors has been studied particularly at the concrete and formal operational stages of development (Dasen & Heron, 1981; Gardiner, Mutter, & Kosmitzki, 1998).

Studies dealing with development at the concrete operational stage have generally focused on the development of conservation. In an early work, Dasen (1972) reviewed cross-cultural findings on conservation task performance and sorted results into four categories:

1. Cultural groups in which conservation appears at about the same time as it does in American and European children (e.g., Nigerians, Zambians, Hong Kong children, Iranian and Australian aborigines)
2. Groups in which conservation generally develops earlier (e.g., Asians)
3. Groups in which conservation appears 2 to 6 years later (e.g., Africans, Americans and Europeans of low socioeconomic status)
4. Groups in which some individuals fail to engage in concrete operations even after reaching adolescence (e.g., Algerians, Nepalese, Amazon Indians, and Senegalese)

A large body of cross-cultural data provides us with convincing evidence that (a) the structures or operations underlying the preoperational period are universal, and (b) the functioning of these structures and the rate at which this might take place are strongly influenced by factors operating within one's culture. Nyiti (1982) concludes that "while children in different cultures may have to deal with different realities, they all apply the same operations or processes of thought" (p. 165). However, some later studies revealed the existence of supplementary stages in the sequence described by Piaget. Saxe (1981, 1982) found evidence for this in a study of the development of number concepts among the Oksapmin of Papua New Guinea, who use a number system based on the names of body parts.

With respect to formal operational thinking, some researchers have expressed the view that individuals in many societies fail to achieve this characteristic of thought (Shea, 1985). Although this is more true for societies in which people do not participate in formal schooling, the evidence for the existence of formal operational thinking is not consistent even among the schooled subjects. Keats (1985) worked with Australian, Malay, Indian, and Chinese students and found formal operational thinking to be present in some subjects within all groups, but not in all subjects within any group. A proportionality training session brought improvement in the performance of all groups. This suggested that differences among groups were largely at the "performance" level.

Tapé's study (1987) brings out the importance of using culturally appropriate situations with nonschooled subjects for the study of formal operational thinking. Saxe (1981) worked with Ponam islanders, who use a system of child naming in which daughters are given a name according to their birth order in relation to their female siblings. The same rule is used in naming sons, but using another series of names. Saxe developed a task of formal operational thinking using the familiar rules of naming boys and girls. The participants were asked to construct hypothetical families in accordance with the rules of naming. Given this situation, the participants were able to resolve questions pertaining to each sex or both sexes, suggesting that they did possess the ability to carry out formal operational thinking.

Piagetian theory has been reconstructed by integrating both structural and contextual aspects. These "neo-Piagetian theories" (Case, 1985; Demetriou, Efklides, & Platsidou, 1993; Fischer, 1980; Pascual-Leone, 1970) focus on the invariance of structure across situations, but insist on the necessity for the inclusion of situational variables. Dasen and de Ribaupierre (1987) have examined the potential of these theories for accommodating cultural and individual differences. They found none of them to be adequate as they are not tested enough cross-culturally.

Specific Skills

The specific skills approach originally was proposed in experimental anthropology (Cole, Gay, Glick, & Sharp, 1971) and does not hold to the existence of a general or central processor. The emphasis is on the study of the relationship between a particular feature of the ecocultural context (e.g., an experience) and a specific cognitive performance (e.g., classification of stimuli). It suggests that "cultural differences in cognition reside more in the situations to which particular cognitive processes are applied than in the existence of a process in one cultural group and its absence in another" (Cole et al., 1971, p. 233). Thus, the approach admits the relationship of cognitive performance with ecocultural features of groups without involving a central processor to mediate the effect of culture on cognition.

Studies carried out with Kpelle farmers in Liberia on estimation of the quantity of rice (Gay & Cole, 1967) provide major support to the above conclusion. The Kpelle are upland rice farmers who often sell surplus rice as a way to supplement their meager income. They store rice in buckets, tin cans, and bags and use a standard minimal measure for rice, called *kopi* (a tin can). This is often used to estimate the amount of rice in day-to-day exchange. The Kpelle adults and children were compared with American working class adults and school-children for their accuracy in estimating different amounts of rice. It was found that Kpelle adults were extremely accurate at this task, averaging only 1% or 2% error compared to the American adults, who overestimated one of the amounts by 100%. This accuracy is not reflected by Kpelle farmers in other situations. Studies on free recall of the Kpelle (Cole et al., 1971), on conservation of mass among children of Mexican potters (Price-Williams, Gordon, & Ramirez, 1969), on pattern reproduction among Zambian and Scottish children (Serpell, 1979), and on understanding of "profit" among Scottish and Zimbabwean children (Jahoda, 1983) also tend to support the notion of "specificity" in cognitive processes.

Similar evidence was obtained in a study of the effect of Vai, Liberia, literacy on cognitive performance (Scribner & Cole, 1981). Vai literacy influenced only some specific test performances (e.g., descriptive communications and grammatical judgments). Such a limited role of literacy was explained in terms of its "restricted" use in the community.

Berry and Bennett (1991) studied the Cree of Northern Ontario in Canada, where the use of literacy is not so restricted as in the Vai. The effect of literacy was evident only for rotation and spatial tasks, that is, the tasks that involved cognitive operations essential for the use of the script. However, the analysis revealed positive intercorrelation among all test scores, suggesting a definite patterning in the data. Patterning in performance has also been reported in another study, in which the effect of a particular cultural experience (weaving) on reproduction of patterns through different media (e.g., pen-cil-paper, sand, wire, and hand positioning) was examined (R. C. Mishra & Tripathi, 1996).

The advocates of this approach have realized some of its difficulties. A major problem is "its failure to account for generality in human behavior" (Laboratory of Comparative Human Cognition, 1983, p. 331). With respect to performance, it is now felt that "skills and knowledge acquired in one setting often do appear in other settings under recognizably appropriate circumstances" (p. 331). In a relatively recent formulation, Cole (1992) has proposed the concept of "modularity." He maintains that psychological processes are domain specific, but considers different domains as modules, which are intricately related to cultural contexts and have inputs that are fed into a central processor that operates on them. With respect to cultural context, Cole (1997) admits

> There is no doubt that culture is patterned, but there is also no doubt that it is far from uniform and that its patterning is experienced in local, face-to-face interactions that are locally constrained. . . . Consequently, anyone interested in the question of culture and cognition must be concerned with the effective units of culture vis a vis mind: They are to be located somewhere between the "perfectly patterned whole" and the "random collection of artifacts." (p. 250)

In a retrospective assessment of his theoretical position, Cole (1996) acknowledged, "What we did not have was a systematic way of thinking about the relation between the psychic reality we created through our research practices and the psychological reality of people in their everyday practices" (p. 97). Research using the "sociohistorical approach" (Vygotsky, 1978) and "everyday cognition" approach (Schliemann & Carraher, chapter 8, this volume; Schliemann, Carraher, & Ceci, 1997) is an attempt to overcome some of these difficulties.

Cognitive Styles

The cognitive styles approach was articulated by Ferguson (1956), who argued that "cultural factors prescribe what shall be learned and at what age; consequently different cultural environments lead to the development of different patterns of ability" (p. 156). Thus, those who use this approach look for interrelationships (patterns) in cognitive performances and postulate that different patterns of abilities tend to develop in different ecocultural settings, depending on the demands placed on an individual's life.

Among various cognitive styles, the field dependent–field independent (FD-FI) style has received substantial attention in research (Witkin & Goodenough, 1981). Cross-cultural studies of FD-FI cognitive style have largely been pursued in an ecocultural framework proposed by Berry (1966, 1976, 1987). In this framework, ecology and acculturation are perceived as two major set of "input" variables, and the culture of groups and behavior of individuals are considered "adaptive to the demands placed on individuals and groups in their respective ecological settings." Witkin and Berry (1975) and Berry (1981, 1991) have presented comprehensive reviews of cross-cultural studies of FD-FI style. Findings generally suggest that the cognitive style of individuals and groups can be predicted from knowledge of their ecocultural and acculturation characteristics (Berry, 1976, 1981).

The study of FD-FI cognitive style, using the ecocultural framework, has generated considerable interest among researchers for decades. D. Sinha (1979, 1980) studied children of nomadic hunting-gathering, transitional, and long-standing agricultural groups of tribal and other cultures. Hunters and gatherers were found to be psychologically more differentiated (FI) than agriculturists. Hill ecology supported by certain cultural practices of the Brahmin group was found to reinforce the process of differentiation among Nepalese children (D. Sinha & Shrestha, 1992). Schooling, urbanization, and industrialization have also been found to promote differentiation among Santhal children (G. Sinha, 1988).

Berry et el. (1986) studied male and female children and adults of the Biaka (Pygmy hunters and gatherers), the Bangandu (mainly agriculturist, but with some hunting and gathering), and the Gbanu (full-fledged agriculturist) cultural groups of central Africa, using eight measures of differentiation in the cognitive domain and three in the social domain. Data obtained from parent and neighbor interviews, child ratings, and observation of parent-child interaction on a specially designed task were used to assess the nature of child socialization. Acculturation was assessed at both the subjective and objective levels.

Findings on the cognitive tests offered support to the notion of cognitive style. Socialization emphases were toward making children independent and self-reliant in both the Biaka and the Bangandu samples, whereas in the Gbanu sample the emphasis was toward interdependence. However, the socialization variables did not relate strongly with cognitive (FD-FI) style of children. On the other hand, both test and contact acculturation significantly influenced test performance in the predicted direction.

In a more recent study, R. C. Mishra et al. (1996) studied parents and children of the Birhor (nomadic hunters-gatherer group), Asur (recent settlers pursuing a mixed economy of hunting-gathering and agriculture), and Oraon (long-standing agriculturists) tribal cultural groups in the state of Bihar in India. In each cultural group, variations among subjects were obtained with respect to a number of variables of contact and test acculturation. Socialization emphases (towards compliance or assertion) of the groups were also assessed through a combination of observation, interview and testing. The findings supported the notion of cognitive styles, and it was possible to predict these styles on the basis of ecocultural and acculturational characteristics of the groups. Parent- or child-reported socialization emphases turned out as weak predictors of children's cognitive style, while variables like parental helping and feedback (extracted from factor analysis) could reliably predict cognitive style in the expected direction. Almost similar results have been obtained in another study carried out with children of hunting-gathering, agricultural, and wage-earning samples of the Tharu culture in the Himalayan region of India (K. Mishra, 1998).

R. C. Mishra (1996) studied unschooled children of the Birjia cultural group in Bihar (India) using Story-Pictorial EFT (Embedded Figures Test) and Indo-African EFT as measures of cognitive style. Distances traveled by children daily away from home (either in the forest or within the village) and their self-directed activities were assessed. In general, children moving into the forests traveled longer distances and engaged in more self-directed activities than those moving in the village surroundings. The children who moved in the forest scored significantly higher on both the measures of cognitive style than the village children, which was attributed to high differentiation demands placed on children in the forest settings.

Thus, studies that adopt a cognitive style approach reveal that the effect of culture on cognition cannot be explored simply by observing the performance of various cultural groups on certain cognitive tasks. An analysis of the cultural life of groups, the behavioral competencies required in their cultural settings, and the way in which they are nurtured in the course of individual development is essential.

Differences exemplified in these approaches point to the various ways in which the relationship between culture and cognition can be addressed in empirical research. As we can see, there is no disagreement on the role of culture in cognition. The difference among approaches lies in how they prefer to approach culture, cognition, and the relationship between the two.

Influence of Culture on Cognitive Processes

In this section, we discuss some studies of cognitive processes to examine how and to what extent the cultural factors can influence them.

Categorization

Our perception gives us very diverse knowledge of the surrounding world. To organize and retain this knowledge, some kind of categorization becomes essential. Do people from different cultures use different principles of category formation, or are the principles the same everywhere? Cross-cultural research on the categorization of colors and objects provides us with some interesting results.

Color Coding and Categorization

Early studies pertaining to color codability (Whorf, 1956) had demonstrated that people in different societies did not have the same array of color terms to partition the color spectrum. Berlin and Kay (1969) argued that, if the philosophy underlying color perception is universal, then there should be agreement on "focal points" for color among those who speak different languages in spite of variations in color vocabulary. Berlin and Kay (1969), however, noted an evolutionary progression in color terms in the sense that culturally simpler societies tended to have fewer basic color terms than culturally complex (e.g., large-scale, industrial) societies. MacLaury's (1991) work also demonstrates the effect of ecocultural factors on color coding. A comprehensive discussion of color-naming studies has been presented by Russell, Deregowski, and Kinnear (1997).

Recent studies provide support for a weak linguistic effect on color categorization. Davies and Corbett (1997) studied speakers of English, Russian, and Setswana languages, which differ in their number of basic color terms and in how the blue-green region is categorized. A set of 65 colors was given to subjects for sorting into groups so that the members of the groups looked similar to each other. Contrary to the expectation, the findings revealed considerable similarity among the patterns of choice of the three samples. At the same time, there were also significant differences among the samples. For example, Setswana speakers (who have a single basic term for blue and green) were more likely to group blue colors with green colors than either English or Russian speakers. On the other hand, Russian speakers (who have two basic color terms for blue) were no more likely than English speakers to group light and dark blue separately. There were also structural differences in grouping among the samples. For example, the samples differed in the level of consensus in grouping, the number of groups formed, and the distribution of the number of colors placed in a group.

Classification of Plants and Animals

Ethnobiology is a discipline in which folk classification systems of plants and animals are examined. It provides some interesting data about the categorization behavior of people. Berlin's (1992) book, *Ethnobiological Classification*, deals with some of the crucial issues. Blount and Schwanenflugel (1993) discussed some of this work at length. The main issue relates to the categorical distinctions that members of traditional societies make among species of plants and animals. A commonsense approach would suggest that plants and animals, which are most important to a society in terms of its survival, are the most likely objects of discrimination and naming. Contrary to this notion, Berlin (1992) claims that the structural and typological consistencies in the classification system of traditional people "can best be explained in terms of human beings' similar perceptual and largely unconscious appreciation of the natural affinities among groupings of plants and animals in their environment" (p. XI). The basic point is that the natural world impinges on all human beings in a common way, and that they all perceive it in highly similar ways.

If this claim is correct, then the question is: Where do cultural influences find a place in the systems of classification and nomenclature? Berlin argues that they appear at the "subgeneric" level, which is largely associated with domesticated species of plants and animals. This means that the increased importance of animals and plants in a society's life will lead to subgeneric conceptual distinctions.

Cross-cultural comparisons suggest considerable variation in categories at the level of "life-form." The economic importance of plants and species is reported as the most significant factor in determining categorization by people. Differences associated with factors like gender, age, and division of labor in the knowledge of categories and nomenclature provide important evidence of cultural influence on classification (Berlin, 1992) as long as these factors account for differential familiarity of people with stimuli as a result of their participation in different settings.

Lopez, Atran, Coley, Medin, and Smith (1997) compared industrialized American and traditional Itzaj-Mayan, Guatemala cultural groups to examine potential universal and cultural features of folk biological taxonomies and inductions. The findings revealed that the American and the Mayan groups built taxonomies of local mammal species that were comparable in many ways. On the other hand, there was also evidence for differences in folk biological taxonomy based largely on the greater weighting of ecological factors by the Mayans. These findings suggest that there is a universal ability to construct taxonomies of living kinds and to use those taxonomies in reasoning. What varies is the knowledge that members of different cultures bring to the process, indicating that there are different paths to the same destination.

Prototypes

Prototypes have largely been studied by psychologists. The approach is mainly based on "prototypicality analysis." In this approach, people from different societies are asked to rate the goodness of an item as an example of a specific category term (e.g., how good "rabbit" is as an example of the category "animal"). Studies provide evidence for some culture-specific and some universal patterns in categorization systems. Schwanenflugel and Rey (1986) compared the prototypical judgments of monolingual Spanish- and English-speaking groups living in Florida. The typicality ratings of the two groups over a large number of categories

were correlated positively (.64); however, differences between them were evident for categories like "bird" and "fruit." On the other hand, Lin and Schwanenflugel (1995) indicate that cross-cultural variations in category structure tend to increase as cultures become more distinct from each other. These findings suggest that differences in categorization and labeling of categories are relative to the cultural experiences of individuals or groups.

Sorting of Objects

Another way to study categorization is to discover how people place various objects in groups. Such studies have often used a "sorting" procedure. Because categories are defined here by shared attributes, the procedure is also called *equivalence sorting* (Segall et al., 1999). Both "constrained" and "free" sorting procedures have been used to explore the dimensions along which differences in categorization can be evaluated. These include taxonomic, functional, perceptual, and structural categorizations. Cultural groups have been found to vary in the preferred dimensions of classification, the ease or difficulty of changing dimensions of categorization, the generality of fineness involved in their sorts, and the verbalization of the dimensions used in sorting (Rogoff, 1981).

R. C. Mishra et al. (1996) studied the categorization behavior of Birhor, Asur, and Oraon tribal groups of Bihar (India). Subjects were presented 29 familiar and locally salient objects that were expected to belong to six familiar categories. A free-sorting procedure was used. The performance was assessed on a number of measures, such as number of categories produced, number of categories conforming to the expected categories, number of subcategories, nature of groupings (conceptual, functional, perceptual, idiosyncratic), and the shifts in the basis of grouping over trials. The findings revealed that Birhors generally sorted objects in fewer categories and produced fewer subcategories than the Asur and Oraon did. Contact acculturation of groups did not influence the overall production of categories, conforming categories, and subcategories. The pattern of results did not change in the regrouping of objects. All the groups sorted objects predominantly on a functional basis, but Asur and Oraon children did this more frequently. The effect of acculturation was significant with respect to conceptual grouping for the Oraon children alone, indicating that other groupings were less under the influence of acculturation.

Wassmann and Dasen (1994) studied classification among the Yupno of Papua New Guinea, whose worldview classifies everything into "hot" and "cold." This highly abstract dimension is not detectable by any visible features. Hence, only experts (sorcerers) can manipulate these states. A sorting task was developed that consisted of 19 objects that could be clearly classified as either hot or cold, but could also be classified according to other criteria such as color, form, function, or taxonomy. It was found that only the sorcerers used the categories hot and cold explicitly. The other older adults used them implicitly through function. Although schooling induced sorting by color, children in general (schooled or unschooled) used it as the basis of sorting. As criteria for classification of objects, form was never used, and taxonomy was used very seldom.

These findings disregard the notion held about the inability of some cultural groups to carry out abstract thinking. Differential familiarity is not the only explanation. Dasen (1984) argues that groups can categorize objects even if they are not familiar with them. Further, they can categorize familiar stimuli in very different ways, depending on their specific experiences with those stimuli and the cultural appropriateness of the technique used to assess the categorization behavior (Wassmann, 1993). The evidence suggests that different cultural groups have similar capacity for information processing.

Learning and Memory

Learning and memory are very important cognitive processes that deal with acquisition and retention of information. Several decades ago, Bartlett (1932) argued that memory skills in preliterate societies developed differently from those in literate societies. The difference was explained on the ground that daily life in nonliterate societies places a high premium on remembering even those details that are a matter of written record in literate societies. Individuals in literate societies may have lost memory skills because of a lack of practice associated with greater reliance on written records (e.g., telephone directories) or other kinds of memory banks (e.g., computers). There is some evidence to show that people reared in societies with strong oral traditions have a strong memory capacity. Ross and Millsom (1970) compared Ghanaian (oral tradition) and American (written tradition) university students for the recall of themes contained in stories read aloud in English. In general, Ghanaian students recalled stories better than American students, even though English was not their first language.

Memory for Stories

Some studies have tried to test the effect of culture on memory by introducing the element of "cultural knowledge" in stories. Reynold, Taylor, Steffensen, Shirley, and Anderson (1982) compared Black and White American students using a story about an incident, which could be interpreted as either a "fight" or a ritualistic game called "sounding." They found that White students interpreted the incident as a fight, whereas Black students interpreted it as a sounding game. These interpretations were consistent with their own cultural knowledge.

Steffensen and Calker (1982) studied American and Australian Aboriginal women's recall of stories about a sick child who was treated by Western medicine in one story and by native medicine in another. The findings revealed that women had better recall of stories that were consistent with their cultural knowledge. Comparison of American and Brazilian (Harris, Schoen, & Lee, 1986), as well as American and Mexican (Harris, Schoen, & Hensley, 1992), cultural groups have provided similar results.

Other studies indicate relatively few differences in the amount or pattern of story recall, suggesting that story structure is a "cultural universal." The classical work of Cole et al. (1971) among the Kpelle of Liberia brings out the importance of story context in memory. Cole and colleagues were interested in assessing if the Kpelle were able to recall in categorical clusters words presented in a random order. It was found that the subjects were able to demonstrate clustering only when the words were presented in the context of stories, a cultural practice to which the subjects were exposed in day-to-day life.

Other Aspects of Memory

The effect of cultural pressures can operate in many other ways to influence memory of individuals. R. C. Mishra and Singh (1992) studied children of the Asur cultural group in India. The Asur manage life without lamps or other sources of light during nights. It was argued that such a life would place great demand on individuals to put things in "fixed" places and to remember them. Children's memory for "locations" and "pairs" of pictures under intentional and incidental learning conditions was assessed. All children showed greater recall accuracy for location than pair of pictures even under an incidental learning condition.

Cultural practices can also predispose people to learn certain kinds of material efficiently and to employ organizational strategies quite easily. R. C. Mishra and Shukla (1999) compared recall and clustering of Tharu children in India with those of other cultural groups. Tharu is a tribal cultural group with music that is characterized by a dominant emphasis on rhythm. A word list characterized by phonetic similarity of items was given to children for learning and recall. It was argued that phonetic similarity among items would generate rhyming and encourage easy encoding by the Tharu children of the items into clusters. The findings supported the prediction. While Tharu children did not employ much clustering on other tasks (e.g., conceptually related list of items), they used it on the phonetic task to the same extent as the other groups did.

Schooling and Literacy

Cross-cultural studies have quite often reported schooling as an important determinant of cognitive test performance. Rogoff (1981) presented a detailed review of these studies. The effect of schooling (more particularly, of literacy) has been interpreted in four different ways (Segall et al., 1999):

1. Schooling produces new cognitive processes.
2. Schooling promotes the application of existing processes to a large array of contexts, including new and unfamiliar ones.
3. Schooling produces only superficial effects that result from positive test-taking attitudes and ease in test situations.
4. Schooling generates effects that are likely to show up only in school-like experimental studies.

Because literacy is typically attained with schooling, it is generally difficult to separate their effects. Scribner and Cole (1981) have distinguished between two kinds of effect of literacy on individuals. One relates to the growth of mind as a function of assimilation of knowledge and information that is transmitted by written texts. Another relates to the content of thought and the processes of thinking.

Goody (1968) has made very strong assertions about the effect of literacy on cognitive functioning, but empirical studies do not support the claim. The effect of Quranic literacy has been particularly analyzed. Wagner (1993) worked with Muslim children in Morocco using a variety of memory tasks. The Quranic students demonstrated better remembering than nonschooled children did, but almost at the same level as the modern school children. However, they were found to rely on "rote" learning (Scribner & Cole, 1978, 1981). Reliance on rote memorization in the pedagogy of a modern Islamic school is held as an important reason for the use of this strategy in test situations.

With respect to the effect of schooling, studies have compared the learning and memory of children attending different qualities of school (e.g., good or poor, high -facility or low-facility schools) or different types of school (e.g., traditional or Western type). Good schools are characterized by enough space for students and staff; transportation; adequate facilities for sports, games, and recreational activities; library and reading room; trained teachers; and use of new teaching technology (R. C. Mishra & Gupta, 1978; D. Sinha, 1977). Ordinary schools are less equipped with these facilities. Such a contrast in schools can be easily observed in countries like India, where many primary schools do not have even the most basic facilities, like blackboard, chalk, and erasers (R. C. Mishra, 1999).

Agrawal and Mishra (1983) compared word learning and recall of children attending better and ordinary schools in Varanasi (India). Findings revealed that, compared to children from better schools, the children from an ordinary school took more trials to learn the task and exhibited less clustering in recall. A. Mishra (1992) studied recall and organization (clustering) of words among children from good and ordinary schools by manipulating the context of item presentation. The overall recall and organization scores of children from ordinary schools were lower than those from the better schools under both uncued and cued recall conditions. When the same items were presented in the context of familiar stories, differences in recall and organization scores of children from good and ordinary schools disappeared. The ability for random and categorical recall was clearly demonstrated by both the school groups, and they could use it with a high degree of flexibility, depending on the demand of the situation.

Studies in which learning strategies of children attending traditional schools have been compared with those of children attending Western-type schools (R. C. Mishra, 1988; R. C.

Mishra & Agrawal, in press; Wagner, 1978, 1983, 1993; Wagner & Spratt, 1987) indicate that rote learning is the dominant learning strategy of children attending traditional school. When an organizational strategy is employed, the "basis" rather than the "level" of organization characterize their differences. R. C. Mishra (1988) found that Sanskrit school children tended to organize the list items according to the "importance of objects." On the other hand, the organization of children attending Western-type schools was based on the "importance of events."

These studies exemplify the role of cultural factors in learning and memory. They point out that not only cultural salience of objects, events, and practices, but also many school-based experiences can account for different outcomes for individual's learning and memory.

Spatial Cognition

Spatial cognition refers to a process through which individuals gain knowledge of objects and events situated in or linked to space (Gauvain, 1993; R. C. Mishra, 1997). Cross-cultural studies of spatial cognition largely focused on how people describe space. Picture description and route description tasks have often been used in these studies. In a study with British and Iranian preschool children, Spencer and Darvizeh (1983) reported that the Iranian children gave more detailed accounts of the site along a route, but less directional information, than the British children. Similarity in the child and adult ways of communicating spatial information in each culture suggested that communicative competence about space is a culturally patterned skill. This competence is greatly facilitated by certain cultural artifacts such as paper-pencil or maps.

Frake (1980) carried out a classical study of spatial orientation in two cultures. He analyzed the use of absolute directions (e.g., east, west, south, north) and contingent directions (e.g., right, left, forward, behind) in Southeast Asia and California. His findings revealed that cultures differ in the use of directional terms, and that terms such as south or north are not the veridical descriptions of the world; instead, they are concepts held by people within a particular cultural framework. For example, in Southeast Asia, south is often used to refer to "seaward" rather than "landward" and virtually never for true south; in California, the Pacific Ocean is said to be to the west, although this is not always true.

Recent studies of spatial cognition focus on the use of language to describe space. Taylor and Tversky (1996) indicate that theorists of spatial language have distinguished three kinds of reference frames, depending on their origins: (a) deictic or viewer centered, (b) intrinsic or object centered, and (c) extrinsic or environment centered. These three frames correspond to Levinson's (1996) distinction among relative, intrinsic, and absolute frames that seems to have gained wide acceptance. Levinson's (1996) work suggests that different language communities preferentially use different reference frames.

Wassmann and Dasen (1998) explored the intricacies of the Balinese geocentric spatial orientation system, its adaptation to topological and historical contexts, its uses in everyday language and behavior, and its influence on the encoding of spatial relationships in memory tasks. The findings suggested that, while most Balinese used the absolute frame of reference provided by their language and culture, a relative (egocentric) encoding was also used. However, the flexibility with which the Balinese could switch from one encoding to the other increased with age. This study provided evidence for moderate linguistic relativity.

Niraula (1998) studied the development of spatial cognition in rural and urban Nepalese children of the Newar cultural group. With increase in child's age, she found a clear switch from relative to absolute encoding. Children who appeared to be psychologically more differentiated (on the story-Pictorial EFT) tended to use the absolute frame of encoding more often than those who were less differentiated. Differences in absolute or relative encoding due to rural or urban upbringing were not significant.

Dasen, Mishra, and Niraula (1999) recently studied village and city children 4 to 14 years old in Varanasi (India) and in Dolakha (Nepal). While village children encoded spatial information predominantly in an absolute frame, city children used a variety of frames (also including the absolute one) in spatial encoding, although both groups speak a common language (i.e., Hindi). In Nepal, on the other hand, a preference for the "uphill-downhill" geocentric frame is most commonly used for spatial encoding. Whether these orientation systems influence children's performance on cognitive tasks seems to be doubtful.

Problem Solving and Verbal Reasoning

Problem solving represents a very important domain of human cognitive functioning. Mathematical problem solving has been particularly addressed in cross-cultural studies. As we know, in all cultures, people do some sort of mathematics; however, in Eastern cultures, where calculators or computers are not commonly used, great emphasis is placed on the development of numerical skills. Hence, it is not surprising that students from these cultures perform better on mathematical achievement measures. Geary, Fan, and Bow-Thomas (1992) compared the performance of Chinese and American children on problems of simple addition and found that Chinese children correctly solved three times more problems than American children, and they also did it with greater speed. Chinese children used direct retrieval and decomposition strategies, whereas American children depended mainly on counting. The excellence of Chinese children was attributed to the involvement of parents and teachers with children during the course of mastery of the basic mathematical skills.

A distinction has been made between formal and informal mathematical thinking. Davis and Ginsburg (1993) compared the performance of African, American, and Korean children. On informal mathematical problems, little difference in their performance was noted. On formal mathematical problems, on the other hand, the Korean children performed better than the other groups. It was argued that classroom instruction and parental training given to Korean children during the school years was responsible for their excellent performance on formal mathematical problems.

Syllogistic reasoning problems have been used for the analysis of cross-cultural differences in some studies. These problems are concerned with logical (necessary) truths that are different from empirical (contingent) truths. Logical truths require comprehension and inference. Empirical truths are learned from one's experiences or from the testimony of others. Luria (1976) did the classical work on syllogistic reasoning. He found that even illiterate peasants in Uzbekistan were able to grasp the empirical truths, but they failed to grasp the logical truths.

Scribner (1979) has made a distinction between "theoretic" and "empiric" answers. The theoretic answers are based on information contained in the problem, whereas the empiric answers are based on information external to the problem. Scribner and Cole (1981) found that schooling contributed significantly to syllogistic reasoning. This indicates that, through

an emphasis on analysis, school education promotes a theoretic orientation to syllogisms. The nature of syllogisms is another factor to influence reasoning process. In a study in India, Dash and Das (1987) found that schooled children performed better on "conjunctive" type syllogisms (e.g., A horse and dog always move together. The dog is moving in the jungle now. What is the dog doing?). The unschooled children performed better on syllogisms of the "contrary-to-experience" type (e.g., If the horse is well fed, it cannot work well. Rama Babu's horse is well fed today. Can it work well today?). These results suggest that nonschooled children can also grasp the logical truths in the same manner as the schooled children do. The difference lies only with respect to the context in which reasoning is carried out.

Creativity

Creativity is one of the most valued cognitive processes; it is measured by the originality, flexibility, and fluency of ideas or products. Unfortunately, this process has been little studied cross-culturally, but studies do bring out the role of environmental supports (Stein, 1991) and ecological context in the development of creativity (Harrington, 1990). Children's relationship with parents, including their supports and stimulation, tend to influence creativity (Simonton, 1987).

Colligan (1983) has done a classical study on the role of cultural pressures and socialization practices in the development of musical creativity. The Samoan, Balinese, Japanese, and Omaha Indian cultures were studied. In the Samoan and Balinese cultures, the dancers are encouraged to recognize their individuality (as a person in Samoa and as a member of a group in Bali); hence, in these cultures, the dancers develop unique individual dancing styles within the basic framework of the art prescribed by their respective societies. On the other hand, the Japanese and Omaha Indian cultures do not sanction innovation and originality. Hence, the dancing style in these cultures has remained relatively unchanged.

Encouraging children to participate in certain games, such as "make believe," can foster creativity (Segall et al., 1999). Creative thinking among children can also be promoted by role-playing (Dasen, 1988). The extent to which such games and play activities form part of the socialization process of children in any culture can predict the influence of culture on creativity.

Conclusion

In this chapter, we examined some of the basic issues pertaining to the relationship between culture and cognition. We also tried to see how different theoretical positions have addressed these issues and what research on various cognitive processes informs us about this relationship. We may realize at this stage that human beings use the same cognitive processes to adapt to the world in which they live. Cultural difference appears in the way these processes are applied to specific contexts. While some of these processes develop as a result of long-term adaptation of individuals or groups to the eco-cultural settings, others develop in the course of adaptation to the new challenges of the changing world. Consequently, we find evidence for continuity, as well as change, in the cognitive processes of individuals, both within and across cultures.

As we observed, the diversity of the findings does not allow us to draw an easy conclusion about the relationship between culture and cognition. As a matter of fact, recent research has added elements of complexity to this relationship. Viewpoints differ with respect to the conceptualization of culture, the structure of cognitive processes, and the means of transmission of both of these to individuals, including their representation and organization in the human system. These differences present us with a variety of alternatives for designing studies to restructure our knowledge in this particular field.

At the same time, we find that culture has been taken more seriously in recent studies than in earlier decades. Researchers have displayed sensitivity to the use of tests, tasks, and experimental situations, but studies still fail to capture the realities of the day-to-day psychological life of individuals. Interest in the study of everyday cognition reflects an attempt to capture this reality. Developments of cultural psychology (Stigler, Shweder, & Herdt, 1990) and indigenous psychologies (Kim & Berry, 1993) in recent years represent other attempts to come to terms to with these realities. Movement toward indigenization of psychology (D. Sinha, 1997) is also evident in many parts of the world. We hope that studies will continue addressing the various issues raised with respect to the culture-cognition relationship. We also hope that different perspectives would come closer to each other to present a more unified approach to the understanding of cognition in the coming years.

References

Agrawal, S., & Mishra, R. C. (1983). Disadvantages of caste and schooling, and development of category organization skill. *Psychologia, 26*, 54–61.

Altarriba, J. (Ed.). (1993). *Cognition and culture: A cross-cultural approach to cognitive psychology.* Amsterdam: Elsevier Science.

Bartlett, F. C. (1932). *Remembering.* London: Cambridge University Press.

Berlin, B. (1992). *Ethnobiological classification: Principles of categorization of plant and animals in traditional societies.* Princeton, NJ: Princeton University Press.

Berlin, B., & Kay, P. (1969). *Basic color terms: Their universality and evolution.* Berkeley: University of California Press.

Berry, J. W. (1966). Temne and Eskimo perceptual skills. *International Journal of Psychology, 1*, 207–229.

Berry, J. W. (1976). *Human ecology and cognitive style: Comparative studies in cultural and psychological adaptation.* New York: Sage/Halsted.

Berry, J. W. (1981). Developmental issues in the comparative study of psychological differentiation. In R. H. Munroe, R. L. Munroe, & B. B. Whiting (Eds.), *Handbook of cross-cultural human development* (pp. 475–498). New York: Garland.

Berry, J. W. (1984). Toward a universal psychology of cognitive competence. *International Journal of Psychology, 19*, 335–361.

Berry, J. W. (1987). The comparative study of cognitive abilities. In S. H. Irvine & S. Newstead (Eds.), *Intelligence and cognition: Contemporary frames of reference* (pp. 393–420). Dordrecht, The Netherlands: Nijhoff.

Berry, J. W. (1991). Cultural variation in field dependence-independence. In S. Wapner & J. Demick (Eds.), *Field dependence-independence: Cognitive style across the life span* (pp. 289–308). Hillsdale, NJ: Lawrence Erlbaum.

Berry, J. W., & Bennett, J. A. (1991). *Cree syllabic literacy: Cultural context and psychological consequences.* Tilburg, The Netherlands: Tilburg University Press.

Berry, J. W., & Dasen, P. (Eds.). (1974). *Culture and cognition.* London: Methuen.

Berry, J. W., Poortinga, Y. H., Segall, M. H., & Dasen, P. (1992). *Cross-cultural psychology: Research and applications.* New York: Cambridge University Press.

Berry, J. W., van de Koppel, J. M. H., Senechal, C., Annis, R. C., Bahuchet, S., Cavalli-Sforza, L. L., & Witkin, H. A. (1986). *On the edge of the forest: Cultural adaptation and cognitive development in Central Africa.* Lisse, The Netherlands: Swets & Zeitlinger.

Blount, B. G., & Schwanenflugel, P. (1993). Cultural bases of folk classification systems. In J. Altarriba (Ed.), *Cognition and culture: A cross-cultural approach to cognitive psychology* (pp. 3–22). Amsterdam: Elsevier Science.

Brunswik, E. (1956). *Perception and the representative design of psychological experiments.* Berkeley: University of California Press.

Burg, B., & Belmont, I. (1990). Mental abilities of children from different cultural backgrounds in Israel. *Journal of Cross-Cultural Psychology, 21,* 90–108.

Carroll, J. B. (1983). Studying individual differences in cognitive abilities: Implications for cross-cultural studies. In S. H. Irvine & J. W. Berry (Eds.), *Human assessment and cultural factors* (pp. 213–235). New York: Plenum.

Case, R. (1985). *Intellectual development: Birth to adulthood.* New York: Academic Press.

Ceci, S. J. (1994). Schooling. In R. J. Strenberg (Ed.), *Encyclopedia of human intelligence* (Vol. 2). New York: Macmillan.

Cole, M. (1992). Context, modularity and the cultural constitution of development. In L. T. Winegar & J. Valsiner (Eds.), *Children's development within social contexts* (Vol. 2, pp. 5–31). Hillsdale, NJ: Lawrence Erlbaum.

Cole, M. (1996). *Cultural psychology: A once and future discipline.* Cambridge: Harvard University Press.

Cole, M. (1997). Cultural mechanisms of cognitive development. In E. Amsel & K. A. Renninger (Eds.), *Change and development: Issues of theory, method, and application* (pp. 245–263). Hillsdale, NJ: Lawrence Erlbaum.

Cole, M., Gay, J., Glick, J., & Sharp, D. (1971). *The cultural context of learning and thinking.* New York: Basic Books.

Colligan, J. (1983). Musical creativity and social rules in four cultures. *Creative Child and Adult Quarterly, 8,* 39–44.

Dasen, P. R. (1972). Cross-cultural Piagetian research: A summary. *Journal of Crosss-Cultural Psychology, 7,* 75–85.

Dasen, P. R. (1984). The cross-cultural study of intelligence: Piaget and the Baoule. *International Journal of Psychology, 19,* 407–437.

Dasen, P. R. (1988). Development psychologique et activites quotidienners chez des enfants africains [Psychological development and everyday activities among African children]. *Enface, 41,* 3–24.

Dasen, P. R., & de Ribaupierre, A. (1987). Neo-Piagetian theories: Cross-cultural and differential perspectives. *International Journal of Psychology, 22,* 793–832.

Dasen, P. R., Heron, A. (1981). Cross-cultural tests of Piaget's theory. In H. C. Trindis & A. Heron (Eds.), *Handbook of cross-cultural psychology* (Vol. 3, pp. 295–342). Boston: Allyn & Bacon.

Dasen, P. R., Mishra, R. C., & Niraula, S. (1999). *Spatial orientation and moderate linguistic relativity.* Unpublished manuscript.

Dash, U. N., & Das, J. P. (1987). Development of syllogistic reasoning in schooled and unschooled children. *Indian Psychologist, 4,* 53–63.

Davies, I. R. L., & Corbett, G. G. (1997). A cross-cultural study of colour grouping: Evidence for weak linguistic relativity. *British Journal of Psychology, 88,* 493–517.

Davis, J. C., & Ginsburg, H. P. (1993). Similarities and differences in the formal and informal mathematical cognition of African, American and Asian children: The role of schooling and social class. In J. Altarriba (Ed.), *Cognition and culture: A cross-cultural approach to cognitive psychology* (pp. 343–360). Amsterdam: Elsevier Science.

Demetriou, A., Efklides, A., & Platsidou, M. (1993). The architecture and dynamics of developing mind: Experiential structuralism as a frame for unifying cognitive developmental theories. *Monographs of the Society for Research in Child Development, 58* (5–6, Serial No. 234).

Ferguson, G. A. (1956). On transfer and abilities of man. *Canadian Journal of Psychology, 10,* 121–131.

Fischer, K. W. (1980). A theory of cognitive development: The control and construction of hierarchies of skills. *Psychological Review, 87,* 477–531.

Frake, C. (1980). The ethnographic study of cognitive systems. In C. Frake (Ed.), *Language and cultural descriptions* (pp. 1–17). Stanford, CA: Stanford University Press.

Gardiner, H. W., Mutter, J. D., & Kosmitzki, C. (1998). *Life across cultures: Cross-cultural human development.* Boston: Allyn & Bacon.

Gauvain, M. (1993). Spatial thinking and its development in socio-cultural context. *Annals of Child Development, 9,* 67–102.

Gay, J., & Cole, M. (1967). *The new mathematics and the old culture.* New York: Holt, Rinehart & Winston.

Geary, D. C., Fan, L., & Bow-Thomas, C. (1992). Numerical cognition: Loci of ability differences comparing children from China and United States. *Psychological Science, 3,* 180–185.

Goody, J. (1968). Literacy in traditional societies. London: Cambridge University Press.

Harrington, D. M. (1990). The ecology of human creativity: A psychological perspective. In M. A. Runco & R. S. Albert (Eds.), *Theories of creativity* (pp. 143–169). Newbury Park, CA: Sage.

Harris, R. J., Schoen, L. M., & Hensley, D. L. (1992). A cross-cultural study of story memory. *Journal of Cross-Cultural Psychology, 23*, 133–147.

Harris, R. J., Schoen, L. M., & Lee, D. J. (1986). Culture-based distortion in memory of stories. In J. L. Armagost (Ed.), *Proceedings of the 20th Mid-American Conference*. Manhattan: Kansas State University Press.

Herrnstein, R. J., & Murray, C. (1994). *The bell curve*. New York: The Free Press.

Irvine, S. H. (1979). The place of factor analysis in cross-cultural methodology and its contribution to cognitive theory. In L. Eckensberger & Y. H. Poortinga (Eds.), *Cross-cultural contributions to psychology* (pp. 330–341). Lisse, The Netherlands: Swets & Zeitlinger.

Irvine, S. H. (1983). Testing in Africa and America: The search for routes. In S. H. Irvine & J. W. Berry (Eds.), *Human assessment and cultural factors* (pp. 45–58). New York: Plenum.

Jahoda, G. (1983). European "lag" in the development of an economic concept: A study in Zimbabwe. *British Journal of Developmental Psychology, 1*, 113–120.

Jahoda, G., & Krewer, B. (1997). History of cross-cultural and cultural psychology. In J. W. Berry, Y. H. Poortinga, & J. Pandey (Eds.), *Handbook of cross-cultural psychology* (Vol. 1, pp. 1–42). Boston: Allyn & Bacon.

Keats, D. M. (1985). Strategies in formal operational thinking: Malaysia and Australia. In I. R. Lagunes & Y. H. Poortinga (Eds.), *From a different perspective: Studies of behavior across cultures* (pp. 306–318). Lisse, The Netherlands: Swets & Zeitlinger.

Kim, U., & Berry, J. W. (Eds.). (1993). *Indigenous psychologies: Research and experience in cultural contexts*. Newbury Park, CA: Sage.

Laboratory of Comparative Human Cognition. (1983). Culture and cognitive development. In P. H. Mussen & W. Kessen (Eds.), *Handbook of child psychology* (Vol. 1, pp. 295–356). New York: Wiley.

Levinson, S. C. (1996). Frames of reference and Molyneux's question: Cross-linguistic evidence. In P. Bloom, M. Peterson, L. Naddel, & M. Garrett (Eds.), *Language and space* (pp. 109–169). Cambridge: MIT Press.

Lin, P. J., & Schwanenflugel, P. J. (1995). Cultural familiarity and language factors in the structure of category knowledge. *Journal of Cross-Cultural Psychology, 23*, 153–168.

Lopez, A., Atran, S., Coley, J. D., Medin, D. L., & Smith, E. E. (1997). The tree of life: Universal and cultural features of folkbiological taxonomies and inductions. *Cognitive Psychology, 32*(3), 251–295.

Luria, A. R. (1976). *Cognitive development: Its cultural and social foundations*. Cambridge: Harvard University Press.

MacLaury, R. E. (1991). Exotic color categories: Linguistic relativity to what extent. *Journal of Linguistic Anthropology, 1*, 26–51.

McShane, D., & Berry, J. W. (1988). Native North Americans: Indian and Inuit abilities. In S. H. Irvine & J. W. Berry (Eds.), *Human abilities in cultural context* (pp. 385–426). New York: Cambridge University Press.

Mishra, R. C. (2000). Perceptual, learning, and memory processes. In J. Pandey (Ed.), *Psychology in India revisited: Developments in the discipline* (Vol. 1, pp. 94–150). New Delhi: Sage.

Mishra, A. (1992). *Role of age, school related differences and contextual change in recall and organization*. Unpublished doctoral thesis, Varanasi Hindu University, India.

Mishra, K. (1998). *Cognitive style of Tharu children in relation to daily life activities and experience of schooling*. Unpublished doctoral thesis, Varanasi Hindu University, India.

Mishra, R. C. (1988). Learning strategies among children in the modern and traditional schools. *Indian Psychologist, 5*, 17–24.

Mishra, R. C. (1996). Perceptual differentiation in relation to children's daily life activities. *Social Science International, 12*, 1–11.

Mishra, R. C. (1997). Cognition and cognitive development. In J. W. Berry, P. R. Dasen, & T. S. Saraswathi (Eds.), *Handbook of cross-cultural psychology* (Vol. 2, pp. 143–175). Boston: Allyn & Bacon.

Mishra, R. C. (1999). Research on education in India. *Prospects, 29*, 335–347.

Mishra, R. C., & Agrawal, A. (in press). Learning strategy of Hindu and Muslim children in traditional and modern schools. *Indian Educational Review*.

Mishra, R. C., & Gupta, V. (1978). Role of schooling and exposure in perceiving pictorial sequence. *Psychologia, 21*, 231–236.

Mishra, R. C., & Shukla, S. N. (1999). *Learning and memory skills of the Tharu children*. Proceedings of the seminar on the Development of Tribal Groups, National Council of Development Communication, Varanasi.

Mishra, R. C., & Singh, T. (1992). Memories of Asur children for locations and pairs of pictures. *Psychological Studies, 37*, 38–46.

Mishra, R. C., Sinha, D., & Berry, J. W. (1996). *Ecology, acculturation and psychological adaptation: A study of Adivasis in Bihar*. New Delhi: Sage.

Mishra, R. C., & Tripathi, N. (1996). Reproduction of patterns in relation to children's weaving experiences. In J. Pandey, D. Sinha, & D. P. S. Bhawuk (Eds.), *Asian contribution to cross-cultural psychology* (pp. 138–150). New Delhi: Sage.

Niraula, S. (1998). *Development of spatial cognition in rural and urban Nepalese children.* Unpublished doctoral dissertation, Banaras Hindu University, India.

Nyiti, R. M. (1982). The validity of "cultural differences explanation" for cross-cultural variation in the rate of Piagetian cognitive development. In D. A. Wagner & H. W. Stevenson (Eds.), *Cultural perspectives on child development* (pp. 146–165). San Francisco: W. H. Freeman.

Pascual-Leone, J. (1970). A mathematical model for the transition rule in Piaget's developmental stages. *Acta Psychologia, 32,* 301–345.

Piaget, J. (1974). Need and significance of cross-cultural studies in genetic psychology. In J. W. Berry & P. R. Dasen (Eds.), *Culture and cognition* (pp. 299–309). London: Methuen.

Price-Williams, D. R., Gordon, W., & Ramirez, M. (1969). Skill and conservation: A study of pottery making children. *Developmental Psychology, 1,* 769.

Reynold, R. E., Taylor, M. A., Steffensen, M. S., Shirley, L. L., & Anderson, R. C. (1982). Cultural schemata and reading comprehension. *Reading Research Quarterly, 3,* 353–366.

Rogoff, B. (1981). Schooling and the development of cognitive skills. In H. C. Triandis & A. Heron (Eds.), *Handbook of cross-cultural psychology* (Vol. 4, pp. 233–294). Boston: Allyn & Bacon.

Ross, B. M., & Millsom, C. (1970). Repeated memory of oral prose in Ghana and New York. *International Journal of Psychology, 5,* 173–181.

Rushton, J. P. (1995). *Race, evolution, and behavior: A life history perspective.* New Brunswik, NJ: Transaction.

Russell, P., Deregowski, J. W., & Kinnear, P. (1997). Perception and aesthetics. In J. W. Berry, P. R. Dasen, & T. S. Saraswathi (Eds.), *Handbook of cross-cultural psychology* (Vol. 2, pp. 107–142). Boston: Allyn & Bacon.

Saxe, G. B. (1981). Body parts as numerals: A developmental analysis of numeration among remote Oksapmin village populations in Papua New Guinea. *Child Development, 52,* 306–316.

Saxe, G. B. (1982). Culture and the development of numerical cognition: Studies among the Oksapmin of Papua New Guinea. In C. J. Brainerd (Ed.), *Children's logical and mathematical cognition* (pp. 157–176). New York: Springer.

Schlieman, A., Carraher, D., & Ceci, S. J. (1997). Everyday cognition. In J. W. Berry, P. R. Dasen, & T. S. Saraswathi (Eds.), *Handbook of cross-cultural psychology* (Vol. 2, pp. 177–216). Boston: Allyn & Bacon.

Schwanenflugel, P. J., & Rey, M. (1986). The relationship between category typicality and concept familiarity: Evidence from Spanish- and English-speaking monolinguals. *Memory and Cognition, 14,* 150–163.

Scribner, S. (1979). Modes of thinking and ways of speaking: Culture and logic reconsidered. In R. O. Freedle (Ed.), *New directions in discourse processing* (pp. 223–243). Norwood, NJ: Ablex.

Scribner, S., & Cole, M. (1978). Literacy without schooling: Testing for intellectual effects. *Harvard Educational Review, 48,* 448–461.

Scribner, S., & Cole, M. (1981). *The psychology of literacy.* Cambridge: Harvard University Press.

Segall, M. H., Dasen, P. R., Berry, J. W., & Poortinga, Y. H. (1999). *Human behavior in global perspective: An introduction to cross-cultural psychology.* Boston: Allyn & Bacon.

Serpell, R. (1979). How specific are perceptual skills? A cross-cultural study of pattern reproduction. *British Journal of Psychology, 70,* 365–380.

Serpell, R. (1989). Dimensions endogenes de l'intelligence chez les A-chewa etautress peuples africains. In J. Retschitzky, M. Bossel-Lagos, & P. R. Dasen (Eds.), *La researche interculturelle* (pp. 164–179). Paris: Harmattan.

Shea, J. D. (1985). Studies of cognitive development in Papua New Guinea. *International Journal of Psychology, 20,* 33–61.

Simonton, D. K. (1987). Developmental antecedents of achieved eminence. *Annals of Child Development, 5,* 131–169.

Sinha, D. (1977). Social disadvantages and development of certain perceptual skills. *Indian Journal of Psychology, 52,* 115–132.

Sinha, D. (1979). Perceptual style among nomadic and transitional agriculturalist Birhors. In L. Eckensberger, W. J. Lonner, & Y. H. Poortinga (Eds.), *Cross-cultural contributions to psychology* (pp. 83–93). Lisse, The Netherlands: Swets & Zeitlinger.

Sinha, D. (1980). Sex differences in psychological differentiation among different cultural groups. *International Journal of Behavioral Development, 3,* 455–466.

Sinha, D. (1997). Indigenizing psychology. In J. W. Berry, Y. H. Poortinga, & J. Pandey (Eds.), *Handbook of cross-cultural psychology* (Vol. 1, pp. 129–169). Boston: Allyn & Bacon.

Sinha, D., & Shrestha, A. B. (1992). Eco-cultural factors in cognitive style among children from hills and plains of Nepal. *International Journal of Psychology, 27,* 49–59.

Sinha, G. (1988). Exposure to industrial and urban environments and formal schooling as factors in psychological differentiation. *International Journal of Psychology, 23,* 707–719.

Spearman, C. (1927). *The abilities of man.* London: Macmillan.

Spencer, C., & Darvizeh, Z. (1983). Young children's place description, map and route findings: A comparison of nursery school children in Iran and Britain. *International Journal of Early Childhood, 15,* 26–31.

Steffensen, M. S., & Calker, L. (1982). Intercultural misunderstandings about health care: Recall of descriptions of illness and treatments. *Social Science and Medicine, 16,* 1949–1954.

Stein, M. (1991). On the sociohistorical context of creativity programs. *Creativity Research Journal, 4,* 294–300.

Sternberg, R. J. (1985). *Beyond I.Q.: A triarchiac theory of human intelligence.* New York: Cambridge University Press.

Sternberg, R. J. (Ed.). (1994). *Encyclopedia of intelligence* (Vol. 1). New York: Macmillan.

Stigler, J. W., Shweder, R. A., & Herdt, G. (Eds.). (1990). *Cultural psychology: Essays on comparative human development.* New York: Cambridge University Press.

Tapé, G. (1987). *Milieu africaiet developpement cognitif: Uneetude raisonnement experimental chez l'adolescent ivoirien.* Unpublished doctoral thesis, University de Caen, France.

Taylor, H. A., & Tversky, B. (1996). Perspective in spatial descriptions. *Journal of Memory and Language, 35,* 371–391.

Vernon, P. E. (1969). *Intelligence and cultural environment.* London: Methuen.

Vygotsky, L. S. (1978). *Mind and society: The development of higher psychological processes.* Cambridge, MA: Harvard University Press.

Wagner, D. A. (1978). Memories of Morocco: The influence of age schooling and environment on memory. *Cognitive Psychology, 10,* 1–28.

Wagner, D. A. (1983). Islamic education: Traditional pedagogy and contemporary aspects. In T. Husen & T. N. Postlethwite (Eds.), *International encyclopedia of education: Research and studies* (pp. 2714–2716). New York: Pergamon.

Wagner, D. A. (1993). *Literacy, culture and development: Becoming literate in Morocco.* New York: Cambridge University Press.

Wagner, D. A., & Spratt, J. E. (1987). Cognitive consequences of contrasting pedagogies: The effects of Quranic preschooling in Morocco. *Child Development, 58,* 1207–1219.

Wassmann, J. (1993). When actions speak louder than words: The classification of food among the Yupno of Papua New Guinea. *Newsletter of the Laboratory of Comparative Human Cognition, 15,* 30–40.

Wassmann, J., & Dasen, P. R. (1994). "Hot" and "cold": Classification and sorting among the Yupno of Papua New Guinea. *International Journal of Psychology, 29,* 19–38.

Wassmann, J., & Dasen, P. R. (1998). Balinese spatial orientation: Some empirical evidence of moderate linguistic relativity. *The Journal of Royal Anthropological Institute, 4,* 689–711.

Whorf, B. (1956). *Language, thought and reality.* Cambridge: MIT Press.

Witkin, H. A., & Berry, J. W. (1975). Psychological differentiation in cross-cultural perspective. *Journal of Cross-Cultural Psychology, 6,* 4–87.

Witkin, H. A., & Goodenough, D. R. (1981). *Cognitive style: Essence and origin.* New York: International University Press.

Wober, M. (1974). Towards an understanding of the Kiganda concept of intelligence. In J. W. Berry & P. R. Dasen (Eds.), *Culture and cognition* (pp. 261–280). London: Methuen.

8

Everyday Cognition

Where Culture, Psychology, and Education Come Together

ANALÚCIA D. SCHLIEMANN & DAVID W. CARRAHER

The study of cognition across cultures is informed not only by work in topic areas that would be considered "traditional" cognition, but also by a burgeoning field of inquiry known as *everyday cognition*. Everyday cognition refers to the cognitive skills developed in everyday activities, especially those unrelated to formal schooling. Known under different denominations over the years, studies of everyday cognition have spanned many topics across many cultures, including navigation skills, tailoring, weaving, horse racing betting, and the like.

In this chapter, Schliemann and Carraher provide an excellent overview of the field of everyday cognition, first comparing and contrasting it with studies of traditional cognitive skills. They successfully argue that studies of cognition that are limited to laboratory or testing situations, often involving abstract skills learned in formal educational systems, may not show a complete picture of cognitive abilities, especially across cultures. They provide a historical context with which to understand the emergence of the field of study of everyday cognition, drawing on sources not only in cross-cultural psychology, but also in anthropology, education, and political science.

While the field of everyday cognition spans a number of different cognitive abilities, in this chapter, Schliemann and Carraher highlight issues related to one specific domain that has been studied: everyday and school mathematics. By reviewing numerous studies from various disciplines, they document how people of different cultures can develop considerable mathematical skills through their everyday life, often without the supposed benefit of formal education. At the same time, however, Schliemann and Carraher discuss objectively the strengths and weaknesses of mathematics learned in everyday life, as well as its relevance. By asking different questions, Schliemann and Carraher deftly refocus concerns about everyday mathematics versus school-based mathematics learning from an emphasis on antagonistic competition between the two approaches to potentialities that arise because of the simultaneous complementation of them.

In looking toward the future, Schliemann and Carraher raise a number of important issues that need to be addressed for this area of cross-cultural psychology to continue to evolve. They suggest, for instance, that new theoretical approaches concerning the nature of knowledge, cognition, intelligence, and cognitive development need to be created, especially those that integrate individual cognitive skills and ecological and sociocultural factors. New theoretical frameworks bring with them multiple research paths and methodologies, especially those that move away from viewing cognition as an individual, decontextualized process and instead toward a focus on sociocultural practices as mediators of cognitive development. These practices include language, cultural tools, and conventional symbolic systems in shaping and transforming mental processes.

Schliemann and Carraher also argue that future theoretical and empirical work needs to redefine context, pointing out that contexts are not just constituted by their physical properties, but involve cultural meanings and interpretations. In particular, their ideas concerning the redefinition of the time frameworks of cognitive development studied and the term they call *situated generalization,* which refers to the tension between abstract and concrete processes, deserve special attention.

A message that Schliemann and Carraher deliver throughout their chapter, especially in the section describing future work, concerns the issue of integration—of new theoretical and empirical approaches; of qualitative, quantitative, ethnographic methods and open-ended interviews with traditional studies of cognition; of viewpoints from anthropology, sociology, psychology, history, and education; and of work involving both school and everyday life, especially concerning the possible synergy created by their interaction. They argue that this integration is necessary if cross-cultural work in this area of psychology will continue to evolve from a field that merely documents interesting and sometimes exotic differences to one that truly captures the rich diversity of cognitive development in multiple contexts. In this vein, their message concerning the integration of theory and method from disparate sources as being vital to the continued evolution of the field is entirely consonant with that given by all authors in this volume.

Studies of cognition reveal that people may perform well on reasoning tasks in natural settings despite the fact that they fail to solve what appear to be similar tasks in laboratory or testing settings. This has led some researchers to question traditional views of cognitive abilities as free from the situations in which they are used. To account for such disparities and to give a broader account of cognitive development, researchers have drawn attention to the role of symbolic systems, cultural practices, and historical events in shaping people's reasoning and behavior. The field of everyday cognition aims at understanding how cognitive abilities emerge in cultural milieus and draw their character from their social origins.

Everyday cognition research has benefited from an unwitting alliance of diverse research and theoretical views about how knowledge develops. Although the Piagetian opus does not generally draw attention to sociocultural factors in cognitive development, it nonetheless provides a wealth of empirical and theoretical findings on children's "spontaneous" development. This work and, more generally, that of developmental psychologists has identified an impressive spectrum of concepts and topics in which children make progress before schools

exert significant influence on their thinking. If learning out of school were simply a matter of getting a head start on formal learning, it might not seem so important. But, again and again, developmental psychologists have noted substantial differences in the quality of children's thinking at different stages of development. Children given "the same" task will consistently construe the issues in diverse ways. In essence, developmental research over the past decades has undermined the empiricist premise that knowledge proceeds through unmediated observation of reality and through the passive assimilation of information provided by others. By drawing attention to the details of children's interpretive processes, researchers have highlighted the extent to which learning takes place in noneducational settings and depends on the outcomes of the children's efforts to comprehend.

Investigations by Cole and his associates constituted an influential landmark in the shift from the use of standardized interviews and tests toward the analysis of cognition in everyday contexts. Their studies of cognitive development among the Kpelle in Africa (Cole, Gay, Glick, & Sharp, 1971; Gay & Cole, 1967) represent a systematic effort to identify practical activities that could serve as models for cognitive tasks or as opportunities for a more appropriate assessment of cognitive skills. Their work opened up new pathways for researching human cognition across cultures and inspired new theoretical and methodological ways of looking at knowledge development in everyday contexts. Through the work of Cole and his associates, the Soviet sociohistorical tradition became a major theoretical influence in the study of cognition and cognitive development. The sociohistorical tradition established by Leontiev (1981), Luria (1976), and Vygotsky (1978) views the development of human psychological processes as "determined by humanity's historically-developing, culturally mediated, practical activity" (Cole, 1988, pp. 137–138). This approach constitutes the core of many recent studies of human knowledge in everyday contexts.

Within the experimental psychological tradition, Neisser (1967, 1976, 1982) appears as a major influence, urging psychologists to study cognition in everyday contexts and lamenting psychology's silence on questions related to cognition in everyday life. Neisser and a new generation of cognitivists promulgated a view that embedded cognition in a larger framework, including the contexts in which cognitive processes take place and the individual's knowledge and feelings about these processes.

Similar developments occurred in the area of cross-cultural psychology, as emic and ecocultural approaches to cross-cultural psychology such as that of Berry (1976) began to appear. Variables intimately linked to everyday activities became the object of cross-cultural studies. In the last decades, we have seen the development of a large number of cross-cultural studies that contrast the everyday knowledge of ordinary people to school, expert, or scientific knowledge (see Berry, Dasen, & Saraswathi, 1997; Dasen & Bossel-Lagos, 1989; and Segall, Dasen, Berry, & Poortinga, 1999).

Now, under different denominations, such as indigenous cognition (Berry, 1993), ethnomathematics (D'Ambrosio, 1985), practical intelligence (Sternberg & Wagner, 1986), situated cognition (Brown, Collins, & Duguid, 1989), cognition in context (Laboratory of Comparative Human Cognition, 1983), socially shared cognition (Resnick, Levine, & Teasley, 1991), or everyday cognition (Rogoff & Lave, 1984), everyday cognition has become a field of study in itself. Researchers have investigated subjects as varied as navigation skills, tailoring,

weaving, shopping, betting on horse racing, weight watching, work in a dairy plant, carpentry, house building, cooking, lottery betting, fishing, market selling, and so on. They have raised new issues, such as the following: What kind of understanding develops in everyday activities? How does the knowledge developed through everyday working activities differ from the knowledge acquired in schools through formal explicit instruction? How does everyday knowledge interact with school experience? Does absence of school instruction limit the development of knowledge in everyday settings? How specific is knowledge acquired in everyday activities? How is it related to performance on psychological tests? How do studies of everyday cognition help clarify issues related to intelligence, learning, or transfer? How do culture, cultural tools, cultural symbolic systems, and social interactions relate to knowledge development?

In the following sections, we describe empirical studies of everyday cognition that helped clarify some of these questions. We first provide a brief account of studies on cognitive performance in laboratory settings versus performance in everyday settings. We then consider the diverse areas researchers have studied in the last decades. Then, by focusing mainly on mathematical knowledge in out-of-school, out-of-laboratory contexts of individuals with restricted school experience, we contrast everyday and school knowledge and discuss the generality, the strengths, and the limitations of knowledge developed in specific everyday settings. Finally, we consider some implications of studies of everyday cognition for cognitive and psychological theories, research methodology, and education. A more detailed review of everyday cognition studies by Schliemann, Carraher, and Ceci (1997) and several edited volumes and chapters on everyday cognition among schooled subjects (see Chaiklin & Lave, 1993; Detterman & Sternberg, 1993; Harris, 1990; Rogoff & Lave, 1984; Sternberg & Wagner, 1986; Voss, Perkins, & Segal, 1991) will complement and expand this review.

Cognition in the Laboratory versus Cognition in Everyday Contexts

Even Piaget recognized the importance of contexts and of one's previous experiences when he stated (Piaget, 1972) that carpenters, locksmiths, and mechanics with limited formal education, who may fail in school-oriented formal operations tasks, might well display formal reasoning in tasks related to their field of experience. Although maintaining the belief that formal operations are logically independent of the reality content to which they are applied, he admitted, "It is best to test the young person in a field that is relevant to his career and interests" (p. 1).

Glick (1981) describes an interesting example of the role of cultural contexts and values on the display of cognitive abilities. The example comes from the 1971 studies of Cole et al. with the Kpelle tribe in Liberia. They constructed a list of objects that could be categorized as foods, clothes, tools, and eating utensils and asked unschooled Kpelle adults to "put together the ones that go together." In contrast to schooled Western subjects, the Kpelle adults did not use overarching categories (tools, foods, etc.), but tended to employ functional categories, stating, for instance, "The knife and the orange go together because the knife cuts the orange." One of the interviewees, who consistently provided "low-level functional" answers, volunteered the observation that his way of classifying the objects reflected how a "wise person" would do it. When the interviewer asked how a "stupid" person would classify the objects, the interviewee answered that a stupid person would group them according to general classes (tools, foods, and so forth). This answer suggests that he could classify familiar items according to Western standards of intelligence, but that it made more sense to him to use the kind of groups that functions in natural settings. As Cole (1988) concludes:

> Cultural differences in cognition reside more in the contexts within which cognitive processes manifest themselves than in the existence of a particular process (such as logical memory or theoretical responses to syllogisms) in one culture and its absence in another. (p. 147)

Ceci and Liker's (1986) study of academic versus nonacademic intelligence illustrates well the contextual nature of reasoning performance. They found that racetrack handicappers' levels of reasoning complexity in handicapping tasks are not correlated with IQ scores. Cognitive development studies also show the effect of contexts on the display of cognitive abilities. Children who fail in the traditional Piagetian conservation, class inclusion, or per-

spective taking tasks demonstrate logical reasoning when the same questions are phrased in more natural and meaningful ways (see, among others, Donaldson, 1978; Light, Buckingham, & Robbins, 1979; McGarrigle & Donaldson, 1974). Microlevel cognitive strategies, such as the temporal calibration of one's psychological clock (Ceci & Bronfenbrenner, 1985), multicausal reasoning (Ceci & Bronfenbrenner; see Ceci, 1990, 1993) and syllogistic reasoning (Dias & Harris, 1988) are also strongly affected by contexts.

The above studies call into question cognitive analysis that relies exclusively on performance in laboratory settings. Researchers have been aware for the last few decades that, to understand cognition and learning better, we need studies of cognition in everyday settings.

Attempts to understand cognition in everyday contexts are found in anthropological studies. Outstanding examples are given by Hutchins in the analysis of inferences in the everyday discourse of the Trobriand Islanders (1980) and description of Micronesian navigation skills (1983). Data from these studies challenged conclusions reached by previous anthropological studies by showing use of logical reasoning among unschooled people in the everyday activities of traditional societies.

Within psychology, studies of child development in the sociocultural context such as those of Rogoff (1990) and Saxe (1991) focus on children's everyday activities as a source of cognitive development. Also, as pointed out by Hatano (1990), studies of conceptual development and change show that, independent of school instruction, children develop a fairly rich body of knowledge about scientific topics through their everyday experiences in the world. Examples of these are the studies of Carey (1985), Gelman (1979), Hughes (1986), Inagaki (1990), Inagaki and Hatano (1987), Resnick (1986), and Vosniadou (1991) and Piaget's analysis of children's understanding of logico-mathematical and scientific concepts.

A few studies, in different cultures, focused on everyday memory. Cole et al. (1971) demonstrated that, although failing in free recall tasks, Liberian Kpelle subjects used categorization and benefited from it in tasks for which items to be memorized were inserted in a story that provided reason for categorization. Neisser's work on everyday memory includes the analysis of the testimony produced by John Dean, a defendant in the American Watergate scandal in 1974 (Neisser, 1981), of children's recollections of the Challenger space shuttle disaster in 1987, and of adults' recollections of their earliest childhood experiences (Usher & Neisser, 1993).

Through a combination of anthropological and psychological approaches, Wassmann (1993) and Wassmann and Dasen (1994) looked at categorization in the everyday activities of the Yupno of Papua New Guinea. They found that most members of the Yupno population know about use of the "hot," "cool," and "cold" categories to describe everything in the Yupno world. However, only sorcerers are allowed to manipulate these categories. As a consequence, members of the population used the categorization system in everyday contexts, but only sorcerers explicitly used the categories in sorting tasks proposed by the researchers.

Everyday syllogistic reasoning was examined by Luria (1976) in relation to educational experience, by Hutchins (1979) in the context of everyday discourse, by Scribner (1977) with illiterate Kpelle farmers in Liberia, and by Dias (1987) with Brazilian bricklayers and engineers. A general conclusion of studies in this area is that schooled subjects use a theoretical approach to syllogistic problems and draw conclusions from the information in the premises, while unschooled subjects tend to adopt an empirical approach and refuse to reason about unknown facts or to reach conclusions contrary to the facts.

The above studies cover a rich variety of content areas and, as such, provide general support for the idea that knowledge develops in everyday settings, and that cognitive performance is associated closely with the everyday meaning of the tasks. However, if we want to have a better understanding of the characteristics of everyday knowledge, we need to focus on the multiple facets of everyday knowledge in one specific area. The many studies on everyday mathematics reviewed next can offer deeper insights into the nature of everyday cognition.

Everyday Mathematics and School Mathematics

Most of the available research on everyday cognition focuses on mathematical understanding and use of mathematical procedures at work, mainly in areas concerned with measurement, geometry, and arithmetic (see reviews by D. W. Carraher, 1991; Nunes, 1992; Nunes, Schliemann, & Carraher, 1993; and Schliemann et al., 1997).

The first studies of everyday mathematics by Cole et al. (1971) shows measurement as a common mathematical activity in the everyday life of groups with limited access to school instruction. Kpelle rice farmers measure the volume of amounts of rice as part of their everyday work; they become very skilled in estimating the volume of rice amounts and perform better than American students in volume estimation tasks (Gay & Cole, 1967). The Oksapmin people of Papua New Guinea use their own system for measuring the depths of string bags widely used in their culture (Saxe & Moylan, 1982). Unschooled farmers in northeastern and southern Brazil use a nonstandard system of measures and formulas to calculate the areas of plots of land (Abreu & Carraher, 1989; Acioly, 1994; Grando, 1988). In addition to Western measures for reckoning time such as hours and minutes, illiterate, semiliterate, and literate adults in India use movements of the sun, the moon, or stars and devices based on shadows or on finely calibrated water containers (Saraswathi, 1988, 1989). Their use of different measuring systems is context oriented: They use standard units when working with heights, depths, distances, short lengths, and area, but prefer to use body measures or nonspecific descriptions when asked to measure medium lengths, girth or perimeter, diameter, incline, and rainfall. Shortly after the metric system was introduced in Nepal, Ueno and Saito (1994) documented market sellers' invented rules for measuring and for converting between the old volume-based measuring system and the government-imposed weight-based metric system.

Despite certain limitations due to the approximate nature of the calculations, the systems of measurement developed in everyday activities allow unschooled individuals to obtain meaningful, and often more adequate, answers than those provided by students. For example, experienced Brazilian carpenters with limited schooling develop better approaches to deal with measurement and computation of volume than carpenter apprentices enrolled in mathematical classes meant to teach them how to compute area and volume (Schliemann, 1985). Similarly, when compared to students, the American dairy workers studied by Scribner (1984, 1986) showed more flexible and effort-saving strategies.

Concerning geometry, Zaslavsky (1973) showed that geometrical concepts are used widely in the design of African geometrical patterns. In Mozambique, fishermen, house builders, and basket weavers, who have no access to the procedures and representations of school mathematics, use geometrical concepts and patterns at work (Gerdes, 1986, 1988a, 1988b). Harris (1987, 1988) showed geometrical reasoning emerging from the activities of women doing needlework or working with textiles at home and in factories. As documented by Millroy (1992), South African carpenters extensively use geometrical concepts such as congruence, symmetry, and straight and parallel lines in their everyday work.

Arithmetic has been the most widely analyzed area of knowledge in everyday cognition studies. The available results on the development and uses of arithmetic in everyday settings help clarify general issues related to cognition, cognitive development, and education. Some of the questions concern the specificity of everyday knowledge and the characteristics, the scope, and the limitations of everyday knowledge as opposed to knowledge developed as a result of school instruction.

Lave (1977; see also Reed & Lave, 1979) showed that, instead of the symbolic manipulation taught in schools, Liberian tailors use mental procedures based on manipulation of quantities to solve arithmetic problems at work. These everyday procedures ensure that no big mistakes with serious practical consequences will occur. Street sellers and other workers with restricted school experience show understanding and use of the properties of the decimal system when they deal with addition and subtraction problems in the context of commercial activities (T. N. Carraher, 1985; T. N. Carraher, Carraher, & Schliemann, 1982, 1985; Saxe, 1991; Schliemann & Acioly, 1989; Schliemann, Santos, & Canuto, 1993).

Street sellers repeated addition strategies to find the price of many items from the price of one item reveal understanding that two variables (namely, price and number of items to be sold) are related proportionally (Schliemann & Carraher, 1992). Use of proportional reasoning by individuals with restricted school experience was also found in the work of construction foremen (T. N. Carraher, 1986), fishermen (Schliemann & Nunes, 1990), and cooks (Schliemann & Magalhães, 1990; McMurchy-Pilkington, 1995).

Besides measurement, geometry, and arithmetic, everyday mathematics can also encompass other content areas, as exemplified by the studies of Schliemann (1988) and Schliemann and Acioly (1989) on use of permutations and probability by lottery bookies in Brazil.

We next discuss the differences between school mathematics and everyday mathematics and the generality, strengths, and limitations of mathematical understanding developed in specific everyday contexts. A more detailed discussion of the same issues is provided by Schliemann (1995) and by D. W. Carraher and Schliemann (in press).

Strengths and Limitations of Everyday Mathematics

Comparisons of street sellers' mathematical abilities across contexts show that, while at work they usually provide correct answers to mathematical problems, the same is not true when they are asked to solve problems at school or in school-like situations. It was argued by T. N. Carraher, Carraher, and Schliemann (1987) that differences in performance across situations could be explained by the use of different procedures. At work, or in worklike situations, oral procedures are the preferred strategy, frequently leading to correct answers. At school, or in school-like situations, written procedures are preferred and frequently lead to wrong results. These findings suggest that the quality and effectiveness of mathematical reasoning depend on the nature of the representations employed.

Street vendors seem to develop the basic logical abilities needed for solving arithmetic problems in their work settings; their difficulties with school arithmetic seem to be related to the mastery of particular symbolic systems adopted by schools. Given the emphasis on fixed steps to manipulate numbers in the solution of any problem, school algorithms set meaning aside. In contrast, arithmetic oral strategies developed at work preserve meaning throughout the solution of problems, thus avoiding nonsense errors.

Analyses of the general characteristics of mathematical knowledge in everyday settings consistently point to meaning as the most important and relevant aspect in everyday problem solving. Moreover, everyday computation strategies may become flexible and understood as part of a general logico-mathematical structure that could fit problems in different contexts, as Schliemann and Nunes (1990) show in a study of the mathematics of fishermen in northeastern Brazil. Schliemann and Magalhães (1990; see also Schliemann & Carraher, 1992) provided further evidence of the generality of the everyday strategies for solving proportionality problems in their study of female cooks enrolled in an adult literacy program.

Everyday knowledge seems to be general enough to allow people to address new problems with strategies they develop in specific everyday situations. However, questions may be raised concerning the scope of everyday mathematics, especially if one considers the wider variety of mathematical situations that could be dealt with in schools as compared to what people naturally encounter in everyday settings. It would be misleading to suggest that people's everyday understanding of mathematics rivals in any way that of a professional mathematician. In view of the available research data, we have to acknowledge the mathematical character of everyday mathematics while recognizing, at the same time, its limitations.

In fact, it seems that the same cultural and social environments that foster construction of mathematical understanding also constrain and limit the kind of knowledge children and adults will come to develop. Understanding of the commutative law for multiplication is a case in point. Petitto and Ginsburg (1982) found that nonschooled Dioula tailors and cloth merchants in Liberia would solve a problem involving 100×6 by adding 100 six times, but did not accept that the same result would apply for the computation of 6×100. Schliemann, Araujo, Cassundé, Macedo, and Nicéas (1994) found similar results among young street sellers with restricted school experience in Brazil. Participants in this study computed the price of many items, given the price of one item, by repeatedly adding the number referring to price as many times as the number denoting the amount of items to be sold. When given problems for which use of commutativity would represent a substantial economy in terms of computation steps (e.g., find the price of 50 items at $3.00 per item), they did not accept adding the number of items as many times as the price of each one to find the total price. Moreover, when compared to schoolchildren who received instruction on multiplication, it was only at a later age that street sellers accepted using commutativity to solve multiplication problems.

Another limitation concerns use of scalar versus functional approaches to solve proportionality problems. Street sellers' procedures to compute the price of many items from the price of a few fall into what Vergnaud (1988) describes as the scalar approach for missing value proportionality problems. In this case, each

variable remains independent of the other, and parallel transformations that maintain the proportional relationship are carried out on both of them. In the school-oriented functional approach, the focus is on the ratio between the starting values of the two variables, which is then applied to the final pair to find the missing value. Exclusive use of the scalar approach may set limits to street sellers' problem-solving ability when the relation between price and number of items (the functional relation) is easier to work out than the relation between the starting and the ending quantities (the scalar relation). While schoolchildren most often focus on the functional relation, street sellers continue to use the scalar strategy, even when this requires cumbersome computations (Schliemann & Carraher, 1992).

A study on negative numbers by T. N. Carraher (1990) also reveals the constraints imposed by everyday solutions to mathematical problems. She found that, from their everyday experience with money, schooled and unschooled subjects were able to solve problems involving the addition of directed numbers by marking the negative numbers as losses or debts. When asked to use the written notation, however, they showed difficulties due to lack of correspondence between their everyday methods and school procedural steps for dealing with directed numbers.

Given the strengths and limitations of everyday mathematics, a natural question immediately raised concerns its relevance to mathematics education. We tried to answer this question in more detail elsewhere (D. W. Carraher & Schliemann, in press). In the next section, we provide a brief account of our views.

Relevance of Everyday Mathematics

If mathematical ideas acquire meaning by virtue of their ties to everyday situations, then how can students come to understand complex concepts that are not used in everyday activities and have very little relation to daily experience? Should mathematical knowledge always be tied directly to everyday contexts?

Everyday activities such as farming, commerce, and astronomy played a fundamental role in the emergence and development of mathematics as a scientific field (Kline, 1962). But, just as a student's understanding of mathematics is not the sum of his or her former everyday experiences, the field of mathematics cannot be reduced to the circumstances that gave rise to its emergence. Once knowledge assumes higher forms, it tends to become relatively autonomous from its origins. This is true for the individual learner, as well as for the scientific community, that receives, as a legacy from former generations, the symbolic tools for formulating and thinking about problems. As we stressed elsewhere (Schliemann, Carraher, & Ceci, 1997), scientific and mathematical reasoning are always indebted to their origins in human activity without becoming enslaved to it.

Participation in everyday simulated activities such as buying and selling may help students establish links between their previous experiences and intuitions and the topics learned in school. But, it would be a mistake to suggest to educators that participation in simulated everyday activities in schools is the main resource they have to promote meaningful learning of mathematics (see Schliemann, 1995, and D. W. Carraher & Schliemann, in press). First, one can establish rich links to out-of-school activities through discussion without re-enacting the activities in the classroom. In addition, children require a range of new activities that will enrich and complement their out-of-school experience. Schools should provide access to new symbolic systems and representations essential for establishing links between concepts and situations that would otherwise remain unrelated. To achieve this, educators need to create situations in which symbolic representations become tools for achieving goals that are different from and probably no less complex than everyday goals.

Everyday Cognition:
New Views on Research,
Theory, and Application

The findings of everyday cognition studies call for new theoretical approaches concerning the nature of knowledge, cognition, intelligence, and cognitive development. Drawing on Ferguson's (1956) analysis, Irvine and Berry (1988) and Berry (1987) proposed that cognitive abilities develop in response to ecological demands, which are in turn modified by skill acquisition. Ceci (1990, 1993) proposes to replace the notion of a general, singular, inherited intelligence by a contextual model of intelligence in which the potential for intellectual achievement develops as a result of one's experience in specific contexts. Rogoff (1990) and Saxe (1991) designed models for cognitive development that attempt to reconcile the notion of individual

cognitive development and prior understandings with sociocultural analysis. Building on the "Soviet" sociohistorical tradition, Wertsch (1991) proposed that individuals create their environments and themselves through the actions they undertake. Cole (1988) brought into discussion the principles of the sociohistorical psychology, reinterpreting results of cross-cultural research and emphasizing the importance of social, historical, political, and economical changes for the organization and development of human activity and modes of cognitive functioning.

Conceptions of cognition as an individual's general ability have been replaced by notions such as situated cognition (Brown et al., 1989; Lave, 1988), shared cognition (Resnick, 1987; Resnick et al., 1991), or distributed cognition (Hutchins, 1993). Cognitive development and learning are now described in terms of the creation of communities of practice through legitimate peripheral participation (Lave & Wenger, 1991), apprenticeship through guided participation (Rogoff, 1990), or social construction of responses (Perret-Clermont, Perret, & Bell, 1991).

The variety of proposed theoretical approaches point to multiple research paths. As researchers moved away from views of cognition as an individual decontextualized process, they focused on sociocultural practices and the role of mediators such as language, cultural tools, and conventional symbolic systems in shaping and transforming mental processes. These new approaches, however, are still far from accounting for how cultural tools and social processes interact with individual reasoning processes to allow cognitive development and learning to occur.

Research and theoretical views of culture and cognition need to find room for contexts that are not simply physical settings or social structures to which the learner is passively submitted. Contexts are not just constituted by their physical properties, but involve issues of meaning and interpretation. Contexts can be insinuated, imagined, alluded to, created on the fly, or carefully constructed over long periods of time.

Since the development of knowledge takes considerable time, we may arrive at different conclusions about the role of cultural practices in the emergence of knowledge depending on the time framework adopted. If we focus on the time period when children are taught, for instance, to "do" division and measurement, the knowledge acquired in one set of situations may appear isolated from and irrelevant to the knowledge acquired in another set of situations. One thus leans toward a strict situated cognition type of analysis. If, on the other hand, one scans a much wider period of time, knowledge acquired in one type of situation may ultimately make substantial contributions in other domains.

Furthermore, we should be skeptical of attempts to classify concepts as contextualized or decontextualized, as abstract or concrete, as formal or informal, as specific or general, or as everyday or school concepts as if these were inherent properties of the concepts. Concrete knowledge acquired in everyday, familiar, specific situations may ultimately play a fundamental role in the development of formal abstract school knowledge. General, abstract concepts are powerful not by their detachment from particular instances and situations, but by their usefulness in explaining and illuminating a wide range of particular phenomena (Cassirer, 1923). The abstract thus is bound inextricably to the concrete. We have coined the expression *situated generalization* (D. W. Carraher, Nemirovsky, & Schliemann, 1995; D. W. Carraher & Schliemann, 1998) to capture this tension.

Since methods and techniques are not isolated from theoretical, educational, and social concerns, the findings of everyday cognition studies also affected research methods in psychology and in education. Qualitative methods, ethnographic methods, and open-ended interviews are now part of the psychological and educational research tradition. The traditional boundaries among anthropology, sociology, psychology, and history are becoming less strict in the search to understand how symbol systems that are part of one's cultural legacy are appropriated and adapted to group and individual needs. Most of all, as culture becomes a central part of cognitive studies, the boundaries between psychology and education tend to disappear as researchers and educators try to understand how children develop and learn as they participate in in-school and out-of-school activities. Cognitive psychology's emphasis on abilities of individuals has provided researchers with disappointingly few insights into the nature and use of goals in classrooms and how they differ from goals in out-of-school situations. This is an area open for studies that will contribute to better educational approaches and to deeper theoretical insights into the nature of cognitive processes. We need to develop cognitive studies in school settings, taking into account the activities and tools to which children have access as they participate in instructional activities.

Concerning educational applications, everyday cognition research shows that failure in school or in formal tests does not imply inability to understand. In the case of mathematical knowledge, children and adults appear to understand and use with flexibility some of the mathematical properties they seem not to comprehend in school. These properties and relations, of course, are represented in very different ways across the two contexts. Mastery of mathematical concepts and relations in school depend intimately on the appropriation of culturally developed symbolic systems that have their own peculiar structure, conventions, and logic. Thus, the questions educators and psychologists must face are not those referring to the development of general psychological structures and stages, but rather the question of what sorts of activity are likely to promote meaningful appropriation of new symbolic systems.

Conclusions

When the expression *everyday cognition* first appeared, it seemed to designate an area of research. However, with time, it has become clear that it represents rather a set of attitudes and methodological bents toward knowledge, reasoning, and learning. Researchers who identify with the area share the premise that learning and thinking develop in social contexts and bear the marks of culture. In the early part of this century, such ideas might have seemed strange to students of mental processes. In the present zeitgeist, one would be hard-pressed to find researchers who would not endorse such ideas. No longer do researchers and educators wonder whether culture exerts an influence on one's thinking.

But, discourse at this level of generality is bound to leave one with the mistaken impression that we now understand the secrets of cognitive development. Nothing could be further from the truth. Consider the relationship of schools to everyday cognition. Schools are part of children's everyday social reality. They involve cultural practices. They bring children into contact with a wide set of symbolic tools—specialized uses of language, tables, writing systems, and registers. Researchers of everyday cognition have often fostered the notion that schools somehow were artificial settings in which pallid and meaningless sorts of knowledge were being foisted on students. It is true that people, children included, often have difficulty understanding how knowledge as presented in school relates to life out of school, but researchers cannot dismiss schools and what takes place in them as lying outside the domain of everyday cognition.

Once we recognize that schools fall into the domain of natural settings, we see that the task before us is very great. There is a small (but growing) body of research about how children reconcile knowledge developed out of school with knowledge developed in school. How does algebraic notation differ from and yet draw on natural language? How does learning about variables draw on what children have learned about relations among quantities in the physical world? How does sharing goods provide a basis for learning about fractions? How do (or how might) the concepts of credit and debt play a role in learning about directed numbers? How do children's experiences of motion and force set the stage for learning physics and the mathematics of calculus? Does thinking ever become autonomous of physical situations? If scientists project themselves onto graphical representations as they interpret them—imagining what happens as one traverses a graphical space— what does this mean, if anything, for how we teach students about graphs? When we note that children naturally think in certain ways— "naturally" meaning, in this case, without specific instruction in school—should educators themselves begin to adopt the children's thinking in their examples? For example, if children naturally approach addition and subtraction problems by breaking up quantities in convenient ways and then regrouping them to find answers, should mathematics instructors spend a lot of time encouraging them to do just that? Would it not be better if educators invested their energies in devising tasks to help children learn mathematics that they would *not* discover on their own? (According to the same logic, we do not bother teaching babies to walk.)

Because we focused here on mathematical thinking, we have failed to deal with most of what qualifies as cognition. We suspect that an everyday cognition that focused, let us say, on history and social sciences would pose issues of quite a different sort. Rather, we leave this as an issue for others.

References

Abreu, G. de, & Carraher, D. W. (1989). The mathematics of Brazilian sugar cane farmers. In C.

Keitel, P. Damerow, A. Bishop, & P. Gerdes (Eds.), *Mathematics, education and society* (Science and Technology Education Document Series No. 35, pp. 68–70). Paris: United Nations Educational, Scientific, and Cultural Organization.

Acioly, N. (1994). *La juste mesure: Une étude des competences mathématiques des travailleurs de la canne a sucre du Nordeste du Brésil dans le domaine de la mesure.* Unpublished doctoral dissertation, Université René Descartes, Paris.

Berry, J. W. (1976). *Human ecology and cognitive styles: Comparative studies in cultural and psychological adaptation.* New York: Sage/Halsted/Wiley.

Berry, J. W. (1987). The comparative study of cognitive abilities. In S. H. Irvine & S. E. Newstead (Eds.), *Intelligence and cognition: Contemporary frames of reference* (pp. 393–420). Dordrecht, The Netherlands: Nijhoff.

Berry, J. W. (1993). Indigenous cognition: A conceptual analysis and an empirical example. In J. Wassmann & P. Dasen (Eds.), *Alltagwissen: Les savoirs quotidiens—Everyday cognition. 11. Kolloquium (1990) der Schweizerischen Akademie der Geistes- und Sozialwissenschaften* (pp. 139–156). Freiburg: Universitatsverlag.

Berry, J. W., Dasen, P. R., & Saraswathi, T. S. (Eds.). (1997). *Handbook of cross-cultural psychology: Vol. 2. Basic processes and developmental psychology* (2nd ed.). Boston: Allyn & Bacon.

Brown, J. S., Collins, A., & Duguid, P. (1989). Situated cognition and the culture of learning. *Educational Researcher, 18*(1), 32–42.

Carey, S. (1985). *Conceptual change in childhood.* Cambridge: MIT Press.

Carraher, D. W. (1991). Mathematics in and out of school: A selective review of studies from Brazil. In M. Harris (Ed.), *Schools, mathematics and work* (pp. 169–201). London: Falmer Press.

Carraher, D. W., Nemirovsky, R., & Schliemann, A. D. (1995). Situated Generalization. In L. Meira & D. Carraher (Eds.), *Proceedings of the 19th International Conference for the Psychology of Mathematics Education* (Vol. 1, p. 234). Recife, Brazil: Program Committee of the 19th PME Conference.

Carraher, D. W., & Schliemann, A. D. (1998, April). *The transfer dilemma.* Symposium presentation at the Annual Meeting of the American Educational Research Association, San Diego, CA.

Carraher, D. W., & Schliemann, A. D. (in press). Is everyday mathematics truly relevant to mathematics education? In J. Moshkovich & M. Brenner (Eds.), *Everyday and Academic Mathemat-*

ics in the Classroom. Monographs of the Journal for Research in Mathematics Education. Reston, VA: National Council of Teachers of Mathematics.

Carraher, T. N. (1985). The decimal system: Understanding and notation. In L. Streefland (Ed.), *Proceedings of the Ninth International Conference for the Psychology of Mathematics Education* (Vol. 1, pp. 288–303). Noordwijkerhout, The Netherlands: State University of Utrecht.

Carraher, T. N. (1986). From drawings to buildings: Working with mathematical scales. *International Journal of Behavioural Development, 9,* 527–544.

Carraher, T. N. (1990). Negative numbers without the minus sign. In *Proceedings of the 14th International Conference for the Psychology of Mathematics Education* (Vol. 3, pp. 223–230). Oaxtepec, Mexico: International Group for the Psychology of Mathematics Education.

Carraher, T. N., Carraher, D. W., & Schliemann, A. D. (1982). Na vida, dez; na escola, zero: Os contextos culturais da educação matemática. *Cadernos de Pesquisa, 42,* 79–86.

Carraher, T. N., Carraher, D. W., & Schliemann, A. D. (1985). Mathematics in the streets and in schools. *British Journal of Developmental Psychology, 3,* 21–29.

Carraher, T. N., Carraher, D. W., & Schliemann, A. D. (1987). Written and oral mathematics. *Journal for Research in Mathematics Education, 18,* 83–97.

Cassirer, E. (1923). *Substance and Function.* New York: Douglas Publications.

Ceci, S. J. (1990). *On intelligence . . . more or less: A bio-ecological treatise on intellectual development.* Englewood Cliffs, NJ: Prentice Hall Century Psychology Series.

Ceci, S. J. (1993). Some contextual trends in cognitive development. *Developmental Review, 13,* 403–435.

Ceci, S. J., & Bronfenbrenner, U. (1985). Don't forget to take the cupcakes out of the oven: Strategic time-monitoring, prospective memory and context. *Child Development, 56,* 175–190.

Ceci, S. J., & Liker, J. (1986). Academic and nonacademic intelligence: An experimental separation. In R. Sternberg & R. Wagner (Eds.), *Practical intelligence: Nature and origins of competence in the everyday world* (pp. 119–142). New York: Cambridge University Press.

Chaiklin, S., & Lave, J. (1993). *Understanding practice: Perspectives on activity and context.* New York: Cambridge University Press.

Cole, M. (1988). Cross-cultural research in sociohistorical tradition. *Human Development, 31,* 137–157.

Cole, M., Gay, J., Glick, J. A., & Sharp, D. W. (1971). *The cultural context of learning and thinking.* New York: Basic Books.

D'Ambrosio, U. (1985). Ethnomathematics and its place in the history and pedagogy of mathematics. *For the Learning of Mathematics, 5*(1), 44–48.

Dasen, P. R., & Bossel-Lagos, M. (1989). L'etude interculturelle des savoirs quotidiens: Revue de la litterature. In J. Retschitzky, M. Bossel-Lagos, & P. R. Dasen (Eds.), *La recherche interculturelle* (pp. 98–114). Paris: L'Harmattan.

Detterman, D. K., & Sternberg, R. S. (1993). *Transfer on trial: Intelligence, cognition, and instruction.* Norwood, NJ: Ablex.

Dias, M. G. (1987). Da lógica do analfabeto à lógica do universitário: Há progresso? *Arquivos Brasileiros de Psicologia, 39*(1), 29–40.

Dias, M. G., & Harris, P. L. (1988). The effect of make-believe play on deductive reasoning. *British Journal of Developmental Psychology, 6,* 207–221.

Donaldson, M. (1978). *Children's minds.* Glasgow, Scotland: Fontana/Collins.

Ferguson, G. A. (1956). On transfer and the abilities of man. *Canadian Journal of Psychology, 10,* 121–131.

Gay, J., & Cole, M. (1967). *The new mathematics and an old culture.* New York: Holt, Rinehart & Winston.

Gelman, R. (1979). Preschool thought. *American Psychologist, 44,* 134–141.

Gerdes, P. (1986). How to recognize hidden geometrical thinking: A contribution to the development of anthropological mathematics. *For the Learning of Mathematics, 6*(2), 10–17.

Gerdes, P. (1988a). On culture, geometrical thinking and mathematics education. *Educational Studies in Mathematics, 19,* 137–162.

Gerdes, P. (1988b). A widespread decorative motive and the Pythagorean theorem. *For the Learning of Mathematics, 8*(1), 35–39.

Glick, J. (1981). Functional and structural aspects of rationality. In I. Sigel, D. Brodzinsky, & R. Golinkoff (Eds.), *New directions in Piagetian theory and practice* (pp. 219–228). Hillsdale, NJ: Lawrence Erlbaum.

Grando, N. (1988). *A matemática na agricultura e na escola.* Unpublished masters thesis, Universidade Federal de Pernambuco, Recife, Brazil.

Harris, M. (1987). An example of traditional women's work as a mathematics resource. *For the Learning of Mathematics, 7*(3), 26–28.

Harris, M. (1988). Common threads—Mathematics and textiles. *Mathematics in School, 17*(4), 24–28.

Harris, M. (Ed.). (1990). *Schools, mathematics and work* (pp. 169–201). London: Falmer Press.

Hatano, G. (1990). The nature of everyday science: A brief introduction. *British Journal of Developmental Psychology, 8,* 245–250.

Hughes, M. (1986). *Children and number.* Oxford: Blackwell.

Hutchins, E. (1979). Reasoning in Trobriand discourse. *Quarterly Newsletter of the Laboratory of Comparative Human Cognition, 1*(2), 13–17.

Hutchins, E. (1980). *Culture and inference.* Cambridge: Harvard University Press.

Hutchins, E. (1983). Understanding Micronesian navigation. In D. Gentner & A. Stevens (Eds.), *Mental models* (pp. 191–225). Hillside, NJ: Erlbaum.

Hutchins, E. (1993). Learning to navigate. In S. Chaiklin & J. Lave (Eds.), *Understanding practice: Perspectives on activity and context* (pp. 35–63). New York: Cambridge University Press.

Inagaki, K. (1990). Young children's use of knowledge in everyday biology. *British Journal of Developmental Psychology, 8,* 281–288.

Inagaki, K., & Hatano, G. (1987). Young children's spontaneous personification as analogy. *Child Development, 58,* 1013–1020.

Irvine, S. H., & Berry, J. W. (Eds.). (1988). *Human abilities in cultural context.* Cambridge: Cambridge University Press.

Kline, M. (1962). *Mathematics: A cultural approach.* Reading, MA: Addison-Wesley.

Laboratory of Comparative Human Cognition. (1983). Culture and cognitive development. In P. H. Mussen (Ed.), *Handbook of child psychology: Vol. 1. History, theory and methods* (pp. 295–356). New York: Wiley.

Lave, J. (1977). Cognitive consequences of traditional apprenticeship training in Africa. *Anthropology and Educational Quarterly, 7,* 177–180.

Lave, J. (1988). *Cognition in practice: Mind, mathematics, and culture in everyday life.* Cambridge: Cambridge University Press.

Lave, J., & Wenger, E. (1991). *Situated learning: Legitimate peripheral participation.* New York: Cambridge University Press.

Leontiev, A. N. (1981). *Problems of the development of the mind.* Moscow: Progress.

Light, P., Buckingham, N., & Robbins, A. (1979). The conservation task as an interactional setting. *British Journal of Educational Psychology, 49,* 304–310.

Luria, A. R. (1976). *Cognitive development: Its cultural and social foundations.* Cambridge: Harvard University Press.

McGarrigle, J., & Donaldson, M. (1974). Conservation accidents. *Cognition, 3,* 341–350.

McMurchy-Pilkington, C. (1995). *Maori women engaging in mathematical activities in Marae kitchens.* Unpublished master's thesis, University of Auckland, New Zealand.

Millroy, W. L. (1992). An ethnographic study of the mathematical ideas of a group of carpenters. *Journal for Research in Mathematics Education* (Monograph no. 5). Reston, VA: National Council of Teachers of Mathematics.

Neisser, U. (1967). *Cognitive psychology.* New York: Apple-Century-Crofts.

Neisser, U. (1976). *Cognition and reality. Principles and implications of cognitive psychology.* New York: W. H. Freeman & Co.

Neisser, U. (1981). John Dean's memory: A case study. *Cognition, 9,* 1–22.

Neisser, U. (Ed.). (1982). *Memory observed. Remembering in natural contexts.* San Francisco: W. H. Freeman & Co.

Nunes, T. (1992). Ethnomathematics and everyday cognition. In D. Grouws (Ed.), *Handbook of research in mathematics education* (pp. 557–574). New York: Macmillan.

Nunes, T., Schliemann, A. D., & Carraher, D. W. (1993). *Street mathematics and school mathematics.* New York: Cambridge University Press.

Perret-Clermont, A.-N., Perret, J.-F., & Bell, N. (1991). The social construction of meaning and cognitive activity in elementary school children. In L. Resnick, J. Levine, & S. Teasley (Eds.), *Perspectives on socially shared cognition* (pp. 41–62). Washington, DC: American Psychological Association.

Petitto, A., & Ginsburg, H. (1982). Mental arithmetic in Africa and America: Strategies, principles and explanations. *International Journal of Psychology, 17,* 81–102.

Piaget, J. (1972). Intellectual evolution from adolescence to adulthood. *Human Development, 15,* 1–12.

Reed, H. J., & Lave, J. (1979). Arithmetic as a tool for investigating relations between culture and cognition. *American Anthropologist, 6,* 568–582

Resnick, L. (1986). The development of mathematical intuition. In M. Perlmutter (Ed.), *Minnesota Symposium on Child Psychology* (Vol. 19, pp. 159–194). Hillsdale, NJ: Erlbaum.

Resnick, L. (1987, December). Learning in school and out. *Educational Researcher,* 13–20.

Resnick, L., Levine, J., & Teasley, S. (Eds.). (1991). *Perspectives on socially shared cognition.* Washington, DC: American Psychological Association.

Rogoff, B. (1990). *Apprenticeship in thinking. Cognitive development in social context.* New York: Oxford University Press.

Rogoff, B., & Lave, J. (Eds.). (1984). *Everyday cognition: Its development in social context.* Cambridge, MA: Harvard University Press.

Saraswathi, L. S. (1988). Practices in identifying (reckoning), measuring and planning for utilization of time in rural Tamil-Nadu (India): Implications for adult education programs. *Journal of Education and Social Change, 2*(3), 125–140.

Saraswathi, L. S. (1989). Practices in linear measurements in rural Tamil-Nadu: Implications for adult education programs. *Journal of Education and Social Change, 3*(1), 29–46.

Saxe, G. B. (1991). *Culture and cognitive development: Studies in mathematical understanding.* Hillsdale, NJ: Lawrence Erlbaum.

Saxe, G. B., & Moylan, T. (1982). The development of measurement operations among the Oksapmin of Papua New Guinea. *Child Development, 53*, 1242–1248.

Schliemann, A. D. (1985). Mathematics among carpenters and carpenters apprentices: Implications for school teaching. In P. Damerow, M. Dunckley, B. Nebres, & B. Werry (Eds.), *Mathematics for all,* (Science and Technology Education Document Series No. 20, pp. 92–95). Paris: United Nations Educational, Scientific, and Cultural Organization.

Schliemann, A. D. (1988). Understanding permutations: Development, school learning, and work experience. *Quarterly Newsletter of the Laboratory of Comparative Human Cognition, 10*(1), 3–7.

Schliemann, A. D. (1995). Some concerns about bringing everyday mathematics to mathematics education. In L. Meira & D. Carraher (Eds.), *Proceedings of the 19th International Conference for the Psychology of Mathematics Education* (Vol. 1, pp. 45–60). Recife, Brazil: Editora da Universidade Federal de Pernambuco.

Schliemann, A. D., & Acioly, N. M. (1989). Mathematical knowledge developed at work: The contribution of practice versus the contribution of schooling. *Cognition and Instruction, 6*(3), 185–221.

Schliemann, A. D., Araujo, C., Cassundé, M. A., Macedo, S., & Nicéas, L. (1994). School children versus street sellers' use of the commutative law for solving multiplication problems. In *Proceedings of the Eighteenth International Conference for the Psychology of Mathematics Education* (Vol. 4, pp. 209–216). Lisbon, Portugal: International Group for the Psychology of Mathematics Education.

Schliemann, A. D., & Carraher, D. W. (1992). Proportional reasoning in and out of school. In P. Light & G. Butterworth (Eds.), *Context and cognition: Ways of learning and knowing* (pp. 47–73). New York: Harvester Wheatsheaf.

Schliemann, A. D., Carraher, D. W., & Ceci, S. J.

(1997). Everyday cognition. In J. W. Berry, P. R. Dasen, & T. S. Sarawathi (Eds.), *Handbook of Cross-Cultural Psychology: Vol. 2. Basic processes and developmental psychology* (2nd ed., pp. 177–215). Boston, Allyn & Bacon.

Schliemann, A. D., & Magalhães, V. P. (1990). Proportional reasoning: From shops, to kitchens, laboratories, and, hopefully, schools. In *Proceedings of the 14th International Conference for the Psychology of Mathematics Education* (Vol. 3, pp. 67–73). Oaxtepec, Mexico: International Group for the Psychology of Mathematics Education.

Schliemann, A. D., & Nunes, T. (1990). A situated schema of proportionality. *British Journal of Developmental Psychology, 8*, 259–268.

Schliemann, A. D., Santos, C. M., & Canuto, S. F. (1993). Constructing written algorithms: A case study. *Journal of Mathematical Behavior, 12*, 155–172.

Scribner, S. (1977). Modes of thinking and ways of speaking. In P. Wason & P. Johnson-Laird (Eds.), *Thinking: Readings in cognitive science* (pp. 483–500). New York: Cambridge University Press.

Scribner, S. (1984). Studying working intelligence. In B. Rogoff & J. Lave (Eds.), *Everyday cognition: Its development in social context* (pp. 9–40). Cambridge: Harvard University Press.

Scribner, S. (1986). Thinking in action: Some characteristics of practical thought. In R. Sternberg & D. Wagner (Eds.), *Practical intelligence. Nature and origins of competence in the everyday world* (pp. 13–30). New York: Cambridge University Press.

Segall, M., Dasen, P., Berry, J., & Poortinga, Y. (1999). *Human behavior in global perspective.* Boston: Allyn & Bacon.

Sternberg, R., & Wagner, D. (Eds.). (1986). *Practical intelligence. Nature and origins of competence in the everyday world.* New York: Cambridge University Press

Ueno, N., & Saito, S. (1994, June). *Historical transformations of mathematics as problem solving in a Nepali bazaar.* Paper presented at the 13th Biennial Meetings of the International Society for the Study of Behavioural Development, Amsterdam.

Usher, J., & Neisser, U. (1993). Childhood amnesia and the beginnings of memory for four early life events. *Journal of Experimental Psychology: General, 122*(2), 155–165.

Vergnaud, G. (1988) Multiplicative structures. In J. Hiebert & M. Behr (Eds.), *Number concepts and operations in the middle grades* (Vol. 2). Reston, VA: Erlbaum/National Council of Teachers of Mathematics.

Vosniadou, S. (1991). Children's naive models and the processing of expository text. In M. Carretero, M. Pope, R.-J. Simons, & J. I. Pozo (Eds.), *Learning and instruction: European research in an international context* (Vol. 3, pp. 325–336). Oxford, England: Pergamon Press.

Voss, J., Perkins, D., & Segal, J. (1991). *Informal reasoning and education.* Hillsdale, NJ: Erlbaum.

Vygotsky, L. S. (1978). *Mind in society.* Cambridge: Harvard University Press.

Wassmann, J. (1993). When actions speak louder than words: The classification of food among the Yupno of Papua New Guinea. *Quarterly*

Newsletter of the Laboratory of Comparative Human Cognition, 15, 30–40.

Wassmann, J., & Dasen, P. R. (1994). "Hot" and "cold": Classification and sorting among the Yupno of Papua New Guinea. *International Journal of Psychology, 29*(1), 19–38.

Wertsch, J. (1991). *Voices of the mind: A sociocultural approach to mediated action.* Cambridge: Harvard University Press.

Zaslavsky, C. (1973). *Africa counts.* Boston: Prindle & Schmidt.

9

Culture and Moral Development

JOAN G. MILLER

No topic is more central to an understanding of culture than perhaps morality. Indeed, it is often difficult to delineate where culture ends and morality begins as culture and morality share an intricate and intimate relationship. In fact, an argument could be (and has been) made that much of culture's contents and the goals of enculturation are to ensure the inscription of culture-specific processes and understanding of morality, justice, and fairness in the individual.

In this chapter, Miller provides us with a comprehensive and excellent overview of the literature in the area of culture and morality. She begins by describing the major mainstream approaches to moral development, including the cognitive developmental perspectives of Piaget and Kohlberg, the distinct domain perspective of Turiel, and the morality of caring perspective of Gilligan. Miller is deft at not only describing in detail the basic tenets of each of the approaches, but also cleverly evaluating each in terms of empirical and theoretical limitations. As Miller notes, each of the three approaches downplays the impact of cultural meanings and practices, shares the assumption that morality is self-constructed in the context of everyday socialization experiences, and assumes fundamentally the same forms in all cultural settings.

Miller then goes beyond the mainstream approaches in discussing cultural approaches to moral development. Focusing on three key issues—culturally inclusive definitions of morality, the nature of cultural meanings, and the cultural grounding of developmental processes—Miller describes key empirical findings in the cross-cultural literature that demonstrate the close interrelationship between culture and morality. The evidence reviewed spans all areas of morality research, including judgments of justice morality, moralities of community and interpersonal relationships, and moralities related to divinity and spirituality and demonstrates convincingly that cultural meanings and practices affect the application of moral codes in everyday situations and also produce qualitative differences in moral reasoning.

Using this review as a platform, Miller argues convincingly for a future research agenda that is well characterized by an integration with other psychological processes, an incorporation of areas of morality previously ignored by mainstream research, and a longitudinal approach to understanding the process of moral development during enculturation. She argues, for example, for the need to understand better the relationship between self and morality, especially in the process of enculturation and in non-Western cultures. She also argues for more work in the areas of personhood and harm, in the relationship between culture and context, and in the area of power. Her comments about culture and context are appropriate not only in the area of morality, but also throughout all topic areas covered in this volume. She also argues for the inclusion of examinations of indigenous approaches to understanding morality and to investigations of the motivational forces of existing cultural systems.

Miller's comments regarding future theoretical and empirical work are consonant with the theme espoused throughout this volume concerning the need for theoretical integration across disciplines and topic areas and for empirical refinement and evolution of technique that involves the incorporation and rapprochement of qualitative and quantitative approaches; of mainstream, cultural, cross-cultural, and indigenous approaches; and of longitudinal approaches. While this type of research is undoubtedly and fundamentally more difficult than that which is currently conducted, the arguments to engage in such endeavors are quite convincingly clear.

Morality represents one of the most central, yet challenging, areas of psychological investigation. Its centrality stems from its pervasive importance in psychological functioning, with moral beliefs closely linked to the development of self. In turn, its challenge lies in the central questions that are raised by the study of morality not only regarding issues of universalism versus relativism, but also regarding the nature of individual agency and the development of self. The existence of systems of morality is universal, with all known cultural groups identifying behaviors that are considered to be moral in the sense of being regarded as based on criteria of perceived right/wrong. Specific moral beliefs and morally relevant behaviors, however, vary markedly within and between cultural communities and across historical cohorts. Key questions arise in determining the degree to which this variation may be considered fundamental and what it implies regarding the processes underlying the development of moral understandings.

This chapter examines the role of culture in the development of morality (for other recent cross-cultural reviews of psychological research on morality, see, e.g., Eckensberger & Zimba, 1997; Edwards, 1994; J. R. Snarey, 1985; J. Snarey & Keljo, 1991). Focus centers on moral reasoning rather than on the broader topic of prosocial behavior. Within this tradition of psychological inquiry, morality tends to be understood as a domain that is based on a perceived natural law rather than on social consensus or personal preference. For example, slavery may be considered as a violation of morality even though it is widely practiced and condoned within a society. It is in this research tradition,

then, that questions about the relativity of morality are raised most centrally since morality is not identified exclusively with normative conformity.

The chapter is organized in three parts. In the first section, examination is undertaken of the mainstream approaches that have dominated psychological work on moral development, with particular attention given to the theoretical assumptions that are made in these approaches that support their universalistic claims. The second section reviews culturally grounded approaches to morality, highlighting respects in which they give greater weight to culture in defining morality and in explaining the nature of everyday moral judgment. Finally, the third section of the chapter identifies directions for future theory and research. It is concluded that there is a need to integrate cultural considerations centrally into psychological research on morality, while developing approaches that are more dynamic, ecologically sensitive, and closely linked to the development of self in cultural context.

Mainstream Approaches to Moral Development

In the following discussion, the focus centers on the core assumptions and central empirical findings associated with the mainstream perspectives on moral development. Consideration is given to the conceptual and methodological contributions of these approaches and to the ways in which each maintains a universalistic emphasis in the face of observable cultural vari-

ation in individuals' reasoning about moral issues.

Cognitive Developmental Perspectives

In one of the earliest approaches to the development of moral reasoning, Piaget formulated a
two-stage model of moral development (Piaget,
1932). It was argued that, with increasing age,
children's viewpoints change from an undifferentiated conception of morality centered on
objective responsibility or heteronomy to a conception of morality centered on subjective responsibility or autonomy. This developmental
change is illustrated in the responses of children to the widely used Piagetian research vignette that portrays an agent either intentionally causing minor harm (e.g., breaking a single
dish) or unintentionally causing more serious
harm (e.g., accidentally causing several dishes
to break). In focusing exclusively on the magnitude of objective consequences, young children
typically judge the second act to represent a
greater violation than the first. In contrast, in
focusing on the subjective property of intentionality, older children typically judge the first
act to represent the more serious violation. Parallel types of shifts from a heteronomous to an
autonomous orientation were documented by
Piaget in the domains of games, with young
children proceeding from a view of the rules
of games as fixed to a view that they represent
social creations. These developmental shifts are
explained in terms of socialization processes,
with young children assumed to construct a
heteronomous morality from their hierarchically structured experiences with adult socialization agents and later an autonomous morality from their egalitarian interactions with
peers.

Whereas research utilizing Piagetian procedures has supported the universality of these
age trends (Eckensberger & Zimba, 1997), the
Piagetian approach itself has been subject to
criticism on both methodological and conceptual grounds. It has been noted that Piagetian
vignettes confound intentions and consequences,
with negative intentions always linked to serious consequences, and positive intentions always linked to minor consequences. The Piagetian approach has also been seen as limited
because of its failure to differentiate fully between conventional and moral rule understandings (e.g., between rules involving games
versus rules involving harm).

Extending and elaborating the approach to
morality of Piaget while retaining its cognitive
developmental assumptions, Kohlberg formulated a justice model of morality that had broad
appeal and widespread impact (Kohlberg, 1969,
1971, 1981, 1984). Kohlberg's theory offered a
sharp break with the behaviorist and psychodynamic approaches that had dominated previous
psychological work on morality (e.g., Aronfreed,
1968; Freud, 1930) and drew a sharp distinction
between morality and social convention. Behaviorist and psychodynamic models define
morality in terms of societal standards of right
or wrong, which are internalized by individuals. Within the Kohlbergian tradition, this stance
was seen as problematic for its passive view of
the agent, who was portrayed as merely absorbing the understandings current in the social
context. Perhaps most seriously, the psychoanalytic and behaviorist approaches were criticized for treating morality in culturally relative
terms, as merely reflecting what is normative
in a given cultural context. The Kohlbergian
model presented a powerful alternative to these
viewpoints.

In the Kohlbergian framework, the individual is portrayed as deducing principles of
morality in a spontaneous self-constructive
process rather than passively absorbing the understandings of his or her society. Morality is
defined in terms of a natural law (i.e., an objective standard that transcends societal norms).
Drawing on the Kantian notion of the categorical imperative, it is argued that a behavior is
moral only if it meets the formal criteria of being
universally applicable, prescriptive, and capable of being applied in an impartial and imper-
sonal manner. This type of stance was seen as
realizable in terms of a morality of justice and
individual rights, in which an individual's
moral worth is treated as intrinsic and as unrelated to the individual's social position, affective ties, or personal characteristics (Rawls,
1971). Importantly, in such a view, role-based
social expectations are judged to lack moral
status in that they are viewed as based exclusively on normative standards rather than on
moral criteria.

The Kohlbergian model charts a six-stage developmental sequence in terms of three broad
levels (Carter, 1980). These include (a) a preconventional level, focused on avoiding punishment (Stage 1) and on instrumental exchange
(Stage 2); (b) a conventional level, focused on
fulfilling social role expectations (Stage 3) and
on upholding the social order and rule of law

(Stage 4); and (c) a postconventional level, focused on general individual rights that have been agreed upon by the whole society (Stage 5) and on self-chosen ethical principles of justice, human rights, and respect for the dignity of individual human beings (Stage 6). The first two levels are based on subjective preferences, either those of individuals at the preconventional level or those held within societies or social groups at the conventional level. In turn, at the postconventional level, reasoning is seen as achieving a moral stance, in that it is assumed that it is only at this level that judgments are based on objective standards, which are grounded neither in social consensus nor in self-serving individual preferences.

In Kohlbergian research, moral judgment is assessed in terms of open-ended responses given to hypothetical moral dilemmas (Colby & Kohlberg, 1987). In the most well known of these scenarios, the Heinz dilemma, for example, a husband is portrayed as stealing medicine from a greedy druggist to save the life of his dying wife, with respondents asked to evaluate the moral adequacy of Heinz's behavior. Subjects' responses are then categorized in terms of their level of moral stage development. Thus, for example, a subject who defended the husband's actions by citing the woman's right to life would be scored as reasoning at the postconventional level, the highest level of moral maturity in the Kohlbergian scheme. In contrast, a subject who defended the husband's actions in terms of his role-related obligations to his wife would be scored as reasoning only at the conventional level, a premoral stage of development according to Kohlbergian criteria.

Whereas a strength of the Kohlbergian methodology is in allowing subjects to formulate their reasoning about moral issues in open-ended ways, the methodology has been criticized for placing great demands on verbal fluency. The vignettes also have been considered limited in assessing hypothetical, rather than real-life, reasoning, and in tapping issues that, in many cases, are somewhat removed from everyday concerns. To address at least some of these methodological issues, a program of contemporary work on moral judgment was undertaken by Rest and his colleagues on the Defining Issues Test, a measure that reduced linguistic demands by turning the task into a recognition rather than a recall procedure (Rest, 1979, 1986; Rest, Narvaez, Bebeau, & Thoma, 1999). The Defining Issues Test presents subjects with abbreviated versions of the Kohlbergian moral dilemmas paired with a set of potential justification responses. Utilizing both rating and ranking procedures, subjects are asked to indicate which responses reflect their moral outlooks.

While initiated in Kohlberg's doctoral dissertation research among middle-class American males (Kohlberg, 1958), research on the Kohlbergian model of moral judgment was quickly broadened to include not only women, but also a range of different cultural and subcultural populations. Over time, there was also the release of a standardized scoring manual (Colby & Kohlberg, 1987), as well as minor shifts in the theory. The final versions of the model, for example, included content distinctions between values (e.g., truth, life, etc.) and elements (e.g., respect for oneself, dignity, autonomy, etc.), as well as between soft or heteronomous and hard or autonomous substages (Kohlberg, Levine, & Hewer, 1994). These changes had an impact on the methods of scoring Kohlbergian protocols; however, they had little impact on the cross-cultural trends observed in Kohlbergian research and did not challenge the fundamental assumptions made in the theory about the universality of a morality of justice.

What has been striking about research in the Kohlbergian tradition is not only the findings of marked cultural skewing in observed levels of moral development, but also the tendency of cognitive developmental researchers to view this variation as compatible with their claims about the universality of a morality of justice and individual rights. For example, Kohlberg (1969) observed, in some of his earliest research, that postconventional levels of moral judgment are linked to Westernization, urbanization, and socioeconomic status and tend to be absent altogether among village populations. Later research confirmed these findings, while revealing, with refined coding schemes, that the observed incidence of postconventional moral reasoning was even less common than first believed. For example, in a review of 45 culturally diverse samples, J. R. Snarey (1985) observed that only approximately 6% of responses reflect a mixture of postconventional and conventional concerns (Stages 4 and 5), with only 2% or less of responses worldwide tending to be purely postconventional. Higher stage responses occurred principally in middle-class Western urban populations, with members of traditional folk societies, such as in Kenya and New Guinea, failing to use either Stage 4/5 or Stage 5 reasoning. Similar trends have been observed in a recently completed review of over 400 Defining Issues Test studies conducted over a 25-year period (Rest et al., 1999), with moral judgment showing a positive relationship to education, urbanization, and Westernization. Evidence of this type led many contemporary cultural critics of Kohlberg to charge that the scheme is culturally bound and reflects a modern Western liberal cultural perspective (Simpson, 1974). It was argued that the model embodies a secular outlook that neglects religious bases of morality and that fails to take into account contrasting cultural views of personhood, such as viewpoints that accord value to all life, not just all human life (Vasudev & Hummel, 1987).

However, rather than accepting the validity of these charges, Kohlberg and his associates regarded the cross-cultural results as highly compatible with their theoretical claims (Kohlberg, 1969, 1971). Embracing the philosophical dictum that no inference can be drawn from "is to ought," the observed cross-cultural distributions of moral responses were not seen as having any implications for how morality is to be defined. Furthermore, findings that levels of moral judgment are related to education and to socioeconomic status were regarded as to be expected given the sophisticated levels of judgment assumed to be required for higher levels of moral judgment (Kohlberg, 1971; Rest et al., 1999).

Notably, the only major revision made by Kohlbergian researchers in their theoretical framework in response to cross-cultural critics was not in reaction to these findings of marked cross-cultural variability in moral judgment or to the charges of cultural bias in the Kohlbergian scheme, but in response to charges by Gilligan and colleagues that a focus on justice and individual rights led to the neglect of concerns with caring (Gilligan, 1977, 1982). In response to this insight, Kohlberg and colleagues in later years acknowledged that morality encompasses not only justice concerns, but also interpersonal responsiveness (Colby & Kohlberg, 1987). Within the Kohlbergian framework, however, such positive responsibilities of caring were viewed as lacking the full moral force of justice obligations in that they are considered as discretionary and as applying only to in-group relationships rather than universally. In embracing in this way Gilligan's argument about the role of caring in morality, Kohlberg and his colleagues, it may be seen, did not abandon their universalistic stance. Broadening their original claims about the scope of morality, they acknowledged that morality encompasses the positive duties of interpersonal responsiveness to family and friends and not only the negative duties of avoiding harm and infringement on the rights of others. However, they continued to view each of these aspects of morality in universal terms.

Distinct Domain Perspective

Complexity was introduced into the Kohlbergian cognitive developmental stage model of moral judgment by the distinct domain approach of Turiel and associates (L. Nucci, 1981; L. P. Nucci & Turiel, 1978; Smetana, 1983; Turiel, 1980, 1983, 1998a). While retaining the universalism of Kohlbergian theory and its assumption that justice and individual rights form the core content of morality, the distinct domain perspective made contrasting claims regarding the self-constructive processes entailed in moral judgment and adopted a methodology for assessing moral reasoning that has yielded contrasting findings regarding its cross-cultural and developmental distribution.

In contrast to the Kolbergian emphasis on logical deduction, the distinct domain perspective stresses the role of social interaction in the construction of morality. Morality is viewed as inductively derived, based on individuals observing the intrinsic consequences of actions (Turiel, 1983). Actions that lead to harm or that infringe on another's rights are seen as moral, such as the act of arbitrarily assaulting another person or of taking another person's belongings without permission. In contrast, it is assumed that other types of social behaviors, such as dress codes, represent social conventions in that the behaviors serve to facilitate social coordination and do not involve matters of justice or harm. Finally, it is assumed that a domain of personal choice and prudence exists that is based exclusively on the individual's subjective preferences and does not involve either moral issues of justice and harm or conventional concerns of social coordination (L. Nucci, 1981; L. Nucci & Lee, 1993). For example, the decision about whom to select as a friend tends to be regarded as a personal matter in that it is seen as based solely on considerations of personal taste and liking.

Methodologically, research within the distinct domain tradition focuses assessment on an individual's intuitive understandings. It is assumed that, just as individuals may be competent speakers of their languages without necessarily being fully aware of or able to articulate its grammar, young children are capable of distinguishing between different types of social rules even if they are not able to justify their judgments in as sophisticated a way as adults. Research in the distinct domain tradition typically proceeds by presenting individuals with short vignettes that portray breach situations involving violations of justice and individual rights in cases designed to tap moral issues, violations of social customs in cases designed to tap social conventional issues, and agents acting on their personal preferences in cases designed to tap personal choice concerns. Criterion probes are administered to assess such issues as whether the behavior is judged to be alterable, culturally relative, and legitimately regulated. Thus, for example, a child would be considered to view a behavior in moral terms if the child considered the behavior as legitimately subject to social regulation (e.g., indicated that it would be all right to have a rule regarding the behavior) and as nonculturally relative (e.g., indicated that it would not be all right to have a different rule regarding the behavior in another social setting).

Just as the Kohlbergian procedures produced findings that were congruent with the then-dominant stage view of cognition of Piagetian theory, the criterion probe methodology is producing findings that are congruent with contemporary models of cognitive development, which have views of children as highly competent cognitively (Kuhn & Siegler, 1998). Thus, for example, studies have shown that even children as young as 2 years old are able to discriminate morality from social convention (Smetana, 1981; Smetana & Braeges, 1990), with this ability evident in diverse cultural populations (Song, Smetana, & Kim, 1994). Findings of this type challenge cognitive developmental claims that morality emerges only late in development. Rather, the conclusion is drawn that the ability to distinguish among morality, social convention, and personal choice is available at young ages. However, whereas work in the distinct domain tradition makes contrasting claims regarding the developmental emergence of moral judgment compared to the Kohlbergian perspective, it retains its universalism. The conclusion is drawn that the content of morality centers in all cultures around issues of justice and individual rights, and that role expectations and religious issues represent social conventional and not moral concerns—a conclusion fundamentally similar to that reached within the Kohlbergian model.

Whereas studies utilizing clear-cut vignette situations provide evidence to suggest that, in all cultures, individuals show considerable agreement on the types of content issues within each domain, research that has utilized less prototypic situations reveals marked cultural and subcultural variation in domain categorization. For example, it has been found that certain issues that are seen as involving matters of personal choice by secular American populations (e.g., whether or not to eat beef) are categorized as moral violations by orthodox Hindu Indian populations (Shweder, Mahapatra, & Miller, 1987).

Within the distinct domain approach, however, this type of cultural variation is interpreted as fully compatible with the assumption that the content of morality is universal. It is argued that what appears to be a cultural difference in moral outlook is merely a cultural difference in background knowledge (Wainryb, 1991). For example, in judging that it is immoral to eat beef, Indians are seen as maintaining a morality of harm. They are viewed as differing from Americans only in their assumptions that a cow is a sacred object deserving of protection from harm and not in their moral assumption that harm should be avoided. In this type of interpretive stance, then, the position is taken that background epistemological knowledge presuppositions (e.g., assumptions about the existence of a spiritual world of sacred objects) should be held constant or parceled out in appraising the cultural universality of morality. These cultural knowledge presuppositions are treated as matters of fact, with validity that can be ascertained rationally, rather than as more arbitrary matters of value.

Morality of Caring Perspective

The morality of caring perspective of Gilligan and colleagues presented a major conceptual challenge to both the cognitive developmental and distinct domain frameworks in terms of a new vision regarding the content of morality, the processes underlying its development, and the impact of gender on its form (Gilligan, 1977, 1982; Gilligan & Wiggins, 1987). Gilligan argued that morality needs to be viewed as extending to issues of caring and interpersonal responsiveness. Challenging the assumption that justice forms the exclusive content of morality, Gilligan maintained that caring represents an integral aspect of morality. In contrast to the cognitive emphasis of the Kohlbergian and distinct domain perspectives, Gilligan argued for the need to understand the development of morality in terms of the affectively based development of self—a process that was seen as gender-related.

Drawing on psychodynamic and attachment formulations (e.g., Ainsworth, 1978; Bowlby, 1969–1980; Chodorow, 1978), Gilligan located the roots of morality in terms of the development of self in early socialization experiences. In naturally identifying with their mothers and in having experiences in family interaction that emphasize interpersonal responsiveness, girls are seen as developing a connected self and an associated morality of caring (Gilligan & Wiggins, 1987). In contrast, in identifying with their fathers, boys are seen as developing an autonomous self and an associated morality of justice.

Methodologically, work from a morality of caring perspective taps moral reasoning as it is reflected in individuals' narrative assessments of their personal experiences (Brown, Tappan, Gilligan, Miller, & Argyris, 1989). Qualitative methodologies are employed that involve multiple interpretive readings of text to distinguish between voices of care and of justice expressed in individuals' open-ended responses.

In its attention to gender-related variation in individuals' sense of self and moral outlook, the morality of caring approach accords greater weight to cultural considerations than do either the cognitive developmental or distinct domain perspectives. Strikingly, however, little or no weight is given to cultural meanings and practices that structure self-related experiences and outlooks. Rather, the claim is made that, whereas cultures vary in their everyday socialization practices, they all embody the same patterns of structural inequalities associated with gender and thus would all lead to fundamentally the same forms of self and of morality. Gilligan and Wiggins make this argument for the universality of the moralities of justice and of caring:

The different dynamics of early childhood inequality and attachment lay the groundwork for two moral visions—one of justice and one of care. . . . Although the nature of the attachment between child and parent varies across individual and cultural settings and although inequality can be heightened or muted by familial or societal arrangements, all people are born into a situation of inequality and no child survives in the absence of adult connection. Since everyone is vulnerable both to oppression and to abandonment, two stories about morality recur in human experience. (p. 281)

Most research from a morality of caring perspective has focused on gender differences in moral judgment. Whereas there was initial support for the claim that males emphasize justice and females emphasize caring, recent evidence indicates that moral reasoning tends not to be gender related (Thomas, 1986; Walker, 1984, 1991). Rather, it appears that gender-related variation in moral reasoning arises primarily from differences in education, occupation, or discourse style or from the types of issues under consideration (e.g., abortion) rather than from gender differences in moral outlook per se.

While rejecting the claim that moral reasoning is gender related, mainstream psychological theorists, however, continue to embrace Gilligan's assertion about the existence of a morality of caring. The conclusion is drawn that caring represents an important aspect of morality for both males and females, with such a morality assuming the same form in all cultural contexts. Interestingly, then, whereas the morality of caring perspective of Gilligan has succeeded in broadening contemporary understandings regarding the scope of morality, it remains within a universalistic framework.

Summary

Work within the mainstream psychological theories of moral development has shown that concerns with justice, individual rights, and welfare are central to morality. Cognitive developmental research indicates that a reflective understanding of justice morality arises late in development and is associated with Westernization and socioeconomic development, whereas research within the distinct domain tradition establishes that the ability to distinguish, on formal grounds, among issues of morality, convention, and personal choice is available early in development. In turn, work from a morality of caring viewpoint establishes that the content of morality extends to interpersonal responsibilities rather than being limited to matters of justice. Downplaying the impact of cultural meanings and practices, the three positions, however, share the assumptions that morality is self-constructed in the context of everyday socialization experiences, and that it assumes fundamentally the same forms in all cultural settings.

Cultural Approaches to Moral Development

As has been seen, a striking feature of the mainstream psychological theories of moral development is that their assumptions that moral orientations assume universal forms is not called into question by evidence of cultural variation in moral judgment and in everyday cultural practices. This suggests that giving greater weight to cultural considerations in theories of moral development requires not only obtaining evidence regarding cultural variation in moral judgment and behavior, but also interpreting this evidence in more culturally grounded ways. It may be seen that this is the type of position taken in recent cultural approaches. Such approaches maintain contrasting assumptions regarding how to define morality, the nature of cultural systems, and the impact of culture on development than those maintained within the mainstream approaches. Below, brief consideration is given first to these contrasting assumptions, followed by an examination of empirical evidence that documents the impact of culture on moral reasoning.

Key Assumptions

Culturally Inclusive Definitions of Morality

Cultural perspectives emphasize the importance of defining morality in ways that accommodate cultural variation. The argument is made that there has been a tendency in the mainstream psychological theories operationally to define morality in terms of criteria that, in fact, reflect culturally specific presuppositions. This process is seen as occurring, for example, in the stance taken within the mainstream psychological theories of excluding religion from the domain of morality and of assuming that role-based concerns lack moral force. Such a stance, it is argued, leads to these approaches treating many issues as not fully moral by definition that individuals from non-Western cultures identify as part of their morality.

Challenging what is regarded as the culturally biased nature of the content-based definitions of morality adopted in the dominant psychological theories, recent cultural viewpoints emphasize the importance of recognizing the open relationship that exists between the formal criteria that define a moral outlook and the content of systems of morality. Formal criteria

include general distinctions that define different domains of thought (Turiel, 1983) and abstract conceptions of harm, personhood, and the like that are relevant to the application of moral standards (Shweder et al., 1987). For example, from the present type of cultural perspective, it would not be assumed that vegetarianism invariably represents a matter of personal preference. Rather, it would be recognized that whether individuals consider eating meat a moral versus a nonmoral issue depends, in part, on their culturally based assumptions about the nature of personhood and of harm (e.g., whether harm includes nonhuman animals, etc.). The present type of stance leads to a position in which the determination that someone is reasoning morally is based on his or her attitude toward the issue in question (e.g., whether they consider it important, non–rule contingent, etc.) and not on the specific–nature of the content issues involved.

Nature of Cultural Meanings

From the perspective of recent cultural approaches, it is also regarded as limited to evaluate cultural differences in moral judgment only after controlling for cultural variation in knowledge presuppositions and associated practices. Such a stance assumes that knowledge presuppositions are fully rational in nature and may be evaluated comparatively according to their relative adequacy. However, many of the epistemological premises entailed in moral judgment are nonrational in nature, and thus their relative adequacy cannot be adjudicated through observation of experience (Shweder, 1984). For example, no advances in science will make it possible to determine when life begins and thus to appraise in absolute terms the moral adequacy of abortion.

Furthermore, from the perspective of recent cultural approaches, attempts to hold cultural beliefs and practices constant while appraising cultural differences in moral values are viewed as obscuring the phenomena of interest. They are seen, in effect, as evaluating cultural differences only after holding constant integral aspects of culture. For example, from this type of analytic stance, a devout Christian who regarded sex before marriage as an immoral violation of God's law and an atheist who regarded sex before marriage as a personal decision would be seen as sharing the same moral outlook with the only difference being their other-worldly beliefs about the existence of God. Efforts of this type, it is argued, yield evidence of highly abstract commonalities in moral outlook, but tend to gloss over important content differences in everyday moral judgment. The argument is made, however, that it is at the level of local understandings and practices that experience is lived and moral outlook is formed, not at a purely abstract analytical level of highly general and somewhat vacuous commonalities.

Cultural Grounding of Developmental Processes

Finally, recent cultural approaches challenge the emphasis on the autonomous construction of morality in the mainstream psychological viewpoints. Like the mainstream psychological viewpoints, cultural approaches maintain that individuals actively contribute meanings to experience. However, they assume that this type of active self-constructive process is always grounded, in part, in culturally based presuppositions. To the extent that moral development reflects, in part, the development of self in cultural variable settings, such development then is anticipated to be culturally variable as well.

Key Empirical Findings

This section presents a select overview of empirical studies that have been conducted by cultural theorists. The empirical evidence reviewed highlights not only respects in which cultural meanings and practices affect the application of moral codes in everyday situations, but also their qualitative impact on the nature of these codes.

Cultural Variability in Justice Morality

Work by cognitive developmental and distinct domain theorists has demonstrated that a concern with justice exists universally. However, even with this universality, culture is found to influence when justice concepts are applied. Such variation, it may be seen, reflects the contrasting adaptive demands of different cultural settings, the relative priority of competing moral obligations, as well as culturally based theories of the self and associated practices.

Cross-cultural evidence indicates, for example, that the findings of marked skewing in levels of Kohlbergian moral stage development reflect, at least in part, the contrasting relevance of justice concepts in different social settings.

In this regard, Harkness and colleagues (Harkness, Edwards, & Super, 1981), for example, found that the moral leaders of a Kipsigis community in Kenya typically score at Stage 3 on Kohlbergian measures, whereas a sample of nonleaders, who were matched for age, education, wealth, and religion with the leaders, tend only to score at Stage 2. They assume that whereas the concrete individual perspective on morality embodied in Stage 2 is most relevant to the everyday concerns of the nonleaders in this community, for the moral leaders, it is important to cultivate the perspective of the interpersonal systems orientation of Stage 3. More generally, cultural theorists maintain that the understanding of social structure entailed in Stages 4 and higher on the Kohlbergian scheme has relevance primarily in contexts that are closely tied to state or national governments—a finding that may explain, at least in part, the association observed cross-culturally between higher levels of Kohlbergian moral stage development and processes of modernization (Edwards, 1975, 1978, 1994; J. R. Snarey, 1985).

Cross-cultural work has also documented that, even in cases in which individuals from different cultures agree on the moral status of justice concepts, their application of these concepts in everyday situations may differ, depending on other moral values that they hold. Thus, it has been shown, for example, that Hindu Indians tend to give greater priority to interpersonal responsibilities relative to competing justice obligations than do European Americans because of their contrasting views of such responsibilities (Miller & Bersoff, 1992). In particular, whereas Americans tend to consider interpersonal responsibilities as discretionary commitments, Indians tend to accord them the same obligatory moral status as justice issues. Similar cross-cultural differences have been observed in research that contrasts the moral judgments of Chinese and Icelandic children (Keller, Edelstein, Fang, & Fang, 1998). When reasoning about moral dilemmas, Chinese children tend to give greater priority to altruistic and relationship concerns, and Icelandic children give greater priority to contractual and self-interested considerations.

Judgments of moral accountability represent another area in which cross-cultural differences obtain, even in cases in which individuals from different cultures agree on the moral status of the issues involved. In maintaining more contextually oriented views of the agent, individuals from cultures that emphasize relational as compared with individualistic beliefs and practices show a greater tendency to consider behavior as under the control of situational influences and are less prone to hold agents morally accountable for them. Thus, for example, Hindu Indians have been found more frequently than European Americans to absolve agents of moral accountability for justice breaches performed under the agent's emotional duress, immaturity, or other potentially extenuating situational factors (Bersoff & Miller, 1993; Miller & Luthar, 1989). Similarly, greater emphasis on contextual sensitivity is found in moral codes grounded in Confucian cultural traditions as compared with those grounded in Judeo-Christian cultural traditions (Dien, 1982). This is reflected, for example, in a tendency to stress reconciliation rather than conflict resolution in dispute settlement.

Finally, as noted briefly in discussion of the distinct domain viewpoint, cultural differences in everyday justice reasoning may occur because of culturally based variation in the content assumptions that individuals make in determining the applicability of particular justice concepts. These cultural differences in background premises may lead to marked variation in everyday moral judgment, with individuals from different cultural communities disagreeing in their assessments of such issues as which entities are assumed to have rights and to be entitled to protection from harm or even regarding what, in fact, constitutes harm. For example, in maintaining a greater cultural emphasis on hierarchy, orthodox Hindu Indian populations consider it as morally justifiable to accord unequal privileges to females relative to males (Shweder et al., 1987).

Moralities of Community

Compelling evidence for the need to give greater weight to cultural considerations in moral development may be seen in work on moralities of community. This research identifies types of postconventional moral outlooks that are not taken into account in the mainstream theories of moral development.

Work in various Chinese cultural populations, for example, points to the contrasting premises that underlie moral outlooks grounded in Confucian and Taoist thought as contrasted with in the Judeo-Christian outlook assumed in the Kohlbergian framework (Dien, 1982; Ma, 1988, 1989, 1992, 1997). Within these cultural traditions, humans are viewed as possessing innate moral tendencies, the preservation and

cultivation of which ensure a harmonious moral order. Central to this outlook is the concept of *jen*, an affectively grounded concept that encompasses such ideas as love, benevolence, and filial piety. The impact of this type of stance on moral judgment is illustrated, for example, in the reaction of a Chinese undergraduate to the Kohlbergian "Joe" dilemma, involving a father who demanded that his son give him money that the son had earned and had been previously promised by the father that he could use for camp. Rather than view this as a situation involving a breach of contract, Chinese subjects emphasized the son's filial duty to his father, which they saw as requiring that the son meet his father's demands. As a Chinese undergraduate argued: "He [the son] should once again work hard to earn money and give the money to his father. Although his father is not right, but because of filial piety, I think he should give the money to his father" (Ma, 1997, p. 99).

Related types of interpersonally oriented moral stances have been documented in a range of other cultural communities. Work on Hindu Indian populations, for example, highlights the centrality to morality of *dharma*, a concept that denotes simultaneously inherent disposition or nature, code for conduct, and natural law. Within such a cultural system, role-related responsibilities to meet the needs of others are treated as matters that possess full moral force rather than as forms of supererogatory justice expectations or of social conventions (Miller, 1994). Importantly, this type of moral outlook embraces the idea of the unity of all life, extending to promoting the welfare of nonhuman animals as well (Vasudev, 1994; Vasudev & Hummel, 1987).

A related, but somewhat contrasting orientation, may be seen in Buddhist cultural traditions, based on such cultural premises as *Dukkha*, or a view of life as suffering and of negative karma as accumulating through transgressions (A. Huebner & Garrod, 1991; A. M. Huebner & Garrod, 1993). From such a perspective, there is assumed to be a moral imperative to act to eliminate the suffering of others, whether human or nonhuman, and to overcome the effects of negative accumulated karma. Closely linked orientations are also observed in the affiliative concern for the social ideal and emphasis on harmony displayed by adult subjects from Cracow, Poland (Niemczynski, Czyzowska, Pourkos, & Mirski, 1988), in the emphasis on a state of harmony with others among the Maisin people of Papua New Guinea (Tietjen & Walker, 1985), and in the moral concern with helping others in the community reported among Black Caribs of British Hondura (Gorsuch & Barnes, 1973), as well as among Nigerian Igbo subjects (Okonkwo, 1997).

The cross-cultural evidence on moralities of community point out serious cultural biases in the cognitive development and distinct domain models, with their linkage of morality exclusively to justice and individual rights and their treatment of role-based obligations exclusively in conventional terms. As J. Snarey and Keljo (1991) conclude, in arguing for the existence of a *Gemeinschaft* voice of community that remains untapped within the Kohlbergian framework:

> There are legitimate forms of conventional and postconventional reasoning that seem to be missing from the current theory and scoring manual. Moreover, these forms of reasoning seem to be consonant with and even characteristic of *Gemeinschaft*. (p. 418)

Whereas there are many important differences between culturally based interpersonal moralities that reflect a Gemeinschaft orientation, certain widely shared characteristics of these types of moral stance can be identified. Such orientations, it may be seen, tend to embody an organic perspective on self, society, and morality. Within this type of communal orientation, role-related expectations and cultural traditions are experienced as approximations of the nature of being or of a perceived natural law rather than as mere societal constructions. Persons are seen as naturally part of the social whole, with their satisfaction perceived as closely linked to the well-being of the community.

A key question arises concerning the extent to which the types of Gemeinschaft communal orientations identified in various non-Western cultural settings relate to the morality of caring framework identified by Gilligan. Gilligan portrayed the morality of caring as universal. However, as discussed above, her approach downplays respects in which culture has an impact on the development of interpersonal morality. A closer reading of morality of caring responses illustrates respects in which the type of morality of caring responses identified by Gilligan embody a somewhat individualistic approach to caring. One individualistic aspect of this morality, for example, is in the weight given to individual choice in deciding whether to respond to the needs of others. As 11-year-old "Amy" argues:

> If you have a responsibility with someone else, then you should keep it to a certain extent, but to the extent that it is really going to hurt you or stop you from doing something that you really, really want, then I think maybe you should put yourself first. (Gilligan, 1982, p. 35)

The individualistic tenor of the morality of caring is also reflected in the emphasis placed on the need to act in a way that is autonomous from conventional role definitions. Embracing such a stance, college student "Claire" describes how she has rejected societal role definitions and begun to act more autonomously in developing a morality of caring:

> I am not necessarily the type of girlfriend I should be or that I've been perceived as, and I'm not necessarily the type of daughter that I've been perceived as. You grow up to find yourself in the way other people see you, and it's very hard, all of a sudden, to start separating this and start realizing that really nobody else can make these decisions. (Gilligan, 1982, p. 52)

Finally, the individualistic tenor of the morality of caring is evident in its eschewing of self-sacrifice and promotion of individuality. As Gilligan describes Claire's adoption of such a stance as she develops a mature morality of caring outlook:

> She has come to observe "faults" in her mother, whom she perceives as endlessly giving, "because she doesn't care if she hurts herself in doing it. . . . . Measured against a standard of care, Claire's ideal of self-sacrifice gives way to a vision of "a family where everyone is encouraged to become an individual and at the same time everybody helps others and receives help from them." (Gilligan, 1982, p. 54)

In sum, whereas Gilligan never explicitly linked the form of the morality of caring to the individualistic assumptions of middle-class European American culture, this type of outlook is evident in the morality of caring responses in her data, with informants emphasizing choice, rejecting role obligations as the basis for moral commitments, and stressing the need to avoid the loss of individuality entailed in stances that appear to involve giving priority to the requirements of the social whole.

Whereas the individualism of the morality of caring orientation is thus reflected in the open-ended caring responses cited by Gilligan, more direct evidence that the morality of caring outlook differs qualitatively from the types of communal outlooks maintained in many collectivist cultures is found in a program of comparative studies undertaken of middle-class European American and Hindu Indian populations (Miller, 1994). This research demonstrates that, whereas European Americans tend to approach morality as freely given commitments or matters of personal choice, Hindu Indians tend to view interpersonal responsibilities as matters of moral duty that extend across a broader range of need and role situations. Compared with Hindu Indians, European Americans also give greater weight to individual tastes and interests in assessing interpersonal responsibilities. Thus, they tend to treat responsibilities to meet the needs of family and friends as dependent on personal affinity and liking for them, whereas Hindu Indians tend to treat such responsibilities as dependent on more immutable role based obligations (Miller & Bersoff, 1998).

For example, whereas European Americans tend to maintain that a person has less responsibility to be responsive to a brother's needs if they personally share few common tastes and interests with the brother and thus do not enjoy each other's company than if they share many common tastes and interests and enjoy being together. In contrast, Hindu Indians tend to maintain that a person's responsibility to a brother is unaffected by such nonmoral self-serving considerations. Furthermore, Hindu Indians consider it morally required, rather than beyond the scope of morality, to give priority to the needs of others in the face of personal hardship or sacrifice, and they show a greater tendency than is shown by European Americans to experience satisfaction in such cases (Miller & Bersoff, 1995).

These cultural differences are illustrated, for example, in prototypic responses to a situation that was presented to informants; the situation involved a wife who remains married to her husband after he is severely injured in a motorcycle accident and becomes depressed and inactive for the rest of his life. Regarding the wife's behavior as both morally required and as highly desirable, a Hindu Indian informant noted the satisfaction that she expected the wife

would experience in being responsive to her husband's welfare and fulfilling her duty as a wife: "She will have the satisfaction of having fulfilled her duty. She helped her husband during difficulty. If difficulties and happiness are both viewed as equal, only then will the family life be smooth" (Miller & Bersoff, 1995, p. 275).

In contrast, considering such behavior as a matter for personal decision making rather than one of morality, an American focused on the dissatisfaction that she expected that the wife would experience in giving insufficient attention to her personal desires: "She is acting out of obligation—not other reasons like love. She has a sense of duty but little satisfaction for her own happiness" (Miller & Bersoff, 1995, p. 275).

In sum, cultural research in this area indicates that there appear to be multiple culturally based moralities of caring that differ qualitatively in significant ways. In particular, the type of morality of caring orientation found among middle-class European American populations is one in which interpersonal responsibilities tend to be approached not only in voluntaristic terms as freely given rather than socially constrained commitments, but also as somewhat delimited in scope in order not to override the agent's personal preferences or to place too many constraints on an individual's freedom of choice. In contrast, whereas there is less emphasis on individual autonomy among Hindu Indians than in the European American case, there tends to be a more robust sense of community within in-group relationships, with interpersonal responsibilities to family and friends regarded as both broader in scope and less contingent on personal preferences.

Moralities of Divinity

Just as role-based responsibilities have tended to be approached exclusively as conventional, rather than moral, concerns within the mainstream psychological theories of moral development, religious or spiritual orientations have tended also to be understood exclusively as matters of convention. Research, however, is increasingly highlighting the importance of religious and spiritual orientations to morality. In an in-depth qualitative study of moral exemplars, Colby and Damon (1992), for example, found that their respondents had deep spiritual commitments on which they drew in grounding their moral behaviors as social activists or humanitarians (see also Walker, Pitts, Hennig, & Matsuba, 1995).

Research conducted in various African cultures documents that religious and spiritual orientations are related integrally to moral judgment through their link with individuals' epistemological presuppositions. Nigerians (Igbo), for example, ground their responses to Kohlbergian moral dilemmas on what they regard as the revealed truth of a superior or divine being rather than on a secular outlook (Okonkwo, 1997). In a related finding, the moral judgments of Algerian respondents to Kohlbergian dilemmas have been found to be based on a belief in God as the creator and supreme authority of the universe (Bouhmama, 1984).

One of the important insights of cultural research in this area is to document that morality may be grounded in spiritually based issues that are orthogonal to concerns with justice or of community (Shweder, Much, Mahapatra, & Park, 1997). Shweder and Much (1987), for example, provide evidence that informants from an orthodox Hindu temple community justify their judgments that it is wrong for the husband to steal in the Heinz dilemma by reference to the negative consequences in suffering and spiritual degradation. Notably, their arguments in such cases frequently make no mention of considerations of justice, individual rights, or welfare. Condemning stealing as a violation of dharma, the Hindu Indian informants regard the act of stealing as resulting in spiritual degradation and automatic suffering, in cycles of future rebirths (for related analysis of Buddhist understandings of dharma and related moral concepts, see Huebner & Garrod, 1991). These types of noncultural presuppositions, it is documented, inform orthodox Hindu Indians' moral reasoning about a wide range of everyday social practices, resulting in moral assessments markedly different from those observed among secular Western populations, with their contrasting epistemological presuppositions. Thus, it is shown, for example, that orthodox Hindu populations tend to consider it a moral violation for a wife to eat with her husband's elder brother or for a widow to eat fish, with their reasoning influenced by such spiritually based epistemological premises and arguments as that "the husband is a moving god and should be treated with comparable respect," and that the "the body is a temple with a spirit dwelling in it. Therefore the sanctity of the temple must be preserved. Therefore impure things must be kept out of and away from the body" (Shweder et al., 1987, pp. 76–77).

Evidence for moralities of divinity that extend beyond justice and welfare have been documented in other cultural populations, including groups from modern Western societies. Haidt and colleagues (Haidt, Koller, & Dias, 1993) demonstrated, for example, that lower class Brazilian children, as well as lower class African American children, tend to treat in moral terms certain disgusting or disrespectful actions, such as eating one's dog, even while viewing actions of this type as harmless. The importance of an orthodox worldview to this type of moral stance has been documented in interviews conducted with both fundamentalist and progressivist U.S. Baptists (Jensen, 1997). Reflecting their assumption that humans relate to each other and to the divine in terms of a hierarchically structured order, fundamentalist Baptist informants consider divorce a sacrilege, with negative repercussions for the afterlife. As one informant reasoned:

> Divorce to me means [that] you slap God in the face. In other words, you bring reproach upon God. Because Jesus Christ and the church are a form of marriage. What we are saying by divorce is that the bride goes away from the husband. Think about what that means. That means that we could lose salvation. [Divorce] breaks down the very essence of our religion and that's why I think divorce is shameful. (Jensen, 1997, p. 342)

Within these spiritual perspectives, the epistemological premises not only differ markedly from the secular premises assumed in the mainstream theories of moral development, but also are integrally linked with moral prescriptions regarding right behavior.

Summary

Cultural meanings and practices have been shown to have a qualitative impact on moral reasoning. Culture has been found to influence the relevance of justice concepts, the weighting of justice issues in solving moral dilemmas, as well as judgments of moral accountability. In regard to interpersonal morality, evidence points to the existence of culturally grounded postconventional moralities of community that differ qualitatively from each other and from the type of individually oriented approach to community embodied in the morality of caring framework of Gilligan. Finally, concerning moralities of divinity, cultural research highlights the role of spiritual epistemological presuppositions in moral judgment, with such presuppositions providing a grounding for moral judgment beyond considerations of either justice or welfare.

Future Directions

In this section, consideration is given to future directions for theory and research in examining cultural influences on moral development. Attention is paid to the need to further understandings of enculturation, as well as to take greater account of cultural influences on the development of self. Consideration is also given to the importance of developing dynamic views of culture that give greater weight to power relations, while at the same time remaining sensitive to cultural variation in views of self and moral outlook.

Cultural Influences on Self and Morality

Greater attention needs to be paid to understanding the processes of enculturation through which culture has an impact on the development of self and morality. Research has shown, for example, that children come to gain an understanding of social rules, in part, through the responses of socialization agents to different types of everyday behavior. Thus, for example, in a serious of studies conducted both in school and free play situations, it has been shown that responses given to moral transgressions typically focus on the hurtful or unjust consequences of the acts, whereas responses given to transgressions of school regulations or of other general conventions typically focus on rules or normative expectations (L. Nucci, 1982; L. P. Nucci & Nucci, 1982; L. P. Nucci & Turiel, 1978; L. Nucci & Weber, 1995). Sociolinguistic research likewise documents that transgressions of different types of social rules tend to be excused in contrasting ways, for example, with moral breaches eliciting talk concerning what was done and conventions eliciting references to conditions and rule formulations (Much & Shweder, 1978).

Whereas some research of this type has been undertaken in non-Western cultural settings (e.g., Edward, 1987), there remains a need for more research to be conducted outside the middle-class European-American settings that, to date, have received most attention. In these efforts, it is important to tap a wider range of issues, including ones that may be culturally specific, such as the central cultural concepts of filial piety and of dharma. Challenges also exist in understanding the enculturation of nonrational aspects of cultural meanings and practices, the validity of which is relatively impervious to disproof by empirical evidence, yet which may have a central impact on moral reasoning, such as concepts of karma or of an afterlife.

In terms of developing more dynamic understanding of enculturation, greater attention needs to be paid to the varied cultural tools and everyday practices that serve to embody and sustain cultural meanings. Thus, for example, it is important to examine ways in which cultural messages are communicated in media, through authorities in the culture, as well as in everyday social routines, such as sleeping arrangements (e.g., Harkness, Super, & Keefer, 1992; Shweder, Jensen, & Goldstein, 1995). The complexity and subtlety of cultural messages also must be accorded greater consideration, with recognition given that certain practices may promote a particular cultural message explicitly, while embodying a contradictory cultural message on an implicit level.

More generally, it is critical to extend the examination of work on morality to issues of culture and the development of self. For example, recent research shows that, for Puerto Rican mothers, the developmental goals of having a child who is loving and who shows proper respect are more salient than are the goals, emphasized among middle-class European American mothers, of having a child who is able to balance autonomy with relatedness (Harwood, Miller, & Irizarry, 1995). In other examples, it has been found that toughening up a child to confront what is perceived to be a relatively harsh world is stressed in the socialization practices of various lower class European American communities (Kusserow, 1999), whereas developing a child with an adjustable nature and sense of social responsibility are emphasized in various Asian and African cultural settings (Harkness & Super, 1996; Miller & Bersoff, 1995). A challenge exists in linking these alternative normative developmental end points to lay conceptions of morally exemplary behavior and of what is meant by morality itself.

It is also important to bring a cultural perspective to bear in exploring the various ways in which personhood and harm are defined. For example, research has demonstrated that American and Brazilian children treat issues of harming the environment in moral terms (Kahn, 1996, 1998, 1999) These types of responses are justified by reference both to anthropocentric concerns, which focus on protecting human welfare, and to biocentric concerns, which treat nature as having intrinsic values, rights, or a teleology. Work of this type valuably can be extended through consideration of the processes of enculturation that promote moral outlooks on environmentalism, such as changing cultural awareness and new laws, as well as by exploring the development of moral conceptions of the natural order in cultural communities that emphasize orthodox religious outlooks.

Culture, Context, and Power

In future work on culture and moral development, effort should also be made to understand cultures in more process-oriented ways that relate to indigenous conceptual viewpoints and that recognize the heterogeneous nature of cultural understandings (Greenfield, 1997; Miller, 1997b). In this regard, greater attention needs to be given to variation that obtains both between and within cultural communities. It must be recognized that cultures exist not only as shared representations, but also include behavioral and material aspects such as customs, everyday routines, patterns of discourse, and artifacts.

While highlighting the need to go beyond stereotypical conceptions of culture, however, it is equally important to avoid stances that assume that there is so little homogeneity to cultural meanings and practices that culture adds no additional force to explanation once contextual variation is taken into account. Adopting the last position, for example, theorists from the distinct domain perspective have concluded that cultural influences can be treated as fundamentally the same as contextual influences (Turiel, 1998a; Wainryb & Turiel, 1995). They also have interpreted findings that persons from collectivist cultures are concerned with issues of self and autonomy, and that persons from individualistic cultures are concerned with social role obligations as evidence against the idea that qualitative differences exist in cultural views of self and associated psychological processes. Challenging such conclusions, the present argument stresses the importance of recognizing that cultural and contextual considerations are interdependent in explanation. Cultural effects, it must be recognized, are always contextually dependent, just as contextual influences depend on the culturally based meanings accorded to contexts

(Miller, 1997a). The present considerations then also imply that it is misguided to treat a concern with social role obligations as evidence of collectivism or a concern with issues of self and autonomy as evidence of individualism. Rather, as illustrated in the research reviewed in this chapter, concerns that may be considered universal at a relatively abstract level are frequently instantiated in culturally variable forms. Thus, it was seen, for example, that all cultures are concerned with issues of community while embodying culturally variable stances toward communitarian moralities, just as all cultures are concerned with personal choice while differing in the weight that it is given in everyday moral judgment.

An additional important direction for future research is to give greater weight to power relations. To date, studies of moral development have been conducted primarily with elite populations. Little attention has been directed to examining the perspectives of women or of minority subgroups, who have limited power or who may be the targets of racism or of other oppressive social policies. However, as recognized in recent work by social domain theorists (e.g., Turiel, 1998a, 1998b), as well in poststructuralist anthropological viewpoints (e.g., Abu-Lughod, 1993; Clifford, 1998), cultural practices frequently constitute instruments of domination, with groups in subordinate positions maintaining a perspective on social practices that contrasts with that of privileged groups. For example, in this regard, research has documented that Druze women in Israel are more prone to consider the power relationships between males and females in the family as morally unfair than are Druze men (Turiel & Wainryb, 1998; Wainryb & Turiel, 1994). Valuably, in future work in this tradition, it will be important to consider a broader range of issues and cultural subgroups, as well as to trace the developmental emergence of children's awareness of issues of social injustice within more diverse cultural settings.

Another challenge for work on the present concerns is to integrate attention to issues of power more fully with cultural views of the self. A concern exists that at times the categories brought to bear in examining power relations fail to take into account local cultural outlooks. Thus, for example, although a concern with individual rights exists universally, such a construct, in certain cases, may be less relevant to family relations in certain cultural communities than is the case among European

Americans. In many Asian and African cultural settings, for example, family relations tend to be conceptualized primarily as hierarchically structured welfare units in which members are mutually interdependent and not primarily as associations of equal and separate individuals with competing claims. Both in the phrasing of research questions and in interpretation of the meaning of findings, studies that assess power dynamics in the former cultural communities then may need to be attentive to respects in which individuals conceptualize family interaction in terms of patron/client relationships rather than in terms of the freedoms and rights of discrete individuals.

Whereas it is important to give greater attention in future research to respects in which individuals in all cultures may challenge the social order, this issue needs to be approached in ways that take into account the motivational force of existing cultural systems. It must be recognized that dissent is frequently directed at relatively superficial or overt aspects of cultural practices, with more fundamental cultural commitments remaining unchallenged. This type of stance was uncovered, for example, in a recent ethnographic study of everyday socialization practices within an orthodox Hindu Brahmin family (Much, 1997). Against the wishes of both his parents and the cultural beliefs of his community, the adolescent son in the family temporarily stopped wearing his Sacred Thread. The son's breach of his duty as a Brahmin to wear this holy symbol reflected his rebellion against the orthodox Hindu view of such behavior as morally required. It expressed his conviction that wearing the Sacred Thread, in fact, represents only an unimportant matter of social convention that identifies him to others as a member of the Brahmin caste. Although questioning the authority of both his parents and of his community in this way, the son, however, remained accepting of deeper commitments of his culture. His challenge to the social order was conducted within the frame of certain orthodox Hindu Indian beliefs that he presupposed as given and never called into question—such as the fundamental principles of hierarchy and of the importance of Brahmin identity.

Summary

In sum, future work on culture and moral development needs to build on the insights of recent developments in culture theory. There is a need to develop more dynamic understandings of the nature of enculturation as well as to examine new questions related to cultural variation in the self. Cultural systems also must be approached in ways that are sensitive to indigenous outlooks and to the affective force of cultural institutions and symbols, while research continues to focus on bringing a concern with power relations into studies of moral development.

Conclusion

As is the case with cultural work in other areas of psychology, cultural research on moral development remains in a peripheral position in the field, with many mainstream investigators downplaying its importance. Still, there are signs of increasing interchange across research traditions as, moving into a post-Piagetian and post-Kohlbergian phase of inquiry, investigations of morality, self, and culture are proceeding in ways that are ecologically sensitive and theoretically rich. Overcoming the parochialism of some of the early theoretical models, research in this area is uncovering qualitative cultural variation in moral outlooks that speak to common concerns with justice, community, and spiritual issues. Investigators are also working to formulate approaches to culture that are dynamic and nuanced and that attend to issues of power, affect, and cultural practices. Far from leading either to an extreme relativism or to a view of individuals as merely passively conforming to existing understandings, research on culture and moral development is pointing the way for understanding moral outlooks as involving individuals acting in ways that are simultaneously highly agentic even as they also are influenced by cultural meanings and practices.

References

Abu-Lughod, L. (1993). *Writing women's worlds: Bedouin stories.* Berkeley: University of California Press.

Ainsworth, M. D. (1978). *Patterns of attachment: A psychological study of the strange situation.* Hillsdale, NJ: Erlbaum.

Aronfreed, J. M. (1968). *Conduct and conscience: The socialization of internalized control over behavior.* New York: Academic Press.

Bersoff, D. M., & Miller, J. G. (1993). Culture, context, and the development of moral accountability judgments. *Developmental Psychology,* *29*(4), 664–676.

Bouhmama, D. (1984). Assessment of Kohlberg's stages of moral development in two cultures. *Journal of Moral Education, 13,* 124–132.

Bowlby, J. (1969–1980). *Attachment and loss.* New York: Basic Books.

Brown, L. M., Tappan, M. B., Gilligan, C., Miller, B. A., & Argyris, D. E. (1989). Reading for self and moral voice: A method for interpreting narratives of real-life moral conflict and choice. In M. J. Packer & R. B. Addison (Eds.), *Entering the circle: Hermeneutic investigation in psychology* (pp. 141–164). Albany: State University of New York Press.

Carter, R. E. (1980). What is Lawrence Kohlberg doing? *Journal of Moral Education, 9*(2), 88–102.

Chodorow, N. (1978). *The reproduction of mothering: Psychoanalysis and the sociology of gender.* Berkeley: University of California Press.

Clifford, J. (1988). *The predicament of culture: Twentieth-century ethnography, literature, and art.* Cambridge: Harvard University Press.

Colby, A., & Damon, W. (1992). *Some do care: Contemporary lives of moral commitment.* New York: Free Press.

Colby, A., & Kohlberg, L. (1987). *The measurement of moral judgment: Vol. 1. Theoretical foundations and research validation. Vol. 2. Standard issue scoring manual.* New York: Cambridge University Press.

Dien, D. S.-F. (1982). A Chinese perspective on Kohlberg's theory of moral development. *Developmental Review, 2,* 331–341.

Eckensberger, L. H., & Zimba, R. F. (1997). The development of moral judgment. In J. W. Berry, P. R. Dasen, & T. S. Saraswathi (Eds.), *Handbook of cross-cultural psychology, Vol. 2: Basic processes and human development* (2nd ed., pp. 299–338) *Handbook of cross-cultural psychology.* Boston: Allyn & Bacon.

Edwards, C. P. (1975). Societal complexity and moral development: A Kenyan study. *Ethos, 3*(4), 505–527.

Edwards, C. P. (1978). Social experience and moral judgment in East African young adults. *Journal of Genetic Psychology, 133*(1), 19–29.

Edwards, C. P. (1987). Culture and the construction of moral values: A comparative ethnography of moral encounters in two cultural settings. In J. Kagan & S. Lamb (Eds.), *The emergence of morality in young children* (pp. 123–151). Chicago: University of Chicago Press.

Edwards, C. P. (1994). Cross-cultural research on Kohlberg's stages: The basis for consensus. In W. Puka (Ed.), *Moral development. A compendium. Vol. 5. New research in moral development* (pp. 373–384). New York: Garland.

Freud, S. (1930). *Civilization and its discontents.* London: Hogarth Press.

Gilligan, C. (1977). In a different voice: Women's conceptions of self and of morality. *Harvard Educational Review, 47*(4), 481–517.

Gilligan, C. (1982). *In a different voice: Psychological theory and women's development.* Cambridge, MA: Harvard University Press.

Gilligan, C., & Wiggins, G. (1987). The origins of morality in early childhood relationships. In J. Kagan & S. Lamb (Eds.), *The emergence of morality in young children* (pp. 277–305). Chicago: University of Chicago Press.

Gorsuch, R. L., & Barnes, M. L. (1973). Stages of ethical reasoning and moral norms of Carib youths. *Journal of Cross-Cultural Psychology, 4,* 283–301.

Greenfield, P. M. (1997). Culture as process: Empirical methods for cultural psychology. In J. W. Berry, Y. H. Poortinga, & J. Pandey (Eds.), *Handbook of cross-cultural psychology: Vol. 1. Theory and method* (2nd ed., pp. 301–346). Boston: Allyn & Bacon.

Haidt, J., Koller, S. H., & Dias, M. G. (1993). Affect, culture, and morality, or is it wrong to eat your dog? *Journal of Personality and Social Psychology, 65*(4), 613–628.

Harkness, S., Edwards, C. P., & Super, C. M. (1981). Social roles and moral reasoning: A case study in a rural African community. *Developmental Psychology, 17*(5), 595–603.

Harkness, S., & Super, C. M. (1996). *Parents' cultural belief systems: Their origins, expressions, and consequences.* New York: Guilford Press.

Harkness, S., Super, C., & Keefer, C. (1992). Learning to be an American parent: How cultural models gain directive force. In R. D'Andrade & C. Strauss (Eds.), *Human motives and cultural models* (pp. 163–178). Cambridge, England: Cambridge University Press.

Harwood, R. L., Miller, J. G., & Irizarry, N. L. (1995). *Culture and attachment: Perceptions of the child in context.* New York: Guilford Press.

Huebner, A., & Garrod, A. (1991). Moral reasoning in a Karmic world. *Human Development, 34,* 341–352.

Huebner, A. M., & Garrod, A. C. (1993). Moral reasoning among Tibetan Monks: A study of Buddhist adolescents and young adults in Nepal. *Journal of Cross-Cultural Psychology, 24*(2), 167–185.

Jensen, L. A. (1997). Different worldviews, different morals: America's culture war divide. *Human Development, 40*(6), 325–344.

Kahn, P. (1996). Environmental views and values of children in an inner city Black community. *Child Development, 66*(5), 1403–1417.

Kahn, P. (1998). Children's moral and ecological reasoning about the Prince William Sound oil spill. *Developmental Psychology, 33*(6), 1091–1096.

Kahn, P. (1999). *The human relationship with nature: Development and culture.* Cambridge: MIT Press.

Keller, M., Edelstein, W., Fang, F.-X., & Fang, G. (1998). Reasoning about responsibilities and obligations in close relationships: A comparison across two cultures. *Developmental Psychology, 34*(4), 731–741.

Kohlberg, L. (1958). *The development of modes of moral thinking and choice in the years 10 to 16.* Unpublished doctoral dissertation, University of Chicago.

Kohlberg, L. (1969). Stage and sequence: The cognitive-developmental approach to socialization. In D. A. Goslin (Ed.), *Handbook of Socialization Theory* (pp. 347–380.). Chicago: Rand McNally.

Kohlberg, L. (1971). From is to ought: How to commit the naturalistic fallacy and get away with it in the study of moral development. In T. Mischel (Ed.), *Cognitive development and epistemology* (pp. 151–236). New York: Academic.

Kohlberg, L. (1981). *The philosophy of moral development: Moral stages and the idea of justice.* (Vol. 1). New York: Harper & Row.

Kohlberg, L. (1984). *The psychology of moral development: The nature and validity of moral stages (Essays on Moral Development, Vol. II).* San Francisco: Harper & Row.

Kohlberg, L., Levine, C., & Hewer, A. (1994). Moral stages: A current formulation and a response to critics: 3. Synopses of criticisms and a reply; 4. Summary and conclusion, In W. Puka (Ed.), *Moral development. A compendium. Vol. 5. New research in moral development* (pp. 126–188). New York: Garland.

Kuhn, D., & Siegler, R. S. (Eds.). (1998). *Handbook of child psychology: Cognition, perception, and language* (Vol. 2). New York: Wiley.

Kusserow, A. S. (1999). De-homogenizing American individualism: Socializing hard and soft individualism in Manhattan and Queens. *Ethos, 27*(2), 210–234.

Ma, H. K. (1988). The Chinese perspective on moral judgment development. *International Journal of Psychology, 23,* 201–227.

Ma, H. K. (1989). Moral orientation and moral judgment in adolescents in Hong Kong, Mainland China, and England. *Journal of Cross-Cultural Psychology, 20,* 152–177.

Ma, H. K. (1992). The moral judgment development of the Chinese people: A theoretical model. *Philosophica, 49,* 55–82.

Ma, H. K. (1997). The affective and cognitive aspects of moral development: A Chinese perspective. In H. Kao & D. Sinha (Eds.), *Asian perspectives on psychology* (pp. 93–109). Thousand Oaks, CA: Sage.

Miller, J. G. (1994). Cultural diversity in the morality of caring: Individually oriented versus duty-based interpersonal moral codes. *Cross-Cultural Research, 28*(1), 3–39.

Miller, J. G. (1997a). Agency and context in cultural psychology: Implications for moral theory. In H. Saltzstein (Ed.), *New directions for child development. No. 76. Culture as a context for moral development: New perspectives on the particular and the universal* (pp. 69–85).). San Francisco: Jossey-Bass.

Miller, J. G. (1997b). Theoretical issues in cultural psychology, In J. W. Berry, Y. H. Poortinga, & J. Pandey (Eds.), *Handbook of cross-cultural psychology: Vol. 1. Theory and method* (2nd ed., pp. 85–128). Boston: Allyn & Bacon.

Miller, J. G., & Bersoff, D. M. (1992). Culture and moral judgment: How are conflicts between justice and interpersonal responsibilities resolved? *Journal of Personality and Social Psychology, 62*(4), 541–554.

Miller, J. G., & Bersoff, D. M. (1995). Development in the context of everyday family relationships: Culture, interpersonal morality, and adaptation. In M. Killen & D. Hart (Eds.), *Cambridge Studies in Social and Emotional Development. Morality in everyday life: Developmental perspectives* (pp. 259–282). New York: Cambridge University Press.

Miller, J. G., & Bersoff, D. M. (1998). The role of liking in perceptions of the moral responsibility to help: A cultural perspective. *Journal of Experimental Social Psychology, 34*(5), 443–469.

Miller, J. G., & Luthar, S. (1989). Issues of interpersonal responsibility and accountability: A comparison of Indians' and Americans' moral judgments. *Social Cognition, 3,* 237–261.

Much, N. C. (1997). A semiotic view of socialization, lifespan development and cultural psychology: With vignettes for the moral culture of traditional Hindu households. *Psychology and Developing Societies, 9*(1), 65–106.

Much, N. C., & Shweder, R. A. (1978). Speaking of rules: The analysis of culture in breach. *New Directions for Child Development, 2,* 19–39.

Niemczynski, A., Czyzowska, D., Pourkos, M., & Mirski, A. (1988). The Cracow study with Kohlberg's moral judgment interview: Data pertaining to the assumption of cross-cultural validity. *Polish Psychological Bulletin, 19*(1), 43–53.

Nucci, L. (1981). Conceptions of personal issues: A domain distinct from moral or societal concepts. *Child Development, 52*(1), 114–121.

Nucci, L. (1982). Children's responses to moral and social conventional transgressions in free-play

settings. *Child Development, 53*(5), 1337–
1342.

Nucci, L., & Lee, J. (1993). Morality and personal
autonomy. In G. Noam & T. E. Wren (Eds.),
*Studies in contemporary German social
thought. The moral self* (pp. 123–148).
Cambridge: MIT Press.

Nucci, L., & Weber, E. K. (1995). Social interactions
in the home and the development of young
children's conceptions of the personal. *Child
Development, 66*(5), 1438–1452.

Nucci, L. P., & Nucci, M. S. (1982). Children's social interactions in the context of moral and
conventional transgressions. *Child Development, 53*(2), 403–412.

Nucci, L. P., & Turiel, E. (1978). Social interactions
and the development of social concepts in preschool children. *Child Development, 49*(2),
400–407.

Okonkwo, R. (1997). Moral development and culture in Kohlberg's theory: A Nigerian (Igbo) evidence. *IFE Psychologia: An International Journal, 5*(2), 117–128.

Piaget, J. (1932). *The moral judgment of the child.*
London: Routledge & Kegan Paul.

Rawls, J. (1971). *A theory of justice.* Cambridge:
Harvard University Press.

Rest, J. (1979). *Development in judging moral issues.* Minneapolis: University of Minnesota
Press.

Rest, J. (1986). *Moral development : advances in research and theory.* New York: Praeger.

Rest, J., Narvaez, D., Bebeau, M. J., & Thoma, S. J.
(1999). *Postconventional moral thinking: A
neo-Kohlbergian approach.* Mahwah, NJ:
Erlbaum.

Shweder, R. A. (1984). Anthropology's romantic rebellion against the enlightenment, or there's
more to thinking than reason and evidence. In
R. A. Shweder & R. A. LeVine (Eds.), *Culture
theory: Essays on mind, self, and emotion* (pp.
27–66). Cambridge: Cambridge University
Press.

Shweder, R. A., Jensen, L. A., & Goldstein, W. M.
(1995). Who sleeps by whom revisited: A
method for extracting the moral goods implicit in practice. *Cultural practices as contexts for development* (pp. 21–39 *New Directions for Child Development*, No. 67). San
Francisco: Jossey-Bass.

Shweder, R. A., Mahapatra, M., & Miller, J. (1987).
Culture and moral development. In J. Kagan &
S. Lamb (Eds.), *The emergence of morality in
young children* (pp. 1–90). Chicago: University of Chicago Press.

Shweder, R. A., & Much, N. C. (1987). Determinants of meaning: Discourse and moral socialization. In W. M. Kurtines & J. L. Gewirtz

(Eds.), *Moral development through social interaction* (pp. 197–244). New York: Wiley.

Shweder, R. A., Much, N. C., Mahapatra, M., &
Park, L. (1997). The "big three" of morality
(autonomy, community, divinity) and the "big
three" explanations of suffering. In A. M.
Brandt & P. Rozin (Eds.), *Morality and health*
(pp. 119–169). New York: Routledge.

Simpson, E. L. (1974). Moral development research: A case study of scientific cultural bias.
Human Development, 17(2), 81–106.

Smetana, J. G. (1981). Preschool children's conceptions of moral and social rules. *Child Development, 52*(4), 1333–1336.

Smetana, J. G. (1983). Social-cognitive development: Domain distinctions and coordinations.
Developmental Review, 3(2), 131–147.

Smetana, J. G., & Braeges, J. L. (1990). The development of toddler's moral and conventional judgments. *Merrill-Palmer Quarterly, 36*(3), 329–
346.

Snarey, J., & Keljo, K. (1991). In a Gemeinschaft
voice: The cross-cultural expansion of moral
development theory. In W. M. Kurtines & J. L.
Gewirtz (Eds.), *Handbook of moral behavior
and development: Vol. 1. Theory. Vol. 2. Research. Vol. 3. Application* (pp. 395–424).
Hillsdale, NJ: Erlbaum.

Snarey, J. R. (1985). Cross-cultural universality of
social-moral development: A critical review of
Kohlbergian research. *Psychological Bulletin,
97*(2), 202–232.

Song, M.-J., Smetana, J. G., & Kim, S. Y. (1994). Korean children's conceptions of moral and conventional transgressions. In W. Puka (Ed.),
*Moral development. A compendium. Vol. 5.
New research in moral development* (pp. 309–
314). New York: Garland.

Thomas, S. J. (1986). Estimating gender differences
in the comprehension and preference of moral
issues. *Developmental Review, 6*, 165–180.

Tietjen, A. M., & Walker, L. J. (1985). Moral reasoning and leadership among men in a Papua
New Guinea society. *Developmental Psychology, 21*(6), 982–992.

Turiel, E. (1980). Distinct conceptual and developmental domains: Social convention and morality. In H. E. Howe & C. B. Keasey (Eds.),
*Nebraska Symposium on Motivation, 1977: So-
cial cognitive development* (Vol. 25, pp. 77–
116). Lincoln: University of Nebraska Press.

Turiel, E. (1983). *The development of social knowledge: Morality and convention.* Cambridge:
Cambridge University Press.

Turiel, E. (1998a). The development of morality. In
N. Eisenberg (Ed.), *Handbook of child psychology: Social, emotional, and personality development* (5th ed., Vol. 3, pp. 863–932). New
York: Wiley.

Turiel, E. (1998b). Notes from the underground: Culture, conflict, and subversion. In J. Langer & M. Killen (Eds.), *The Jean Piaget symposium series. Piaget, evolution, and development* (pp. 271–296). Mahwah, NJ: Erlbaum.

Turiel, E., & Wainryb, C. (1998). Concepts of freedoms and rights in a traditional, hierarchically organized society. *British Journal of Developmental Psychology, 16*(3), 375–395.

Vasudev, J. (1994). Ahimsa, justice, and the unity of life: Postconventional morality from an Indian perspective. In M. E. Miller & S. R. Cook-Greuter (Eds.), *Transcendence and mature thought in adulthood: The further reaches of adult development* (pp. 237–255). Lanham, MD: Rowman & Littlefield.

Vasudev, J., & Hummel, R. C. (1987). Moral stage sequence and principled reasoning in an Indian sample. *Human Development, 30*(2), 105–118.

Wainryb, C. (1991). Understanding differences in moral judgments: The role of informational assumptions. *Child Development, 62*(4), 840–851.

Wainryb, C., & Turiel, E. (1994). Dominance, subordination, and concepts of personal entitlements in cultural contexts. *Child Development, 65*(6), 1701–1722.

Wainryb, C., & Turiel, E. (1995). Diversity in social development: Between or within cultures? In M. Killen & D. Hart (Eds.), *Cambridge studies in social and emotional development. Morality in everyday life: Developmental perspectives* (pp. 283–313). New York: Cambridge University Press.

Walker, L. J. (1984). Sex differences in the development of moral reasoning: A critical review. *Child Development, 55*(3), 677–691.

Walker, L. J. (1991). Sex differences in moral reasoning. In W. M. Kurtines & J. L. Gewirtz (Eds.), *Handbook of moral behavior and development* (pp. 333–364). Hillsdale, NJ: Erlbaum.

Walker, L. J., Pitts, R. C., Hennig, K. H., & Matsuba, M. K. (1995). Reasoning about morality and real-life moral problems. In M. Killen & D. Hart (Eds.), *Cambridge studies in social and emotional development. Morality in everyday life: Developmental perspectives* (pp. 371–407). New York: Cambridge University Press.

10

Culture and Emotion

DAVID MATSUMOTO

Emotions are a central part of our lives and, as such, have been the focus of much cross-cultural research in psychology. Indeed, the work documenting the universal basis of a set of facial expressions of emotion, reviewed in this chapter, arguably serves as one of the most influential findings in the history of cross-cultural psychology to date. Emotions give key clues to understanding cognition, motivation, and people in general and in that role are a rich and diverse area of cross-cultural inquiry.

In this chapter, Matsumoto provides an overview of the cross-cultural work conducted in this area. Beginning with a description of the study of emotion and culture in historical perspective, he discusses especially the relevance and importance of this line of work for contemporary psychology. Indeed, this line is noteworthy as almost all contemporary research on emotion in mainstream psychology has its roots in the cross-cultural work documenting expression universality.

Matsumoto then presents a brief overview of cross-cultural work on various facets of emotion, including expression, antecedents, appraisal, subjective experience, emotion concepts, and its physiological correlates. This review amply demonstrates that all aspects of emotion were well studied across cultures over the past two decades and have produced a plethora of new findings.

The bulk of the review presented in this chapter focuses on work related to the recognition and judgment of emotion across cultures, indeed, because it is the most well-studied area of culture and emotion. Matsumoto presents in detail much of the cultural similarities and differences reported in the cross-cultural literature on this aspect of emotions. In particular, he highlights the way in which the most recent studies of cultural differences in judgments (of intensity) have attempted not only to document the existence of cultural differences, but also to test multiple hypotheses about why those differences occur; he does this through the incorporation of the assessment of cultural dimensions of variability in the research. These methodological changes agree with the evolution of theory and method in cross-cultural psychology discussed in the introduction to this book, and throughout this volume, as studies begin to replace the global, abstract concept of culture with well-defined, measurable constructs that can be tested in terms of their contribution to cultural differences.

The chapter ends with a detailed discussion of four areas of possible future research on culture and emotion. A strong element of the message in this section is one of integration—of the need to incorporate issues of context in research and theory in culture and emotion and of the need to link judgments of emotion with other psychological processes. As Matsumoto suggests, many areas of study in psychology are fragmented from other areas; consequently, we know relatively less about how judgments on emotion function in concert with other psychological processes within a total, integrated, synthesized, living person than we do about judgments on emotion obtained in a vacuum in an artificial laboratory setting. While laboratory experiments of course are valuable, we need to put Humpty Dumpty back together again. As cross-cultural research in this and other areas continues to evolve and integrate other topics, methods, and disciplines, it promises to play a major role in putting those pieces of life that have been fragmented by academia back together again.

Emotions are arguably some of the most important aspects of our lives, and psychologists, philosophers, and social scientists for many years have been concerned with them. Emotions give meaning to life, serve as important motivators for our behaviors, and color our thoughts and cognitions. They are, indeed, the basic psychological fuel for growth, development, and action.

In this chapter, I review some of the major cross-cultural research that has been conducted on emotion. I begin with an overview of the study of emotion and culture in a historical perspective and discuss the impact of this research on contemporary psychology. Then, I present a very brief review of a wide range of cross-cultural studies on emotion, spanning emotional expression, perception, experience, antecedents, appraisal, physiology, and the concepts and definitions of emotion. I then focus on one area of study—cross-cultural research on emotion judgments—and provide a much more in-depth review of this area, highlighting what is known to date. Using this as a platform, I then provide four suggestions for future research in this area before concluding the chapter. My goal is not only to provide the reader with a detailed review of this area of psychology, but also to encourage scientists to get out of their boxes when thinking about this, and other, areas of research.

Emotion and Culture in Historical Perspective: Their Impact on Contemporary Psychology

Emotion and culture have been objects of study and fascination by not only contemporary psychologists in recent history, but also by philosophers and other thinkers for centuries. Indeed, emotions played a large role in the thinking and writing of Aristotle and Socrates (Russell, 1994) and were also well represented in the third century Sanskrit text Rasadhyaya (Shweder & Haidt, 2000). Emotion was also central to many thinkers who were influential to modern psychology, such as Freud, Darwin, Erikson, Piaget, Bowlby, and many others.

Most modern day studies of emotion and culture, however, find their roots in the work of Darwin. One reason for this was that Darwin inspired work on the expression of emotion and, as such, offered scientists a platform with which to measure emotions objectively, going beyond basic self-report, which psychologists tend to consider unreliable. Darwin's thesis, summarized in his work, *The Expression of Emotion in Man and Animals* (Darwin, 1872/1998), suggested that emotions and their expressions have evolved across species and are evolutionarily adaptive, biologically innate, and universal across all human and even nonhuman primates. According to Darwin, all humans, regardless of race or culture, possess the ability to express emotions in exactly the same ways, primarily through their faces.

Darwin's work, while influential and provocative, was not without criticism. One main issue raised about his ideas, for example, was the lack of hard evidence that supported his claims. Indeed, many of Darwin's original ideas were supported only through his own observations and descriptions of emotional expression in humans and other animals. Albeit done in painstaking detail, such descriptions would not be accepted as scientific proof for his universality thesis.

Between the time of Darwin's original writing and the 1960s, a handful of scientists attempted to address this gap in our knowledge by conducting more formalized and systematic research on the issue. In fact, only a total of seven studies appeared in the literature during this time. These studies, however, were methodologically flawed in a number of ways, so that unequivocal data speaking to the issue of the possible universality of emotional expression did not emerge (reviewed in Ekman, Friesen, & Ellsworth, 1972).

It was not until the mid-1960s when psychologist Sylvan Tomkins, a pioneer in modern studies of human emotion, joined forces independently with Ekman and Izard to conduct what has become known today as the *universality studies*. These researchers conducted studies in many cultures and obtained judgments of faces thought to express emotions panculturally (see Ekman, 1973, and C. Izard, 1971, for reviews). The findings from these studies demonstrated the existence of six universal expressions—anger, disgust, fear, happiness, sadness, and surprise—as judges all around the world agreed on the emotion that was portrayed in the faces.

Yet, the judgment studies in literate cultures conducted by Ekman and Izard were not the only evidence that came to bear on the question of emotion universality. Ekman and his colleague Friesen also conducted studies that demonstrated that judgments of members of preliterate cultures were also consistent with the notion of universality, as were judgments of expressions posed by members of preliterate cultures (see Ekman, 1973, for a review). They also showed that the expressions that spontaneously occurred in reaction to emotion-eliciting films were universal (Ekman, 1972). Moreover, other scientists have shown that the same expressions occur in nonhuman primates and congenitally blind individuals (Charlesworth & Kreutzer, 1973; Ekman, 1973) and correspond to similarities in emotion taxonomies in different languages around the world (Romney, Boyd, Moore, Batchelder, & Brazill, 1996; Romney, Moore, & Rusch, 1997). And, since the original universality studies in the late 1960s, many studies have replicated the universal recognition of these expressions (see below and reviews in Ekman, 1982). Thus, the universal basis for emotional expression is no longer debated in contemporary psychology and is considered a pancultural aspect of psychological functioning.

We also know, however, that people modify their expressions on the basis of *cultural display rules* (Ekman, 1972; Ekman & Friesen, 1969;

Friesen, 1972). These are culturally prescribed rules, learned early in life, that dictate the management and modification of the universal expressions, depending on social circumstance. The existence of these display rules was demonstrated empirically in Ekman and Friesen's (Ekman, 1972) study of American and Japanese participants viewing stressful films alone and in the presence of an experimenter. When alone, they displayed the same expressions of disgust, anger, fear, and sadness. When with the experimenter, however, there were dramatic differences. While the Americans tended to continue to show their negative feelings, many Japanese invariably smiled to conceal their negative feelings. Ekman and Friesen reckoned that cultural display rules in the Japanese culture were operating that prevented the free expression of negative emotions in the presence of another person. Today, the existence of both universality and cultural display rules is well accepted in mainstream psychology (see also Fridlund's 1997 view of display rules).

The discovery of the universal basis for emotional expression has had an enormous impact on contemporary psychology as expressions provided an objective and reliable signal of emotion. Using universality as a platform, both Ekman and Izard developed methods of measuring facial behaviors validly and reliably. In particular, Ekman and Friesen's (1978) Facial Action Coding System (FACS) is widely recognized as the most comprehensive tool to analyze facial movements. It involves the identification of the appearance changes associated with over 40 separate and functionally independent anatomical units that can move in the face at any one time. Using it, researchers can code the muscles involved in any facial expression, along with their timing characteristics (onset, apex, offset), intensity, and laterality.

The development of techniques like FACS, along with the theoretical contributions of universal emotions, has led to a plethora of new research, theories, and applications in psychology in the past 30 years. Notions concerning the universality of emotion and facial measurement techniques have made enormous contributions to studies in all areas of psychology, particularly social, personality, and developmental psychology. Studies using facial expressions of emotion as markers have addressed decades-old questions concerning the role and function of physiology in emotion; we now know that each of the universal emotions is associated with a distinct and unique physiological pattern in response (Ekman, Levenson, & Friesen, 1983). Studies involving faces and emotions have also made substantial contributions to a number of areas of psychology, with applications in clinical, forensic, industrial, and organizational psychology. An increasing number of universities are offering programs that specialize in the study of emotion, and funding sources are increasing to provide specialized training to pre- and postdoctoral candidates to develop further research in the area. All of this has been made possible through the contributions of the original cross-cultural research on emotional expressions.

The Breadth of Cross-Cultural Research on Emotion

The original universality studies not only had a considerable impact on mainstream, contemporary psychology, but also served as an important platform for continued work investigating the relation between culture and emotion. As mentioned above, for example, many studies since Ekman and Izard's original research have tested the recognition of emotion in facial expressions across cultures, replicating the universality findings. As one can see from the listing and summary of studies investigating emotion recognition across cultures, there is considerable evidence for the universality of the set of six emotional expressions originally reported by Ekman and Izard (see Table 10.1).

But, other aspects of emotion have also received considerable attention. For instance, a number of recent cross-cultural studies have examined cultural differences in emotional expression and cultural display rules. Waxer (1985), for example, examined American and Canadian cultural differences in spontaneous emotional expressions of participants in television game shows and found that Americans tended to be judged as more expressive than the Canadians despite no differences in actual behaviors. Matsumoto and colleagues examined cultural display rule differences between Japan and the United States (Matsumoto, 1990) and among the United States, Poland, and Hungary (Biehl, Matsumoto, & Kasri, in press), suggesting that cultural display rules differ systematically according to individualistic versus collectivistic differences in the meaning of relationships of the self with the in-group and the self with the out-group. Matsumoto (1993) also tested differences in cultural display rules among four ethnic groups within the United States.

More recent research has gone beyond the mere documentation of cultural differences to test the degree to which cultural dimensions such as individualism and collectivism (IC) account for differences among the United States, Japan, Korea, and Russia in display rules (Matsumoto, Takeuchi, Andayani, Kouznetsova, & Krupp, 1998); in this study, the IC dimension accounted for about 30% of the between-country variation in display rules. Other research has also documented cross-cultural differences in expression among five European countries (Edelmann et al., 1987).

A number of studies of the past decade have also examined the antecedents of emotions across cultures. Led mainly by a large-scale study conducted by Scherer and colleagues, over 3,000 participants in 37 countries described a situation or event in which they experienced each of the universal emotions (Scherer & Wallbott, 1994; Scherer, Wallbott, & Summerfield, 1983). Trained raters coded the situations described by participants into general categories such as good news and bad news, temporary and permanent separation, success or failure in achievement situations, and the like. No culture-specific antecedent category was necessary to code the data, indicating that all categories of events generally occurred in all cultures to produce each of the emotions studied. These studies and others (e.g., Boucher & Brandt, 1981; Brandt & Boucher, 1985; Buunk & Hupka, 1987; Galati & Sciaky, 1995; R. I. Levy, 1973) have reported evidence of considerable cross-cultural similarity in emotion antecedents. To be sure, cross-cultural differences in the differential usage of emotion antecedent categories have also been reported (Scherer, Matsumoto, Wallbott, & Kudoh, 1988; see also review by Mesquita & Frijda, 1992).

Closely related to the issue of emotion antecedents is the topic of emotion appraisal, and a number of studies have examined cultural similarities and differences in this aspect of emotion as well. Perhaps the largest cross-cultural study on emotion appraisal processes is Scherer et al.'s large-scale study reported in Scherer (1997a, 1997b). After describing situations in which they experienced one of seven emotions, respondents answered a series of questions designed to assess their appraisals of the events, including questions concerning novelty-expectation, intrinsic pleasantness, goal conduciveness, fairness, coping potential, norms, and self-ideals. Two studies reporting the analyses of these data (Scherer, 1997a, 1997b)

Table 10.1   Contemporary Cross-Cultural Studies that Examine the Recognition of Universal Facial Expressions of Emotion

Citation	Judge Cultures	Stimuli	Judgment Task	Major Findings
Biehl, et al., 1997	Hungarians, Poles, Japanese, Sumatrans, Americans, and Vietnamese	56 expressions from Matsumoto and Ekman (1988)	Forced-choice emotion categories	For all expressions, judges selected the intended emotion category at well above chance levels
Bormann-Kishkel, Hildebrand-Pascher, Stegbauer, 1990	Germans 4, 5, and 6 years old and adults	Seven Ekman and Friesen (1976) photos and two photos from Bullock and Russell (1984)	Matching with emotion category	4-year-olds correctly identified six emotions above chance levels; 5-year-olds correctly identified seven emotions above chance levels; 6-year-olds and university students correctly identified all emotions tested
Boucher and Carlson, 1980	Americans and Malays	25 American photos meeting Ekman criteria and 42 photos of Malays with approximate criteria	Forced-choice emotion categories	Across all photos, judges selected the intended emotion category at well above chance levels
Chan, 1985	Hong Kong Chinese	9 photos from Izard (1977)	Forced-choice emotion categories	Judges selected the intended emotion category at well above chance levels for all six universal emotions, as well as interest and shame
Ducci, Arcuri, W/ Georgies, and Sineshaw, 1982	Ethiopian high school students	28 photos from Ekman and Friesen (1976)	Forced-choice emotion categories (seven)	Judges selected the intended emotion category at well above chance levels for each of the six universal emotions
Ekman et al., 1987	College students from Estonia, Germany, Greece, Hong Kong, Italy, Japan, Scotland, Sumatra, Turkey, and the United States	18 photos from Ekman and Friesen (1976)	Forced-choice emotion categories and multiple scalar ratings of emotion categories	All judges selected the intended emotion category at well above chance levels and gave the intended emotion category the highest intensity rating
Haidt and Keltner, 1999	Americans and East Indians	Universal emotions based on Ekman criteria and other expressions	Free-response and forced-choice emotion categories	For all universal expressions except contempt judged by Americans, judges selected the intended emotion category above chance levels; similar findings obtained using free response
Kirouac and Dore, 1982	French-speaking Quebec individuals	110 photos from Ekman and Friesen (1976)	Forced-choice emotion categories	Judges selected the intended emotion category at well above chance levels for all universal emotions

(continued)

Table 10.1 *Continued*

Citation	Judge Cultures	Stimuli	Judgment Task	Major Findings
Kirouac and Dore, 1983	French-speaking students in Quebec	96 photos from Ekman and Friesen (1976)	Forced-choice emotion categories	Judges selected the emotion category intended by the expressions well above chance levels for all emotions
Kirouac and Dore, 1985	French-speaking individuals in Quebec	96 photos from Ekman and Friesen (1976)	Forced-choice emotion categories	Judges selected the emotion category intended by the expressions well above chance levels for all emotions
Leung and Singh, 1998	Hong Kong Chinese children	24 photos from Ekman and Friesen (195)	Matching with emotion-associated stories	Percentage of judges matching the expression with the emotion intended in the stories was well above chance levels for all six emotions tested
McAndrew (1986)	Americans and Malays	30 photos from Ekman and Friesen (1975) presented tachistoscopically at 10 exposure times	Forced choice of six emotion categories	At 800 milliseconds, all judges selected the intended emotion category well above chance levels
Mandal, Saha, and Palchoudhury, 1986	Indians	Photos from Ekman and Friesen (1976)	Forced-choice emotion categories in Procedure 1, multiple scalar ratings of emotion categories in Procedure 2	For all six universal emotions, the percentage of judges selecting the intended emotion category (Procedure 1) or giving the intended emotion the highest intensity rating (Procedure 2) was well above chance levels
Markham and Wang, 1996	Chinese and Australian children	18 photos from Ekman and Friesen (1976) and 18 Chinese facial expressions developed by Wang and Meng (1986)	Situation discrimination task and a situational inference task	Children from both cultures recognized the six universal emotions above chance levels
Matsumoto, 1990	Americans and Japanese	14 expressions from Matsumoto and Ekman (1988)	Forced-choice emotion categories	Judges selected the intended emotion category at well above chance levels
Matsumoto, 1992a	Americans and Japanese	56 expressions from Matsumoto and Ekman (1988)	Forced-choice emotion categories	Judges selected the intended emotion category at well above chance levels
Matsumoto and Assar, 1992	Americans and Indians	56 expressions from Matsumoto and Ekman (1988)	Forced-choice emotion categories	Judges selected the intended emotion category at well above chance levels
Matsumoto and Ekman, 1989	Americans and Japanese	56 expressions from Matsumoto and Ekman (1988)	Multiple scalar ratings on emotion categories	Judges gave the highest intensity rating to the intended emotion category for all universal emotions except one

Table 10.1 *Continued*

Citation	Judge Cultures	Stimuli	Judgment Task	Major Findings
Matsumoto, Kasri, et al. 1999	Americans and Japanese	56 expressions from Matsumoto and Ekman (1988)	Forced-choice emotion categories	Judges selected the intended emotion category at well above chance levels
Mazurski and Bond, 1993, Experiment 2	Australians	110 photos from Ekman and Friesen (1976)	Forced-choice emotion categories	Judges selected the intended emotion category for all universal emotions well above chance levels
Mehta, Ward, and Strongman, 1992	Maori and Pakeha individuals	Maori and Pakeha poses of seven emotions and a neutral (coded by Ekman and Friesen's FACS)	Forced-choice from 11 emotion categories	All emotions and neutral expressions were recognized accurately at above chance levels
Russell, Suzuki, and Ishida, 1993	Canadians, Greeks, and Japanese	7 slides from Matsumoto and Ekman (1988)	Open-ended emotion categories	For all emotions except contempt, the proportion of judges producing the intended emotion category was substantially greater than chance levels
Toner and Gates, 1985	Australians	110 slides from Ekman and Friesen (1976)	Six emotion categories and neutral	Overall, judges selected the intended emotion term well above chance levels for all emotions
Wallbott, 1991	Germans	28 slides from Ekman and Friesen (1976)	Scalar ratings of seven emotion categories	The proportion of judges rating the intended emotion category most intense was well above chance levels for each of the seven emotions tested
Wolfgang and Cohen, 1988	South and Central Americans, Canadians, Israelis, and Ethiopians	Wolfgang Interracial Facial Expressions Test (produced according to Ekman and Friesen criteria)	Forced-choice emotion categories	Overall, judges in all four groups selected the intended emotion term well above chance levels for all emotions
Yik, Meng, and Russell, 1998	English-speaking Canadians, Cantonese-speaking Hong Kong Chinese, and Japanese-speaking Japanese	13 still photographs of facial expressions of babies	Freely produced emotion categories	Judges in all three groups produced the intended emotion category for happy photos, but not for any of the five other emotions
Yik and Russell, 1999	English-speaking Canadians, Cantonese-speaking Hong Kong Chinese, and Japanese-speaking Japanese	Six photos from Ekman and Friesen (1976), one photo from Matsumoto and Ekman (1988)	10 emotion categories statements	Judges in all three groups selected the intended emotion category significantly above chance levels

Note. The inclusion criteria used in assembling these studies were as follows: (1) The study must have used full-face presentations of emotion with no distortion, using Ekman and Friesen or Izard related stimuli or other stimuli provided there was a methodological check on the validity of the expressions to portray emotions. (2) The study must have included data from at least one non-U.S. sample; no within-country ethnic difference studies were included. (3) The study must have reported data for which recognition levels can be compared against chance. (4) The judges must not have been mentally impaired.

177

indicated that, while differences existed between both emotions and countries, the differences according to country were much smaller than the differences according to emotion. That is, there were much more cultural similarities in emotion appraisal processes than there were cultural differences. Cultural similarities in emotion appraisal processes have also been reported by Roseman, Dhawan, Rettek, Nadidu, and Thapa (1995) and by Mauro, Sato, and Tucker (1992). Cultural differences were also reported in each of these studies; Roseman et al. (1995), in fact, suggest that cultural similarities may occur on more "primitive" dimensions of appraisal, while cultural differences may occur on more "complex" dimensions.

Scherer et al.'s large-scale studies have also been the most comprehensive to examine cultural influences on subjective emotional experience (Scherer & Wallbott, 1994; Scherer et al., 1983). In their study, participants provided self-report data concerning subjective feeling states (e.g., intensity, duration, etc.), physiological symptoms, and behavioral reactions (e.g., nonverbal behaviors, verbal utterances, etc.). While cultural differences existed, the differences among the emotions were much larger than the differences between cultures; that is, emotions appeared to share a more or less universal experiential base across cultures (see reviews in Scherer & Wallbott, 1994; Wallbott & Scherer, 1986). To be sure, a number of writers take a more "functionalist" approach to describing emotional experience, suggesting that emotion is a set of "socially shared scripts" composed of physiological, behavioral, and subjective components that develop as individuals are enculturated (e.g., Kitayama & Markus, 1994, 1995; Markus & Kitayama, 1991; Shweder, 1993; Wierzbicka, 1994). Such a view argues against notions of universality in experiential basis as emotions have to be as distinct as each culture is different. In reality, however, I do not view these approaches as mutually exclusive.

The topic of cultural similarities and differences in the concept of emotion has also received considerable attention in the literature. A number of writers, for instance, have suggested that there are substantial differences in the concept and definition of emotion across cultures, and that some cultures have no concept of emotion as we do in the American English language (R. I. Levy, 1973, 1983; Lutz, 1983; Russell, 1991b). Cultures also apparently differ in the kinds of feeling states and words they use to describe and categorize emotions,

in the location of emotions, and in the meaning of emotions to people, interpersonal relationships, and behavior (see review by Russell, 1991b). While these notions have been used to argue against the concept of universality in emotional expression, again, I do not believe that these are mutually exclusive. Universality in a small set of emotional expressions, and their underlying feeling states, can coexist with substantial cultural differences in the linguistic coding of emotion via language across cultures.

A final, relatively new but equally important area of cross-cultural research on emotion concerns the influence of culture on human physiology during emotional reactions. The specificity of physiological response in emotion is a topic that has been debated widely in psychology for decades, with views varying as extremely on the one hand to suggest that physiological responses are not necessary at all (e.g., Mandler, 1984) and, on the other hand, to associate each emotion with a specific physiological response pattern (e.g., James, 1890). Using universal facial expressions as markers, Ekman et al. (1983) found the first systematic evidence for a distinct autonomic response for each of the six emotions tested in a sample of American participants. Levenson and colleagues have since extended these findings to include individuals from other groups, including Chinese Americans and the Minangkabau of Sumatra (Levenson, Ekman, Heider, & Friesen, 1992; Tsai & Levenson, 1997). Future research in this area promises to extend this line of inquiry further, investigating also the possibility of specific patterning of central nervous system activity.

As seen from this very quick review, cross-cultural studies on emotion have spanned a wide range of topics and have contributed important information to the literature on this aspect of human functioning. In the next section, I focus more specifically on a review of cross-cultural studies of the recognition and judgment of emotional expressions as it is arguably the most well-studied area of culture and emotion, producing many new and exciting findings over the past two decades.

Recognition and Judgments of Emotion across Cultures

Even within this area of research, there is a wide range of studies, many differing in the nature of the stimuli that are used as a basis to make emotion judgments. A number of studies, for example, have examined the recognition of emotion in voice and vocal cues (e.g., Albas, McCluskey, & Albas, 1976; Beier & Zautra, 1972; Guidetti, 1991; Hatta & Nachshon, 1988; Matsumoto & Kishimoto, 1983; McCluskey & Albas, 1981; McCluskey, Albas, Niemi, Cuevas, & Ferrer, 1975; Van Bezooijen, Otto, & Heenan, 1983). In general, these studies have demonstrated that emotions can be recognized to a considerable degree in vocal cues and characteristics, although it is often difficult to distinguish specific and discrete emotional states via voice. A handful of other studies has also examined cultural differences in judgments of body postures (e.g., Kudoh & Matsumoto, 1985; Matsumoto & Kudoh, 1987; Sogon & Masutani, 1989); these studies have indicated that emotional states can be inferred to some degree from body postures, although discriminations finer than gross dimensions of pleasantness-unpleasantness or approach-avoidance are difficult to make.

By far, the greatest bulk of research in this area has been conducted using facial expressions of emotion as stimuli. Given the original findings of emotion universality based on facial expressions and the wealth of evidence summarized in Table 10.1 that subsequently replicated them, it is no wonder that cross-cultural research on emotion recognition continues to be dominated by research on the face. Facial expressions offer many advantages over other channels of study. First, years of research on the face provide more than ample basis for conducting new studies and extending previous findings. Second, the notion of universality offers theorists and researchers alike a conceptual basis by which to understand cultural similarities and differences in facial expressions. Third, the face can display discrete emotional states, providing specific information about people that can be studied from the viewpoint of motivation, as well as communication. Fourth, developments such as Ekman and Friesen's (1978) FACS, described above, have shown the face to be one of the most complex and intricate signal systems available, lending itself to rich and productive areas of study.

In the remainder of this chapter, I review the major findings in the area of culture and emotion judgments involving facial expressions, describing first studies that show how countries and cultures are similar to, and then how they are also different from, each other when judging emotions. Collectively, they give us further insights to the biological and environmental processes that underlie facial expressions and emotion. I then discuss the implications of these findings for future empirical and theoretical work on emotion and emotion judgments, giving researchers and students of emotion new ideas for unique and innovative research on emotion in the future.

Cultural Similarities in Emotion Judgments

Other Universal Expressions

Although I mentioned above that the original universal expressions included six emotions, these included only those that both Ekman and Izard had agreed were universal. In fact, Izard (1971, 1978) also suggested that several other expressions were universal, including interest-excitement and shame-humiliation. Some controversy, however, existed as to whether these were actually facial expressions or were more reflective of head position or gaze direction. In fact, the studies reviewed in Table 10.1 were not equivocal in their support for the universality of expressions other than the six described above.

In the last decade, however, a number of studies have reported the existence of a seventh universal facial expression of emotion: contempt. Initial evidence from 10 countries, including West Sumatra (Ekman & Friesen, 1986; Ekman & Heider, 1988), was later replicated by Matsumoto (1992b) in 4 countries, 3 of which were different from Ekman and Friesen's original 10. This finding received considerable attention and criticism (C. E. Izard & Haynes, 1988; Russell, 1991a, 1991c). Russell (1991a, 1991c), for example, suggested that the context in which the expression was shown influenced results in favor of universality. In his study, the contempt expression was more often labeled either disgust or sadness when shown either alone or after showing a representing disgust or sad (Russell, 1991a). Ekman, O'Sullivan, and Matsumoto (1991a, 1991b), however, reanalyzed their data and found no effect of context. Biehl et al. (1997) also tested and found no effects for other methodological confounds, and Rosenberg and Ekman (1995) suggested that people understand the emotional connotations of the expression even if they do not freely produce an emotion label for it.

A recent study by Haidt and Keltner (1999) also raises the possibility of a universal expression of embarrassment. These researchers showed American and Indian judges such an expression, which involved a smile, a lip press, a gaze and head movement down, and a face touch. Judges gave both a free-response and a forced-choice selection of emotion categories. Both methods produced cross-cultural agreement that was well above chance levels and was comparable to the data obtained for the other universal emotions.

Relative Intensity Ratings

When comparing expressions, people of different countries agree on which is more strongly expressed. Ekman et al. (1987) compared intensity ratings between paired expressions of the same emotion across 10 countries and found that, 92% of the time, the 10 countries in their study agreed on which was more intense. Matsumoto and Ekman (1989) extended this finding by including comparisons across different poser types, including Caucasian and Japanese posers. Looking separately for each emotion, within country across gender and then within gender across country, Americans and Japanese agreed on which photo was more intense 80% of the time. These findings suggest that cultures judge emotions on a similar basis, despite differences in facial physiognomy, morphology, poser race, poser sex, or culturally prescribed rules governing the expression and perception of faces.

Association between Perceived Expression Intensity and Inferences about Subjective Experience

There is a strong, positive relationship between how strongly judges rate an expression and how much they believe the poser is feeling it. Matsumoto, Kasri, and Kooken (1999) showed Japanese and American observers 56 expressions posed by Japanese and Caucasians. The observers judged what emotion the poser was expressing and then the strength of both the external display and internal experience. Correlations between the two intensity ratings were computed twice, first across observers separately for each expression and second across expressions for each observer. The correlations for both were high and positive for both countries and all expressions, suggesting commonality in that linkage across culture. This link is a topic of considerable importance in contemporary theories of emotion. Some authors have claimed that the linkage between expression and experience is unfounded (e.g.,

Fernandez-Dols & Ruiz-Belda, 1997; Russell, 1997). Others, however, have argued that expressions and experience are intimately linked with each other, but need not always be coupled (Rosenberg & Ekman, 1994; see also the literature on the facial feedback hypothesis, reviewed by Matsumoto, 1987; Winton, 1986). The data from Matsumoto, Kasri, et al. (1999) clearly support notions of linkage.

Second Mode of Response in Emotion Recognition

People of different countries agree on the secondary emotions portrayed in an expression. Observers in the 1987 study of Ekman et al. judged not only which emotion was portrayed in the faces, but also the intensity of each of seven emotion categories. This task, therefore, allowed observers to report multiple emotions or no emotion instead of being forced to select an emotion to describe the face. While previous studies showed universality in the first mode of response, countries may have differed in which emotion is next most prevalent. Analyses supported cross-national agreement. For every country in the 1987 study of Ekman et al., the secondary emotion for the disgust expressions was contempt, and for fear expressions, it was surprise. For anger, the second mode varied depending on the photo, with disgust, surprise, and contempt as the second responses. Matsumoto and Ekman (1989) and Biehl et al. (1997) replicated these findings, suggesting pancultural agreement in the multiple meanings derived from universal faces. This agreement may exist because of overlap in the semantics of the emotion categories, in antecedents and elicitors of emotion, or in the facial configurations themselves.

Perceived Expressivity

People of different countries have similar stereotypes about the expressivity of other countries (Pittam, Gallois, Iwawaki, & Kroonenberg, 1995). In the study of Pittam et al., Australian and Japanese subjects completed a questionnaire regarding overall level of expressivity of Australians and Japanese. The Japanese were rated as less expressive than the Australians by judges of both countries, indicating that people of different countries believe that there are differences in intensity of emotion expression, and that they agree about who is more or less expressive. A study by Waxer (1985) described above also speaks to this point.

Cultural Differences in Emotion Judgments

Emotion Recognition

Although the original universality research showed that subjects recognized emotions at rates well over chance, no study ever reported perfect cross-national agreement. Matsumoto (1992a) formally tested Japanese and American judgments of emotion categories and found that recognition rates ranged from 64% to 99%. Americans were better at recognizing anger, disgust, fear, and sadness than the Japanese, but accuracy rates did not differ for happiness or surprise. These differences were consistent with data reported in earlier universality studies. And, in fact, many of the studies listed in Table 10.1, while presenting recognition data at well above chance levels, also report statistically significant differences in absolute levels of agreement across cultures. Thus, while the universal expressions are recognized at levels considerably higher than chance and at high agreement across cultures, cultures also differ in the absolute level of agreement.

Some writers have used cross-national differences in emotion recognition to argue against universality, criticizing the methodology used in judgment studies (Russell, 1991b, 1994, 1995), interpretations (Russell, 1994), and the use of language-specific terms for facial expressions of emotion (Wierzbicka, 1995). Russell (1994), for example, raised several criticisms of the methods employed, including the nature and presentation of the stimuli and the response format. He reanalyzed judgment data across a number of studies, separating studies by method and also employing a Western/non-Western distinction to demonstrate that the methods employed may have biased responses in favor of Western cultures.

Wierzbicka (1995) suggested that reference to emotions should not be in terms of the six (or seven) basic emotions because they are language-specific terms. Alternatively, she suggests that we should only speak of universals in terms of "conceptual primitives." For example, she suggests that, when a person is recognizing a smile of happiness, he or she is reading the face as, "I think: Something good is happening, I feel something good because of this." Her position, therefore, is that while facial expressions of emotion may indeed be universal, the methods that we have used to study them, including the use of emotion terms as response alternatives in judgment tasks, are bound by the culture in which those terms arise and cannot possibly be universal.

These concerns have been addressed by a number of writers. Ekman (1994b) and C. E. Izard (1994), for example, both point out that Russell's (1994) article paid selective attention to those studies that helped to support his thesis and failed to cite studies that controlled for the various flaws that he raised. His thesis was also flawed in that he used criticisms about only one of several types of evidence for universality to argue against the entire basis of universality, and he failed to mention studies on nonhuman primates and with infants and the congenitally blind, all of which strongly support the universality notion. A recent study by Geen (1992), for example, reported that rhesus monkeys reared in isolation showed "more or less normal-appearing facial expressions" (p. 277) when they were later placed with other monkeys. Hauser (1993) found evidence that, in rhesus monkeys as in humans, emotion expression is lateralized in the right hemisphere of the brain. In a review of studies conducted with blind children, Charlesworth and Kreutzer (1973) concluded that spontaneous expressions of blind children did not differ from the expressions of sighted children who had been exposed to visual examples of expressions for their entire lives. And, Rosenberg and Ekman (1995) presented data to suggest that, even though judges cannot produce a discrete emotion category label that corresponds to the one intended by the researchers, they often understand the emotional connotations of the expression in the manner intended.

Wierzbicka's thesis is also not without criticism. Winegar (1995) is somewhat critical of Wierzbicka's conceptual primitives as they are also constrained by culture and suggests that one cannot ever avoid cultural specificity in studying psychological phenomena, and that even if we could agree on the universality of evaluation, we would not be able to avoid the effect of culture in our theory building. VanGeert (1995) agrees that there is a need for a coding procedure for universal emotions similar to Wierzbicka's conceptual primitives, and that we need a more precise measure, one in which each universal has a "specific physical definition" (p. 265). He presents three dimensions on which universals can be named and organized. In one, he suggests a distinction between what he calls "experiential" and "technical" universals. He believes that

> Emotions are experiential universals, that is, all people are in principle able to entertain a set of similar subjective experiences called the universal emotions. But the only way to refer to such shared emotions is by means of a technical language. (p. 206)

Finally, recent research demonstrating pancultural universality in emotion taxonomies challenge Wierzbicka's assumption that emotion language cannot possibly be universal.

One important point to remember is that universality and cultural relativity are not mutually exclusive; the perception of emotion can be both universal and culture specific, depending on the aspect of perception being discussed. Elsewhere (Yrizarry, Matsumoto, & Wilson Cohn, 1998), we have suggested at least five sources that would produce cultural differences in emotion perception even though the expression being judged may be universal. They include (a) semantic overlap in the linguistic categories and mental concepts related to emotion that are used in the judgment process, (b) overlapping facial components in the expressions, (c) cognitive overlap in events and experiences related to emotion, (d) personality biases in social cognition, and (e) culture. Future research needs to tease out the separate and interactive effects of all of these sources on the nature of the judgment process.

Instead of challenging the basis of universality, in fact, several studies have attempted to uncover possible explanations for cross-national differences in judgments of emotion categories. For instance, Matsumoto (1992a) suggested that the differences in recognition rates are due to cultural differences in socially learned rules about how emotions could be recognized. Specifically, cultural differences between Japan and the United States in the allowance for individuality or conformity may have contributed to their findings. In Japan, emotions that threaten group harmony and conformity may be discouraged. Therefore, a Japanese person would be careful not to show negative emotions and would have a tendency not to recognize these expressions in others. In contrast, the United States, a country that encourages individuality, would encourage both the expression and perception of negative emotions. Such a view allows for the examination

of the influence of dimensions of culture on emotion judgments, a view that has received support from research described below.

Cross-National Differences in Emotion Recognition Rates and Cultural Dimensions

To broaden the base of cultural dimensions that could explain cross-national differences in agreement levels, Matsumoto (1989) selected recognition data from 15 cultures reported in four studies and ranked each country on Hofstede's dimensions (1980). These included *power distance* (PD), the degree to which differences in power are maintained by culture; *uncertainty avoidance* (UA), the degree to which a culture develops institutions and rituals to deal with the anxiety created by uncertainty; *individualism* (IN), the degree to which a culture encourages the sacrificing of group goals for the individual; and *masculinity* (MA), the degree to which a culture emphasizes sex differences (Hofstede, 1980, 1983). The dimensions were then correlated with recognition accuracy levels. The results supported the claim that Americans (individualistic culture) are better at recognizing negative emotions than Japanese (collectivistic culture).

Differences in emotion perception as a function of culture were also found in a metanalysis (Schimmack, 1996). Individualism was a better predictor of recognition of happiness than ethnicity (operationalized as Caucasian/non-Caucasian), supporting the notion that sociocultural dimensions account for differences in the perception of emotion. They also support the notion that people of different cultures learn ways of perception management via cultural decoding rules.

Biehl et al. (1997) also reported cross-national differences in agreement (and in intensity ratings). These differences could not be explained adequately according to a Western/non-Western dichotomy, a division consistent with regional/country and racial/ethnic approaches to making culture operational. Rather, Biehl et al. discussed these differences in terms of possible underlying sociopsychological variables (i.e., those postulated by Hofstede in 1980 and 1983) and the dimensional approach to culture advanced by Matsumoto (1989, 1990). Theoretical explanations and further testing of the relationship between culture and recognition should define culture according to meaningful sociopsychological dimensions above and beyond country, region, race, or ethnicity.

Attributions of Personality Based on Smiles

The smile is a common signal for greeting, for acknowledgment, or for showing acceptance. It is also employed to mask emotions, and cultures may differ in the use of smiles for this purpose. This was the case in Friesen's (1972) study, in which Japanese and American men watched disgusting video clips with an experimenter in the room. The Japanese men used smiles to cover up their negative expressions much more often than the American men (Ekman, 1972; Friesen, 1972).

To investigate further the meaning of those differences, Matsumoto and Kudoh (1993) obtained ratings from Japanese and Americans on smiling versus nonsmiling (i.e., neutral) faces with regard to intelligence, attractiveness, and sociability. Americans rated smiling faces more intelligent than neutral faces; the Japanese, however, did not. Americans and Japanese both found smiling faces more sociable than neutral faces, but for the Americans, the difference was greater. These differences suggest that cultural display rules cause Japanese and Americans to attribute different meanings to the smile and serve as a good explanation for perceived major differences in communication styles across cultures.

Attributions of Intensity

The 1987 study of Ekman et al. of 10 countries was the first to document cross-national differences in the intensity attributed to the facial expressions. Although overall recognition data supported universality, Asians gave significantly lower intensity ratings on happiness, surprise, and fear. These data suggested that the judges were acting according to culturally learned rules about how to perceive expressions, especially given the fact that all posers were Caucasian. But, it could also be that the Asians rated the Caucasian posers less intensely out of politeness or ignorance.

To address this question, Matsumoto and Ekman developed a stimulus set comprised of Asian and Caucasian posers (Matsumoto & Ekman, 1988) and presented them to judges in the United States and Japan (Matsumoto & Ekman, 1989). For all but one emotion, Americans rated the expressions more intensely than the Japanese, regardless of the race of the poser. Because the differences were not specific to the poser, Matsumoto and Ekman (1989) interpreted the differences as a function of cultural decoding

rules. Since then, a number of studies have replicated the existence of cultural differences in intensity ratings (e.g., Biehl et al., 1997; Matsumoto, 1990).

Matsumoto's (1989) study described above also investigated the relationship between Hofstede's (1980) dimensions of culture and emotion intensity ratings. Two important findings emerged. First, there was a negative correlation between PD and intensity ratings of anger, fear, and sadness, suggesting that cultures that emphasize status differences rate these emotions less intensely. Secondly, IN was correlated positively with intensity ratings of anger and fear; individualistic cultures gave higher ratings. These results suggest that understanding dimensions of culture could be a key to explaining cross-national differences in the perception of negative emotions.

Ethnic Differences in Intensity Ratings

Matsumoto (1993) examined ethnic differences in affect intensity, emotion judgments, display rule attitudes, and self-reported emotional expression among four ethnic groups in the United States. African Americans perceived anger more intensely than Asian Americans and perceived disgust more intensely than Caucasian Americans and Asian Americans; Hispanic Americans perceived Caucasian faces more intensely than did Caucasian Americans and Asian Americans; and African Americans perceived female expressions more intensely than did Asian Americans. These findings compel us to reevaluate the way we conceptualize culture, and they stress the importance of psychologically meaningful dimensions of culture that are independent of ethnicity or country. Most cross-cultural research assumes that a person living in a country is a member of its primary culture. The finding of differences within an American sample (which is nearly always the comparison group in cross-cultural studies) clearly demonstrates otherwise, and we are urged to consider meaningful psychological dimensions (e.g., individualism-collectivism, status differentiation) to explain cultural and individual differences in emotion expression and perception.

Inferences about Emotional Experiences Underlying Facial Expressions of Emotion

Although cultures differ in their intensity ratings of external display, it was unclear as to whether they also differ in their inferences about underlying experience and, if so, whether these differences were similar to judgments of external display. Matsumoto, Kasri, et al. (1999) tested this notion by comparing American and Japanese judgments in which separate ratings were obtained for expression intensity and inferred subjective experience. Americans rated external display more intensely than the Japanese, replicating previous findings. The Japanese, however, rated internal experience more intensely than Americans. Within-country analyses indicated no significant differences between the two ratings for the Japanese. Americans, however, consistently rated external display more intensely than subjective experience. These findings were totally unexpected. Previously, we suggested that American-Japanese differences occurred because the Japanese suppressed their intensity ratings, as they do their expressions. Contrarily, however, it was the Americans who exaggerated their external display ratings relative to subjective experience, not the Japanese who suppressed.

A recent study by Matsumoto, Consolacion, et al. (1999) has extended these findings. In the study described immediately above, observers viewed expressions portrayed at 100% intensity. In Matsumoto, Consolacion, et al., however, American and Japanese judges saw expressions at 0%, 50%, 100%, and 125% intensities. The data for the 100% and 125% expressions replicated the previous findings; Americans rated external display significantly higher than internal experience, while there were no differences for the Japanese. Also, there were no differences between external and internal ratings for either Americans or Japanese on 0% expressions, which were expected. On 50% expressions, however, the findings were intriguing. While there was no difference between external and internal ratings for the Americans, the Japanese rated internal experience higher than external display. Matsumoto, Consolacion, et al. interpreted these findings as suggesting that, for weaker expressions, Japanese may assume that a display rule is operating and may thus infer more emotion being felt than is actually displayed. When Americans see a weak expression, however, there need not be any such assumption; thus, they interpret the same amount of emotion felt as expressed. For strong expressions, Japanese may assume that the context was such that the expression was justified; thus, they infer a level of emotion felt that is commensurate with what is shown. When Amer-

icans see a strong expression, however, they know that there is a display rule to exaggerate one's feelings; thus, they compensate for this display rule by inferring less emotion felt.

Contribution of Cultural Dimensions to Cross-National Differences in Emotion Judgments

Most cross-cultural work in this area, as well as others, has really been cross national, with culture made operational by country. Although this approach is standard practice, it limits our ability to interpret differences when observed. That is, when culture is made operational by country and differences are found, they can only be interpreted by making assumptions about the nature of cultural differences underlying the countries because culture was never actually measured in the study. Recently, however, several writers have called for a move away from such practices and toward research that "unpackages" the culture effects on psychological variables (e.g., Bond & Tedeschi, chapter 16, this volume; Poortinga, van de Vijver, Joe, & van de Koppel, 1987; van de Vijver & Leung, 1997). *Unpackaging* refers to the identification of specific, psychological dimensions of culture that may account for between-country differences in the variable of interest, their inclusion and measurement, and the statistical estimation of the degree to which they actually account for between-country differences. Thus, specific, measurable dimensions of culture on the psychological level replace the global, nonspecific construct we know as *culture*.

When such dimensions are included and actually measured in research, they allow researchers to demonstrate empirically that participants differ (or not) on these constructs, eliminating the need to assume so. Researchers need not rely on impression, anecdote, or stereotype in interpreting differences as measurement provides a methodological check on intended cultural operations. Measurement also allows for an assessment of the relationship between culture and the dependent variables by quantitatively assessing the degree to which culture contributes to between-country differences. Thus, researchers can ask not only whether constructs such as IC contribute to cross-national differences, but also how much. The inclusion of these types of measures in future cross-cultural studies is a necessary evolution in the field if researchers wish to specify exactly what about culture produces differences and why.

The study of Matsumoto, Consolacion et al. (1999) was unique in that not only were judgments of faces obtained, but also data from the respondents were obtained that assessed individual-level differences in two major cultural constructs—IC and status differentiation (SD). IC has been used to explain many cross-national and cross-cultural differences in behavior and is arguably the most well-known, well-studied, and important dimension of culture that exists today (Triandis, 1994, 1995). Individualistic cultures tend to emphasize the individual, fostering uniqueness, separateness, autonomy, and individuality. Collectivistic cultures value in-groups over individuality and foster harmony, cohesion, and cooperation. SD refers to the degree to which cultures differentiate their behaviors toward others on the basis of the status differences that exist between them and their interactants. Some cultures make large differentiations on the basis of status, affording people of higher status more power; others make smaller differentiations, treating people more or less the same regardless of status differences. Like IC, how cultures differentiate and use status and power has been shown to be a major dimension of cultural variability (Hofstede, 1983, 1984).

To investigate the contribution of IC and SD to the cross-national differences in emotion judgments reported above, Matsumoto, Consolacion, et al. (1999) compared separately the effect sizes associated with the differences between external and internal ratings for Americans and Japanese between analyses with and without the IC and SD ratings as covariates (these same procedures were used to examine the contribution of IC to cross-national differences in display rules reported in Matsumoto et al., 1998). These analyses indicated that approximately 90% of the variance in the rating differences was accounted for by these two cultural variables. Subsequent follow-up analyses further indicated that IC may contribute independent variance to this prediction. Thus, this study was the first to demonstrate empirically that the differences between Americans and Japanese on judgments of external and internal intensity may be almost entirely accounted for by cultural differences in IC and SD between the two cultures.

Summary

The evidence available to date suggests that perception can have both universal and culture-specific elements. Elsewhere (Matsumoto, 1996), I have suggested a mechanism similar to Ekman and Friesen's neurocultural theory of expression to describe how cultural similarities and differences in emotion perception or judgment can be obtained. This mechanism implies that judgments of emotion are affected by (a) a facial affect recognition program that is innate and universal (similar to Ekman and Friesen's facial affect program) and (b) culture-specific decoding rules that intensify, deintensify, mask, or qualify the perception (cf. Buck, 1984). When we perceive emotions in others, the expression is recognized through a process analogous to template matching with the universal facial prototypes of emotion. Before a judgment is rendered, however, that stimulus is also joined by learned rules about perceiving such expressions in others. The most recent research suggests that these rules may differ according to stable sociocultural dimensions such as IC and SD. This mechanism may be as basic to emotion communication across cultures as Ekman and Friesen's original neurocultural theory of expression.

A Research Agenda on Culture and Emotion Judgments for the Future

Many of the findings described above lend themselves neatly to research questions that should be addressed. For instance, the five suggestions of Yrizarry et al. (1998) for the possible reasons why cultural differences in agreement levels in emotion recognition judgment data occur should be examined, and the contribution of each of those, and other, sources should be elucidated. Future research can examine further the social meanings of facial expressions of emotion and differences in those meanings across cultures. And, new studies on ratings of intensity across different cultures are needed to extend those previous findings beyond comparisons of the United States and Japan.

In the remainder of this section, I explore a number of other areas, however, that I hope serve as a platform for new areas of research in this area of psychology. These, of course, are not all encompassing; instead, they highlight some of what I consider are pressing theoretical and empirical needs in the very near future that go beyond mere extensions of the existing work.

The Search for Other Universals

As mentioned, the fact that the six emotions—anger, disgust, fear, happiness, sadness, and surprise—were documented originally as universal, then later as contempt, and then perhaps as embarrassment does not preclude the possibility of the existence of other universal expressions. Ekman (1994a) suggests that 12 other emotions, including amusement, awe, contentment, embarrassment, excitement, guilt, interest, pride in achievement, relief, satisfaction, sensory pleasure, and shame, are strong candidates for universality. These, and other, candidates should be examined in the future. Albeit not conclusive, initial data that support universality are relatively easy to obtain through judgment studies across a wide range of cultures. If other emotions are found to be universally expressed and recognized, that finding would have a profound impact on theories of emotion, notions of evolution, theories of social learning, social cognition, communication, and many research endeavors on emotion.

The Need to Investigate the Boundaries of Emotion Judgments

To date, the bulk (although not, of course, all) of cross-cultural research has examined cross-cultural similarities and differences in emotion recognition, presenting college student judges with full-face displays of emotion and asking them to select an emotion category they feel represents the emotion displayed (Table 10.1). While this type of study has had its place in the area, future studies need to give strong consideration to modifying the parameters of this research to examine the boundaries of the judgments.

For example, studies involving intensity ratings conducted in the past 10 years have provided a wealth of new information about cultural similarities and differences that was not available through the forced-choice method of emotion category selection. In the future, similar modifications to the type of judgment made will extend the current literature in important ways. Judgments of behavioral intentions or underlying personality traits, for instance, would help to tease out the social and personal meanings of emotional expressions in communication.

Future studies also need to give strong consideration to modifications to the nature of the stimuli used in research. Because almost all of the cross-cultural research conducted to date has used full-face presentations of emotions, we have little knowledge of how people interpret blends or partial expressions and how cultures differ in these judgments. Such research is needed. In addition, most research to date has utilized static poses of expressions presented via photograph or slide. Future research will need to employ the use of more spontaneously occurring expressions in fluid and dynamically occurring contexts. The availability of computer and video technology now makes these potentials much more of a realistic possibility than in the past.

Of special consideration also are the possible changes to the nature of the judges typically involved in judgment research. Like so many other areas of psychology, the overwhelming majority of judges who have participated in emotion judgment studies have been college students. Future studies need to examine the judgment of emotion across ages, occupations, social economic status, ethnicity, and a host of other demographic variables as well.

The Need to Incorporate Context

Perhaps the most pressing need for future cross-cultural research on emotion judgments is the need to incorporate context into the judgment process. Indeed, the bulk of the studies conducted to date have presented stimuli to judges in a rather artificial environment, often without context information or manipulation. The degree to which judgments obtained in this fashion is indicative of judgments made across different contexts and cultural differences in these differentials is an empirical question that is yet to be addressed systematically in research. How do judgments differ according to differences in whom one is with, the place of the event, the target of the emotion, the time of day, and the like?

The issue of context is not merely an empirical one; it raises important theoretical questions about the very nature of culture. Many writers in cross-cultural psychology (e.g., authors of this volume) view culture as a conglomeration of attitudes, values, beliefs, and behaviors across a wide variety of contexts. To the extent that enculturation occurs originally through context-specific learning that is generalized across contexts over time, culture *is* context. In this sense, the considerable influence of culture on emotion judgments (and on other psychological processes, for that matter) cannot be gauged comprehensively without incorporating judgments across multiple contexts. While judgments of expressions given out of context may be important to establishing universality, judgments of expressions embedded within context are necessary to investigate cultural influences on the judgment process.

Indeed, the field has made some headway regarding this important question. A number of studies have investigated the effects of the context of the judge, generally manipulating what was shown to the judge prior to the judgment on a target face (e.g., Biehl et al., 1997; Russell, 1991a, 1991c; Russell & Fehr, 1987; Tanaka-Matsumi, Attivissimo, Nelson, & D'Urso, 1995; Thayer, 1980a, 1980b). Other studies have examined the effect of the context of the poser on the judgment, manipulating information about the context in which the expression is occurring (e.g., Carroll & Russell, 1996; Fernandez-Dols, Wallbott, & Sanchez, 1991; Knudsen & Muzekari, 1983; Munn, 1940; Muzekari, Knudsen, & Evans, 1986; Nakamura, Buck, & Kenny, 1990; Spignesi & Shor, 1981; Wallbott, 1988a, 1988b). In general, these studies have shown that context has some degree of influence, but the exact nature of this influence is not known.

One of the major limitations of previous research on context and emotion judgments has been the lack of a systematic manipulation of the specific parameters of context that may influence judgments—the who, what, when, where, why, and how of context. One of the reasons why this limitation exists is because researchers have not been careful to define and delineate these context parameters and to investigate systematically which of these are most important to emotion judgments. This research is necessary as its findings will guide which context parameters are most important to include in future comprehensive studies that will systematically vary context to examine its effects on judgments. These studies will then lend themselves to cross-cultural work, allowing scientists to examine whether the same context parameters have the same meanings in different cultures, as well as the same or different influences on the judgment process.

The Need to Link Judgments with Other Psychological Processes

Cross-cultural research on emotion judgments to date has basically explored emotion judgments in a vacuum, studying them to the exclusion of other psychological processes in the same study. Future research will need to incorporate emotion judgments in combination with other psychological processes, such as display rules, emotional expression, stereotype and category formation, person perception, social cognition, brain function, and the like. While some studies have examined the relationship between expressing and perceiving emotions in the same individuals within the United States (e.g., Lanzetta & Kleck, 1970; P. K. Levy, 1964; Zuckerman, Hall, DeFrank, & Rosenthal, 1976; Zuckerman, Larrance, Hall, DeFrank, & Rosenthal, 1979), for instance, I know of no research in which this relationship is examined crossculturally. Also, given the large role that emotion judgment processes should play in person perception, studies that examine the relationship between emotion judgments and other judgments, especially as related to intercultural interaction (e.g., stereotyping, etc.), should be investigated across cultures.

Of particular interest in the future are studies that examine the brain correlates of emotion recognition. If emotional expressions are universal, they imply the existence during recognition tasks of brain processes that are also constant across cultures. This research is yet to be done. The investigation of the brain correlates of face recognition has a long history in neuroscience (e.g., Bruyer, 1979; Levine, Banich, & Koch-Weser, 1988; Ley & Bryden, 1979), and recent research has indicated the existence of areas of the brain that are specific to recognizing faces (Bruce & Humphreys, 1994; Farah, 1996; Nachson, 1995). Other new studies also suggest that the recognition of facial expressions of emotion may also be localized further (e.g., Streit et al., 1999). The merging of this line of study with the knowledge and methods of universal facial expressions may extend this knowledge even further.

Tying research on emotion judgments with other areas of psychology is important conceptually as well. Many areas of study in psychology are fragmented from each other. Consequently, we know relatively much less about how a process such as emotion judgments functions in concert with other psychological processes within a total, integrated, synthesized, living person than we do about emotion judgments obtained in an artificial vacuum. Somewhere, somehow, we need to put Humpty Dumpty back together again. As the process of emotion judgments is a basic and important one, it most logically has ties to many other psychological processes. We need to flesh out these ties and examine cultural similarities and differences in them in the future.

Summary

Of course, there are many other ideas that are worthy of strong consideration for future research. I offer these not only as my suggestions for future research, but also as an encouragement to all students of culture and emotion to get outside the box we often paint ourselves into when we do a lot of research in one area of psychology. By doing so, we will raise, and address, important questions about those areas, and linkages of those areas with others, that we would have never been able to if we merely kept our noses too close to the proverbial grindstone.

Conclusion

Cross-cultural research over the past 30 years and more has been pivotal in demonstrating the universality and culture specificity of the expression and perception of emotion. These studies have had an enormous impact not only in the area of emotion, but also on psychology in general as the pancultural expression and perception of emotion has come to be considered a fundamental and universal aspect of human psychological functioning. Cross-cultural findings in this area have served as the platform for new areas of research based on emotion in all other areas of psychology, and much of the information we have today on emotions in development, clinical work, psychopathology, social interaction, personality, and the like find their roots in the original universality studies. The study of emotion has been well accepted in mainstream psychology, and pre- and post-doctoral training programs exist to develop new scientists in this important area of study.

The next two decades promise to be even more exciting for research on culture and emotion. Interesting programs have sprung up all around the world and in all disciplines of psychology. New technologies for mapping culture as a psychological construct on the individual level are being developed, as well as ways to measure precisely moment-to-moment changes in our brains and bodies when we feel or judge emotion. Collectively, these endeavors will tell us more in the future about the relationship between culture and the physiology of emotion, the representation of display and decoding rules, emotion perception, and culture itself in the brain. Research is also currently being done that elucidates the nature of the social meaning of emotions across cultures (e.g., Kitayama, Markus, & Matsumoto, 1995; cf. Kemper, 1978)

and the differential and relative contribution of emotion and other factors in social interaction. In particular, the role of emotion and its perception in intercultural adjustment and adaptation is now being examined systematically, and preliminary evidence suggests that they are key to successful living, working, and playing across different cultural milieus (e.g., Bennett, 1993; Gudykunst et al., 1996; Matsumoto, Le-Roux, et al., 1999). Future research will also examine the contributions of folk psychology and other theories of mind that can aid in developing more comprehensive theories of display and decoding rules than are available today.

Emotion is one of the most exciting areas of study in psychology and is central to our understanding of people around the world. While we share emotions with nonhuman primates and other primitive relatives, it is our most endearing human quality, and future research will undoubtedly capture its place in our lives even better than we can today. Cross-cultural research in the future will certainly play a leading role toward this end.

References

Albas, D. C., McCluskey, K. W., & Albas, C. A. (1976). Perception of the emotional content of speech: A comparison of two Canadian groups. *Journal of Cross-Cultural Psychology, 7,* 481–490.

Beier, E. G., & Zautra, A. J. (1972). Identification of vocal communication of emotions across cultures. *Journal of Consulting and Clinical Psychology, 39,* 166.

Bennett, M. J. (1993). Towards ethnorelativism: A developmental model of intercultural sensitivity. In R. M. Paige (Ed.), *Education for the intercultural experience* (pp. 1–50). Yarmouth, ME: Intercultural Press.

Biehl, M., Matsumoto, D., Ekman, P., Hearn, V., Heider, K., Kudoh, T., & Ton, V. (1997). Matsumoto and Ekman's Japanese and Caucasian Facial Expressions of Emotion (JACFEE): Reliability data and cross-national differences. *Journal of Nonverbal Behavior, 21,* 3–22.

Biehl, M., Matsumoto, D., & Kasri, F. (in press). Culture and emotion. In U. Gielen and A. L. Comunian (Eds.)., *Cross-cultural and international dimensions of psychology.* Trieste, Italy: Edizioni Lint Trieste S.r.1.

Bormann-Kischkel, C., Hildebrand-Pascher, S., & Stegbauer, G. (1990). The development of emotional concepts: A replication with a German sample. *International Journal of Behavioural Development, 13,* 355–372.

Boucher, J. D., & Brandt, M. E. (1981). Judgment of emotion: American and Malay antecedents. *Journal of Cross-Cultural Psychology, 12,* 272–283.

Boucher, J. D., & Carlson, G. E. (1980). Recognition of facial expression in three cultures. *Journal of Cross-Cultural Psychology, 11,* 263–280.

Brandt, M. E., & Boucher, J. D. (1985). Judgment of emotions from antecedent situations in three cultures. In I. Lagunes & Y. Poortinga (Eds.), *From a different perspective: Studies of behavior across cultures* (pp. 348–362). Lisse, The Netherlands: Swets & Zeitlinger.

Bruce, V., & Humphreys, G. W. (Eds.). (1994). Object and face recognition [Special issue]. *Visual Cognition, 1*(2/3).

Bruyer, R. (1979). The brain and the visual recognition of human faces. *Acta Psychiatrica Belgica, 79,* 113–143.

Buck, R. (1984). *The communication of emotion.* New York: Guilford Press.

Bullock, M., & Russell, J. A. (1984). Preschool children's interpretation of facial expressions of emotion. *International Journal of Behavioral Development, 7*(2), 193–214.

Buunk, B., & Hupka, R. B. (1987). Cross-cultural differences in the elicitation of sexual jealousy. *Journal of Sex Research, 23,* 12–22.

Carroll, J. M., & Russell, J. A. (1996). Do facial expressions signal specific emotions? Judging emotion from the face in context. *Journal of Personality and Social Psychology, 70,* 205–218.

Chan, D. W. (1985). Perception and judgment of facial expressions among the Chinese. *International Journal of Psychology, 20,* 681–692.

Charlesworth, W. R., & Kreutzer, M. A. (1973). Facial expressions of infants and children. In P. Ekman (Ed.), *Darwin and facial expression* (pp. 91–168). New York: Academic Press.

Darwin, C. (1872/1998). *The expression of emotion in man and animals.* New York: Oxford University Press.

Ducci, L., Arcuri, L., W/Georgis, T., & Sineshaw, T. (1982). Emotion recognition in Ethiopia: The effect of familiarity with western culture on accuracy of recognition. *Journal of Cross-Cultural Psychology, 13,* 340–351.

Edelmann, R. J., Asendorpf, J., Contarello, A., Georgas, J., Villanueva, C., & Zammuner, V. (1987). Self-reported verbal and non-verbal strategies for coping with embarrassment in five European cultures. *Social Science Information, 26,* 869–883.

Ekman, P. (1972). Universals and cultural differences in facial expressions of emotion. In J. Cole (Ed.), *Nebraska Symposium of Motivation, 1971: Vol. 19* (pp. 207–283). Lincoln: University of Nebraska Press.

Ekman, P. (1973). *Darwin and facial expression.* New York: Academic Press.

Ekman, P. (Ed.). (1982). *Emotion in the human face* (2nd ed.). Cambridge: Cambridge University Press.

Ekman, P. (1994a). All emotions are basic. In P. Ekman & R. J. Davidson (Eds.), *The nature of emotion: Fundamental questions* (pp. 15–19). New York: Oxford University Press.

Ekman, P. (1994a). Strong evidence for universals in facial expressions: A reply to Russell's mistaken critique. *Psychological Bulletin, 115,* 268–287.

Ekman, P., & Friesen, W. V. (1969). Nonverbal leakage and clues to deception. *Psychiatry, 32,* 88–106.

Ekman, P., & Friesen, W. V. (1975). *Unmasking the face: A guide to recognizing emotions from facial clues.* New York: Prentice-Hall.

Ekman, P., & Friesen, W. V. (1976). Pictures of facial affect. Palo Alto, CA: Consulting Psychologists Press.

Ekman, P., & Friesen, W. V. (1978). *Facial action coding system.* Palo Alto, CA: Consulting Psychologists Press.

Ekman, P., & Friesen, W. V. (1986). A new pan-cultural facial expression of emotion. *Motivation and Emotion, 10,* 159–168.

Ekman, P., Friesen, W. V., & Ellsworth, P. (1972). *Emotion in the human face.* New York: Cambridge University Press.

Ekman, P., Friesen, W. V., O'Sullivan, M., Chan, A., Diacoyanni-Tarlatzis, I., Heider, K., Krause, R., LeCompte, W. A., Pitcairn, T., Ricci-Bitti, P. E., Scherer, K., Tomita, M., & Tzavaras, A. (1987). Universals and cultural differences in the judgment of facial expressions of emotion. *Journal of Personality and Social Psychology, 53,* 712–717.

Ekman, P., & Heider, K. G. (1988). The universality of a contempt expression: A replication. *Motivation and Emotion, 12,* 303–308.

Ekman, P., Levenson, R., & Friesen, W. V. (1983). Autonomic nervous system activity distinguishes between emotions. *Science, 221,* 1208–1210.

Ekman, P., O'Sullivan, M., & Matsumoto, D. (1991a). Confusions about context in the judgment of facial expression: A reply to "The contempt expression and the relativity thesis." *Motivation and Emotion, 15,* 169–184.

Ekman, P., O'Sullivan, M., & Matsumoto, D. (1991b). Contradictions in the study of contempt: What's it all about? Reply to Russell. *Motivation and Emotion, 15,* 293–296.

Farah, M. J. (1996). Is face recognition "special"? Evidence from neuropsychology. *Behavioural Brain Research, 76,* 181–189.

Fernandez-Dols, J. M., & Ruiz-Belda, M. A. (1997).

Spontaneous facial behavior during intense emotional episodes: Artistic truth and optical truth. In J. A. Russell & J. M. Fernandez-Dols (Eds.), *The psychology of facial expression* (pp. 255–274). New York: Cambridge University Press.

Fernandez-Dols, J. M., Wallbott, H., & Sanchez, F. (1991). Emotion category accessibility and the decoding of emotion from facial expression and context. *Journal of Nonverbal Behavior, 15*, 107–123.

Fridlund, A. J. (1997). The new ethology of human facial expressions. In J. A. Russell, & J. M. Fernandez-Dols (Eds.), *The psychology of facial expression* (pp. 103–129). New York: Cambridge University Press.

Friesen, W. V. (1972). *Cultural differences in facial expressions in a social situation: An experimental test of the concept of display rules.* Unpublished doctoral dissertation, University of California, San Francisco.

Galati, D., & Sciaky, R. (1995). The representation of antecedents of emotions in northern and southern Italy. *Journal of Cross-Cultural Psychology, 26*, 123–140.

Geen, T. (1992). Facial expressions in socially isolated nonhuman primates: Open and closed programs for expressive behavior. *Journal of Research in Personality, 26*, 273–280.

Gudykunst, W. B., Matsumoto, Y., Ting-Toomey, S., Nishida, T., Kim, K., & Heyman, S. (1996). The influence of culture, individualism-collectivism, self construals, and individual values on communication styles across cultures. *Human Communication Research, 22*, 510–543.

Guidetti, M. (1991). Vocal expression of emotions: A cross-cultural and developmental approach. *Annee Psycholgique, 91*, 383–396.

Haidt, J., & Keltner, D. (1999). Culture and facial expression: Open-ended methods find more expressions and a gradient of recognition. *Culture and Emotion, 13*, 225–266.

Hatta, T., & Nachshon, I. (1988). Ear differences in evaluating emotional overtones of unfamiliar speech by Japanese and Israelis. *International Journal of Psychology, 23*, 293–302.

Hauser, M. (1993). Right hemisphere dominance for the production of facial expression in monkeys. *Science, 261*, 475–477.

Hofstede, G. (1980). *Culture's consequences.* Beverly Hills, CA: Sage.

Hofstede, G. (1983). Dimensions of national cultures in fifty countries and three regions. In J. Deregowski, S. Dziurawiec, & R. Annis (Eds.), *Expiscations in cross-cultural psychology.* Lisse, The Netherlands: Swets & Zeitlinger.

Hofstede, G. (1984). *Culture's consequences: International differences in work-related values.* Newbury Park, CA: Sage.

Izard, C. (1971). *The face of emotion.* New York: Appleton-Century-Crofts.

Izard, C. E. (1977). Human emotions. New York: Plenum Press.

Izard, C. E. (1978). Emotions as motivations: An evolutionary-developmental perspective. In R. A. Dienstbier (Ed.), *Nebraska Symposium on Motivation: Vol. 26* (pp. 163–200). Lincoln: University of Nebraska Press.

Izard, C. E. (1994). Innate and universal facial expressions: Evidence from developmental and cross-cultural research. *Psychological Bulletin, 115*, 288–299.

Izard, C. E., & Haynes, O. M. (1988). On the form and universality of the contempt expression: A challenge to Ekman and Friesen's claim of discovery. *Motivation and Emotion, 12*, 1–16.

James, W. (1890). *Psychology.* New York: Holt and Company.

Kemper, T. D. (1978). *A social interactional theory of emotions.* New York: Wiley.

Kirouac, G., & Dore, F. Y. (1982). Identification des expressions facials emotionalles par un echantillon Quebecois Francophone. *International Journal of Psychology, 17*, 1–7.

Kirouac, G., & Dore, F. Y. (1983). Accuracy and latency of judgment of facial expressions of emotions. *Perceptual and Motor Skills, 57*, 683–686.

Kirouac, G., & Dore, F. Y. (1985). Accuracy of the judgment of facial expression of emotions as a function of sex and level of education. *Journal of Nonverbal Behavior, 9*, 3–7.

Kitayama, S., & Markus, H. R., (1994). *Emotion and culture: Empirical studies of mutual influence.* Washington, DC: American Psychological Association.

Kitayama, S., & Markus, H. R. (1995). Culture and self: Implications for internationalizing psychology. In N. R. Goldberger and J. B. Veroff (Eds.), *The culture and psychology reader.* New York: New York University Press.

Kitayama, S., Markus, H. R., & Matsumoto, H. (1995). Culture, self, and emotion: A cultural perspective on "self-conscious" emotions. In J. P. Tangney, & K. W. Fischer (Eds.), *Self-conscious emotions: The psychology of shame, guilt, embarrassment, and pride* (pp. 439–464). New York: Guilford Press.

Knudsen, H. R., & Muzekari, L. H. (1983). The effects of verbal statements of context on facial expressions of emotion. *Journal of Nonverbal Behavior, 7*, 202–212.

Kudoh, T., and Matsumoto, D. (1985). A cross-cultural examination of the semantic dimensions of body postures. *Journal of Personality and Social Psychology, 48,* 1440–1446.

Lanzetta, J. T., & Kleck, R. E. (1970). Encoding and decoding of nonverbal affect in humans. *Journal of Personality and Social Psychology, 16,* 12–19.

Leung, J. P., & Singh, N. N. (1998). Recognition of facial expressions of emotion by Chinese adults with mental retardation. *Behavior Modification, 22,* 205–216.

Levenson, R. W., Ekman, P., Heider, K. & Friesen, W. V. (1992). Emotion and autonomic nervous system activity in the Minangkabau of West Sumatra. *Journal of Personality and Social Psychology, 62,* 972–988.

Levine, S. C., Banich, M. T., & Koch-Weser, M. P. (1988). Face recognition: A general or specific right hemisphere capacity? *Brain and Cognition, 8,* 303–325.

Levy, P. K. (1964). The ability to express and perceive vocal communications of feeling. In J. R. Davitz (Ed.), *The communication of emotional meaning.* New York: McGraw-Hill.

Levy, R. I. (1973). *Tahitians.* Chicago: University of Chicago Press.

Levy, R. I. (1983). Introduction: Self and emotion. *Ethos, 11,* 128–134.

Ley, R. G., & Bryden, M. P. (1979). Hemispheric differences in processing emotions and faces. *Brain and Language, 7,* 127–138.

Lutz, C. (1983). Parental goals, ethnopsychology, and the development of emotional meaning. *Ethos, 11,* 246–262.

Mandal, M. K., Saha, G. B., & Palchoudhury, S. (1986). A cross-cultural study on facial affect. *Journal of Psychological Researches, 30,* 140–143.

Mandler, G. (1984). *Mind and body: Psychology of emotion and stress.* New York: W. W. Norton.

Markham, R., & Wang, L. (1996). Recognition of emotion by Chinese and Australian children. *Journal of Cross-Cultural Psychology, 27,* 616–643.

Markus, H. R., & Kitayama, S. (1991). Culture and the self: Implications for cognition, emotion, and motivation. *Psychological Review. 98,* 224–253.

Matsumoto, D. (1987). The role of facial response in the experience of emotion: More methodological problems and a meta-analysis. *Journal of Personality and Social Psychology, 52,* 769–774.

Matsumoto, D. (1989). Cultural influences on the perception of emotion. *Journal of Cross-Cultural Psychology, 20,* 92–105.

Matsumoto, D. (1990). Cultural similarities and differences in display rules. *Motivation and Emotion, 14,* 195–214.

Matsumoto, D. (1992a). American and Japanese cultural differences in the recognition of universal facial expressions. *Journal of Cross-Cultural Psychology, 23,* 72–84.

Matsumoto, D. (1992b). More evidence for the universality of a contempt expression. *Motivation and Emotion, 16,* 363–368.

Matsumoto, D. (1993). Ethnic differences in affect intensity, emotion judgments, display rule attitudes, and self-reported emotional expression in an American sample. *Motivation and Emotion, 17,* 107–123.

Matsumoto, D. (1996). *Unmasking Japan: Myths and realities about the emotions of the Japanese.* Stanford, CA: Stanford University Press.

Matsumoto, D., & Assar, M. (1992). The effects of language on judgments of facial expressions of emotion. *Journal of Nonverbal Behavior, 16,* 85–99.

Matsumoto, D., Consolacion, T., Yamada, H., Suzuki, R., Franklin, B., Paul, S., Ray, R., & Uchida, H. (1999). *American-Japanese cultural differences in judgments of emotional expressions of different intensities.* Manuscript submitted for publication.

Matsumoto, D., & Ekman, P. (1988). *Japanese and Caucasian Facial Expressions of Emotion (JACFEE) and Neutral Faces (JACNeuF)* [Slides]. (Available from Human Interaction Laboratory, University of California, San Francisco, 401 Parnassus Avenue, San Francisco, CA, 94143)

Matsumoto, D., & Ekman, P. (1989). American-Japanese differences in intensity ratings of facial expressions of emotion. *Motivation and Emotion, 13,* 143–157.

Matsumoto, D., Kasri, F., & Kooken, K. (1999). American-Japanese cultural differences in judgments of expression intensity and subjective experience. *Cognition and Emotion, 13,* 201–218.

Matsumoto, D., & Kishimoto, H. (1983). Developmental characteristics in judgments of emotion from nonverbal vocal cues. *International Journal of Intercultural Relations, 7,* 415–424.

Matsumoto, D., & Kudoh, T. (1987). Cultural similarities and differences in the semantic dimensions of body postures. *Journal of Nonverbal Behavior, 11,* 166–179.

Matsumoto, D., & Kudoh, T. (1993). American-Japanese cultural differences in attributions of personality based on smiles. *Journal of Nonverbal Behavior, 17,* 231–243.

Matsumoto, D., LeRoux, J., Ratzlaff, C., Tatani, H., Uchida, H., Kim, C., & Araki, S. (in press). Development and validation of a measure of intercultural adjustment potential in Japanese sojourners: The Intercultural Adjustment

Potential Scale (ICAPS). *International Journal of Intercultural Relations.*

Matsumoto, D., Takeuchi, S., Andayani, S., Kouznetsova, N., & Krupp, D. (1998). The contribution of individualism-collectivism to cross-national differences in display rules. *Asian Journal of Social Psychology, 1,* 147–165.

Mauro, R., Sato, K., & Tucker, J. (1992). The role of appraisal in human emotions: A cross-cultural study. *Journal of Personality and Social Psychology, 62,* 301–317.

Mazurski, E. J., & Bond, N. W. (1993). A new series of slides depicting facial expressions of affect: A comparison with the Pictures of Facial Affect Series. *Australian Journal of Psychology, 45,* 41–47.

McAndrew, F. T. (1986). A cross-cultural study of recognition thresholds for facial expressions of emotion. *Journal of Cross-Cultural Psychology, 17,* 211–224.

McCluskey, K. W., & Albas, D. C. (1981). Perception of the emotional content of speech by Canadian and Mexican children, adolescents, and adults. *International Journal of Psychology, 16,* 119–132.

McCluskey, K. W., Albas, D. C., Niemi, R., Cuevas, C., & Ferrer, C. (1975). Cross-cultural differences in the perception of the emotional content of speech: A study of the development of sensitivity in Canadian and Mexican children. *Developmental Psychology, 11,* 551–555.

Mehta, S. D., Ward, C., & Strongman, K. (1992). Cross-cultural recognition of posed facial expressions of emotion. *New Zealand Journal of Psychology, 21,* 74–77.

Mesquita, B., & Frijda, N. H. (1992). Cultural variations in emotions: A review. *Psychological Bulletin, 112,* 197–204.

Munn, N. L. (1940). The effect of knowledge of the situation upon judgment of emotion from facial expressions. *Journal of Abnormal and Social Psychology, 35,* 324–338.

Muzekari, L. H., Knudsen, H., & Evans, T. (1986). Effect of context on perception of emotion among psychiatric patients. *Perceptual and Motor Skills, 62,* 79–84.

Nachson, I. (1995). On the modularity of face recognition: The riddle of domain specificity. *Journal of Clinical and Experimental Neuropsychology, 17,* 256–275.

Nakamura, M., Buck, R., & Kenny, D. A. (1990). Relative contributions of expressive behavior and contextual information to the judgment of the emotional state of another. *Journal of Personality and Social Psychology, 59,* 1032–1039.

Pittam, J., Gallois, C., Iwawaki, S., & Kroonenberg, P. (1995). Australian and Japanese concepts of expressive behavior. *Journal of Cross-Cultural Psychology, 26,* 451–473.

Poortinga, Y. H., van de Vijver, F. J. R., Joe, R. C., & van de Koppel, J. M. H. (1987). Peeling the onion called culture: A synopsis. In C. Kagitcibasi (Ed.), *Growth and progress in cross-cultural psychology* (pp. 22–34). Berwyn, PA: Swets North America.

Romney, A. K., Boyd, J. P., Moore, C. C., Batchelder, W. H., & Brazill, T. J. (1996). Culture as shared cognitive representations. *Proceedings from the National Academy of Sciences, 93,* 4699–4705.

Romney, A. K., Moore, C. C., & Rusch, C. D. (1997). Cultural universals: measuring the semantic structure of emotion terms in English and Japanese. *Proceedings of the National Academy of Sciences, 94,* 5489–5494.

Roseman, I. J., Dhawan, N. Rettek, S. I., Nadidu, R. K., & Thapa, K. (1995). Cultural differences and cross-cultural similarities in appraisals and emotional responses. *Journal of Cross-Cultural Psychology, 26,* 23–48.

Rosenberg, E. L., & Ekman, P. (1994). Coherence between expressive and experiential systems in emotion. *Cognition and Emotion, 8,* 201–229.

Rosenberg, E. L., & Ekman, P. (1995). Conceptual and methodological issues in the judgment of facial expressions of emotion. *Motivation and Emotion, 19,* 111–138.

Russell, J. A. (1991a). The contempt expression and the relativity thesis. *Motivation and Emotion, 15,* 149–184.

Russell, J. A. (1991b). Culture and the categorization of emotions. *Psychological Bulletin, 110,* 426–450.

Russell, J. A. (1991c). Negative results on a reported facial expression of contempt. *Motivation and Emotion, 15,* 281–291.

Russell, J. A. (1994). Is there universal recognition of emotion from facial expression? A review of cross-cultural studies. *Psychological Bulletin, 115,* 102–141.

Russell, J. A. (1995). Facial expressions of emotion: What lies beyond minimal universality? *Psychological Bulletin, 118,* 379–391.

Russell, J. A. (1997). Reading emotions from and into faces: Resurrecting a dimensional-contextual perspective. In J. A. Russell, & J. M. Fernandez-Dols (Eds.), *The psychology of facial expression* (pp. 295–320). New York: Cambridge University Press.

Russell, J. A., & Fehr, B. (1987). Relativity in the perception of emotion in facial expression. *Journal of Experimental Psychology: General, 116,* 223–237.

Russell, J. A., Suzuki, N., & Ishida, N. (1993). Canadian, Greek, and Japanese freely produced emotion labels for facial expressions. *Motivation and Emotion, 17,* 337–351.

Scherer, K. (1997a). Profiles of emotion antecedent-appraisal: Testing theoretical predictions across cultures. *Cognition and Emotion, 11*, 113–150.

Scherer, K. (1997b). The role of culture in emotion-antecedent appraisal. *Journal of Personality and Social Psychology, 73*, 902–922.

Scherer, K., Matsumoto, D., Wallbott, H., & Kudoh, T. (1988). Emotional experience in cultural context: A comparison between Europe, Japan, and the USA. In K. Scherer (Ed.), *Facets of emotion: Recent research* (pp. 5–30). Hillsdale, NJ: Erlbaum.

Scherer, K. R., & Wallbott, H. G. (1994). Evidence for universality and cultural variation of differential emotion response patterning. *Journal of Personality and Social Psychology, 66*, 310–328.

Scherer, K. R., Wallbott, H. G., & Summerfield, A. B. (Eds.). (1983). *Experiencing emotion: A cross-cultural study.* Cambridge: Cambridge University Press.

Schimmack, U. (1996). Cultural influences on the recognition of emotion by facial expressions: Individualist or Caucasian cultures? *Journal of Cross-Cultural Psychology, 27*, 37–50.

Shweder, R. A. (1993). Liberalism as destiny. In B. Puka (Ed.), *Moral development: A compendium. Vol. 4. The great justice debate: Kohlberg criticism* (pp. 71–74). New York: Garland.

Shweder, R. A., & Haidt, J. (2000). The cultural psychology of the emotions: Ancient and new. In M. Lewis and J. Haviland (Eds.), *The handbook of emotions.* New York: Guilford Press.

Sogon, S., & Masutani, M. (1989). Identification of emotion from body movements: A cross-cultural study of Americans and Japanese. *Psychological Reports, 65*, 35–46.

Spignesi, A., & Shor, R. E. (1981). The judgment of emotion from facial expressions, contexts, and their combination. *Journal of General Psychology, 104*, 41–58.

Streit, M., Ioannides, A. A., Liu, L., Woelwer, W., Dammers, J., Gross, J., Gaebel, W., & Mueller-Gaertner, H. W. (1999). Neurophysiological correlates of the recognition of facial expressions of emotion as revealed by magnetoencephalography. *Cognitive Brain Research, 7*, 481–491.

Tanaka-Matsumi, J., Attivissimo, D., Nelson, S., & D'Urso, T. (1995). Context effects on the judgment of basic emotions in the face. *Motivation and Emotion, 19*(2), 139–155.

Thayer, S. (1980a). The effect of expression sequence and expresser identity on judgments of the intensity of facial expression. *Journal of Nonverbal Behavior, 5*(2), 71–79.

Thayer, S. (1980b). The effect of facial expression sequence upon judgments of emotion. *Journal of Social Psychology, 111*, 305–306.

Toner, H. L., & Gates, G. R. (1985). Emotional traits and recognition of facial expressions of emotion. *Journal of Nonverbal Behavior, 9*, 48–66.

Triandis, H. C. (1994). *Culture and social behavior.* New York: McGraw-Hill.

Triandis, H. C. (1995). *Individualism and collectivism.* Boulder, CO: Westview Press.

Tsai, J. L., & Levenson, R. W. (1997). Cultural influences of emotional responding: Chinese American and European American dating couples during interpersonal conflict. *Journal of Cross-Cultural Psychology, 28*, 600–625.

Van Bezooijen, R., Otto, S., & Heenan, T. (1983). Recognition of vocal expressions of emotion. *Journal of Cross-Cultural Psychology, 14*, 387–406.

Van de Vijver, F. J. R., & Leung, K. (1997). *Methods and data analysis for cross-cultural research.* Newbury Park, CA: Sage.

VanGeert, P. (1995). Green, red, and happiness: Towards a framework for understanding emotion universals. *Culture and Psychology, 1*, 259–268.

Wallbott, H. G. (1988 a). Faces in context: The relative importance of facial expression and context information in determining emotion attributions. In K. R. Scherer (Ed.), *Facets of emotion* (pp. 139–160). Hillsdale, NJ: Erlbaum.

Wallbott, H. G. (1988 b). In and out of context: Influences of facial expression and context information on emotion attributions. *British Journal of Social Psychology, 27*, 357–369.

Wallbott, H. G. (1991). Recognition of emotion from facial expression via imitation? Some indirect evidence for an old theory. *British Journal of Social Psychology, 30*, 207–219.

Wallbott, H. G., & Scherer, K. (1986). How universal and specific is emotional experience? Evidence from 27 countries on five continents. *Social Science Information, 25*, 763–795.

Wang, L., & Meng, Z. (1986). A preliminary study of discrimination on facial expressions of adults. *Acta Psychologica Sinica, 18*(4), 349–355.

Waxer, P. H. (1985). Video ethology: Television as a data base for cross-cultural studies in nonverbal displays. *Journal of Nonverbal Behavior, 9*, 111–120.

Wierzbicka, A. (1994). Semantic universals and primitive thought: The question of the psychic unity of humankind. *Journal of Linguistic Anthropology, 4*, 23.

Wierzbicka, A. (1995). Emotion and facial expression: A semantic perspective. *Culture and Psychology, 1*, 227–258.

Winegar, L. (1995). Moving toward culture-inclusive theories of emotion. *Culture and Psychology, 1*, 269–277.

Winton, W. M. (1986). The role of facial response in self-reports of emotion: A critique of Laird. *Journal of Personality and Social Psychology, 50*, 808–812.

Wolfgang, A., & Cohen, M. (1988). Sensitivity of Canadians, Latin Americans, Ethiopians, and Israelis to interracial facial expressions of emotions. *International Journal of Intercultural Relations, 12*, 139–151.

Yik, M. S. M., Meng, Z., & Russell, J. A. (1998). Adults' freely produced emotion labels for babies' spontaneous facial expressions. *Cognition and Emotion, 12*, 723–730.

Yik, M. S. M., & Russell, J. A. (1999). Interpretation of faces: A cross-cultural study of a prediction from Fridlund's theory. *Cognition and Emotion, 13*, 93–104.

Yrizarry, N., Matsumoto, D., & Wilson Cohn, C. (1998). American and Japanese multi-scalar intensity ratings of universal facial expressions of emotion. *Motivation and Emotion, 22*, 315–327.

Zuckerman, M., Hall, J. A., DeFrank, R. S., & Rosenthal, R. (1976). Encoding and decoding of spontaneous and posed facial expressions. *Journal of Personality and Social Psychology, 34*, 966–977.

Zuckerman, M., Larrance, D. T., Hall, J. A., DeFrank, R. S., & Rosenthal, R. (1979). Posed and spontaneous communication of emotion via facial and vocal cues. *Journal of Personality, 47*, 712–733.

11

Gender and Culture

DEBORAH L. BEST & JOHN E. WILLIAMS

All cultures of the world must deal with the division of labor between the sexes, and exactly how they do this has been the topic of much research and debate. Like culture, the awareness and recognition of sex and gender differences, and of course similarities, have played a prominent role in the development of contemporary knowledge in psychology. This recognition is complemented by an abundance of studies in cross-cultural psychology and anthropology that have been concerned with the relationship between culture and gender, which forms the basis for much of the work reviewed here.

In this chapter, Best and Williams provide a comprehensive overview of the current state-of-the-art knowledge that exists concerning culture and gender. After first defining key terms, they describe research that examines gender at the individual adult level, including their own and others' research on sex role ideology, gender stereotypes, and self-concept. They go on to describe research on relations between women and men, including mate preferences, love and intimacy, harassment and rape, and work-related values. Using these findings as a platform, they discuss different factors that may contribute to the development of differences between genders, including biological determinism, sociobiological factors, sexual dimorphism, cultural influences, and socialization practices.

Best and Williams also review contemporary research that has examined gender differences in four psychological constructs: nurturance, aggression, proximity to adults, and self-esteem. They then present an excellent and detailed analysis of factors that contribute to the development of differences on the cultural level, including gender roles and stereotypes, theories of gender-related learning, and cultural practices that influence the behaviors of males and females. Their discussion of the interplay of social, psychological, cultural, political, historical, and economic forces reveals the depth and complexity of gender differences across cultures.

Given the vast number of areas in which gender has been studied and the rather complex relationship between multiple factors that contributes to its ontogeny, how can future research help develop models that will improve our understanding of how qualitative differences in the lives of males and females occur? Best and Williams suggest that improvements in our theories and methods for studying gender and culture need to occur. In particular, previous simplistic theories of gender will need to become multifactorial, recognizing the complexities of gender and the factors that influence it across cultures in various sociocultural systems. The incorporation of new and old methods of inquiry from other subfields of psychology, such as the five-factor model from personality research and the semantic differential in psychocultural linguistics, may also be important to broadening our understanding of culture and gender. Refining and improving our understanding of culture itself promises to be a key to improving our understanding of cultural influences on gender, especially in relation to the continued contextualization of culture and psychology. And, the examination of gender-related concepts across time and age in longitudinal studies will need to be given strong consideration.

The suggestions of Best and Williams for future research and theory strike a constant chord with the messages of the other authors of this volume. The integration of theories and methods from other branches of psychology is important to begin to put the fragmented pieces of psychology back together as a whole. Integration is not limited to other branches of psychology; indeed, Best and Williams suggest that anthropologists and psychologists must learn more from each other, a message that is also consistent with the message of many others in this volume. Future research will need to be fundamentally different from the past, including bridges between cultural and cross-cultural psychology, if it is to help knowledge in this area of culture and psychology to continue to evolve in a progressive fashion. Although Best and Williams suggest that it is reasonable to think in terms of a pancultural model of culture and gender, they also recognize the lack of adequate pancultural theories in the area, and the surprising fact that much gender-related cross-cultural work is not theory driven. The ideas presented here, however, promise to alleviate that concern.

One of the more striking variations observed when traveling in different countries is that some societies emphasize the differences between women and men, while other societies show less interest in such diversity. Highlighting sex differences leads to the expectation that gender must be an important determinant of human behavior. However, it is essential to remember that, anatomically and physiologically, human males and females are much more similar than different. Consequently, they are mostly interchangeable with regard to social roles and behaviors, with childbearing being the fundamental exception. As recent cross-cultural research related to gender is reviewed, the reader may be surprised to see how little difference gender makes when considered against the broad background of variability in psychological characteristics across cultural groups.

This chapter concerns gender in the cross-cultural context; it extends from the individual to the cultural level and examines topics such as gender roles and stereotypes, relationships between men and women, the roles of biology and socialization, and theories of gender role development. The focus is on the general areas of developmental, personality, and social psychology that deal with how males and females

view themselves and one another, as well as the way they should and do interact. Before reviewing the literature, some basic gender-related terms are defined to avoid conceptual confusion.

Definitions of Gender-Related Concepts

- *Sex* refers to the anatomical and physiological differences between males and females and the implication of those differences in procreation.
- *Gender* is also used to distinguish the male and female members of the human species, but with emphasis on social, rather than biological, factors.
- *Gender roles* refer to the social roles, including familial, occupational, and recreational activities, that men and women occupy with differential frequency.
- *Sex role ideology* designates beliefs concerning appropriate relationships between the genders and varies along a dimension ranging from a traditional, male-dominant or antifemale view to a modern or egalitarian view.

- *Gender stereotypes* refer to the psychological traits and behaviors that are believed to occur with differential frequency in the two gender groups (i.e., men are more "aggressive," women are more "emotional"). Stereotypes provide support for traditional sex role assignments and may serve as socialization models for children.
- *Masculinity/femininity* (M/F) represents the degree to which men and women have incorporated traits into their self-perceptions that are considered in their culture to be "womanlike" or "manlike."

With these definitions in mind, the discussion now turns to the individual and the role of gender in the cross-cultural context. Cross-cultural studies of gender are concerned with both the degree to which psychological processes and behaviors are relatively invariant across cultures and how they vary systematically with cultural influences.

Gender at the Individual Adult Level

Sex Role Ideology

In virtually all human groups, women have greater responsibility for "domestic" activities, while men have greater responsibility for "external" activities. These pancultural similarities originate, primarily, in the biological differences between the sexes, particularly the fact that women bear and, in most societies, nurse the offspring (Williams & Best, 1990b). However, recently in many societies these socially assigned duties are being shared, with men engaging in more domestic activities and women in more external, particularly economic, activities. The gender division of labor is reviewed below, while here the beliefs and attitudes about appropriate role behaviors for the two sexes are discussed.

Most researchers classify sex role ideologies along a continuum ranging from traditional to modern. Traditional ideologies assert that men are more "important" than women, and that it is proper for men to control and dominate women. In contrast, modern ideologies represent a more egalitarian view, sometimes labeled a *feminist position*, in which women and men are equally important, and dominance of one gender over the other is rejected.

Sex roles have been studied extensively in India, where contemporary Indian culture juxtaposes traditional and modern ideologies. When male and female Indian and American university students were asked what qualities women in their culture should and should not possess, Indian students expressed more traditional views than American students. Women in both groups were more modern, or liberal, than were men (Agarwal, Lester, & Dhawan, 1992; Rao & Rao, 1985). University women with nontraditional sex role attitudes came from nuclear families, had educated mothers, and were in professional or career-oriented disciplines (Ghadially & Kazi, 1979).

Similarly, education and professional managerial work are strong predictors of sex role attitudes for both Japanese and American women (Suzuki, 1991). American women with jobs, no matter what sort, had more egalitarian attitudes than women without jobs. In contrast, Japanese women with career-oriented professional jobs were more egalitarian than all other women, with or without jobs.

Gibbons, Stiles, and Shkodriani (1991) capitalized on a unique research opportunity and studied attitudes toward gender and family roles among adolescents from 46 different countries attending schools in the Netherlands. Countries of origin were grouped into two categories based on Hofstede's cultural values: the wealthier, more individualistic countries and the less wealthy, more collectivistic countries. Students from the second group of countries had more traditional attitudes than students from the first group of countries, and girls generally responded less traditionally than boys.

In a number of sex role ideology studies, Americans served as a reference group and were usually found to be more liberal, suggesting that Americans may be unusual in this respect. However, Williams and Best (1990b) did not find this to be true in their 14-country study of sex role ideology with university students. The most modern ideologies were found in European countries (the Netherlands, Germany, Finland, England, Italy). The United States was in the middle of the distribution, and the most traditional ideologies were found in African and Asian countries (Nigeria, Pakistan, India, Japan, Malaysia). Generally, women had more modern views than men, but not in all countries (e.g., Malaysia and Pakistan). However, there was high correspondence between men's and women's scores in a given country. Overall, the effect of culture was greater than the effect of gender.

Before concluding that observed variations between countries are due to cultural factors, the variations must be shown to relate to cultural comparison variables. Williams and Best (1990b) found a substantial relationship between men's and women's sex role ideology and economic-social development; that is, sex role ideology tended to be more modern in more developed countries. Sex role ideology also was more modern in more heavily Christian countries, in more urbanized countries, and in countries in the higher latitudes.

Gender Stereotypes

Related to sex role ideology, and often used as justifications for those beliefs, are gender stereotypes, the psychological traits believed to be more characteristic of one gender than the other. In their research, Williams and Best (1990a) presented the 300 person-descriptive adjectives from the Adjective Checklist (ACL; Gough & Heilbrun, 1980) to university students in 27 countries and asked them to indicate whether, in their culture, each adjective was associated more frequently with men, associated more frequently with women, or not differentially associated by gender. There was substantial agreement across all 27 countries concerning the psychological characteristics differentially associated with men and with women. Male and female stereotypes differed most in the Netherlands, Finland, Norway, and Germany and least in Scotland, Bolivia, and Venezuela. Stereotypes of men and women differed more in Protestant than in Catholic countries, in more developed countries, and in countries where Hofstede's male work-related values were relatively high in individualism (Williams & Best, 1990a, appendix D).

In each country, the high-agreement male and female stereotype items were scored using an affective meaning scoring system, and in all countries, the male stereotype items were more active and stronger than the female stereotype items. Interestingly, there was no pancultural effect for favorability, with the male stereotype being more positive in some countries (e.g., Japan, South Africa, Nigeria) and the female stereotype in others (e.g., Italy, Peru, Australia). Using a second scoring system (Transactional Analysis Ego States) indicated that, in all countries, the Critical Parent and Adult ego states were more characteristic of men, while the Nurturing Parent and Adapted Child ego states were more characteristic of women; the Free Child ego state was not associated differentially. A third scoring system based on 15 psychological needs revealed that, across all countries, dominance, autonomy, aggression, exhibition, and achievement were associated with men, while nurturance, succorance, deference, and abasement were associated with women. A recent reanalysis of the stereotype data in terms of the Five-Factor Model of personality revealed that the pancultural male stereotype was higher in extraversion, conscientiousness, emotional stability, and openness, while the female stereotype was higher only in agreeableness (Williams, Satterwhite, & Best, 1999).

Within these general similarities, there was also variation between countries. For example, strength and activity differences between male and female stereotypes were greater in socioeconomically less-developed countries, in countries where literacy was low, and in countries where the percentage of women attending the university was low. Perhaps economic and educational advancement are accompanied by a reduction in the tendency to view men as stronger and more active than women. However, the effects were merely reduced—not eliminated.

The high degree of cross-cultural similarity in gender stereotypes leads to the conclusion that the psychological characteristics differentially associated with men and women follow a pancultural model, with cultural factors producing minor variations around general themes (see Williams & Best, 1990a, pp. 241–244, for a more detailed description of such a model). In brief, Williams and Best's model proposes that biological differences set the stage (e.g., females bear children, males have greater physical strength) and lead to a division of labor, noted above, with women responsible for child care and other domestic activities and men for hunting (providing) and protection. Gender stereotypes evolved to support this division of labor. Stereotypes contend that each gender has or can develop characteristics congruent with the assigned role. Once established, stereotypes serve as socialization models that encourage boys to become independent and adventurous and girls to become nurturant and affiliative. Thus, the model demonstrates how people in widely different cultures come to associate one set of characteristics with men and another set with women with only minor variations around these central themes.

Masculinity/Femininity of Self-Concepts

Manlike or womanlike are the essential meanings of the paired concepts of masculinity/femininity (M/F). A person might be masculine or feminine in a variety of ways, including dress, mannerisms, or tone of voice. Here, the definition is restricted to self-concepts and the degree to which they incorporate traits that are associated differentially with women or men. Within this restricted concept of masculinity/femininity, researchers have used different measurement techniques. Some have used self-descriptive questionnaire items (Gough, 1952), some analyze only socially desirable characteristics (Bem, 1974; Spence & Helmreich, 1978), and others examine gender-associated characteristics without reference to social desirability (Williams & Best, 1990b).

Regarding measurement, cross-cultural studies of masculinity/femininity should address emic or culture-specific considerations. Problems arise when a masculinity/femininity scale (e.g., Spence & Helmreich, 1978) developed in one country, often the United States, is translated into another language and administered to persons in other cultures. Scores are interpreted as if they represent comparative degrees of masculinity/femininity in the different cultures, and there is little emic consideration. Cross-culturally, some items in translated scales may be inappropriate due to content, whereas others may be poorly translated.

Williams and Best (1990b) employed culture-specific measures of masculinity/femininity in a study with university students in 14 countries. Each participant described himself/herself and his/her ideal self using the 300 ACL adjectives, and these descriptions were scored relative to the local gender stereotypes determined in an earlier study (Williams & Best, 1990a). Men in all countries were found to be more masculine than women, hardly a surprising result. In contrast, for the ideal self, both gender groups wished to be "more masculine" than they thought they were.

While some cultural variation in self-concepts was found, there were no substantial associations with cultural comparison variables, such as economic/social development. Across cultural groups, relative to their own culture's definition of femininity and masculinity, there was no evidence that women in some societies were more feminine than women in others, or that men in some societies were more masculine than men in others.

In contrast, when self-concepts were examined in terms of affective meaning scores, there were substantial differences across countries in self and ideal self-concepts, and these corre-

lated with cultural comparison variables. For example, the differences in the self-concepts of men and women were less in more developed countries, when women were employed outside the home, when women constituted a large percentage of the university population, and where a relatively modern sex role ideology prevailed.

Thus, an interesting paradox occurs. When using the masculinity-femininity scoring system, which seems methodologically superior due to its reliance on culture-specific definitions, there is scant evidence of cross-cultural variation and greater evidence of pancultural similarity in definitions of masculinity/femininity. On the other hand, when using the affective meaning scoring system, which is based on ratings by persons in the United States and may be culturally biased, there are a number of robust relationships with cultural comparison variables. This paradox cannot be resolved easily.

Relations between Women and Men

This section reviews cross-cultural studies dealing with the relationships between men and women. Readers interested in cross-cultural variations in human sexual behavior are referred to D. L. Davis and Whitten (1987), Hatfield and Rapson (1993, 1995), and Reiss (1986).

Mate Preferences

The most extensive investigation of mate preferences was conducted by Buss and associates (Buss, 1989, 1990; Buss et al., 1990), who gathered data from 37 samples totaling over 10,000 respondents from 33 countries. Buss and coworkers note that, although social scientists often assume that mate preferences are highly culture bound and arbitrary, their findings are contrary.

On two similar lists of potential mate characteristics, Buss asked participants to indicate their preferences by rating or ranking the items. The most striking finding was the remarkable degree of agreement in preference for mate characteristics between men and women. Both genders ranked "kind and understanding" first, "intelligent" second, "exciting personality" third, "healthy" fourth, and "religious" last. Despite the overall gender similarity, women generally valued good earning capacity in a potential mate slightly more than did men, whereas men generally valued physical appearance slightly more than did women, providing modest support for sociobiological views (e.g., Wilson, 1975).

Conversely, cultural differences were found for virtually every item, and on some items, there was great variation across cultures. The greatest cultural effect occurred for chastity, with northern European groups viewing it as largely unimportant, while groups from China, India, and Iran placed great emphasis on it. Men valued chastity in a prospective mate more than did women.

Buss et al. (1990) concluded that there were substantial commonalities among all samples, suggesting substantial unity in human mate preferences that may be regarded as "species typical." On the other hand, no sample was exactly like any other sample—each displayed some uniqueness in the ordering of mate preference characteristics, reflecting modest degrees of cultural variation.

Romantic Love and Intimacy

As with mate preferences, romantic love and intimacy are assumed to be influenced by culture. Generally, romantic love is valued highly in less-traditional cultures with few strong extended family ties and is less valued in cultures in which strong family ties reinforce the relationship between marriage partners. For example, Japanese university students value romantic love less than do West German students, with the value placed by American students between the other two societies (Simmons, Kolke, & Shimizu, 1986). Compared with Swedish young adults, American young adults differentiate love and sex more strongly (Foa et al., 1987).

Interestingly, Vaidyanathan and Naidoo (1990/1991) found that Asian Indian immigrants to Canada show generational changes in attitudes toward love and marriage. Although 63% of first-generation immigrants had arranged marriages, a large proportion of them believed that "love marriages" were an option for their offspring. More than 70% of the second generation wanted more freedom in mate selection and believed that love should precede marriage.

Dion and Dion (1993) examined the concepts of love and intimacy in individualistic (Canada, United States) and collectivistic (China, India, Japan) countries and reported some paradoxical findings. Individualistic societies emphasize romantic love and personal fulfillment

in marriage, but individualism makes realization of these outcomes difficult. In contrast, collectivism fosters a receptiveness to intimacy, but intimacy is likely to be diffused across a network of family relationships. Broude (1987) suggests that intimacy is likely to occur when individuals have no social support outside marriage.

Buunk and Hupka (1987) surveyed over 2,000 students from seven industrialized nations (Hungary, Ireland, Mexico, the Netherlands, the former Soviet Union, the United States, Yugoslavia) with regard to behaviors that elicit jealousy. Within a general picture of cross-cultural similarities, there were some interesting differences. Flirting in Yugoslavia evokes a more negative response than in any other country, but kissing and sexual fantasies elicit the least negative reactions. In the Netherlands, sexual fantasies are less accepted than in any other country, but kissing, dancing, and hugging arouse less jealousy than in most other countries. Culture seems to play a critical role in the interpretation of cross-gender close relationships.

Harassment and Rape

Among the few cross-cultural studies of male harassment and hostility toward women is a study by Kauppinen-Toropainen and Gruber (1993), who examined professional and blue collar women in the United States, Scandinavia, and the former Soviet Union. Americans reported the most woman-unfriendly experiences. Scandinavians had fewer job-related or psychological problems, more autonomy, and better work environments than Americans. Former Soviet professionals reported more unfriendly experiences than workers, but less than their peers in other regions.

Rozeé (1993), in a random sample of 35 world societies from the Standard Cross Cultural Sample, found rape occurs in all societies. Generally, respondents blamed both criminal and victim less than do Americans, emphasizing instead the circumstances surrounding the offense (L'Armand, Pepitone, & Shanmugam, 1981).

The most comprehensive cross-cultural study of attitudes toward rape victims was conducted with university students in 15 countries by a network of researchers led by Ward from Singapore (Ward, 1995). Relatively favorable attitudes toward rape victims were found in the United Kingdom, Germany, and New Zealand, while relatively unfavorable attitudes were found in Turkey, Mexico, Zimbabwe, India, and, particularly, Malaysia. Attitudes toward rape victims mirror attitudes toward women more generally, with more favorable attitudes in countries with more modern sex role ideologies and less favorable attitudes in countries with a lower percentage of female labor force participation and lower literacy rates.

Masculine Work-Related Values

In the area of more general values, Hofstede (1980) compared work-related values in 40 countries using attitude survey data collected from thousands of employees of IBM, a large, multinational, high-technology business organization. One scale derived from Hofstede's factor analysis concerned the extent to which values of assertiveness, money, and things prevail in a society rather than the values of nurturance, quality of life, and people. While the scale might have easily been named *Materialism*, Hofstede named the scale *Masculinity* (MAS) because male employees assign greater weight to the first set of values, whereas females assign greater weight to the second set. Calling the scale Masculinity leads to the expectation that variations on these values might be associated with cross-country variations in other gender-related concepts, such as those discussed above.

Hofstede computed a MAS index for each of the 40 countries in his study. The five countries with the highest MAS indices were Japan, Austria, Venezuela, Italy, and Switzerland; the five countries with the lowest MAS indices were Sweden, Norway, Netherlands, Denmark, and Finland. Hofstede (1980) made extensive comparisons among country MAS scores with data from other sources and found a large number of interesting relationships. For example, in countries with high MAS, there is greater belief in independent decision making as opposed to group decision making, stronger achievement motivation, and higher job stress, and work is more central in people's lives.

While it is clear that the MAS dimension is a significant one, the appropriateness of designating this value system as Masculinity remains somewhat doubtful. Best and Williams (1994; 1998) found no relationship between the cross-country variations in their sex stereotypes and masculinity/femininity scores and the cross-country variations in Hofstede's MAS scores. Likewise, Ward (1995) notes that, while attitude toward rape scores covary with Hof-stede's power distance scores, they are unrelated to his MAS scores.

Developmental Influences

Having seen the influence of gender on the behavior and relationships of adults, it is natural to wonder about the development of gender-related beliefs and behaviors and the role of biological and cultural influences across ontogeny.

Biological Determinism

Researchers studying gender differences in behavior often cite similarities across cultures as support for the role of genes and hormones, implying complete genetic or biological determinism. Biological determinism assumes that any biological influence or bias always leads to an irreversible sex difference, making biology both the necessary and sufficient cause of sex differences. Biology is neither. The long-standing nature-nurture controversy within developmental psychology has shown that biology does not cause behavior, and that such thinking is quite naive.

Sex chromosomes or sex hormones are neither necessary nor sufficient to cause behaviors; they simply change the probability of occurrence of certain behaviors (Hoyenga & Hoyenga, 1993; Stewart, 1988). The gene-behavior pathway is bidirectional (Gottlieb, 1983), and somewhat like people inherit genes, they may "inherit" environments by living close to parents and family.

Sociobiology, Evolutionary Psychology, Economic Anthropology

Looking at the interplay between biology and environment, sociobiologists (e.g., Daly & Wilson, 1978; Wilson, 1975), evolutionary psychologists (e.g., Buss, 1990; Nisbett, 1990), and economic anthropologists (Fry, 1987) suggest that some behavioral mechanisms have evolved in response to selection pressures. Diversity in gender roles reflects the fact that different circumstances trigger different behavioral responses, each of which are biologically prepared.

Gilmore (1990) proposes that the male macho behavior pattern is an adaptation to extreme risk associated with economic necessities. The dramatic difference in gender roles between two South Pacific islands, Truk and Tahiti, illustrate Gilmore's hypothesis. Trukese males are competitive, violent fighters and are sexually promiscuous, while females are expected to be submissive and protected by the men. In contrast, Tahitian men are not interested in material pursuits or in competition and are expected to be passive and submissive, while the women are generally known to be sexually active. Gilmore (1990) accounts for these variations by the dramatic difference in obtaining food. Tahitians fish in a protected lagoon where there is little risk, and fish are plentiful. Trukese must fish in the open ocean with the genuine possibility of not returning after a day at sea. Thus, the macho style may be an adaptation to danger that encourages Trukese men to face great peril.

While some notions of sociobiology are consistent with the interactive view of nature and nurture, the theory has been criticized on many levels (Gould & Lewontin, 1979). Indeed, many of its assumptions are not supported by empirical data (Travis & Yeager, 1991).

Sexual Dimorphism

While biology is not destiny, biological influences are certainly important contributors to the development of gender differences. The term *biological* is often used to refer to genes, in this case, sex chromosomes, but biological should also include the influence of an organism's prenatal and postnatal environments, and often the activities in those environments are culturally determined. For example, lengths of sleep bouts are modified by culturally determined demands on mothers' time, and the course of sitting and walking by infants are influenced by culturally defined child care practices (Super & Harkness, 1982).

Compared with females, at birth males are larger and have a higher activity level (Eaton & Enns, 1986), higher basal metabolism, more muscle development, and higher pain threshold (Rosenberg & Sutton-Smith, 1972). During the preadolescent years (ages 3–10), there are few gender differences in morphology or hormonal states, but those that are observed are consistent with the sexual dimorphism that is found later (Tanner, 1961, 1970).

By adulthood, males attain greater height, have a more massive skeleton, higher muscle-to-fat ratio, higher blood oxygen capacity, more body hair, and different primary and secondary sex characteristics (D'Andrade, 1966; Tanner,

1961). The first of these differences is related to the greater physical strength and stamina of the male and seem to be related to the longer growth period of boys and the hormonal changes that appear after age 8 (Ember, 1981). However, these differences only hold within populations, not between, and they apply only to group means, not individual comparisons (Munroe & Munroe, 1975/1994). Many women are stronger and more active than many men.

Cultural Influences

Even though biological factors may impose predispositions and restrictions on development, sociocultural factors are important determinants of development (Best & Williams, 1993; Munroe & Munroe, 1975/1994; Rogoff, Gauvain, & Ellis, 1984). Culture has profound effects on behavior, prescribing how babies are delivered, how children are socialized, how children are dressed, what is considered intelligent behavior, what tasks children are taught, and what roles adult men and women will adopt. The scope and progression of the children's behaviors, even behaviors that are considered biologically determined, are governed by culture. Cultural universals in gender differences are often explained by similarities in socialization practices, while cultural differences are attributed to differences in socialization.

One of the best known, although often questioned, examples of cultural diversity in gender-related behaviors is Margaret Mead's classic study of three tribes in New Guinea (Mead, 1935). Mead reported that, from a Western viewpoint, these societies created men and women who are both masculine and feminine and who reversed the usual gender roles.

The pervasive nature of sex differences in behaviors was poignantly illustrated in the Israeli kibbutz, established in the 1920s, where there was a deliberate attempt to develop egalitarian societies (Rosner, 1967; Snarey & Son, 1986; Spiro, 1956). Initially, there was no sexual division of labor. Both women and men worked in the fields, drove tractors, and worked in the kitchen and in the laundry. However, as time went by and the birth rate increased, it was soon discovered that women could not undertake many of the physical tasks of which men were capable. Women soon found themselves in the same roles from which they were supposed to have been emancipated—cooking, cleaning, laundering, teaching, caring for children. The kibbutz attempts at equitable division of labor seemed to have little effect on the children. Carlsson and Barnes (1986) found no cultural or sex differences between kibbutz-raised children and Swedish children regarding how they conceptualized typical female and male sex role behaviors or in their sex-typed self-attributions.

Socialization of Boys and Girls

For boys and girls, many behavioral differences are attributed to differences in socialization. Barry, Bacon, and Child (1957) examined socialization practices in over 100 societies and found that boys are generally raised to achieve and to be self-reliant and independent, while girls are raised to be nurturant, responsible, and obedient. However, Hendrix and Johnson (1985) reanalyzed these data and did not replicate the male-female difference in socialization. Indeed, the instrumental-expressive components were not polar opposites, but were orthogonal, unrelated dimensions with similar emphases in the training of boys and girls.

In their metanalysis, Lytton and Romney (1991) found that, in 158 North American studies of socialization, the only significant effect was for the encouragement of sex-typed behaviors. In the 17 additional studies from other Western countries, there was a significant sex difference for physical punishment, with boys receiving a greater portion than girls. Differential treatment of boys and girls decreased with age, particularly for disciplinary strictness and encouragement of sex-typed activities.

Overall, these socialization findings suggest that there may be subtle differences in the ways that boys and girls are treated by parents. In research, these differences are only occasionally significant, perhaps due to the categories used to quantify behaviors. Even if parents do not differentiate between daughters and sons due to biological differences or preexisting preferences, the same parental treatment may affect girls and boys differently.

Task Assignment

Examination of children's learning environments in various cultural groups yields a better understanding of how cultural differences in socialization processes affect children's development. Learning environments were investigated in the Six Culture Study (Edwards & Whiting, 1974; Minturn & Lambert, 1964; E.

Whiting & Edwards, 1973), which examined aggression, nurturance, responsibility, and help and attention-seeking behaviors of children aged 3 to 11 years in Okinawa, Mexico, the Philippines, India, Kenya, and the United States. Fewer gender differences were found in the three samples (the United States, the Philippines, Kenya) in which both boys and girls cared for younger siblings and performed household chores. In contrast, more differences were found in the samples (India, Mexico, Okinawa) in which boys and girls were treated dissimilarly, and girls were asked to assume more responsibility for siblings and household tasks. Indeed, the fewest gender differences were found in the American sample, in which neither girls nor boys were assigned many child care or household tasks.

Bradley (1993) examined children's labor in 91 Standard Cross-Cultural Sample cultures (Murdock & White, 1969) and found that children less than 6 years of age perform little work, whereas children more than 10 years old perform work much like that of same-gender adults. Both boys and girls do women's work (e.g., fetching water) more frequently than men's (e.g., hunting), and children tend to do work that adults consider demeaning or unskilled. Women monitor children's labor that socializes them and helps the mother. Along with providing care in parents' old age, children's labor is one of the important benefits of having children.

Caretaking

Weisner and Gallimore (1977) analyzed data from 186 societies and found that mothers, female adult relatives, and female children are the primary caretakers of infants. However, when those infants reach early childhood, responsibilities are shared among both sex peer groups. Sibling caretakers are a predominant source of socialization in societies in which 2- to 4-year-olds spend more than 70% of every day with their child nurses. Mothers in such societies spend much of their time in productive activities and are not devoted exclusively to mothering (Greenfield, 1981; Mintern & Lambert, 1964), although children in all cultures see mothers as responsible for children.

Indeed, in 20% of 80 cultures surveyed (Katz & Konner, 1981; West & Konner, 1976), fathers were rarely or never near their infants. Father-infant relationships were close in only

4% of the cultures, but even when close, fathers spent only 14% of their time with their infants and gave only 6% of the actual caregiving. In most societies, play characterized paternal interactions with children (R. L. Munroe & Munroe, 1994).

Absence of a father has been associated with violent or hypermasculine behaviors (Katz & Konner, 1981; Segall, 1988; B. B. Whiting, 1965). When fathers are absent for extended periods of time due to war (Stolz, 1954) or lengthy sea voyages (Gronseth, 1957; Lynn & Sawrey, 1959), their sons display effeminate overt behaviors, high levels of dependence, excessive fantasy aggression, as well as some overly masculine behaviors.

Fathers also pay less attention to female offspring than to males and encourage sex-typed activities more than mothers (Lytton & Romney, 1991). Mothers are equally important as caretakers of sons and daughters, but fathers tend to be more important as caretakers of sons (Rohner & Rohner, 1982). Mackey observed parents and children in public places in 10 different cultures and found that girls were more often in groups with no adult males, while boys were frequently found in all-male groups; these differences intensified with age (Mackey, 1985; Mackey & Day, 1979).

Peers

Throughout childhood and adolescence, peers play an important role in socialization. Peer influence increases as children grow older, helping to structure the transition between childhood and adulthood (Edwards, 1992).

Analysis of peer interactions of children 2 to 10 years old from the Six Culture Study and six additional samples (Edwards, 1992; Edwards & Whiting, 1993) showed a cross-culturally universal and robust tendency for same gender preference to emerge after age 2. By middle childhood, gender segregation is found frequently. Edwards speculates that same-gender attraction may be motivated by a desire for self-discovery, making same gender agemates the best mirrors. Agemates resemble the child in abilities and activity preferences, but they also provide the greatest opportunity for competition and conflict.

Adolescent initiation rites found in many cultures are designed to detach the initiate from the family; to socialize them to culturally appropriate sexuality, dominance, and aggression; to create peer group loyalty; and to solidify political ties. Collective rituals are more common for boys than girls and are found more frequently in warrior societies, which emphasize gender differences in men's and women's activities (Edwards, 1992). Although Western education has begun to change initiation rites, vestiges remain.

Education

Educational settings also greatly influence children's behaviors. Observations of fifth graders in Japan and in the United States indicate that teachers in both countries paid more attention to boys, particularly negative attention, and the greater attention was not attributable to off-task or bad behavior (Hamilton, Blumenfeld, Akoh, & Miura, 1991).

Parental beliefs about academic performance can also have profound impact on children's achievements. Serpell (1993) found that education was considered more important for Zambian boys than girls, and fathers assumed responsibility for arranging schooling even though mothers were primarily responsible for child care. In China, Japan, and the United States, mothers expect boys to be better at mathematics and for girls to be better at reading (Lummis & Stevenson, 1990), although both sexes perform equally well in some aspects of both disciplines.

Gender Differences in Male and Female Behaviors

Together, biological and cultural influences lead to differences in the behaviors of males and females. Four areas of cross-cultural gender differences have been found and are reviewed briefly: nurturance, aggression, proximity to adults, and self-esteem.

Nurturance

In the Six Culture Study, Edwards and Whiting (1980) found that between ages 5 and 12 years, gender differences in nurturance were most consistent in behavior directed to infants and toddlers rather than in behavior directed toward mothers and older children. Since infants elicit more nurturant behavior than do older children, girls, who spent more time with infants, demonstrated more nurturance than boys, who were not engaged in as much infant interaction.

Barry, Bacon, and Child (1957) found that, compared with boys, girls were socialized to be more nurturant (82% of cultures), obedient (35% of cultures), and responsible (61% of cultures). Boys, on the other hand, were socialized to be more achieving (87% of cultures) and self-reliant (85% of cultures) than girls. In 108 cultures, Welch, Page, and Martin (1981) found more pressure for boys to conform to their roles than girls, who also had greater role variability.

Aggression

Cross-cultural studies of prepubertal children have consistently shown that boys have higher levels of aggression, competitiveness, dominance seeking, and rough-and-tumble play than do girls (Ember, 1981; Freedman & DeBoer, 1979; Strube, 1981). Examining data from the Six Culture Study and additional African samples, B. B. Whiting and Edwards (1988) found sex differences in aggression and dominance, but unlike their earlier findings, aggression did not decrease with age and was more physical among the oldest boys. Omark, Omark, and Edelman's (1975) playground observations in Ethiopia, Switzerland, and the United States showed that boys were more aggressive than girls, and Blurton-Jones and Konner's (1973) study had similar findings in four !Kung bush people villages and in London. In their observations in four nonindustrial cultures, Munroe and colleagues (R. L. Munroe, Hulefeld, Rodgers, Tomeo, & Yamazaki, 2000) found more frequent aggression in boys than girls. While both boys and girls segregated by sex, aggregation by sex was associated most strongly with episodes of aggression by boys.

The Six Culture Study indicated that mothers generally react similarly to aggression by boys and girls, but there was some evidence of differential aggression training in Okinawa and the United States, which suggested that fathers may play an important role in socializing aggression in boys (Minturn & Lambert, 1964). Acceptance of aggression is similar for males and females in western European countries, but there are gender differences in the forms of aggressive acts. Males initially are more restrained, but when they act, they are more violent (Ramirez, 1993), while females are more emotional and use shouting and verbal attacks (Burbank, 1987).

Moving to the other end of the spectrum, Boehnke and colleagues (Boehnke, Silbereisen, Eisenberg, Reykowski, & Palmonari, 1989) examined the development of prosocial motivation in schoolchildren from West Germany, Poland, Italy, and the United States. By age 12, but not before, girls demonstrated more mature motives in their responses to hypothetical situations, which provided opportunity for prosocial action.

Proximity to Adults and Activity

Observing the play of children 5 to 7 years old in eight cultures (Australian Aboriginal, Balinese, Ceylonese, Japanese, Kikuyu, Navajo, Punjabi, Taiwanese), Freedman (1976) found that boys ran in larger groups, covered more physical space, and did more physical and unpredictable activities, while girls were involved in more conversations and games with repeated activities. Girls are usually found closer to home (Draper, 1975; R. L. Munroe & Munroe, 1971; B. Whiting & Edwards, 1973). Task assignment (B. Whiting & Edwards, 1973) and behavioral preferences may contribute to these gender differences (Draper, 1975). Boys tend to interact more with other boys, while girls tend to interact more with adults (Blurton Jones & Konner, 1973; Omark et al., 1975; B. Whiting & Edwards, 1973).

Children's drawings reflect a gender segregation similar to that in play, with boys drawing more pictures of boys and girls of girls (Freedman, 1976). Perhaps reflecting gender differences in what children like, boys in nine cultures drew more vehicles, monsters, and pictures with violent themes than did girls, who drew more flowers.

Self-Esteem

Although gender role attributions are similar, girls seem less satisfied with being girls than boys are with being boys (Burns & Homel, 1986), and boys perceive themselves to be more competent than girls (van Dongen-Melman, Koot, & Verhulst, 1993). However, the dissatisfaction of girls is not consistently manifested in lower self-esteem (Calhoun & Sethi, 1986). Compared with boys, adolescent girls in Nepal, the Philippines, and Australia had lower opinions of their physical and mathematical abilities, but girls in Australia and Nigeria felt more competent in reading (Watkins & Akande, 1992; Watkins, Lam, & Regmi, 1991). Nigerian boys believed they were more intelligent than did girls (Olowu, 1985).

In sum, differences between boys and girls in nurturance, aggression, and mobility are robust and consistently found across cultures (Ember, 1981), while self-esteem differences are less consistent. Culture shapes the social behaviors of children by selecting the company they keep and the activities that engage their time. Such experiences can maximize, minimize, or even eliminate gender differences in social behaviors.

Gender Roles and Stereotypes

Within the context of cultural stereotypes about male-female differences, gender roles and knowledge develop. Research in the United States indicates that, as early as 2 years of age, children stereotype objects as masculine or feminine (Thompson, 1975; Weinraub et al., 1984), and by 3 to 4 years of age, children use stereotypic labels accurately with toys, activities, and occupations (Edelbrook & Sugawara, 1978; Guttentag & Longfellow, 1977).

Similar gender stereotyping of toys is found in Africa, where girls play with dolls, and boys construct vehicles and weapons (Bloch & Adler, 1994). By age 4 to 5 years, Sri Lankan village children demonstrate gender differences in play similar to those found with British children (Prosser, Hutt, Hutt, Mahindadasa, & Goonetilleke, 1986). Boys exhibit more negative behaviors and more fantasy object play, while girls display more fantasy person play. Even though cultural factors determine the content of children's play, the form of only a few behaviors seem to be culturally specific.

Development of Sex-Trait Stereotypes

Research in the United States indicates that children acquire knowledge of sex-trait stereotypes somewhat later than stereotypic knowledge of toys and occupations (Best et al., 1977; Reis & Wright, 1982; Williams & Best, 1990a). Using the Sex Stereotype Measure (SSM) to assess children's knowledge of adult-defined stereotypes, research conducted with European American children revealed a consistent pattern of increasing knowledge from kindergarten through high school, similar to a typical learning curve. The most dramatic increases in stereotype knowledge occurred in the early elementary school years, with scores reaching a

plateau in the junior high years. African American children's scores increased with age, but were lower than those of the European American children, perhaps reflecting subcultural variation in stereotype knowledge.

Cross-Cultural Findings

Williams, Best, and colleagues (1990a) administered the SSM II to 5-, 8-, and 11-year-olds in 25 countries. Across all countries, the percentage of stereotyped responses rose from around 60% at age 5 to around 70% at age 8. Strong, aggressive, cruel, coarse, and adventurous were consistently associated with men at both age levels, and weak, appreciative, softhearted, gentle, and meek were consistently associated with women.

Both male and female scores were unusually high in Pakistan and relatively high in New Zealand and England. Scores were atypically low in Brazil, Taiwan, Germany, and France. Although there was variation among countries in the rate of learning, there was a general developmental pattern in which the acquisition of stereotypes begins prior to age 5, accelerates during the early school years, and is completed during the adolescent years.

Boys and girls learned the stereotypes at the same rate, although there was a tendency for male stereotype traits to be learned somewhat earlier than female traits. In 17 of the 24 countries studied, male stereotype items were better known than female items. Germany was the only country where there was a clear tendency for the female stereotype to be better known than the male. In contrast, female stereotype items were learned earlier than male items in Latin/Catholic cultures (Brazil, Chile, Portugal, Venezuela), where the adult-defined female stereotype is more positive than the male (Neto, Williams, & Widner, 1991; Tarrier & Gomes, 1981).

In predominantly Muslim countries, 5-year-olds associate traits with the two sexes in a more highly differentiated manner, and they learn the stereotypes, particularly the male items, at an earlier age than in non-Muslim countries. Children in predominantly Christian countries are slower in their initial learning of the stereotypes, perhaps reflecting the less-differentiated nature of the adult stereotypes, particularly in Catholic countries.

Using a combined measure of traits and roles, Albert and Porter (1986) examined the gender stereotypes of 4- to 6-year-olds in the United States and South Africa and found stereotyping increased with age. South African children stereotyped the male role more than did U.S. children, but there were no country differences for the female role. South African children from liberal Christian and Jewish backgrounds stereotyped less than children from more conservative religious groups. In the United States, religious background was not a factor.

Looking at older children (11 to 18 years of age), Intons-Peterson (1988) found that Swedish children attributed more instrumental qualities to women than did American children. Gender stereotypes were more similar in Sweden than in the United States, perhaps reflecting Swedish cultural philosophy. Surprisingly, in Sweden, ideal occupational choices did not overlap; young Swedish women were interested in service occupations, such as flight attendant, hospital worker, and nanny, and young Swedish men were interested in business occupations. In contrast, ideal occupations for the sexes overlapped in the United States, with both groups listing doctor/dentist/attorney and business executive as their top choices. Considering the similarities found across diverse countries and the differing measures used, sex stereotypes appeared to be universal, with culture modifying the rate of learning and minor aspects of content. These findings are consistent with the general pancultural model of gender stereotypes discussed above and suggest that pancultural stereotypes could be considered to be *variform universals* (Lonner, 1980).

Cross-Cultural Theories of Gender-Related Learning

Most theories of gender role learning emphasize gender information readily available in the culture even though the theories were devised primarily in the United States.[1] Each theory can be adapted to explain cross-cultural patterns of development.

Social Learning Theories

Social learning theories (Bandura, 1969; Bussey & Bandura, 1984; Mischel, 1970) consider sex role development to be the result of cumulative experience. Parents, teachers, peers, and other socialization agents shape children's gender-related behaviors through reinforcement and punishment of gender-appropriate and inappropriate behaviors, modeling, expectations,

toy choices, and other differential treatment of boys and girls. Research in the United States has shown same-sex and opposite-sex parents react differently to their children, with fathers showing more differential behavior (Maccoby & Jacklin, 1974). Interestingly, the few studies conducted in other countries (Bronstein, 1984, 1986; Lamb, Frodi, Hwang, Frodi, & Steinberg, 1982; Russell & Russell, 1987; Sagi, Lamb, Shoham, Dvir, & Lewkowicz, 1985) do not show differential treatment of boys and girls.

Best and colleagues (Best, House, Barnard, & Spicker, 1991) observed parents and their preschool children in public parks and playgrounds in France, Germany, and Italy and found that parent-child interactions varied across both gender and country. Italian and French parents and children were more interactive than German parent-child dyads, and French and Italian children showed and shared more objects with their fathers than mothers, with the pattern reversed for German children. These interactional differences may be related to the cultural differences in sex stereotype learning noted above. Perhaps female characteristics are learned earlier by German children as a result of greater interaction with mothers than fathers, a pattern that was not found in the other countries.

While there is substantial cross-cultural evidence that social forces play an important part in gender role learning, social learning by itself does not provide a sufficient explanation. Differential treatment of boys and girls varies greatly across cultures and is not consistently tied to differential behavior (Bronstein, 1984; Lamb et al., 1982; Russell & Russell, 1987). Tasks assigned to children, as well as role models in the larger culture, provide opportunities for them to learn differential roles and behaviors. The salient aspects of culture that contribute to children's gender role learning and behaviors should be systematically addressed.

Cognitive Developmental Theory

The other prominent theory of gender role learning, cognitive developmental theory (Kohlberg, 1966; Ruble, 1987), emphasizes the role of external forces on children's developing gender role orientation. The impact of these factors, however, is governed by the child's emerging cognitive structures. Children progress through stages in acquiring gender knowledge, and their level of understanding structures their experiences.

Slaby and Frey (1975) identified four stages in the development of American children's understanding of gender. Initially, children do not distinguish between the sexes, but by the second stage, they begin to use gender categories based on superficial physical characteristics. In the last two stages, achieved by age 4½ to 5 years, children understand that gender is stable across time and is consistent.

In testing cognitive developmental theory, R. H. Munroe, Shimmin, and Munroe (1984) expected to find cultural differences in progression through the gender stages related to the degree to which societies emphasize distinctions between males and females. Contrary to expectation, these culture-specific predictions were not supported. Children in the sex-differentiating cultures, Kenya and Nepal, did not attain gender classification at an earlier age than did children in Belize and Samoa. In fact, Kenyan children reached this stage at an older age than did Samoan children, and Nepalese children did not differ from the other groups. As predicted, the later stages that depend on cognitive structural factors showed little variation across cultures. R. H. Munroe and Munroe (1982) suggest that gender understanding develops slowly in cultures in which young children have little contact with male figures, such as more traditional cultures in which child care is almost completely a maternal responsibility.

Bussey (1983) has found that gender constancy is not an important antecedent for the development of sex-typed behaviors. For boys, there is a two-process model, acceptance of masculine behavior and rejection of feminine behavior; there is a one-process model for girls, acceptance of same-sex behavior without rejection of other-sex behavior. Hence, it is acceptable for young girls to be "tomboys," but not for boys to be "sissies."

Taken as a whole, these findings indicate the dominant contribution of cognitive developmental factors and the concomitantly small contribution of culture-specific factors in the development of gender concepts.

Gender Schema Theory

Recently, a variant of cognitive developmental theory and social learning theory has evolved, gender schema theory (Bem, 1981; Liben & Signorella, 1980, 1987; Signorella, Bigler, & Liben, 1993). A *schema* is a set of ideas used for organizing information, filtering new information, and directing cognitive processing. Gender sche-

ma theory assumes that the primacy of the gender concept within a particular culture serves as a basis for organizing information (Jacklin, 1989), although there is little evidence for this assumption from cultures other than the United States.

Cultural Practices that Influence Behaviors of Males and Females

This section examines broader cultural influences on gender mentioned briefly in sections of the chapter above: the status of women, gender division of labor, religious beliefs and values, economic factors, and political participation.

Status of Women

Ethnographic evidence suggests that women's "status" is multidimensional and includes economic indicators, power, autonomy, prestige, and ideological dimensions (Mukhopadhyay & Higgins, 1988; Quinn, 1977). Proposed determinants of the asymmetry in status between men and women include women's reproductive roles, secondary sexual characteristics, greater male aggression and strength, sexual division of labor, complexity of the society (Berry, 1976; Ember, 1981), socialization, education, and religious beliefs.

Gender Division of Labor

What is considered masculine and feminine may be culturally variable, but the literature suggests two possible cultural universals: To some degree, every society assigns traits and tasks on the basis of gender (R. L. Munroe & Munroe, 1975/1994); in no society is the status of women superior to that of men, while the reverse is quite common (Hoyenga & Hoyenga, 1993; Population Crisis Committee, 1988; Whyte, 1978). D'Andrade (1966) analyzed ethnographic records of jobs and tasks in 244 different societies and found that men were involved with hunting, metal work, weapon making, and travel further from home, while women were responsible for cooking and food preparation, carrying water, caring for clothing, and making things used in the home. Women participated in subsistence activities consistent with child-rearing responsibilities (Brown, 1970; Segal, 1983), and men had major responsibilities for child rearing in only 10% of the 80 cultures examined (Katz & Konner, 1981).

Decreases in infant mortality and fertility have reduced the proportion of women's life-span spent in rearing children. Indeed, technology has made it possible to separate childbearing from child rearing (Huber, 1986), permitting women to participate in the labor force outside the home. Paid employment, however, does not provide a full picture of women's economic contributions to the family (Dixon, 1978).

Looking at trends across 56 countries from 1960 to 1980, Jacobs and Lim (1992) found women experienced a decline in occupational opportunities and greater segregation. Surprisingly, measures of modernization, such as per capita gross national product and women's education, were related positively to sex segregation, but as expected, women's labor force participation and fertility rate were related inversely. Compared with men, women remain economically disadvantaged and are paid less than their male counterparts (Ottaway & Bhatnagar, 1988). Women prefer traditionally female jobs and those that offer the greatest possibilities for contact with other people, while men prefer jobs with the highest income and the greatest possibilities for promotion (Loscocco & Kalleberg, 1988; Mullet, Neto, & Henry, 1992).

Even in societies in which women have moved actively into the labor force, there has not been a commensurate reduction in their household duties (Population Crisis Committee, 1988). In the United States, Switzerland, Sweden, Canada, Italy, Poland, and Romania, the overwhelming majority of household work is performed by women, regardless of the extent of their occupational demands (Calasanti & Bailey, 1991; Charles & Höpflinger, 1992; Lupri, 1983; Vianello et al., 1990; Wright, Shire, Hwang, Dolan, & Baxter, 1992). Presence of children and larger homes are associated with less male participation in domestic chores. However, in all countries, blue collar workers hold more traditional views of the sexual division of labor, which suggests that more egalitarian views emerge with increases in education and social class (Vianello et al., 1990).

Gender inequity, however, does not completely disappear with greater job opportunities for women or with greater education. In four western countries (the United States, Great Britain, West Germany, and Austria), N. J. Davis and Robinson (1991) found that well-educated people and women with employed husbands were less favorable toward efforts to reduce gender inequality than were less-educated people or women without a male wage earner.

Religious Beliefs and Values

Religious beliefs and culturally based views of family honor also influence views of women and their working outside the home (Rapoport, Lomski-Feder, & Masalia, 1989). Latin America and the Middle East share many ideals of personal and family honor that link the manliness of men (machismo, *muruwwa*) with the sexual purity of women (*vergüenza, 'ird*) and influence roles and the division of labor in the family (Youssef, 1974). In both cultures, there is strong resentment against married women participating in the labor force, and if they do work, they must have few public contacts with men. Despite similar levels of economic development, female participation in the labor force is strikingly higher in Latin America than in the Middle East. The powerful male-based family kinship structure in the Middle East tightly controls women's labor force participation, but the power of male kin has been diffused in Latin American by the central role of priests (Youssef, 1974). However, education leading to prestigious positions overcomes barriers for women in both cultures.

Economic Factors

Economic factors appear to influence gender-related cultural practices. Bride price is a form of compensation for the loss of a daughter's economic contributions to her family (Heath, 1958) and is found more frequently when her contributions are substantial. Dowry accompanies the bride when her economic contributions to her family are relatively small.

Cronk (1993) theorized that when parents have high socioeconomic status, males are favored, but when parents have low status, females are favored. For example, the Mukogodo in Kenya are at the bottom of the regional hierarchy of wealth, prestige, and ultimately marital and reproductive opportunities. Due to their low status, it is hard for the Mukogodo men to find wives because they do not have bride wealth to pay for a bride. Because men can have as many wives as they can afford, women are always in short supply, so Mukogodo women easily find husbands, often among their wealthier and higher status neighbors.

Economic conditions also may influence sex-biased parental investment in children. Among the Mukogodo, the birth ratio of males to females is typical, but the 1986 census recorded 98 girls and 66 boys under 4 years of age. While there is no evidence of male infanticide, it is likely that the higher death rate for boys is due to favoritism shown toward girls. Compared with sons, daughters are breast-fed longer, are generally well fed, and visit the doctor more often. Parents invest more in offspring who provide the greater economic or reproductive success (Trivers & Willard, 1973).

Among the nomadic Kanjar of Pakistan and northern India, women provide more than half of the income of most families, dominating public life and private affairs (Cronk, 1993). Bride wealth payments are high, and it is easy to see why the birth of a girl is greeted with fanfare, but boys are greeted with little interest.

These cultural practices contrast sharply with those found in other traditional parts of the world (e.g., India, China, Turkey, Korea), where boys are highly valued by their families and their births lead to great rejoicing (Kagitcibasi, 1982). Female infanticide (Krishnaswamy, 1988), wife beating (Flavia, 1988), and bride burning (Ghadially & Kumar, 1988) are cultural practices that attest to the lack of concern for women in some traditional Indian cultures. Preference for boys continues to be strong in the United States (Oakley, 1980; Pooler, 1991) and in non-Western countries (Hammer, 1970), even though many of the religious traditions and economic circumstances that created the preference for sons no longer apply to contemporary culture.

Female Political Participation

Cross-culturally, men are more involved in political activities and wield greater power than women (Ember, 1981; Masters, 1989; Ross, 1985, 1986). In a sample of 90 preindustrial societies, women were found to have more political involvement when there was high internal conflict and violence within a society and low external warfare (Ross, 1986).

The long-standing stereotyped dichotomy of public/male versus private/female suggests that men are in the public eye and active in business, politics, and culture, while women stay at home and care for home and family (Peterson & Runyan, 1993). However, cross-cultural studies do not support this dichotomy, with women actively working and in public life outside the home, and men more involved with their families (Vianello et al., 1990).

Indeed, Gibbons and colleagues (Gibbons et al., 1991, 1993) have shown that adolescents in a variety of cultures conceptualize the female gender role to encompass both homemaking and employment outside the home. Adolescents' images of women reflect the change in conditions and attitudes toward women around the world.

Questions and Challenges for the Future

The question of sex differences has fascinated social scientists for decades, and with the growing interest in culture, it seems safe to assume that questions regarding the joint effects of these variables will continue to intrigue researchers. In spite of the fact that males and females are biologically more similar than different, persons in traditional or modern, industrialized societies can expect to live qualitatively different lives based on whether they are male or female. Consequently, psychologists will continue to explore the reasons for these differences both within and between cultures.

Theories and Methods for Studying Gender

Future research concerning the interface of gender and culture will need cogent theories and new methodologies to examine the complexities of gender in various sociocultural systems. In the United States, recent theories addressing masculine and feminine attributes have become multifactorial (Ashmore, 1990; Spence, 1993), and empirical research has supported such an approach by showing little or no relationship between different aspects of gender (Twenge, 1999). At present, the multifactorial approach has not been examined in other cultural groups to see how the relationships between various aspects of gender, such as personality traits, occupational choices, leisure activities, and personal and social relationships, may be influenced by culture.

A promising new method in personality assessment may provide a valid way to examine gender-related concepts across cultural groups.

The Five Factor Model of personality (McCrae & Costa, 1990, 1997) proposes that most significant variation in human personality can be explained by five "super traits": extraversion, agreeableness, conscientiousness, emotional stability, and openness to experience. The model has been applied successfully in a variety of other societies (Church & Lonner, 1998) and recently was used to study sex stereotypes in 27 countries (Williams et al., 1999; Williams, Satterwhite, Best, & Inman, 2000). Indeed, the model could be used to examine other gender-related concepts, such as self and ideal self descriptions of men and women, ideal wife and husband, or father and mother. Using a method from general personality research to study gender concepts provides links with existing theory and permits comparisons across different studies and across different conceptual domains.

Another method with wide applicability across conceptual areas that has been used in 23 language/cultural groups is the semantic differential devised by Osgood and associates (Osgood, May, & Miron, 1975; Osgood, Suci, & Tannenbaum, 1957). This procedure assesses affective or connotative meaning associated with a particular "target" (e.g., person, concept, event, object) and yields scores on evaluation (favorability), potency (strength), and activity.

Finally, the Adjective Checklist (Gough & Heilbrun, 1980), a collection of 300 person-descriptive adjectives that has been translated into more than 20 languages, was used by Williams and Best (1990a, 1990b) in the research described above.[2] This method has broad applicability for cross-cultural comparison of gender concepts.

Evaluating Cultural Effects

Individual cultures, like individual persons, are unique—no two are exactly alike. Beyond description or ad hoc speculation, conventional science does not deal well with uniqueness, focusing instead on commonalities, such as systems of classification. To study the effects of culture as an antecedent or independent variable, researchers have categorized societies in a number of ways. For example, societies have been classified according to residence patterns (e.g., patrilocal, neolocal), cultural values (e.g., individualism-collectivism by Hofstede, 1980; autonomy-conservation, hierarchy-mastery by Schwartz, 1990), and interpersonal relations (e.g., horizontal-vertical by Triandis, 1995). Us-

ing such classifications, culture can be treated as an overarching explanatory framework for a number of phenomena or as a set of values, norms, or beliefs. In either case, culture is assumed to have direct or indirect effects on behavior (Lonner & Adamopoulos, 1997).

Classifications systems have been criticized for being too general and failing to consider situational variables. For example, a person may behave individualistically in some situations (e.g., at work) and collectivistically in others (e.g., with family), which demonstrates the importance of the situation. Matsumoto and colleagues (Matsumoto, Weissman, Preston, Brown, & Kupperbusch, 1997) have responded to this objection by combining the examination of culture and situation, evaluating an individual's behaviors relative to individualism/collectivism in four different social contexts. Similar refinements in defining culture are needed to understand better how culture and specific cultural practices may influence behavior.

Developmental Questions

Future studies of gender concepts across cultural groups should address how social relationships and behaviors change with age. In the United States, Maccoby (1990) reports that, by 33 months of age, boys were unresponsive to the vocal prohibitions of female partners. She speculates that girls find it aversive to interact with unresponsive partners, so they avoid them. This leads to same-sex playmate preferences, a finding that has been demonstrated across a variety of cultural groups (R. L. Munroe et al., 2000). However, the reasons for such preferences have not been examined in a cross-cultural context.

Furthermore, Maccoby (1990) reports that male social groups are more concerned with dominance and competitiveness, and boys frequently use threats, commands, and boasts of authority. Girls, in contrast, are more likely to express agreement and to pause to give their partner a chance to speak. Maccoby speculates that familial processes have been given too much credit or blame for the relational aspects of sex typing, and she emphasizes the importance of peer group influences. The range of variation and diversity in familial and peer relationships seen across cultural groups provides an exceptional opportunity for examining gender-related social development. Cross-cultural researchers have only begun to explore these social and behavioral issues with children in other societies.

Conclusions

In view of the amount and variety of material reviewed in this chapter, any final observations must be very general. Most striking is the central finding that pancultural similarities in sex and gender greatly outweigh cultural differences. Indeed, the manner in which male-female relationships are organized is remarkably similar across social groups. The relatively minor biological differences between the sexes can be amplified or diminished by cultural practices and socialization, making gender differences in roles and behaviors generally modest, but in some cases culturally important. To use an athletic metaphor, gender does not constitute a new ball game in each culture, but rather some relatively minor variations on a very old ball game. Hence, it is reasonable to think in terms of a pancultural model with degrees of variation created by various cultural influences.

It is somewhat surprising that more of the gender-related cross-cultural research is not theory driven, although there are some studies that are consistent with various hypotheses generated from existing theories. To refine understanding of sex and gender further, future research should examine theoretical concerns relevant to cultural influences on behavior. Indeed, longitudinal studies in societies undergoing rapid socioeconomic development could address whether gender concepts change in theoretically expected directions.

Finally, studies in the various areas of social and behavioral science often seem to have evolved in isolation. Few researchers have studied the relationship between cultural practices, such as initiation rites—a typical topic for anthropologists—and the development of the individual, a topic usually confined to the psychological domain. In their efforts to understand the impact of culture on behavior, anthropologists and psychologists must learn more from each other. Perhaps the growing field of cultural psychology, together with cross-cultural psychology, will provide a bridge between disciplines, recognizing that culture serves as both an independent and an organizing variable.

Notes

1. Although psychoanalytic theory was quite influential in early studies of cross-cultural gender differences (see Burton & Whiting, 1961; Freud, 1939; Mead, 1949; Munroe & Munroe, 1994; R. L. Munroe, Munroe, & Whiting, 1981), it has received little recent attention and is not reviewed in this chapter.

2. Inquiries regarding ACL translations should be sent to Deborah L. Best, Department of Psychology, Box 7778, Wake Forest University, Winston-Salem, NC 27109 or best@wfu.edu.

References

Agarwal, K. S., Lester, D., & Dhawan, N. (1992). A study of perception of women by Indian and American students. In S. Iwawaki, Y. Kashima, & K. Leung (Eds.), *Innovations in cross-cultural psychology* (pp. 123–134). Amsterdam, The Netherlands: Swets & Zeitlinger.

Albert, A. A., & Porter, J. R. (1986). Children's gender role stereotypes: A comparison of the United States and South Africa. *Journal of Cross-Cultural Psychology, 17,* 45–65.

Ashmore, R. D. (1990). Sex, gender, and the individual. In L. A. Pervin (Ed.), *Handbook of personality theory and research* (pp. 486–526). New York: Guilford Press.

Bandura, A. (1969). Social learning theory of identificatory process. In D. A. Goslin (Ed.), *Handbook of socialization theory and research* (pp. 213–262). Chicago: Rand McNally.

Barry, H., III, Bacon, M. K., & Child, I. L. (1957). A cross-cultural survey of some sex differences in socialization. *Journal of Abnormal and Social Psychology, 55,* 327–332.

Bem, S. L. (1974). The measurement of psychological androgyny. *Journal of Consulting and Clinical Psychology, 42,* 155–162.

Bem, S. L. (1981). Gender schema theory: A cognitive account of sex-typing. *Psychological Review, 88,* 354–364.

Berry, J. W. (1976). Sex differences in behaviour and cultural complexity. *Indian Journal of Psychology, 51,* 89–97.

Best, D. L., House, A. S., Barnard, A. E., & Spicker, B. S. (1991). Parent-child interaction in France, Germany, and Italy: The effects of gender and culture. *Journal of Cross-Cultural Psychology, 25,* 181–193.

Best, D. L., & Williams, J. E. (1993). Cross-cultural viewpoint. In A. E. Beall & R. J. Sternberg (Eds.), *Perspectives on the psychology of gender* (pp. 215–248). New York: Guilford Press.

Best, D. L., & Williams, J. E. (1994). A cross-cultural examination of self and ideal self descriptions using transactional analysis ego states.

In I. R. Lagunes & Y. H. Poortinga (Eds.), *From a different perspective: Studies of behavior across cultures* (pp. 213–220). Lisse, The Netherlands: Swets & Zeitlinger.

Best, D. L., & Williams, J. E. (1998). Masculinity/femininity in the self and ideal self descriptions of university students in fourteen countries. In G. Hofstede (Ed.), *Masculinity and femininity: The taboo dimension of national cultures* (pp. 106–116). Thousand Oaks, CA: Sage. (Reprinted from *Journeys into cross-cultural psychology* (pp. 297–306), by A.-M. Bouvy, F. J. R. van de Vijver, P. Boski, & P. Schmitz, Eds., Amsterdam, The Netherlands: Swets & Zeitlinger.

Best, D. L., Williams, J. E., Cloud, J. M., Davis, S. W., Robertson, L. S., Edwards, J. R., Giles, H., & Fowles, J. (1977). Development of sex-trait stereotypes among young children in the United States, England, and Ireland. *Child Development, 48*, 1375–1384.

Bloch, M. N., & Adler, S. M. (1994). African children's play and the emergence of the sexual division of labor. In J. L. Roopnarine, J. E. Johnson, & F. H. Hooper (Eds.), *Children's play in diverse cultures* (pp. 148–178). Albany: State University of New York Press.

Blurton-Jones, N. B., & Konner, M. (1973). Sex differences in behavior of London and Bushman children. In R. P. Michael & J. H. Crook (Eds.), *Comparative ecology and behavior of primates* (pp. 690–749). London: Academic.

Boehnke, K., Silbereisen, R. K., Eisenberg, N., Reykowski, J., & Palmonari, A. (1989). Developmental pattern of prosocial motivation: A cross-national study. *Journal of Cross-Cultural Psychology, 20*, 219–243.

Bradley, C. (1993). Women's power, children's labor. *Cross-Cultural Research, 27*, 70–96.

Bronstein, P. (1984). Differences in mothers' and fathers' behaviors toward children: A cross-cultural comparison. *Developmental Psychology, 20*, 995–1003.

Bronstein, P. (1986). Children's social behavior: A cross-cultural comparison. *International Journal of Behavioral Development, 9*, 153–173.

Broude, G. J. (1987). The relationships of marital intimacy and aloofness to social environment: A hologeistic study. *Behavior Science Research, 21*, 50–69.

Brown, J. K. (1970). A note on the division of labor by sex. *American Anthropologist, 72*, 1073–1078.

Burbank, V. K. (1987). Female aggression in cross-cultural perspective. *Behavior Science Research, 21*(1–4), 70–100.

Burns, A., & Homel, R. (1986). Sex role satisfaction among Australian children: Some sex, age, and cultural group comparisons. *Psychology of Women Quarterly, 10*, 285–296.

Burton, R. V., & Whiting, J. W. M. (1961). The absent father and cross-sex identity. *Merrill-Palmer Quarterly, 7*(2), 85–95.

Buss, D. M. (1989). Sex differences in human mate preferences: Evolutionary hypotheses tested in 37 cultures. *Behavioral and Brain Sciences, 12*, 1–49.

Buss, D. M. (1990). Evolutionary social psychology: Prospect and pitfalls. *Motivation and Emotion, 14*, 265–286.

Buss, D. M., Abbott, M., Angleitner, A., Biaggio, A., Blanco-Villasenor, A., BruchonSchweitzer, M., & 45 additional authors. (1990). International preferences in selecting mates. *Journal of Cross-Cultural Psychology, 21*, 5–47.

Bussey, K. (1983). A social-cognitive appraisal of sex-role development. *Australian Journal of Psychology, 35*, 135–143.

Bussey, K., & Bandura, A. (1984). Influence of gender constancy and social power on sex-linked modeling. *Journal of Personality and Social Psychology, 47*, 1292–1302.

Buunk, B., & Hupka, R. B. (1987). Cross-cultural differences in elicitation of sexual jealousy. *Journal of Sex Research, 23*, 12–22.

Calasanti, T. M., & Bailey, C. A. (1991). Gender inequality and the division of household labor in the United States and Sweden: A socialist-feminist approach. *Social Problems, 38*, 34–53.

Calhoun, G., Jr., & Sethi, R. (1987). The self-esteem of pupils from India, the United States, and the Philippines. *Journal of Psychology, 121*, 199–202.

Carlsson, M., & Barnes, M. (1986). Conception and self-attribution of sex-role behavior: A cross-cultural comparison between Swedish and kibbutz-raised Israelian children. *Scandinavian Journal of Psychology, 27*, 258–265.

Charles, M., & Höpflinger, F. (1992). Gender, culture, and the division of household labor: A replication of U.S. studies for the case of Switzerland. *Journal of Comparative Family Studies, 23*, 375–387.

Church, A. T., & Lonner, W. J. (1998). The cross-cultural perspective in the study of personality: Rationale and current research. *Journal of Cross-Cultural Psychology, 29*, 32–62.

Cronk, L. (1993). Parental favoritism toward daughters. *American Scientist, 81*, 272–279.

Daly, M., & Wilson, M. (1978). *Sex, evolution, and behavior.* North Scituate, MA: Duxbury.

D'Andrade, R. G. (1966). Sex differences and cultural institutions. In E. E. Maccoby (Ed.), *The development of sex differences* (pp. 174–204). Stanford, CA: Stanford University Press.

Davis, D. L., & Whitten, R. G. (1987). The cross-cultural study of human sexuality. *Annual Review of Anthropology, 16,* 69–98.

Davis, N. J., & Robinson, R. V. (1991). Men's and women's consciousness of gender inequality: Austria, West Germany, Great Britain, and the United States. *American Sociological Review, 56,* 72–84.

Dion, K. K., & Dion, K. L. (1993). Individualistic and collectivistic perspectives on gender and the cultural context of love and intimacy. *Journal of Social Issues, 49,* 53–69.

Dixon, R. B. (1978). *Rural women at work: Strategies for development in South Asia.* Baltimore, MD: Johns Hopkins University Press.

Draper, P. (1975). Cultural pressure on sex differences. *American Ethnologist, 2*(4), 602–616.

Eaton, W. O., & Enns, L. R. (1986). Sex differences in human motor activity level. *Psychological Bulletin, 100,* 19–28.

Edelbrook, C., & Sugawara, A. I. (1978). Acquisition of sex-typed preferences in preschool-aged children. *Developmental Psychology, 14,* 614–623.

Edwards, C. P. (1992). Cross-cultural perspectives on family-peer relations. In R. D. Parke & G. W. Ladd (Eds.), *Family-peer relationships: Modes of linkages.* Mahwah, NJ: Erlbaum.

Edwards, C. P., & Whiting, B. B. (1974). Women and dependency. *Politics and Society, 4,* 343–355.

Edwards, C. P., & Whiting, B. B. (1980). Differential socialization of girls and boys in light of cross-cultural research. *New Directions for Child Development, 8,* 45–57.

Edwards, C. P., & Whiting, B. B. (1993). "Mother, older sibling, and me": The overlapping roles of caretakers and companions in the social world of 2–3 year olds in Ngeca, Kenya. In K. MacDonald (Ed.), *Parent child play: Descriptions of implications* (pp. 305–329). Albany: State University of New York Press.

Ember, C. R. (1981). A cross-cultural perspective on sex differences. In R. H. Munroe, R. L. Munroe, & B. B. Whiting (Eds.), *Handbook of cross-cultural human development* (pp. 531–580). New York: Garland.

Flavia. (1988). Violence in the family: Wife beating. In R. Ghadially (Ed.), *Women in society: A reader* (pp. 151–166). New Delhi: Sage.

Foa, U. G., Anderson, B., Converse, J., Jr., Urbansky, W. A., Cawley, M. J., III, Muhlhausen, S. M., & Tornblom, K. Y. (1987). Gender-related sexual attitudes: Some cross cultural similarities and differences. *Sex Roles, 16,* 511–519.

Freedman, D. G. (1976). Infancy, biology, and culture. In L. P. Lipsitt (Ed.), *Developmental psychology.* New York: Halsted, Wiley.

Freedman, D. G., & DeBoer, M. M. (1979). Biological and cultural differences in early child development. *Annual Review of Anthropology, 8,* 579–600.

Freud, S. (1939). *Moses and monotheism.* New York: Vintage Books.

Fry, D. P. (1987). What human sociobiology has to offer economic anthropology and vice versa. *Journal of Social and Biological Structures, 10,* 37–51.

Ghadially, R. (Ed.). (1988). *Women in Indian society: A reader.* New Delhi: Sage.

Ghadially, R., & Kazi, K. A. (1979). Attitudes toward sex roles. *Indian Journal of Social Work, 40,* 65–71.

Ghadially, R., & Kumar, P. (1988). Stress, strain, and coping styles of female professionals. *Indian Journal of Applied Psychology, 26*(1), 1–8.

Gibbons, J. L., Lynn, M., Stiles, D. A., de Berducido, E. J., Richter, R., Walker, K., & Wiley, D. (1993). Guatemalan, Filipino, and U.S. adolescents' images of women as office workers and homemakers. *Psychology of Women Quarterly, 17,* 373–388.

Gibbons, J. L., Stiles, D. A., & Shkodriani, G. M. (1991). Adolescents' attitudes toward family and gender roles: An international comparison. *Sex Roles, 25,* 625–643.

Gilmore, D. D. (1990). *Manhood in the making.* New Haven, CT: Yale University Press.

Gottlieb, G. (1983). The psychobiological approach to developmental issues. In P. H. Mussen (Series Ed.) & M. M. Harth & J. J. Campos (Vol. Eds.), *Handbook of child psychology: Vol. 2. Infancy and developmental psychobiology* (pp. 1–26). New York: Wiley.

Gough, H. G. (1952). Identifying psychological femininity. *Educational and Psychological Measurement, 12,* 427–439.

Gough, H. G., & Heilbrun, A. B., Jr. (1980). *The Adjective Check List manual.* Palo Alto, CA: Consulting Psychologists Press.

Gould, S. J., & Lewontin, R. C. (1979). The spandrels of San Marco and the Panglossian paradigm: A critique of the adaptionist programme. *Proceedings of the Royal Society of London, B, 205,* 581–598.

Greenfield, P. M. (1981). Child care in cross-cultural perspectives: Implications for the future organization of child care in the United States. *Psychology of Women Quarterly, 6,* 41–54.

Gronseth, E. (1957). The impact of father absence in sailor families upon the personality structure and social adjustment of adult sailor sons. Part I. In N. Anderson (Ed.), *Studies of the family* (Vol. 2, pp. 97–114). Gottingen, Germany: Vandenhoeck & Ruprecht.

Guttentag, M., & Longfellow, C. (1977). Children's social attributions: Development and change. In C. B. Keasy (Ed.), *Nebraska symposium on motivation* (pp. 305–341). Lincoln: University of Nebraska Press.

Hamilton, V. L., Blumenfeld, P. C., Akoh, H., & Miura, K. (1991). Group and gender in Japanese and American elementary classrooms. *Journal of Cross-Cultural Psychology, 22*, 317–346.

Hammer, J. (1970). Preference for a male child: Cultural factors. *Journal of Individual Psychology, 26*, 54–56.

Hatfield, E., & Rapson, R. L. (1993). Historical and cross-cultural perspectives on passionate love and sexual desire. *Annual Review of Sex Research, 4*, 67–97.

Hatfield, E., & Rapson, R. L. (1995). *A world of passion: Cultural perspectives on love and sex.* New York: Allyn & Bacon.

Heath, D. B. (1958). Sexual division of labor and cross-cultural research. *Social Forces, 37*, 77–79.

Hendrix, L., & Johnson, G. D. (1985). Instrumental and expressive socialization: A false dichotomy. *Sex Roles, 13*, 581–595.

Hofstede, G. (1980). Culture's consequences: International differences in work-related values. Beverly Hills, CA: Sage.

Hoyenga, K. B., & Hoyenga, K. T. (1993). *Gender-related differences: Origins and outcomes.* Boston: Allyn & Bacon.

Huber, J. (1986). Trends in gender stratification, 1970–1985. *Sociological Forum, 1*, 476–495.

Intons-Peterson, M. J. (1988). *Gender concepts of Swedish and American youth.* Hillsdale, NJ: Erlbaum.

Jacklin, C. N. (1989). Female and male: Issues of gender. *American Psychologist, 44,* 127–133.

Jacobs, J. A., & Lim, S. T. (1992). Trends in occupational and industrial sex segregation in 56 countries, 1960–1980. *Work and Occupations, 19*, 450–486.

Kagitcibasi, C. (1982). Old-age security value of children: Cross-national socioeconomic evidence. *Journal of Cross-Cultural Psychology, 13*, 29–42.

Katz, M. M., & Konner, M. J. (1981). The role of the father: An anthropological perspective. In M. E. Lamb (Ed.), *The role of the father in child development* (pp. 155–185). New York: Wiley.

Kauppinen-Toropainen, K., & Gruber, J. E. (1993). Antecedents and outcomes of woman-un-friendly experiences. *Psychology of Women Quarterly, 17*, 543–562.

Kohlberg, L. (1966). A cognitive-developmental analysis of children's sex role concepts and attitudes. In E. E. Maccoby (Ed.), *The development of sex differences* (pp. 82–173). Stanford, CA: Stanford University Press.

Krishnaswamy, S. (1988). Female infanticide in contemporary India: A case-study of Kallars of Tamilnadu. In R. Ghadially (Ed.), *Women in Indian society: A reader* (pp. 186–195). New Delhi: Sage.

Lamb, M. E., Frodi, A. M., Hwang, C. P., Frodi, M., & Steinberg, J. (1982). Mother- and father-infant interaction involving play and holding in traditional and nontraditional Swedish families. *Developmental Psychology, 18*, 215–221.

L'Armand, K., Pepitone, A., & Shanmugam, T. E. (1981). Attitudes toward rape: A comparison of the role of chastity in India and the United States. *Journal of Cross-Cultural Psychology, 12*(3), 284–303.

Liben, L. S., & Signorella, M. L. (1980). Gender-related schemata and constructive memory in children. *Child Development, 51*, 11–18.

Liben, L. S., & Signorella, M. L. (Eds.). (1987). *Children's gender schemata.* San Francisco: Jossey-Bass.

Lonner, W. J. (1980). The search for psychological universals. In H. C. Triandis & W. W. Lambert (Eds.), *Handbook of cross-cultural psychology* (Vol. 1, pp. 143–204). Boston: Allyn & Bacon.

Lonner, W. J., & Adamopoulos, J. (1997). Culture as antecedent to behavior. In J. W. Berry, Y. H. Poortinga, J. Pandey, P. R. Dasen, T. S. Saraswathi, M. H. Segall, & C. Kagitcibasi (Series Eds.) & J. W. Berry, Y. H. Poortinga, & J. Pandey (Vol. Eds.), *Handbook of cross-cultural psychology. Vol. 1: Theory and Method* (2nd ed., pp. 43–83). Boston: Allyn & Bacon.

Loscocco, K. A., & Kalleberg, A. L. (1988). Age and the meaning of work in the United States and Japan. *Social Forces, 67*, 337–356.

Lummis, M., & Stevenson, H. W. (1990). Gender differences in beliefs and achievement: A cross-cultural study. *Developmental Psychology, 26*, 254–263.

Lupri, E. (Ed.). (1983). *The changing position of women in family and society: A cross-national comparison.* Leiden, The Netherlands: E. J. Brill.

Lynn, D. B., & Sawrey, W. L. (1959). The effects of father-absence on Norwegian boys and girls. *Journal of Abnormal Social Psychology, 59*, 258–262.

Lytton, H., & Romney, D. M. (1991). Parents' differential socialization of boys and girls: A meta-analysis. *Psychological Bulletin, 109,* 267–296.

Maccoby, E. E. (1990). Gender and relationships: A developmental account. *American Psychologist, 45,* 513–520.

Maccoby, E. E., & Jacklin, C. N. (1974). *The psychology of sex differences.* Stanford, CA: Stanford University Press.

Mackey, W. C. (1985). *Fathering behaviors: The dynamics of the man-child bond.* New York: Plenum.

Mackey, W. C., & Day, R. (1979). Some indicators of fathering behaviors in the United States: A cross-cultural examination of adult male-child interaction. *Journal of Marriage and the Family, 41,* 287–299.

Masters, R. D. (1989). Gender and political cognition: Integrating evolutionary biology and political science. *Political and Life Sciences, 8,* 3–39.

Matsumoto, D., Weissman, M. D., Preston, K., Brown, B. R., & Kupperbusch, C. (1997). Context-specific measurement of individualism-collectivism on the individual level: The Individualism-Collectivism Interpersonal Assessment Inventory. *Journal of Cross-Cultural Psychology, 28,* 743–767.

McCrae, R. R., & Costa, P. T. (1990). *Personality in adulthood.* New York: Guilford Press.

McCrae, R. R., & Costa, P. T. (1997). Personality trait structure as a human universal. *American Psychologist, 52,* 509–516.

Mead, M. (1935). *Sex and temperament in three primitive societies.* New York: Morrow.

Mead, M. (1949). *Male and female.* New York: New American Library.

Minturn, L., & Lambert, W. W. (1964). *Mothers of six cultures: Antecedents of child rearing.* New York: Wiley.

Mischel, W. (1970). Sex-typing and socialization. In P. H. Mussen (Ed.), *Carmichael's manual of child psychology* (pp. 3–72). New York: Wiley.

Mukhopadhyay, C. C., & Higgins, P. J. (1988). Anthropological studies of women's status revisited: 1977–1987. *Annual Review of Anthropology, 17,* 461–495.

Mullet, E., Neto, F., & Henry, S. (1992). Determinants of occupational preferences in Portuguese and French high school students. *Journal of Cross-Cultural Psychology, 23,* 521–531.

Munroe, R. H., & Munroe, R. L. (1982). The development of sex-gender constancy among children in four cultures. In R. Rath, H. S. Asthana, D. Sinha, & J. B. P. Singha (Eds.), *Diversity and unity in cross-cultural psychol-* ogy (pp. 272–280). Lisse, The Netherlands: Swets & Zeitlinger.

Munroe, R. H., Shimmin, H. S., & Munroe, R. L. (1984). Gender understanding and sex role preference in four cultures. *Developmental Psychology, 20,* 673–682.

Munroe, R. L., Hulefeld, R., Rodgers, J. M., Tomeo, D. L., & Yamazaki, S. K. (2000). Aggression among children in four cultures. *Cross-Cultural Research, 34,* 3–25.

Munroe, R. L., & Munroe, R. H. (1971). Effect of environmental experiences on spatial ability in an East African society. *Journal of Social Psychology, 83,* 3–10.

Munroe, R. L., & Munroe, R. H. (1994). *Cross-cultural human development.* Prospective Heights, IL: Waveland Press. (Original work published 1975)

Munroe, R. L., Munroe, R. H., & Whiting, J. W. M. (1981). Male sex-role resolutions. In R. H. Munroe, R. L. Munroe, & B. B. Whiting (Eds.), *Handbook of cross-cultural human development* (pp. 611–632). New York: Garland.

Murdock, G. P., & White, D. R. (1969). Standard cross-cultural sample. *Ethnology, 8,* 329–369.

Neto, F., Williams, J. E., & Widner, S. C. (1991). Portuguese children's knowledge of sex stereotypes: Effects of age, gender, and socioeconomic status. *Journal of Cross-cultural Psychology, 22,* 376–388.

Nisbett, R. E. (1990). Evolutionary psychology, biology, and cultural evolution. *Motivation and Emotion, 14,* 255–263.

Oakley, A. (1980). *Becoming a mother.* New York: Schocken Books.

Olowu, A. A. (1985). Gender as a determinant of some Nigerian adolescents' self-concepts. *Journal of Adolescence, 8,* 347–355.

Omark, D. R., Omark, M., & Edelman, M. (1975). Formation of dominance hierarchies in young children: Action and perspective. In T. Williams (Ed.), *Psychological anthropology* (pp. 289–315). The Hague: Mouton.

Osgood, C. E., May, W. H., & Miron, M. S. (1975). *Cross-cultural universals of affective meaning.* Urbana: University of Illinois Press.

Osgood, C. E., Suci, G. J., & Tannenbaum, P. H. (1957). *The measurement of meaning.* Urbana: University of Illinois Press.

Ottaway, R. N., & Bhatnagar, D. (1988). Personality and biographical differences between male and female managers in the United States and India. *Applied Psychology: An International Review, 37,* 201–212.

Peterson, V. S., & Runyan, A. S. (1993). *Global gender issues.* Boulder, CO: Westview Press.

Pooler, W. S. (1991). Sex of child preferences among college students. *Sex Roles, 25,* 569–576.

Population Crisis Committee. (1988, June). *Country rankings of the status of women: Poor, powerless, and pregnant* (Issue Brief No. 20). Washington, DC: Author.

Prosser, G. V., Hutt, C., Hutt, S. J., Mahindadasa, K. J., & Goonetilleke, M. D. J. (1986). Children's play in Sri Lanka: A cross-cultural study. *British Journal of Developmental Psychology, 4,* 179–186.

Quinn, N. (1977). Anthropology studies of women's status. *Annual Review of Anthropology, 6,* 181–225.

Ramirez, J. M. (1993). Acceptability of aggression in four Spanish regions and a comparison with other European countries. *Aggressive Behavior, 19,* 185–197.

Rao, V. V. P., & Rao, V. N. (1985). Sex-role attitudes across two cultures: United States and India. *Sex Roles, 13,* 607–624.

Rapoport, T., Lomski-Feder, E., & Masalia, M. (1989). Female subordination in the Arab-Israeli community: The adolescent perspective of "social veil." *Sex Roles, 20,* 255–269.

Reis, H. T., & Wright, S. (1982). Knowledge of sex-role stereotypes in children aged 3 to 5. *Sex Roles, 8,* 1049–1056.

Reiss, I. L. (1986). *Journey into sexuality: An exploratory voyage.* Englewood Cliffs, NJ: Prentice-Hall.

Rogoff, B., Gauvain, M., & Ellis, S. (1984). Development viewed in its cultural context. In M. H. Bornstein & M. E. Lamb (Eds.), *Developmental psychology: An advanced textbook* (pp. 533–571). Hillsdale, NJ: Erlbaum.

Rohner, R. P., & Rohner, E. C. (1982). Enculturative continuity and the importance of caretakers: Cross-cultural codes. *Behavior Science Research, 17,* 91–114.

Rosenberg, B. G., & Sutton-Smith, B. (1972). *Sex and identity.* New York: Holt, Rinehart, & Winston.

Rosner, M. (1967). Women in the kibbutz: Changing status and concepts. *Asian and African Studies, 3,* 35–68.

Ross, M. H. (1985). Female political participation: A cross-cultural explanation. *American Anthropologist, 88,* 843–858.

Ross, M. H. (1986). The limits to social structure: Social structural and psychocultural explanations for political conflict and violence. *Anthropological Quarterly, 59,* 171–176.

Rozée, P. D. (1993). Forbidden or forgiven? Rape in cross-cultural perspective. *Psychology of Women Quarterly, 17,* 499–514.

Ruble, D. N. (1987). The acquisition of self-knowledge: A self-socialization perspective. In N. Eisenberg (Ed.), *Contemporary topics in developmental psychology* (pp. 243–270). New York: Wiley.

Russell, G., & Russell, A. (1987). Mother-child and father-child relationships in middle childhood. *Child Development, 58,* 1573–1585.

Sagi, A., Lamb, M. E., Shoham, R., Dvir, R., & Lewkowicz, K. (1985). Parent-infant interaction in families on Israeli kibbutzim. *International Journal of Behavioral Development, 8,* 273–284.

Schwartz, S. H. (1990). Individualism-collectivism: Critique and proposed refinements. *Journal of Cross-Cultural Psychology, 21,* 139–157.

Segal, E. S. (1983). The structure of division of labor: A tentative formulation. *Behavior Science Research, 18,* 3–25.

Segall, M. (1988). Psycho-cultural antecedents of male aggression: Some implications involving gender, parenting, and adolescence. In N. Sartorious, P. Dasen, & J. W. Berry (Eds.), *Psychological implications for healthy human development* (pp. 71–92). Beverly Hills, CA: Sage.

Serpell, R. (1993). *The significance of schooling: Life-journeys in an African society.* New York: Cambridge University Press.

Signorella, M. L., Bigler, R. S., & Liben, L. S. (1993). Developmental differences in children's gender schemata about others: A meta-analytic review. *Developmental Review, 134,* 147–183.

Simmons, C. H., Kolke, A. V., & Shimizu, H. (1986). Attitudes toward romantic love among American, German, and Japanese students. *Journal of Social Psychology, 126,* 327–336.

Slaby, R. G., & Frey, K. S. (1975). Development of gender constancy and selective attention to same-sex models. *Child Development, 46,* 849–856.

Snarey, J., & Son, L. (1986). Sex-identity development among kibbutz-born males: A test of the Whiting hypothesis. *Ethos, 14,* 99–119.

Spence, J. T. (1993). Gender-related traits and gender ideology: Evidence for a multifactorial theory. *Journal of Personality and Social Psychology, 64,* 624–635.

Spence, J. T., & Helmreich, R. L. (1978). *Masculinity and femininity: Their psychological dimensions, correlates, and antecedents.* Austin: University of Texas Press.

Spiro, M. (1956). *Kibbutz: Venture in utopia.* New York: Schocken Books.

Stewart, J. (1988). Current themes, theoretical issues, and preoccupations in the study of sexual differentiation and gender-related behaviors. *Psychobiology, 16*, 315–320.

Stolz, L. M. (1954). *Father relations of warborn children.* Palo Alto, CA: Stanford University Press.

Strube, M. J. (1981). Meta-analysis and cross-cultural comparison. *Journal of Cross-Cultural Psychology, 12*, 3–20.

Super, C. M., & Harkness, S. (1982). The infants' niche in rural Kenya and metropolitan America. In L. L. Adler (Ed.), *Cross-cultural research at issue* (pp. 47–55). New York: Academic Press.

Suzuki, A. (1991). Predictors of women's sex role attitudes across two cultures: United States and Japan. *Japanese Psychological Research, 33*(3), 126–133.

Tanner, J. M. (1961). *Education and physical growth.* New York: International Universities Press.

Tanner, J. M. (1970). Physical growth. In P. H. Mussen (Ed.), *Carmichael's manual of child psychology* (Vol. 1). New York: Wiley.

Tarrier, N., & Gomes, L. (1981). Knowledge of sex-trait stereotypes: Effects of age, sex, and social class on Brazilian children. *Journal of Cross-Cultural Psychology, 12*, 81–93.

Thompson, S. K. (1975). Gender labels and early sex role development. *Child Development, 46*, 339–347.

Travis, C. B., & Yeager, C. P. (1991). Sexual selection, parental investment, and sexism. *Journal of Social Issues, 47*, 117–129.

Triandis, H. C. (1995). *Individualism and collectivism.* Boulder, CO: Westview.

Trivers, R. L., & Willard, D. E. (1973). Natural selection of parental ability to vary the sex ratio of offspring. *Science, 179*, 90–92.

Twenge, J. M. (1999). Mapping gender: The multifactorial approach and the organization of gender-related attributes. *Psychology of Women Quarterly, 23*, 485–502.

Vaidyanathan, P., & Naidoo, J. (1990/1991). Asian Indians in Western countries: Cultural identity and the arranged marriage. In N. Bleichrodt & P. J. D. Drenth (Eds.), *Contemporary issues in cross-cultural psychology* (pp. 37–49). Amsterdam/Lisse: Swets & Zeitlinger.

van Dongen-Melman, J. E. W. M., Koot, H. M., & Verhulst, F. C. (1993). Cross-cultural validation of Harter's self-perception profile for children in a Dutch sample. *Educational and Psychological Measurement, 53*, 739–753.

Vianello, M., Siemienska, R., Damian, N., Lupri, E., Coppi, R., d'Arcangelo, E., & Bolasco, S. (199). *Gender inequality: A comparative study of discrimination and participation.* Newbury Park, CA: Sage.

Ward, C. (1995). *Blaming victims: Feminist and social psychological perspectives on rape.* London: Sage.

Watkins, D., & Akande, A. (1992). The internal structure of the self description questionnaire: A Nigerian investigation. *British Journal of Educational Psychology, 62*, 120–125.

Watkins, D., Lam, M. K., & Regmi, M. (1991). Cross-cultural assessment of self esteem: A Nepalese investigation. *Psychologia, 34*, 98–108.

Weinraub, M., Clemens, L. P., Sockloff, A., Etheridge, T., Gracely, E., & Myers, B. (1984). The development of sex-role stereotypes in the third year: Relationships to gender labeling, gender identity, sex-typed toy preference, and family characteristics. *Child Development, 55*, 1493–1503.

Weisner, T. S., & Gallimore, R. (1977). My brother's keeper: Child and sibling caretaking. *Current Anthropology, 18*, 169–190.

Welch, M. R., Page, B. M., & Martin, L. L. (1981). Sex differences in the ease of socialization: An analysis of the efficiency of child training processes in preindustrial societies. *Journal of Social Psychology, 113*, 3–12.

West, M. M., & Konner, M. J. (1981). The role of the father: An anthropological perspective. In M. E. Lamb (Ed.), *The role of the father in child development* (2nd ed., pp. 155–186). New York: Plenum Press.

Whiting, B., & Edwards, C. P. (1973). A cross-cultural analysis of sex differences in the behavior of children aged 3 to 11. *Journal of Social Psychology, 91*, 171–188.

Whiting, B. B. (1965). Sex identity conflict and physical violence: A comparative study. *American Anthropologist, 67* (Special publication), 123–140.

Whiting, B. B., & Edwards, C. P. (1988). *Children of different worlds: The formation of social behavior.* Cambridge: Harvard University Press.

Whyte, M. K. (1978). *The status of women in preindustrial societies.* Princeton: Princeton University Press.

Williams, J. E., & Best, D. L. (1990a). *Measuring sex stereotypes: A multination study.* Newbury Park, CA: Sage.

Williams, J. E., & Best, D. L. (1990b). *Sex and psyche: Gender and self viewed cross-culturally.* Newbury Park, CA: Sage.

Williams, J. E., Satterwhite, R. C., & Best, D. L. (1999). Pancultural gender stereotypes revisited: The five factor model. *Sex Roles, 40*(7/8), 1–13.

Williams, J. E., Satterwhite, R. C., Best, D. L., & Inman, G. L. (2000). *Gender stereotypes in 27 countries examined via the five factor model.*

Unpublished manuscript, Georgia State University, Atlanta.

Wilson, E. O. (1975). *Sociobiology: The new synthesis.* Cambridge: Harvard University Press.

Wright, E. O., Shire, K., Hwang, S.-L., Dolan, M., & Baxter, J. (1992). The non-effects of class on the gender division of labor in the home: A comparative study of Sweden and the United States. *Gender and Society, 6,* 252–282.

Youssef, N. H. (1974). *Women and work in developing societies.* Berkeley, CA: Institute of International Studies.

Part III: Culture and Personality

This section of the book presents four chapters that address basic issues broadly classified under the topic of personality. In reality, however, many of the issues discussed in these chapters cut across sections, including discussions of many basic psychological processes, as well as social issues. Thus, the reader is cautioned not to attempt to pigeonhole or characterize these chapters (or any in this volume, for that matter) as being relevant for any single, isolated topic area in psychology.

In chapter 12, Yamaguchi presents a unique and insightful analysis of the issue of control, greatly expanding its utility and scope for use in cultures in which autonomy and primary, direct, personal control may not be the preferred mode of control. In reconceptualizing the issue of control, Yamaguchi suggests that differing cultural values may lead to differential usage of control strategies, each leading to their own sense of psychological well-being. The implications of these ideas to innovations in future theory and research on personality across cultures and to the creation of a pancultural psychology are enormous.

In chapter 13, Peng, Ames, and Knowles describe three major theoretical approaches that have informed and guided cross-cultural research on human inference, and they provide a comprehensive review of research in the area. They propose an integrated model that synthesizes all three approaches into a single, universal model of cultural influences on human in-

ference and suggest the need for an integration of approach and method in the future if research in this area is to continue to evolve.

In chapter 14, Tanaka-Matsumi provides a comprehensive review of the cross-cultural literature on mental disorders and a discussion of this area of study in a historical perspective. By illustrating findings from both etic and emic approaches in the literature, as well as discussing the advantages and disadvantages of each, she argues for an integration of both approaches in concept, theory, and method for future research. She also argues for culture to be put into context and made operational to help cross-cultural work in this line of inquiry to continue to evolve and transition.

In chapter 15, Lee and Sue discuss the monocultural nature of traditional approaches in clinical psychology against the growing awareness of the importance of culture in assessment, psychopathology, and treatment. Their review of issues surrounding testing and treatment is particularly unique, and they argue for integration and rapprochement across approaches and disciplines for future work in this area to continue to expound on the important and pervasive nature of cultural influences in clinical psychology.

Once again, these chapters provide excellent presentations of the vision of the continued evolution of cross-cultural psychology and the methodological revisions and improvements that are necessary to achieve that vision.

12

Culture and Control Orientations

SUSUMU YAMAGUCHI

How individuals exercise control over themselves, others, and their environments in their daily lives is an issue that strikes at the heart of individual psychology. Indeed, as described in this chapter, research from mainstream psychology has amply demonstrated that personal, primary control over self-related outcomes is related intimately to autonomy, individuality, self-concept, and self-esteem. Control processes are central to self-construals and are closely related to core social and cultural values we all have that serve as guiding principles in our lives.

In this chapter, Yamaguchi presents an excellent analysis of the issue of control. He takes us far beyond the simple notions of control typically presented in mainstream psychology by outlining not only direct, personal control (which is the type of control typically discussed in mainstream psychology), but also three other types of control agents: indirect, proxy, and collective control. Yamaguchi suggests that these other types of control agents are more prevalent in cultures that value interpersonal harmony over autonomy and individual agency and suggests that core cultural values encourage the development and use of differential control strategies as individuals attempt to master and adapt to their environments.

Yamaguchi also describes two different types of control targets—primary and secondary—and four subtypes for each. As he describes, in primary control, the target of control is existing external realities in one's physical and social environment. In secondary control, however, the target of control is oneself. Previous authors have claimed that East Asians attempt primary control less and secondary control more than do Americans. According to Yamaguchi, however, while this analysis is theoretically clear, the existing research does not support these claims. Instead, Yamaguchi presents a reconceptualization of these concepts and suggests that primary control would have functional primacy over secondary control only when an individual's biological needs are urgent or in a culture in which psychological well-being depends largely on a sense of autonomy. In particular, Yamaguchi's second illustration depicts how differing roads to psychological well-being may exist in different cultures, each with its own set of paths.

Needless to say, the analysis presented here by Yamaguchi is unique, intriguing, and insightful. In presenting his ideas and models, Yamaguchi is essentially arguing for a reconceptualization of major psychological concepts such as self-esteem, self-concept, and self-construals within a multicultural model. He specifies different paths to essentially being, depending on the cultural context and core psychological values that are associated with those contexts, and demonstrates how individuals can move on one or more paths, depending on culture and values. This reconceptualization has major implications for redefining and recasting all research related to self and well-being across cultures, including, but not limited to, such topics as self-enhancement and self-efficacy. While couched in the framework of East-West distinctions, the models and ideas presented are applicable across cultures.

Yamaguchi's ideas also have multiple important ramifications for innovations in future empirical work. Testing ideas concerning collective self-efficacy, for example, would require designing ways of creating and measuring collective action and dealing with collective influences on individual data, for which current psychological methods and data analytic techniques fall far short. His ideas also force us to reexamine definitions of autonomy, well-being, and self-efficacy and, as such, may bring about necessary changes in the conduct of research on these constructs as well.

As Yamaguchi states, the two paths that he uses as examples in his important second illustration are not incompatible or mutually exclusive. As such, they bring with them the possibility that these paths, and others, coexist simultaneously in each individual, and people use the multiple paths differentially according to context and culture. If true, this would signify a major revision in our understanding of self and personality across cultures and would be a major step toward the creation of a pan-cultural psychology that resonates with the major theme of this volume.

At fifteen, I set my heart on learning.

. . . .

At seventy, I followed my heart's desire without overstepping the line.
(Confucius/Lau, *Analects*, 1979, p. 63)

It is a Confucian ideal that individuals can naturally fit well with the environment. Confucianism views humans as integral parts of an orderly universe who have an innate moral sense to maintain harmony. According to this view, mature individuals such as Confucius can live a comfortable life without experiencing conflicts between their inner demands or wishes and the external world, thus representing the Asian value of maintaining harmony with the world. In U.S. culture, an individual's independence and self-sufficiency have been valued to a greater extent than harmony with the environment (Sampson, 1977, 1988). In the U.S. value system, individuals attempt to acquire an ability to keep important societal and material resources under their control so they can verify and enjoy their independence and self-sufficiency. Thus, an ideal relationship between the self and the environment in the United States would take a quite different form from that which Confucian philosophy would preach (Kim, 1994; Triandis, 1994). Hence, the main purpose of this chapter is to understand how these differences in the core values between the United States and Asia

can affect the way that individuals adjust their relationship with the environment.

Before proceeding to the details of the cultural effects on the control orientations of individuals, we digress briefly to verify that East Asians actually prescribe to harmony with the environment to a greater extent than autonomy, whereas the reverse is true with Westerners.

Harmony versus Autonomy

At the value level, Schwartz (1992) demonstrated in his value survey that social harmony (i.e., conformity, security, and tradition) is valued higher in a communal society like Taiwan than in a contractual society like New Zealand. On the other hand, the value of mastery, defined as "active mastery of the social environment through self-assertion" (Schwartz, 1994, p. 103), is valued more highly in the United States than in East Asian countries. Kwan, Bond, and Singelis (1997) showed that relationship harmony is a more important determinant of college student's self-esteem in Hong Kong than in the United States.

Not only do people in East Asia endorse harmony, the maintenance of harmony serves as an important guiding principle in their daily lives, such as teaching, filial piety, advertisements, discussions, and conflict resolutions.

Shigaki (1983) found that the most important value among Japanese nursery school teachers is to foster harmonious relationships. Sung (1994) compared filial motivation among Korean and American caregivers of elderly relatives. For Koreans, family harmony was an important motivation for caregiving to elderly relatives, whereas it was not mentioned by Americans. Han and Shavitt (1994) found that magazine advertisements in the United States appealed to individual benefits and preferences, whereas in Korea, advertisements appealed to in-group benefits, harmony, and family integrity. They also demonstrated in a follow-up experiment that ads emphasizing family or in-group benefits were less persuasive in the United States than in Korea.

Prunty, Klopf, and Ishi (1990a,b) found that Japanese university students were less argumentative, valued group harmony, and shunned controversy more than their American counterparts. According to Trubisky, Ting-Toomey, and Lin (1991), Taiwanese students prefer to resolve a conflict within an in-group by "obliging (e.g., going along with the suggestions of the group member)," "avoiding (e.g., staying away from disagreement with the group member)," "integrating (e.g., integrating ideas with the group member or coming up with a decision jointly)," and "compromising (e.g., trying to find a middle course to resolve an impasse)" compared to American students.

Leung and Lind (1986) also showed that undergraduates in the United States preferred the adversary procedure to the nonadversary procedure in conflict resolution, whereas such a difference was not found for Chinese undergraduates. Similarly, Ohbuchi, Fukushima, and Tedeschi (1999) asked American and Japanese college students to recall an experience of conflict and rate the episode on dimensions such as goal orientation, goal attainment, and tactics in their attempts at conflict resolution. Japanese students tended to avoid a confrontation with the other party, whereas American students tended to assert their request strongly. They found further that the most important goal for the Japanese students was to maintain a positive relationship with the other party, whereas restoration of fairness was the most important goal for the American students. Leung (1988) showed that Hong Kong Chinese tended to pursue a conflict less than Americans when a potential disputant is an in-group member. Leung (1987) further demonstrated that Hong Kong adults tended to perceive that mediation and

bargaining could reduce animosity between disputants and preferred those procedures to a greater extent than American adults.

The foregoing brief review indicates that a core value in East Asia is the maintenance of harmony rather than autonomy. Although the maintenance of both interpersonal harmony and autonomy must be important in any culture, when the two values come into conflict, East Asians tend to value harmony more than autonomy. The main thrust of this chapter, therefore, is to understand control orientations among people, such as East Asians, who value a harmonious relationship with the social and physical environment in contrast with those who value autonomy to a greater extent than harmony, like North Americans.

More specifically, I focus on how the two cultural values affect individuals' choice regarding who acts as an agent of control and what they attempt to change. As to the agent of control, it does not have to be the self. It can be another person or a collective of which one is a member. For example, individuals can repair their car in three different ways, depending on who does the job. First, one can fix the car by himself or herself. Second, one can bring it to a car dealer and ask them to fix it. Third, one can repair it collectively with family members or friends. In the following sections, I argue that one's choice of agent is affected by the two cultural values that I discussed above. The target of control is also affected by cultural values. People's target of control can be either themselves or the environment (Rothbaum, Weisz, & Snyder, 1982). Researchers have claimed that East Asians attempt to change themselves rather than the environment, whereas Westerners attempt to influence existing realities (e.g., Weisz, Rothbaum, & Blackburn, 1984). I conceptually analyze the contentions of Rothbaum and Weisz and review relevant literature. Then, an agenda for future research is presented.

Concept of Control

Although control appears a very simple concept, there has not been a consensus among researchers regarding its definition (for a review, see Skinner, 1996). For example, it is defined cognitively by Thompson (1981) as the belief that one has at one's disposal a response that can influence the aversiveness of an event (p. 89), whereas Skinner, Chapman, and Baltes (1988) defined control as the extent to which an agent can produce desired outcomes (p. 118).

As Skinner (1996) concluded after a comprehensive review of the control-related constructs, the prototype of control is personal control, in which the agent of control is the self. Thus, most researchers in this area may mean personal control when they simply refer to control. However, because the agent of control is not limited to the self, the prototypicality of personal control may reflect a cultural value that personal control is more desirable than other types of control due to its facilitative effect on one's autonomy. Therefore, I simply mean "causing an intended event" (Weisz et al., 1984, p. 958) when I refer to control because this definition is free of cultural values.

Agent of Control

An agent of control, in the present context, refers to a person or a collective who can cause a particular outcome. As such, the agent can be the self, powerful other(s), or a collective such as a group or organization. I discuss how considerations about autonomy and harmony would affect one's choice of the agent.

Personal Control

Direct Personal Control

People who value autonomy are assumed to prefer personal control, in which the self acts as an agent. Individuals would especially feel themselves more self-efficacious when their agency is made explicit, thus allowing them to feel their autonomy to a greater extent than otherwise. I refer to this type of control as *direct personal control*, as contrasted with *indirect personal control*, in which one's agency is hidden or played down (Table 12.1).

Previous theoretical and empirical research in North America has emphasized the impor-

tance of self-efficacy, which can be attained by successful direct personal control and can serve as the basis for one's sense of autonomy. White (1959) argued that people have an effectance motivation, which is satisfied by production of effective changes in the environment. His theory posits that individuals attempt to be agentic toward the environment, and when they are successful as an agent, they can feel satisfaction, a process that is called a *feeling of efficacy*. Bandura (1977) advanced this line of thought and argued that expectation of self-efficacy affects one's coping behavior. If one has confidence in his or her self-efficacy, he or she will initiate and persist in coping behavior and consequently attain autonomy. More generally, one's beliefs in self-efficacy, which is defined as "people's beliefs about their capabilities to exercise control over events that affect their lives" (Bandura, 1989, p. 1175), determines subsequent motivation, affect, and action (Bandura, 1989). In the cognitive domain, beliefs in self-efficacy lead one to set a higher goal and commit oneself in the attainment of that goal (e.g., Wood and Bandura, 1989). Motivationally, the belief in self-efficacy leads one to put more effort in one's enterprise (e.g., Bandura & Cervone, 1983), whereas in terms of emotion, those with high belief in self-efficacy feel less anxious in a stressful situation (e.g., Averill, 1973). Furthermore, Langer and Rodin (Langer & Rodin, 1976; Rodin & Langer, 1977) demonstrated that a feeling of control even can contribute to longevity. In their field study at a nursing home, mortality was found to be lower among aged residents who had been given the freedom to make choices and the responsibility of taking care of a plant relative to those who had not been given such choices and responsibility.

Not only do people bolster beliefs in their ability to control in response to successful con-

Table 12.1   Agency in Control Strategies and Their Likely Effect on Autonomy and Interpersonal Harmony

Control Strategies	Agency	Effect on Autonomy and Harmony	
		Autonomy	Harmony
Personal control			
Direct	The self acts as an agent explicitly	Positive	Neutral or negative
Indirect	The self's agency is hidden	Negative	Positive
Proxy control	Someone else acts as an agent	Negative	Positive
Collective control	A collective acts as an agent	Negative	Positive

trol of an event, but also they hold an unwarranted belief that they can control chance events in some circumstances. Langer (1975) showed that people perceive an illusion of control over chance events, which are uncontrollable by definition. In one of her experiments, adult male and female office workers were asked if they wished to purchase a lottery ticket costing $1, by which the winner could earn $50. After having agreed to enter the lottery, participants in the choice condition were allowed to select the ticket that they wanted, whereas the other participants in the no-choice condition were not given such a choice. On the morning of the lottery drawing, the participants were asked if they would like to sell their ticket to someone who wanted to get into the lottery. The mean price the participants named was $8.67 in the choice condition, and it was only $1.96 in the no-choice condition. This result indicates that participants in the choice condition had an illusion of control that they could choose the winning lottery ticket.

Given the compelling theoretical reasons and overwhelming empirical evidence indicating the prevalence of direct personal control attempts, there remains little room for questioning a strong orientation among Westerners toward direct personal control of the environment. Indeed, as noted above, personal control of one's physical and social environment is thought to be a prototype of control (Skinner, 1996). When it comes to East Asians, however, the story becomes more complicated due to the importance of interpersonal harmony.

Indirect Personal Control

Direct personal control attempts often cause interpersonal confrontations, which East Asians attempt to avoid (Ohbuchi et al., 1999; Trubinsky et al., 1991). For this reason, people who value interpersonal harmony would prefer indirect personal control to direct personal control when direct personal control of the environment is undesirable, but there is still a need or wish to control the environment. In *indirect personal control*, individuals hide or play down their agency by pretending that they are not acting as an agent while they are actually doing so. Kojima (1984) provided an excellent example of this kind of control attempt:

Suppose that a *rakugo* (comic story) master is annoyed by his disciple, who is singing a song too loudly. Instead of issuing a direct reprimand to stop it, he says, "How well you

sing a song!" For a moment, the disciple is proud, taking his master's statement at its face value, but soon he becomes aware of the true meaning of the message. (p. 972)

In this episode, the rakugo master pretended that he was not acting as an agent, although he actually attempted to stop his disciple from singing. He hid his real intention and "praised" how well his disciple was singing. The rakugo master's indirect attempt to stop his disciple from singing has the merit of maintaining their close relationship by letting him become aware of it by himself. The disciple was not forced to stop his singing and thus could maintain his face.

The prevalence of such an attempt at indirect control is suggested by Muramoto and Yamaguchi (1997) with some empirical evidence. We found that Japanese attempt to enhance self-evaluation indirectly by group serving attributions. In the previous research, it is well known that people make self-serving attributions in which they attribute success to their ability and attribute failure to an external cause, such as luck or task difficulty (Bradley, 1978; Miller & Ross, 1975), to attain positive self-evaluation.

Muramoto and Yamaguchi found that Japanese make self-effacing attributions about their performance, whereas they make group-enhancing attributions for their group's performance. This result indicates that Japanese do not always make self-effacing attributions. Rather, the result can be interpreted as an attempt to raise their self-evaluation indirectly by praising their in-group, while maintaining harmonious relationships with others by self-effacing attribution.

As social identity theory (Tajfel, 1982) posits, evaluation of one's in-group affects his or her *social identity*, which is defined as "that part of an individual's self-concept that derives from the individual's knowledge of his or her membership in a social group (or groups) together with the value and emotional significance attached to that membership" (p. 255). Because social identity is equivalent to one's "self-conception as a group member" (Abrams & Hogg, 1990), one can enhance one's self-evaluation by favorable evaluations of one's in-group. In this way, individuals can raise one's self-evaluation without disrupting group harmony.

Consistent with this interpretation, Muramoto and Yamaguchi (1999) have found that Japanese participants tend to evaluate their personal contribution to group success as equal to or greater than that of the average group member, although they may not express this self-evaluation to their in-group members. This finding suggests that Japanese attempt to enhance self-esteem, albeit indirectly. This result also indicates that Japanese pretend that they are not acting as an agent, although in actuality they are acting agentically to enhance their self-esteem. If one can assume that the cost of direct personal control of self-evaluation is high, as suggested by previous research, then one would understand why Japanese indirectly attempt to enhance or protect their self-esteem. When it comes to group performance, one's agency is diluted among in-group members; thus, attribution of group success is less agentic than attribution of personal performance. Muramoto and Yamaguchi's findings indicate that Japanese do strive for higher self-evaluation, but through another route in which one's agency is played down; thus, disruption of interpersonal harmony is less likely. It is quite conceivable that, in Japanese culture, one's need for higher self-evaluation is masked by an even stronger need for maintenance of harmony and is fulfilled indirectly through group enhancement rather than self-enhancement.

Self-effacing attribution for one's performance is not limited to Japanese. Researchers have maintained that humility is a norm in Chinese societies as well (for a review, see Leung, 1996). Farh, Dobbins, and Cheng (1991) have found, in line with Muramoto and Yamaguchi (1997), that Chinese employees in Taiwan rated their job performance less favorably than their supervisors did. In addition, Wan and Bond (1982) found that such self-effacing tendencies among Chinese disappeared in a public situation as far as luck is concerned, suggesting that the self-effacing attribution is an impression management tactic.

This empirical evidence suggests, despite recent arguments by Heine and his colleagues for lower self-concept among Japanese relative to North Americans (Heine, Lehman, Markus, & Kitayama, 1999; Heine, Takata, & Lehman, 2000), that expressed low self-concept among Japanese and Chinese needs to be taken with reservations. They may just be following the humility norm prevalent in their societies and attempting to heighten their self-evaluation indirectly by showing that they are competent enough to understand and follow the cultural norm.

The previous research suggests, as a whole, that those who value interpersonal harmony would tend to choose indirect personal control in the fear that direct personal control attempts may cause interpersonal confrontations. For those who value autonomy, on the other hand, indirect personal control would not be an attractive choice because it is not conducive to their sense of autonomy even when it is implemented successfully. It becomes their choice, however, when direct personal control is unavailable. Lopez and Little (1996) reported that dependent children of U.S. military personnel in Germany tended to use indirect coping strategies (i.e., indirect control attempts) when they were faced with uncontrollable events.

Proxy Control

When exercise of personal control is neither readily available nor encouraged, one might well relinquish his or her direct control attempts and seek "security in proxy control" (Bandura, 1982, p. 142). *Proxy control* means control by someone else for the benefit of the person (Table 12.1).

For example, in third-party interventions, intermediaries are called in to regulate interpersonal relationships between parties with potential or actual conflict of interests. With the help of those intermediaries, people can gain a desired outcome without acting agentically. In this sense, those people are thought to use proxy control in third-party interventions. As the foregoing analysis of the reluctance of East Asians to use direct personal control suggests, third-party interventions would be preferred to a greater extent in East Asia than in the West. Indeed, according to Bian and Ang's (1997) survey of 1,008 Chinese workers and 512 workers in Singapore, when a worker changes his or her job, intermediaries play an important role by bridging the job changers and their new employer.

Proxy control is essential for survival of those who are in a weaker position and thus are unable to change their environment to their liking. Because they do not have enough skills, knowledge, and power to bring about their desired outcome or avoid an undesired outcome in the environment, they cannot afford a means to control their environment other than proxy control. Thus, it would be of paramount importance for those in a weaker position, such as children and subordinates in an organization, to develop an ability to locate powerful others who can be induced to act in their benefit. For example, parents are powerful persons who can bring about a desired outcome for children.

Thus, a child would ask his or her parents to buy him or her an expensive toy. Likewise, a subordinate may ask his or her boss to negotiate with the chief executive officer of the company for a promotion. In those situations, people who seek proxy control are unable to exercise direct personal control. The child cannot afford to buy expensive goods, and the subordinate does not have a chance to negotiate with the chief executive officer regarding his or her promotion. Thus, they need to use proxy control if they wish to bring about a desired outcome in their environment.

Prevalence of proxy control in Asian contexts is reflected in a Japanese indigenous concept, *Amae*, which has been suggested by a Japanese psychoanalyst, Doi (1977), to be a key concept to understanding the Japanese mentality. In everyday use, Amae involves a person's behavior that is not necessarily acceptable (Taketomo, 1986). More precisely, individuals can presume that their inappropriate behavior would be accepted by their counterpart if they are in a close relationship with the counterpart. This presumption is called Amae among the Japanese (Yamaguchi, 1999).

For example, the child may expect his or her parents to buy an expensive toy because the parents love the child. The subordinate in a company, who wishes to be promoted, may expect his or her superior to accept a request for promotion because they have been in a friendly relationship, although the subordinate may not deserve promotion. In those examples, the requests are normally perceived as inappropriate by the counterparts. Nevertheless, the requesters or solicitors are attempting to get what they desire through a powerful other, such as parents, husband, or superordinate, because the counterparts are in a close relationship with them. It is important to note here that Amae typically involves a close relationship, such as with a close friend or a child-parent or husband-wife type of relationship. In close relationships, even inappropriate behaviors are often accepted, albeit within some limits. Thus, Amae among Japanese can be considered an attempt at proxy control, in which a benefactor accepts an inappropriate behavior or request that would hardly be accepted in other relationships.

Obviously, Amae or other types of proxy control will not foster the sense of self-efficacy in attaining the goal of control. Individuals in a proxy control situation have to relinquish their direct control over the environment and for-

go an opportunity to acquire requisite skills (Bandura, 1982). A resulting low self-efficacy may well foster dependence on proxy control, which further reduces opportunities to build the skills needed for efficacious action (Bandura, 1997, p. 17). Thus, as far as one subscribes to the value of autonomy, proxy control is definitely undesirable because of its deteriorating effect on one's autonomy.

However, if one gives priority to maintenance of harmony, a bright side of proxy control, including Amae, will emerge: Proxy control can have a beneficial effect on interpersonal relationships. If the benefactor successfully handles the situation for the requester's benefit, it will foster a feeling of trust on the benefactors. The benefactor would also be able to feel that he or she is valued and trusted by the requester because the requester relinquished control and asked the benefactor for a favor.

Even in terms of self-efficacy, proxy control may not necessarily be detrimental. It can foster a feeling of self-efficacy in managing interpersonal relationships because proxy control entails social skills to locate a powerful other and induce the person to work on behalf of the requester. In this sense, proxy control should be distinguished from mere relinquishment of control. It can be conceived as a control attempt in which the real agent (i.e., self) is hidden. In proxy control, individuals know what they want, and they often use well-developed social skills to induce a potential benefactor to work on their behalf. For this reason, the situation is typically under the requester's control rather than that of the benefactor. By using proxy control, individuals may get even what they normally cannot afford when they attempt personal control, as in the case of Amae.

Indeed, Kim and Yamaguchi (2001) have found that Japanese understand the double-edged sword nature of Amae: a detrimental effect on autonomy and a facilitative effect on interpersonal relationship. We asked more than 1,000 Japanese, including junior high, senior high, and college students, as well as adults, to answer questions about Amae in an open-ended questionnaire. The results indicated, as expected, that Japanese acknowledge both positive and negative aspects of Amae and consequently have an ambivalent attitude toward it. Japanese respondents associated positive feelings with Amae, such as like/love, acceptance, or trust, as well as negative feelings such as dependency, unpleasantness, selfishness, or childishness. The respondents also answered that, in allowing Amae, there are positive aspects, such as a closer relationship and reciprocal benefit, as well as negative aspects, such as immaturity and trouble for the provider of benefit.

The Japanese respondents accepted Amae only in certain situations. As Taketomo (1986) maintained, Amae would be welcome and accepted only when both interactants agree. That is, acceptability of Amae would depend on closeness of the interpersonal relationship and context in which Amae is made. Amae appears to be a useful way to control individuals' physical and social environments, at least in Japan. Successfully implemented, Amae will enable powerless individuals to change their environment while maintaining interpersonal harmony.

Collective Control

In addition to indirect personal control and proxy control, there is another type of control that does not come into conflict with interpersonal harmony. In *collective control*, one attempts to control the environment as a member of a group or collective, which serves as an agent of control. Thus, members do not have to worry about maintenance of interpersonal harmony among in-group members because they share the goal of control (Table 12.1).

In East Asia, the unit of survival has been a group or collective rather than isolated individuals or nuclear families (Triandis, 1994). As the unit of survival, groups or collectives may well be autonomous agents. Indeed, Menon, Morris, Chiu, and Hong (1999) argue that East Asians perceive collectives as autonomous. They demonstrated, consistent with their argument, that East Asians tend to attribute the cause of various events more readily to group properties rather than personal properties. Chinese in Hong Kong attributed the cause of organizational scandals to group properties rather than individual properties, whereas their American counterparts showed the reverse tendencies.

In collective control, responsibility, as well as agency, will be diffused among actors (Latane & Darley, 1970). If everyone in a collective is responsible for the outcome to the same extent, no one will have to take responsibility for a negative outcome personally. Although no one can claim responsibility for a positive outcome either, it would be exactly what East Asians prefer. Muramoto and Yamaguchi (1997) showed that Japanese prefer to attribute success to their group members, indicating that Japanese do not claim personal responsibility for their successful performance in a group. People can maintain harmony among in-group members by sharing responsibilities for the outcome regardless of its valence.

Not only are groups perceived as agents, but also East Asians have a belief that they are more efficacious as a collective than as a person (Earley, 1989, 1993). Earley (1989) asked managerial trainees from the United States and the People's Republic of China to work on an additive task (Steiner, 1972), such as writing memos and making priorities for client interviews. He predicted and found that social loafing (i.e., reduced effort in a collective task as compared with an individualized task) appeared among individualistic Americans, as shown by Latané, Williams, and Harkins (1979), whereas it did not appear among collectivistic Chinese. It was also found that the Chinese participants worked harder in a group than when working alone, especially in settings with high shared responsibility in which the participants were given a specified group goal. He interpreted the results as indicating that Chinese give priority to group goals and collective action rather than their self-interests, whereas the reverse would be the case with Americans.

Earley (1993) advanced this line of interpretation and further demonstrated that nonoccurrence of social loafing among Chinese is related to an individual's perceived group efficacy, which is defined as a person's expectation about a group's capability. In this experiment, managers from the United States and China were asked to perform simulated managerial activities as in Earley's 1989 study under one of three conditions of group membership: alone, in-group, or out-group. In the in-group and out-group conditions, the participants were led to believe that they were working with either in-group members or out-group members. For the Chinese participants, performance was significantly higher in the in-group condition than in the out-group or alone condition, whereas for the American participants, performance was significantly higher in the alone condition than in the other two conditions. Corresponding to the result on performance, the Chinese participants perceived group efficacy in the in-group condition was higher than that of the American participants. Hence, the results suggest that the Chinese participants worked harder in the in-group condition because they have a belief in group efficacy.

Such beliefs in collective efficacy may well lead people to create an illusion of collective control among them. Yamaguchi (1998) hypothesized that Japanese would tend to estimate risk unjustifiably lower in a collective setting than when they are alone. In the first experiment, Japanese female participants were asked to estimate a risk level in fictitious situations described in a vignette with a varied number of risk companions who are exposed to the same risk source. For example, the participants were asked to estimate the probability of getting cancer assuming that they were drinking water contaminated with carcinogens either alone or with a small number or a large number of risk companions. As the reader should be aware by now, there is absolutely no normative ground to expect that the number of risk companions affects the probability that one gets cancer. Nevertheless, the participants estimated that the risk level would be lower with more risk companions. In the second study, the finding was successfully replicated in a laboratory setting in which participants were exposed to a real risk of electric shocks. This group diffusion effect of risk perception has been replicated in Hong Kong using essentially the same vignettes (Amy & Leung, 1998).

Yamaguchi, Gelfand, Mizuno, and Zemba (1997) examined more directly if Japanese overestimate their collective efficacy and Americans, especially males, overestimate self-efficacy. We predicted that Japanese hold a belief that their collective control is more efficacious than their personal control, whereas Americans, especially males, would hold the opposite belief, that their personal control is more efficacious than their collective control.

In the experiment, participants were told that the experiment was concerned with the effect of an unpleasant experience on the subsequent task performance. Ostensibly for this purpose, the participants were told that they would be assigned either to a control condition or to an unpleasant experience condition, depending on the result of lottery drawings. It was explained that they would be asked to take a bitter drink in the unpleasant experience condition, whereas they would not have to take the drink in the control condition.

Actually, there were two conditions: alone and group. In the alone condition, each participant was asked to draw four lottery tickets, on each of which a one-digit number was given. In the group condition, on the other hand, the participant was told that he or she was a member of a four-person group with the other three participants in the other rooms. An experimenter explained that each of the four members of the group would draw one lottery ticket. It was explained both in the alone and group conditions that the participant's assignment to the conditions would be determined by the sum of the four numbers given on the four lottery tickets. That is, the experimental situation was controlled so that in both the alone and group conditions the chance level of getting into the unpleasant condition was the same. The participants in the alone condition drew four tickets alone, whereas the participants in the group condition were led to believe that each of the four members would draw one lottery ticket. As in Yamaguchi (1998), there was no normative ground for the participants to believe that the sum of the four digits would be affected by who drew the lottery tickets. The dependent variable was the participant's estimate of the likelihood that they would eventually be assigned to the unpleasant condition and have to take a bitter drink.

The results indicated, as expected, that the Japanese participants in the group condition estimated their likelihood of being assigned to the unpleasant condition was lower than those in the alone condition, whereas the reverse tendency was the case with American male participants. The American female participants showed the same tendency as their Japanese counterparts: They overestimated their collective efficacy relative to their self-efficacy.

Although the result for the American females may appear perplexing, it can be explained in terms of the value to which American females subscribe. Gilligan (1993) argued that females in the United States value interpersonal relatedness to a greater extent than males, and they are less psychologically separated from others compared with American males. Consistent with Gilligan's argument, Beutel and Marini (1995) reported that, among U.S. high school seniors between 1977 and 1991, female respondents were more likely than male respondents to express concern and responsibility for the well-being of others and less likely than male respondents to accept materialism and competition. It is conceivable, therefore, that females in the United States are more like East Asians in the sense that they value maintenance of interpersonal relationships and care for others. Such orientations may well lead American females to foster general beliefs in collective efficacy. The issue of gender difference in control orientations is discussed again in the final section.

Developmentally, a sense of self-efficacy is fostered in one's socialization process (Bandura, 1989, 1997). When a baby is born, the baby does not have any sense of self-efficacy. Infants gradually develop a sense of self-efficacy based on the contingency between their behavior and outcome. Because the contingency between behavior and its outcome is often influenced by parents, teachers, or other powerful adults, one's sense of self-efficacy is thought to be influenced by the cultural milieus in which he or she is raised. If the contingency between infants behavior and outcome is constructed or emphasized as in the United States, they will grow up with a high sense of self-efficacy. On the other hand, if adults stress and construct a contingency between collective behavior and outcome, children will develop a relatively stronger sense of collective efficacy (i.e., that collectives are more efficacious in influencing the environment). Once established, this sense of collective efficacy would function as a self-fulfilling prophecy. Thus, Chinese tend to believe in collective efficacy and put more effort in collective settings than when alone (Earley, 1993), which makes the collective more efficacious than the individual.

In sum, it appears quite reasonable for East Asians to prefer collective control to personal control for at least three reasons. First, in collective control, individuals are not perceived as an agent, and thus they can avoid interpersonal conflicts. Second, they hold a self-fulfilling belief that a collective effort is more efficacious than that of individuals. Third, collective control can facilitate interpersonal harmony with in-group members because their personal goals are compatible with the group goals.

As to the agency of control, three possibilities were suggested in addition to direct personal control, which has been claimed to be important in Western cultural milieus. As summarized in Figure 12.1, emphasis on the maintenance of interpersonal harmony would lead individuals to adopt the lower route through indirect personal control, proxy control, and collective control strategies. On the other hand, emphasis on autonomy would encourage one to adopt the upper route through direct personal control strategies. Previous research and present discussions suggest that the upper route is more prevalent among people who value autonomy, whereas the lower route is preferred among people who tend to value interpersonal harmony more than individual autonomy.

Target of Control

Individuals in any culture need to adjust their relationship with the physical and social environments for their physiological and psychological well-being. In doing so, individuals attempt to change either the physical and social environments or themselves. Rothbaum et al. (1982) and Weisz et al. (1984) proposed an important distinction between the two kinds of control attempt, *primary control* and *secondary control*. In primary control, the target of control is existing external realities in one's physical and social environments. Individuals attempt to "enhance their rewards by influencing existing realities (e.g., other people, circumstances, symptoms, or behavior problems)" by means of "personal agency, dominance, or even aggression" (Weisz et al., 1984, p. 955). In secondary control, on the other hand, the target of control is oneself. Individuals attempt to "enhance their rewards by accommodating to existing realities and maximizing satisfaction or goodness of fit with things as they are without changing the existing realities" (Weisz et al., 1984, p. 955).

By extending the meaning of control to include secondary control, they made a seminal contribution to the advancement of conceptual and empirical research in this area. Specifically, in the present context, they applied the distinction to cultural differences in control orientations. Weisz et al. (1984) argued that primary control plays an important role in everyday life in the United States, whereas secondary control does so in Japan. As to the differences in control orientations in the East and West, the arguments of Weisz et al. (1984) suggest that (a) East Asians would attempt primary control to a lesser extent because they perceive primary control as both less feasible and less desirable than do Americans, and (b) East Asians would attempt to exert secondary control to a greater extent than do Americans. In the following sections, available evidence is examined after the meaning of the two kinds of control is elaborated.

Primary Control

According to Rothbaum et al. (1982), both primary and secondary control includes four types

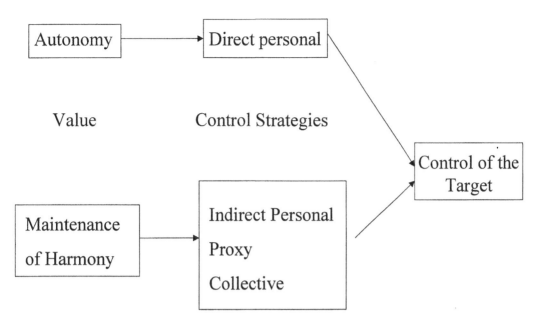

Figure 12.1   Relationship between Value and Control Strategies

of control: predictive, illusory, vicarious, and interpretive (Table 12.2). In *predictive primary control*, individuals attempt to predict events so that they will succeed at them. An example of this type of control would be to predict the next move that one's opponent will make in a chess game. By predicting the opponent's move correctly, one will have a better chance to beat the opponent. In *illusory primary control*, individuals attempt to control an uncontrollable event like an event determined by chance. The superstitious behavior of gamblers would be included in this category. A gambler may continue to wear a dirty hat that he or she wore 10 years ago at the time of a big winning bet in the belief that the hat brings good fortune. *Vicarious primary control* is equivalent to proxy control in that it includes an attempt to manipulate powerful others. Last, *interpretive primary*

control refers to attempts at understanding problems to solve or master them.

In discussing primary control, it should be noted that proxy control, or vicarious primary control in the terminology of Rothbaum et al. (1982), is included in the original classification of primary control attempts (Rothbaum et al., 1982). Proxy control is unique in that the agent is some powerful other(s) rather than oneself. Because proxy control is detrimental for development of skills required for personal control and thus would neither be valued nor preferred in the United States (Bandura, 1997), the argument of Weisz et al. (1984) that primary control is more prevalent in the United States than in Japan appears logically untenable. Indeed, available empirical evidence indicates that the suggestion of Weisz et al. (1984) face a serious problem when examined empirically.

Table 12.2   Primary Control Strategies

Strategy	Example
Predictive	Predict an opponent's move to win a game
Vicarious (proxy)	Manipulate a powerful other to obtain something
Illusory	Gambler's superstitious behavior
Interpretive	Understand a problem to solve it

By using their scale of primary and secondary control, Seginer, Trommsdorff, and Essau (1993) compared control beliefs of Malaysian students with those of North American and German students. Their Malaysian sample consisted mostly of Iban and Malay students, whose religions emphasize the importance of harmonious interpersonal relationships (Seginer et al., 1993). Thus, their Malaysian participants are thought to endorse the value of harmonious relationships. Their result did not provide support for the suggestion of Weisz et al. (1984). In terms of total primary control beliefs, contrary to the expectation of the researchers, Malaysians scored higher than Germans, and no difference was found between Malaysians and North Americans. Furthermore, it was found that the Malaysian students scored higher than both the North American and German students on the vicarious primary control (i.e., proxy control) dimension. This result indicates, as the foregoing discussion suggests, that Malaysians tend to control the environment through someone else (proxy control) rather than directly.

In one of Weisz's empirical studies, McCarty et al. (1999) compared stress coping strategies of 6- to 14-year-olds in Thailand and the United States. Because the Thai child is taught from an early age not to "disturb their personal equilibrium by expressing one's own feelings or wishes overtly" (p. 810), the results from Thai children are thought to be suggestive of East Asian coping strategies. Regarding primary control, they found no difference between children in the two cultures. One important result again was that Thai children reported more than twice as much covert (i.e., indirect) coping as their American counterparts. This result indicates that Thai children exert indirect personal control rather than giving up their influence on the realities, as Japanese students enhance self-evaluation indirectly (Muramoto & Yamaguchi, 1999). Such results led McCarty et al. (1999) to conclude

> Thai youngsters were more likely than Americans to use covert coping methods when interacting with adults, but they were not more likely than Americans, in these situations, to adopt secondary control goals or to relinquish control. In other words, it would not be correct to assume that the deferent, subtle, indirect forms of coping employed by Thai youth in these situations imply a lack of investment in exerting influence or causing events to turn out as they wish. A more accurate view may be that Thai youth

> were following the social norms of appropriate outward behavior towards adults while maintaining goals that involved just as much primary control as those of American youth. (p. 816)

Nakamura and Flammer (1998) compared control orientations of Swiss students and Japanese students. When it comes to active problem-solving strategies, which can be classified as interpretive primary control, Swiss students had a higher orientation than their Japanese counterparts. This result indicates that, in a specific primary control strategy such as interpretive primary control, Japanese are less inclined to use primary control relative to Westerners.

Overall, previous empirical research is scarce and has not demonstrated that Japanese or East Asians are motivated to use primary control in general to a lesser extent relative to Americans or Westerners. Although undoubtedly cultural milieus affect individuals' choice of control strategies, we should not ignore the fact that individuals in any culture need to pursue control over the environment for their subsistence. Hence, it is not surprising that the concept of primary control cannot appropriately differentiate control orientations in the East and West. Differences in primary control orientations in the East and West would not reside in its prevalence in one culture relative to others, but in the type of agents and ways individuals can afford or prefer in their respective cultural milieu, as suggested in previous sections.

The claim of Weisz et al. (1984) would be most appropriately taken as suggesting the relative prevalence of direct personal control of the environment in the United States rather than primary control in general. Although this interpretation of the argument of Weisz et al. is inconsistent with their original definition of primary control, subsequent researchers appear to have adopted it already. For example, when Heckhausen and Shultz (1995) characterized primary control as involving "direct action on the environment" (p. 285), they undoubtedly departed from the original definition of Rothbaum et al. (1982) by excluding vicarious primary control and illusory primary control. Heckhausen and Shultz essentially meant personal control of the environment by primary control.

A more viable hypothesis, therefore, would be that direct personal control of the environment is more prevalent in the West than in East Asia. That is, Westerners would prefer to exert direct personal control much more than East

Asians when the target of control is the environment. This hypothesis is discussed in more detail below.

Secondary Control

The second component of the arguments of Weisz et al. (1984) was that secondary control would be more prevalent in East Asian cultures relative to American culture. To examine the validity of this hypothesis appropriately, it is again essential that we take a closer look at the nature of secondary control. Weisz et al. suggested four kinds of secondary control as in primary control (Table 12.3).

Predictive secondary control refers to the accurate prediction of events and conditions so that one can control their psychological impact on the self. For example, one may attempt to know how a dentist will treat his or her decayed tooth before visiting the dentist to reduce the negative impact of the treatment. In this case, the target of control is fear or other negative feelings that may accompany a dental treatment. Generally, the target of predictive secondary control is the psychological impact of external events.

In *vicarious secondary control*, on the other hand, individuals attempt to gain a feeling of self-efficacy by aligning with powerful others or groups who can make accomplishments that the individual cannot afford. In this type of control, the target is one's feeling of self-efficacy. A good example of this type of control is provided by Cialdini et al. (1976). They demonstrated that college students tend to show their associations with successful others. In one of their experiments, college students were found to wear school-identifying apparel after the victory of the football team. By basking in reflected glory (BIRGing), the college students could foster a sense of self-efficacy, albeit illusory. This type of control can be considered proxy control of internal states, in this case, a feeling of self-efficacy.

As to *illusory secondary control*, the definitions of Rothbaum et al. (1982) and Weisz et al. (1984) are not consistent. In Rothbaum et al., this type of control was defined as a person's attempt to align themselves with the force of chance so that they may share in the control exerted by that powerful force (p. 17). According to this definition, the control target was once again one's sense of self-efficacy as in vicarious secondary control. On the other hand, illusory secondary control was defined by Weisz et al. as an individual's attempts to associate or get into synchrony with chance to enhance comfort with and acceptance of one's fate (p. 957). According to this new definition, the target of control is one's feelings associated with acceptance of his or her fate. For example, a dying cancer patient may accept his or her fate and stop fighting against it. By doing so, the patient will be able to control emotions, such as fear of death, and restore his or her peace of mind. If illusory secondary control refers to this type of coping, it would be more appropriately termed *accommodative secondary control* because it does not involve any illusion about control, and most likely the goal of control is to restore one's peace of mind.

Finally, in *interpretive secondary control*, individuals attempt to derive a meaning or purpose from existing realities and thereby enhance their satisfaction with those realities. An extreme case of such control would be an attempt by a Japanese Zen priest named Kaisen in the medieval period. When he was executed by fire, he reportedly uttered, "If you train your mind to disregard agony, you will find even fire cool." In more ordinary life, when we make a mistake or fail at something, we would attempt to derive a meaning from the mistake or failure and justify it. For example, a student who failed a final exam may think, "It is all right that I did not get credit for the course. I have learned a lot in the class anyway." Thus, in interpretive secondary control, the target of

Table 12.3   Target in Secondary Control Strategies

Strategy	Target
Predictive	Psychological impact of external events
Vicarious (proxy)	One's feeling of self-efficacy
Illusory	One's feeling of self-efficacy (Rothbaum et al., 1982)
	One's feelings associated with acceptance of fate (Weisz et al., 1984)
Interpretive	Psychological impact of one's experience

control is the psychological impact of one's experience.

The extant empirical evidence on cultural differences in secondary control is again scarce, and the results are mixed. Seginer et al. (1993) found that secondary control beliefs are stronger among Malaysian adolescents than German or North American adolescents. In Nakamura and Flammer's (1998) comparison between problem-solving strategies of Swiss and Japanese students, reinterpretation strategies, which can be classified as interpretive secondary control, were found more often among Japanese students than Swiss students. However, McCarty et al. (1999) did not find any consistent secondary control attempts among Thai youths compared to American youths.

In an attempt to compare control orientations directly among Americans and Japanese, Morling (2000) asked questions of participants in aerobics classes in Japan and the United States. Being asked what they would do in a class when the moves get too difficult, both Japanese and American participants answered that they were most likely to try harder to keep up with the instructor. Because the author operationally defined this response as the measure of their secondary control attempt, the result indicates that secondary control was dominant in the aerobics class in both cultures. The second most reported response, however, was more frequently primary control (i.e., to change the move to something they like) among Americans than Japanese.

In all, the previous research on cultural differences in secondary control strategies provides mixed results and thus does not allow us to draw any conclusion. Perhaps the conceptual ambiguity of secondary control and resulting diversity in its operationalization are responsible for the mixed results. Because the specific target in the four types of secondary control is diverse (see Table 12.3), we need to examine which cognitive or emotional component of the self individuals would wish to control in each culture. For example, in the case of vicarious secondary control, one is not motivated to accommodate the self to the existing realities. In this type of control, the goal is supposed to be to maintain one's sense of self-efficacy and to continue to believe that he or she has a capability to influence the reality. Such a control strategy would be more preferred by those who value autonomy.

Although the distinction of Weisz et al. (1984) between primary and secondary control is conceptually clear, this dichotomy cannot be readily applicable to cultural differences in control orientations. As we have seen, their claim that "primary control is more valued and prevalent in the United States, whereas in Japan secondary control has been more central in everyday life" (p. 955), cannot be sustained conceptually or empirically. It is not primary control per se that is valued in the United States. Nor is it secondary control per se that is valued in Japan particularly or East Asia in general. Primary and secondary control need to be distinguished from cultural values.

Primacy of Primary Control or Secondary Control

The present review has implications for recent debates on the primacy of primary control over secondary control (Gould, 1999; Heckhausen & Shultz, 1995, 1999). Heckhausen and Shultz (1995) argued in their theory of lifetime development that primary control has functional primacy over secondary control. Because the target of primary control is one's environment, they maintained that "it enables individuals to shape their environment to fit their particular needs and developmental potential" (p. 286). On the other hand, they argued, the adaptive value of secondary control is limited to its compensatory function (Heckhausen & Shultz, 1995). When people experience a threat to self-esteem or self-efficacy due to failed or unavailable primary control, secondary control is assumed to ameliorate the negativity of this threat and "preserve and rekindle the individual's motivational resources for maintaining and enhancing primary control in the future" (Heckhausen & Shultz, 1995, p. 286). According to their view, "the primacy of primary control is invariant across cultures and historical time" (p. 286).

Before we discuss their claim for the primacy of primary control, it would be appropriate to remind the reader that Heckhausen and Shultz (1995) characterized primary control as involving "direct action on the environment" (p. 285). That is, they did not include proxy control, in which someone else attempts to control the environment. Thus, they essentially argued for the primacy of direct primary control over secondary control rather than primacy of primary control in general.

More recently, Gould (1999) criticizes Heckhausen and Shultz (1995), arguing that they constructed their theory largely in biologically driven terms (p. 600) and ignored cultural perspectives. Obviously, control over the environment is essential for human survival. Hence, one can legitimately advance an argument that primary control is indispensable for human subsistence. It does not follow, however, that direct primary control is more adaptive than secondary control in any cultures or in any situations. Gould and my foregoing analysis suggest that secondary control can be more adaptive than direct personal control of the environment (which Heckhausen & Shultz, 1995, meant by primary control) in East Asia for at least two reasons. First, secondary control can contribute to the advancement of individual's mental and biological strength. For example, Chang, Chua, and Toh (1997) have found that the tendency to use secondary control is associated with lower test anxiety among those in Singapore. It is quite conceivable that successful control of one's emotions would be associated with lower test anxiety. In addition, when individuals have some specific goal, they would attempt to improve their abilities to catch up with the standard set by an expert. American and Japanese participants in an aerobics class, who attempted to catch up with their instructor (Morling, 2000), must have improved their ability in aerobics over those who exerted primary control and moved to a lower level class that matched their present ability of aerobics. Undoubtedly, results of secondary control such as improved ability, resilient personality, mental stamina, and increased physical strength, would be beneficial for one's adaptation in the future.

Second, secondary control would also make a contribution to the advancement of psychological well-being by fostering a sense of self-efficacy in terms of controlling oneself and maintaining interpersonal harmony. When individuals have successfully controlled their internal state, such as their desires or emotions, it may well foster a sense of self-efficacy in terms of controlling oneself, which would heighten one's psychological well-being. In addition, if one can maintain harmonious relationships with the environment as a result of successful secondary control, the sense of self-efficacy in maintaining harmony will also be fostered and thus would advance the person's sense of psychological well-being. That is, an individual's psychological well-being can be heightened by the sense of self-efficacy in self-control and maintenance of harmonious relationships with the environment, as far as they

subscribe to the value of harmonious relationships with the environment, which will be arguably facilitated by secondary control. Indeed, in Korea, Kim and Park (1998) developed a scale to measure the sense of self-efficacy in maintaining interpersonal relations and social harmony based on Bandura's (1997) conceptualization. They found that their Relational Efficacy and Social Harmony Efficacy Scale is correlated positively with life satisfaction and negatively correlated with stress among Korean high school students. It is important that psychological well-being can be gained without the risk of direct confrontations by using secondary control. Thus, in a culture in which people value harmonious interpersonal relationships, secondary control can be more adaptive if immediate biological needs are not at issue.

Probably the most important assumption in the theory of Heckhausen and Shultz (1995) is that psychological well-being is dependent solely on one's sense of autonomy, which is closely related to his or her sense of self-efficacy and self-esteem. Although they did not state this explicitly, it appears at least to the present author that their argument makes use of an assumption that is shared by many Western researchers. If a theorist stipulates the indispensability of the sense of autonomy for psychological well-being, it would follow that one's psychological well-being can be enhanced only in response to one's direct and personal control attempt, which had brought about desired outcomes in the environment. On the other hand, if a theorist assumes only that a sense of successful adaptation is enough for one's psychological well-being, any primary or secondary control strategies can be claimed to bring about one's psychological well-being.

Figure 12.2 illustrates the two alternative routes to psychological well-being. The upper route describes a route that would be chosen by those who value autonomy. Alternatively, the lower route describes a route to psychological well-being through a strategy of successful adaptation that does not require autonomy. The lower route does not entail changes in one's environment for increased psychological well-being, although it does not exclude primary control. As far as direct personal control attempts do not disrupt harmony, individuals who value harmony would exert such attempts. For example, they will not hesitate to open a window in their room when they feel hot, although they may hesitate to do so when they are not alone in

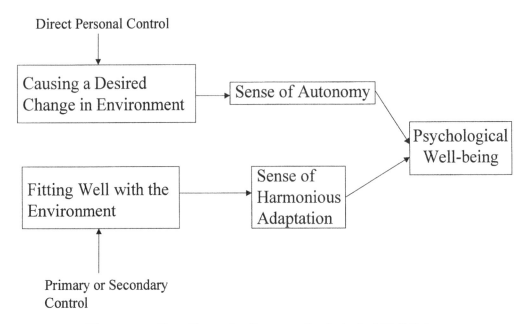

Figure 12.2   Two Alternative Routes to Psychological Well-Being

the room and are uncertain about how others feel about the room temperature.

Primary control would have functional primacy over secondary control only when an individual's biological needs are urgent or when they are in a culture in which their psychological well-being depends largely on their sense of autonomy, which can be bolstered by their capability in exerting direct and personal control over the environment. On the other hand, when an individual's biological needs are not urgent or they are in a culture in which their psychological well-being is determined primarily by their ability to fit well in the environment, secondary control would be able to heighten one's psychological well-being if the individual values harmony with the environment.

Future Agenda for Empirical Research

Admittedly, this chapter has raised more questions than it has answered. The lack or scarcity of empirical evidence in this area, however, should not be taken as indicating that the area is infertile and does not deserve empirical research. On the contrary, many important empirical questions await our merited research attentions. Some of these questions are highlighted in the following section.

Agency and Target of Control

I have suggested in this chapter that we need to broaden our framework beyond the now-popular primary-secondary control distinction so it can incorporate control orientations of those who value harmony more than autonomy. One of my suggestions is that indirect personal control, proxy control, and collective control strategies are available and actually used in place of direct personal control when individuals attempt to control the environment. Based on the foregoing discussions, one can predict cross-cultural, as well as individual, differences in the choice of control strategies: (a) East Asians, who tend to value harmony more than autonomy, would use control strategies other than direct personal control, which in turn would be preferred to a greater extent by North Americans, who tend to value autonomy relative to interpersonal harmony; (b) the more individuals value interpersonal harmony relative to autonomy, the more they would tend to use control strategies other than direct personal control. These predictions suggest an interesting possibility that the apparent cross-cultural and gender differences in control orientations can be reduced to individual differences in subscribed values.

The effect of each control strategy on one's sense of autonomy and interpersonal harmony would be invariant across cultures. That is, the likely effect of successful control attempts presented in Table 12.1 would be applicable to any culture, as well as the effect of secondary control. In any culture, successfully implemented indirect personal control, proxy control, and collective control would contribute to the maintenance of interpersonal harmony. This possibility would deserve future empirical attention as well.

We would also need to identify targets of secondary control in future research so we can understand the motivations underlying secondary control attempts. Depending on the situation, one's control attempts would be targeted at different aspects of an individual's cognition or emotions. For example, if one is motivated to heighten his or her sense of self-efficacy, he or she may well attempt to do so vicariously, as shown in the BIRGing phenomenon. This type of secondary control needs to be differentiated from other types of secondary control attempts, which may be aimed at restoring one's peace of mind.

Self-Efficacy and Autonomy

It is evident that direct personal control can foster a sense of self-efficacy. That is, direct personal control will certainly foster one's belief that he or she is capable of exercising control over important life events. However, the effect of other types of control on one's sense of self-efficacy is not so clear. I have suggested that a specific sense of self-efficacy can be fostered by other types of control: self-efficacy in managing interpersonal relationships (proxy control), self-efficacy in self-control (secondary control), and self-efficacy in maintaining harmony (secondary control). Because indirect personal control, proxy control, and collective control are thought to be conducive to the maintenance of harmony, they may also foster a sense of self-efficacy in maintaining harmony. One might ask if these specific senses of self-efficacy are the same as the kind of self-efficacy bolstered by direct personal control. As to the sense of self-efficacy in maintaining interpersonal harmony, Kim, Park, and Kwak (1998) have developed a scale and found that it is positively correlated with life satisfaction. This result indicates that it makes sense to discuss self-efficacy in relation to maintaining harmony, although its relationship to one's general self-efficacy has yet to be explored empirically.

The existence of the other kinds of self-efficacy remains a question for future research as well. In addition to self-efficacy in self-control and managing interpersonal relationships, one might wonder if collective efficacy means collective self-efficacy, which may mean self-efficacy in collectively controlling events. It would also be challenging to design empirical research to answer this question.

The relationship between various types of self-efficacy and autonomy is another issue that needs to be examined. It is quite conceivable that one's self-efficacy bolstered by direct personal control can promote his or her sense of autonomy. However, how about the effect of the other types of self-efficacy on one's sense of autonomy? For example, if one has a sense of self-efficacy in maintaining interpersonal harmony, does it mean that he or she can feel autonomous? Because autonomy means that one is not being controlled by others and can make an independent judgment, it remains uncertain if mere capability to maintain interpersonal harmony makes a person free from influence of others.

Motivations Underlying Control Attempts

The foregoing discussions suggest that control attempts, in both the East and the West, would be affected by considerations other than a mere desire to control the environment or the self. As shown in Figure 12.2, in the lower route to psychological well-being, individuals would be motivated to maintain harmony with the environment while they adjust their relationships with the social and physical environments. On the other hand, in the upper route, psychological well-being would entail a sense of autonomy. In both routes, it is assumed that individuals are motivated to attain psychological well-being in addition to the immediate target of control (i.e., of the self or the environment). Interesting predictions might be derived from this model.

First, the model suggests that a sense of autonomy is not a requirement for one's psychological well-being as far as one takes the lower route of Figure 12.2. Although autonomy may constitute an essential ingredient of adaptation in the West, this model suggests that one can attain psychological well-being without it. For people who take the lower route, a harmonious relationship with the environment is assumed to be more important than the sense of autonomy. Thus, it is plausible that one's self-concept is affected by one's ability in attaining harmonious relationships rather than autonomy. If so, one's self-esteem may be determined by his or her ability to keep harmonious relationships with the environment rather than a capability to change the environment.

Second, desirability of behavior would depend on the route that one chooses. If one takes the upper route of Figure 12.2, one would need to achieve control of the environment personally to obtain the sense of autonomy. Thus, the kind of behavior that maximizes the chance of bringing about changes personally would be most preferred. On the other hand, in the lower route, the kind of behavior that maximizes the chance of a harmonious relationship with the environment would be most preferred as far as one's biological needs are not emergent.

Third, the model suggests a possibility that one does not have to stick to one route. That is, one may try both routes to psychological well-being or change the route, depending on the situation. For example, Uichol Kim (personal communication, February 17, 2000) has found that self-efficacy in maintaining interpersonal harmony, as measured by his scale, is correlated positively with life satisfaction among Germans, as well as Koreans. This result suggests that Germans can attain psychological well-being through the lower route of Figure 12.2, as well as probably the upper route. It might be more adaptive if one could pursue both routes to his or her psychological well-being. Although East Asians are typically supposed to pursue the lower route to psychological well-being, they could also pursue the upper route. Because both autonomy and harmony with the environment must be important in any culture, the two routes described in Figure 12.2 are not incompatible. It would be a challenging idea that both routes are available to individuals regardless of the cultural milieus in which they have been raised.

Conclusion

In this chapter, I critically reviewed theoretical and empirical research on cultural differences in control orientations. In doing so, I attempted to understand the differences in terms of the cultural values of autonomy and harmony to which people subscribe. Although the available evidence is as yet too sparse for strong conclusions to be made, some similarities and differences in control orientations between those who subscribe to autonomy versus those who

subscribe to harmony are suggested. The general conclusion of this chapter is that a broader perspective would be necessary for comprehensive understanding of control orientations across cultures. The model illustrated in Figure 12.2 is a first step toward this end.

Note

This chapter is based on research supported by a grant-in-aid from the Japanese Ministry of Education, Science, Sports, and Culture (10610099). I thank Richard Bradshaw, Emiko Kashima, Yoshi Kashima, Zita Meijor, Michael Morris, Fumio Murakami, Romin Tafarodi, and Yuriko Zemba, in addition to David Matsumoto, the editor of this volume, for their helpful comments on earlier versions of this chapter.

References

Abrams, D., & Hogg, M. A. (1990). An introduction to the social identity approach. In D. Abrams & M. A. Hogg (Eds.), *Social identity theory: Constructive and critical advances*, (pp. 1–9). Hertfordshire, England: Harvester Wheatsheaf.

Amy, H. S. Y., & Leung, K. (1998). Group size effects on risk perception: A test of several hypotheses. *Asian Journal of Social Psychology, 1*, 133–145.

Averill, J. R. (1973). Personal control over aversive stimuli and its relationship to stress. *Psychological Bulletin, 80*, 286–303.

Bandura, A. (1977). Self-efficacy: Toward a unifying theory of behavioral change. *Psychological Review, 84*, 191–215.

Bandura, A. (1982). Self-efficacy mechanism in human agency. *American Psychologist, 37*, 122–147.

Bandura, A. (1989). Human agency in social cognitive theory. *American Psychologist, 44*, 1175–1184.

Bandura, A. (1997). *Self-efficacy: The exercise of control*. New York: Freeman.

Bandura, A., & Cervone, D. (1983). Self-evaluative and self-efficacy mechanisms governing the motivational effects of goal systems. *Journal of Personality and Social Psychology, 45*, 1017–1028.

Beutel, A. M., & Marini, M. M. (1995). Gender and values. *American Sociological Review, 60*, 436–448.

Bian, Y., & Ang, S. (1997). Guanxi networks and job mobility in China and Singapore. *Social Forces, 75*, 981–1005.

Bradley, G. W. (1978). Self-serving biases in the attribution process: A reexamination of the fact or fiction question. *Journal of Personality and Social Psychology, 36*, 56–71.

Chang, W. C., Chua, W. L., & Toh, Y. (1997). The concept of psychological control in the Asian context. In K. Leung, U. Kim, S. Yamaguchi, & Y. Kashima (Eds.), *Progress in Asian Social Psychology*, (Vol. 1, pp. 95–117). Singapore: Wiley.

Cialdini, R. B., Borden, R. J., Thorne, A., Walker, M. R., Freeman, S., & Sloan, L. R. (1976). Basking in reflected glory: Three (football) field studies. *Journal of Personality and Social Psychology, 34*, 366–375.

Confucious. (1979). *The Analects* (D. C. Lau, Trans.). London: Penguin Books.

Doi, T. (1977). *The anatomy of dependence.* Tokyo: Kodansha.

Earley, C. P. (1989). Social loafing and collectivism: A comparison of the United States and the People's Republic of China. *Administrative Science Quarterly, 34*, 565–581.

Earley, C. P. (1993). East meets West meets Mideast: Further explorations of collectivistic and individualistic work groups. *Academy of Management Journal, 36*, 219–348.

Farh, J., Dobbins, G. H., & Cheng, B. (1991). Cultural relativity in action: A comparison of self-rating made by Chinese and U.S. Workers. *Personnel Psychology, 44*, 129–147.

Gilligan, C. (1993). *In a different voice.* Cambridge: Harvard University Press.

Gould, S. J. (1999). A critique of Heckhausen and Schulz's (1995) life-span theory of control from a cross-cultural perspective. *Psychological Review, 106*, 597–604.

Han, S., & Shavitt, S. (1994). Persuasion and culture: Advertising appeals in individualistic and collectivistic societies. *Journal of Experimental Social Psychology, 30*, 326–350.

Heckhausen, J., & Schulz, R. (1995). A life-span theory of control. *Psychological Review, 102*, 284–304.

Heckhausen, J., & Schulz, R. (1999). The primacy of primary control is a human universal: A reply to Gould's (1999) critique of the life-span theory of control. *Psychological Review, 106*, 605–609.

Heine, S. J., Lehman, D. R., Markus, H. R., & Kitayama, S. (1999). Is there a universal need for positive self-regard? *Psychological Review, 106*, 766–794.

Heine, S. J., Takata, T., & Lehman, D. R. (2000). Beyond self-presentation: Evidence for self-criticism among Japanese. *Personality and Social Psychology Bulletin, 26*, 71–78.

Kim, U. (1994). Individualism and collectivism: Conceptual clarification and elaboration. In U. Kim, H. C. Triandis, C. Kagitcibasi, S. C. Choi, & G. Yoon (Eds.), *Individualism and collectivism: Theory, method, and applications* (pp. 19–40). Thousand Oaks, CA: Sage.

Kim, U., Park, Y. S., & Kwak, K. J. (1998). Hanguk Chungsonyunui Saenghwalmanjokdowa Stress Hyungsung yoin: Doshiwa Nongchon chungsonyunul Jungsimuro [Factors influencing stress and life-satisfaction level of Korean adolescents: Comparison of urban and rural students]. *Korean Journal of Health Psychology, 3*, 79–101.

Kim, U., & Yamaguchi, S. (2001). *Amae.* Manuscript in preparation.

Kojima, H. (1984). A significant stride toward the comparative study of control. *American Psychologist, 39*, 972–973.

Kwan, V. S. Y., Bond, M. H., & Singelis, T. M. (1997). Pancultural explanations for life satisfaction: Adding relationship harmony to self-esteem. *Journal of Personality and Social Psychology, 73*, 1038–1051.

Langer, E. J. (1975). The illusion of control. *Journal of Personality and Social Psychology, 32*, 311–328.

Langer, E. J., & Rodin, J. (1976). The effects of choice and enhanced personal responsibility for the aged: A field experiment in an institutional setting. *Journal of Personality and Social Psychology, 34*, 191–198.

Latané, B., & Darley, J. M. (1970). *The unresponsive bystander: Why doesn't he help?* New York: Appleton-Century-Crofts.

Latané, B., Williams, K., & Harkins, S. (1979). Many hands make light the work: The causes and consequences of social loafing. *Journal of Personality and Social Psychology, 37*, 822–832.

Leung, K. (1987). Some determinants of reactions to procedural models for conflict resolution: A cross-national study. *Journal of Personality and Social Psychology, 53*, 898–908.

Leung, K. (1988). Some determinants of conflict avoidance. *Journal of Cross-Cultural Psychology, 19*, 125–136.

Leung, K. (1996). The role of beliefs in Chinese culture. In M. H. Bond (Ed.), *The handbook of Chinese Psychology* (pp. 247–262). Hong Kong: Oxford University Press.

Leung, K., & Lind, E. A. (1986). Procedural justice and culture: Effects of culture, gender, and investigator status on procedural preferences. *Journal of Personality and Social Psychology, 50*, 1134–1140.

Lopez, D. F., & Little, T. D. (1996). Children's action—control beliefs and emotional regulation in the social domain. *Developmental Psychology, 32*, 299–312.

McCarty, C. A., Weisz, J. R., Wanitromanee, K., Eastman, K. L., Suwanlert, S., Chaiyasit, W., & Band, E. B. (1999). Culture, coping, and context: Primary and secondary control among Thai and American youth. *Journal of Child Psychology and Psychiatry, 40*, 809–818.

Menon, T., Morris, M. W., Chiu, C. Y., & Hong, Y. Y. (1999). Culture and the construal of agency: Attribution to individual versus group dispositions. *Journal of Personality and Social Psychology, 76*, 701–717.

Miller, D. T., and Ross, M. (1975). Self-serving biases in the attribution of causality: Fact or fiction? *Psychological Bulletin, 82*, 213–225.

Morling, B. (2000). "Taking" an aerobics class in the U.S. and "entering" an aerobics class in Japan. *Asian Journal of Social Psychology, 3*, 73–85.

Muramoto, Y., & Yamaguchi, S. (1997). Mouhitotsu no self-serving bias: Nihonjin no kizoku ni okeru jikohige—shudanhoushi keikou no kyozon to sono imini tsuite [Another type of self-serving bias: Coexistence of self-effacing and group-serving tendencies in attribution in the Japanese culture]. *Japanese Journal of Experimental Social Psychology, 37*, 65–75.

Muramoto, Y., & Yamaguchi, S. (1999, August). *An alternative route to self-enhancement among Japanese*. Paper presented at the Third Conference of the Asian Association of Social Psychology, Taipei, Taiwan.

Nakamura, Y., & Flammer, A. (1998, August). *Control beliefs and self-construals in Japanese and Swiss adolescents*. Paper presented at the 25th Congress of the International Association for Cross-Cultural Psychology, Bellingham, WA.

Ohbuchi, K., Fukushima, O., & Tedeschi, J. T. (1999). Cultural values in conflict management: Goal orientation, goal attainment, and tactical decision. *Journal of Cross-Cultural Psychology, 30*, 51–71.

Prunty, A. M., Klopf, D. W., & Ishii, S. (1990a). Argumentativeness: Japanese and American tendencies to approach and avoid conflict. *Communication Research Reports, 7*, 75–79.

Prunty, A. M., Klopf, D. W., & Ishii, S. (1990b). Japanese and American tendencies to argue. *Psychological Reports, 66*, 802.

Rodin, J., & Langer, E. J. (1977). Long-term effects of a control-relevant intervention with the institutionalized aged. *Journal of Personality and Social Psychology, 35*, 897–902.

Rothbaum, F., Weisz, J. R., & Snyder, S. S. (1982). Changing the world and changing the self: A two-process model of perceived control. *Journal of Personality and Social Psychology, 42*, 5–37.

Sampson, E. E. (1977). Psychology and the American ideal. *Journal of Personality and Social Psychology, 35*, 767–782.

Sampson, E. E. (1988). The debate on individualism: Indigenous psychologies of the individual and their role in personal and societal functioning. *American Psychologist, 43*, 15–22.

Schwartz, S. H. (1992). Universals in the content and structure of values: Theoretical advances and empirical tests in 20 countries. In M. P. Zanna (Ed.), *Advances in experimental social psychology* (Vol. 25, pp. 1–65). San Diego, CA: Academic Press.

Schwartz, S. H. (1994). Beyond individualism and collectivism: New cultural dimensions of values. In U. Kim, H. C. Triandis, C. Kagitcibasi, S. C. Choi, & G. Yoon (Eds.), *Individualism and collectivism: Theory, method, and applications* (pp. 85–119). Thousand Oaks, CA: Sage.

Seginer, R., Trommsdorff, G., & Essau, C. (1993). Adolescent control beliefs: Cross-cultural variations of primary and secondary orientations. *International Journal of Behavioral Development, 16*, 243–260.

Shigeki, I. S. (1983). Child care practices in Japan and the United States: How do they reflect cultural values in young children. *Young Children, 38*(4), 13–24.

Skinner, E. A. (1996). A guide to constructs of control. *Journal of Personality and Social Psychology, 71*, 549–570.

Skinner, E. A., Chapman, M., & Baltes, P. B. (1988). Control, means-ends, and agency beliefs: A new conceptualization and its measurement during childhood. *Journal of Personality and Social Psychology, 54*, 117–133.

Steiner, I. D. (1972). *Group processes and productivity*. New York: Academic Press.

Sung, K. (1994). A cross-cultural comparison of motivations for parent care: The case of Americans and Koreans. *Journal of Aging Studies, 8*, 195–209.

Tajfel, H. (1982). *Human groups and social categories*. New York: Cambridge University Press.

Thompson, S. C. (1981). Will it hurt less if I can control it? A complex answer to a simple question. *Psychological Bulletin, 90*, 89–101.

Triandis, H. C. (1994). Theoretical and methodological approaches to the study of collectivism and individualism. In U. Kim, H. C. Triandis, C. Kagitcibasi, S. C. Choi, & G. Yoon (Eds.), *Individualism and collectivism: Theory, method, and applications* (pp. 41–51). Thousand Oaks, CA: Sage.

Trubisky, P., Ting-Toomey, S., & Lin, S. (1991). The influence of individualism-collectivism and self-monitoring on conflict styles. *International Journal of Intercultural Relations, 15*, 65–84

Wan, K. C., & Bond, M. H. (1982). Chinese attributions for success and failure under public and anonymous conditions of rating. *Acta Psychologica Taiwanica, 24*, 23–31.

Weisz, J. R., Rothbaum, F. M., & Blackburn, T. C. (1984). Standing out and standing in: The psychology of control in America and Japan. *American Psychologist, 39*, 955–969.

White, R. W. (1959). Motivation reconsidered: The concept of competence. *Psychological Review, 66*, 297–333.

Wood, R., & Bandura, A. (1989). Impact of conceptions of ability on self-regulatory mechanisms and complex decision making. *Journal of Personality and Social Psychology, 56*, 407–415.

Yamaguchi, S. (1998). Biased risk perception among Japanese: Illusion of interdependence among risk companions. *Asian Journal of Social Psychology, 1*, 117–131.

Yamaguchi, S. (1999). Nichijyougo to shiteno Amae kara Kangaeru [Thinking about "Amae" as an everyday word]. In O. Kitayama (Ed.), *Nihongo Rinsho [Clinical Japanese]*, (Vol. 3, pp. 31–46). Tokyo: Seiwa Shoten.

Yamaguchi, S., Gelfand, M., Mizuno, M., & Zemba, Y. (1997, August). *Illusion of collective control or illusion of personal control: Biased judgment about a chance event in Japan and the U.S.* Paper presented at the Second Conference of the Asian Association of Social Psychology, Kyoto, Japan.

13

Culture and Human Inference

Perspectives from Three Traditions

KAIPING PENG, DANIEL R. AMES, & ERIC D. KNOWLES

Human inference—that is, the ability to make judgments—is a basic psychological process that cuts across areas of study in psychology, from perception and cognition through social behavior and reasoning. It is an area that has been well studied not only in mainstream psychology in the United States, but also across many other cultures of the world, by psychologists, anthropologists, and philosophers alike.

In this chapter, Peng, Ames, and Knowles provide a comprehensive review of the cross-cultural literature on human inference. They first describe three major perspectives that have provided much of the impetus for the work conducted to date—the value, self, and theory tradition. In particular, they describe the basic tenets of each tradition and highlight their contributions to the conduct of research and theoretical understanding of human inference.

A major part of their chapter presents a state-of-the-art review of the cross-cultural research in specific domains of inference, including domains in inductive reasoning, as well as deductive and formal reasoning. Their review of these areas is superb and draws attention to the major findings in the field, which cut across cognitive, personality, and social psychology.

The major contribution of the work of Peng et al., however, is their attempt to integrate the three major perspectives into a single, synthesized model of cultural influence on human inference. They point out, and correctly so, that mainstream psychology is too quick to latch on to single viewpoints, examining psychological processes solely from those single viewpoints to the exclusion of other views of the same process. One is quickly reminded from their points here about the story of different people viewing a different part of the same elephant or of the Humpty Dumpty story as described in a previous chapter in this book. Peng et al. also point out that such an exclusive focus on single perspectives of psychological phenomena runs the danger of becoming fragmented into more pieces, further shattering the whole into more unidentifiable parts.

Instead, Peng et al. distill an integrated theory of cultural influences on human inference, suggesting the ways in which the value, self, and theory traditions may all be true and all work together in a collectively efficient manner to influence human inference. While they describe for the reader different traditions of thought among Western linear thought, logical determinism, and Eastern holism and contradiction and how these influence human inference, at the same time they provide an important lesson about cultural influences on theory construction as they employ a framework of holism and synthesis to a field that is fragmented. In this way, there are two lessons to be learned from their approach, one concerning the content of their work (i.e., about their model of human inference) and the other concerning their method of theory construction.

Given their synthesized view of human inference, Peng et al. suggest clearly that the most important challenge for future study in this area concerns the need for methodologies that are meaningful at both psychological and cultural levels, that are both tractable and precise, while at the same time nuanced and sensitive. They call for a rapprochement between the methods and theories of cross-cultural and cultural psychology, at the same time espousing the guiding methodological principles of mainstream research, including concerns for objectivity, validity, generalization, and causal explanation. Their call for rapprochement and integration among theories, methods, and approaches, including quantitative and qualitative ones, strikes a chord similar to the message provided by many other authors in this volume and is necessary if cross-cultural psychology will be able to continue to evolve in the creation of universal models of psychological processes, as Peng et al. have proposed, and to test them adequately.

Two decades ago, American social psychologists Nisbett and Ross (1980) published their now classic book, *Human Inference*, a broad survey of how judgments, particularly about the social world, unfold from evidence and reasoning. D'Andrade, a notable cognitive anthropologist, read the book and pronounced it a "good ethnography." The authors were dismayed: They thought they had written a universal account of inference and cognition, describing social judgment processes in a relatively timeless and culture-free way. Most of their colleagues at the time agreed. However, in the ensuing 20 years, cultural psychology has blossomed, some of it pursued by Nisbett and Ross. The accumulating evidence on cultural differences in inference is clear, and Nisbett and Ross now agree that their original work amounts to something of an ethnographic study of inference in a single culture, the United States (see Nisbett, Peng, Choi, & Norenzayan, in press).

What has happened in the past two decades that changed the minds of these and other psychologists studying human judgment, leading them to believe previous efforts on human inference are useful, but culturally bound? What has cultural psychology revealed about the role of culture in human inference? In this chapter, we review an ongoing revolution that examines the cultural nature of judgment and thinking. Evidence suggests that so-called basic processes such as attribution and categorization do not play out in the same ways among all human groups—and the differences go beyond

superficial variety in content. A variety of empirical studies on culture and inference, mostly works completed in the past decade, is utilized to illustrate the cultural characteristics of human inference. But, before reviewing this evidence, we examine three prominent psychological approaches to studying culture: the well-established *value* and *self* traditions and the emerging *theory* tradition. Each has a distinct way of conceiving culture and makes different kinds of claims about the relationship between culture and inference. Our brief introduction of these traditions lays the groundwork for an overview of psychological research findings. After recounting the findings, we return to the traditions and propose an integrated way for thinking about the rich and wide-ranging connections between culture and human inference.

Perspectives on Culture and Human Inference

It is no great exaggeration to suggest that the biggest challenge to culture-oriented scholars of human inference is the issue of the independent variable, "What is culture?" Wide-ranging answers are available from a host of disciplines, variously including shared meaning systems, cultural personality or ethos, practices and habits, institutions and social structures, artifacts and tools, and everything that takes place in human psychological life and interaction beyond what is dictated by our genes. However, for psychological researchers to gain traction on the issue of human inference, they must "unpack" culture and adopt a position on how to define and reflect culture in their work (Ames & Peng, 1999b; Betancourt & Lopez, 1993; Rohner, 1984; Whiting, 1976).

There is likely no single best definition of culture or way of studying the effects of culture. Rather, research psychologists highlight various aspects of culture, adopting inevitably imperfect, but workable, assumptions about what culture is. In psychological work related to human inference, there have been two dominant traditions over the last 20 years: one that arranges cultures by their distinct value systems and one that contrasts cultures in terms of their conceptions of selfhood. More recently, another tradition has emerged that describes cultures in terms of a variety of widely shared implicit folk theories. We review each of these perspectives in turn, but note that they have many assumptions and techniques in common; individual scholars—and even individual studies—may draw on several or all of these approaches.

Value Tradition

Many people who have traveled or lived outside their home country have a sense that people in other cultures possess values different from their own. In some way, these values could be taken as defining culture itself, and systematic differences in values—especially in a small collection of "core" values—could be seen as providing some structure for thinking about cultural differences. This, broadly, is the approach advocated by a large number of cultural psychologists (e.g., P. B. Smith & Bond, 1999, p. 69).

A pioneering figure from these ranks is Hofstede (1980), who some 20 years ago compiled an almost unparalleled data set: He administered a survey of values to nearly 120,000 IBM employees in 40 countries. Hofstede factor analyzed the data at the country level (as a proxy for culture) and found four dimensions, which he labeled *power distance* (willingness to tolerate differences in power and authority), *individualism* (versus collectivism; orientation toward individual or group), *masculinity* (versus femininity; the former stressing achievement and material success, the latter stressing harmony and caring), and *uncertainty avoidance* (willingness to tolerate ambiguity). Hofstede's

approach has been pursued by a number of other scholars, including Schwartz (1991; Schwartz and Sagiv, 1995), who argues that 10 important values (such as tradition, security, power, and stimulation) form a universal structure across two dimensions: openness to change/conservation and self-transcendence/self-enhancement. According to Schwartz, any given culture has an identifiable position in this value space that allows it to be compared with other cultures.

A number of scholars have examined cross-cultural differences in inference and judgment by focusing on particular value dimensions. Shweder (1995), for instance, explored the value of spiritual purity among Hindu Indians. Meanwhile, Leung (1997) examined how East Asian harmony values affect justice perceptions and decisions, such as reward allocation. However, the most widespread research program in the value tradition has focused on one of the dimensions identified by Hofstede: individualism-collectivism. This dimension reflects an orientation toward one's own needs and impulses (individualism) or toward the needs and dictates of one's social groups, such as families and communities (collectivism).

Individualism-collectivism has drawn a great deal of attention from cross-cultural researchers, and some observers see it as the most overarching theory of cultural psychology (Triandis, 1995). Scholars have made this dimension operational at both the country level (assigning "individualism scores" to countries) and at the individual level (with studies gauging individual participants' values). Most often, East Asians are seen as more collectivist, while North Americans and Europeans are viewed as individualist.

How does the value tradition prepare us to think about cultural differences in inference? Three main points emerge. First, in frequently highlighting individualism-collectivism as a central dimension, the value approach draws our attention to inferences that concern judgments about groups and about how individuals relate to groups. If a main source of cultural differences occurs in the attitudes of members about their groups and group relations, we would expect to find considerable accompanying cultural variance in inferences related to groups and membership.

Second, and more broadly, the value tradition underscores the importance of prescriptive stances in construal and judgment. Scholars in this tradition do not simply make causal claims about values that affect other values and choices (such as claims about a general stance of individualism that affects a narrow attitude toward wanting to take credit for some good outcomes). Rather, claims are made that connect values to inferences and resulting beliefs (e.g., between individualism and the belief that a single person is the cause for a good performance). What is the connection between these prescriptive and descriptive stances? How do norms shape inferences from evidence? The value tradition draws attention to such questions.

A third, and related, consideration prompted by the values approach is a pragmatic or functionalist one: What are the consequences of certain inferences in, for example, a collectivist culture? If collectivism describes a system of norms, those norms comprise an important part of the environment in which inferences must be "lived out." Thus, the value approach prompts consideration of how inferences are shaped by the consequences they might entail in particular cultural contexts. We return to this issue of consequences, as well as to the issue of prescription-description, in our concluding analysis of the three traditions.

Self Tradition

Beginning a century ago with James (1890), the construct of "self" has been widely regarded by scholars as playing a key role in much psychological functioning (see Markus & Cross, 1990, for a review). Although James and many of his Western intellectual heirs have voiced the caveat that the self may be experienced differently in various cultural systems, there has been little psychological research on this issue until recently. Is self a cultural concept? A chorus of researchers answers "Yes" and suggests it is perhaps the most important cultural concept.

Contemporary thinking about culture and self has been led by Markus and Kitayama (1991), who suggest not only that the psychology of self varies across cultures, but also that self-conceptions may be at the very heart of what culture is. Markus, Kitayama, and others have described culturally driven ways of "being" a self, focusing specifically on two types of self: independent and interdependent. An independent construal of self, prevalent in the West, is characterized by a sense of autonomy, of being relatively distinct from others. In contrast, the interdependent construal of self, prevalent in Asia, is characterized by an emphasis on the interrelatedness of the individual to oth-

ers; self-identity is more diffused socially across important others rather than strictly bounded with the individual. There is an obvious similarity between these self-concepts and individualism-collectivism. However, it is worth noting the descriptive, as well as the prescriptive, nature of these positions. We might crudely characterize the slogan of collectivism as "My in-group is important," while an interdependent self might be described as "My in-group is who I am."

A host of research by Markus and Kitayama (e.g., 1991), Heine and Lehman (e.g., 1995, 1997), Singelis (e.g., 1994), and others has explored this cultural dimension of selfhood. Other scholarship on culture and self has emerged as well, including Shweder's (1995) description of divinity in selfhood among Hindu Indians; in this case, self is not so much distributed socially across other persons (as with an interdependent self), but distributed spiritually across reincarnations and all living things.

What guidance does the self tradition provide regarding cultural differences in human inference? Two major considerations emerge. First, understanding the social network that could potentially be implicated in a perceiver's self-concept becomes critical. A perceiver's attention to others in this network may be driven by his or her self-concept; the self-concept would likely also affect how others in this network are treated in judgments. Second, highlighting the self-concept encourages us to expand our view of the domains of inference in which self-construal matters. In other words, the impact of self-concept can be found in domains beyond self-judgment. Cognitive dissonance, for instance, might seem unrelated to the self, but Heine and Lehman (1997) argue that Japanese experience less dissonance than Canadians because of how they understand social contexts and the self.

Theory Tradition

The traditions of value and self have attracted many cultural psychologists over the last 20 years. These perspectives have revealed many insights and continue to do so. However, an increasing amount of cultural scholarship is not based on a person's notions of self or value systems, but on various folk theories and beliefs shared by a culture's members. There is no single theme of content (like "individualism") that unifies this emerging tradition, but rather there is an inclination to identify and measure implicit folk theories at a rather specific level—a level, moreover, that ties directly into inference and judgment. Work in this tradition does not attempt to measure culture in its entirety, but rather selects particular domains and attempts to describe judgments by culturally driven beliefs.

Members of a culture share a variety of widespread stances that scholars have described in terms of cultural models (Holland & Quinn, 1987); cosmologies (Douglas, 1982); social representations (Moscovici, 1984; Wagner, 1997); cultural representations (Boyer, 1993; Sperber, 1990); naive ontologies and epistemologies (Ames & Peng, 1999b; Peng & Nisbett, 1999); and folk psychologies, biologies, sociologies, and physics (e.g., Ames, 1999; Atran, 1990; Fiske, 1992; Lillard, 1998; Peng & Knowles, 2000; Vosniadou, 1994).

One way of describing these stances is to consider them implicit theories (Dweck, Chiu, & Hong, 1995; Vallacher & Wegner, 1987) about the world that persons in particular communities have in common to varying degrees. The particular theories studied vary widely. Chiu, Hong, and Dweck (1997), for instance, examined implicit theories about personality change: Americans tend to assume considerable constancy in personality, while Hong Kong Chinese often expect malleability. Elsewhere, Ames and Peng (1999a) showed that, compared to Americans, Chinese are guided by more holistic theories of impression evidence in getting to know a target person. The research of Menon, Morris, Chiu, and Hong (1999) suggests that Americans' theories of groups lead them to assign less causality and responsibility at the group level, while Chinese, led by different theories, are more willing to make such attributions.

Given this variety of topics, the theory approach to culture is identifiable by a common set of assumptions and methodologies—stances largely shared with the emerging implicit theories perspective in psychology in general (Dweck, 1996; Wegner & Vallacher, 1977). Some of these assumptions are shared with scholarship in the self and value traditions, but the theory tradition seems distinct in its specificity of constructs and variety of domains.

What distinct insights does the theory tradition offer regarding culture and the psychology of inference? Two novel points emerge. First, the implicit theory approach offers compelling ways for describing variance across persons and groups and change across time. Personality psychologists are increasingly using implicit

theories to capture the differences between individuals (e.g., Dweck, 1996); some developmental psychologists, meanwhile, describe the course of cognitive development in terms of theory adoption and use (e.g., Gopnik & Meltzoff, 1997). At the culture level, the theory approach offers dynamic models for describing how widespread beliefs are transmitted, flourish, and fade—and for what kinds of beliefs might be likely to prosper (Boyer, 1993; Moscovici, 1984; Sperber, 1990; Strauss & Quinn, 1997). The implicit theory approach also lends itself readily to cultural differences within a given geographic region, such as within a country.

A second contribution is that the theory approach points toward comparatively precise models of culturally influenced psychological process. Culture is made operational at a representational level as a knowledge structure (a folk theory) that supports and guides inference. As Ames and Peng (1999b) note, implicit theories can play a direct role in inferences, with perceivers invoking a theory to go beyond the information given (e.g., use of a stereotype in which a target's gender yields an inference about their aggressive tendencies). Theories can also play a management role in inference, guiding how evidence and other theories are recruited and used (Ames & Peng, 1999b). For instance, an epistemological theory about the value of contextual evidence does not itself yield a conclusion, but can guide a perceiver's attention toward certain aspects of the environment. The effect of culture no doubt can be seen working at both these levels.

Cultural Research on Human Inference

These three traditions take different approaches to studying culture and human inference. What does each reveal about cultural differences in inference? Can they be integrated into some overarching framework? Are they somehow at odds with one another—and is one more preferable than the others? Before we answer these questions, we proceed first by reviewing evidence for cultural differences. We organize our review around two major domains of inference: induction and deduction. Here, we are concerned with findings rather than traditions, and we include as much relevant empirical work as possible. After this review of findings, we return to the issue of the three traditions and, based on the evidence, search for an overarching framework.

Inductive Reasoning

As a working definition, we take *induction* to be the human ability to reach useful generalizations based on limited experience and information. These generalizations come in multiple forms, ranging from the apprehension of correlations between phenomena in the environment to the attribution of causes for physical and social events, and from the inference of a target person's personality traits and mental states to the formation and use of categories. In this section, we argue that culture plays a role in each of these types of inductive inference.

Covariation Judgment

Since the birth of behaviorism, psychologists have viewed the ability to perceive covariations between environmental stimuli accurately as a fundamental type of human inference (Alloy & Tabachnik, 1984). Perhaps because the processes that rely on covariation judgment (e.g., classical conditioning) are seen as so basic to human cognition, psychologists have only recently begun investigating the influence of culture on people's ability to detect and evaluate associations. In one of the few studies to address this issue, Ji, Peng, and Nisbett (1999) examined covariation judgment among Chinese and Americans. Reasoning that the dialectical epistemology of Asians would make them especially sensitive to relations between stimuli, these researchers predicted that Asians would exceed Americans in their ability to evaluate the magnitude of associations between stimuli. Chinese and American participants were shown pairs of arbitrary figures on a computer screen; particular stimuli were correlated to varying degrees, and participants were asked to judge the degree of association.

The results provide preliminary evidence for the influence of culture on covariation detection. Chinese were more confident than Americans about their covariation judgments, and their confidence judgments were better calibrated with the actual degree of covariation between figures. In addition, American participants showed a strong primacy effect, making predictions about future covariations that were more influenced by the first pairings they had seen than by the overall degree of covariation to which they had been exposed. In contrast, Chinese participants showed no primacy effect at all and made predictions about future covariation that were based on the covariation they had actually seen.

Causal Attribution

Covariation judgment is undeniably important to human survival; very often, however, people are not satisfied by merely estimating the magnitude of associations between environmental phenomena. People typically go further, assigning phenomena to their presumed *causes*. Lay causal analysis—or causal attribution—has been one of the most thoroughly studied areas in psychology. Below, we review evidence that, in both the social and physical domains, people's attributions are influenced by culture.

Social Domain   The last two decades have seen a growing acknowledgment that culture guides people's attributions for social phenomena (i.e., the social behavior of others). Prior to this recognition, however, psychologists often assumed that the findings of studies conducted in Western settings would generalize across cultures. One of most widely reported findings in (Western) attribution research is that people tend to see behavior as a product of the actor's dispositions, while ignoring important situational causes of behavior.

In an early demonstration of dispositional bias, Jones and Harris (1967) asked perceivers to infer a target's attitude on a controversial political topic based on an essay written by the target. Participants were also given information about situational determinants of the target's behavior that suggested against the usefulness of the speech in ascertaining the target's true attitude—specifically, that the target had been required to write the essay by an authority figure. Despite having information about the power of the situation, most participants were willing to infer a behavior-correspondent attitude.

After this and other classic demonstrations, confidence in the universality of dispositional bias ran high—so high, in fact, that psychologists dubbed the bias the "fundamental attribution error" (Ross, 1977). The assumption of universality is reflected in theoretical accounts of attribution, which portray dispositional inference as the product of gestalt (Heider, 1958; Jones, 1990) or ecological (Baron & Misovich, 1993) perceptual processes presumed to be similar across cultures.

Work by Miller (1984) first suggested that the fundamental attribution error might not be so fundamental. She found that, whereas Americans explained the behavior of others predominantly in terms of traits (e.g., recklessness or kindness), Hindu Indians explained comparable behaviors in terms of social roles, obligations, the physical environment, and other contextual factors. This finding calls into question the universality of dispositional bias and, by extension, attribution theories that link dispositional inference to universal perceptual mechanisms. Miller's work instead suggested that attributions for social events are largely the product of culturally instilled belief systems that stress the importance of either dispositional or situational factors in producing social behavior. Numerous researchers have extended Miller's (1984) basic finding—in which Asians focus more on situational factors in explaining behavior than do Westerners—to a wide range of cultures and social phenomena. While we cannot present an exhaustive review of cross-cultural attribution research (see Choi, Nisbett, & Norenzayan, 1999, for a more extensive treatment), we survey some representative studies below.

American explanations for events such as mass murders were shown by Morris and Peng (1994; see also Morris, Nisbett, & Peng, 1995) to focus almost entirely on the presumed mental instability and other negative dispositions of the murderers, whereas Chinese accounts of the same events referred more to situational and societal factors. The researchers then replicated this cultural difference using visual stimuli that depicted animal movements. Participants were presented with cartoon displays of a target fish moving relative to the school in a variety of ways. Each pattern of movement was ambiguous in that the movement of the target fish could be attributed to dispositional causes (e.g., the fish is a leader) or situational causes (e.g., the fish is being chased by the school). As expected, Chinese participants were more likely to see the behavior of the individual fish as being produced by situational factors than were Americans.

Other researchers have documented cultural diversity in attributions for more mundane, everyday events. For instance, F. Lee, Hallahan, and Herzog (1996) found that sports editorial writers in Hong Kong focused on situational explanations of sports events, whereas American sports writers were more likely to prefer explanations that involved the dispositions of individual team members. Choi et al. (1999) found that Korean participants, unlike American participants, did not underutilize consensus information (i.e., information about the behavior of other people) when making attributions—information that logically should be used to gauge the power of situational factors. Likewise, Norenzayan, Choi, and Nisbett (1999) found that Korean participants were more responsive to contextual factors when making predictions about how people in general would behave in a given situation and, much more than American participants, made use of their beliefs about situational power when predicting the behavior of a particular individual.

Choi and Nisbett (1998) duplicated the basic conditions of the Jones and Harris (1967) study, adding a condition in which, before making judgments about the target's attitude, participants were required to write an essay and were allowed no choice about which side to take. It was made clear to participants that the target had been through the same procedure the participants had. Participants were then asked to judge the target's true attitude. The American participants in this condition made inferences about the target's attitude that were as strong as those made by participants in the standard no-choice condition. Korean participants, in contrast, made much less extreme inferences. Thus, Korean participants, presumably by virtue of seeing the role that the situation played in their own behavior, recognized the power of the context and made attributions about others accordingly. Similar results were obtained by Kitayama and Masuda (1997) in Japan. These researchers duplicated the procedure of Gilbert and Jones (1986), in which participants were paired with a confederate and told one of them would be randomly assigned to read an essay written by a third person. After the confederate was chosen to read the essay, American observers assumed that the target individual actually held the position advocated in the speech. Although Masuda and Kitayama found strong attitude inferences in line with the speech for Japanese subjects in the standard no-choice condition, they found none at all when it was made clear that the target individual was simply reading an essay written by someone else.

Physical Domain   Unlike attributions for social phenomena, relatively little research has examined the influence of culture on lay explanations for physical events. Nonetheless, there is reason to believe that folk theories of physical causality differ between Western and Asian cultures, and that these differences may lead to culturally divergent interpretations of physical phenomena. Many scholars have argued that Asian folk physics is relational and dialectical, stressing conceptions of "field" and "force over distance" (Capra, 1975; Needham, 1954, 1962; Zukav, 1980). On the other hand, Western folk physics is seen as preferring internal and dispositional causes, explaining physical phenomena in terms of "the nature of the object concerned" rather than the relation of objects to the environment (Lewin, 1935, p. 28). Peng and Knowles (2000) presented evidence that this difference in intellectual tradition may affect everyday interpretations of physical events. These researchers presented Chinese and American individuals with physical interactions involving "force-over-distance" causality resembling hydrodynamic, aerodynamic, or magnetic phenomena. In explaining these events, Chinese participants were more likely to refer to the field, whereas Americans were more likely to refer solely to factors internal to the object. The researchers concluded that development within Asian cultures instilled individuals with a relational, field-oriented folk physics, while Western cultures instilled their members with a more dispositional, analytic folk physics (also see Peng & Nisbett, 1996).

Person Perception

Our inferences about other persons are crucial to our everyday lives. We frequently and fluidly make judgments about those around us: what they're like, how they're feeling, what they want. These judgments are certainly related to attribution, but differ in an important way: Whereas attribution concerns assigning cause and responsibility to events, person perception concerns assigning qualities to persons. For instance, if Beth's new assistant Andrew acts aggressively toward her, Beth might consider attributing the behavior to Andrew's dispositional aggression or to some other event that made Andrew angry—a case of both attribution and person perception. However, if Beth is deciding whether or not to ask Charles to be her new assistant and gets letters of recommendation from Charles' teachers and former employers and also interviews Charles, integrating this information to form a judgment is more a case of person perception ("solving for a person") than attribution ("solving for an event").

Not surprisingly, person perception inferences take on different forms in different cultures. Here, we only briefly review selected findings in two areas of person perception: impression formation and the inference of mental states.

Impression Formation   What kinds of impressions do we form about persons? One theme that emerges is the willingness to see personal qualities as fixed and enduring or malleable and changing (Dweck, 1996). This difference seems to map well onto the cultural dimension of independent and interdependent selves: The former notion features a more fixed self, the latter describes a changeable, context-based self. This connection was pursued by C. Y. Chiu, Hong, and Dweck (1997) in their comparison of dispositional judgments by American and Hong Kong perceivers. As the literature on the self would predict, these researchers found a main effect of culture: American perceivers were more willing than Hong Kong perceivers to ascribe fixed, enduring traits to targets. Dweck, Chiu, and Hong (1995) also measured the individual theories of the perceivers about the nature of dispositions: A high score on their dispositionalism scale indicated a belief in fixed, unchanging traits. There was a culture difference in dispositionalism, with Americans scoring higher. Following in the theory tradition, Dweck and colleagues demonstrated that this implicit theory of dispositionalism mediated the effect of culture on perceivers' trait judgments.

It appears that perceivers in the East may be less oriented toward making ascriptions of dispositions to targets. Are there also differences in the kinds of evidence that are sought out and used in forming impressions? Research by Ames and Peng (1999a) suggests there are. Following from cultural research on self, dispositionalism, and dialecticism, Ames and Peng proposed that Americans would be more focused on evidence directly from or about a target (e.g., a self-description), while Chinese would be more focused on contextual evidence (e.g., a description of the target by a friend, a description of the target's friend). Across a variety of studies, just such a pattern emerged. Americans expressed greater preference for target-focused evidence and made greater use of target self-descriptions in their evaluations of targets.

Inference of Mental States   How is it that we know what others are thinking, feeling, and wanting? Recent work suggests that mental state epistemologies may differ by culture.

Knowles and Ames (1999) suggested that Western cultures stress a "norm of authenticity" such that a person's external actions and displays should be consistent with their internal attitudes. "Saying what's on your mind" and "straight talk" are sought-after qualities in the West. Eastern cultures, meanwhile, may view such displays as impolite and potentially bizarre. The role of hosts in many Asian countries, for instance, is to intuit a guest's unspoken needs, while guests are often expected to defer and not betray self-centered desires.

Knowles and Ames (1999) collected initial evidence documenting such an epistemic difference in the United States and China. When asked how important various pieces of evidence are in determining what someone is thinking, Americans, on average, rate "what they say" as more important than "what they do not say," while Chinese show the reverse preference. The same pattern holds for determining what someone is feeling or wanting. Mental state epistemology in the West may be as simple as listening: It is not uncommon to wish targets disclosed less about their beliefs, desires, intentions, and so forth. Reading minds in the East, however, may take other routes, such as nonverbal behavior.

Categorization

Categorization is one of the most ubiquitous and important human mental activities and provides efficiency in memory and enables communication. Moreover, categories aid survival by allowing us to make educated guesses about the unseen properties of categorized objects ("That rustling behind the bush must be Johnny's new pit bull. I bet it has a bad temper."). Categorization is one of the most well-studied areas of psychology, as well as the closely allied field of cognitive anthropology. Researchers have distinguished between three related questions. First, where do categories get their structure (the question of category coherence)? Second, how and when do people use categories to make inductions about unseen properties of objects (the question of category use)? Finally, how do individuals acquire new categories (the question of category learning)? There is growing evidence that culture is part of the answer to each of these questions.

Category Coherence   Of all the infinitely many ways one could divide the world, why do people show a decided preference for some categories (e.g., "dog") and not others (e.g., "apple

or prime number")? In other words, what makes some categories hang together or cohere? In her recent review of category coherence research, Malt (1995) noted a shift in psychologists' thinking concerning the source of category coherence. Early psychological work tended to suppose that structure inherent in the environment determines which categories people will form. Most notably, Rosch and colleagues (Rosch & Mervis, 1975; Rosch, Mervis, Gray, Johnson, & Boyes-Braem, 1976) argued that perceptible features in the world are not distributed randomly across entities, but rather occur in clusters—for instance, "fur," "four legged," and "barks" tend to occur together. People take advantage of this environmental structure by grouping entities that share clusters of features into categories; for instance, entities in which fur, four legged, and barks cooccur are grouped into the category "dog." While it is true that the human perceptual system must place constraints on which feature correlations people notice (Murphy & Medin, 1985), the work of Rosch and colleagues emphasizes the role of environmental structure in determining category coherence. A corollary of this view is that, to the extent the human perceptual system is the same everywhere, classification systems will be relatively impervious to the influence of higher level cognitive structures—such as those instilled by culture.

More recent work, while not denying the role of environmental structure in lending coherence to taxonomic categories like "dog" and "fern," points to the contribution of high-level cognitive structures in determining coherence of nontaxonomic categories. Barsalou (1983, 1985) drew attention to a class of categories that could not exist simply by virtue of their mapping onto environmental structures such as correlations between perceptible features. Specifically, "goal-based" categories are coherent because their members serve a common goal; for example, pencils and calculators, despite sharing few features, could both be grouped into the category "things used to take to a math exam." Goal-based categories are highly susceptible to cultural influence since cultures undeniably shape the goals adopted by their members. To illustrate, things to take to a math exam is a coherent category for Western youths, but not for members of preliterate societies, whose members lack the goal of taking math exams.

Work in cognitive anthropology and cross-cultural psychology suggests that culture even plays a role in the coherence of taxonomic categories. Malt (1995) reviewed a number of ethnobiological studies that indicated that the degree to which a society subcategorizes a plant or animal domain corresponds in part to the cultural importance of that domain. Folk categorizers direct their attention disproportionately to domains of the most practical importance to their culture (e.g., edible plants and domesticated or dangerous animals) and as a result create narrower subordinate categories within those domains. This finding parallels psychological evidence that individuals with a history of allocating a disproportionate amount of attention to a particular domain—for instance, birdwatchers or dog aficionados—may develop "expertise" in that domain. Experts create more subdivisions within their domain of expertise than do nonexperts and categorize within the domain more quickly (Tanaka & Taylor, 1991). In sum, culture may affect the deployment of attention to different taxonomic domains, lending coherence to increasingly subordinate categories.

Other anthropological and psychological research suggests that culture influences category coherence not only by directing attention, but also by changing the kinds of features used to bind categories together. López, Atran, Coley, Medin, and Smith (1997) found that, while Americans tended to categorize animals on the basis of size and ferocity, Itzaj-Mayan animal categories were based largely on relational—specifically, ecological—features, such as habitat and food consumption. Likewise, Atran and Medin (1997) found that Itzaj-Mayan informants grouped arboreal mammals partly according to the nature of their interactions with plants.

Experimental research suggests that such a relational style of categorization plays an important role in Chinese culture. In 1972, L.-H. Chiu showed Chinese and American children sets of three pictures drawn from various domains and asked them to pick the two that went together. The dominant style of categorization for Chinese children was "relational-contextual." For instance, shown a picture of a man, a woman, and a child, Chinese children were likely to group the woman and child together because "the mother takes care of the baby." In contrast, American children were more likely to group objects on the basis on isolable properties, such as age (e.g., grouping the man and woman together because "they are both grownups").

Category-Based Induction   In addition to organizing the world for purposes of memory and communication, categories serve the vital function of allowing people to go "beyond the information given." Once an object has been categorized, category membership may be used as the basis for inferences about the object's unseen or invisible properties; this process is referred to as *category-based induction*. For instance, knowing that an animal is a mammal allows one to infer that it probably bears live young and regulates its own body temperature.

Work by Choi, Nisbett, and Smith (1997) suggests that category representations are less chronically accessible for Koreans than for Americans and thus are less readily used in category-based induction. In keeping with previous research on category-based induction (e.g., Osherson, Smith, Wilkie, López, and Shafir, 1990), Choi and colleagues made operationalized category-based induction using a premise-conclusion format. For instance, individuals might be presented with the following argument:

Hippos have ulnar arteries.
Hamsters have ulnar arteries.
. . . .
Dogs have ulnar arteries.

Participants are then asked the extent to which they believe the conclusion given the premises. In the above example, participants might use the premises to infer that mammals have ulnar arteries and thus place great confidence in the conclusion. The researchers increased category salience by mentioning the category in the conclusion (that is, participants made an inference about "mammals" rather than dogs). This manipulation had no effect on Americans, but increased the degree to which Koreans performed category-based induction. This suggests that categories have a lower chronic accessibility for Koreans and are thus more susceptible to priming.

Category Learning   There is evidence that culture may influence the processes through which people acquire new categories. Norenzayan, Nisbett, Smith, and Kim (2000), adopting a procedure used by Allen and Brooks (1991), presented East Asians and Americans with cartoon extraterrestrial creatures, indicating some were from Venus and some were from Saturn. One group of participants was asked to examine a series of creatures and make guesses, with feedback, about the category to which each belonged. Other participants went through a more formal, rule-based category-learning procedure. In this condition, participants were told to pay attention to five different properties of the animals and were told that if the animal had any three of these properties, it was from Venus; otherwise, it was from Saturn. Although Asian and American participants performed equally well at the exemplar-based categorization task, the response times of Asian participants were slower in the rule-based condition. Most telling, when presented with an animal that met the formal criteria for a certain category, but more closely resembled animals in the other category—thus placing rule-based and exemplar-based criteria in conflict—Asians made more classification errors than did Americans.

The Category of Self   The idea of "self" being a category like "mammal" or "hammer" may seem peculiar at first glance, but after considering cultural differences, seeing self as a culturally varying category becomes something of an obligation. Considerable research attention has been directed at how perceivers in the West and East describe themselves. The results reveal several themes, most notably that perceivers in the West see the self as more bounded and concrete, while perceivers in the East see the self as more socially diffused, changeable, and context bound. In 1998, A. P. Fiske, Kitayama, Markus, and Nisbett reviewed much of the relevant research and showed that Americans are more likely to describe themselves in abstract, fixed ways (e.g., using trait terms such as "friendly"), while Koreans, Japanese, and Chinese are more likely to refer to social roles and other people (e.g., "I am Jane's friend"). Elsewhere, Shweder (1995) explored the Hindu Indian self-concept. Whereas Americans appear to possess an independent view of self, and Southeast Asians seem to see the self as more socially distributed, Shweder argued that the Indian notion of self invokes notions of divinity. With beliefs in reincarnation, karma, and the interconnectedness of all living things, the category of self comes to include multiple lifetimes and life forms.

Deduction and Formal Reasoning

In this section, we review findings about the role of culture in deduction and formal reasoning. Deduction has a rather well-accepted meaning: moving from information that is given to information that follows with certainty or necessity (e.g., given that all donuts have holes, if X is a donut, then it must have a hole). By formal reasoning, we mean to broaden our scope somewhat to include a variety of judgments based on propositions or highly distilled arguments. Here, we note selected cultural research on syllogistic reasoning and dialectical reasoning, particularly in the domain of thinking about contradiction. Historically, it was often assumed that such abilities were universal—or at least took on a single form such that cultural differences could be ascribed to performance or intellectual differences (see Cole, 1996). However, a host of scholars have revealed culture-specific concepts and approaches, differences that seem much more reflective of fundamental epistemologies and cultural assumptions than individual competence.

Syllogistic Reasoning

Russian psychologist Luria (1931) was an early explorer of syllogistic reasoning and culture. In his studies in remote areas of Russia, participants were given what most Western scholars would view as a straightforward task of deduction. Participants were told that all bears in the North are white, and that a particular village was in the North. Participants were then asked the color of the bears in the village. Most failed to answer the question—and many questioned the basic premises of the task, suggesting, for instance, that the researcher go to the village and find out firsthand.

Cole (1996) replicated part of Luria's (1931) work in Africa and similarly found that many participants did not engage the question at the theoretical level. Participants were given premises such as, "If Juan and Jose drink a lot of beer, the mayor of the town gets angry," and, "Juan and Jose are drinking a lot of beer now." In this case, participants were asked to judge if the mayor was angry with Juan and Jose. Some participants treated the question theoretically, but many others saw it as an empirical issue and gave answers such as, "No, so many men drink beer, why should the major get angry?"

A century ago, such supposed "deficits" of reasoning might have been seen as evidence of lack of intelligence and cultural development. Now, most scholars would agree that such performance is not a deficit, but rather highlights distinct cultural models of reasoning (D'Andrade, 1995). Indeed, Luria (1931) and Cole (1996) came to stress practical, everyday activity and cultural artifacts as central to culture-specific reasoning: It may be useless, and perhaps harmful, to presume that abstract Western tasks such as syllogistic reasoning are the gold standard of reasoning and deductive ability.

D'Andrade (1995) suggested that reasoning relies on learned cultural models (such as inference rules) and may also incorporate physical cultural artifacts (like an abacus). Using the Wason task, a widely employed puzzle that putatively tests logical reasoning, D'Andrade showed that successful performance depends overwhelmingly on how the puzzle is framed in terms of everyday knowledge and ordinary domains. Framed as an abstract issue in a "label factory," participants do poorly; framed as a question about the drinking age, participants excel. Such real-world grounding has similar effects across a variety of syllogistic and other kinds of reasoning tasks (D'Andrade, 1995).

Dialectical Reasoning

While few people share the logician's ability and enthusiasm for formal reasoning, it is tempting to characterize most everyday thinkers as broadly adhering to some core tenets of argument that have been mobilized since Aristotle's time—for instance, the "law of noncontradiction," which implies that no statement can be both true and false. However, Peng and Nisbett (Peng, 1997; Peng & Nisbett, 1999) have shown that such a characterization might best be limited to Western thinkers; East Asians, they argue, subscribe to a different epistemology, with different rules for constructing arguments and making judgments. This work highlights the fact that deductive and other kinds of reasoning hinge on underlying epistemological assumptions about what knowledge and truth are and how one can know them—assumptions that can vary by culture.

Peng and Nisbett (1999) describe Western reasoning as embracing three core laws. The law of *identity* (A = A) denotes that everything must be identical with itself. The law of the *excluded middle* (A is either B or not-B) implies that any statement is either true or false; there are no half-truths. The law of *noncontradiction* (A is not equal to not-A) proposes that no statement can be both true and false. On their face, such notions seem to fit with a variety of Western psychological phenomena, such as naive realism (e.g., Ross & Ward, 1996) and essentialism (e.g., Gelman & Medin, 1993), as well as a seeming abhorrence of vacillation and falsehood.

Following various philosophers and historians of the East and West (Liu, 1974; Lloyd, 1990; Needham, 1954, 1962; Zhang & Chen, 1991), Peng and Nisbett (1999) argued that a different approach obtains in Eastern folk thinking: a dialectical epistemology. This folk dialecticism differs from the rarified ("dialectical") philosophies of Hegel and Marx in that these approaches often assume or insist on some original contradiction or opposition that is then resolved; the Eastern folk dialectical epistemology Peng and Nisbett describe accepts and even embraces contradiction rather than attempting to "fix" or resolve it.

Peng and Nisbett (1999) described three assumptions that underpin the Eastern dialectical epistemology. First, the *principle of change* suggests that reality is a dynamic process; something need not be identical with itself because reality is fluid and changing. Second, the *principle of contradiction* notes that, since change is constant, contradiction is constant; the very nature of the world is such that old and new, good and bad, exist at the same time in the same object or event. Third, the *principle of holism* holds that, since change and contradiction are constant, nothing in human life or nature is isolated and independent; rather, all things are related, and attempts to isolate elements of a larger whole can only be misleading.

Peng and Nisbett (1999) claimed that these sets of assumptions form two kinds of folk epistemologies: a dialectical epistemology that is more widespread in the East and a more linear/logical epistemology that is more widespread in the West. Of course, elements from each epistemology are shared by many or all cultures, but the comparative prevalence of these implicit theories suggests cross-cultural studies might reveal how culture-specific epistemologies affect inference. We turn now to evidence on culture and dialectical thinking.

Folk Wisdom on Dialectical Thinking Peng and Nisbett (1999) examined folk knowledge as embodied in books of proverbs. They found that dialectical proverbs that pose a contradiction or assertion of instability (e.g., "Too humble is half-proud") were more common among Chinese proverbs than among English ones. When nondialectical (e.g., "Half a loaf is better than none") and dialectical proverbs were selected from among Chinese and English proverbs equally and given to Chinese and American undergraduates to evaluate, Chinese participants had a greater preference for the dialectical proverbs than did American participants. The same pattern of preference emerged with Yiddish proverbs, stimuli equally unfamiliar to both Chinese and Americans.

Dialectical Resolution of Social Contradictions
Peng and Nisbett (1999) presented Chinese and American students with a variety of contradictions drawn from everyday life. For example, participants were asked to analyze conflicts between mothers and their daughters and between having fun and going to school. American responses tended to come down clearly in favor of one side or the other (e.g., mothers should respect their daughters' independence). Chinese responses were more likely to find a middle way that attributed fault to both sides and attempted to reconcile the contradiction (e.g., both the mothers and the daughters failed to understand each other).

Dialecticism and Preferred Argument Form   In a study examining argument preferences, Peng (1997) gave Chinese and American participants two different types of arguments—a logic-based one refuting contradiction and a dialectical one—for several issues. In one case, participants read arguments against Aristotle's proposition that a heavier object falls to the ground first. The logical argument summarized Galileo's famous thought experiment: If a heavy object is joined to a lighter one, they now have a weight greater than the lighter object alone and hence should fall faster; on the other hand, extending Aristotle's view, the lighter object should act as a brake and therefore the combined object should fall more slowly. Since these entailments form a contradiction, it is possible to reject the original proposal that objects of a different weight fall at different speeds. The dialectical argument, meanwhile, was based on a holistic approach to the problem: Since Aristotle isolated objects from possible surrounding factors (e.g., wind, weather, and height), the proposition must be wrong. For several such issues, Chinese expressed a greater preference for the dialectical arguments, while Americans were drawn to the linear, logical arguments.

Tolerance of Apparent Contradiction   One of the strongest implications of the notion that Westerners adhere to a logical analysis of problems is that, when presented with contradictory propositions, they should be inclined to reject one in favor of the other. Easterners, on the other hand, might be inclined to embrace both propositions, finding them each to have merit. In one study, Peng and Nisbett (1999) presented participants either with one proposition or with two propositions that were seemingly contradictory. For instance, one proposition used was, "A developmental psychologist studied adolescent children and asserted that those children who were less dependent on their parents and had weaker family ties were generally more mature." In some cases, this was paired with a second, apparently contradictory statement: "A social psychologist studied young adults and asserted that those who feel close to their families have more satisfying social relationships." Participants read one, the other, or both of these and then rated the plausibility of the statements they read.

Across five issues, Chinese and American participants agreed on which of the two statements offered was more plausible (i.e., a main effect of statement). However, when reading the statements in pairs, Americans found the predominantly plausible statement even more plausible than when reading it alone: They bolstered their belief in the plausible statement that it was presented along with a contradiction (cf. Lord, Ross, & Lepper, 1979). In contrast, Chinese participants expressed lower plausibility ratings for the predominant statement when it was paired with a contradiction, seemingly compromising between the two perspectives.

Conclusions

Two decades ago, cognitive anthropologist Edwin Hutchins, like Nisbett and Ross, published a book. His was titled *Culture and Inference* (1980), and it contains a careful ethnography of reasoning among the Trobriand Islanders. Hutchins was working against arguments that the Trobrianders and other such cultures lacked concepts of causality and logic (D. D. Lee, 1940, 1949). Thus, Hutchins, ironically enough, was making something of a universalist argument: Sophisticated inferences are not the kind of thing that only members of "civilized" cultures can do. However, in the process of showing that complex reasoning, such as *modus tollens* and *plausible inference*, existed among the Trobrianders, Hutchins also delivered important conclusions about the ways in which inferences differ across cultures: Reasoning, he concluded, is inseparably intertwined with cultural models. What is universal is our capacity to infer and judge, but this is always and only done in light of cultural models (see D'Andrade, 1995).

Over the last 20 years, cultural psychologists have done much to qualify, interpret, and expand on the ideas of both Nisbett and Ross and Hutchins. Those in cultural psychology know much now about how inference unfolds in different ways in various cultures—and they are poised to learn even more. The differences reviewed in this chapter defy simple summation, but the highlights deserve to be recounted briefly. After doing so, we consider cultural differences in inference in light of the value, self, and theory traditions.

Lessons on Cultural Differences

Findings on cultural differences in inference can be grouped into two broad categories: induction and deduction.

Induction

Covariation detection is a basic form of induction: Given evidence of the cooccurrence of various events and features, how and when do perceivers infer a connection? Research that focuses on the holistic, dialectical epistemology associated with Chinese culture shows that Chinese may be more attuned to relations among stimuli in a field: They show fewer primacy effects than Americans, and compared to Americans, their confidence in judging covariation tracks better with their actual accuracy.

Attribution has enjoyed considerable attention from cultural researchers, in part because of the compelling differences that emerge. In the domain of social attribution, scholars have repeatedly shown that Americans tend to isolate single individuals as causes, while Asians and other collectivists comparatively stress situations and groups as causes. Similarly, in the physical domain, Chinese are more likely to highlight the role of the field in explanations, whereas Americans tend to focus on the internal properties of objects.

Cultural differences emerge in judgments about persons as well, including inferences about their personalities and their mental states. Americans appear to share a dispositionalist folk theory, such that they see individuals as having stable, internal, enduring dispositions, whereas Asians are more likely to see persons as changeable and context bound. Likewise, in forming impressions of a target person,

Americans tend to prefer information directly from that person, while Chinese are comparatively more interested in others' views of the target and information about the target's context. Further, Americans seem to expect that mental states are more readily inferred by a person's own statements; Chinese seem to base inferences of mental states more heavily on other, unspoken cues.

In the realm of categorization, culture shapes category coherence by directing attention to culturally important phenomena; as the priorities of cultures differ, so do their categories. Further, Asians seem more likely than Americans to categorize things by their relations, such as social obligations, rather than isolable features. Compared to Americans, Asians may also be less attuned to categories in their inferences and category learning. These findings are perhaps more intriguing in light of cultural research on the category of self. Considerable scholarship shows that Asian concepts of self are more socially diffused and context and relationship bound, while American concepts of self are more concrete and abstract.

Deduction

Given premises in some logical relation, do people in all cultures draw the same inference? Studies of culture and syllogistic reasoning suggest that this question needs to be reconsidered. Namely, what count as premises and logical relations depends on the culture-specific models. Within a culture, framing logical questions with ordinary knowledge rather than abstractions has a massive difference on performance. It seems safe to conclude that people in all cultures are capable of making complex inferences, but each culture does so within its own models.

Cultural studies have also highlighted diversity in basic epistemologies of what counts as evidence and the nature of truth—and differences in epistemology give rise to different styles of reasoning and deduction. Chinese appear to share a dialectical epistemology that stresses the changing nature of reality and the enduring presence of contradiction. This stands in contrast to a Western linear epistemology built on notions of truth, identity, and noncontradiction. As a result, some scholars argue, Chinese prefer to seek a compromise in the face of contradiction, whereas Americans pursue more exclusionary forms of truth and resolution.

The Three Traditions: Relation to Culture and Inference

In the beginning of this chapter, we reviewed three perspectives for approaching culture: the value tradition, the self tradition, and the theory tradition. The value tradition, for instance, has shown that individualists tend to isolate single persons as causes. The self tradition, for example, has revealed that the category of self differs substantially across cultures. And, the theory tradition can be seen in work on the role of culturally bound epistemologies in reasoning. Each tradition, then, has shed light on the question of culture and inference, but is there some way of integrating these perspectives? Do scholars and concerned readers have to place their loyalty in one tradition to the exclusion of the others? We suggest that a synthesis is both possible and preferable, at least at the level of describing how the phenomena targeted by each tradition might relate. The result is a rich way for thinking about how culture and inference relate.

A starting point for building the synthesis is to consider what folk theories do and their origin. Virtually by definition, theories (whether implicit folk ones or scientific ones) support inferences: They guide how evidence is collected and interpreted and support judgments that go beyond immediate data. Indeed, it would be nearly impossible to describe everyday inference in a psychologically rich way without resorting to some folk knowledge structures like implicit theories. Thus, to understand cultural effects on inference in a proximal sense implies understanding how cultural theories are at work in ordinary judgment.

But what is the origin of theories? It seems quite clear that cultural values must be an important source for theories: Values guide our attention to what is good and important. Our views of what the world is like are shaped by what we think the world should be like. Asian norms about the importance of groups and social relations, for instance, no doubt yield rich folk theories about those entities. The dynamic seems to be at work within the tradition of the self as well, for norms about how to be a "good" self are seen as yielding beliefs about what the self "is." And, as James (1890) notes, self concepts have a wide-ranging role in psychological processes, so concepts of self are likely intertwined with a host of other beliefs, such as beliefs about others.

In short, implicit theories may play something of a mediating role between values and the concept of self on the one hand and inferences on the other. Values and concepts of self may have a more removed, distal effect on inferences, but a more proximal impact on beliefs. This mediating model may seem complete, but it fails to address a final important question: What are inferences for? As S. T. Fiske (1992) and others have observed, thinking is always *for* something; we would add that what thinking is for differs across cultures. Why is it, for instance, that people judge causes? On occasion, it might be a private act, meant to be shared with no one. More often, though, such inferences are shared and put to use in some kind of action. Take the example of a transgression: We seek an explanation in order to act—to prevent, to punish, to forgive, and so on. Our implicit theories may guide an attribution inference, but the inference is not alone in shaping action. Action is also shaped by cultural values and concepts of self. In the case of transgressions, Western theories may isolate a single person as a cause, and Western values may imply some form of person-directed retributive justice. East Asian theories, meanwhile, might identify a group or situation as a cause, and East Asian harmony values might prescribe collective responsibility as an outcome.

Values and concepts of self thus play a dual role: First, they shape the theories that, in turn, drive inferences; second, they shape the contexts in which the resulting inferences are turned into action (see Figure 13.1). In this scheme, it makes no sense to ask which of the three traditions is the "best" approach to studying culture and inference. Rather, these three traditions target different parts of a system of the influence of culture on inference. Isolating one set of relationships at a time (for instance, between theories and inferences or between values and theories) is a practical, and perhaps necessary, research strategy, but scholars are well served to acknowledge the broader system of the relationship of culture with inference. A full story of how culture affects inference must address each of these components.[1]

Looking Ahead

What is next for the cultural psychology of human inference? Several challenges emerge from our review of findings. The traditions of value and self each contain differing perspectives, but each has also been dominated by a central construct, individualism-collectivism in the case

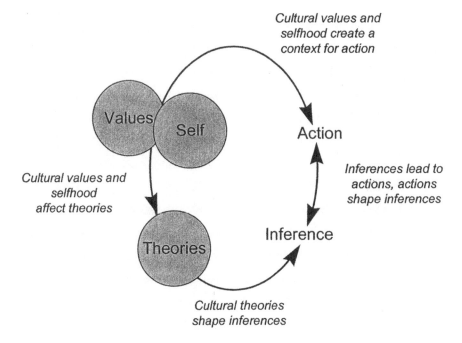

Figure 13.1   A Model of Cultural Influence on Human Inference

of values and independent-interdependent selves in the tradition of self. One challenge for these traditions will be to expand these dimensions. The 1996 work of Nisbett and Cohen on the "culture of honor," for instance, suggests an important alternative to the constructs of value and self.

For its part, the theory tradition continues to grow. As it does, it may face the danger of becoming fragmented. While it holds the promise of being psychologically precise and rich in terms of describing cultural effects on inference, it runs the risk of targeting an ad hoc collection of representations detached from broader cultural patterns. Scholars in this tradition are challenged to describe connections, both among the implicit theories they are studying and between those theories and other cultural constructs (such as values).

All these traditions are challenged to study inference with new populations. Most work to date has been done in the United States and Asia. More work needs to explore inference in other parts of the world, such as Africa. As Nisbett and Cohen (1996) have shown, research on values and judgments can also fruitfully examine cultural differences within countries. As globalization and immigration continue, cultural clashes in inferences deserve increased attention, as does the issue of acculturation.

Perhaps the most important challenge for the study of culture and human judgment is one shared with other areas of cultural psychological work: the need for methodologies that are meaningful at both the psychological and cultural levels (Peng, Nisbett, & Wong, 1997). This general challenge requires approaches that are tractable and precise and, at the same time, nuanced and sensitive. Current approaches vary in their strengths and weaknesses, and it seems clear there is no single superior perspective. Postmodern approaches stress the uniqueness of cultures, but sometimes eschew opportunities for fruitful cross-cultural comparisons. Cultural system approaches focus on the important everyday ecology of practices and institutions, but may omit descriptions of the mediating psychology of cultural members. Dimensional or typological approaches stress important factors for arraying cultures, but run the risk of glossing over rich systems of sense-making that have psychological reality. Many theory and value approaches helpfully focus on psychologically important aspects of culture, but may leave the broader picture undescribed.

As psychological research moves to embrace the role of culture, it will do well to retain its guiding methodological principles. Among others, these include objectivity (attempting to observe and describe with a minimal influence of personal bias), validity (a consistent concern with measures and operationalizations), generalization (attempting to go beyond single cases to reveal lawlike mechanisms and processes of psychology), and causal explanation (a focus on the causal relationships between factors). Yet, perhaps new principles will need to be integrated as well, including holism (seeing the important connections between cultural components of sense-making), suprapersonal levels of analysis (moving beyond the individual), and qualitative approaches (reflecting the richness of culture). It may be that a combination of approaches is required to satisfy all these principles—and so flexibility may itself become the most important principle of all.

Looking back, an impressive amount of compelling scholarship has emerged on the topic of culture and inference in the past few decades. The topic and some basic tenets have come into focus, yet there is much more to do. We hope and expect that 20 years hence our current understanding will look well intentioned but naive in the face of accumulating insights on how culture shapes human inference.

Notes

This project was supported by the Regents' Junior Faculty Research Fellow Award by the University of California to the first author. We thank Sanjay Srivastava, Michael Shin, Coline McConnel, and other members of the U. C. Berkeley Culture and Cognition Lab for their comments and suggestions

1. Note that this system resembles what philosophers and developmental psychologists have called *belief-desire psychology* (see, e.g., Dennett, 1987; Searle, 1983; Wellman, 1990). This view holds that the keys to understanding everyday human action (e.g., "Carl eats celery") are desires (e.g., "Carl wants to lose weight") and beliefs ("Carl believes that celery aids weight loss"). Similarly, this system suggests that cultural values, like desires, shape action goals, while cultural theory-driven inferences yield beliefs relevant to actions.

References

Allen, S. W., & Brooks, L. R. (1991). Specializing the operation of an explicit rule. *Journal of Experimental Psychology (General), 120,* 3–19.

Alloy, L. B., & Tabachnik, N. (1984). Assessment of covariation by human and animals: The joint influence of prior expectations and current situational information. *Psychological Review, 91,* 112–149.

Ames, D. (1999). *Folk psychology and social inference: Everyday solutions to the problem of other minds.* Unpublished doctoral dissertation, University of California, Berkeley.

Ames, D., & Peng, K. (1999a). *Culture and person perception: Impression cues that count in the US and China.* Manuscript in preparation, University of California, Berkeley.

Ames, D., & Peng, K. (1999b). *Psychology of meaning: Making sense of sense making.* Manuscript in preparation, University of California, Berkeley.

Atran, S. (1990). *Cognitive foundations of natural history.* New York:

Atran, S., & Medin, D. (1997). Knowledge and action: Cultural models of nature and resources management in Mesoamerica. In M. Z. Bazerman & D. Messick (Eds.), *Environment, ethics, and behavior: The psychology of environmental valuation and degradation* (pp. 171–208). San Francisco: New Lexington Press.

Baron, R. M., & Misovich, S. J. (1993). Dispositional knowing from an ecological perspective. *Personality & Social Psychology Bulletin, 19,* 541–552.

Barsalou, L. W. (1983). Ad-hoc categories. *Memory and Categories, 11,* 211–227.

Barsalou, L. W. (1985). Ideals, central tendency, and frequency of instantiation as determinants of graded structure in categories. *Journal of Experimental Psychology: Learning, Memory, and Cognition, 11,* 629–654.

Betancourt, H., & Lopez, S. R. (1993). The study of culture, ethnicity, and race in American psychology. *American Psychologist, 48,* 629–637.

Boyer, P. (1993). *The naturalness of religious ideas.* Berkeley: University of California Press.

Capra, F. (1975). *The tao of physics.* Berkeley, CA: Shambala.

Chiu, C. Y., Hong, Y. I., & Dweck, C. S. (1997). Lay dispositionism and implicit theories of personality. *Journal of Personality and Social Psychology, 73,* 19–30.

Chiu, L.-H. (1972). A cross-cultural comparison of cognitive styles in Chinese and American children. *International Journal of Psychology, 7,* 235–242.

Choi, I., & Nisbett, R. E. (1998). Situational salience and cultural differences in the correspondence bias and in the actor-observer bias. *Personality and Social Psychology Bulletin, 24,* 949–960.

Choi, I., Nisbett, R., & Norenzayan, A. (1999). Causal attribution across cultures: Variation and universality. *Psychological Bulletin, 125,* 47–63.

Choi, I., Nisbett, R. E., & Smith, E. E. (1997). Culture, category salience, and inductive reasoning. *Cognition, 65*, 15–32.

Cole, M. (1996). *Cultural psychology: A once and future discipline.* Cambridge: Belknap Press of Harvard University Press.

D'Andrade, R. G. (1995). *The development of cognitive anthropology.* Cambridge: Cambridge University Press.

Dennett, D. C. (1987). *The intentional stance.* Cambridge: MIT Press.

Douglas, M. (1982). *In the active voice.* London: Routledge & Kegan Paul.

Dweck, C. S. (1996). Capturing the dynamic nature of personality. *Journal of Research in Personality, 30*, 348–362.

Dweck, C. S., Chiu, C. Y., & Hong, Y. I. (1995). Implicit theories and their role in judgments and reactions: A world from two perspectives. *Psychological Inquiry, 6*, 267–285.

Fiske, A. P. (1992). The four elementary forms of sociality: Framework for a unified theory of sociality. *Psychological Review, 99*, 689–723.

Fiske, A. P., Kitayama, S., Markus, H. R., & Nisbett, R. E. (1998). The cultural matrix of social psychology. In D. T. Gilbert, S. T. Fiske, & G. Linzey (Eds.), *Handbook of social psychology* 4th ed.) (pp. 915–981). Boston: McGraw-Hill.

Fiske, S. T. (1992). Thinking is for doing. Portraits of social cognition from daguerreotype to laserphoto. *Journal of Personality and Social Psychology, 63*, 877–889.

Gelman, S. A., & Medin, D. L. (1993). What's so essential about essentialism? A different perspective on the interaction of perception, language, and conceptual knowledge. *Cognitive Development, 8*, 157–167.

Gilbert, D. T., & Jones, E. E. (1986). Perceiver-induced constraint: Interpretations of self-generated reality. *Journal of Personality and Social Psychology, 50*, 269–280.

Gopnk, A., & Meltzoff, A. (1997). *Words, thoughts, and theories.* Cambridge: MIT Press.

Heider, F. (1958). *The psychology of interpersonal relations.* New York: Wiley.

Heine, S., & Lehman, D. R. (1995). Cultural variation in unrealistic optimism: Does the West feel more invulnerable than the East? *Journal of Personality and Social Psychology, 68*, 595–607.

Heine, S., Lehman, D. R. (1997). Culture, dissonance, and self-affirmation. *Personality and Social Psychology Bulletin, 23*, 389–400.

Hofstede, G. (1980). *Culture's consequences: International differences in work-related values.* Beverly Hills, CA: Sage.

Holland, D., & Quinn, N. (1987). *Cultural models in language and thought.* Cambridge: Cambridge University Press.

Hutchins, E. (1980). *Culture and inference.* Cambridge: Harvard University Press.

James, W. (1890). *The principles of psychology.* New York: Holt.

Ji, L., Peng, K., & Nisbett, R. E. (2000). Culture, control, and perception of relationships in the environment. *Journal of Personality and Social Psychology, 78*(5), 943–955.

Jones, E. E., & Harris, V. A. (1967). The attribution of attitudes. *Journal of Experimental Social Psychology, 3*, 1–24.

Kitayama, S., & Masuda, T. (1997). Shaiaiteki ninshiki no bunkateki baikai model: Taiousei bias no bunkashinrigakuteki kentou [Cultural psychology of social inference: The correspondence bias in Japan]. In K. Kashiwagi, S. Kitayama, & H. Azuma (Eds.), *Bunkashinrigaju: riron to jisho* [Cultural psychology: Theory and evidence]. Tokyo: University of Tokyo Press.

Knowles, E. D., and Ames, D. R. (1999). *The mentalistic nature of folk person concepts: Individual and trait term differences.* Manuscript in preparation, University of California, Berkeley.

Lee, D. D. (1940). A primitive system of values. *Journal of Philosophy, 7*, 355–379.

Lee, D. D. (1949). Being and value in a primitive culture. *Journal of Philosophy, 48*, 401–415.

Lee, F., Hallahan, M., & Herzog, T. (1996). Explaining real life events: How culture and domain shape attributions. *Personality and Social Psychology Bulletin, 22*, 732–741.

Leung, K. (1997). Negotiation and reward allocations across cultures. In P. C. Earley & M. Erez (Eds.), *New perspectives on international industrial/organizational psychology* (pp. 640–675). San Francisco: Jossey-Bass.

Lewin, K. (1935). *A dynamic theory of personality.* New York: McGraw-Hill.

Lillard, A. (1998). Ethnopsychologies: Cultural variations in theories of mind. *Psychological Bulletin, 123*, 3–32.

Liu, S. H. (1974). The use of analogy and symbolism in traditional Chinese philosophy. *Journal of Chinese Philosophy, 1*, 313–338.

Lloyd, G. E. R. (1990). *Demystifying mentalities.* New York: Cambridge University Press.

Lopez, A., Atran, S., Coley, J. D., Medin, D. L., & Smith, E. E. (1997). The tree of life: Universal and cultural features of folkbiological taxonomies and inductions. *Cognitive Psychology, 32*, 251–295.

Lord, C., Ross, L., & Lepper, M. (1979). Biased assimilation and attitude polarization: The effects of prior theories on subsequently considered evidence. *Journal of Personality and Social Psychology, 37*, 2098–2109.

Luria, A. R. (1931). Psychological expedition to Central Asia. *Science, 74*, 383–384.

Malt, B. (1995). Category coherence in cross-cultural perspective. *Cognitive Psychology, 29*, 85–148.

Markus, H. R., & Cross, S. (1990). The interpersonal self. In L. A. Pervin (Ed.), *Handbook of personality: Theory and research* (pp. 576–608). New York: Guilford.

Markus, H. R., & Kitayama, S. (1991). Cultural variation in the self-concept. Culture and self: Implications for cognition, emotion and motivation. *Psychological Review, 98*, 224–253.

McCloskey, M. (1983). Intuitive physics. *Scientific American, 248*, 122–130.

Menon, T., Morris, M., Chiu, C. Y., & Hong, Y. I. (1999). Culture and the construal of agency: Attribution to individual versus group dispositions. *Journal of Personality and Social Psychology, 76*, 701–727.

Miller, J. G. (1984). Culture and the development of everyday social explanation. *Journal of Personality and Social Psychology, 46*, 961–978.

Morris, M. W., Nisbett, R. E., & Peng, K. (1995). Causal understanding across domains and cultures. In D. Sperber, D. Premack, & A. J. Premack (Eds.), *Causal cognition: A multidisciplinary debate* (pp. 577–612). Oxford: Oxford University Press.

Morris, M. W., & Peng, K. (1994). Culture and cause: American and Chinese attributions for social and physical events. *Journal of Personality and Social Psychology, 67*, 949–971.

Moscovici, S. (1984). The phenomenon of social representations. In R. Farr & S. Moscovici (Eds.), *Social representations*. Cambridge: Cambridge University Press.

Murphy, G. L., & Medin, D. L. (1985). The role of theories in conceptual coherence. *Psychological Review, 92*, 289–316.

Needham, J. (1954). *Science and civilization in China* (Vol. 1). Cambridge: Cambridge University Press.

Needham, J. (1962). *Science and civilization in China: Vol. 4. Physics and physical technology*. Cambridge: Cambridge University Press.

Nisbett, R. E., & Cohen, D. (1996). *Culture of honor: The psychology of violence in the South*. Boulder, CO: Westview Press.

Nisbett, R. E., & Ross, L. (1980). Human Inference: Strategies and Shortcomings of Social Judgment. Englewood Cliffs, New Jersey: Prentice-Hall.

Nisbett, R. E., Peng, K., Choi, I., & Norenzayan, A. (2001). Culture and system of thought: Holistic versus analytic cognition. *Psychological Review, 108*, 1–20.

Norenzayan, A., Choi, I., & Nisbett, R. (1999). Eastern and western perceptions of causality for social behavior: Lay theories about personalities and social situations. In D. Prentice & D. Miller (Eds.), *Cultural divides: Understanding and overcoming group conflict* (pp. 239–272). New York: Sage.

Norenzayan, A., Nisbett, R. E., Smith, E. E., & Kim, B. J. (2000). Rules vs. similarity as a basis for reasoning and judgment in East and West. Unpublished manuscript, University of Illinois.

Osherson, D. N., Smith, E. E., Wilkie, O., López, A., & Shafir, E. (1990). Category-based induction. *Psychological Review, 97*, 185–200.

Peng, K. (1997). *Naive dialecticism and its effects on reasoning and judgment about contradiction*. Unpublished doctoral dissertation, University of Michigan, Ann Arbor.

Peng, K., & Ames, D. (in press). Psychology of dialectical thinking. In N. J. Smelser & P. B. Baltes (Eds.), *International encyclopedia of the social and behavioral sciences*. Oxford, England: Elsevier Science.

Peng, K., & Knowles, E. (2000). Culture, ethnicity and attribution of physical causality. *Personality and social psychology bulletin* (under review).

Peng, K., & Nisbett, R. E. (1996). Cross-cultural similarities and differences in the understanding of physical causality. In G. Shields & M. Shale (Eds.), *Science and culture: Proceedings of the seventh interdisciplinary conference on science and culture*. Frankfort, KY: University Graphics.

Peng, K., & Nisbett, R. E. (1999). Culture, dialectics, and reasoning about contradiction. *American Psychologist, 54*, 741–754.

Peng, K., Nisbett, R., & Wong, N. Y. C. (1997). Validity problems comparing values across cultures and possible solution. *Psychological Methods, 2*, 329–344.

Rohner, R. (1984). Toward a conception of culture for cross-cultural psychology. *Journal of Cross-Cultural Psychology, 15*, 111–138.

Rosch, E., & Mervis, C. B. (1975). Family resemblances: Studies in the internal structure of categories. *Cognitive Psychology, 7*, 573–605.

Rosch, E., Mervis, C. B., Gray, W. D., Johnson, D., & Boyes-Braem, P. (1976). Basic objects in natural categories. *Cognitive Psychology, 8*, 382–439.

Ross, L. (1977). The intuitive psychologist and his shortcomings. In L. Berkowitz (Ed.), *Advances in experimental social psychology* (Vol. 10) (pp. 172–200). New York: Academic Press.

Schwartz, S. H. (1991). The universal content and structure of values: Theoretical advances and empirical tests in 20 countries. *Advanced in Experimental Social Psychology, 25*, 1–65.

Schwartz, S. H., & Sagiv, L. (1995). Identifying culture-specifics in the content and structure of value. *Journal of Cross-Cultural Psychology, 26*, 92–116.

Shweder, R. (1995). Cultural psychology: What is it? In N. R. Goldberger & J. B. Veroff (Eds.), *The culture and psychology reader* (pp. 41–86). New York: New York University Press.

Searle, J. R. (1983). *Intentionality, an essay in the philosophy of mind*. New York: Cambridge University Press.

Singelis, T. M. (1994). The measurement of independent and interdependent self-construals. *Personality and Social Psychology Bulletin, 20*, 580–591.

Smith, P. B., & Bond, M. H. (1999). *Social psychology across cultures*. Needham Heights, MA: Allyn & Bacon.

Sperber, D. (1990). The epidemiology of beliefs. In C. Fraser & G. Gaskell (Eds.), *The social psychological study of widespread beliefs* (pp. 24–44). Oxford, England: Clarendon Press.

Stich, S. (1990). *The fragmentation of reason*. Cambridge: MIT Press.

Strauss, C., & Quinn, N. (1997). *A cognitive theory of cultural meaning*. Cambridge: Cambridge University Press.

Tanaka, J. W., & Taylor, M. E. (1991). Categorization and expertise: Is the basic level in the eye of the beholder? *Cognitive psychology, 23*, 457–482.

Triandis, H. C. (1995). *Individualism and collectivism*. Boulder, CO: Westview Press.

Vallacher, R. R., & Wegner, D. M. (1987). What do people think they're doing? Action identification and human behavior. *Psychological Review, 94*, 3–15.

Vosniadou, S. (1994). Universal and culture-specific properties of children's mental models of the earth. In L. A. Hirschfeld & S. A. Gelman (Eds.), *Mapping the mind: Domain specificity in cognition and culture*. New York: Cambridge University Press.

Wagner, W. (1997). Local knowledge, social representations and psychological theory. In K. Leung; U. Kim, S. Yamaguchi, & Y. Kashima (Eds.), *Progress in Asian social psychology*. Singapore: Wiley.

Wegner, D. M., & Vallacher, R. R. (1977). *Implicit psychology: An introduction to social cognition*. New York: Oxford University Press.

Wellman, H. M. (1990). *The child's theory of mind*. Cambridge: MIT Press.

Whiting, B. B. (1976). The problem of the packaged variable. In K. F. Reigel & J. A. Meacham (Eds.), *The developing individual in a changing world*. The Hague: Mouton.

Zhang, D. L., & Chen, Z. Y. (1991). *Zhongguo Siwei Pianxiang* [The orientation of Chinese thinking]. Beijing: Social Science Press.

Zukav, G. (1980). *The dancing Wu Li masters: An overview of the new physics*. New York: Quill Morrow.

14

Abnormal Psychology and Culture

JUNKO TANAKA-MATSUMI

Questions about abnormal behavior and deviance in the cross-cultural context have been raised for decades, undoubtedly fueled by the undeniable fact that what may appear to be entirely inappropriate and abnormal from one cultural perspective may be entirely normal and expected from another. Abnormal behavior and psychopathology have been the focus of much research and study not only by psychologists, but also by anthropologists and physicians for decades.

In this chapter, Tanaka-Matsumi provides an excellent, comprehensive review of cross-cultural research and theory in the area of abnormal behaviors. Beginning with a presentation of cross-cultural mental health research in a historical context, she goes on to describe the ways in which diagnostic methods have been studied and standardized across cultures. In particular, she examines the U.S.-U.K. Diagnostic Project as a starting point for discussing etic approaches to diagnosis, the emic-based critiques of these approaches, and the reformulations that currently exist that attempt to address both universalist and culturally relativist (that is, both etic and emic) approaches in making diagnoses of mental disorders across cultures, including the American Psychiatric Association's *Diagnostic and Statistical Manual of Mental Disorders,* 4th edition (*DSM-IV*), and the World Health Organization's *International Classification of Diseases, 10th Revision* (*ICD-10*). While these reformulations appear to be steps in the right direction, continued research in the future will be needed to test and confirm further their cross-cultural validity.

Tanaka-Matsumi then goes on to review major cross-cultural findings on three mental disorders: depression, schizophrenia, and anxiety. For each, research exemplifying both etic and emic approaches, as well as contemporary attempts at combinations of the two, are described in great detail. In particular, she describes work that begins to demonstrate sensitivity to culturally relevant views of abnormal behavior and its diagnoses in indigenous contexts and discusses how they inform traditional cross-cultural findings using standardized methods across cultures. In my experience, this review of this literature is one of the finest, most comprehensive, and most efficient (in terms of its brevity) to be found today.

While the quality of the literature review presented throughout the chapter, and the discussion of its implications, is stellar, Tanaka-Matsumi's ideas concerning future directions for research deserve considerable attention in their own right. In particular, she describes seven questions that future cross-cultural researchers should ask when formulating, conducting, and interpreting research in the future. In raising these questions, Tanaka-Matsumi inherently argues for an integration of varying and diverse approaches to the study of psychopathology across cultures. She argues, on the one hand, for example, for the adoption of strict guidelines for culturally adapting various instruments to establish equivalence across cultures, while on the other hand, she also argues for the development of more emically derived measures. In doing so, she argues for the blending and merging of the objectivity of traditional psychometrics and research methodology with the vision and content that can be supplemented by culturally relevant, indigenous, emic approaches. While previous research has provided us with a wealth of information on the topic, it has typically excluded one or the other focus. In the future, however, both need to be incorporated into a single, comprehensive line of inquiry so that psychopathology can be examined and understood not only in a quantitatively different fashion, but also in a qualitatively different fashion.

At the same time, Tanaka-Matsumi also argues for the incorporation and consideration of four concepts that further elaborate on the nature of culture itself in the study of psychopathology across cultures. As she rightly points out, while pathological outcomes have been compared across national, racial, and ethnic groups in many studies, the specific cultural-contextual factors contributing to their differential rates, etiologies, and outcomes have not been addressed empirically. Future research needs to address the contribution of specific, measurable cultural variables to psychopathological differences across cultures if cross-cultural theory and research in this area is going to be able to make the transition from merely documenting differences in incidence rates to truly addressing what it is about culture that produces differences in abnormal behavior and why. In this sense, Tanaka-Matsumi's points about the integration of methods and concepts, along with the contextualization of culture and its operationalization in research here, are entirely consonant with the message provided by so many others in this volume.

The goal of this chapter is to appraise the current state of knowledge on the relationship between culture and psychopathology. The most relevant domains of psychology and allied disciplines are abnormal and clinical psychology, psychiatry, anthropology, and epidemiology. I examine how the dramatic changes in approaches to psychiatric research over the past three decades have provided a basis for studying mental disorders in a global, cross-cultural, or multicultural context (Desjarlais, Eisenberg, Good, & Kleinman, 1995; Marsella, 1998). Two major changes include the development of standardized diagnostic assessments of mental disorders since the early 1970s and contextual approaches to assessing abnormal behaviors in different cultures. These developments are frequently characterized as reflecting the universalist and culture relativist perspectives in cross-cultural mental health research.

History and Emic and Etic Perspectives to Cross-Cultural Mental Health Research

Formulations and findings on the interplay of abnormal behavior and culture are rooted in one of three general orientations: absolutist, universalist, and culturally relativist (Berry, Poortinga, Segall, & Dasen, 1992). From the absolutist perspective, culture is thought to play no role in the concepts and meanings of normality and abnormality, expressions and consequences of abnormal patterns of behavior. The absolutist orientation would advocate the biological model of psychopathology with invariant symptoms across cultures. However, the literature is in agreement that culture exerts varying degrees of influence on psychopathological processes and manifestations (Al-Issa, 1995; Draguns, 1980; Tanaka-Matsumi & Draguns, 1997). Therefore, the most plausible positions to study abnormal behavior and culture are the etic and emic positions. The universalist and cultural relativist viewpoints overlap greatly with the etic and emic positions (Berry, 1969). As Segall, Lonner, and Berry (1998) explained, contemporary cross-cultural psychologists

typically expect both biological and cultural factors to influence human behavior, but, like relativists, assume that the role of culture in producing human variation both within and across groups (especially across groups) is substantial. (p. 1104)

In this chapter, *culture* is defined as "the set of attitudes, values, beliefs, and behaviors, shared by a group of people, communicated from one generation to the next via language or some other means of communication" (Matsumoto, 1994, p. 4).

In relation to psychopathology, the etic or universalist view emphasizes comparability of cross-culturally or even globally applicable dimensions or categories. Frequently, but not always, these categories are equated with the major entries of the Western Kraepelinian diagnostic system. Historically, Kraepelin's (1904) observational accounts from Java of the universality of mental disorders (such as "dementia praecox" and "manic-depressive psychosis") inspired Western psychiatric researchers to study psychopathology in non-Western cultures. These pioneers include Brody (1967), Devereux (1961), Draguns (1973), Kiev (1972), Lin (1953), H. B. M. Murphy (1982a), J. M. Murphy and Leighton (1965), Pfeiffer (1970), Wittkower and Rin (1965), and Yap (1974), among others. Throughout the major part of this century, cross-cultural researchers have pursued the same questions posed originally by Kraepelin: Are there universals in psychopathology? What are the sources of "very remarkable differences" (Kraepelin, 1904) in forms of psychopathology?

Cross-cultural research is believed to enhance our understanding of psychopathology with regard to prevalence rates, risk factors, protective factors, and the possible etiology of particular disorders (Leff, 1988). To this end, the universalist perspective has inspired research on the cross-cultural validity and reliability of psychiatric diagnosis (Draguns, 1980).

Emic or culturally relativist investigators, on the other hand, eschew comparison and categorization. The word *emic*, in fact, has come to mean "culture-specific" (Brislin, 1983, p. 382). Emic researchers focus on the local context of a phenomenon within a culture and investigate indigenous, culturally based meanings of concepts such as idioms of distress. The key to conducting emic research is collecting ethnographic or culturally grounded data without imposing a priori definitions and ideas of the researcher. Emic researchers believe that the dialectical interaction of biological and cultural processes shape abnormal behavior and its communication (Kleinman, 1988; Littlewood, 1990).

Historically, Sarbin and Juhasz (1982) have analyzed the broadening of theoretical approaches to mental disorders that lead away from the ethnocentrism of the colonial era to a cultural relativism, beginning with the contribution of anthropologists such as Mead (1935) and Benedict (1934). Much later, in the 1960s, some aspects of cultural relativism were reflected strongly in the works of Foucault (1965), Goffman (1961), Sarbin (1969), Scheff (1966), Szasz (1961), and Ullmann and Krasner (1969). All these scholars advanced a view that the standard of what is normal and abnormal is culturally variable. Many people who would be considered abnormal in one culture would be considered quite normal in another culture due to differences in values and norms for certain behaviors. By the mid-1960s, the majority of abnormal psychology textbooks published in the United States referred to cultural relativity views of abnormal behavior (Tanaka-Matsumi & Chang, 1999). For example, J. M. Murphy (1976) used local informants and compared labeling practices of two widely separated and distinctly contrasting non-Western groups of Eskimos of northwest Alaska and Yorubas of rural, tropical Nigeria. Both cultures were reported by J. M. Murphy to use indigenous labels to describe similar patterns of behaviors (e.g., seeing, hearing, and believing things that were not seen, heard, and believed by others) that were linked to the local concept of insanity. Labeling, however, depended on the degree to which culturally deviant behaviors were controlled (e.g., self-control) and used for a specific social function (e.g., shamanism). Rejecting the psychiatric-medical model of abnormal behavior, Ullmann and Krasner (1969, 1975) viewed psychiatric diagnosis as a value-laden social act involving the patient and the observer in a specific context.

Tanaka-Matsumi and Chang (1999) noted, however, that during the past four decades, the authors of the abnormal psychology textbooks have almost invariably followed the disorder categories based on the *Diagnostic and Statistical Manual of Mental Disorders* (*DSM*) published by the American Psychiatric Association (1980, 1987, 1994). We have yet to see an active infusion of etic categories of mental disorders with emic information according to a combined etic-emic approach (Brislin, 1983) in the majority of our mainstream abnormal psychology textbooks. Thus, comprehensive review of the literature on culture and psychopathology by Draguns (1980) cautioned that three factors have complicated the problem of identifying cultural universals and cultural particulars in psychopathology: (a) the application of Kraepelinian categories throughout the world, (b) the exportation of Western psychiatric institutions to other cultures, and (c) the imitation of "Western" symptoms and complaints by patients in cultures undergoing modernization.

The purpose of this chapter is to review theoretical and methodological developments in studies of culture and psychopathology and to appraise the field in terms of future research questions. I apply a combined etic-emic perspective (Brislin, 1983) with a hope of illuminating derived etics (Berry, 1969) in psychopathology and cultural particulars in the content of human distress, its antecedents, communication, and social consequences.

Standardization of Diagnosis across Cultures: Etic Approaches, Emic Critiques, and Reformulations

The U.K.-U.S. Diagnostic Project: A Beginning of Modern Cross-Cultural Mental Health Research

As a starting point of modern, prototypical cross-cultural research on psychopathology, I examine the U.S.-U.K. Diagnostic Project (Cooper et al., 1972). This project provided an important impetus toward identifying sources of cultural variance in diagnostic outcome and the subsequent development of standardized assessment methods to compare abnormal behavior patterns across cultures. There were three parts to the project. First, Cooper et al. confirmed earlier reports that comparisons of hospital diagnoses of first admissions to the mental hospitals in New York and London revealed striking contrasts for nearly every major diagnostic category. Most notably, there were far more patients with initial diagnoses of schizophrenia in the New York sample, and more patients were diagnosed with depressive psychoses in the London sample. Second, Cooper et al. demonstrated that these diagnostic differences disappeared greatly when British and American project psychiatrists diagnosed the patients with the stan-

dardized diagnostic system (*International Classification of Diseases, 8th Revision* [*ICD-8*]) of the World Health Organization (WHO). Finally, the U.S.-U.K. Project examined if American and British psychiatrists used different symptom criteria when evaluating videotaped interviews of both American and British patients. The cross-national agreement was high for prototypical cases. However, for mixed cases, American psychiatrists had a broader concept of schizophrenia, and British psychiatrists had a broader concept of manic depressive illness. Further, both groups of experienced raters expressed confidence in their conflicting diagnoses.

At that time, these significant cross-national differences in diagnostic practices were attributed to a variety of factors, including cultural differences in the threshold for the perception of various abnormal behaviors and value judgments of psychiatrists, as well as training-related variables. The triple interactive factors of the patient, observer, and context were considered relevant to the process and outcome of psychiatric diagnosis (Draguns, 1973; Rosenhan, 1973). Many cross-cultural differences typically attributed to patient behavior (e.g., hallucinations) may also be influenced by factors due to observers (e.g., psychiatrists), treatment settings (e.g., psychiatric hospital), and communities (e.g., urban versus rural setting). Clinicians evaluate deviant and distressful behaviors based on their training model (e.g., psychoanalytic versus behavioral model) and professional experience within a particular setting or context of observation. The act of identifying, describing, labeling, and developing a treatment plan involves a complex sociocultural process (Westermeyer, 1987). Thus, there was a great deal of interest in investigating not only the characteristics of the individual disturbance, but also the context of its occurrence (Kleinman, 1978). Contexts of abnormal behaviors include the cultural reference group (e.g., family), local community and institution, and their respective norms and values (Tanaka-Matsumi & Higginbotham, 1996; Tanaka-Matsumi, Seiden, & Lam, 1996).

Dramatic and major developments have since taken place in cross-cultural psychopathology. Questions raised by the U.S.-U.K. Diagnostic Project have led to two competing pathways. The first is the development and field testing of standardized diagnostic instruments across cultures. The second is refocusing on each individual culture and avoiding cross-cultural comparisons. In the first etic pathway, cross-cultural variance due to diagnosticians was to be eliminated since it interfered with a reliable assessment of patient differences. Major efforts went into the development of explicit diagnostic criteria and standardized diagnostic systems according to biomedical models of mental illness. Today, for every major psychiatric disorder, we can identify standardized diagnostic instruments (Sartorius & Janca, 1996).

The standardized systems have contributed to investigating universality of mental disorders across different cultures and have produced an enormous amount of new literature on cross-cultural psychopathology (Tanaka-Matsumi & Draguns, 1997). Unfortunately, the assessment of culture of the diagnostician has received minimum research attention, as did the cultural context of abnormal behavior (Fabrega, 1987; Kleinman, 1988; Rogler, 1999; Thakker & Ward, 1998; Whaley, 1997). As a consequence, various scholars have cautioned that cross-cultural mental health research has lacked specification of cultural factors and culture-relevant hypotheses in research design (Betancourt & Lopez, 1993; Canino, Lewis-Fernandez, & Bravo, 1997; Phinney, 1996; Sue & Zane, 1987).

Those who were intrigued by cultural factors in the practice of psychiatric diagnosis have gone on to develop a separate and emic path of cultural research. Kleinman's (1977) paper on the "category fallacy" marked the beginning of the new cross-cultural psychiatry. Kleinman (p. 4) stated that psychiatric categories are bound to the context of professional psychiatric theory and practice in the West. The cultural relativist position has produced descriptive and ethnographic studies on cultural idioms of distress, contextual descriptions of culture-bound syndromes, and cultural interpretation of major disorders such as depression (Kleinman & Good, 1985).

In studying race differences in psychiatric diagnoses, Whaley (1997) clarified diagnostic questions as harboring two different propositions: (a) the clinician bias hypothesis and (b) the cultural relativity hypothesis. Similarly, López (1989) proposed specific factors contributing to overdiagnosing and underdiagnosing of certain psychiatric disorders, such as paranoid schizophrenia in African Americans. These views suggest that, in cross-cultural contexts, diagnosticians have their own baselines for psychopathologies for different groups, and they are influenced by their own normative judgments (Adebimpe, 1981). Therefore, indigenous diagnostic practices do continue to differ across cultures, while the project diagnoses increase precision in judgment.

Methodological Innovations in Epidemiology

The U.S.-U.K. Diagnostic Project (Cooper et al., 1972) stimulated the development of (a) diagnostic criteria to define specific psychiatric disorders, (b) the use of standardized structured interview schedules by trained diagnosticians, and (c) the development of face-to-face interviews for large-scale community surveys. In the United States, the Epidemiological Catchment Area (ECA) study used the advanced epidemiological method (Robins & Regier, 1991) and involved five centers located in St. Louis, Missouri; Baltimore, Maryland; New Haven, Connecticut; Durham, North Carolina; and Los Angeles, California. The ECA survey has generated epidemiological research data according to ethnicity, age, gender, and socioeconomic status. Over 20,000 randomly selected community residents were interviewed using the Diagnostic Interview Schedule (DIS) for case identification. The DIS assesses major psychiatric disorders described in the *DSM-III* to determine lifetime and current diagnoses based on a set of explicit diagnostic criteria (Robins, Helzer, Croughan, & Ratcliff, 1981). The DIS was translated into Spanish. In the validation study (Burman, Karno, Hough, Escobar, & Forsythe, 1983), however, the Spanish DIS tended to underdiagnose depression and affective disorders and overdiagnose alcohol abuse when compared with trained clinicians' diagnoses using the *DSM-III*.

The ECA data suggest the importance of assessing the direct and indirect effects of ethnicity and acculturation status on the prevalence of affective disorders. For example, the lifetime prevalence of affective disorders was 11.0% for non-Hispanic Whites and 7.8% for Mexican Americans (Karno et al., 1987). In comparison with Mexican American women, the rate of major depressive episode was 2.5 times higher for non-Hispanic White women under 40 years of age. However, Mexican Americans born in the United States resembled the non-Hispanic Whites in exhibiting increased rates for specific symptoms of major depression (e.g., dysphoria, appetite disturbances, sleep disturbances, etc.) (Golding, Karno, & Rutter, 1990). The rates for Mexican Americans born in Mexico were lower in eight of the nine symptom categories examined. Some of these ECA findings may be the result of confounding of ethnicity with acculturation and acculturative stress. In the ECA study, birthplace and language served as the index of acculturation status. With acculturation, Mexican Americans may learn to experience and/or express depression through more cognitive and affective symptoms rather than through the somatic channel.

Internationally, the DIS was translated widely into different languages and was used in major psychiatric epidemiological surveys in general populations of different countries in the 1980s. Theoretically, these comparisons hold the promise of establishing normative baselines for different disorders across cultures. Baselines in the general populations would serve important functions when we compared the thresholds for abnormal behavior in different cultures. The outcomes of six major epidemiological surveys from six countries were compared by Hwu and Compton (1994): Puerto Rico (Canino et al., 1987), Canada (Bland, Newman, & Orn, 1988), Korea (C. K. Lee et al., 1990), Taiwan (Hwu, Yeh, & Chang, 1989), and New Zealand (Wells, Bushnell, Hornblon, Joyce, & Oakley-Browne, 1989). Hwu and Compton (1994) made post hoc cross-national comparisons of the lifetime prevalence rates of different disorders according to such variables as urban versus rural areas and gender. In cross-cultural comparisons, the ratio of the greatest prevalence ratio to the lowest prevalence ratio of each specific disorder varied widely, from a low of 2.6% for pathological gambling to a high of 83.8% for drug abuse/dependence.

Cultural variations were evident for major disorders as defined by the *DSM-III*. The lifetime prevalence rates for the majority of disorders, except alcohol abuse/dependence in Korea, were generally lower in Asian samples (Korea and Taiwan) than in American, Caucasian, and Hispanic samples. Helzer and Canino (1992) compared the DIS data involving 48,000 respondents from 10 cultures in North America, Europe, and Asia. They found that, in every culture investigated, men had higher rates of alcohol abuse/dependence than did women, particularly in Taiwan, China, and Korea. Within the United States, only 10% of men and women who met the *DSM-III* diagnosis of alcohol abuse/dependence in the ECA study sought treatment (Robins, Locke, & Regier, 1991). This alone suggests that the differentiation of normal and abnormal drinking is difficult to establish

both within and across cultures (Bennett, Janca, Grant, & Sartorius, 1993).

Cross-cultural differences in the prevalence rates of mental disorders might be explained by such factors as biological vulnerability, culturally determined protective factors, threshold for reporting symptoms, social stigma, and demographic risk factors (e.g., divorce) (Hwu & Compton, 1994). These are plausible hypotheses that warrant empirical testing in future research.

DSM-IV *and the Inclusion of Cultural Formulation*

Current editions of the *ICD* (*ICD-10*; WHO, 1992) and *DSM-IV* (American Psychiatric Association, 1994) have further promoted the use of standardized diagnostic systems around the world (Mezzich, Fabrega, Mezzich, & Goffman, 1985). The principal criteria for inclusion of a behavior pattern in *DSM-IV* are *distress* and *disability*. In addition to these two hallmarks, the current definition of mental disorder also posits "increased risk of suffering death, pain, disability, or an important loss of freedom" (American Psychiatric Association, 1994, p. xxi). By restricting mental disorder to those dysfunctions that primarily occur within the individual, these inclusion criteria attempt to differentiate mental disorder from social deviance.

To increase the cross-cultural applicability of *DSM-IV*, its authors have taken several new steps: (a) presentation of information in the text regarding cultural variations in the clinical manifestations of the disorders, (b) a description of 25 culture-bound syndromes in an appendix, and (c) an outline of cultural formulation for the evaluation of the individual's cultural context. More specifically, the cultural formulation was designed to provide a review of (a) the individual's cultural background, (b) cultural explanations of the individual's illness (e.g., cultural idioms of distress), (c) cultural factors related to the psychosocial environment and levels of functioning, (d) cultural elements of the relationship between the individual and the clinician, and (e) the overall cultural assessment necessary for diagnosis and care.

These modifications hold the promise of contributing toward a culturally more sensitive, reliable, and informative diagnosis of the individual. However, the cross-cultural applicability of *DSM-IV* remains to be tested (Thakker & Ward, 1998). In fact, both Kleinman (1988) and Rogler (1999), and many others, argue that standardization of categories is itself a form of "cultural suppression" because category contents are selected by rational decision to conform to the procedural norms of scientific and professional guidelines rather than the indigenous, local norms.

To remedy the situation, the journal *Culture, Medicine and Psychiatry* has initiated the "Clinical Cases Section" to provide a testing ground for the cultural formulation by emphasizing an ideographic assessment of the patient in his or her relevant sociocultural environment. Instead of relying exclusively on the fixed format of the *DSM-IV*, the journal encourages a narrative approach (Lewis-Fernandez, 1996). Narratives include (a) clinical case history, (b) cultural formulation, (c) cultural identity, (d) cultural explanation of the illness, (e) cultural factors related to psychosocial environment and levels of functioning, (f) cultural elements of the clinician-patient relationship, and (g) overall cultural assessment. Complete case analyses from African Americans, American Indians, Asian Americans, and Latinos are available and should benefit all clinicians who treat culturally diverse clients (Mezzich, Kleinman, Fabrega, & Parron, 1996).

Beyond the culture-specific critiques of *DSM-IV*, some generic diagnostic problems remain to be addressed (Tanaka-Matsumi & Draguns, 1997): (a) What are the defining criteria of normal and abnormal functioning of the individual in different cultural contexts? (b) How does the diagnostician recognize whether a behavior disorder is clinically significant within the unique cultural context of the individual? *DSM-IV* does not provide a generic set of decision rules to be applied across all of the diagnostic categories. Thus, the authors of *DSM-IV* explicitly recognize that cross-cultural diagnostic decisions will continue to be based on clinical judgment. *DSM-IV* may not, in fact, provide a universal diagnostic framework that may be used across diverse cultures. Everything known about the cross-cultural manifestation of most psychological disturbances strongly suggests not (Canino et al., 1997; Draguns, 1990).

In summary, the development of standardized diagnostic instruments has dramatically altered the nature of cross-cultural research by attempting to use the same criteria for case identification across cultures. I now review substantive findings of cross-cultural mental health research with a primary focus on schizophrenia, depression, and anxiety.

Substantive Findings on Major Disorders

Depression

Historically, themes of personal and communal loss, role disruption, and sudden changes in one's environment have been linked to states of dejection, anger, and even severe melancholia (Jackson, 1986). Yet, cultural studies of depressive experiences have been hampered by both conceptual and methodological differences among researchers (Fabrega, 1974; Marsella, 1980). The cross-cultural literature on depression has been noted for value-laden observations of colonial, ethnomedical investigators. For example, Carothers (1953) wrote that African natives did not have the capacity to feel depressed because the size of their frontal lobe was much smaller, hence inferior, to the Westerners.

During this time, cultures were identified in the literature with qualifiers such as simple and primitive. Prince (1968) then published a major review article on depressive syndromes in Africa and questioned if the sudden increase in the prevalence of depression in sub-Saharan Africa after the mid-1950s reflected a "fact or diagnostic fashion." The anthropologist Field (1960) issued a definitive statement, based on her fieldwork in rural Ghana with Ashanti women, that depression is actually common in Africa. Her fieldwork suggested that the Western biomedical model and its ethnocentric method would miss depressed Africans because the investigator is not informed of indigenous cultural practices of depressed roles. In the 1970s, several scholarly reviews of the literature on culture and depression were published (e.g., Fabrega, 1974; Singer, 1975).

Marsella (1980) integrated the literature on "depressive experience and disorder across cultures" and concluded that the problem is one of conceptualization. He further stated that, "There appears to be no universal conception of depression," (p. 274) and "Even among those cultures not having conceptually equivalent terms, it is sometimes possible to find variants of depressive disorders similar to those found in Western cultures" (p. 274). Although different cultures may have different words that describe subjective experiences of what is called depression in English, connotative meanings of these words can be widely different (Tanaka-Matsumi & Marsella, 1976).

In the ECA study, nearly 30% of the U.S. adults interviewed in the community reported experiencing dysphoria lasting at least 2 weeks at some point during their lifetime (Weissman, Bruce, Leaf, Florio, & Holzer, 1991). Women reported more of all symptoms than men did. Whites reported more dysphoria, sleep changes, fatigue, guilt, diminished concentration, and thoughts about death, whereas blacks reported more appetite change and psychomotor agitation or retardation relative to other ethnic groups

A number of international studies have published prevalence estimates of "major depression." Lifetime prevalence estimates using the DIS varied across studies, ranging from a low of 3.3% in Seoul, Korea, to a high of 12.6% in Christchurch, New Zealand (Hwu & Compton, 1994). However, even within the United States, the estimates of lifetime prevalence varied depending on the instrument used. For example, the ECA study estimated the lifetime prevalence of 5.8%, while the National Comorbidity Survey (Kessler et al., 1994) estimated it at 17.1%. These differences might be explained by methodological factors such as the specificity and sensitivity of the diagnostic instruments used and age compositions of the samples studied. Thus, a better research design is a simultaneous case finding and assessment using the same instrument with demonstrated reliability.

A prototypically etic study of depression is the international project of WHO (1983) on the diagnosis and classification of depression in Switzerland, Canada, Japan, and Iran. The goal was to test the feasibility of using standardized instruments. Patients ($N = 573$) were diagnosed using the Schedule for Standardized Assessment of Depressive Disorders (WHO/SADD) by project psychiatrists. The WHO/SADD examines 39 symptoms of depression. Its overall reliability was .96, with no specific item reliability falling below .90. WHO (1983) found that more than 76% of the depressed patients reported core depressive symptoms that included "sadness, joylessness, anxiety, tension, lack of energy, loss of interest, loss of ability to concentrate, and ideas of insufficiency" (p. 61). Suicidal ideation was present in 59% of patients. The WHO project also discovered cross-cultural variation in the expression of depression. Specifically, 40% of patients displayed "other symptoms," such as somatic complaints and obsessions, that were not part of the original 39 symptoms of depression measured by the WHO/SADD. Variations existed both within and across cultures. Marsella, Sartorius, Jablensky, and Fenton (1985) interpreted these findings as a strong demonstration of cultural factors.

The topic of guilt and depression has been subject to both theoretical and methodological inquires in cross-cultural research. In the WHO project, guilt was defined as "painful awareness of having committed offenses against one's moral code, or having failed to perform a duty or a task" (WHO, 1983, p. 137). It is important to note that guilt feelings were probed and elicited according to semistructured interviews and were not necessarily expressed spontaneously by patients. Specific probe questions included those regarding religious, social, and familial duties. It was observed by both H. B. M. Murphy (1982a) and Jackson (1986) that personal guilt is historically associated with the development of individualism in the Judeo-Christian tradition in the West. Reports from several East Asian and South Asian cultures converge in suggesting that guilt is differently experienced, conceptualized, and communicated in these settings than in the West (Kimura, 1967; Pfeiffer, 1994; Rao, 1973; Yap, 1971). According to Sow (1980), the rarity of spontaneous reports about guilt among African people is a consequence of the social orientation of self that is prone to attribute blame to "exogenous persecution," hence avoiding explanation through self-blame or guilt. Cross-cultural investigations should find variable content and expressions of guilt feelings since such complaints are readily influenced by the different conceptualization of self and value orientations according to locus of responsibility (H. B. M. Murphy, 1982a).

Both etic and emic studies of depression have succeeded in developing instruments to measure depression and its cultural equivalents. As a model of an emic study of depression, Manson, Shore, and Bloom's (1985) research on the development of the American Indian Depression Scale (AIDS) demonstrates the importance of using local words and concepts to describe depression. Through interviews with informants, the authors came up with five Hopi illness categories that are relevant to depression. The categories were translated as (a) worry sickness, (b) unhappiness, (c) heartbroken, (d) drunken-like craziness, and (e) disappointment. The AIDS included questions on the five indigenous categories of illness and the National Institute of Mental Health DIS (NIMH-DIS) items representing depression, alcohol abuse, and somatization. The AIDS was administered to the clinical index group and a matched community group of Hopis. The majority of subjects said that they could not find a single Hopi word equivalent to the term *depression*, even though all of them were familiar with the five Hopi illness categories. The various Hopi categories of illness were differently related to the major *DSM-III* criteria of depression. Unhappiness was most strongly associated with the *DSM-III* criterion of dysphoric mood. The indigenous category of heartbroken was more broadly marked by "weight loss, disrupted sleep, fatigue, psychomotor retardation and agitation, loss of libido, a sense of sinfulness, shame, not being likable, and trouble thinking clearly" (Manson et al. 1985, p. 350).

Epidemiological surveys indicate that the general population reports symptoms of depression rather frequently. The pioneering work by Brown and Harris (1978) on the "social origin" of depression among working class women in London found significant predictors of depression in a prospective study. The experience of loss of parent(s) early in life, not having someone to confide in, and husband's unemployment status were all risk factors for depression. Cronkite and Moos (1995) advocate that "the degree of social integration may have a direct relationship to mental health because it reflects the extent of one's engagement within the larger society" (p. 576). Low levels of social integration characterize people who are depressed or who have a recurrent course of depression. They further state that the behaviors and symptoms associated with depression may detract from the formation and maintenance of social ties and social integration. Conversely, strong social ties seen in collectivistic societies (e.g., Japan) may alleviate certain symptoms of depression (e.g., inability to make decisions) as compared to individualistic societies (e.g., Australia) (Radford, Nakane, Ohta, Mann, & Kalucy, 1991). In fact, social support and coping are postulated as protective factors against depression (Coyne & Downey, 1991; Cronkite & Moos, 1995). Cross-cultural research should therefore offer an excellent opportunity to test the social support and coping model of depression in individualistic versus collectivistic cultures.

Schizophrenia

Schizophrenia is a concept applied to a cluster of most socially debilitating symptoms involving disorders of thought, perception and attention, motor symptoms, and affective symptoms (Davison & Neale, 1998). Kraepelin's (1904) original concept, dementia praecox, literally meant early onset (praecox) and progressive intellectual deterioration (dementia). He focused on both course and symptoms of this disorder. Later, Bleuler (1902) coined the term *schizophrenia*. In contrast to Kraepelin, he believed that the disorder did not necessarily have an early onset, and that it did not follow a degenerative course requiring a lifetime institutionalization. With deinstitutionalization of psychiatric patients over the past 30 years, the assumption that individuals with schizophrenia will be found in treatment settings has become obsolete.

The ECA study (Keith, Regier, & Rae, 1991) has estimated a lifetime prevalence rate of 1.3% for schizophrenia in the general population in the United States, with the highest concentrations of schizophrenia among those 18–29 years old, which occurs without significant gender difference. The schizophrenic disorders are two to three times higher among those never married (2.1%) and divorced/separated (2.9%) groups than among those married (1.0%) or widowed (0.7%). More people diagnosed with schizophrenia are unemployed than are those without this diagnosis in the community. In the United States, schizophrenia is almost five times more common at the bottom of the socioeconomic ladder than at the top. As for race-ethnicity, the lifetime rate for Blacks (2.1%) is significantly higher than that found for both White/Anglo (1.4%) and Hispanic (0.8%) groups. However, when controlled for age, gender, marital status, and most importantly, socioeconomic status, the significant difference between Black and White prevalence rates disappears. The correlations between socioeconomic status and the diagnosis of schizophrenia are consistent, but their causal interpretations are difficult. Thus, both the sociogenic hypothesis and the social drift theory of schizophrenia offer plausible explanations (Davison & Neale, 1998).

In the cross-cultural domain, the idea of comparing traditional versus modern or developing versus developed societies has reached a high point with the WHO's (1973, 1979) International Pilot Study of Schizophrenia (IPSS). In the last 30 years at 20 research centers in 17 countries, WHO has conducted three major studies on the course and outcome of schizophrenia. Prominent features of the WHO schizophrenia program include (a) simultaneous case finding and data collection, (b) standardized instruments, (c) trained project psychiatrists, (d) the combined clinical and computer-based reference categorization of the case, and (e) multiple follow-up assessments (Jablensky, 1989).

In the IPSS (WHO, 1973), 1,202 patients were evaluated at nine centers in Africa (Nigeria), Asia (India, Taiwan), Europe (Czech Republic, Denmark, Russia, the United Kingdom), Latin America (Colombia), and North America (the United States). The purpose of the IPSS was to develop and test a standardized method of diagnosis using the Present State Examination (PSE; Wing, Cooper, & Sartorius, 1974). WHO (1973) reported universality in the core symptoms of schizophrenia. These symptoms included lack of insight, predelusional signs (such as delusional mood, ideas of reference, perplexity), flatness of affect, auditory hallucinations, and experiences of control.

In a 2-year follow-up study (WHO, 1979) that investigated the course and outcome of schizophrenia, project psychiatrists interviewed 75.6% of the patients. Across most centers, the subjects lacked positive psychotic symptoms such as delusions and hallucinations. However, they exhibited negative psychotic symptoms such as flatness of affect, lack of insight, and difficulties in cooperation. Acute undifferentiated and catatonic cases of schizophrenia were more prevalent in developing countries.

The prognosis for schizophrenia was made operational as the percentage of the follow-up period characterized by psychosis. Prognosis was better for patients in developing countries (Colombia, Nigeria, and India) than for those in developed countries (the United States, Great Britain, and Denmark). During the follow-up period, 48% of the subjects in Aarhus, Denmark; 47% in Washington, DC; and 36% in Prague, Czech Republic, were still psychotic more than 75% of the time. During this same period, only 7% and 19% of the subjects in Cali, Colombia, and Agra, India, respectively, were judged to be psychotic. Social isolation and unmarried status were associated with a poor outcome in both developed and developing countries (WHO, 1979). High educational status was predictive of chronicity in non-Western and developing countries, but not in the West. For example, in rural Agra, India, the outcome for schizophrenia was worse among the better educated. Warner (1994) explained that the educated men in the Third World are affected adversely by the greater labor market stresses. Although Jablensky (1989) concluded

that "schizophrenia is highly malleable by internalized or extrinsic environmental influences (or both)" (p. 521), the authors of the IPSS offered only tentative suggestions that better outcome may stem from the community support and family ties found in rural settings.

In a more ambitious project, WHO has also conducted a prospective epidemiological study to compare the true prevalence of schizophrenia across cultures (Jablensky et al., 1992). In this case-finding project, 1,379 subjects were evaluated at 12 centers in 10 countries: Aarhus, Denmark; Agra and Chandigarh, India; Cali, Colombia; Dublin, Ireland; Ibadan, Nigeria; Moscow, Russia; Nagasaki, Japan; Nottingham, England; Prague, Czech Republic; and Honolulu, Hawaii, and Rochester, New York in the United States. The project identified all individuals who contacted "helping agencies" for the first time over two consecutive years in specified geographical catchment areas. Identified persons were then screened for symptoms of a functional psychosis. The helping agencies included indigenous healers and religious institutions. The incidence rates were found to be comparable in developed and developing countries. However, more patients in the developing countries had an acute onset of schizophrenia.

The second purpose of the WHO case-finding study was to investigate the role of stressful life events occurring 2 to 3 weeks preceding the development of schizophrenic episodes (Day et al., 1987). Patients at six of the nine centers had a similar mean number of stressful life events, which were coded into five categories (personal, livelihood, family/household, social network, and additional). The subjects in the three remaining centers (Agra, Chandigarh, and Ibadan) reported lower rates of stressful events within these categories. These results suggest that specific events described by the subjects from developing countries may not be easily classified into predetermined categories.

Much literature exists on the association between stressful events and the onset of schizophrenic episodes. The focus of H. B. M. Murphy (1982b) was on faulty information processing as a risk factor for developing schizophrenia. Faulty information processing develops through "(1) mistraining in information processing, (2) the complexity of the information to which one is exposed, (3) the degree to which decisions are expected on the basis of complex or unclear information, and (4) the degree to which schizophrenia-bearing families are discouraged or encouraged to have children" (p. 223). It was proposed by H. B. M. Murphy that the noted high prevalence rate of schizophrenia among Irish Catholics and Irish immigrants in Canada was due to the complicated communication style of Irish people. It is of note, however, that Bateson's double-bind communication theory of schizophrenia has produced little empirical support in the research literature due to the difficulty of making the concept operational (Neale & Oltmanns, 1980).

Methodological critiques of the WHO schizophrenia project concern patient selection and differences in access to hospitals across countries. Cohen (1992) attributes the differences in prognosis to differing rates of hospital contact rather than to illness. In Cohen's view, the greater proportion of acute cases in developing countries merely reflects differing access to modern psychiatric centers. Waxler-Morrison (1992), however, found that differential access could not account for prognostic findings in her 5-year follow-up study of hospitalized schizophrenics in Sri Lanka. Other researchers (e.g., Hopper, 1992) have pointed to the standardized procedures and exhaustive follow-up evaluation of the patients in the WHO study as safeguards against contamination by artifacts. Jablensky and Sartorius (1988) concluded that "the position of cultural relativism vis-à-vis the identification of schizophrenia in different populations finds little support" (p. 68). Kleinman (1988), however, cautioned that the sample homogeneity based on the imposed case identification criteria eliminated those who do not fit the category criteria, thus the WHO project was designed to identify universality and systematically eliminate important cultural variations.

Cultural Interpretation
of Schizophrenia:
Research Questions

Empirical cross-cultural studies of schizophrenia suggest that the course of the disorder is highly variable depending on the social environment. In an attempt to account for the prognostic differences, K. Lin and Kleinman (1988) compared and contrasted Western and non-Western societies according to a number of factors, including family structure, social support, work environment, communication styles, and attribution of mental illness. These cultural explanations remain elusive since the contrasts in culture were not based on a priori, verifiable

hypotheses or ethnographic assessment of cultural differences.

Expressed emotion (EE) by the family of the schizophrenic patient has offered a promising lead into the prediction of relapse in the West (Leff & Vaughn, 1986). Using the Cumberwell Family Interview protocol, these researchers confirmed that the level of the relative's EE at the interview was the best predictor of the patient's symptomatic relapse in the 9 months following discharge from the hospital. Specifically, the best predictor was the number of critical remarks made about the schizophrenic patient by the relative when the relative was interviewed alone (Leff & Vaughn, 1986). The authors compared the Indian data from Chandigarh center and similar data collected in London, Los Angeles, and Pittsburgh in the WHO study. They identified large differences between the Chandigarh relatives and the Anglo Americans. The Indian relatives made a mean of 3.6 times less critical comments than the Los Angeles relatives of schizophrenic patients did.

One major concern of the EE measurement for cross-cultural research purposes is the cultural validity of using the frequency of negative verbal remarks as EE. Based on the cross-cultural research literature on emotion and its communication, cultures differ greatly in the perception and expression of negative emotions verbally or nonverbally (Matsumoto, Kudoh, Scherer, & Wallbott, 1988; Tanaka-Matsumi, 1995). Furthermore, Jenkins and Karno (1992) argue that the expressed emotion construct itself taps primarily into cross-culturally variable features of family response to an ill relative. Without probing into family communication style and the range of culturally relevant emotion vocabularies, we may not develop culturally valid hypotheses to explain course and outcome of schizophrenia.

Finally, Desjarlais et al. (1995) have advanced several important hypotheses about how social and cultural factors might contribute to a better course of schizophrenia. Among them, conceptions of the cause and course of schizophrenia held by the members of a social group should influence the course of illness. Internal versus external attribution of illness should also predict chronicity, such that attributing cause of illness to the self should lead to chronicity. When internal attribution is combined with the nuclear family environment in a highly competitive, technologically developed society, lack of firm support should also increase chronicity. In developed societies, iatro-

genic effects of institutional treatment may reinforce dependency of patients on the aide staff
and increase chronicity (Ullmann & Krasner,
1975).

Anxiety Disorders

A review of the literature on culture and anxiety
by E. Good and Kleinman (1985) stated that,
"Anxiety and disorders of anxiety are universally present in human societies" (p. 298). They
also cautioned that, "The phenomenology of
such disorders, the meaningful forms through
which distress is articulated and constituted as
social reality, varies in quite significant ways
across cultures" (p. 298). Ample evidence has
been provided by J. A. Russell (1991) and Mesquita and Frijda (1992) that categories and
meanings of emotions vary across cultures. Individualistic and collectivistic cultures should
differ in antecedents and consequences of specific emotions and in the specificity and quantity of direct communication (Triandis, 1994).
The languages of emotion words and their natural taxonomies are of enormous variety across
cultures (J. A. Russell, 1991). Barlow (1988) has
proposed a biopsychosocial model of anxiety
disorders with contributing factors of cue-pro-
voked physiological arousal, cognitive interpretation, and approach-avoidance coping behavior and its consequence.

It thus poses a major challenge for cross-
cultural researchers to investigate anxiety disorders, although probably nobody would disagree
that anxiety and fear are human universals. In
fact, the literature is in agreement that there is
great cross-cultural variability for ambulatory
anxiety disorders (Tanaka-Matsumi & Draguns,
1997). One question concerns which disorders
within this category deviate from the normative
behavior of the general population.

Hwu and Compton's (1994) comparison of
the major six major epidemiological surveys
suggests that the lifetime prevalence rates of the
DIS-derived specific anxiety disorders greatly
depend both on the disorder (e.g., generalized
anxiety disorder, panic disorder, etc.) and ethnic culture. The greatest prevalence ratios varied from a low of 2.9% for generalized anxiety
disorder to a high of 7.3% for panic disorder
when the DIS data were compared from Taiwan, Korea, the United States, Canada, New
Zealand, and Puerto Rico. These data clearly
indicate that cultures define different thresholds for symptoms of anxiety disorders. Only
a few studies, however, have included both

normal and clinical samples in research studies
on anxiety disorders.

Tseng et al. (1990) investigated the symptomatology of patients with "neuroses, situational adjustment reaction or acute emotional
reaction" (p. 252) at five research centers in
Asia. The sites included Ching-Mai, Thailand;
Bali, Indonesia; Kao-Hsiung, Taiwan; Shanghai, China; and Tokyo, Japan. The study assessed the similarities and differences between
normal and clinical populations within the
same culture and then compared data across
cultures. Symptom profiles of the patients in
each city deviated from the profiles of the normal subjects toward exaggeration. In addition,
there was cross-cultural variability across the
five centers, together with a greater similarity
between the Taiwan and mainland China groups
than between any other centers.

Differences in diagnostic practices account
in part for cross-cultural differences in reported
symptoms of neurosis. Tseng, Xu, Ebata, Hsu,
and Cui (1986) had psychiatrists in Beijing,
Tokyo, and Honolulu diagnose six videotaped
Chinese patients undergoing a mental status
examination. Psychiatrists from Beijing diagnosed the patients with neurasthenia when
their colleagues in Tokyo and Honolulu diagnosed them with adjustment reactions. Tseng,
Asai, Kitanishi, McLaughlin, and Kyomen (1992)
also compared diagnostic judgments of Japanese psychiatrists in Tokyo and American psychiatrists in Honolulu. Patients with the project
diagnosis of social phobia were presented on
videotape. The diagnostic agreement of the Japanese psychiatrists was greater than that of the
American psychiatrists for the Japanese cases of
social phobia (*taijin kyofusho*). The agreement
rate of the Japanese psychiatrists for the two
American cases was only 6.5%. Tseng's two
international studies demonstrate that diagnostic practices contribute to cross-cultural variability in observed symptoms. For this reason,
researchers endorse the use of a standardized
diagnostic system to control for differences in
diagnostic practice.

To the extent that anxiety disorders reflect
an exaggeration of a culture's baseline (Draguns, 1980; Lambert et al., 1992; Tseng & Hsu,
1980), standardization of diagnostic criteria
may miss culturally unique deviations and
meanings ascribed to the subjective experiences of anxiety and fear in cultural contexts.
Culture-bound disorders such as taijin kyofusho in Japan (J. G. Russell, 1989; Tanaka-Matsumi, 1979), and *koro* (Tseng, Mo, et al., 1992)

in Southern China and Southeast Asia demonstrate the importance of assessing the cultural values of specific symptoms and cultural responses to the individuals exhibiting these anxiety-based disorders. Similarly, the cultural idiom of distress, *attaque de nervios*, in Latin American populations (Guarnaccia, Rivera, Franco, & Neighbors, 1996), is reported to occur in culturally stressful and familiar settings such as during a funeral or at the scene of an accident. As Kirmayer (1991) stated, "Cultural beliefs or rules and patterns of interaction are constitutive of the disorder. . . . There is no way to intelligibly describe the problem without invoking cultural particulars" (p. 26).

Cultural Idioms of Distress: Indigenous Models of Psychopathology

The development of "indigenous psychologies" has contributed to a diversity of views, particularly from Third World countries, and has infused the emic approach with new vitality (Sinha, 1997). Indigenous views and concepts of distress are considered fundamental to understanding the cultural context of illness behaviors (Kirmayer, 1984). Investigators of the emic orientation have studied psychopathology in relation to the sociocultural context (B. J. Good, 1992; Jenkins, 1994; Kleinman, 1980, 1986; Marsella & White, 1982). These researchers seek to investigate (a) the meanings of indigenous idioms of distress (Nichter, 1981); (b) culture-specific classifications of disorders; (c) the role of culture in identifying and shaping the form and meaning of antecedent risk factors; and (d) attributions for consequences of illness (Marsella & Dash-Scheur, 1988; M. G. Weiss & Kleinman, 1988).

The Explanatory Model Interview Catalogue

As an alternative to standardized diagnostic assessment, the Explanatory Model Interview Catalogue (EMIC) was designed by M. G. Weiss et al. (1992) to identify culture-specific idioms of distress, perceived causes of illness, and help-seeking behavior. The EMIC refers to a framework for semistructured interviews to gather data, and it was originally used in a cultural study of leprosy and mental health in India. Reported interrater agreement of the EMIC items using kappa ranged from .62 to .90. Five areas of inquiry for EMIC interviews were de-

scribed by M. G. Weiss et al. (1992): (a) patterns of distress, (b) perceived causes, (c) help seeking and treatment, (d) general illness beliefs, and (e) disease-specific queries. These large domains are questioned using a semistructured interview format based on (a) empowering introduction, (b) open-ended queries, (c) screening queries focused on categories of interest, (d) summary judgment comparing multiple responses, and (e) prose elaboration. In 1997, M. Weiss identified 21 research studies that used the EMIC explanatory model interviews to investigate various disorders, such as leprosy, depression, ataque de nervios, alcohol abuse and dependence, depression and somatoform disorders, and neurasthenia and chronic fatigue syndrome, in various parts of the world.

To illustrate, Guarnaccia et al. (1996) analyzed narrative accounts of the most recent ataques de nervios of 145 Puerto Ricans. Symptoms of nervios include trembling, headaches, sleeping disorder, dizziness, stomach ailments, and dysphoric emotions (fear, worry, anxiety, and rage). The lifetime prevalence of ataques de nervios in Puerto Rico was 16%, making it the second most prevalent psychiatric disorder after generalized anxiety disorder (18%). The data were coded according to several themes, including the core feature, social contexts, emotional experiences, symptoms, and action tendencies, among others. Together, these domains of narrative data help illuminate the "particular and full constellation of experiences" (Guarnaccia et al., 1996) of ataques de nervios frequently reported by community residents in Puerto Rico.

The EMIC project is a work in progress (M. Weiss, 1997) and holds the promise of developing comparable explanatory model interviews across cultures. Culture-specific data generated by the EMIC may also contribute to identifying universals in contextual factors associated with major disorders.

Somatization, Neurasthenia, and Depression

Somatization is a common problem across cultures and is associated with significant health problems, including chronic disease, anxiety disorders, depression, and occupational or social disability. The question concerns the cultural meaning of somatic complaints (Tung, 1994). As White (1982), Kirmayer (1984), and Kleinman (1986) point out, it may be ethnocentric to view bodily complaints as the simple result of a lack of "psychological mindedness"

(Draguns, 1996). Different cultures may selectively encourage or discourage the reporting of psychological or physiological components of the stress response. The focus on psychologization versus somatization has been particularly salient in the literature on Chinese mental health (Cheung, 1989; Draguns, 1996; Lam, 1999; T. Y. Lin, 1989; Seiden, 1999).

Neurasthenia is a very common diagnosis in China. In China, neurasthenia is called *shenjing shuairuo*, literally meaning neurological weakness. Symptoms of neurasthenia include bodily weakness, fatigue, tiredness, headaches, dizziness, and a range of gastrointestinal and other complaints (Kleinman & Kleinman, 1985). Kleinman (1982), with the assistance of a Chinese psychiatrist, interviewed 100 Chinese patients with the diagnosis of shenjing shuairuo. He used the Chinese language version of the Schedule of Affective Disorders and Schizophrenia (SADS) modified to yield *DSM-III* diagnoses. Kleinman reported that 93 neurasthenic patients met the criteria for depressive disorder, of whom 87 patients met the criteria for major depressive disorder. "Depressed" patients spontaneously complained of headaches (90%), insomnia (78%), dizziness (73%), pain (48%), and loss of or poor memory (43%), among other things. However, when Kleinman specifically asked the patients about psychological and affective symptoms, they acknowledged dysphoric mood (100%), trouble concentrating (84%), anhedonia (61%), hopelessness (50%), and low self-esteem (60%). In Shanghai, Zhang (1989) demonstrated that the primary "Western" diagnostic status of Chinese-diagnosed neurasthenia (shenjing shuairuo) varies between depressive and anxiety disorders, depending on the particular Western-derived standardized instruments employed.

In a more recent survey, S. Lee and Wong (1995) determined that the most common perceived symptoms of shenjing shuairuo among undergraduate students in Hong Kong were anxiety, insomnia, depression, fright, and inability to concentrate. They presented a psychological construal of shenjing shuairuo in contrast to the more somatic orientation portrayed in the literature. According to the authors, Chinese culture itself has undergone changes in Hong Kong toward a more Westernized and urban lifestyle among young people. Thus, the contextual meaning of this popular folk illness category has come to assume a more psychological meaning in recent years.

From an emic standpoint, the discrepancy between spontaneous expression of somatic complaints and elicited symptoms (e.g., dysphoria) suggests that cultural meanings of symptoms are altered by interpretations based on Western-derived standardized instruments and imposed criteria. Elicited symptoms may not conform to culturally accepted ways of expressing distress. Somatic complaints are less stigmatized among Chinese, and somatization justifies an acceptable medical intervention. Chinese in Hong Kong, Taiwan, and China do not readily recognize psychological symptoms as problems that justify seeking help in a medical setting (Cheung, 1989). The setting (e.g., general medical versus psychiatric clinic) and problem conceptualization influence reasons given for help-seeking behavior and reported symptoms.

Using functional assessment, Seiden (1999) has demonstrated the reliability of cross-cultural behavioral case formulation of Chinese neurasthenia. He presented Chinese-American and European-American clinicians with videotaped behavioral interviews conducted by a Chinese behavior therapist. Patients were four Chinese-American immigrants with symptoms of neurasthenia. On the basis of the video material, each clinician made functional assessment decisions for one of the four videotaped patients (e.g., regarding problems, their antecedents and consequences, and suggested treatments). Clinical decision content demonstrated majority consensus both within and between clinician cultures on specific cross-culturally validated categories.

In Seiden's (1999) study, the two clinician groups also demonstrated expected cross-cultural differences in their clinical decisions. For example, proportionally more Chinese American than European American clinicians targeted problems involving somatization (e.g., somatization of emotional problems), whereas proportionally more European American than Chinese American clinicians targeted cognitive problems (e.g., intrusive thoughts about adjustment to the United States). In addition, proportionally more Chinese American than European American clinicians targeted stress-related antecedents (e.g., stress at work) and social environmental consequences (e.g., extra attention from family members and relief from household responsibilities) as being functionally related to the patients' problems. Although each of the four patients experienced the somatic symptoms associated with neurasthenia, the content of agreed-upon intervention targets and treatments varied from patient to patient. This indicated that neurasthenia is not a unitary phenomenon and highlighted the usefulness of functional assessment in generating context-rich data necessary for individualized treatment planning.

Cultural Relocation, Acculturation, and Psychopathology

With an upsurge in migration around the world, there has been an increased interest in the mental health status of migrants. *World Mental Health* (Desjarlais et al., 1995) offers a serious, data-based overview of the mental health situation in the Third World. The authors regard poverty, social disorganization, inequity, and repression as the main sources of mental health problems and contend that the successful service programs take into consideration cultural traditions and resources, especially support systems. A "call to action" and research agenda presented in *World Mental Health* underscore the need for a unifying conceptual scheme that can accommodate a complex set of variables deemed relevant to assess cross-cultural transitions and adjustment.

Adaptation problems develop through the interactive effects of many factors, including the conditions in the host culture, upbringing in the country of origin, and the experience of voluntary migration versus forced migration (Berry & Kim, 1988; Ward & Kennedy, 1994). Berry and Sam (1997) present conceptual frameworks for acculturation and mental health according to integration, assimilation, separation, and marginalization modes applied to the predicament of the acculturating individual. There are differences in the preferred mode of acculturation and in associated mental health problems. Berry, Kim, Minde, and Mok (1987) studied a total of 1,197 acculturating individuals in Canada (native peoples, refugees, sojourners, immigrants, and ethnic groups) during the 1969–1979 period. Native peoples of Canada and refugees scored the highest on the acculturative stress measure, while the immigrants reported the least amount of stress. Education was a consistent predictor of low stress. Moyerman and Forman's (1992) metanalytic study of acculturation and adjustment based on 49 re-

ports found that lower socioeconomic status was associated with acculturative stress.

Liebkind (1996) tested Berry's model of migration contingencies and acculturative stress for the two-generation sample of young Vietnamese refugees, their parents, and caregivers in Finland. The model assessed four classes of predictor variables on the Indochinese versions of the Hopkins Symptom Checklist. The four classes of predictor variables were (a) the premigration experiences, (b) ethnic composition of the community, (c) postmigration acculturative experiences, and (d) acculturation attitudes and degree of acculturation. The results presented a complex and differential outcome, depending on the gender and generation. Different significant predictors emerged in separate regression analyses for the four groups of subjects (males, females, boys, and girls). Premigration traumatic experiences predicted the frequency of anxiety symptoms of the adult females, but the effects disappeared with positive acculturation attitudes. For the girls, the presence of coethnics in the community was a most significant negative predictor of anxiety symptoms. For the boys, adherence to the traditional Vietnamese family values was a negative predictor of anxiety symptoms, while the premigration traumatic experience was a significant positive predictor. For the men, the postmigration acculturative experiences of length of time in Finland and the experience of prejudice and discrimination predicted their anxiety scores. The result demonstrated that the postmigration factors exerted more impact on stress symptoms than the premigration traumatic experiences. The study confirmed the importance of assessing the conflicts of particular cultural values in the acculturation process (Liebkind, 1996; Szapocznik & Kurtines, 1993).

Ward and Kennedy (1994) distinguished psychological and sociocultural adjustment during cross-cultural transitions. Ward and Rana-Deuba (1999) found empirical support for differential predictions of these two types of adjustment over time as a function of Berry's four acculturation modes (integration, separation, marginalization, and assimilation) and the two basic dimensions of acculturation (host and conational identification). Conceptual integration of acculturation models and efforts to develop effective measures of acculturation, therefore, have produced empirical results that could be used to develop programs to assist those undergoing or expecting cross-cultural transitions.

Conclusions and Future Directions for Research

Culture exerts a major influence on the identification, labeling, course, and outcome of maladaptive behaviors. Culture provides context for abnormal behaviors. Kraepelin's question posed at the turn of the 20th century regarding universality of major categories of psychiatric disorders and interpretation of cultural differences in their symptoms has generated heated conceptual debates and theory-guided methods of investigation. The field of culture and psychopathology is now characterized by methodologically sophisticated research, which has increasingly incorporated culture-oriented anthropological and ethnographic information. Throughout this chapter, I have reviewed both conceptual and methodological developments in cross-cultural research on culture and psychopathology and have presented research questions and hypotheses. I now focus more specifically on future directions for culturally informed research.

Culturally Informed Research

The following seven questions are relevant when we study culture and psychopathology:

1. What is the phenomenon under investigation (e.g., depression) and how is it defined by the profession and by the indigenous culture?
2. What words and concepts are used to describe the phenomenon?
3. Are different words and concepts equivalent?
4. What aspects are known to be culturally similar and variable?
5. What would account for cultural similarities and differences?
6. How does one communicate different types of distress to others in the same culture?7. What are the implications of universality and cultural relativity for the theory of psychopathology?

The investigator asking these questions would refrain from imposing diagnostic categories and criteria developed in one culture on another. These questions immediately call for testing and establishing the cultural validity of diagnostic categories and their criteria. In the last three decades, the field has produced reliable assessment instruments for various psychopathologies; however, reliability per se does not guarantee cultural validity. Therefore, more active research efforts will be directed toward culturally adapting various instruments to establish equivalence across cultures (Geisinger, 1994; Lam, 1999). The literature on cross-cultural measurement describes empirical means of establishing cross-cultural normative assessment, including translation and adaptation concerns (Church & Lonner, 1998). These strict guidelines should be encouraged in cross-cultural psychopathology (Lam, 1999).

I also expect the development of more emically derived measures. Contextual approaches to diagnostic assessment such as the EMIC framework (M. Weiss, 1997) will generate culturally informed data. For example, although the *DSM-IV* lists culture-bound disorders, we are yet to identify functional relationships between culture-relevant antecedents and consequences for adopting those cultural roles described in ethnographic accounts. The cultural formulation proposed in *DSM-IV* also serves as an initial step for collecting culture-relevant data for all disorders.

Explanation of Culture

A combined etic-emic approach will gain more acceptances. Based on the present literature review, I expect that culturally informed researchers will incorporate the following four concepts more actively in future research: (a) self-orientation, (b) values, (c) family structure and social support, and (d) individualism and collectivism orientations. Although these concepts have been the direct targets of productive, empirical investigations in cross-cultural and cultural psychology (Lonner & Adamopoulos, 1997), they have not been systematically adopted in the design of studies concerning culture and psychopathology. In other words, psychopathology outcomes have been compared across nations (as in WHO projects on schizophrenia or depression) or racial and ethnic groups (as in the ECA study), but cultural-contextual factors frequently have not been compared empirically. Throughout this chapter, I have called attention to self-orientation, family structure, individualism-collectivism dimensions, and values as possible explanatory factors for similarities and differences in abnormal behavior across cultures. The field needs to conduct a more rigorous, a priori assessment of these important cultural variables. I am suggesting that empirical measures of "culture" be included in cross-cultural psychopathology.

Finally, application of culturally sensitive and valid assessment of psychopathology will produce important literature on the prevention and treatment of various disorders; this literature will be tailored to meet the needs of members of specific ethnic and cultural groups (Sue, 1998; Tanaka-Matsumi, Seiden, & Lam, 2001). The field of cross-cultural psychopathology is in great need of empirical research that evaluates the utility of culture-accommodating assessment and treatment practices.

References

Adebimpe, V. R. (1981). Overview: White norms and psychiatric diagnosis of black patients. *American Journal of Psychiatry, 138*, 279–285.

Al-Issa, I. (1995). Culture and mental illness in international perspective. In I. Al-Issa (Ed.), *Handbook of culture and mental illness: An international perspective* (pp. 3–49). Madison, CT: International Universities Press.

American Psychiatric Association. (1980). *Diagnostic and statistical manual of mental disorders* (3rd ed.). Washington, DC: Author.

American Psychiatric Association. (1987). *Diagnostic and statistical manual of mental disorders* (3rd ed., rev.). Washington, DC: Author.

American Psychiatric Association. (1994). *Diagnostic and statistical manual of mental disorders* (4th ed.). Washington, DC: Author.

Barlow, D. H. (1988). *Anxiety and its disorders: The nature and treatment of anxiety and panic.* New York: Guilford.

Benedict, R. (1934). Culture and the abnormal. *Journal of Genetic Psychology, 1*, 60–64.

Bennett, L. A., Janca, A., Grant, B. F., & Sartorius, N. (1993). Boundaries between normal and pathological drinking. *Alcohol, Health and Research World, 17*, 190–195.

Berry, J. W. (1969). On cross-cultural comparability. *International Journal of Psychology, 4*, 119–128.

Berry, J. W., & Kim, U. (1988). Acculturation and mental health. In P. Dasen, J. W. Berry, & N. Sartorius (Eds.), *Health and cross-cultural psychology: Towards applications* (pp. 207–236). Newbury Park, CA: Sage.

Berry, J. W., Kim, U., Minde, T., & Mok, D. (1987). Comparative studies of acculturative stress. *International Migration Review, 11*, 491–510.

Berry, J. W., Poortinga, Y. H., Segall, M. H., & Dasen, P. J. (1992). *Cross-cultural psychology: Research and applications.* Cambridge: Cambridge University Press.

Berry, J. W., & Sam, D. (1997). Acculturation and adaptation. In J. W. Berry, M. H. Segall, & C. Kagitcibasi (Eds.), *Handbook of cross-cultural psychology: Vol. 3. Social behavior*

and applications (pp. 291–326). Boston: Allyn & Bacon.

Betancourt, H., & López, S. R. (1993). The study of culture, ethnicity and race in American psychology. *American Psychologist, 48*, 629–637.

Bland, R. C., Newman, S. C., & Orn, H. (1988). Epidemiology of psychiatric disorders in Edmonton. *Acta Psychiatrica Scandinavica, 77*(Suppl. 338), 1–80.

Bleuler, E. (1902). Dementia praecox. *Journal of Mental Pathology, 3*, 479–498.

Brislin, R. W. (1983). Cross-cultural research in psychology. *Annual Review of Psychology, 34*, 363–400.

Brody, E. B. (1967). Transcultural psychiatry, human similarities and socio-economic evolution. *American Journal of Psychiatry, 124*, 616–622.

Brown, G. W., & Harris, T. O. (1978). *Social origins of depression: A study of psychiatric disorders in women.* London: Tavistock.

Burman, M. A., Karno, R. L., Hough, J. I., Escobar, J. I., & Forsythe, A. B. (1983). The Spanish Diagnostic Interview Schedule. *Archives of General Psychiatry, 40*, 1189–1196.

Canino, G. J., Bird, H. R., Shrout, P. E., Rubio-Stipec, M., Bravo, M., Martinez, R., Sesman, M., & Guevara, L. M. (1987). The prevalence of specific psychiatric disorders in Puerto Rico. *Archives of General Psychiatry, 44*, 727–735.

Canino, G., Lewis-Fernandez, R., & Bravo, M. (1997). Methodological challenges in cross-cultural mental health research. *Transcultural Psychiatry, 34*, 163–184.

Carothers, J. C. (1953). *The African mind in health and disease* (Monograph No. 17). Geneva: World Health Organization.

Cheung, F. M. C. (1989). The indigenization of neurasthenia in Hong Kong. *Culture, Medicine and Psychiatry, 13*, 227–241.

Church, A. T., & Lonner, W. J. (1998). The cross-cultural perspective in the study of personality: Rationale and current research. *Journal of Cross-Cultural Psychology, 29*, 32–62.

Cohen, A. (1992). Prognosis for schizophrenia in the Third World: A reevaluation of cross-cultural research. *Culture, Medicine and Psychiatry, 16*, 53–75.

Cooper, J. E., Kendell, R. E., Gurland, B. J., Sharpe, L., Copeland, J. R. M., & Simon, R. (1972). *Psychiatric diagnosis in New York and London.* London: Oxford University Press.

Coyne, J. C., & Downey, G. (1991). Social factors and psychopathology. *Annual Review of Psychology, 42*, 401–425.

Cronkite, R. C., & Moos, R. H. (1995). Life context, coping processes, and depression. In E. E. Beckman & W. R. Leber (Eds.), *Handbook of depression* (2nd ed., pp. 569–590). New York: Guilford.

Davison, G. C., & Neale, J. M. (1998). *Abnormal psychology. An experimental clinical approach* (7th ed.). New York: Wiley.

Day, R., Nielsen, J. A., Korten, A., Ernberg, G., Dube, K. C., Gebhart, J., Jablensky, A., Leon, C., Marsella, A. J., Olatawura, M., Sartorius, N., Stromgren, E., Takahashi, R., Wig, N., & Wynne, L. C. (1987). Stressful life events preceding the acute onset of schizophrenia: A cross-national study from the World Health Organization. *Culture, Medicine and Psychiatry, 11*, 123–205.

Desjarlais, R., Eisenberg, L., Good, B., & Kleinman, A. (1995). *World mental health: Problems and priorities in low-income countries*. New York: Oxford University Press.

Devereux, G. (1961). *Mohave ethnopsychiatry and suicide: The psychiatric knowledge and the psychic disturbances of an Indian tribe* (No. 1975). Washington, DC: Smithsonian Institution, Bureau of American Ethnology.

Draguns, J. G. (1973). Comparisons of psychopathology across cultures: Issues, findings, directions. *Journal of Cross-Cultural Psychology, 4*, 9–47.

Draguns. J. G. (1980). Psychological disorders of clinical severity. In H. C. Triandis & J. G. Draguns (Eds.), *Handbook of cross-cultural psychology: Vol. 6. Psychopathology* (pp. 99–174). Boston: Allyn and Bacon.

Draguns, J. G. (1990). Normal and abnormal behavior in cross-cultural perspective: Specifying the nature of their relationship. In J. J. Berman (Ed.), *Nebraska Symposium on Motivation, 1989: Vol. 37. Cross-cultural perspectives* (pp. 235–278). Lincoln: University of Nebraska Press.

Draguns, J. G. (1996). Abnormal behavior in Chinese societies: Clinical, epidemiological, and comparative studies. In M. Bond (Ed.), *Handbook of psychology of the Chinese people* (pp. 395–411). Hong Kong: Oxford University Press.

Fabrega, H. (1974). Problems implicit in the cultural and social study of depression. *Psychosomatic Medicine, 36*, 377–398.

Fabrega, H. (1987). Psychiatric diagnosis: A cultural perspective. *Journal of Nervous and Mental Disease, 175*, 383–394.

Field, M. (1960). *Search for security: An ethnopsychiatric study of rural Ghana*. Evanston, IL: Northwestern University Press.

Foucault, M. (1965). *Madness and civilization: A history of insanity in the age of reason*. New York: Pergamon.

Geisinger, K. F. (1994). Cross-cultural normative assessment: Translation and adaptation issues influencing normative interpretation of assessment instruments. *Psychological Assessment, 6*, 304–312.

Goffman, E. (1961). *Asylums*. Chicago: Aldine.

Golding, J. M., Karno, M., & Rutter, C. M. (1990). Symptoms of major depression among Mexican-American and non-Hispanic whites. *American Journal of Psychiatry, 147*, 861–866.

Good, B., & Kleinman, A. (1985). Culture and anxiety: Cross-cultural evidence for the patterning of anxiety disorders. In A. H. Tuma & J. D. Maser (Eds.), *Anxiety and anxiety disorders* (pp. 297–324). Hillsdale, NJ: Erlbaum

Good, B. J. (1992). Culture and psychopathology: Directions for psychiatric anthropology. In T. Schwartz, G. M. White, & C. A. Lutz (Eds.), *New directions in psychological anthropology* (pp. 181–205). Cambridge: Cambridge University Press.

Guarnaccia, P. J., Rivera, M., Franco, F., & Neighbors, C. (1996). The experiences of *ataques de nervios*: Towards an anthropology of emotions in Puerto Rico. *Culture, Medicine and Psychiatry, 20*, 343–367.

Helzer, J. E., & Canino, G. J. (1992). Comparative analysis of alcoholism in 10 cultural regions. In J. E. Helzer & G. J. Canino (Eds.), *Alcoholism in North America, Europe, and Asia* (pp. 289–308). New York: Oxford University Press.

Hopper, K. (1992). Cervantes' puzzle: A commentary on Alex Cohen's "Prognosis for schizophrenia in the Third World: A reevaluation of cross-cultural research." *Culture, Medicine and Psychiatry, 16*, 89–100.

Hwu, H. G., & Compton, W. M. (1994). Comparison of major epidemiological surveys using the diagnostic interview schedule. *International Review of Psychiatry, 6*, 309–327.

Hwu, H. G., Yeh, E. K., & Chang, L. Y. (1989). Prevalence of psychiatric disorders in Taiwan defined by the Chinese diagnostic interview schedule. *Acta Psychiatrica Scandinavica, 79*, 136–174.

Jablensky, A. (1989). Epidemiology and cross-cultural aspects of schizophrenia. *Psychiatric Annals, 19*, 516–524.

Jablensky, A., & Sartorius, N. (1988). Is schizophrenia universal? *Acta Psychiatrica Scandinavica, 78*, 65–70.

Jablensky, A., Sartorius, N., Ernberg, G., Anker, M., Korten, A., Cooper, J. E., Day, R., & Bertelsen, A. (1992). *Schizophrenia: Manifestations, incidence, and course in different cultures: A World Health Organization 10 Country Study* (Psychological Medicine Monograph Supplement 20). Cambridge: Cambridge University Press.

Jackson, S. W. (1986). *Melancholia and depression*. New Haven, CT: Yale University Press.

Jenkins, J. H. (1994). Culture, emotion, and psychopathology. In S. Kitayama & H. R. Markus (Eds.), *Emotion and culture: Empirical studies of mutual influence* (pp. 307–338). Washington, DC: American Psychological Association.

Jenkins, J. H., & Karno, M. (1992). The meaning of expressed emotion: theoretical issues raised by cross-cultural research. *American Journal of Psychiatry, 149*, 9–21.

Karno, M., Hough, R. L., Burman, A., Escobar, J. I., Timbers, D. M., Santana, F., & Boyd, J. H. (1987). Lifetime prevalence of specific psychiatric disorders among Mexican Americans and non-Hispanic whites in Los Angeles. *Archives of General Psychiatry, 44*, 695–701.

Keith, S. J., Regier, D. A., & Rae, D. S. (1991). Schizophrenic disorders. In L. N. Robins & D. A. Regier (Eds.), *Psychiatric disorders in America: The Epidemiologic Catchment Area Study*. New York: Free Press.

Kessler, R. C., McGonagle, K. A., Zhao, S., Nelson, C. B., Hughes, M., Eshleman, S., Wittchen, H. U., & Kendler, K. S. (1994). Lifetime and 12-month prevalence of *DSM-III-R* psychiatric disorders in the United States: Results from the National Comorbidity Survey. *Archives of General Psychiatry, 51*, 8–19.

Kiev, A. (1972). *Transcultural psychiatry*. New York: Free Press.

Kimura, B. (1967). Phänomenologie des Schulderlebnisses in einer vergleichenden psychiatrischen Sicht. In N. Petriolowitsch (Ed.), *Beiträge zue vergleichenden Psychiatrie* (Vol. 11, pp. 54–83). Basel: Karger.

Kirmayer, L. J. (1984). Culture, affect, and somatization: Parts 1 and 2. *Transcultural Psychiatric Research Review, 21*, 159–262, 237–262.

Kirmayer, L. J. (1991). The place of culture in psychiatric nosology: Taijin Kyofusho and *DSM-III-R*. *Journal of Nervous and Mental Disorder, 179*, 19–28.

Kleinman, A. (1977). Depression, somatization, and the "New Cross-Cultural Psychiatry." *Social Science and Medicine, 11*, 3–9.

Kleinman, A. (1978). Clinical relevance of anthropological and cross-cultural research: Concepts and strategies. *American Journal of Psychiatry, 135*, 427–431.

Kleinman, A. (1980). *Patients and healers in the context of culture*. Berkeley: University of California Press.

Kleinman, A. (1982). Neurasthenia and depression: A study of somatization and culture in China. *Culture, Medicine, and Psychiatry, 6*, 117–189.

Kleinman, A. (1986). *Social origins of distress and disease: Depression, neurasthenia, and pain in modern China*. New Haven, CT: Yale University Press.

Kleinman, A. (1988). *Rethinking psychiatry: From cultural category to personal experience*. New York: Free Press.

Kleinman, A., & Good, B. (Eds.). (1985). *Culture and depression: Studies in the anthropology and cross-cultural psychiatry of affect and disorder*. Berkeley: University of California Press.

Kleinman, A., & Kleinman, J. (1985). Somatization: The interconnections in Chinese society among culture, depressive experiences, and the meaning of pain. In A. Kleinman & B. Good (Eds.), *Culture and depression* (pp. 429–490). Berkeley: University of California Press.

Kraepelin, E. (1904). *Vergleichende Psychiatrie. Zentralblatt für Nervenheilkunde und Psychiatrie, 15*, 433–437.

Lam, K. (1999). *An etic-emic approach to validation of the Chinese version of the Children's Depression Inventory*. Unpublished doctoral dissertation, Hofstra University, Hempstead, NY.

Lambert, M. C., Weisz, J. R., Knight, F., Desrosiers, M. F., Overly, K., & Thesiger, C. (1992). Jamaican and American adult perspectives on child psychopathology: Further exploration of the threshold model. *Journal of Consulting and Clinical Psychology, 60*, 146–149.

Lee, C. K., Kwak, Y. S., Yamamoto, J., Rhee, H., Kim, Y. S., Han, J. H., Choi, J. K., & Lee, Y. H. (1990). Psychiatric epidemiology in Korea. Part I: Gender and age differences in Seoul. *Journal of Nervous and Mental Disease, 178*, 242–246.

Lee, S., & Wong, K. C. (1995). Rethinking neurasthenia: The illness concepts of shenjing shuairuo among Chinese undergraduates in Hong Kong. *Culture, Medicine and Psychiatry, 19*, 91–111.

Leff, J. (1988). *Psychiatry around the globe: A transcultural view*. London: Gaskell.

Leff, J., & Vaughn, C. (1986). *Expressed emotion in families: Its significance for mental illness*. New York: London.

Lewis-Fernandez, R. (1996). Cultural formulation of psychiatric diagnosis. *Culture, Medicine and Psychiatry, 20*, 133–144.

Liebkind, K. A. (1996). Acculturation and stress. Vietnamese refugees in Finland. *Journal of Cross-Cultural Psychology, 27*, 161–180.

Lin, K., & Kleinman, A. (1988). Psychopathology and clinical course of schizophrenia: A cross-cultural perspective. *Schizophrenia Bulletin, 14*, 555–567.

Lin, T. Y. (1953). A study of the incidence of mental disorders in Chinese and other cultures. *Psychiatry, 16*, 313–336.

Lin, T. Y. (1989). Neurasthenia revisited: Its place in modern psychiatry. *Culture, Medicine and Psychiatry, 13*, 105–129.

Littlewood, R. (1990). From categories to contexts: A decade of the new cross-cultural psychiatry. *British Journal of Psychiatry, 156,* 308–327.

Lonner, W. J., & Adamopoulos, J. (1997). Culture as antecedent to behavior. In J. W. Berry, Y. H. Poortinga, & J. Pandey (Eds.), *Handbook of cross-cultural psychology: Vol. 1. Theory and method* (pp. 43–84). Boston: Allyn & Bacon

López, S. R. (1989). Patient variable biases in clinical judgment: Conceptual overview and methodological considerations. *Psychological Bulletin, 106,* 184–204.

Manson, S. M., Shore, J. H., & Bloom, J. D. (1985). The depressive experience in American Indian communities: A challenge for psychiatric theory and diagnosis. In A. Kleinman & B. Good (Eds.), *Culture and depression* (pp. 331–368). Berkeley: University of California Press.

Marsella, A. J. (1980). Depressive experience and disorder across cultures. In H. C. Triandis & J. G. Draguns (Eds.), *Handbook of cross-cultural psychology: Vol. 6. Psychopathology* (pp. 233–262). Boston: Allyn & Bacon

Marsella, A. J. (1998). Toward a "global psychology": New directions in theory and research. *American Psychologist, 53,* 1282–1291

Marsella, A. J., & Dash-Scheur, A. (1988). Coping, culture, and healthy human development: A research and conceptual overview. In P. Dasen, J. W. Berry, & N. Sartorius (Eds.), *Cross-cultural psychology and health: Toward applications* (pp. 162–178). Newbury Park, CA: Sage.

Marsella, A. J., Sartorius, N., Jablensky, A., & Fenton, F. (1985). Cross-cultural studies of depressive disorders: An overview. In A. Kleinman & B. Good (Eds.), *Culture and depression: Studies in the anthropology and cross-cultural psychiatry of affect and disorders* (pp. 299–324). Berkeley: University of California Press.

Marsella, A. J., & White, G. (Eds.). (1982). *Cultural conceptions of mental health and therapy.* Hingham, MA: D. Reidel (Kluver).

Matsumoto, D. (1994). *Cultural influence on research methods and statistics.* Pacific Grove, CA: Brooks/Cole.

Matsumoto, D., Kudoh, T., Scherer, K., & Wallbott, H. (1988). Antecedents of and reactions to emotions in the United States and Japan. *Journal of Cross-Cultural Psychology, 19,* 267–286.

Mead, M. (1935). *Sex and temperament in three primitive societies.* New York: Morrow.

Mesquita, B., & Frijda, N. H. (1992). Cultural variations in emotion: A review. *Psychological Bulletin, 112,* 179–204.

Mezzich, J. E., Fabrega, H., Mezzich, A. C., & Goffman, G. A. (1985). International experience with *DSM-III. Journal of Nervous and Mental Disease, 173,* 738–741.

Mezzich, J. E., Kleinman, A., Fabrega, H., & Parron, D. L. (1996). *Culture and psychiatric diagnosis: A DSM-IV perspective.* Washington, DC: American Psychiatric Press.

Moyerman, D. R., & Forman, B. D. (1992). Acculturation and adjustment: A meta-analytic study. *Hispanic Journal of Behavioral Sciences, 14,* 163–200.

Murphy, H. B. M. (1982a). *Comparative psychiatry: The international and intercultural distribution of mental illness.* Berlin: Springer-Verlag.

Murphy, H. B. M. (1982b). Culture and schizophrenia. In I. Al-Issa (Ed.), *Culture and psychopathology* (pp. 221–250). Baltimore, MD: University Park Press.

Murphy, J. M. (1976). Psychiatric labeling in cross-cultural perspective. *Science, 182,* 1019–1027.

Murphy, J. M., & Leighton, A. H. (Eds.). (1965). *Approaches to cross-cultural psychiatry.* Ithaca, NY: Cornell University Press

Neale, J. M., & Oltmanns, T. F. (1980). *Schizophrenia.* New York: Wiley.

Nichter, M. (1981). Idioms of distress. *Culture, Medicine, and Psychiatry, 5,* 379–408.

Pfeiffer, W. (1970). *Transkulturelle Psychiatrie: Ergebnisse und Probleme.* Stuttgart: Thieme.

Pfeiffer, W. (1994). *Transkulturelle Psychiatrie* (2nd ed.). Stuttgart: Thieme.

Phinney, J. S. (1996). When we talk about American ethnic groups, what do we mean? *American Psychologist, 51,* 918–927.

Prince, R. H. (1968). The changing picture of depressive syndromes in Africa: Is it fact or diagnostic fashion? *Canadian Journal of African Studies, 1,* 177–192.

Radford, M. H. B., Nakane, Y., Ohta, Y., Mann, L., & Kalucy, R. S. (1991). Decision making in clinically depressed patients: A transcultural social psychological study. *Journal of Nervous and Mental Disease, 179,* 711–719.

Rao, A. V. (1973). Depressive illness and guilt in Indian cultures. *Indian Journal of Psychiatry, 23,* 213–221.

Robins, L. N., Helzer, J. E., Croughan, J. L., & Ratcliff, K. (1981). The NIMH Diagnostic Interview Schedule: Its history, characteristics and validity. *Archives of General Psychiatry, 38,* 381–389.

Robins, L. N., Locke, L. N., & Regier, D. A. (1991). An overview of the psychiatric disorders in America. In L. N. Robins & D. A. Regier (Eds.), *Psychiatric disorders in America: The Epidemiologic Catchment Area Study* (pp. 328–366). New York: Free Press.

Robins, L. N., & Regier, D. A. (Eds.). (1991). *Psychiatric disorders in America: The Epidemiologic Catchment Area Study.* New York: Free Press.

Rogler, L. H. (1999). Methodological sources of cultural insensitivity in mental health research. *American Psychologist, 54*, 424–433.

Rosenhan, D. L. (1973). On being sane in insane places. *Science, 179*, 250–258.

Russell, J. A. (1991). Culture and categorization of emotions. *Psychological Bulletin, 110*, 426–450.

Russell, J. G. (1989). Anxiety disorders in Japan: A review of the Japanese literature on Shinkei-shitsu and Taijin Kyofusho. *Culture, Medicine, and Psychiatry, 13*, 391–403.

Sarbin, T. R. (1969). The scientific status of the mental illness metaphor. In S. C. Plog & R. B. Edgerton (Eds.), *Changing perspectives in mental illness* (pp. 9–30). New York: Holt, Rinehart & Winston.

Sarbin, T. R., & Juhasz, J. B. (1982). The concept of mental illness: A historical perspective. In I. Al-Issa (Ed.), *Culture and psychopathology* (pp. 71–122). Baltimore, MD: University Park Press.

Sartorius, N., & Janca, A. (1996). Psychiatric assessment instruments developed by the World Health Organization. *Social Psychiatry and Psychiatric Epidemiology, 31*, 55–69.

Scheff, T. J. (1966). *Being mentally ill: A sociological theory.* Chicago: Aldine.

Segall, M. H., Lonner, W. J., & Berry, J. W. (1998). Cross-cultural psychology as a scholarly discipline. *American Psychologist, 53*, 1101–1110.

Seiden, D. Y. (1999). *Cross-cultural behavioral case formulation with Chinese neurasthenia patients.* Unpublished doctoral dissertation, Hofstra University, Hempstead, NY.

Singer, K. (1975). Depressive disorders from a transcultural perspective. *Social Science and Medicine, 9*, 289–301.

Sinha, D. (1997). Indigenizing psychology. In J. W. Berry, Y. Poortinga, & J. Pandey (Eds.), *Handbook of cross-cultural psychology: Vol. 1. Theory and method* (pp. 129–170). Boston: Allyn & Bacon.

Sow, I. (1980). *Anthropological structures of madness in Black Africa.* New York: International Universities Press.

Sue, S. (1998). In search of cultural competence in psychotherapy and counseling. *American Psychologist, 532*, 440–448.

Sue, S., & Zane, N. (1987). The role of culture and cultural techniques in psychotherapy: A critique and reformulation. *American Psychologist, 42*, 37–45.

Szapocznik, J., & Kurtines, W. M. (1993). Family psychology and cultural diversity. *American Psychologist, 48*, 400–407.

Szasz, T. S. (1961). *The myth of mental illness.* New York: Paul B. Hoeber.

Tanaka-Matsumi, J. (1979). Taijin Kyofusho: Diagnostic and cultural issues in Japanese psychiatry. *Culture, Medicine and Psychiatry, 3*, 231–245.

Tanaka-Matsumi, J. (1995). Cross-cultural perspectives on anger. In H. Kassinove (Ed.), *Anger disorders: definition, diagnosis and treatment* (pp. 80–89). Washington, DC: Francis & Taylor.

Tanaka-Matsumi, J., & Chang, R. (1999, August). What questions arise when studying cultural universals in depression? In H. Kassinove (Chair), *Are there cultural universals in psychopathology?* Symposium conducted at the annual meeting of the American Psychological Association, Boston.

Tanaka-Matsumi, J., & Draguns, J. G. (1997). Culture and psychopathology. In J. Berry, M. H. Segall, & C. Kagitcibasi (Eds.), *Handbook of cross-cultural psychology: Vol. 3. Social psychology* (2nd ed., pp. 449–491). Boston: Allyn & Bacon.

Tanaka-Matsumi, J., & Higginbotham, N. H. (1996). Behavioral approaches to cross-cultural counseling. In P. B. Pedersen, J. G. Draguns, W. J. Lonner, & J. E. Trimble (Eds.), *Counseling across cultures* (4th ed., pp. 266–292). Newbury Park, CA: Sage.

Tanaka-Matsumi, J., & Marsella, A. J. (1976). Cross-cultural variations in the phenomenological experience of depression: I. Word association studies. *Journal of Cross-Cultural Psychology, 7*, 379–396.

Tanaka-Matsumi, J., Seiden, D. Y., & Lam, K. (1996). Cross-cultural functional analysis: A strategy for culturally-informed clinical assessment. *Cognitive and Behavioral Practice, 2*, 215–233.

Tanaka-Matsumi, J., Seiden, D. Y., & Lam, K. (2001). Translating cultural observations into psychotherapy: A functional approach. In J. F. Schumaker & T. Ward (Eds.), *Cognition, Culture and Psychopathology* (pp. 193–212). Westport, CT: Praeger.

Thakker, J., & Ward, T. (1998). Culture and classification: The cross-cultural application of the *DSM-IV. Clinical Psychology Review, 18*, 501–529.

Triandis, H. C. (1994). Major cultural syndromes and emotion. In S. Kitayama & H. Markus (Eds.), *Emotion and culture: Empirical studies of mutual influence* (pp. 285–306). Washington, DC: American Psychological Association.

Tseng, W.-S., Asai, M., Jieqiu, L., Wibulswasd, P., Suryani, L. K., Wen, L.-K., Brennan, J., & Heiby, E. (1990). Multicultural study of minor psychiatric disorders in Asia: Symptom manifestations. *International Journal of Social Psychiatry, 36*, 252–264.

Tseng, W.-S., Asai, M., Kitanishi, K., McLaughlin, D., & Kyomen, H. (1992). Diagnostic patterns of social phobia: Comparison in Tokyo and Hawaii. *Journal of Nervous and Mental Disease, 180*, 380–385.

Tseng, W.-S., & Hsu, J. (1980). Minor psychological disturbances of everyday life. In H. C. Triandis & J. G. Draguns (Eds.), *Handbook of cross-cultural psychology: Vol. 6. Psychopathology* (pp. 61–98). Boston: Allyn & Bacon.

Tseng, W.-S., Mo, K.-M., Li, L.-S., Chen, G.-Q., Ou, L.-W., & Zheng, H.-B. (1992). Koro epidemics in Guangdong, China: A questionnaire survey. *Journal of Nervous and Mental Disease, 180*, 117–123.

Tseng, W.-S., Xu, N., Ebata, K., Hsu, J., & Cui, Y. (1986). Diagnostic pattern of neurosis among China, Japan and America. *American Journal of Psychiatry, 143*, 1010–1014.

Tung, M. P. M. (1994). Symbolic meanings of the body in Chinese culture and "somatization." *Culture, Medicine and Psychiatry, 18*, 483–492.

Ullmann, L. P., & Krasner, L. (1969). *A psychological approach to abnormal behavior* (1st ed.) Englewood Cliffs, NJ: Prentice-Hall.

Ullmann, L. P., & Krasner, L. (1975). *A psychological approach to abnormal behavior* (2nd ed.) Englewood Cliffs, NJ: Prentice-Hall.

Ward, C., & Kennedy, A. (1994). Acculturation strategies, psychological adjustment, and sociocultural competence during cross-cultural transitions. *International Journal of Intercultural Relations, 18*, 329–343.

Ward, C., & Rana-Deuba, A. (1999). Acculturation and adaptation revisited. *Journal of Cross-Cultural Psychology, 30*, 422–442.

Warner, R. (1994). *Recovery from schizophrenia: Psychiatry and political economy* (2nd ed.). New York: Routledge.

Waxler-Morrison, N. E. (1992). "Prognosis for schizophrenia in the Third World: A reevaluation of cross-cultural research": Commentary. *Culture, Medicine and Psychiatry, 16*, 77–80.

Weiss, M. (1997). Explanatory Model Interview Catalogue (EMIC): Framework for comparative study of illness. *Transcultural Psychiatry, 34*, 235–263.

Weiss, M. G., Doongaji, D. R., Siddhartha, S., Wypij, D., Pathare, S., Bhatawdekar, M., Bhave, A., Sheth, A., & Fernandes, R. (1992). The Explanatory Model Interview Catalogue (EMIC) contribution to cross-cultural research methods from a study of Leprosy and mental health. *British Journal of Psychiatry, 160*, 819–830.

Weiss, M. G., & Kleinman, A. (1988). Depression in cross-cultural perspective: Developing a cultur-

ally informed model. In P. Dasen, J. W. Berry, & N. Sartorius (Eds.), *Cross-cultural psychology and health: Toward applications* (pp. 179–206). Newbury Park, CA: Sage.

Weissman, M. M., Bruce, M., Leaf, P., Florio, L., & Holzer, C. (1991). Affective disorders. In L. Robins & E. Regier (Eds.), *Psychiatric disorders in America* (pp. 53–80). New York: Free Press.

Wells, J. E., Bushnell, J. A., Hornblon, A. R., Joyce, P. R., & Oakley-Browne M. A. (1989). Christchurch psychiatric epidemiology study, Part I: Methodology and lifetime prevalence for specific psychiatric disorders. *Australian and New Zealand Journal of Psychiatry, 23*, 315–326.

Westermeyer, J. (1987). Cultural factors in clinical assessment. *Journal of Consulting and Clinical Psychology, 55*, 471–479.

Whaley, A. L. (1997). Ethnic/race paranoia, and psychiatric diagnoses: Clinician bias versus sociocultural differences. *Journal of Psychopathology and Behavioral Assessment, 19*, 1–20.

White, G. (1982). The role of cultural explanations in "somatization." *Social Science and Medicine, 16*, 1519–1530.

Wing, J. K., Cooper, J. E., & Sartorius, N. (1974). *Measurement and classification of psychiatric symptoms. An instruction manual for the PSE and CATEGO program.* Cambridge: Cambridge University Press.

Wittkower, E. D., & Rin, H. (1965). Transcultural psychiatry. *Archives of General Psychiatry, 13*, 387–394.

World Health Organization. (1973). *Report of the International Pilot Study of Schizophrenia.* Geneva: Author.

World Health Organization. (1979). *Schizophrenia: An international follow-up study.* Geneva: Author.

World Health Organization. (1983). *Depressive disorders in different cultures: Report of the WHO collaborative study of standardized assessment of depressive disorders.* Geneva: Author.

World Health Organization. (1992). *The ICD-10 classification of mental and behavioural disorders: Clinical descriptions and diagnostic guidelines.* Geneva: Author.

Yap, P. M. (1971). Guilt and shame, depression and culture: A psychiatric cliché reexamined. *Community Contemporary Psychology, 1*, 35–53.

Yap, P. M. (1974). *Comparative psychiatry: A theoretical framework.* Toronto: University of Toronto Press.

Zhang, M.-Y. (1989). The diagnosis and phenomenology of neurasthenia: A Shanghai study. *Culture, Medicine and Psychiatry, 13*, 147–161.

15

Clinical Psychology and Culture

JAYNE LEE & STANLEY SUE

We close this section of the book with an examination of cultural influences on clinical psychology. Indeed, the goals of psychology as a whole include not only the science of studying and understanding human behavior, but also the use of psychological principles and knowledge to intervene in people's lives to improve them. This enterprise of psychology, in fact, sets psychology apart from many other scientific disciplines and is associated with real consequences for the nature of scientific truth and principles generated in research. As cross-cultural research over the years has continually highlighted the importance of culture in understanding human behavior, so therefore does its importance in understanding and treating mental disorders loom larger.

As Lee and Sue point out in this chapter, the entire field of clinical psychology is now grappling with many pressing and important issues that cultures bring to bear on the work of clinicians. They begin their chapter with an overview of the underpinnings of clinical psychology and describe the founding and growth of clinical psychology as a field. As a primarily and uniquely American enterprise from the beginning, Lee and Sue correctly point out that the general orientation and approach of clinical psychology reflected much American, and to a lesser extent, western European influence. This has led in general to monoculturalism in clinical psychology.

The continued growth of cross-cultural psychology and the implications of its findings for mainstream psychological theories, however, and the development of greater awareness of race and ethnic relations in the United States have led to a much greater promotion of cross-cultural issues in clinical psychology in the past few decades. As a result, the enterprise of clinical psychology, not only in the United States, but also worldwide, has gradually evolved from a generally monocultural orientation to one that recognizes the unique needs and issues that people of diverse cultural backgrounds bring with them. Cultural influences are now well recognized in three main foci of work in clinical psychology: assessment, psychopathology, and treatment. And, as Lee and Sue highlight in their review, research and theory have made particularly insightful inroads to the development of knowledge and methods in these areas with respect to the incorporation of culture.

The reader is especially encouraged to examine how Lee and Sue present their brief review of cultural influences on pathology. While overlapping in content to some degree with Tanaka-Matsumi's chapter, the points they raise and issues they highlight reflect a unique concern about cultural influences in relation to treatment issues. And, their review of cultural issues related to various areas and types of treatments is superb and highlights the important, yet complex, relationship among culture, society, biology, and psychology. In particular, their analysis of the core issues of individualism, self-reliance, and self-awareness, which may underlie many psychotherapeutic approaches based in the American or western European culture yet may not be equally applicable to people of other cultures, is poignant and significant. Their discussion of culturally sensitive treatment approaches also is excellent.

In closing their chapter, Lee and Sue offer eight issues that they deem important for future work in this area to continue. Their suggestions include the notion that empirical and theoretical work in clinical psychology needs to incorporate, even more than in the past, the examination and psychologies of peoples outside the United States. In doing so, researchers themselves, along with therapists and clinicians, need to become more culturally competent, and they need to go beyond giving pro forma statements about the need to test different populations and actually do the work. Greater integration among traditional psychotherapeutic approaches along with culturally specific folk healers needs to occur, and the methods that can be used to study these collectively and simultaneously in an unbiased manner across cultures need to be developed. Integration of new methodologies (quantitative and qualitative), as well as rapprochement between molecular (i.e., biological) and molar (cultural) ways of understanding and investigating human behavior, also needs to be given consideration. These ideas are especially important for work in clinical psychology as there is no other area in psychology that has a direct impact on the lives of so many people around the world than this area. For that reason, we ought to get it right.

Our interest in culture and clinical psychology is derived from our involvement with ethnic minority groups in the United States. We have been impressed with how African Americans, Asian Americans, Hispanics, Native Americans, and White Americans exhibit differences, as well as similarities, in the rate and distribution of mental disorders, etiological factors in psychopathology, and the effective means to treat and prevent disorders. Furthermore, most of the ethnic/cultural principles and issues confronting different populations within the United States are applicable to populations outside the United States.

In this chapter, we reflect on the development of the field of clinical psychology and the slow, but steady, appreciation for the importance of culture, as revealed in the various tasks in the domain of the field—namely, assessing, understanding etiology, and devising effective treatment/preventive interventions. To place the field's development in perspective, we begin with a historical account of clinical psychology, which was established in the United States. As we shall see, the formal field of clinical psychology was (a) established in the United States; (b) guided by national needs, especially needs for psychological testing and assessment; (c) largely an American enterprise;

and (d) culturally dominated by the United States.

Underpinnings of Clinical Psychology

Clinical Psychology: Historical Perspective

Throughout history, human beings in all cultures have experienced emotional distress and have attempted to alleviate this condition. It was in the United States that clinical psychology was established in 1896 to address problems of assessment, emotional distress, and treatment. Lightner Witmer, a psychologist who studied under Wilhelm Wundt, founded the first psychological child guidance clinic at the University of Pennsylvania. There, he offered courses and training in clinical method in psychology. At this time, clinical psychology functioned mainly from a research and evaluation standpoint.

In its nascent form, clinical psychology did not receive a warm reception from psychiatrists, who did not want this "new" field of psychology to infringe on their territory, nor was it supported by other psychologists, who saw no need for the application of psychology. Psychology was upheld as a "pure" science (Reisman, 1991). Increasingly, clinical psychologists grew in number and began to form associations, the first being the independent American Association of Clinical Psychology (AACP) in 1917. This dissolved and reformulated into the first clinical section of the American Psychological Association (APA) in 1919. Internationally, the first child guidance clinic in England was formed in 1919. Likewise, in the same year, Alfred Adler organized the first child guidance clinic in Vienna, Austria.

Psychological testing became widespread, particularly with the use of mental tests for United States army recruits during World War I. In 1919, Robert Yerkes, then president of the American Psychological Association, became chair of a committee of five experimental psychologists working within the medical department of the army. They were given the responsibility of devising methods to classify the men according to their abilities. Various intelligence tests were used, one with a verbal scale, known as Army Alpha, and one with a nonverbal scale, known as Army Beta. Results from these tests were alarming. Of the 1,726,000 men tested during the war, over 500,000 were found to be illiterate, and about 8,000 were recommended for discharge on the basis of low intelligence (Reisman, 1991).

These findings fueled the development and implementation of psychological tests to assess individuals. The demand for testing, especially within school systems, was immediate and pressing. In the United States, the shortage of trained psychologists to administer and interpret intelligence scales resulted in teachers and principals taking on the roles of psychological examiners. In response to this need for clinical psychologists, the number of psychological clinics increased. By 1919, clinical psychology had attained status as a science and as a profession.

Testing became implemented at a feverish rate. Few children could escape these mental tests. Equipped with a few diagnostic tools, school psychologists were given instruction to differentiate between those children who could not and those who would not learn. Despite the complexities surrounding such a difficult decision, many schools relied heavily on the information derived from these psychological tests. Testing was adopted in the field of vocational and industrial guidance as well. Although the need for trained psychologists was rapidly growing, there was also growing discontent among clinical psychologists. Their status became that of "mental testers" as opposed to clinicians. Top-tier positions, such as heads of clinics and bureaus, were given to psychiatrists, whereas clinical psychologists were relegated to "second-string" jobs. This was due to a lack of standards, regulations, and a prescribed training program for clinical psychologists was to blame (Wallin, 1929).

To address this problem, the Section of Clinical Psychology of the APA in 1931 made an effort to establish a prescribed training program in clinical psychology that would be accepted by the universities. The Committee on Standards of Training for Clinical Psychologists was created to develop the program. The committee recommended that, to obtain the title of clinical psychologist, a person should be required to have a doctor of philosophy (PhD) degree and a year of supervised experience.

Just as programs evolved, the domain of clinical psychology also began to evolve. Kazarian and Evans (1998) track the evolution of the term itself. During the post–World War II era, the definition of clinical psychology was expanded to include methods and procedures to promote the welfare of the individual person and to increase the mental well-being of the individual. Shakow (1976) defined clinical psychology as

A body of knowledge growing out of both correlational and experimental techniques which are based on general, cryptic, psychobiological and psychosocial principles. The skills of assessment and therapy which derive from this knowledge can be used to help persons with behavior disabilities and mental disorders to achieve better adjustment and self-expression. (p. 559)

Fox (1982) expanded the definition to emphasize the improvement and effectiveness of human behavior and coping skills.

By including general health issues, clinical psychologists were now able to help people with physical health problems in addition to mental and emotional problems (Kazarian & Evans, 1998). The American Psychological Association assumed the responsibility of determining which programs satisfied standards and merited support. Furthermore, graduate programs in clinical psychology were required to provide training in psychotherapy, assessment, and research. The new objective of the American Psychological Association was to advance psychology as a science *and* as a means of promoting human welfare (Reisman, 1991).

The 1940s marked a significant increase in graduate education in clinical psychology. The scientist-practitioner model (also known as the Boulder model) was embraced as a training approach that required an empirical scientific base, high academic qualifications, and effective interventions. Clinical psychologists were finally being trained as scientists and practitioners, yet complaints were voiced with respect to the high value placed on research skills, whereas clinical work was less regarded. Concern was expressed that psychotherapy and diagnostic assessment could not be taught properly in an atmosphere that was so richly steeped in academia.

In 1965, Kenneth Clark proposed a professional model (doctor of psychology, PsyD) in which greater focus could be placed on professional practice and less on academic training. Endorsement of this professional model occurred in 1973 at the Vail Conference (Kazarian & Evans, 1998). Despite the growth of the professional model, the scientist-practitioner model continues to be the dominant form of professional training for North American psychologists. In other countries of the world, there was comparatively little professional activity, and what little there was centered on teaching, research, and diagnostic testing. Indeed, in many Asian countries today, psychologists hold roles primarily in testing and assessment, as was the case in the United States decades ago.

In the 1960s, clinical psychology was still largely an American phenomenon. While the United States had thousands of clinicians, it was estimated that there were 345 in the United Kingdom, 60 in Yugoslavia, several in Egypt and Lebanon, 1 in Syria, 6 in Iraq, a few hundred in Japan, and several hundred in Canada and Latin America (Reisman, 1991). Research conducted in the United States, which accounted for the majority of empirical knowledge in clinical psychology, had slowly filtered to other parts of the world. An exchange of cultural ideas was generated. More international scholars began attending American doctoral programs. Other countries began to embrace formal clinical psychology, integrating American models with indigenous concepts (e.g., neurasthenia in China). The U.S. model became the standard from which others evolved.

Clinical Psychology: Cultural Perspective

Because clinical psychology first evolved in the United States, the cultural orientation of the field reflected American influence. Properly speaking, the United States is composed of many different cultures. However, it is largely Western (i.e., western European), as opposed to Eastern (e.g., Asian) in perspective. Not surprisingly, the theoretical underpinnings of clinical psychology were grounded on Western figures such as Freud and Watson. Freud's *Interpretation of Dreams* (1900) was published. Underlying this book was the assumption of psychic determinism, in which an individual's thoughts and behaviors are products of natural laws as opposed to freely willed. For Freud, thoughts or acts could be unconscious and upon analysis, might reveal causes or motives of which the person is unaware. These unconscious processes interfere with, and are a part of, the ordinary functioning of "normal" people. Thus, Freud began to develop psychoanalysis as a treatment (Reisman, 1991). Disagreements arose regarding specific aspects of Freud's theory. For example, the critics could not understand why he insisted that sexual motivation was so very important. Even Jung, who was a protégé of Freud, wrote to him recommending a more discrete approach to the "unsavory topic" of sex. Despite such disagreements, for the most part, psychoanalytic theory was highly regarded, and its popularity increased with time. The use of introspection gained in popularity as well.

In 1913, Watson published his manifesto, "Psychology as the Behaviorist Views It." In this manuscript, he proposed that psychology should focus on predicting and controlling behavior. He contended that all psychology had to concern itself with were stimuli and responses. Given the stimuli, investigators should discover the responses. Given the responses, they should discover the stimuli. The method of introspection would be minimal.

With the introduction of behaviorism, psychology shifted from the study of consciousness to the study of behavior. Enthusiasm for behaviorism increased. People did not want to regard psychology as an abstract intellectual notion. They were interested in practical applications of knowledge. Response to the extreme notion of behaviorism lent itself to a search to clarify the extent to which human behavior is learned (Reisman, 1991). The concept of culture became a key component in learning, although most behaviorists at the time simply examined the immediate antecedents and consequences of behavior rather than longer term socialization processes involving culture. With behaviorism came an increasing interest in scientific research methods based on observable, operational definitions, hypothesis testing, control groups, and the like.

From psychoanalytic and behavioral traditions, a number of other important theoretical positions emerged, including the neo-Freudian, client/person centered, existential, gestalt, cognitive, and cognitive behavioral perspectives. For the most part, however, the ideological basis for the positions shared two characteristics: They were typically Western, and cultural influences were not emphasized.

Cultural anthropologists also demonstrated interest in behavior. Many were making use of psychological research in their attempts to specify which forms of behavior might be universal, which forms seemed to be inherited, and which were acquired. Linton (1938) pointed out that no individual could possibly learn all the nuances and subtle shades of meaning that comprise his or her culture. Furthermore, he claimed that by understanding an individual's culture, a foundation for predicting behavior would develop. Anthropologists realized that individuals need to be studied against their cultural and ecological backgrounds. The United States gradually became more integrated culturally, particularly with the resurgence of immigrants that occurred as a result of immigration laws, such as the 1965 amendments to the McCarran-Walter Act, which permitted sizable Asian immigration (U.S. Commission on Civil Rights, 1992).

Culture has been defined in a number of ways. Kroeber and Kluckhohn (1952) suggest that culture represents patterns of behaviors that are transmitted by symbols that denote the distinct achievements of human groups. Culture can also be viewed as a set of rules and norms that promote stability and harmony within a society. For the purposes of this chapter, we employ this definition of culture in our discussion of clinical psychology.

Monoculturalism in Clinical Psychology

A number of psychologists recognized the importance of cultural influences, and organizations such as the International Association of Applied Psychology and the International As-

sociation of Cross-Cultural Psychology were established. However, mainstream American psychology in general and clinical psychology in particular failed to address cultural issues adequately. Because theories and methodologies were derived primarily from Euroamerican culture, the field was dominated by this culture—a phenomenon called an *imposed etic* (Segall, Lonner, & Berry, 1998). This can be seen from the relative absence of diverse cultural content in clinical psychology programs and resources. Similarly, attempts to address the inadequacies in meeting psychological service needs of people from diverse cultures have only just begun (Kazarian & Evans, 1998).

Two developments were important in promoting cross-cultural issues. First, a number of researchers in the cross-cultural and cross-national areas demonstrated the importance of culture in socialization practices, personality, manifestations of mental disorders, means of treating disorders, and other behaviors. Triandis and Brislin (1984) pointed to advantages that cross-cultural research had in the development of psychological theory. By testing one's theory in different societies and cultures, the relevance and validity of the theory for human beings in general can be established. They also noted that cross-cultural research could have other benefits, such as the ability to increase the range of variables studied. For example, assume that a researcher is interested in the relationship between collectivism and moral development. Because different cultures vary in the degree of collectivism, by including different cultural groups in the study, the investigator can find a wider range of collectivism among the research participants. Similarly, cultures can be found to differ in variables that, for ethical or practical reasons, are difficult to manipulate as independent variables (e.g., the effects of certain human values on sexual aggression).

Second, given the history of race and ethnic relations in the United States, investigators began to study racial or ethnic differences in intelligence, personality, stereotyping, emotional disturbance, achievements, and mental health services. Increasingly, the needs of ethnic minority populations (especially African Americans, Asian Americans, Hispanics, and Native Americans) for services of clinical psychologists and the inability of psychologists to meet those needs (American Psychological Association Office of Ethnic Minority Affairs, 1993) were recognized. There was a large body of data that showed the lack of cultural consideration in clinical practice. For example, Dahlquist and Fay (1983) cited the failure of the mental health professions to meet the needs of the multicultural society adequately; Padilla, Ruiz, and Alvarez (1975) urged for training of Spanish-speaking students in mental health professions; S. Sue (1998) advocated for the delivery of culturally appropriate services; Korchin (1980) urged for commitment to training larger numbers of qualified ethnic minority psychologists; Howard et al. (1986) found that ethnic minorities were poorly represented in the mental health field. Obviously, ethnic minority issues were not identical with those of cross-cultural psychology. While both are concerned with cultural matters, ethnic minority psychology is also interested in race and ethnic relations between the dominant and minority groups in the United States.

Because clinical psychology experienced its birth in the United States, the value orientations were derived from the dominant North American (Anglo American) paradigm (Ho, 1985; McHolland, Lubin, & Forbes, 1990; S. Sue, 1983). From an international perspective, the dominance of the U.S. paradigm led to cultural restructuring of clinical psychology in other parts of the world. In 1985, Ho stated that, "Clinical psychology is not an indigenous outgrowth but a foreign transplantation into the community" (p. 1214). For example, he notes that in China, there is a basic contradiction between the traditional moralistic-authoritarian orientation and the psychological-therapeutic orientation of clinical psychology. Consequently, the task of the clinician then becomes one of delicately balancing the psychological-therapeutic orientation with the traditional values of a given culture.

Another dilemma stems from the contradiction between the concepts of individualism and collectivism. The mainstream Western psychology, which has its roots in the Judeo-Christian tradition of individualism, places an emphasis on qualities such as self-reliance, uniqueness, autonomy, and freedom. Ho (1985) argues that this ideological bias underlies the traditional approaches to intervention (i.e., counseling and psychotherapy). In contrast, collectivism places an emphasis on social action, preservation, and enhancement of well-being of the group. The strategies for prevention and intervention are suggested through support systems rooted in the culture. In this way, cultural forces can be utilized to help people through difficulties.

Because of the growing appreciation of the importance of culture, American psychology has attempted to address issues concerning ethnic minority groups, such as the establishment in the APA of various governance groups (e.g., Committee on the Equality of Opportunity in Psychology, Board of Ethnic Minority Affairs, Office of Ethnic Minority Affairs, and the Society for the Psychological Study of Ethnic Minority Issues). In 1993, the APA established guidelines for providers of psychological services to ethnic, linguistic, and culturally diverse populations (see American Psychological Association Office of Ethnic Minority Affairs, 1993).

In other countries, attempts have been made to modify clinical psychology from an American model to ones that meet the needs of particular cultures. For instance, Ho (1985) argued that, in most Asian and other Third World countries, "it makes more sense to develop solid training programs at the master's level rather than attempting to follow the American doctor of philosophy or doctor of psychology models, at least during the initial stages of professional development." (p. 1215) In many developing and underdeveloped countries, professional progress is dependent on careful consideration of socioeconomic factors. The long path to obtaining a doctorate not only restricts the number of clinical psychologists available, but also does not ensure remuneration commensurate with an advanced degree. With respect to psychological research, the Western mainstream paradigm follows an etic approach in research and training, which emphasizes the "universals" and core human similarities. In contrast, cultural psychology focuses on the emic approach, which places an emphasis on culture specificity and influence of culture on human behavior (Kazarian & Evans, 1998).

In summary, clinical psychology was first established in the United States. Its practices and principles understandably reflected American (largely western Anglo-Saxon European) interests and needs. Because many ethnic minority populations felt that their needs and cultural perspectives were not being well served and because of the growing international interest in clinical psychology, the field has gradually recognized the importance of cultural influences and the necessity of dealing with cultural issues.

The growing interest and concern over cultural influences are revealed in the three main foci of clinical psychology: (a) assessment, (b) psychopathology, and (c) treatment. Some of the important issues in each of the three areas are as follows: What are the problems in conducting valid assessments and evaluations of mental disorders across cultures? How can the validity of assessment be improved? In what ways are emotional disorders influenced by culture? Are there differential patterns of cause and course of disorders? Are treatment methods effective across cultures? What kinds of treatments can be found among different cultures?

Assessment

Problems and Issues in Assessment

One of the important, yet unresolved, issues in assessment and psychopathology is whether cultural variations in symptoms are better conceptualized as Western identified disorders that differ in symptom expressions across cultures or whether cultural variations represent distinctly different disorders. In the early 1900s, Emil Kraepelin, who is considered the father of descriptive psychiatry, discovered that illnesses found in the West, such as dementia praecox (now known as schizophrenia), are found in non-Western countries as well. The incidence and symptomatology, however, differed. He also noted culture-specific syndromes such as *amok*, a dissociative state characterized by outbursts of unrestricted violence associated with homicidal attacks found prevalent in Indonesian and Malaysian males. Despite finding these cultural differences, Kraepelin believed these syndromes to be indicative of Western illnesses (Al-Issa, 1995).

The problem in addressing the issue includes the difficulty in trying to examine cultural phenomena without being biased by one's culture. Kleinman (1995) observed that research in psychiatry is motivated to show that a psychiatric disorder is like any other disorder and therefore will be found everywhere in the world with the same diagnostic techniques. International studies on schizophrenia are indicative of this. One study, the International Pilot Study of Schizophrenia (IPSS) funded by the National Institute of Mental Health (NIMH), examined groups of patients in India, Nigeria, Colombia, Denmark, the United Kingdom, the former Soviet Union, and the United States. The samples of psychiatric patents were indeed found to display similar symptoms, thus supporting the notion of a "universal" disorder.

However, striking differences were also found, namely, that the course of schizophrenia was better for patients in the less-developed societies and worse for those in industrially advanced societies. In the mental health field, this finding was emphasized only secondarily to the finding that core schizophrenic symptoms could be found at all sites (Kleinman, 1995).

Likewise, the World Health Organization (WHO) launched the Determinants of Outcome Study, also funded by the NIMH (Sartorius & Jablensky, 1983). Twelve centers in countries such as India, Japan, Nigeria, Colombia, Denmark, the United Kingdom, and the United States studied over 1,300 cases collectively. The researchers found that, in all locations, patients with schizophrenia share many features at the level of symptomatology. Nevertheless, important differences were found as well. In the developed countries, catatonic schizophrenia was rarely found, while in the developing countries, it was diagnosed in 10% of the cases. Similarly, in developing countries, the acute subtype diagnosis was used almost twice as often as the diagnosis of the paranoid subtype. In contrast, the hebephrenic subtype diagnosis was used over three times as often in developed countries as in developing countries. Despite these important cross-cultural differences, the conclusions of the study focused on the universality of schizophrenic symptoms (Kleinman, 1995). In addressing these conclusions, Kleinman stated, "There is, then, a tacit professional ideology that exaggerates what is universal in psychiatric disorder and de-emphasizes what is culturally particular" (p. 636).

Diagnosticians themselves may disagree because of their cultural backgrounds or ethnicity. In a study to evaluate the influence of culture on the diagnostic approach of therapists, five Chinese American and five White American male therapists rated the functioning of Chinese and White male clients during a videotaped interview (Li-Repac, 1980). The results revealed an interaction effect on the therapists' clinical judgments involving ethnicity of the therapist and client. While White therapists rated Chinese American clients as anxious, awkward, confused, and nervous, Chinese therapists perceived the same clients as alert, ambitious, adaptable, honest, and friendly. In the case of White American clients, White therapists rated them as affectionate, adventurous, sincere, and easygoing, while Chinese therapists judged the same clients to be active, aggressive, rebellious, and outspoken. Furthermore, White therapists rated Chinese clients as more depressed, more inhibited, less socially poised, and less capable of interpersonal relationships than did Chinese therapists. Chinese therapists rated White clients as more severely disturbed than did White therapists. These findings suggest that judgments about psychological functioning depend at least in part on the ethnic similarity (and presumably the cultural backgrounds) of therapists to their clients.

Other sources of bias involve assessment procedures. Most psychological assessment instruments have items that are developed in a vernacular that is not inherently translatable to other languages Kleinman (1995). For example, diagnostic instruments in the United States use terms like "feeling blue" or "feeling down" to represent depressive affect. In many non-Western languages, direct translation of these terms would yield nonsensical expressions. In order to capture cultural differences fully, researchers must identify specific expressions of distress and include them in standard questionnaires. In other words, equivalence is often lacking when a measure is developed in one culture and used in another.

Brislin (1993) outlines three areas in which the equivalence of measures can be problematic in cross-cultural assessment research: (a) translation equivalence, (b) conceptual equivalence, and (c) metric equivalence. Potential problems in translation, conceptual, and metric equivalence have been sufficiently great that some researchers even go so far as to refrain from making any inference from the results of quantitative comparisons of a given measure between subjects from two different cultures (e.g., Hui, 1988).

Problems in translation equivalence often occur when questionnaires or instructions from one language group are used with another language group. When the descriptors and measures of psychological concepts cannot be translated adequately across languages, there is nonequivalence. To test the translation equivalence of a measure developed in a particular culture, it is first translated by a bilingual expert to another language, then "back-translated" from the second language to the first by an independent bilingual translator. The two versions of the measure in the original language are then compared to discern which words or concepts seem to "survive" the translation procedures, with the assumption that the concepts that survive are translation equivalent. This procedure can be used to discover which psychological concepts appear to be culture specific or culture common.

Conceptual equivalence refers to a functional aspect of the construct that serves the same purpose in different cultures, although the specific behavior or thoughts used to measure the construct may be different. For example, one aspect of good decision making in the Western cultures may be typified by an ability to make a personal decision without being unduly influenced by others, whereas good decision making may be understood in Asian cultures as an ability to make a decision that is best for the group. These different behaviors pertaining to making decisions are equivalent in that they comprise the very definition of the construct (good decision making) as used by individuals in the different cultures. Yet, the actual behaviors considered as good decision making are strikingly different. The lack of conceptual equivalence means that a particular construal of good decision making in one culture may be a poor way of construing the concept in another culture.

Finally, metric equivalence refers to whether scores on a measure achieved by persons from different cultures have the same scalar meaning and can be compared directly. For example, a score of 100 on a certain scale or measure used with one population may not be equivalent to a score of 100 on the same measure when used with a different population or when translated into another language. The lack of metric equivalence is especially apparent when cutoff scores are derived from one culture and then applied to another. For example, if a certain score on a measure is indicative of clinical depression, the same score for someone from a different culture may not be indicative of clinical depression. Many factors influence metric equivalence, including translation and conceptual equivalence, response sets, norms for clinical depression, and the like.

Attempts at Solutions

In 1996, S. Sue outlined several ways to address cultural bias in assessment: Devise new tests and measures, evaluate tests and revise to make them cross-culturally valid, and study the nature of bias.

Devise New Tests and Measures New psychological tests and measures that are appropriate for different ethnic or cultural populations need to be developed. For example, Cheung (in press) is developing a measure of personality for use in Chinese societies. Her measure is based not only on Western concepts and items, but also on more indigenous concepts derived from Chinese culture. In this way, a culture-specific measure will be available for Chinese societies.

Zane (1999) believes that certain personal constructs may be more culturally salient for some groups than others. One significant personality attribute that affects interpersonal interactions is "face." *Loss of face* (defined as the threat or loss of one's social integrity) is an important interpersonal dynamic in Asian social relations. Many individuals fear the loss of face or their social integrity, particularly Asian Americans who come from face cultures. To assess this construct accurately, Zane has developed a measure of loss of face (LOF). The 21-item measure reflects four face-threatening areas involving social status, ethical behavior, social propriety, and self-discipline. Findings indicate that the measure has good reliability and validity. It is positively correlated with other-directedness, self-consciousness, and social anxiety and negatively correlated with extraversion and acculturation level of Asian Americans. Furthermore, Asian Americans score higher on the measure than do Whites. LOF is able to predict, independent of social desirability, certain behaviors, such as assertiveness and help-seeking behaviors. The findings may have direct implications for conceptualization of personality.

In the United States, researchers have discovered five orthogonal personality factors, called the "Big Five" (Goldberg, 1981), which include characteristics such as agreeableness, conscientiousness, and emotional stability. While the Big Five appears to be applicable in different cultures, the degree of salience of the factors differs across cultures (Yang & Bond, 1990). If LOF is a strong predictor of behavior in certain cultural groups and is relatively orthogonal to the Big Five factors, then the conceptualization of personality into the Big Five factors has limitations as a universal way of construing personality.

Evaluate Tests and Revise to Make Them Cross-Culturally Valid In the past, tests and measures were developed in Western societies. In the assessment of individuals from non-Western cultures, the typical practice was simply

to use these existing measures, sometimes in translated or slightly modified forms. For example, intelligence tests (e.g., the Wechsler Adult Intelligence Scale [WAIS]), personality inventories (e.g., Minnesota Multiphasic Personality Inventory, 2nd revision [MMPI-2]), and survey instruments (e.g., Diagnostic Interview Schedule) have been used to study ethnic minorities or cross-national groups.

The problem is the instruments may be inappropriate not only because of translation nonequivalence and item unfamiliarity, but also because of assumptions concerning the meaning of responses to items. With respect to meaning of responses, Rogler, Malgady, and Rodriguez (1989) note that, in Puerto Rican culture, spiritualism is practiced and answering affirmatively to MMPI items (such as "Evil spirits possess me at times") may not be indicative of pathology. Under such circumstances, the instruments should be modified to enhance their validity, or local norms can be established with different populations. Such efforts are important in that they provide a standard by which to compare different groups and yield insights into what aspects or items of a measure are cross-culturally appropriate or inappropriate and what modifications may be necessary to strengthen validity and to interpret test results more accurately.

Study the Nature of Bias One potentially fruitful research area that has been largely ignored in cross-cultural assessment is that of bias. By studying bias, it may be possible to gain insight into how cultural processes influence responses to assessment instruments. With this insight, it provides directions for how to control for bias among culturally different populations. That is, by understanding the cultural processes underlying responses to assessment instruments—processes and principles that may have generality across different assessment tools—it is then possible to attempt to eliminate bias.

Sue is examining if ethnic differences in responses to measures can be predicted by cultural response sets. Once cultural factors are identified, it will be possible to evaluate any measure as to the extent of bias on these factors and to attempt to control bias and increase the validity of instruments. Therefore, existing instruments can still be used while controlling for the identified cultural factors. This approach has been used to control for response sets such as social desirability on the MMPI.

In summary, because of inherent problems in directly using a measure developed and validated in one culture and employing it for another culture, a number of strategies have been used, including language translation and development of norms for other groups using the instrument, modifying the instrument to reflect the local culture, devising measures that can assess constructs that are particularly salient to a cultural group, and studying the nature of cultural bias and correcting for it. The field of cross-cultural psychology has developed greater understanding of the importance of cultural influences on assessment and has attempted to control for bias.

Cultural Influences on Psychopathology

Developing culturally applicable diagnostic instruments is important for the accurate assessment of individuals. What exactly are these tools assessing? In the previous section, we examined the influence of culture on mental health assessment. To focus our attention on the role of cultural factors in explaining psychopathology, we need to understand the theoretical perspectives from which psychopathology is based. From the universalistic perspective, cultural features represent just the exterior layer of psychopathology. Once this outer layer is removed, the core of psychopathology is displayed in its pure form. In contrast, the cultural relativists assert that abnormal manifestations, expressions, and experiences are malleable. What can be construed as pathological in one society could be epitomized in another (Draguns, 1995).

Research on culture and psychopathology mirror these viewpoints. The etic view encompasses the universalistic perspective by emphasizing the pervasiveness of abnormal experience. Examples of this approach to cultural research are the WHO studies (1973, 1979) on schizophrenia. In these studies, the comparisons among cultures assume the existence of schizophrenia across cultures. While acknowledging the importance of culture in influencing specific symptoms or content of symptoms (e.g., the content of delusions) or in accounting for the rate and distribution of particular disorders, the etic perspective maintains that disorders and their processes are the same across cultures.

Even if we assume that disease symptomology is universal and can be assessed with the same diagnostic instruments across cultures, what is the meaning of culture-bound syndromes? According to American Psychiatric Association guidelines (1994), culture-bound syndromes denote recurrent, locality-specific patterns of aberrant behavior and troubled experiences. They do not fit into contemporary diagnostic and classification systems such as those of the *Diagnostic and Statistical Manual of Mental Disorders, Fourth Edition* (*DSM-IV*) (1994) and the *International Classification of Diseases* (*ICD*). Examples of these syndromes are amok, *shenjing shuairuo*, and *ataque de nervios* (American Psychiatric Association, 1994).

Amok is a dissociative episode characterized by a period of brooding, followed by outbursts of violent, aggressive, or homicidal behavior directed at people and objects. The episode tends to be precipitated by a perceived insult and seems to be prevalent only among males. The episode is often accompanied by persecutory ideas, amnesia, exhaustion, and a return to premorbid state following the episode. Amok is found in Malaysia, Laos, Philippines, Polynesia, Papua New Guinea, and Puerto Rico and among the Navajo.

Ataque de nervios is a condition among Latinos from the Caribbean, but is recognized in many Latin American and Latin Mediterranean groups. Commonly reported symptoms include uncontrollable shouting, attacks of crying, trembling, heat in the chest that rises into the head, verbal or physical aggression, and feelings of being out of control. Ataques de nervios frequently occur as a direct result of a stressful event relating to the family.

Shenjing shuairuo ("neurasthenia") is a condition in China characterized by physical and mental fatigue, dizziness, headaches, other pains, concentration difficulties, sleep disturbance, and memory loss. Other symptoms include gastrointestinal problems, sexual dysfunction, irritability, excitability, and various signs that suggest disturbance of the autonomic nervous system. In many, but not all, cases, the symptoms would meet the criteria for a *DSM-IV* mood or anxiety disorder. This disorder is discussed in more detail below.

Are culture-bound syndromes just cultural representations of the same underlying symptoms? By applying only one theoretical framework for assessing diseases (namely, the Western one), clinicians may be unable to recognize the existence of a culture-bound syndrome (Aderibigbe & Pandurangi, 1995). For example, amok is traditionally sanctioned in Malaysia, where it is prevalent. In contrast, no country in the West would tolerate such aggressive and sometimes homicidal behavior. Thus, to remove the constraints of differing ideologies from assessment, expressions of distress need to be evaluated without theoretical bias. Is this possible, however, when our current understanding of disease and illness is by nature a product of culture? Consider, for example, the concept of somatization. Fabrega (1990) defines *somatization* as "illness pictures in which bodily symptoms are overly dominant" (p. 653). Information regarding Western biomedical psychology has been derived via experiments and controlled observation of individuals shaped by Western cultural psychology. Thus, it might not be possible to learn fully of what the "culture-free" elements of brain, body, or disease consist. Fabrega (1990) notes, "If one looks at the phenomena of illness as individuals experience, describe and display this in social behavior, few cross cultural uniformities between disease and illness can be expected" (p. 668).

The emic view is based on the cultural relativist perspective. This research orientation addresses the concept of cultural uniqueness. The abnormal experience is defined within a cultural context, and disorders in one culture may not have equivalence in other cultures. As noted above, culture-bound syndromes may not have counterparts in different cultures. Although presentations conforming to the major *DSM-IV* categories can be found throughout the world, the particular symptoms, course, and social response are very often influenced by local cultural factors.

The relationship between culture and psychopathology in the United States has added complexity due to the multicultural diversity of U.S. communities. The context of culture must be equated with the history and experience of inequality within the group (Draguns, 1995). It is important for these factors to be considered within their historical context as opposed to attributed to fundamental characteristics of the group. Furthermore, ethnic identity becomes intermixed with issues such as acculturation status and affiliation to host country. Studying the effects of ethnic culture on psychopathology is complicated by the pervasive American identity. Thus, the challenge is to incorporate clinical sensitivity with cultural competency without resorting to stereotyping.

Draguns (1995) reviews findings on the cross-cultural psychology of abnormal behavior, which mainly come from research on schizophrenia and depression. The WHO (1973) study found core symptoms of schizophrenia in nine participating countries. Examples of these symptoms were withdrawal, confusion, and reality distortion. A later WHO study (1983) yielded similar findings of core symptoms in depression, such as sad affect, loss of enjoyment, and ideas of worthlessness. Despite these universal symptoms of mental disorder, important cultural differences were also found in these international studies. A more benign course of schizophrenia was found for developing countries (WHO, 1979).

Thus, it appears that, to determine cultural differences in psychopathology, there needs to be a series of sequential, standardized, and cross-cultural investigations. In the case of depression, reported symptoms have been manifested differently across cultures (American Psychiatric Association, 1994; Kaiser, Katz, & Shaw, 1998; Kleinman, 1986). For example, there is an underemphasis on guilt-related symptoms in depression in East Asia and Africa (Draguns, 1995). Somatization is a channel for experiencing psychic distress in China (Kleinman, 1982). Expression of abnormal behavior becomes further complicated by the cultural conception of "normal." For example, the tendency for Native Americans to depend on the environment for solutions may be seen as abnormal to Anglo Americans, who look to treatment in the forms of medicine and therapy (Kaiser et al., 1998).

Despite the ongoing research in cross-cultural clinical psychology, there are still many unanswered questions. For example, an unresolved issue concerns the conceptualization of mental disorders. Are disorders best conceptualized as fundamentally the same with culture serving to affect symptom manifestations, or can disorders be essentially different because of cultural influences? Furthermore, biological explanations have been used to refute the influence of culture on psychopathology; however, biology and culture are not opposite and mutually exclusive. How can the relationship between biology and culture be explained? The continued investigation of somatization that focuses on the body, but is shaped by culture, may be an appropriate path in examining the biocultural relationship. Likewise, there is a lack of information on specific cultural variables that may enhance resilience and hardiness in the face of stress. What unique elements may serve to prevent or counteract psychopathology? In analyzing culture and psychopathology, how do we determine the causal relationship? We know that culture shapes the expression and direction of psychopathology, but how does it contribute to the causes as well (Draguns, 1995)? The evolution of the disease entity itself within the context of culture is important when examining the cultural influences on psychopathology. The history of the disorder neurasthenia illustrates some of the seemingly arbitrary nature of diagnostic categories and the changes that occur with culture.

Neurasthenia

Neurasthenia (or shenjing shuairuo) has been closely associated with the American neurologist George Beard (Costa e Silva & Girolamo, 1990). Found in medical dictionaries as a synonym for "nervous weakness," it was associated with profound physical and mental fatigability. Beard asserted that the causes of neurasthenia stemmed from a weakening of the nervous force, which in turn weakened the nervous system. He believed that this weakness was created by the industrialized lifestyle of the American people, in which they were forced to expend great amounts of energy without proper recuperation. For a time, many physicians in continental Europe readily accepted it. During World War I, neurasthenia was diagnosed so often that the British Army instituted a training program that specifically studied the disease. Graduates of the disease were given the title "neurasthenia expert" (Costa e Silva & Girolamo, 1990). After this time, neurasthenia began to disappear from Western nosology.

The symptoms of neurasthenia were thought to be overinclusive, until eventually it became largely submerged with depression (Adams & Victor, 1985). In fact, neurasthenia did not even appear in the *DSM-I* (American Psychiatric Association, 1952). Unexpectedly, it appeared in *DSM-II* (American Psychiatric Association, 1968), in which it was characterized by chronic weakness, easy fatigability, and sometimes exhaustion. Its reappearance was short-lived, however, and it was not included in *DSM-III* (American Psychiatric Association, 1980) or *DSM-III-R* (American Psychiatric Association, 1987). Only the *ICD* of WHO retains neurasthenia (Costa e Silva & Girolamo, 1990). Occasionally in European countries, it is diagnosed in place of reactive depression. Kleinman and

Kleinman (1985) note how strongly widespread the diagnosis is in China and Taiwan. Indeed, in non-Western countries, neurasthenia is still widely used, and is more culturally appropriate than terms such as *depression* or *anxiety* (Good & Kleinman, 1985). Hence, a mental disorder that was once thought to have its origin in industrialized America has now faded in the West and yet has gathered force in non-Western countries.

Influence of the Western World on Psychopathology

Kleinman (1987) stresses that a classification of psychopathology that is relevant for one culture might not be relevant for another. Examples of this are anorexia nervosa, agoraphobia, and borderline personality disorder. These disorders, mainly found in North America and western Europe are rarely seen in non-Western countries (Paris, 1991). Thus, we stand to gain valuable information about a particular mental disturbance by knowing the degree to which that disorder varies or does not vary from one culture to another.

There has been reluctance in the Western world to recognize cultural variables in psychopathology. In recent years, Schumaker (1996) has identified two major trends that have emerged in the field of clinical psychology. First, the popularity of cognitive psychology has been growing. From the cognitive view, psychopathology is seen as a consequence of mental processes operating largely on the part of the individual. Second, there has been a shift toward biologically based models of psychopathology. Both of these theoretical formulations of psychopathology are individual focused and tend to deemphasize cultural factors.

Cognitive theorists typically implicate the individual in producing his or her own cognitions. However, this notion of individual responsibility is not applicable to all cultures. For instance, the Toraja of South Sulawesi in Indonesia have belief systems by which anger evokes the punishment of supernatural forces. Thus, cognitions concerning anger control originate at the level of culture, not the individual (Schumaker, 1996). Because entire societies are devoid of Western-style depression, we must explore the possibility that cultural factors can override biological predisposition toward depression. One example can be found in the diagnosis of postpartum depression. In the West, approximately 20% of women develop clinical depression at mild to moderate levels following childbirth (Hopkins, Marcus, & Campbell, 1984). Etiological models suggest that postpartum depression results from a hormonal imbalance, specifically, a decrease in estrogen and progesterone, which is proposed to underlie depression. Despite such an important finding, there are very few references to cultural factors related to postpartum depression in the literature. By focusing on specific groups from the non-Western world, it is possible to show the close interaction of culture and psychopathology and to assess the emphasis of Western therapists on individual factors.

Treatments

Biological Treatments

As illustrated in the previous section, the relationship between biology and culture is complex. From a prevention perspective, it is important to examine the factors surrounding the causal relationship between culture and biology. In doing so, we can then begin to take advantage of those cultural variables that serve to counteract or prevent psychopathologies. From a treatment perspective, delineating cultural variables that can potentially influence the effectiveness of psychotropic drugs is vital. Variations in drug treatment effectiveness across cultures further complicate the culture-biology relationship. Lin and Shen (1991) assert that pharmacokinetic and pharmacodynamic profiles of various psychotropic medications may be different in Asian than non-Asian patients, leading to differences in dosage requirements and side-effect profiles.

Even among different Asian subcultural groups, there are some important common traits that could influence drug responses significantly. For example, Clark, Brater, and Johnson (1988) found that the consistency of many Asian diets can affect the metabolism rates of certain prescribed drugs. Despite such similarities, there is also important heterogeneity among different Asian groups as well. An example of these important differences is the distribution of the "slow" acetaldehyde dehydrogenase, a specific enzyme that results in significant facial flushing after small amounts of ethanol are ingested. This enzyme is found in close to 50% of Chinese, Japanese, and Vietnamese, yet only in about one-third of Koreans. Furthermore, this facial flushing is comparatively lower in Asians of Malay and Thai descent. In fact, in these populations, the distribution of the slow acetaldehyde dehydrogenase mirrors that of Caucasian populations (Lin & Shen, 1991).

These differences found between Asian and non-Asian populations have important treatment implications. For example, monoamine oxidase inhibitors (MAOIs) have been demonstrated to be useful in the treatment of "atypical depression" and panic disorders. They have also been found to be effective in the control of some post-traumatic stress disorder symptoms. Yet, MAOIs are infrequently used with Asian patients because of possible complications due to interactions with common Asian food, such as soy sauce, fish sauce, or fermented foods. Also, the anticholinergic properties of traditional herbal medicines can cause atropic psychosis when simultaneously taken with tricyclic antidepressants or low potency neuroleptics (Lin & Shen, 1991). The use of these herbal medicines is extremely popular and extensive in many Asian countries.

Another common psychotropic treatment is the use of benzodiazepines (BZPs), which have become among the most frequently prescribed medications (Smith & Wesson, 1985). Ethnicity has been identified as an important factor in determining BZP responses. Rosenblat and Tang (1987) surveyed prescriptive patterns of 21 North American psychiatrists and found that compared to Caucasians, Asians were more sensitive to various psychotropic effects.

With the variability found in biological treatments across cultures, the notion of a "universal" treatment seems unlikely. Thus, the challenge is to isolate those elements of treatment that are optimal for the specific cultures presented.

Psychotherapeutic Treatments

Just as biological treatments vary across cultures, the use of psychotherapy varies as well. Beutler and Crago (1991) investigated 40 different psychotherapy programs across North America and Europe. They found four dimensions in which regions and programs diverged: (a) process versus outcome focus, (b) the theoretical models of psychotherapy considered for investigation, (c) the modality of service delivery studied, and (d) the methodologies preferred. For example, geographic distributions of the utilization of psychodynamic methods revealed that Germany and the coastal regions of North America are heavily psychodynamically oriented. The endorsement of client-centered therapy in Europe contrasts with the tendencies toward cognitive therapies in North America. Thus, the nature of the therapist-client relationship, complete with roles and expectations, is important to consider when observing variances in psychotherapeutic treatments. Most therapists value clients who speak openly about their experiences and difficulties. Yet, there are varying cultural approaches to this notion of self-disclosure (Toukmanian & Brouwers, 1998). These cultural differences in disclosure tendencies are important to consider when examining psychotherapy.

Disclosure is an important aspect of traditional North American psychotherapy. Commonly, treatment strategies will follow an insight-oriented approach. This type of orientation may not be appropriate for non-Western individuals. For example, Ting-Toomey (1991) found that members of Western cultures demonstrate more disclosure tendencies than do members of non-Western cultures. Disclosure of psychological distress centralizes negative thoughts and emotions, which is discouraged in Eastern cultures. In contrast, Western cultural practices, with the encouragement of insight orientation, embody this self-disclosure process.

Individualism and collectivism are important factors to consider in an individual's willingness to disclose. Disclosing psychological distress could result in an undesired presentation of the self or family (Toukmanian & Brouwers, 1998).

Psychodynamic, cognitive behavioral, and humanistic-existential orientations are the three most widely used approaches to psychotherapy practice. Each perspective contains distinct components, and yet they are also simultaneously linked by a common ideological core. All three theoretical frameworks are constructed from a base that utilizes individualism, self-reliance, and self-awareness as its tools. Self-initiated action is implemented to resolve intra- and interpersonal conflicts. This will ensure a productive level of functioning. Despite this emphasis on the self, it is not prudent to suggest that psychotherapy is ineffective for non-Western cultures (Toukmanian & Browers, 1998). For example, the humanistic existential perspective appears to be flexible, making this approach potentially more adaptive for clients from different cultural backgrounds.

The task of identifying those elements of psychotherapy that are effective or ineffective for certain populations is not a small one. In the United States, D. W. Sue and D. Sue (1999) found that certain characteristics inherent in the structure of traditional psychotherapy practice are not effective. For example, it is expected that clients will actively self-disclose and approach issues from an expressive yet objective standpoint. These expectations are incompatible with the norms and patterns of social behavior found in many non-Western cultures. Furthermore, cultural issues can arise from a disconnect between the value orientations of the client and therapist.

In 1987, S. Sue and Zane found that the inability of therapists to provide culturally competent treatment explains many of the problems in service delivery. For example, S. Sue (1977) obtained records from 14,000 clients in 17 community mental health centers in the greater Seattle, Washington, area. Analyses indicated that while Blacks and Native Americans were overrepresented in centers, Asian Americans and Hispanics were underrepresented. In addition, all ethnic/minority groups had higher dropout rates than Whites, regardless of utilization rates. Treatment dropout after one session was higher for ethnic/minority clients (about half) than for Whites (30%). The startling conclusion was that ethnic minorities in the United States are not faring well in the mental health system. The role of culture and cultural techniques in psychotherapy is a difficult issue confronting the mental health field. Cultural knowledge and techniques generated by this knowledge are frequently applied in inappropriate ways (S. Sue & Zane, 1987).

One danger is that therapists can act on insufficient knowledge of a culture. Alternatively, another danger is that therapists can overgeneralize what they have learned about culturally dissimilar groups. Building a database of knowledge about cultures is necessary, but not sufficient, when working with ethnic/minority groups. The relevance of this knowledge does not control for individual differences among members of a particular ethnic group.

Culturally Oriented Treatments

Culturally oriented treatment has grown in the past 30 years. The ultimate goals of therapy and counseling are to resolve problems, eliminate stress, and enhance personal efficacy and quality of life. In the mid-1900s, self-actualization, based on the individual's ultimate goal of self-awareness (Maslow, 1950), was a popular theme in the United States. Thus, this ideology directed the course of psychotherapeutic counseling. This interpretation of self-experience, however, does not translate across cultures. It is a dangerous assumption that self-actualization, as deemed desirable for a particular cultural sample, is the ideal for all humans. Self-reflection and self-expression can be markedly different across individuals (Landrine, 1992; Markus & Kitayama, 1991). The implications of these different kinds of self-experience are important when developing therapeutic operations. For example, a family-oriented approach would be more favored with a self that encompasses others and is not a separate entity in isolation. On the contrary, a more individual-oriented approach may be more appropriate for a self that is separated, encapsulated, and the controller of behavior.

The expanding diversity in the United States has resulted in awareness of differences in self-presentation, patterns of communication, expectations of help, and interpersonal relationships (e.g. Abel, Metraux, & Roll, 1987; Pedersen, Sartorius, & Marsella, 1984; S. Sue & Zane, 1987). Cross-cultural therapy developed from the need to address the unique issues of nonmainstream clients.

Different approaches to cross-cultural treatment have been formulated. The etic approach compiles what the therapist has learned, and been trained in within a particular culture, and then extends/modifies interventions in culturally different therapy encounters. The applicability across cultures is tentatively assumed, and it is the responsibility of the culturally competent therapist to modify accordingly. The emic approach to cross-cultural therapy is based on experiences that are unique to the client's culture. This process entails a careful analysis of the values and practices of that culture. Therapeutic techniques can incorporate all of these different components (Draguns, 1995). Higginbotham, West, and Forsyth (1988) describe culture accommodation as a way to bridge the gulf between cultures for the planning and delivery of mental health services. Culture accommodation involves intensive preparation before developing culturally appropriate programs in a new cultural setting. Various elements need to be taken into account, including needs as perceived by the members of the culture, leaders, and representatives; and conflicts, insecurities, and preferences regarding services. The use of culture accommodation has been effective in different cultures such as Southeast Asia where culturally meaningful

intervention has developed from American and Australian models.

Specific issues that are relevant to the treatment of ethnic minorities have been identified. Gopaul-McNicol and Brice-Baker (1998) discuss important questions to consider in the early stages of therapy, for example, the choice of labels: How does the client want the therapist to refer to the ethnic group to which the client belongs? Furthermore, how important to the client is racial or ethnic similarity between therapist and client? In 1991, S. Sue, Fujino, Hu, Takeuchi, and Zane studied the effects of ethnic match between clients and therapists in psychotherapy in the Los Angeles County mental health system in California. They found that African American, American Indian, Asian American, Mexican American, and White clients had lower premature termination rates, more sessions, or better treatment outcomes when matched with ethnically similar therapists. It was suggested that ethnic match might be an important factor to consider in the treatment; however, individual differences in the effects of match appear to be important as well. Ethnic match may be important for some, but not all, clients.

Another important question to address in the early stages of therapy is how the family is defined (Gopaul-McNicol & Brice-Baker, 1998). What is the power structure within the family? How are the roles of men, women, and children defined? How are the elderly perceived and treated? Answers to some of these questions can help therapists identify important family members to include in sessions. Also, this knowledge could be instrumental in creating the appropriate therapeutic environment (i.e., arrangement of chairs, addressing commentary to the appropriate person, etc.). In addition, the use of translators is another key issue to think about in the early stages of therapy. Often, nonclinical people serve as translators in mental health settings due to lack of resources. This can result in poor quality of translation due to unfamiliarity with clinical nomenclature. Also, problems can arise such as unwillingness of the client to disclose information in the presence of a nonprofessional.

The result of focusing on all of these specific cultural variables in therapy has led to a number of dilemmas. For instance, the development of specific services targeting ethnic minority populations has ignited the heated notion of segregation (S. Sue, 1998). While the tailoring of services is effective for some underserved populations, this is not an excuse for removal of ethnic services from mainstream treatment programs. On the contrary, tailored services were designed to complement existing services.

Despite the fact that difficult issues such as segregation emerge with the implementation of ethnic matching, it is imperative to address such cultural variables in the treatment of ethnic minorities. Furthermore, the international research on biological and psychotherapeutic treatment seem to suggest that there is no universal treatment to psychopathology that has the very same effects for individuals from different cultures. Thus, culture must be considered in every step of the process of analyzing psychopathology.

Future Trends

In this chapter, we pointed to some major issues in cross-cultural clinical psychology. The field of clinical psychology began in the United States and eventually spread throughout the world. Because of its origin, it reflected the needs and perspectives of Americans in the areas of assessment, conceptualizations of mental disorders, and treatment. Later, as the influence of culture was increasingly appreciated, complex issues were recognized. How can valid assessment instruments be developed that have cross-cultural utility? Are mental disorders fundamentally the same, displaying differences only in symptoms, across cultures, or can disorders be distinct in different cultures? How can effective treatment strategies be developed with different cultural groups? While the field is continuing to grapple with these issues, let us speculate on future trends and issues.

First, culture and ethnicity offer challenges to our understanding of human beings. If psychological science is to discover general principles of human behavior, it must include the study of different cultural groups. Because of the dominance of American psychology, most of the research has included Americans as subjects of the research. Yet, Americans represent less than 5% of the world's population. In the future, it is likely that researchers will increasingly study populations other than Americans. Cross-cultural research has grown, and its importance is continuing to be recognized (Segall et al., 1998). Greater research expertise will develop in other countries, and cross-cultural comparisons will increasingly be conducted to test the generality and applicability of findings. Indigenous theories, ones that are generated from within a particular culture, are likely to grow as non-Western cultures begin to articulate their differences with American psychology. Within the United States, the study of different cultural groups will also increase.

Second, one important implication of the greater emphasis on cultural research is that psychology training programs must be able to educate and train psychologists on issues such as cultural bias, cross-cultural methodologies, and cultural differences/similarities. The ability to recognize cultural limitations in measurement instruments, etic-versus-emic approaches, means of devising cross-cultural research strategies, and so on are going to be essential in the repertoire of researchers. That is, the researchers must become culturally competent.

Third, researchers have to identify more clearly the generality or specificity of findings and theories, depending on the cultural groups studied. Currently, research reports often contain the admonishment that the reported results need to be tested on different populations. This pro forma statement is likely to acquire more real meaning as a principle because of the growth of cross-cultural research. Theories that are cross-validated with different populations will acquire more stature and respect than those theories based on one population.

Fourth, it is likely that there will be greater reliance on scientific research findings in developing treatment and preventive interventions. In the United States, there is an "empirically guided" movement, by which the evaluation of treatments and programs is based on empirical results. For example, researchers have identified treatments that are empirically supported as being effective. This trend in using research to guide clinical practice will increase both in the United States and throughout the world. However, there will be inevitable clashes between the perspectives of scientists and cultural folk healers, who may base their practice on intuition, spirituality, and faith rather than scientific research.

Fifth, difficulties in making cross-cultural comparisons and in determining cultural influences have given rise to new methodologies or approaches that can better tease out cultural phenomena. For example, Matsumoto (1999) has challenged some of the ideas of Markus and Kitayama (1991) regarding culture and self. He argues that, to test cultural explanations, innovative methodologies need to be adopted. These strategies include the following: greater use of qualitative methodologies that provide more flexibility in studying different cultures; creation of multimethod strategies that incorporate self-reports, behaviors, and observations on the individual level, while at the same time allowing for the inclusion of extraindividual factors such as economic, religious, demographic, and social variables. Immersion in other cultures also provides opportunities for genuine collaboration and mutual learning among researchers from different cultures.

Sixth, less polarity should develop between molar (e.g., cultural) and molecular (e.g., individual or biological) levels of investigating human behavior. Research findings that indicate the importance of both levels will stimulate more integrative and imaginative theories of behavior and well-being.

Seventh, the study of cultures and societies will probably continue to be controversial. We have seen major debates over issues such as assessment bias, the fundamental nature and universality of mental disorders, effectiveness of treatment, and more. When we add to these debates heated issues such as ethnocentrism and imposed emics, inequities in the delivery of mental health services, racial and ethnic stereotypes among mental health service providers, and other issues, the theories, policies, and practices in cross-cultural clinical psychology will be severely challenged.

Finally, just as the field is facing challenges, there are also possibilities to reduce ethnocentrism and cultural bias. Immersion in cultural issues can produce a more balanced perspective of the ethnocentrism and bias. Indeed, a necessary (but not sufficient) condition for understanding bias and one's own culture is to begin to understand other cultures.

References

Abel, T. M., Metraux, R., & Roll, S. (1987). *Psychotherapy and culture.* Albuquerque: University of New Mexico Press.

Adams, R. D., & Victor, M. (1985). *Principles of neurology* (3rd ed.). New York: McGraw-Hill.

Aderibigbe, Y., & Pandurangi, A. (1995). Comment: The neglect of culture in psychiatric nosology: The case of culture bound syndromes. *International Journal of Social Psychiatry, 4,* 235–241.

Al-Issa, I. (1995). *Handbook of culture and mental illness: An international perspective.* Madison, CT: International Universities Press.

American Psychiatric Association. (1952). *Diagnostic and statistical manual of mental disorders* (1st ed.). Washington, DC: Author.

American Psychiatric Association. (1968). *Diagnostic and statistical manual of mental disorders* (2nd ed.). Washington, DC: Author.

American Psychiatric Association. (1980). *Diagnostic and statistical manual of mental disorders* (3rd ed.). Washington, DC: Author.

American Psychiatric Association. (1987). *Diagnostic and statistical manual of mental disorders* (3rd ed., rev.). Washington, DC: Author.

American Psychiatric Association. (1994). *Diagnostic and statistical manual of mental disorders* (4th ed.). Washington, DC: Author.

American Psychological Association Office of Ethnic Minority Affairs. (1993). Guidelines for providers of psychological services to ethnic, linguistic, and culturally diverse populations. *American Psychologist, 48,* 45–48.

Beutler, L., & Crago, M. (Eds.). (1991). *Psychotherapy research: An international review of programmatic studies.* Washington, DC: American Psychological Association.

Brislin, R. W. (1993). *Understanding culture's influence on behavior.* New York: Harcourt Brace Jovanovich.

Cheung, F. M. (in press). Universal and indigenous dimensions of Chinese personality. In K. S. Kurasaki, S. Okazaki, & S. Sue (Eds.), *Asian American mental health: Assessment theories and methods.* Dordrecht, The Netherlands: Kluwer Academic Publishers.

Clark, W. G., Brater, D. G., & Johnson, A. R. (Eds.) (1988). *Goth's medical pharmacology* (12th ed.). St. Louis, MO: C. V. Mosby.

Costa e Silva, J. A., & Girolamo, G. (1990). Neurasthenia: history of a concept. In N. Sartorius, D. Goldberg, D. DeGirolamo, J. A. Costa e Silva, Y. Lecrubier, & H. Wittchen (Eds.), *Psychological disorders in general medical settings* (pp. 69–81). Goettingen, Germany: Hogrefe & Huber.

Dahlquist, L. M., & Fay, A. S. (1983). Cultural issues in psychotherapy. In C. E. Walker (Ed.), *The handbook of clinical psychology: Theory, research and practice* (pp. 1210–1255). Homewood, IL: Dow-Jones Irwin.

Draguns, J. G. (1995). Cultural influences upon psychopathology: Clinical and practical implications. *Journal of Social Distress, 4*(2), 79–103.

Fabrega, H. (1990). The concept of somatization as a cultural and historical product of Western medicine. *Psychosomatic Medicine, 52,* 653–672.

Fox, R. E. (1982). The need for a reorientation of clinical psychology. *American Psychologist, 37,* 1051–1057.

Freud, S. (1900). *The interpretation of dreams.* New York: Avon, 1965.

Goldberg, L. R. (1981). Language and individual differences: The search for universals in personality lexicons. In L. Wheeler (Ed.), *Reviews of personality and social psychology* (Vol. 2, pp. 141–165). Beverly Hills, CA: Sage.

Good, B., & Kleinman, A. (1985). Culture and anxiety: Cross-cultural evidence for the patterning of anxiety disorders. In A. Hussain Tuma & J. Maser (Eds.), *Anxiety and the anxiety disorders* (pp. 297–324). Hillsdale, NJ: Lawrence.

Gopaul-McNicol, S., & Brice-Baker, J. (1998). The treatment of culturally diverse clients. In *Cross-cultural practice: Assessment, treatment and training* (pp. 73–86). New York: Wiley.

Higginbotham, H. N., West, S. G., & Forsyth, D. R. (1988). *Psychotherapy and behavior change: Social, cultural, and methodological perspectives* (1st ed.). New York: Pergamon Press.

Ho, D. (1985). Cultural values and professional issues in clinical psychology: Implications from the Hong Kong Experience. *American Psychologist, 40*(11), 1212–1218.

Hopkins, J., Marcus, M., & Campbell, S. B. (1984). Postpartum depression: A critical review. *Psychological Bulletin, 95*(3), 498–515.

Howard, A., Pion, G. M., Gottfredson, G. D., Flattau, P. E., Oskamp, S., Pfaffin, S. M., Bray, D. W., & Burstein, A. G. (1986). The changing face of American psychology: A report from the committee on employment and human resources. *American Psychologist, 41*, 1311–1327.

Hui, C. H. (1988). Measurement of individualism-collectivism. *Journal of Research in Personality, 22*, 17–36.

Kaiser, A. S., Katz, R., & Shaw, B. (1998). Cultural issues in the management of depression. In S. Kazarian & D. Evans (Eds.), *Cultural clinical psychology* (pp. 177–214). New York: Oxford University Press.

Kazarian, S., & Evans, D. (Eds.). (1998). *Cultural clinical psychology*. New York: Oxford University Press.

Kleinman, A. (1982). Neurasthenia and depression: A study of somatization and culture in China. *Culture, Medicine, and Psychiatry, 6*, 117–190.

Kleinman, A. (1986). Illness meanings and illness behavior. In S. McHugh & T. M. Vallis (Eds.), *Illness behavior: A multidisciplinary model* (pp. 149–160). New York: Plenum Press.

Kleinman, A. (1987). Culture and clinical reality: Commentary on culture-bound syndromes and international disease classifications. *Culture, Medicine and Psychiatry, 11*(1), 49–52.

Kleinman, A. (1995). Do psychiatric disorders differ in different cultures? The methodological questions. In N. R. Goldberger & J. B. Veroff (Eds.), *The culture and psychology* (pp. 631–651). New York: New York University Press.

Kleinman, A., & Kleinman, J. (1985). Somatization: The interconnections in Chinese society among culture, depressive experiences, and the meanings of pain. In A. Kleinman & B. Goods (Eds.), *Culture and depression* (pp. 420–490). Berkeley: University of California Press.

Korchin, S. J. (1980). Clinical psychology and minority problems. *American Psychologist, 35*, 262–269.

Kroeber, A. L., & Kluckhohn, C. (1952). Culture: A critical review of concepts and definitions. Papers. *Peabody Museum of Archaeology and Ethnology, 47*(1).

Landrine, H. (1992). Clinical implications of cultural differences: The referential versus the indexical self. *Clinical Psychology Review, 12*, 401–415.

Lin, K. M., & Shen, W. W. (1991). Pharmacotherapy for Southeast Asian psychiatric patients. *Journal of Nervous and Mental Disease, 179*, 346–350.

Linton, R. (1938). Culture, society, and the individual. *Journal of Abnormal and Social Psychology, 33*, 425–436.

Li-Repac, D. (1980). Cultural influences on clinical perception: A comparison between Caucasian and Chinese-American therapists. *Journal of Cross-Cultural Psychology, 11*, 327–342.

Markus, H. R., & Kitayama, S. (1991). Culture and the self: Implications for cognition, emotion, and motivation. *Psychological Review, 2*, 224–253.

Maslow, A. H. (1950). Self-actualizing people: A study of psychological health. *Personality, 1*, 11–34.

Matsumoto, D. (1999). Culture and self: An empirical assessment of Markus and Kitayama's theory of independent and interdependent self-construals. *Asian Journal of Social Psychology, 2*(3), 289–310.

McHolland, J., Lubin, M., & Forbes, W. (1990). Problems in minority recruitment and strategies for retention. In G. Stricker, E. Davis-Russell, E. Bourg, E. Duran, W. R. Hammond, J. McHolland, K. Polits, & B. E. Vaughn (Eds.), *Toward ethnic diversification in psychology education and training* (pp. 137–152). Washington, DC: American Psychological Association.

Padilla, A. M., Ruiz, R. A., & Alvarez, R. (1975). Community mental health services of the Spanish speaking/surnamed population. *American Psychologist, 30*, 892–905.

Paris, J. (1991). Personality disorders, parasuicide, and culture. *Transcultural Psychiatric Research Review, 28*, 25–39.

Pedersen, P. B., Sartorius, N., & Marsella, A. J. (1984). *Mental health services: the cross-cultural context*. Beverly Hills, CA: Sage.

Reisman, J. M. (1991). *A history of clinical psychology* (2nd ed.). New York: Hemisphere.

Rogler, L. H., Malgady, R. G., & Rodriguez, O. (1989). *Hispanics and mental health: A framework for research*. Malabar, FL: Krieger.

Rosenblat, R., & Tang, S. (1987). Do Oriental psychiatric patients receive different dosages of psychotropic medication when compared with Occidentals? *Canadian Journal of Psychiatry, 32*(4), 270–274.

Sartorius, N., & Jablensky, A. (1983). *Depressive disorders in different cultures*. Geneva: World Health Organization.

Schumaker, J. F. (1996). Understanding psychopathology: Lessons from the developing world. In S. Carr & J. Schumaker (Eds.), *Psychology and the developing world* (pp. 180–190). Westport, CT: Praeger/Greenwood.

Segall, M. H., Lonner, W. J., & Berry, J. W. (1998). Cross-cultural psychology as a scholarly discipline: On the flowering of culture in behavioral research. *American Psychologist, 53*, 1101–1110.

Shakow, D. (1976). What is clinical psychology? *American Psychologist, 29*, 553–560.

Smith, D. E., & Wesson, D. R. (1985). *The benzodiazepines: Current standards for medical practice*. Boston: MTP Press.

Sue, D. W., & Sue, D. (1999). *Counseling the culturally different: Theory and practice* (3rd ed.). New York: Wiley.

Sue, S. (1977). Community mental health services to minority groups: Some optimism, some pessimism. *American Psychologist, 32*, 616–624.

Sue, S. (1983). Ethnic minority issues in psychology: A reexamination. *American Psychologist, 38*, 583–593.

Sue, S. (1996). Measurement, testing, and ethnic bias: Can solutions be found? In G. Sodowsky & J. C. Impara (Eds.), *Multicultural assessment in counseling and clinical psychology* (pp. 7–37). Lincoln, NE: Buros Institute of Mental Measurements.

Sue, S. (1998). In search of cultural competence in psychotherapy and counseling. *American Psychologist, 53*, 440–448.

Sue, S., Fujino, D., Hu, L. Takeuchi, D. T., & Zane, N. W. S. (1991). Community mental health services for ethnic minority groups: A test of the cultural responsiveness hypothesis. *Journal of Consulting and Clinical Psychology, 59*, 533–540.

Sue, S., & Zane, N. (1987). The role of culture and cultural techniques in psychotherapy: A critique and reformulation. *American Psychologist, 42*(1), 37–45.

Ting-Toomey, S. (1991). Intimacy expressions in three cultures: France, Japan, and the United States. *International Journal of Intercultural Relations, 15*, 29–46.

Toukmanian, S. G., & Brouwers, M. C. (1998). Cultural aspects of self-disclosure and psychotherapy. In S. S. Kazarian & D. R. Evans (Eds.), *Cultural clinical psychology* (pp. 106–124). New York: Oxford University Press.

Triandis, H. C., & Brislin, R. W. (1984). Cross-cultural psychology. *American Psychologist, 39*, 1006–1016.

U.S. Commission on Civil Rights. (1992). Introduction. In *Civil rights issues facing Asian Americans in the 1990s* (pp. 1–21). Washington, DC: Author.

Wallin, J. E. W. (1929). The nature of G, as seen by the clinical psychologist. *Psychological Clinic, 18*, 196–198.

Watson, J. B. (1913). Psychology as the behaviorist views it. *Psychological Review, 20*, 158–179.

World Health Organization. (1973). *The international pilot study of schizophrenia* (Vol. 1). Geneva: Author.

World Health Organization. (1979). *Schizophrenia: An international follow-up study*. New York: Wiley.

World Health Organization. (1983). *Depressive disorders in different cultures*. Geneva: Author.

Yang, K. S., & Bond, M. H. (1990). Exploring implicit personality theories with indigenous or imported constructs: The Chinese case. *Journal of Personality and Social Psychology, 58*, 1087–1095.

Zane, N. (1999, August). The many faces of loss of face—research and implications. Paper presented at the annual convention of the American Psychological Association, Boston.

Part IV: Culture and Social Behavior

No area of psychology has been studied as much cross-culturally as the broad area defined by social psychology. The issues cross-cultural psychology raise about social behavior are intense, intricate, and complex; yet, they represent some of the most important and pressing issues facing mainstream and cross-cultural psychology today.

In this light, in chapter 16, Bond and Tedeschi provide a framework future cross-cultural research on social psychological issues can use to help develop universal theories of social behavior. Focusing on the process of unpackaging cultural effects, they suggest that the inclusion of specific, measurable variables in lieu of global and abstract concepts of culture is necessary to force improvements in theory and method. While they use the area of aggression as an example, their points are applicable to all areas of social behavior and are consonant with the message provided throughout this volume.

In chapter 17, using a comprehensive review of the cross-cultural literature on social cognition as a platform, Kashima argues for the creation and development of theoretical models of the social cognition of cultural dynamics. He argues forcefully that past and current research in the area has been biased by an individualistic conception of meaning, in terms of both social cognition and culture, and suggests that alternative meanings of both need to be incorporated in future research and theory.

In chapter 18, presenting a comprehensive review of three areas, Smith describes the contributions that cross-cultural research and theory has made to our understanding of how people influence the behaviors of others. He argues quite convincingly that future research will need to go beyond current efforts in exploring the ways in which individuals behave in intercultural situations and within different types of groups. These efforts will require fundamental changes in research methodology, but are necessary if work in this area will continue to evolve in our increasingly diversifying world.

In chapter 19, Leung and Stephan present a comprehensive review of the cross-cultural literature on three areas of justice—distributive, procedural, and retributive—as well as the literature on perceptions of injustice. They argue for the development of a universal theory of justice that allows for the simultaneous consideration of abstract constructs and rules with context-specific situations based on functionality. The implications of work in this area to all arenas affected by intercultural conflict are enormous.

Finally, in chapter 20, Ward synthesizes three large perspectives to the study of acculturation—culture learning, stress and coping, and social identification—providing a comprehensive review and future directions in each. She argues forcefully and convincingly, however, for an integrated, synthesized view of acculturation theories and research in the future, the message of which is applicable not only to acculturation, but also to all areas covered in this book and more.

As with all other chapters in this book, the chapters presented in this section each and collectively provide strong messages about the vision of the continued evolution of cross-cultural psychology to the creation of universal theories of social behavior. Perhaps more so than others, these chapters highlight the difficulties and complexities that are inherent in that evolution, however. Yet, the integration of concept and the incorporation of previously ignored methods are necessities that we must face to ensure the achievement of that vision.

16

Polishing the Jade

A Modest Proposal for Improving the Study of Social Psychology across Cultures

MICHAEL HARRIS BOND & JAMES T. TEDESCHI

The area of social psychology has provided cross-cultural research and theory with a natural niche in which to flourish over the past few decades, undoubtedly due to the fact that investigations of social behavior lend themselves most neatly to the study of cultural influences. Thus, the study of issues and processes that would typically be considered social psychological in nature has dominated, and continues to dominate, the cross-cultural literature (while, of course, cross-cultural work in all other areas of psychology has also flourished, as witnessed in all the other chapters and sections of this volume).

And yet, as Bond and Tedeschi note in the beginning of their chapter, social psychologists who grapple with culture may often feel frustrated by the difficulty of achieving a sense of closure, most likely because the influence of culture on social processes is enormous, and it is often difficult to get a handle on all the factors that influence social behavior. This frustration is most likely due also to the fact that the field is yet to develop truly universal theories that incorporate cultural variables to explain cultural differences in behavior. Thus, when the field develops such models, and creates and conducts "scientifically defensible and theoretically plausible research about socially significant problems," only then will social psychologists interested in culture begin to feel a sense of closure on issues of importance.

In this first chapter in the section on social behavior, Bond and Tedeschi offer suggestions for how to achieve this sense of closure by demonstrating how future cross-cultural research and theory on social psychological issues can be conducted. They focus on the issue of unpackaging culture, in which the global, abstract concept of culture that is often referred to in research is replaced by specific, objective, and measurable psychological (and other) traits and characteristics (called *context variables*). This approach forces theorists to think about what it is specifically about culture that produces differences and why. When measured, they allow researchers to go beyond making presumptions about cultural differences in their samples to actual testing of the degree to which the specific cultural variables account for the variance in their data. This approach, while not new in concept, is still not wholeheartedly utilized in the field, and Bond and Tedeschi suggest, and correctly so, that such procedures in theorizing and conducting studies need to be given strong consideration in the future.

Bond and Tedeschi offer a review of cross-cultural research in the area of aggression to demonstrate and highlight their views. Early research on this topic, including their own, involved simple cross-cultural comparisons without the inclusion of such context variables that unpackage culture. Thus, although the interpretations of those data were interesting and provocative, Bond and Tedeschi suggest that those types of studies remain "incomplete social science." Instead, future research needs to explicate those variables that may account for cultural differences, measure them, and directly test the degree to which they account for variations.

Yet, while this concept may be easy to grasp, it may be very difficult to place into practice. Bond and Tedeschi offer a number of conceptual difficulties and traps that make the consideration of context variables difficult. In particular, there are a number of nonpsychological variables that need to be considered when accounting for cultural differences in social behavior, including weather and climate, geography, political systems, socioeconomic status, and so forth. Also, how societal values play out and interact with individual psychology is an area of consideration that needs further elaboration if future research is truly able to make a dent in this problem.

While not easy, however, the approach advocated by Bond and Tedeschi clearly represents a fundamental improvement over current approaches to cross-cultural research on social behavior and promises to bring us closer to the development of universal theories of social processes and the creation of the "scientifically defensible and theoretically plausible research" for which they argue in the introduction. In this sense, the argument in favor of revisions in research design and methodology for the ultimate goal of developing panculturally valid theories of behavior is consonant with the message found in the entire book.

Now the general who wins a battle makes
many calculations in his temple ere the battle is fought.
The general who loses a battle makes
but few calculations beforehand.
It is by attention to this point that I can
foresee
who is likely to win or lose.
(Sun Tzu, *The Art of War*,
Book 1, Vol. 26, L. Giles, Trans.)

It is intellectually exciting to study about culture's influence on behavior: the sweep of culture is so wide, its complexity so great, and its forms so varied. One is never bored, although one frequently feels frustrated by the difficulty of achieving a satisfying sense of closure as a social psychologist grappling with culture. For us, that sense of closure will occur when the discipline produces and fleshes out universal theories that incorporate cultural variables to explain cultural variations in social behavior. Satisfaction will also be enlarged when the discipline does scientifically defensible and theoretically persuasive research about socially significant problems. We want to quarry jade, not quartz, and then to polish this jade into works of precision and luster.

This chapter presents our current assessment about what and how—what sort of model is needed to link culture to behavior and how to proceed to develop models that are persuasive to the mainstream of social psychologists. We sense that they regard the efforts of cross-cultural psychologists as those of quirky amateurs, amusing and provocative, but somewhat disorganized and romantic. With some thought and care at the outset, however, we maintain that psychologists dealing with culture can challenge this understandable, but unhappy, reputation by attending to the issues raised below.

We grapple with the problem of how cross-cultural differences can be explained by social psychological theories. To ground our presentation, we use a recent theory of aggression (Tedeschi, 1983; Tedeschi & Felson, 1994) as an example of how this integration may be articulated. This topic of aggression (Tedeschi & Bond, 2001) is socially significant and presents in bold relief all the challenges that characterize the growing field of culture and social behavior. Finally, we examine the rationale and possible outcomes of trying to identify psychological mediators of cultural differences in social behavior.

Explaining Cultural Differences

> In the practical art of war, the best thing of all
> is to take the enemy's country whole and intact;
> To shatter and destroy it is not so good.
> (Sun Tzu, *The Art of War*,
> Book 3, Vol. 1, L. Giles, Trans.)

Cross-cultural research begins with the observation of differences in the frequency of behavior across cultural groups, either in outcomes, like homicide (Robbins, DeWalt, & Pelto, 1972), or in routes to those outcomes, like the use of insults directed toward a targeted individual (Felson, 1978) or members of the target's group (Semin & Rubini, 1990). For present purposes, such behavioral differences have interest only insofar as they stimulate scientific thought about the reason for those differences. Provoked, researchers then attempt to identify that feature of the cultures in question that is associated with, and hence may account for, the observed differences in the frequency of the behavioral outcome.

That feature of the culture must, however, be translated into individual, psychological characteristics that generate the behavior. These psychological characteristics could be beliefs, habits, values, self-construals, personality dispositions, emotions, attributions about oneself or another person, or whatever. The point is that its level varies across persons in any society and relates to the target behavior in persons from all cultures. If this linkage between psychological variable and behavior is found in all cultural groups investigated, then the relationship may be proposed as a "universal."

"Unpackaging" Culture Psychologically

Having unearthed this psychological characteristic, regression equations may be run to determine if the differences across the cultural groups in frequency of the target behavior may be explained as arising from variations in the level of that psychological attribute found in persons from those cultural groups (Bond, 1998b). The answer may be yes, no, or partly. If yes, one might shift focus to examine the features of a culture that give rise to higher or lower average levels of the psychological characteristic in its members. If no, one would probably continue either refining the psychological measure for multicultural work or searching for other psy-

chological explanations. If partly, then the search for additional psychological factors would continue.

This process of explaining the different levels of the target behavior across cultural groups is called *unpackaging* culture at the level of individuals (Clark, 1987; Whiting, 1976). As a result of successful unpackaging, the empty, categorical variable of "culture" is replaced by a measurable, psychological variable as the causal agent (see, e.g., Singelis, Bond, Sharkey, & Lai, 1999). Culture now enters the model as a "positioning factor," a set of influences that affect the typical level of that psychological variable in its members.

Once this goal has been achieved, researchers can then move their attention to the cultural dynamics by which persons in different cultural groups end up with different levels of the operative psychological variable. So, for example, being socialized for aggression by parents relates to male aggressive behavior cross-culturally (Segall, Ember, & Ember, 1997). This socialization press in a cultural system may be driven by the group's need to wage war (Ember & Ember, 1994) that arises in part from resource scarcity. So, different levels of homicide across cultural groups may be related to stronger socialization of sons for aggressiveness by parents, a socialization that arises from the cultural need to prepare men to wage war.

Cross-Cultural Research on Aggression without Unpackaging

Bond, Wan, Leung, and Giacalone (1985) were interested in how the cultural dynamics of collectivism and high power distance (Hofstede, 1980, chapter 3) would shape the individual response to an insult. They presented Chinese (Hong Kongese) and American respondents with a scenario in which one member of a management team insulted another for incompetent performance. The target of this insult was either a superior or a subordinate in the organization and either a member of the same work group or of another work group.

As predicted, Bond et al. (1985) found that the insulter was rated less negatively by the Chinese (from a collectivist, high power distance culture) when he insulted a subordinate from the in-group. The authors argued that the in-group superior in Chinese culture had a closer connection to his group (via cultural collectivism) and enjoyed the prerogative of the superior to counterattack his subordinate (via cultural high power distance) relative to an American superior.

The authors' theoretical reasoning from the cultural dynamics of collectivism and power distance was persuasive and tantalizing. The full scientific logic of their position, however, required that they provide an individual-level measure for both collectivism and power distance that would relate to derogation of the insulter both within and across American and Chinese respondents. This they did not do. Without such an individual-level linkage, their conclusion remains provocative, but incomplete, social science (Bond, 1995).

Cultures of Violence

There has been some fascinating cross-cultural research on aggression that addresses the hypothesis that certain cultural groups socialize their members for violence. A review of this research shows the usefulness of unpackaging as a strategy for improving the persuasiveness of argumentation in social science.

This work concerns differential homicide rates across cultures and across subcultures. It could have begun, as is so often the case in cross-cultural work, with scattered observations about differences in this dramatic form of aggression: So, for example, homicide appears to have been more frequent in the Aztec empire as opposed to the Incan empire (Prescott, 1961); it was higher in Italy than in Spain after the World War II (Archer & Gartner, 1984); it is committed much more frequently by men than by women, especially in certain cultural areas like Afghanistan (Adler, 1981). These fragmented observations can later be brought into the ambit of cross-cultural psychology once a broad, comparable measure of homicide is produced.

The United Nations requires its members to give annual reports of many social indicators, including homicide rates. These can be found in the *Demographic Yearbook* (United Nations, annual) and have been used in cross-national studies, such as that by Robbins et al. (1972), which linked murder rates to heat-humidity. In addition, most large democracies, such as the United States, gather homicide rates from their constituent political units. Given that each of the 50 states in the American union has a different culture of schooling, legal institutions, economic activity, and so forth, cross-state studies can be run to assess hypotheses about variables associated with their different homicide rates. So, for example, Wilkinson, Kawachi, and Kennedy (1998) have shown that those states with higher inequalities in income distribution have higher murder (and assault) rates.

Cohen (1996) has linked the higher rates of homicide in the American South to a more permissive legal code surrounding violence in these states, including less-restrictive laws concerning the owning and use of guns, spousal abuse, defense of property and of self, and to a wider application of capital and corporal punishment. Cohen and Nisbett (1994) have argued that these laws developed out of herding cultures with low levels of policing and enforcement of property rights that characterized the South. In this social ecology, cultures of honor (Peristiany, 1965) emerged in which members were socialized to intervene personally and decisively to stop theft of their property. By social extension, one's reputation for toughness was a part of one's property and useful social capital as well, so one was socialized to counterattack vigorously when insulted. This "prickliness" or hypersensitivity in response to insult persists today, so that cycles of perceived attack and counterattack more readily develop, sometimes escalating into homicide (Felson, 1978).

In addition, contemporary southern states carry a history of slavery and the cultural sequelae associated with the systematic and normative practice of containing, disciplining, and punishing slaves. These would include a sharpened sensitivity to affront or challenge, combined with a normative code that endorses strong countermeasures to reestablish one's authority when challenged. Together, this legal code and historical legacy contribute to a "southern culture of violence" (SCV) in which attacks on others are legitimized as a defense of one's honor or reputation. This cultural element in the context of the wider American social logic leads to higher rates of homicide (and assault).

This is a plausible argument, grounded in subsistence economies, legal institutions, and socialization practices, and eventually personal dispositions of the actors involved, to account for differences in homicide rates across the American states and possibly across cultural or national groups. There are, however, two problems, one of concept and one of translation.

The first is conceptual. The differences in homicide rates are also linked to at least two other factors that distinguish states from one another: their average temperatures (Anderson & Anderson, 1998) and their levels of relative inequality in the distribution of income (Wilkinson et al., 1998). With respect to temperature, Anderson and Anderson have shown that, after controlling for temperature, a societal-level measure they developed for the SCV no longer relates to the homicide rate of a given state. So, the operative societal variable may be ambient average temperature and not its level of SCV. Perhaps the same may also be shown for levels of relative economic inequality. Or, it may be demonstrated that the effects of temperature are reduced or eliminated when relative economic inequality is controlled.

For our present purposes, however, these contentious societal-level results leave researchers unsure about which psychological variables they should be exploring as factors related to individual acts labeled as "murder"—those individual-level factors related to SCV, to temperature, or to relative inequality.

The second problem concerns the need to translate the predictive factor at the societal level into an operative factor at the psychological level. It is not a nation, a culture, or a state, but an individual who murders another person, and only certain individuals kill others. Social psychologists want to isolate and study the psychological variables that are linked to homicide. Here, we confront the happy frustration that homicide is an extremely rare act that would never be provoked in a laboratory situation. So, inventive researchers have developed a number of laboratory paradigms that stimulate surrogate homicides, such as the delivery of intense electrical shock in the teacher-learner scenario (e.g., Milgram, 1974), verbal retaliation following gratuitous insults (e.g., Bond & Venus, 1991), dominance assertion through verbal exchanges (Cohen, Nisbett, Bowdle, & Schwartz, 1996), and so forth. The admissibility of these surrogate actions in the study of homicide depends on the plausibility of the linkage between these surrogates and homicide provided by reconstructions of homicidal acts (e.g., Gilligan, 1996; Toch, 1969) or by theory (e.g., the social interactionist theory of coercive actions of Tedeschi & Felson, 1994).

Psychological Representations of a Culture of Violence

Let us assume that an SCV is at least part of a societal complex relating to higher homicide rates in the United States. What might be the psychological variable that would derive from the SCV and relate to a homicide surrogate? Herein lies a key problem for our model of how cross-cultural social psychology should be done: As Anderson and Anderson (1998) claim,

"There has not yet been a clear statement of what values and attitudes constitute the culture of honor, so there has not been an individual difference measure developed to assess culture of honor" (p. 291). Of course, the operative psychological variable could equally well be the attribution that another intends to harm you (Tedeschi & Felson, 1994), a higher propensity for violence in response to the other's norm violation (Caprara, Barbaranelli, & Zimbardo's 1996 positive evaluation of violence), the assessment that third parties believe you should retaliate against the other's insult (Vandello & Cohen, 1998), or some other psychological construct.

However the researcher chooses to measure the SCV at the individual level, this scale score should be shown to predict the homicide surrogate. It must also unpackage or explain the difference in this homicide surrogate between persons from regions strong and weak in an SCV (Anderson & Anderson, 1998; Tedeschi & Bond, 2001). Cohen and collaborators have done a series of studies attempting to identify what might be the individual-level variable that distinguishes American southerners from northerners in their reactions to insult (e.g., Vandello & Cohen, 1998). Unfortunately, the Cohen team has only compared group averages in the hypothesized mediating psychological variable; they have not reported the correlational analyses linking this mediator to the homicide surrogate. This additional step is needed to unpackage the difference between southerners and northerners in the homicide surrogate.

Whenever discovered, this individual-level measure of an SCV may also constitute an effective measure for other cultures of violence. There are countries of the world other than the United States (e.g., China, Brazil) where substantial regional variation in subsistence and other practices may permit the differential growth of cultures of violence within the same national borders. Likewise, there are similar variations from country to country that would favor differential development of such cultures (Peristany, 1965). An individual-level measure that could unpackage these regional and national differences in homicide surrogates would be an essential support for a universal, social psychological theory of homicide.

Cultural Variation in the Strength of the Mediator

The psychological mediator of the relationship between culture and the homicide surrogate may be found to vary in its predictive strength from culture to culture. As an example, Diener and Diener (1995) examined the relationship between self-esteem and life satisfaction in 31 national samples. They argued that persons from individualistic cultural systems are socialized to attend more closely to their internal attributes, like self-esteem, in assessing their life situations. Consistent with their argument, a nation's level of individualism was shown to moderate the strength of the linkage between the self-esteem mediator and the life satisfaction of its members (see also Kwan, Bond, & Singelis, 1997).

So, variations in cultural dynamics may result in a universal factor in behavior exercising a stronger or weaker effect on that behavior. Triandis (1980) has proposed a general model of behavior based on the relative strength of three factors: social concerns, affect toward the behavior, and perceived consequences arising from the behavior. He argues that behavior in individualistic cultures is influenced more strongly by affect associated with the behavior and consequences attached to the act; in collectivist cultural systems, social norms about appropriate behavior in this setting are relatively more determinative.

Yamagishi, Cook, and Watabe (1998) have applied reasoning like this to design experiments on commitment formation comparing (individualistic) Americans and (collectivist) Japanese. They describe Japan as an "institutional" culture with "systems of mutual monitoring and sanctioning to curtail free riding" (pp. 167–168), which thereby promote cooperation. Social norms are relatively more powerful in this collectivist culture. Those in the individualistic American culture avoid implementing these social controls, but instead generate cooperation by socializing members for greater general trust. Consequences attached to the act of trusting are relatively more powerful in this individualistic culture. In consequence, Japanese cooperate more than Americans when social monitoring is in place; Americans cooperate more than Japanese when social monitoring is absent.

Designing Social Psychological Theories to Include Culture

So, culture may work to affect social behaviors in two ways: It may increase socialization pressures for a certain psychological outcome, thereby increasing the general strength of a mediating variable that affects behavior (the cultural positioning effect). Or, it may increase the relative weight attached to a psychological variable in influencing behavior (the cultural linkage effect). To determine which of these two cultural processes is occurring, we must first expend thought and energy toward developing culturally equivalent measures (see Van de Vijver & Leung, 1997) for both the social behaviors of interest and their psychological predictors. Then, we must do cross-cultural studies to determine how the mediating psychological variables operate to increase or decrease the likelihood of our target social behavior.

The development of such theories would help address Messick's (1988) concern that our discipline needs to make scientifically defensible, psychological sense out of cultural differences in behavior:

> Whatever it is that we mean by culture—institutions, attitudes, personality traits, social environments, expectations, and so forth—what are the processes by means of which it influences behavior? This challenge involves an examination of what culture means psychologically, and the mechanisms and processes that express culture through action. (p. 289)

Unpackaging culture requires that we deploy the creativity and skill necessary to elaborate and measure these mechanisms and processes. The processes by which "these mechanisms and processes" operate can only be determined once they have been identified. But what are these mechanisms, and how do we identify them? We now turn to this fundamental question.

An Extended Example: Explaining Cultural Differences in Aggressive Behavior

> Soldiers when in desperate straits lose the sense of fear.
> If there is no place of refuge, they will stand firm.
> If they are in the heart of a hostile country, they will show a stubborn front.
> If there is no help for it, they will fight hard.
> (Sun Tzu, *The Art of War*, Book 11, Vol. 24, L. Giles, Trans.)

The history of cross-cultural research has often involved the strategy of replicating studies, usually done first in the United States. As P. B. Smith and Bond (1998, chapter 2) have documented, this research sometimes failed to replicate findings across cultures. These "failures," however, stimulated the search for explanations of the inconsistencies. Similarly, some early work of anthropologists attempted to assess the universality of theories. They, too, encountered surprises. For example, the child care practices among the Trobriand Islanders, which consisted of passing children from uncle to uncle in the village, undermined Freud's views on the Oedipus complex (Malinowski, 1927). Mead's (1949) work showed that sex roles across three tribes in New Guinea were so different as to constitute role reversals; this undermined biological theories of gender differences. These sorts of discovery led to cross-cultural theorizing and research on gender socialization (e.g., Barry, Child, & Bacon, 1959).

Researchers in each of these disciplines have discovered provocative results and generated new puzzles to solve. However, another strategy for testing knowledge is to examine a rather general theory in terms of how cultural variables affect the processes postulated by the theory. The idea is that what may appear to be failures of predictions by a theory when tests are conducted may instead represent differences in levels or in strengths of individual processes that vary systematically and understandably across cultures. We examine this strategy in some detail using the social interactionist theory of aggression proposed by Tedeschi (1983) and elaborated by Tedeschi and Felson (1994).

Social Interaction Theory of Aggressive Behavior

The social interaction theory of aggressive behavior proposes that actors have three motives that lead them to threaten others and to act in a punitive fashion: motives for social control, for justice, and for identity. The motive for social control is the basic one of influencing others. Its fundamental assumption is that people are interdependent with respect to outcomes. Hence, it is necessary to get others to do what one wants to obtain reinforcements and avoid punishments. Material rewards, love, respect, status, safety, and other valued outcomes are mediated by other people. Many forms of influence are used to induce others to mediate desired outcomes, including persuasion, prom-

ises, exhortations, rewards, threats, and punishments.

Tedeschi and Felson (1994) propose that threats and punitive acts occur (typically) when more positive forms of influence are expected to, or actually do, fail, and the outcome pursued is too desirable for the actor to give up its pursuit. People who lack resources, expertise, credibility, attractiveness, and status, which are important power bases, are not likely to be confident that they can effectively use positive forms of influence. They are uneducated and inarticulate and not able to encode and transmit persuasive communications successfully to more knowledgeable people—those who usually control the desired outcomes. Their lack of credibility and/or attractiveness detracts from the believability of their communications, so the targets of their influence attempts will remain unpersuaded. Thus, "powerless" people are those who are left with no other means to influence others than to use some form of coercion or force.

Conflict situations, which usually involve competition for scarce resources, tend to make positive forms of influence ineffective. When two or more people want the same resource and only one can have it, we have the prototypical case of conflict. In such conflicts a person can either try to take the resource from the other, let the other have the resource, or try to find some compromise and share the resource. In conflicts, attempts to use positive forms of influence tend to be distrusted, since each party knows that the other person wants what only one of them can have (Deutsch, 1994). Competition and coercion have been shown to be the preponderant mode of interaction in such zero-sum conflicts (see Tedeschi, Schlenker, & Bonoma, 1973).

As postulated by social interactionist theory, a second motive for using threats and punishments is the desire to restore justice. When people perceive that they have been treated unfairly, they become angry. The emotion of anger is associated with a desire to restore justice or, more simply, a desire to get even with the wrongdoer. Justice can be restored if the perpetrator makes restitution or perhaps through an apology that admits the wrong, gives a promise not to do it again, and affirms the grievant's values and norms. Justice can also be restored by imposing the same amount of harm on the perpetrator as was done to the grievant—the principle of *lex talionis*.

While advanced societies have legal and social institutions to act as intermediaries of justice-related disputes, there are many occasions when grievants must simply engage in self-help (Black, 1983). For example, the high incidence of violence among African Americans may be based on distrust of the legal system. When African Americans experience injustice, they may be hesitant to seek help from the legal system and instead engage in punitive acts toward those they hold responsible for the wrong done to them. This logic would also apply in societies in which historical developments have led to a mistrust of the legal system because of its underdevelopment or its influenceability by political and social considerations. Similarly, punitive actions within the family, including spouse and child abuse, are instances of self-help in rule- or norm-violating circumstances in which it is not usual for third parties to intervene.

The third motive postulated by adherents of social interactionist theory is a desire to promote and defend valued identities. The use of coercion to promote identities is associated with a desire to be perceived as powerful, strong, courageous, and masculine. The image of the American gunslinger or the Japanese samurai, who know no fear and seek out physically dangerous situations in which to demonstrate their prowess, represents a proactive use of coercion to establish a desired identity. Police officers, neighborhood toughs, and soccer rowdies may attack others or provoke them into fights to demonstrate to others how tough they are.

Social interactionist theory also stipulates that a major motivation for punitive actions toward others is to defend personal and group identities. When an identity is threatened or attacked (for example, as occurs when insults are used), the person can either accept the lowered power and status implied by silence or can restore status by putting the other person down. Such retaliation leads to a "character contest" in which both parties are motivated to avoid looking weak and ineffective and to maintain positive identities. The interdependent dynamics of a character contest lead to escalation and often to assaults and homicides (Felson & Steadman, 1983). Unlike a justice-related motive, for which the goal is to get even, individuals in a character contest are motivated by a desire to "win."

Cultural Variables and Social Control Motivation

Tedeschi and Felson (1994) proposed that threats and punitive acts are often used to con-

trol the behavior of others. In this sense, aggressive acts are simply aversive forms of social influence and serve the power interests of the controlling individual. The individual who issues threats wants compliance from target individuals for compliance mediates some outcome for the threatener. This form of coercion is usually a nonpreferred form of influence because it carries high costs in terms of possible retaliation and negative social reactions by others.

Among the factors the individual considers when making a decision whether to use coercive tactics is the procedural value attached to such actions. Mahatma Ghandi abhorred the use of violent means to protest, but was not above using nonviolent coercive tactics. Amish and Quaker subcultures teach and practice nonviolence and use shunning as a severe form of punishment against offending members. Studies in developmental psychology have shown that, as compared to nonaggressive boys, aggressive boys believed that coercion would be effective in controlling others (Boldizar, Perry, & Perry, 1989). The implication is that such beliefs about the efficacy and acceptability of coercive tactics increase the frequency of aggression.

Cultural differences in aggressive behavior may then be unpackaged in terms of the procedural value attached to such actions. There is some reason to believe that procedural values to some extent are incorporated into a person's self-concept. Kim and colleagues have found that respondents higher in interdependent self-construals report more reluctance to impose on or hurt others during conversation than do those who are higher in independent construals (Kim et al., 1996; Kim, Sharkey, & Singelis, 1994). Thus, a cultural variation in aggressive verbal behavior appears to be related to whether it is given negative value in terms of one's self-construal. Similar connections for culturally related self-construals may be found for strategies of conflict resolution (see e.g., Bond, Leung, & Schwartz, 1992) and other social behaviors involved in managing interdependencies harmoniously.

Recent theorizing about the cultural dimensions of the self may also be tied to the goals and tactics of individuals in social conflict situations. Markus and Kitayama's (1991) ideas about collectivism and individualism focused on the concepts of independent and interdependent selves. They argued that

> For many cultures of the world, the Western notion of the self as an entity containing

significant dispositional attributes, and as detached from context, is simply not an adequate description of selfhood. Rather, in many construals, the self is viewed as interdependent with the surrounding context, and it is the other or the "self-in-relation-to-other" that is focal in individual experience. (p. 225)

Ohbuchi and Tedeschi (1998) have found that Japanese and Americans have different goals and preferred tactics in social conflict situations. These differences may be mediated by the self-construals of the respondents. The Japanese, who represent a collectivist culture and presumably tend to have more interdependent self-construals, report a strong motivation to maintain social relationships with the person with whom they are in conflict. They also tend to use indirect means to resolve the conflict, such as seeking third-party mediators and offering conciliatory initiatives. Americans, who represent an individualistic culture, are more oriented toward finding a just individual solution to social conflicts with others and tend to use more confrontational tactics. If interdependent self-construals are linked to the promotion of social harmony, and if independent self-construals are linked to the promotion of individual interests (and perhaps a devaluing of interdependent interests), then cultural differences in the propensity to use coercive tactics (e.g., aggressive behavior) may be unpacked in terms of self-construals.

The value of specific resources and their scarcity vary across cultures. Hence, what outcomes will motivate an individual to try to influence others and what will be a source of competition and conflict will also differ. Among the Mbuti of Africa, men fight over hunting territories (Turnbull, 1965). The scarcity of women is a major source of fighting among the Yananomo of Brazil (Chagnon, 1976). In societies in which property is shared, conflicts seldom develop over property (Knauft, 1987).

Cultural Variables and Justice Motivation

The judgment that another person is responsible and blameworthy for an action that breaks a rule or violates a norm causes the perceiver to become angry. Perceived injustice jump-starts the justice process that often evokes punitive actions by the grievant. Since the norms and laws are not the same in all societies, what will constitute a norm violation will be different

across cultures (see, e.g., Argyle, Henderson, Bond, Iizuka, & Contarello, 1986). Hence, the specific triggering event for the justice process will vary across cultures. Subcultural differences within a society may also be attributed to diversity of norms. It has been found, for example, that Muslims and Hindus within India responded in dissimilar ways to 21 situations depicted as norm violations (Ghosh, Kumar & Tripathi, 1992).

Tedeschi et al. (in preparation) are examining the causes of anger and forms of anger expression in four cultures: Hong Kong, Japan, Germany, and the United States. They suggest that, in multicultural societies, there are more conflicts over norms and misinterpretations of ambiguous actions by individuals who represent different ethnic groups, and hence there is more potential for anger-provoking circumstances. Thus, it might be expected that anger would be experienced more frequently in the United States and Hong Kong than in Japan and Germany, especially in response to out-group members; there is just a lot more social interaction with out-group members and hence more opportunity to experience negative consequences. On the other hand, individuals in more homogeneous cultures might perceive out-group members as more threatening to ingroup values and thus may experience a higher level of anger and be less inhibited in expressing it against out-group members.

Cultural norms may also regulate the expression of anger. The expression of anger is perceived as antisocial by the Gebusi of New Guinea and by Central Eskimo groups of North America (Knauft, 1987). Inhibition of anger in these groups may be unpacked by the expected social costs of anger expression. The concealment of grievances does not imply that nothing is done to restore justice by the grievant, however. The Gebusi may not publicly express their grievances, but they have an extremely high homicide rate (Knauft, 1987). Failure to express grievances makes it unlikely that nonviolent redress in the form of restitution or apology can occur and thus may result in extremely violent retribution.

Cultural Variables and Identity Motivation

Any cultural variables that heighten a person's sensitivity to identity threats will lower the threshold for engaging in character contests. Cultural variables, such as those suggested by the culture of honor hypothesis (see, e.g., Cohen, Vandello, & Rantilla, 1998), may also make it more likely that physically violent reactions will be evoked by identity threat. If we view identity threat as an individual-level mediator of retaliatory behavior, then it may be concluded that events leading to identity threat result in retaliatory behavior across persons from the four cultural groups that are being studied by Tedeschi et al. (in preparation). Perceived identity threat should explain the average differences in identity-defensive retaliatory aggression across the four cultural groups (American, Hong Kong Chinese, Japanese, and German).

Unpackaging requires sensitivity to the possibility that cultural variables may affect both cognitions and actions. A person might be very sensitive to identity threats, but be very inhibited about responding overtly to defend the self. Tedeschi et al. (in preparation) hypothesize that philosophical traditions and historical subsistence practices have led these four cultures to differ in their levels of collectivism. This collectivism results in socialization practices that encourage a high value for social harmony. It might be expected that insults would be more frequently issued in individualistic cultures, in which there is less concern for social harmony, and as a consequence people are more confrontational. People in individualistic cultures might be less inhibited about responding aggressively to defend identities against attacks by others. However, it might also be predicted that people in collectivist societies may be more sensitive to threats against group identity and may react more aggressively to defend the group than would people in individualistic societies. A lower tendency to counterattack short-circuits the cycle of escalation (Felson & Stedman, 1983). The implication from the above analysis is that Japanese would be less prone than Americans to commit homicides within the in-group, but they might be much more intense in attacking out-group members who threaten them.

Putting the Theory to the
Cross-Cultural Test

The advantage of using a mainstream theory to explain cross-cultural differences is that the theory provides a set of well-established mediators and moderators of social behavior that can be articulated with already identified cultural variables. Initially, this enterprise is an exercise in ad hoc thinking since the social psychologist is merely speculating about how well each cul-

tural factor might articulate with the processes postulated by the theory. The theorizing must then be tested through the process of cross-cultural unpackaging. So, for example, the likelihood of engaging in personal retribution for unjust actions by another are plausibly linked to perceptions that social agents or their institutions will act to redress the injustice. These perceptions may be measured and linked to both cultural group membership and retributive activity.

In this way, theories focus our attention on operative psychological variables that can be measured and tested cross-culturally. We can then learn how our theories apply in culturally diverse settings and work toward an understanding of how cultural variables affect these psychological processes.

Mediators and Moderators of Cross-Cultural Differences

> Whether the object be to crush an army, to storm a city,
> Or to assassinate an individual, it is always necessary to begin
> By finding out the names of the attendants, the aides-de-camp,
> The door-keepers and sentries of the general in command.
> Our spies must be commissioned to ascertain these.
>
> (Sun Tzu, *The Art of War*, Book 13, Vol. 20, L. Giles, Trans.)

As we have attempted to show, mediators and moderators play a key role in helping us understand psychologically the role that culture plays in shaping behavior. Identifying and then linking the hypothesized mediator or moderator variable to social behavior is not, however, an easy task. In the area of aggression, D. Cohen (personal communication, 1999) reports that he and his collaborators have measured many likely mediators for homicide surrogates in their research on the SCV. They have examined various measures, such as the belief that one's masculine reputation is diminished after one was insulted. Unfortunately, none has yet been correlated with their various outcome measures. So, we do not know what psychological process is mediating the aggressive behaviors they have been examining.

In discussing North-South differences, Cohen (1997) notes that

In terms of magnitude, the weakest North-South differences we found were on the attitude surveys. . . . People were acting out the culture of honor much more easily and readily than they were able to articulate the culture of honor. (p. 126)

This finding raises the possibility that mediators may be difficult to identify. As Cohen surmises, cultural differences in behavior may be most pronounced precisely where they are most automatic:

But, because they are either so overlearned (or were never explicitly taught in the first place), they may bypass conscious processing altogether. Our verbal reports and judgments are most clearly tied to conscious levels of processing, and so they may never get connected with the cultural rules embedded in our preconscious. (p. 126)

The consequence of this argument is that many cultural differences in behavior may not be mediated by measures of conscious processes linked to the behavior itself. We may have to cast a wider net to enmesh a construct less apparently connected to the target behavior. Comprehensive measures of personality dimensions, like the NEO-PI-R (NEO Personality Inventory Revised), may be helpful in this regard since they are composed of a congeries of items that tap values, beliefs, and self-reports on classes of behavior, broad trait labels, and the like. Indeed, if Cohen's argument is sound, we may even have to look for new types of mediator, like constellations of habits (Cattell's 1965 habit systems) or use of scripts (see, e.g., Wierzbica's 1994 work on linguistic scripts) to unpackage cultural differences in behavior.

Promising Psychological Mediators

In a more encouraging vein, cross-cultural studies to date have yielded a cornucopia of potential mediators. These mediators have fulfilled the necessary requirement of showing metric equivalence (Van de Vijver & Leung, 1997) in the various cultural groups in which they have been applied. These mediators have three origins: those from theorizing about culture, those from a core of items that define a universal range of items to measure the construct of interest, and through use of measures developed in one place and applied successfully elsewhere.

The first are those developed out of theorizing about culture itself. Markus and Kitayama's (1991) ideas about collectivism, individualism, and interdependent and independent selves were used by Singelis (1994) to create measures of these two types of self-construal. His measures have proved transportable to other cultural groups and effective in unpackaging cultural differences, as mentioned above. Gudykunst et al. (1996) have developed a similar set of self-construal measures using Bond's (1988) method for deriving etics from a multicultural data set. They found that their two self-construal measures predicted a variety of communication styles, such as indirection, appreciation of silence, and the use of feelings, unpackaging differences in some of these measures across five cultural groups. Matsumoto, Weissman, Preston, Brown, and Kupperbusch (1997) built on Triandis's theorizing about collectivism to develop the Individualism-Collectivism Interpersonal Assessment Inventory. This instrument has demonstrated its reliability and validity in a number of cultural groups and so may be useful in future attempts to unpackage cultural differences in social behavior. Triandis et al. (1993) identified six factors that measure aspects of his theorizing about collectivism in persons from 10 cultural groups. These factors included separation from in-groups, independence, and personal competence. Each could be used to test hypotheses within or across cultures related to these constructs. So, too, could measures of horizontal and vertical individualism and collectivism (Triandis & Gelfand, 1996).

At the level of relational constructs, Kwan et al. (1997) argued that the collectivist cultural dynamic emphasizes the social security arising out of achieving harmonious, interpersonal relationships. In that light, relationship harmony should be a mediator of life satisfaction, just like self-esteem. They developed a measure of relationship harmony and showed that it was a significant additional mediator of life satisfaction in both American and Hong Kongese respondents. Kwan et al. demonstrated empirically that relationship harmony could be used along with self-esteem to explain the higher level of satisfaction with life found in their American sample. Here, then, is a different type of useful mediator developed out of thinking about culture itself.

Second, researchers have used cultural groups and their variability as a filtering device to detect a core of items that defines a universal range of items to measure the construct of interest. So, for example, Schwartz (1992) tested the composition of his 10 value domains from 32 samples in 20 countries. He selected only those values to define the 10 domains that were grouped together in two thirds of his national groups. Bond (1988) used a multicultural averaging technique to identify two broad value factors derived from the Chinese Value Survey (Chinese Culture Connection, 1987). Likewise, Leung and Bond (1998) have developed a culture-general measure of social axioms, selecting items to define their five factors that survive a multicultural filtering procedure.

Third, potential mediators have been identified through surviving the time-honored pattern of "safari research," by which a fruitful measure developed in the West, usually America, is translated and "sent hunting" in other cultural groups. Typically, these measures tap an important construct or set of constructs in a well-developed theory with universal aspirations. McCrae and Costa (1997) have demonstrated the applicability of their measure of the Big Five personality dimensions in a number of cultural/language groups. So has Schwarzer (1993) for Bandura's (1977) concept of self-efficacy; Diener and Diener (1995) for Rosenberg's (1965) concept of self-esteem; Campbell et al. (1996) for their concept of self-concept clarity; Sidanius, Pratto, and Rabinowitz (1994) for Sidanius's (1993) concept of social dominance; and Mauro, Sato, and Tucker (1992) for C. A. Smith and Ellsworth's (1985) analysis of the situational dimensions used to construe emotions.

The citation dates for these three sources of universal mediators suggest a recent emergence of these important tools. It is generally within the last decade that these measures have been tested broadly for their applicability outside the West. Their availability now enables the discipline of social psychology to test its theories for universality and to theorize about culture in scientifically defensible ways. Of course, the behavior to be explained will dictate the mediator to be used, and those mediators already available will undoubtedly need to be supplemented with tailor-made additions.

Nonpsychological Mediators

It is possible that psychological mediators will need to be supplemented by other mediators when cross-cultural psychologists are unpackaging cultural differences in some behaviors. Bond (1998a) has argued that the construction

of role relationships is one way in which cultural groups will differ. If so, then a given cultural difference, say in the perception of insulting persons (Bond et al., 1985), may arise because of the different constructions of the role being instantiated by the insulter. If a teacher insults a student in a more egalitarian culture, this behavior may be sanctioned and generate greater counterattack. The sanctioning and counterattack, however, may have little to do with the psychological characteristics of the insulted person and much to do with how the teacher-student relationship is structured in that cultural group. So, by including the mediator of role egalitarianism, for example, one might be able to unpackage a cultural difference in derogation of the insulter without resort to psychological mediators (for example, the rater's score on the personality dimension of agreeableness).

Seeman (1997) has lamented the lack of attention accorded the social situation in social psychology. The few attempts to assess dimensions of the situation (e.g., Wish, Deutsch, & Kaplan, 1976) have instead assessed psychological reactions to those situations. An exception is the work of Marwell and Hage (1970), who asked respondents to rate role relationships on a variety of objective measures, such as the frequency of meetings, the presence of other persons during the meetings, and so forth. McAuley (1999) has refined and supplemented these measures and is using them to compare Hong Kongese and Australian constructions of common role relationships. It will probably be shown that these two cultural groups construe some role relationships differently. If so, then it will be possible for a nonpsychological mediator, role constructions, to explain some of the differences in behavior observed across cultures.

Another example is provided by the work of Morris, Podolny, and Ariel (2000). They have asserted that

> The subjectivist tradition has not had very good tools for analyzing the moderating variables that really matter—the social contexts that condition the operation of particular action rules, ultimately resulting in culturally varying actions. (p. 82)

These investigators propose and develop measures of relational networks that surround employees in a large multinational company across four cultures representing instances of Parson's typology of universalism—particularism and ascription—achievement. Morris et al. assess the network size and density, upward orientation, same-unit coworkers befriended, interaction beyond that officially required, affective closeness, and longevity characterizing the work relations of employees in Spain, Hong Kong, Germany, and the United States. They report a number of tantalizing differences. This recent research provides theoretically grounded and carefully instrumented measures of equivalent nonpsychological, but social, variables with rich promise for unpacking cultural differences in individual behavior.

Obviously, the use of role or relational mediators is only appropriate for the exploration of interpersonal behavior in specified contexts. Relatively little cross-cultural work has focused on interpersonal behavior, but has instead reflected the dominant emphasis in the field on issues of social cognition. As we essay more interpersonal exchanges, such as conversation and aggression, situational mediators may become more useful in explaining cultural differences and building models of social behavior.

A Conclusion as a Beginning

> After that comes tactical maneuvering,
> Than which there is nothing more difficult.
> (Sun Tzu, *The Art of War*,
> Book 7, Vol. 3, L. Giles, Trans.)

Specifying a desirable goal is one thing; achieving it, another. How might one go about developing, then testing, universal theories of social behavior? Here, we move into the areas of skill development and knowledge acquisition that form the presumed basis for doing such demanding work in cross-cultural psychology. In these regards, there are helpful resources available for mastering the methodological aspects of cross-cultural research (Brislin, Lonner, & Thorndike, 1973; Van de Vijver & Leung, 1997) and for acquiring the current information base in cross-cultural social psychology (Smith & Bond, 1998).

As for the motivation to grapple with the frustrations, ambiguities, and demands of practicing cross-cultural social psychology, that is a much more personal matter. The curiosity and tolerance for ambiguity connected to a high level of openness to experience helps, as does the daily puzzlement and irritation provided by living in a foreign culture (Bond, 1997). The courage to take a risk with one's career may contribute, too, since cross-cultural work re-

quires more preparation and execution time than does monocultural research (Gabrenya, 1988).

On a more optimistic note, the age of diversity is flowering around us. As we write this chapter, many countries are celebrating the 50th anniversary of the signing of the Declaration of Human Rights. This continuing growth of concern about human rights includes an insistence on protecting cultural distinctiveness and an interest in understanding how our different heritages can be integrated. So, we believe that cross-cultural social psychology has an assured future because of the increasing importance attached to cultural group memberships and intergroup harmony. However, it will require a jump-cut improvement in the standard of our theorizing and testing of these theories for us to claim a voice in this multiparty conversation.

> Hence the saying: If you know the enemy and know yourself,
> You need not fear the result of a hundred battles.
> If you know yourself but not the enemy, for every victory gained you will also suffer a defeat.
> If you know neither the enemy nor yourself,
> You will succumb in every battle.
> (Sun Tzu, *The Art of War*,
> Book 3, Vol. 18, L. Giles, Trans.)

Note

We wish to express our appreciation to Drs. Dov Cohen and David Matsumoto, whose comments on an earlier version of this chapter helped us improve its readability, accuracy, and insightfulness.

References

Adler, F. (Ed.). (1981). *The incidence of female criminality in the contemporary world.* New York: New York University Press.

Anderson, C. A., & Anderson, K. B. (1998). Temperature and aggression: Paradox, controversy, and a (fairly) clear picture. In R. G. Geen & E. Donnerstein (Eds.), *Human aggression* (pp. 248–298). New York: Academic Press.

Archer, D., & Gartner, R. (1984). *Violence and crime in cross-national perspective.* New Haven, CT: Yale University Press.

Argyle, M., Henderson, M., Bond, M. H., Iizuka, Y., & Contarello, A. (1986). Cross-cultural variations in relationship rules. *International Journal of Psychology, 21,* 287–315.

Bandura, A. (1977). Self-efficacy: Toward a unifying theory of behavioral change. *Psychological Review, 84*, 191–215.

Barry, H., Child, I., & Bacon, M. (1959). Relation of child training to subsistence economy. *American Anthropologist, 61*, 51–63.

Black, D. (1983). Crime as social control. *American Sociological Review, 48*, 34–45.

Boldizar, J. P., Perry, D. G., and Perry, L. C. (1989). Outcome values and aggression. *Child Development, 60*, 571–579.

Bond, M. H. (1988). Finding universal dimensions of individual variation in multi-cultural studies of values: The Rokeach and Chinese value surveys. *Journal of Personality and Social Psychology, 55*, 1009–1015.

Bond, M. H. (1995). Doing social psychology cross-culturally: Into another heart of darkness. In G. G. Brannigan & M. R. Merrens (Eds.), *The social psychologists: Research adventures* (pp. 186–205). New York: McGraw-Hill.

Bond, M. H. (1997). Preface: The psychology of working at the interface of cultures. In M. H. Bond (Ed.), *Working at the interface of cultures: Eighteen lives in social science* (pp. xi–xix). London: Routledge.

Bond, M. H. (1998a). Managing culture in studies of communication: A futurescape. *Asia Pacific Journal of Communication, 8*, 31–49.

Bond, M. H. (1998b). Social psychology across cultures: Two ways forward. In J. G. Adair, D. Belanger, & K. Dion (Eds.), *Proceeding of the 26th International Congress of Psychology: Vol. 1. Advances in psychological science: Social, personal and cultural aspects* (pp. 137–150). Hove, UK: Psychology Press.

Bond, M. H., Leung, K., & Schwartz, S. (1992). Explaining choices in procedural and distributive justice across cultures. *International Journal of Psychology, 27*, 211–225.

Bond, M. H., & Venus, C. K. (1991). Resistance to group or personal insults in an ingroup or outgroup context. *International Journal of Psychology, 26*, 83–94.

Bond, M. H., Wan, K. C., Leung, K., & Giacalone, R. (1985). How are responses to verbal insult related to cultural collectivism and power distance? *Journal of Cross-Cultural Psychology, 16*, 111–127.

Brislin, R., Lonner, W., & Thorndike, R. M. (1973). *Cross-cultural research methods.* New York: Wiley.

Campbell, J. D., Trapnell, P. D., Heine, S. J., Katz, I. M., Lavallee, L. F., & Lehman, D. R. (1996). Self-concept clarity: Measurement, personality correlates, and cultural boundaries. *Journal of Personality and Social Psychology, 70*, 141–156.

Caprara, G. V., Barbaranelli, C., & Zimbardo, P. G. (1996). Understanding the complexity of human aggression: Affective, cognitive, and social dimensions of individual differences in propensity toward aggression. *European Journal of Personality, 10*, 133–155.

Cattell, R. B. (1965). *The scientific analysis of personality.* Baltimore, MD: Penguin.

Chagnon, N. A. (1976). *Yanomamo, the fierce people.* New York: Holt, Rinehart & Winston.

Chinese Culture Connection. (1987). Chinese values and the search for culture-free dimensions of culture. *Journal of Cross-Cultural Psychology, 18*, 143–164.

Clark, L. A. (1987). Mutual relevance of mainstream and cross-cultural psychology. *Journal of Consulting and Clinical Psychology, 55*, 461–470.

Cohen, D. (1996). Law, social policy, and violence: The impact of regional cultures. *Journal of Personality and Social Psychology, 70*, 961–978.

Cohen, D. (1997). Ifs and thens in cross-cultural psychology. In R. S. Wyer, Jr. (Ed.), *The automaticity of everyday life* (pp. 121–131). Mahwah, NJ: Erlbaum.

Cohen, D., & Nisbett, R. E. (1994). Self-protection and the culture of honor: Explaining southern violence. *Personality and Social Psychology Bulletin, 20*, 551–567.

Cohen, D., Nisbett, R. E., Bowdle, B. F., & Schwarz, N. (1996). Insult, aggression, and the southern culture of honor: An "experimental ethnography." *Journal of Personality and Social Psychology, 70*, 945–960.

Cohen, D., Vandello, J., & Rantilla, A. K. (1998). The sacred and the social: Cultures of honor and violence. In P. Gilbert & B. Andrews (Eds.), *Shame, interpersonal behavior, psychopathology, and culture* (pp. 261–282). New York: Oxford University Press.

Deutsch, M. (1994). Constructive conflict resolution: Principles, training, and research. *Journal of Social Issues, 50*, 13–32.

Diener, E., & Diener M. (1995). Cross-cultural correlates of life satisfaction and self-esteem. *Journal of Personality and Social Psychology, 68*, 653–663.

Ember, C. R., & Ember, M. (1994). War, socialization, and interpersonal violence: A cross-cultural study. *Journal of Conflict Resolution, 38*, 620–646.

Felson, R. B. (1978). Aggression as impression management. *Social Psychology Quarterly, 41*, 205–213.

Felson, R. B., & Steadman, H. J. (1983). Situational factors in disputes leading to criminal violence. *Criminology, 21*, 59–74.

Gabrenya, W. B., Jr. (1988). Social science and social psychology: The cross-cultural link. In

M. H. Bond (Ed.), *The cross-cultural challenge to social psychology* (pp. 48–66). Newbury Park, CA: Sage.

Ghosh, E. S. K., Kumar, R., & Tripathi, R. C. (1992). The communal cauldron: relations between Hindus and Muslims in India and their reactions to norm violations. In R. DeRidder & R. C. Tripathi (Eds.), *Norm violation and intergroup relations* (pp. 70–89). Oxford: Clarendon Press.

Gilligan, J. (1996). *Violence: Our deadly epidemic and its causes*. New York: G. P. Putnam.

Gudykunst, W. B., Matsumoto, Y., Ting-Toomey, S., Nishida, T., Kim, K., & Heyman, S. (1996). The influence of cultural individualism-collectivism, self-construals, and individual values on communication styles across cultures. *Human Communication Research, 22*, 510–543.

Hofstede, G. (1980). *Culture's consequences: International differences in work-related values*. Beverly Hills, CA: Sage.

Kim, M. S., Hunter, J. E., Miyahara, A., Horvath, A. M., Bresnahan, M., & Yoon, H. J. (1996). Individual- versus culture-level dimensions of individualism and collectivism: Effects on preferred conversational styles. *Communication Monographs, 63*, 29–49.

Kim, M. S., Sharkey, W. F., & Singelis, T. (1994). The relationship between individual's self-construals and perceived importance of interactive constraints. *International Journal of Intercultural Relations, 18*, 1–24.

Knauft, B. M. (1987). Reconsidering violence in simple human societies: Homicide among the Gebusi of New Guinea. *Current Anthropology, 28*, 457–497.

Kwan, V. S. Y., Bond, M. H., & Singelis, T. M. (1997). Pancultural explanations for life satisfaction: Adding relationship harmony to self-esteem. *Journal of Personality and Social Psychology, 73*, 1038–1051.

Leung, K., & Bond, M. H. (1998, August). *Cultural beliefs about conflict and peace*. Paper presented at the 24th International Congress of Applied Psychology, San Francisco, CA.

Malinowski, B. (1927). *Sex and repression in savage society*. London: Humanities Press.

Markus, H., & Kitayama, S. (1991). Culture and the self: Implications for cognition, motivation, and emotion. *Psychological Review, 98*, 224–253.

Marwell, G., & Hage, J. (1970). The organization of role relations: A systematic description. *American Sociological Review, 35*, 884–900.

Matsumoto, D., Weissman, M. D., Preston, K., Brown, B. R., & Kupperbusch, C. (1997). Context-specific measurement of individualism—collectivism on the individual level: The Individualism-Collectivism Interpersonal Assessment Inventory. *Journal of Cross-Cultural Psychology, 28*, 743–767.

Mauro, R., Sato, K., & Tucker, J. (1992). The role of appraisal in human emotions: A cross-cultural study. *Journal of Personality and Social Psychology, 62*, 301–317.

McAuley, P. C. (1999). *The construction of role relationships in two cultural groups*. Master's thesis, Chinese University of Hong Kong.

McCrae, R. R., & Costa, P. T. (1997). Personality trait structure as a human universal. *American Psychologist, 52*, 509–516.

Mead, M. (1949). *Male and female*. New York: Morrow.

Messick, D. M. (1988). Coda. In M. H. Bond (Ed.), *The cross-cultural challenge to social psychology* (pp. 286–289). Newbury Park, CA: Sage.

Milgram, S. (1974). *Obedience to authority: An experimental view*. New York: Harper Row.

Morris, M. W., Podolny, J. M., & Ariel, S. (2000). Missing relations: Incorporating relational constructs into models of culture. In P. C. Earley, & H. Singh (Eds.), Innovations in international and cross-cultural management (pp. 52–90). Thousand Oaks, CA: Sage Publications.

Ohbuchi, K., & Tedeschi, J. T. (1998). Multiple goals and tactical behaviors in conflict situations. *Journal of Applied Social Psychology, 27*, 2177–2199.

Peristiany, J. G. (Ed.). (1965). *Honor and shame: The values of Mediterranean society*. London: Weidenfeld and Nicolson.

Prescott, W. (1961). *The conquest of Peru*. New York: Mentor.

Robbins, M. C., DeWalt, B. R., & Pelto, P. J. (1972). Climate and behavior: A biocultural study. *Journal of Cross-Cultural Psychology, 3*, 331–344.

Rosenberg, M. (1965). *Society and the adolescent self-image*. Princeton, NJ: Princeton University Press.

Schwartz, S. H. (1992). The universal content and structure of values: Theoretical advances and empirical tests in 20 countries. In M. Zanna (Ed.), *Advances in Experimental Social Psychology, 25*, 1–65. New York: Academic Press.

Schwarzer, R. (1993). Measurement of perceived self-efficacy. *Psychometric scales for cross-cultural research*. Berlin: Freie Universität.

Seeman, M. (1997). The elusive situation in social psychology. *Social Psychology Quarterly, 60*, 4–13.

Segall, M. H., Ember, C. R., & Ember, M. (1997). Aggression crime, and warfare. In J. H. Berry, M. H. Segall, & C. Kagitcibasi (Eds.), *Handbook of cross-cultural psychology* (Vol. 3, pp. 213–254). Needham Heights, MA: Allyn & Bacon.

Semin, G. R., & Rubini, M. (1990). Unfolding the concept of person by verbal abuse. *European Journal of Social Psychology, 20*, 463–474.

Sidanius, J. (1993). The psychology of group conflict and the dynamics of oppression: A social dominance perspective. In W. McGuire & S. Iyengar (Eds.), *Current approaches to political psychology* (pp. 183–219). Durham, NC: Duke University Press.

Sidanius, J., Pratto, F., & Rabinowitz, J. L. (1994). Gender, ethnic status and ideological asymmetry: A social dominance interpretation. *Journal of Cross-Cultural Psychology, 25*, 194–216.

Singelis, T. M. (1994). The measurement of independent and interdependent self-construals. *Personality and Social Psychology Bulletin, 20*, 580–591.

Singelis, T. M., Bond, M. H., Sharkey, W. F., & Lai, S. Y. (1999). Self-construal, self-esteem, and embarrass ability in Hong Kong, Hawaii, and Mainland United States. *Journal of Cross-Cultural Psychology, 30*, 315–341.

Smith, C. A., & Ellsworth, P. C. (1985). Patterns of cognitive appraisal in emotion. *Journal of Personality and Social Psychology, 48*, 813–838.

Smith, P. B., & Bond, M. H. (1998). *Social psychology across cultures* (2nd ed.). London: Prentice-Hall.

Tedeschi, J. T. (1983). Social influence theory and aggression. In R. Geen & E. Donnerstein (Eds.), *Aggression: Theoretical and empirical reviews* (pp. 135–162). New York: Academic Press.

Tedeschi, J. T., & Bond, M. H. (2001). Aversive behavior and aggression in cross-cultural perspective. In R. Kowalski (Ed.), *Behaving badly: Aversive behaviors in interpersonal relationships* (pp. 257–293). Washington, DC: APA Books.

Tedeschi, J. T., & Felson, R. B. (1994). *A theory of coercive actions: A social analysis of aggression and violence*. Washington, DC: American Psychological Association.

Tedeschi, J. T., Quigley, B. M., Ohbuchi, N., Mikula, G., & Bond, M. H. (in preparation). *Aggressive behavior in four cultural groups*.

Tedeschi, J. T., Schlenker, B. R., & Bonoma, T. V. (1973). *Conflict, power, and games*. Chicago: Aldine.

Toch, H. H. (1969). *Violent men: An inquiry into the psychology of violence*. Chicago, IL: Addine-Atherton.

Triandis, H. C. (1980). Values, attitudes and interpersonal behavior. In H. Howe & M. Page (Eds.), *Nebraska Symposium on Motivation: Vol. 27* (pp. 196–260). Lincoln: University of Nebraska Press.

Triandis, H. C., & Gelfand, M. (1996). Converging measurement of horizontal and vertical individualism and collectivism. *Journal of Personality and Social Psychology, 74*, 118–128.

Triandis, H. C., McCusker, C., Betancourt, H., Iwao, S., Leung, K., Salazar, J. M., Setiadi, B., Sinha, J. B., Touzard, H., & Zaleski, Z. (1993). An etic-emic analysis of individualism and collectivism. *Journal of Cross-Cultural Psychology, 24*, 366–383.

Turnbull, C. (1965). *Wayward servants: The two worlds of the African Pygmies*. Garden City, NY: Natural History.

United Nations, Department of Economic and Social Affairs, Statistics Office. (annual). *Demographic Yearbook*. New York: United Nations.

Vandello, J., & Cohen, D. (1998). *Endorsing, enforcing, or distorting? How southern norms about violence are perpetuated*. Unpublished manuscript, University of Illinois, Urbana.

Van de Vijver, F., & Leung, K. (1997). Methods and data analysis for cross-cultural research. In J. W. Berry, Y. H. Poortinga, & J. Pandey (Eds.), *Handbook of cross-cultural psychology: Vol. 1. Theoretical and methodological perspectives* (2nd ed., pp. 257–300). Boston, MA: Allyn & Bacon.

Whiting, B. B. (1976). The problem of the packaged variable. In K. F. Reigel & J. A. Meacham (Eds.), *The developing individual in a changing world* (pp. 303–309). The Hague: Mouton.

Wierzbica, A. (1994). Cultural scripts: A semantic approach to cultural analysis and cross-cultural communication. In M. Putz (Ed.), *Language contact, language conflict* (pp. 69–87). Amsterdam: John Benjamins.

Wilkinson, R. G., Kawachi, I., & Kennedy, B. P. (1998). Mortality, the social environment, crime and violence. *Sociology of Health and Illness, 20*, 578–597.

Wish, M., Deutsch, M., & Kaplan, S. J. (1976). Perceived dimensions of interpersonal relations. *Journal of Personality and Social Psychology, 33*, 409–420.

Yamagishi, T., Cook, K. S., & Watabe, M. (1998). Uncertainty, trust, and commitment in the United States and Japan. *American Journal of Sociology, 104*, 165–194.

17

Culture and Social Cognition

Toward a Social Psychology of Cultural Dynamics

YOSHIHISA KASHIMA

Social cognition, broadly defined as human thought about social behavior, has received considerable attention in the literature since the cognitive revolution of the 1960s and, indeed, has become one of the most important areas of study in mainstream psychology. Within this large area, cross-cultural research on social cognition has come to play an extremely important role in defining issues and in influencing research and theory.

In this chapter, Kashima presents a comprehensive overview of the area of culture and social cognition. He first begins with an excellent discussion of the concept of culture in psychology, distinguishing the concept of *culture as meaning* from cultural dynamics. As Kashima suggests, cultural dynamics has to do with the paradoxical phenomenon of cultural stability and change, which arises from two contemporary views of culture: system oriented and practice oriented. These definitions and discussions about the concept of culture are essential to Kashima's later points about the necessity for the development and creation of theories and research on cultural dynamics, which represent a further evolution of research and thinking about social cognition, and an integration of approaches and knowledge from various disciplines.

The bulk of Kashima's chapter is devoted to a state-of-the-art review of research on culture and social cognition. This review promises to be one of the most comprehensive reviews on this topic. He begins with a treatment of the historical context of early social cognition research and with a presentation of background studies in the area. His detailed review spans such topics as availability of concepts, causal attributions, self-concepts, social and personal explanation, self-evaluation, and others. He delineates many of the issues that are highlighted through his thorough evaluation of the research literature, pointing out both what we know and what we do not in each area. The reader is sure to view this area of his chapter as an important resource for this line of inquiry.

Using his review of the literature as a platform, Kashima delineates his ideas concerning future research and theoretical work in the area. With regard to future empirical work, he suggests that two topics in the area of culture and social cognition—the explanation of social action and the maintenance of self-regard—deserve closer scrutiny and further research in the future. In particular, while much is known about what North Americans tend to do with regard to these topics, relatively much less is known about other people around the world, leaving this area ripe for investigation. In particular, the holistic approach and worldview perspective of East Asians may bring insights into this area of psychological functioning that heretofore were unconsidered.

Clearly, however, the major thrust of Kashima's argument for future work concerns the creation of what he terms the social cognition of cultural dynamics. As he explains at the beginning of his chapter and throughout his literature review, much of the early social cognition research and theories were characterized by an individualistic conception of meaning, according to which meaning is constructed solely within an individual person's mind. There are many reasons for these biases in the literature, including the fact that most research was done in the United States by American researchers. Even research that was conducted outside the United States was often conducted by researchers who were trained in the United States (and thus influenced by Western educational dogma) or influenced by these factors. In the future, however, greater emphasis will need to be placed on the development of a theoretical framework that incorporates both cognitive and communicative processes in understanding cultural dynamics—that is, the processes by which cultural meanings are constructed in ongoing social activities among multiple individuals, as well as within an individual's mind. This view of social cognition is inherently more complex, involving relational, collective, and individual issues, including the incorporation of context and history, as well as future and present time orientations. For these reasons, the development of such a theoretical viewpoint will necessitate fundamental changes in the ways in which we do research, which will ultimately lead to ways in which we understand human behavior in potentially profoundly different ways than now. This development of new theories and methodologies to ensure the continued evolution of knowledge in this area of psychology is commensurate with a message given by all authors throughout this volume.

Until recently, culture has been a neglected concept in social cognition. Most theories, at worst, have ignored culture entirely or, at best, assumed that culture is connected unproblematically to the traditional social psychological concepts such as attributions and attitudes. To wit, the first edition of the *Handbook of Social Cognition* (Wyer & Srull, 1984) has no entries of culture, and this marginal status of the culture concept continued until the 1990s, as seen in the absence of culture in the second edition of the *Handbook* (Wyer & Srull, 1994). However, culture emerged recently as a major theme in social cognition. There is an increase in publication on culture and social cognition according to my recent search of the literature from 1989 to 1997 of the computer database PSYCINFO (Y. Kashima, 1998b).

The main aim of this chapter is to make a case for a perspective that I call a social psychology of cultural dynamics. It attempts to understand global dynamics of culture as generated from cognitive and communicative processes of individuals in interaction with each other in social contexts. The chapter is divided into four sections. In the first section, the concept of culture is examined, and major meta-

theoretical tenets of a social psychology of cultural dynamics are derived. In the second section, traditional metatheoretical and theoretical characteristics of social cognition are reviewed. The third section reviews the recent explosion of research on culture and social cognition that past reviews (e.g., Fletcher & Ward, 1988; J. G. Miller, 1988; Semin & Zwier, 1997; Zebrowitz-McArthur, 1988) did not cover. In the last section, empirical and theoretical directions of future research are suggested.

Culture Concept in Psychology

To clarify the perspective of a social psychology of cultural dynamics, it is necessary to clarify the concept of culture. The culture concept, despite its popularity and long history in social sciences, is multifaceted, and often ambiguous.

Culture as Meaning

Culture is analytically separable from concepts such as society and social system (e.g., Giddens, 1979; Parsons, 1951; Rohner, 1984; for a more recent discussion, see Y. Kashima, 2000a). On one hand, society is an organized collection of individuals and groups, and *social system* refers to an enduring pattern of interpersonal, intergroup, and person-group relationships within a society. On the other hand, *culture* is a set of meanings shared, or at least sharable, among individuals in a society. Therefore, questions regarding power, resources, and friends have to do with social systems. In contrast, culture has to do with questions about what it means to have power and resources and what it means for a person to be a friend of another.

The concept of meaning, however, is complex. At this stage, let us approximate meaning to the use of symbols, that is, material objects (including sound, light, and other chemical characteristics that are discernible by human senses) that are used to stand for something else. Obviously, words have meanings in this sense. Nevertheless, this sense of meaning goes beyond linguistic meaning. When a nonverbal gesture stands for other ideas (e.g., vertically stretched index and middle fingers standing for victory), this involves a meaning. When a toddler uses a round object as a steering wheel of a car, the child is engaged in a meaningful activity.

Nonetheless, what it stands for does not exhaust the meaning of a symbol. The denotative (extensional) meaning is that to which a symbol refers (i.e., its referent). However, there is more to meaning than reference. As Frege (1984) noted long ago, if the referent of a phrase such as *morning star* or *evening star* is all there is to meaning, then a statement like "The morning star is the evening star" is a meaningless tautology. Yet, this statement can have a rich meaning given that humans had not known for a long time that the morning star and the evening star referred to the same object, Venus. Frege called this extra component of meaning *sense*. Meaning thus has at least two aspects, reference and sense.

It is important to note that referential meaning should include not only literal meaning, but also figurative meaning. For instance, Lakoff and Johnson (1979) noted that a number of abstract concepts in English were based on metaphors. English sentences such as, "That meeting was a waste of time," can be understood in terms of a metaphor that likens time to money. Just as money is wasted, time can be wasted, too. In 1994, Y. Kashima (also see Y. Kashima & Callan, 1994; Shore, 1996) argued that cultural metaphors provide rich meanings

for the experience of mental and social activities. In addition, narratives may also play an important role in the production and maintenance of cultural meanings (Bruner, 1990; Y. Kashima, 1998a).

Cultural Dynamics

Cultural dynamics has to do with the paradoxical phenomenon of cultural stability and change, that is, how some aspects of a culture are maintained in the midst of constant change, and cultural change continues despite strong forces of cultural maintenance. This question arose from a tension between two contemporary views of culture, system oriented and practice oriented (Y. Kashima, 2000a; also see Matsumoto, Kudoh, & Takeuchi, 1996). A *system-oriented view* treats culture as a relatively enduring system of meaning. Culture is conceptualized as a repository of symbolically coded meanings shared by a group of people, which provides structure to their experience. In contrast, a *practice-oriented view* regards culture as signification process in which meanings are constantly produced and reproduced by concrete individuals' particular activities in particular situations. The system-oriented view highlights the stability of culture, whereas the practice-oriented view focuses on the fluid nature of culture in flux.

The *culture-as-meaning-system view* was expressed by a number of cross-cultural psychologists and anthropologists. Most notably, when Triandis (1972) defined *subjective culture* as a "cultural group's characteristic way of perceiving the man-made part of its environment" (p. 4), he was highlighting the enduring and systemic aspect of culture. A well-known anthropologist, Geertz (1973), characterized culture as "interworked systems of construable signs . . . something within which [social events, behaviors, institutions, or processes] can be intelligibly . . . described" (p. 14). Geertz's formulation, called *symbolic anthropology*, likens culture to a text, which is publicly accessible and in need of reading and interpretation. Despite a difference between the views of culture of Triandis and Geertz, there is an underlying similarity. They both treat culture as a system of meanings that is shared within a group of people.

For example, theorists who take this perspective often characterize a culture by using a global concept such as individualism or collectivism (Hofstede, 1980; Triandis, 1995), implying that a relatively stable system of beliefs and values is shared in a society. Similarly, when Geertz (1984, p. 126) characterized the Western conception of the person as "a bounded, unique, more or less integrated motivational and cognitive universe," he implied that this conception was shared by people in the West.

The *culture-as-signification-process view* was put forward by a variety of psychologists influenced by Vygotsky (1978; for an explication of Vygotsky, see Wertsch, 1985) and other thinkers of the Russian cultural-historical school. These include Cole (1996), Greenfield (1997), Lave and Wenger (1991), Rogoff (1990), Valsiner (1989), and Wertsch (1991). Although their theory of culture has progressed beyond Vygotsky's original formulation, they view culture as a collection of concrete everyday practices that occur in everyday life (e.g., basket weaving, estimating amounts of rice). Boesch's (1991) symbolic action theory and Poortinga's (1992) context-specific cross-cultural psychology are similarly concerned with concrete activities as they occur within symbolic, physical, and social contexts. In anthropology, researchers influenced by Bourdieu (1977; *habitus*) and Giddens (1979; *structuration*) or by contemporary Marxist thoughts often take a similar view. Ortner (1984), a neo-Geertzian, also approaches culture from a similar viewpoint.

An example of this approach is provided by a conceptualization of schooling (for a recent review, see Rogoff & Chavajay, 1995). For instance, Cole (1996) views schooling as a collection of context-specific and domain-specific cognitive and motor activities (e.g., reading and writing, remembering a list of words) that influence children's cognitive task performance, such as recall and syllogistic reasoning. In other words, instead of explaining cultural differences in syllogistic reasoning performance in terms of differences in cognitive style (e.g., logical versus prelogical reasoning), this approach suggests that people from Western cultures tend to perform syllogistic reasoning tasks better than illiterate people because the reasoning tasks resemble activities that the former are used to at school.

The two conceptions of culture differ on a number of metatheoretical dimensions. First, they differ in time perspective. The system-oriented view tends to see culture from a long-term perspective and attempts to capture stable aspects of a culture within a historical period (decades or centuries). In contrast, the practice-oriented view tends to construe culture from a short-term perspective and tries to identify activities (that is, people doing things together with tools) that recur in specific contexts. In other words, a unit of time is longer for a system-oriented investigation than for a practice-oriented analysis.

Second, they differ in context specificity and domain specificity. The system-oriented view is generally concerned with culture viewed as a whole, as a context-general and domain-general meaning system that is carried and realized by a group of individuals. Culture, then, is abstracted from specific contexts of social action. Culture is often regarded as present, although it may lay dormant, in all contexts of social activities and all domains of life. The practice-oriented view, on the other hand, is interested in culture as particular activities that use particular artifacts (i.e., tools and other material objects) in particular contexts. This is a view of culture as a collection of context-specific signification activities. To the extent that a domain of meaning is often associated with a particular context (e.g., things to do at school or at home), this view tends toward a view that cultural meanings are domain specific.

Third, they differ in unit of analysis. The system-oriented view takes a group of individuals as a unit of analysis, and culture is a phenomenon closely associated with the collectivity. In a way, culture is regarded as a property of the group. In contrast, the practice-oriented view takes a practice (a pattern of activities carried out by people) as a unit of analysis. In this perspective, culture is a property of situated activities, that is, people acting in context. It should be noted that this notion of practice and situated activities includes not only individuals, but also routine activities that take place in space and time.

Neither view alone can provide a complete picture about cultural dynamics. One view's strength is the other's weakness. On one hand, the system-oriented view takes culture as given for a collective in a historical period. Culture in this sense becomes a "cause" or an independent variable in a quasi-experimental design of typical cross-cultural studies. In fact, comparative investigations must by necessity treat culture as stable systems and compare the slices of cultural traditions. However, this view often looks for factors external to culture as engines of cultural change (e.g., technology, material wealth, and ecology). Creative activities within a culture as a basis for cultural change tend to fall outside the scope of this perspective.

On the other hand, the practice-oriented view takes culture as constantly produced and reproduced. As such, both stability and change are part and parcel of culture. Developmental psychologists, who are concerned with how children are enculturated to become full-fledged participants of a culture, are necessarily interested in context-specific activities. After all, children must learn culture not by osmosis, but from concrete everyday activities. However, it is unclear in this view how one can determine theoretically which aspects of situated activities are to persist and which are to change. Furthermore, while this view provides detailed analyses of particular activities, it fails to shed light on a general pattern, a cultural theme, or something like a context-general meaning system that seems to cut across a number of domains of activities (e.g., see Jahoda's 1980 criticism of Cole's 1996 approach).

Thus, the system-oriented and practice-oriented views of culture provide complementary perspectives on cultural dynamics. The culture-as-system view highlights the persistence of culture over time, whereas the culture-as-practice view focuses on the fluctuation of cultural meaning across contexts and over time. Nonetheless, both local fluctuations and global stability characterize culture. My contention is that we must investigate how both can be true. From the present perspective, the central question of cultural dynamics is how individuals' context-specific signification activities can generate, under some circumstances, something stable that may be called a context-general meaning system and, under other circumstances, a rapid and even chaotic change.

Culture and Social Cognition: Historical Context of Early Social Cognition Research

Despite some early attempts at incorporating culture into human psychology (e.g., Wundt's *Völkerpsychologie*), culture, broadly defined as shared meanings, has been outside the scope of academic psychology for much of the first half of the 20th century under the dogmatic and restrictive reign of logical positivism as a philosophy of science and behaviorism as its psychological counterpart. Behaviorism, in particular, banished any talk of human thought from the academic discourse of psychology. The cognitive revolution of the 1960s, in which human thought was reclaimed as a central concern of psychology, failed to bring meaning, and therefore culture, back into the mainstream of academic psychology (Bruner, 1990).

Social cognition emerged as an attempt at bringing cognition into social psychology. The 1960s saw publications of classic texts in attribution theories (e.g., Jones & Davis, 1965; Kelley, 1967), and social psychology was flooded with research on attribution processes in the 1970s. A more self-conscious effort to draw on cognitive psychology began as well, making use of prototypically cognitive psychological methods such as recall and recognition memory, reaction time, and the like (e.g., Hastie et al., 1980, on person memory). The significance of social cognition in social psychology is undeniable. Some have gone as far as to claiming that social psychology is largely represented by social cognition (H. Markus & Zajonc, 1985). All the while, however, social cognition research emulated the cognitive psychology, pursuing a universal model of human cognitive processes at the expense of culture.

It is intriguing to note that social cognition of the 1970s and 1980s was characterized by its dual emphasis on the individual person as a central focus. On one hand, much of the work was largely concerned about the process by which people form cognitive representations about themselves and other individuals. One enduring question has been how one comes to construe a person (either another individual or oneself) in terms of his or her dispositional characteristics, such as personality traits (e.g., as described by adjectives such as introverted and extraverted) or attitudes (e.g., stances with regard to social issues such as Castro's Cuba or abortion; for a review, see S. T. Fiske & Taylor, 1991). On the other hand, theories of social cognition paid exclusive attention to the individual person's cognitive processes, that is, the encoding of incoming information into cognitive representations, and the storage and retrieval of them for further use. These theories were social only to the extent that they dealt with social stimuli (i.e., other people). In other words, social cognition then exemplified the individualist conception of the person in terms of its subject matter and theoretical assumption.

What underlay the early social cognition research was an individualist conception of meaning. According to this view, the individual constructs meaning by operating on cognitive representations stored in his or her own mind. To be sure, an individual person equipped with the capacity to encode perceptual information into cognitive representations can also decode such individual representations into symbolic codes that are understandable to other individuals. Nonetheless, this individualist model of cognition makes for a model of communication that regards interpersonal communication as mere transmission of information (Clark, 1985). At an extreme, social cognitive minds can be likened to computers that send signals back and forth through rules of syntax and semantics. In this case, culture can be reduced to a "codebook" in which rules can be found to translate between cognitive codes and symbolic codes.

During the Great Leap Forward of social cognition, however, metatheoretical, theoretical, and empirical challenges to the mainstream social psychology began to cumulate. Metatheoretically, Gergen (1973) argued that social psychology cannot hope to "discover" natural laws of social behavior, but only acquire historically contingent knowledge. Although social psychology may develop a theory of social behavior at one point in time, once it is disseminated to the general public, people can try to develop patterns of behaviors that differ from, or even contradict, it. In other words, humans are self-constituting in that our collective attempt at characterizing ourselves can end up influencing ourselves. Gergen's argument that humans are self-constitutive and the products of history that we ourselves have created echoes the point made by the counter-Enlightenment thinkers, such as Vico and Herder, who opposed the Enlightenment thought that regarded human nature as largely fixed and governed by universal natural laws (for a more detailed discussion, see Y. Kashima, 2000a).

Theoretically, some of the central concepts in social psychology began to be scrutinized. For instance, social psychologists began to examine concepts such as personality traits and social attitudes, which were presumed to describe the underlying dispositions of people or consistency in their behavior. Most fundamentally, the capacity of the dispositional characteristics to predict specific behavior was questioned (see Mischel, 1968, for personality traits and Wicker, 1969, for attitudes). Based on these challenges, cognitively oriented researchers such as Shweder and D'Andrade (1979) and Cantor and Michel (1979) began to formulate theories of personality traits that treated them as indicating perceived, as opposed to actual, consistency in behavior. In other words, an individual does not necessarily possess a disposition, but merely appear to do so. This trend reached its peak when Ross (1977) used the term *fundamental attribution error* to refer to North American participants' tendency to attribute personality dispositions to an actor despite contextual information suggesting otherwise. When attribution of a disposition is regarded as an error, social psychology can hardly take its dispositional concepts seriously.

Empirically, drawing on the past literature on culture and social behavior (e.g., for a review, see Triandis & Brislin, 1980), cross-cultural psychology began to mount empirical challenges to social psychology by presenting evidence that there is some significant cultural variability in social behavior (Bond, 1988). Amir and Sharon's (1987) was among the most memorable contributions. They sampled several North American studies published in major journals of social psychology and systematically replicated the experimental procedures in Israel. They reported that, although main effects could be replicated, some of the fine-grain interaction effects could not be, despite their importance for the main theoretical claims of the original papers. Within the context of the globalization of economy and the rapid change in the world order, such as the political and economic collapse of the Communist bloc and the emergence of newly industrializing nations (e.g., Japan, South Korea, Taiwan, Hong Kong, and Singapore), these cross-cultural challenges began to attract the attention of mainstream researchers.

Cross-Cultural Research in Social Cognition

Background

The current popularity of culture and social cognition research owes much to Hofstede (1980) and Shweder and Bourne (1984). Hofstede's research was based on his work value surveys around the world. In this massive, empirically driven work, he extracted dimensions on which cultures can be placed. The individualism dimension attracted the greatest attention partly because of the importance of the individualism concept in social sciences in general. A number of social scientists (e.g., Tönnies' (1955), Gemeinschaft and Gesellschaft; Durkheim's (1964) mechanical and organic solidarity) used related concepts to characterize the transformation of Continental Europe from its medieval past to the modern era. Close-knit communities in which everyone had known everyone else broke down, and there emerged modern nation states in which a central government controls the trade, police, and military might. The emphasis shifted from the community to the individual, with the gradual strengthening of individual rights. Collectivism characterizes the traditional sociality, whereas the modern social relationship is individualistic. An empirical finding that fueled the interest was probably its correlation with 1970 per capita gross national product. Country-level individualism positively correlated with per capita gross national product at .82. Richer countries in North America and western Europe are individualist, whereas poorer countries in Asia and South America tend to be collectivist.

Hofstede's (1980) finding clearly showed that there was a significant relationship between cultural values and economic activities, which is generally consistent with the accepted view of modernization, that is, from traditional communities to modern societies. His work provided a conceptual framework in which to interpret and understand myriad cross-cultural studies on beliefs, attitudes, and values. The concepts of collectivism and individualism also refocused theoretical attention on a central issue of social sciences, that is, the relationship between the collective and the individual.

Shweder and Bourne's study (1982), in contrast, was an ambitious, theoretically driven project. They posited three major theoretical orientations in interpreting cross-cultural diversity. *Universalism* looks for human universals in diversity by attempting to identify a higher order generality or by concentrating on a clearly defined band of data. *Evolutionism* rank orders cultural patterns relative to a normative model (e.g., the cannon of propositional calculus, Bayes' rule of probabilistic reasoning) in terms of their deviation from the norm. It typically treats cultures as progressing toward the normative ideal. *Relativism* seeks to interpret each cultural pattern as an inherently meaningful pattern by itself and to maintain the equality among them.

Against the background of the literature arguing for western Europeans' abstractness relative to other cultures, such as Bali and Gahuku-Gama of New Guinea, Shweder and Bourne (1984) conducted interviews and showed that middle-class Euro-American participants, compared to Oriyan participants from a traditional city of Bhubaneswar in India, tended to use abstract dispositional characterizations (e.g., "He is a leader" as opposed to "He lends people money"), and that their descriptions tended not to be put into context (e.g., "He is verbally abusive" as opposed to "He is verbally abusive to his father-in-law whenever they meet at his home"). Oriyas's contextualized person description, they argued, is a sign of their holistic, sociocentric conception of the relationship of the individual to society.

In adopting this relativist view, Shweder and Bourne (1984) argued against evolutionist interpretations. They showed that Oriyas adopted a contextual person description regardless of formal education, literacy, or socioeconomic status. According to them, this provides evidence against evolutionist explanations. Evolutionists would explain relative concreteness in Oriyas's person description in terms of some cognitive deficit associated with a lack of education, literacy, or socioeconomic background. Oriyas do have abstract traitlike words in their language and are capable of generating those abstract concepts in an interview. This argues against the possibility that Oriyas lack abstract categories with which to describe people abstractly or lack a general capacity to do so. It is unlikely that North Americans encounter their target persons in more diverse settings and therefore are more likely to be able to abstract their dispositional characteristics. There is no evidence to suggest that North Americans live in a more heterogeneous social environment to prompt more abstract patterns of thinking.

These two lines of work were drawn together into a single focus around 1990 by two major papers on culture and self, which triggered the avalanche of cross-cultural research in social cognition. Triandis (1989) theorized about cultural antecedents of the prevalence and access of self-concepts. He postulated that there are three types of self-concepts: private, public, and collective. The *private self-concept* is concerned with people's conceptions about their own personal goals; the *public self-concept* has to do with people's concerns about how others view them; and the *collective self-concept* is about people's involvement in their in-groups. Every culture contains these different self-concepts, but characteristics such as individualism, cultural complexity, and affluence determine the prevalence of the three types of self-concepts. Private self-concepts may be prevalent in individualist cultures, whereas public and collective self-conceptions may be prevalent in collectivist cultures. Cultural complexity and affluence may promote the prevalence of private self-conceptions as well. Furthermore, different self-concepts may be more accessible in different social situations in different cultures according to Triandis.

In 1991, H. R. Markus and Kitayama proposed a theory about psychological consequences when different self-concepts are accessed. In this influential formulation, they postulated that there is the universal aspect of the self, which is the self as a physically distinct body in time and space. However, the self can be construed in two different ways, independent and interdependent. *Independent self-construals* are characterized by their emphasis on the uniqueness and separateness of the individual self in contrast to others. In contrast, *interdependent self-construals* are characterized by their interpenetrations with significant others. That is, selves are conceived to be in interdependent social relationships with other people. They suggested that these self-construals, when accessed, would influence cognitive, affective, and motivational processes.

Although Hofstede's (1980) and Shweder and Bourne's (1984) studies were not without their critics (for instance, see Y. Kashima, 1987, on Hofstede and see Spiro, 1993, on Shweder and Bourne), their contributions suggested that there are significant cultural differences, which may be examined empirically in terms of the contrast between worldviews that emphasize sociality (e.g., collectivist, sociocentric, interpersonal, and interdependent) and those that emphasize individuality (e.g., individualist, egocentric, personal, and independent). Triandis (1989) and H. R. Markus and Kitayama (1991) focused research attention on the self. Generally drawing on the then-current literature on social cognition of self-processes and cross-cultural psychology, they launched a theory that suggested that self-concepts mediate the effect of culture on psychological processes.

Nonetheless, there were important differences. First, they differed in the unit of analysis. Hofstede (1980) used countries or cultures as the unit of analysis, computing cultural averages on surveys, whereas Shweder and Bourne (1984), as well as H. R. Markus and Kitayama (1991), treated individuals as the unit of analysis. Triandis (1989) attempted to connect the two using the self-concept as a central mediator. They also differed in their focus on self or person in general. Triandis's and Markus and Kitayama's contributions were concerned with self-concepts. However, Shweder and Bourne's contribution was about conceptions of the person observed from people's verbal descriptions of their acquaintances. Finally, they differed in operationalization of the constructs. Hofstede made individualism and collectivism operational in terms of importance of personal independence from the organizational context, while Shweder and Bourne made egocentric and sociocentric views of the person operational in terms of abstractness of person descriptions. Triandis and Markus and Kitayama treated them as reflecting the same underlying self-conceptions. In the current literature of culture and social cognition, these differences are generally glossed over or even ignored. But, is it warranted?

Conceptual Advances

Some theoretical advances since the early 1990s have significant implications for culture and social cognition.

Availability, Accessibility, and Applicabilty of Concepts

Higgins (1996) defined availability, accessibility, and applicability of concepts and provided a comprehensive review and discussion of the literature on knowledge activation. The *availability* of a concept refers to whether the concept is stored in an individual's memory, whereas the *accessibility* of a concept means the "activation potential" of the available concept or the ease with which the concept already available in the mind is activated for use. The accessibility of a concept may vary chronically or temporarily due to factors such as motivation and frequency and recency of activation. Bargh, Bond, Lombardi, and Tota (1986) showed that chronic and temporary sources of accessibility are additively combined to produce effects. When accessible concepts are applicable to a given stimulus, the concepts are applied to the stimulus to interpret it. Much of recent research shows that concepts may be activated automatically and used without conscious awareness (Bargh, 1996).

Hong, Chiu, and Kung (1997) provided an example of *priming* cultural concepts, in which the accessibility of concepts was increased temporarily. Hong et al. showed Hong Kong Chinese students pictures of objects that symbolized either Chinese or American culture and had the participants answer short questions such as, "What does this picture symbolize?" A short while later, in an allegedly unrelated study, the participants rated the importance of traditional Chinese values. The participants endorsed the traditional Chinese values more in the Chinese picture condition than in the American picture condition. Pictures that symbolized a culture may have activated concepts and knowledge structures associated with the culture, which influenced subsequent cognitive processes in the experiments.

The availability and accessibility of concepts may be associated closely with the language people use. This is one way of interpreting what is known as the *Whorfian hypothesis*, the idea that language determines thought (Chiu, Krauss, & Lee, 1999; for a recent review on the Whorfian hypothesis, see Hunt & Agnoli, 1991). Hoffman, Lau, and Johnson (1986) provided an example consistent with this thinking. They identified English and Chinese terms for which there were no equivalent economical words or phrases in the other language. Behavioral descriptions were developed for each term. English monolingual and Chinese-English bilingual individuals were given these person descriptions with the aim of forming distinct impressions. The bilingual individuals read them either in English or in Chinese. The bilingual individuals' impressions of the target individuals and recognition memory were influenced by the concepts available in the language used in the experiment, although recall was not.

In examining cultural differences in social cognition, it is important to consider the availability, accessibility, and applicability of a relevant concept in cultures concerned. If a culture does not provide a concept of importance, people from that culture could not use it (unless they invent it on the spot); if a concept is available in the cultures concerned, they may differ in accessibility and therefore may result in differences in cognitive processes; even if a concept is equally available and accessible in the cultures concerned, it may not be equally applicable in both. What is an intriguing possibility is that cultural concepts that are not consciously available, accessible, or applicable may still exert influences on social cognitive processes without awareness of the members of the culture. When a culture is going through a major change and its members are actively attempting to forget or discredit its past cultural practices, there may emerge a discrepancy between conscious awareness about concepts (explicit cognition) and automatically activated concepts (implicit cognition; see also Hetts, Sa-

kuma, & Pelham, 1999). A good example of this is perhaps once-prevalent stereotypes in the contemporary culture of political correctness (e.g., Devine, 1989).

A Variety of Causal Attributions

Another class of theoretical advances in social cognition has to do with the meaning of causal attribution. In the classical attribution theories, it has commonly been assumed that personal and situational attributions perfectly correlate negatively. That is, attributing a behavior to a person means that the context of the behavior is not causally implicated. Alternatively, saying that a behavior is situationally caused means that the person is not causally responsible. This hydraulic assumption of personal and situational causation (Heider, 1958) has been called into question by some empirical studies (F. D. Miller, Smith, & Uleman, 1981). At least North American participants may regard personal and situational causation as two independent forces.

In line with this, current theories of attribution (e.g., Gilbert & Malone, 1995; Krull, 1993; Trope, 1986) draw a distinction between the attribution of a disposition and the adjustment of a dispositional inference on the basis of the contextual factors that may constrain the action. To put it differently, the cognitive process responsible for a dispositional inference is distinguished from the contextualization of the dispositional inference. These theories developed in North America suggest that, when faced with information about a behavioral episode, people first categorize the action into a dispositional category (e.g., personality trait, attitudes), and the implication of this categorization is then adjusted in light of the information about the contextual constraints. If the context is likely to hinder the enactment of the action, the dispositional inference is curtailed, albeit insufficiently, by some normative standards. Obviously, whether the same processes apply around the world needs to be examined by cross-cultural investigations. Nonetheless, the conceptual distinction between disposition and contextualization is highly pertinent to the discussion of cross-cultural research on social cognition, as discussed below.

Two types of personal attribution, *dispositional attributions* (using personality traits to describe and explain a behavior) and *agentic attributions* (saying that a person is responsible for the behavior), have been assumed to be equivalent conceptually in the classical attribution literature. However, recent research has shown that a distinction needs to be made between them. Semin and Marsman (1994) and D. J. Hilton, Smith, and Kin (1995) showed that attributing to a person abstract dispositional characteristics is psychologically different from attributing agency to the person. To put it differently, to describe a person by a certain personality trait on the basis of an observed behavior is not the same as saying that this person is responsible for the behavior.

Individual, Relational, and Collective Selves

Although the pioneering work in culture and social psychology contrasted the individual-centered and sociocentered worldviews (individualist, egocentric, personal, independent vs. collectivist, sociocentric, interpersonal, interdependent), Y. Kashima's (1987) and Oyserman's (1993) exploratory factor analyses (also see Trafimow, Triandis, & Goto, 1991), as well as Singelis's (1994) confirmatory factor analysis, suggested that the individual-centered and sociocentered conceptions of the self are two independent concepts.

More recently, Y. Kashima et al. (1995) further differentiated the sociocentered self into relational and collective facets, making distinctions among individual, relational, and collective self-conceptions. The existing theories of culture and self often conflate two types of sociality: one primarily concerned with the self-other relationship and the other about the relationship of the self with the in-group. Whereas the interpersonal relationship between the self and other individuals may provide a significant basis of sociality, the relationship between the self and its in-group constitutes another social aspect of the self, which requires separate treatment. They showed that measures of these three aspects of the self had relatively small correlations among themselves, and that, more importantly, individual and collective self-conceptions differentiated East Asian (Japanese and Korean) and English-speaking (Australian, American) cultures with Hawaiians in between, but relational self-conceptions differentiated men and women regardless of their cultural background. The finding that collective and relational self-conceptions had different relationships with culture and gender suggests

that they are indeed conceptually separable. Brewer and Gardner (1996) also theorized about the conceptual separation among individual, relational, and collective aspects of the self.

In line with the tripartite distinction among individual, relational, and collective aspects of the self, cross-cultural research on social cognition is reviewed according to whether the individual, relationship, or group is the target of conception.

Individual as Target

Social cognition researchers have traditionally maintained a clear distinction between cognitions about the self (e.g., H. Markus, 1977) and those about others. This conceptual separation was to some extent based on the preconception that the self is a special psychological phenomenon that is uniquely different from any other psychological phenomena, as seen, for instance, in the assertion of Descartes about one's privileged access to one's self-knowledge (i.e., "Cogito ergo sum"). This assumption has been reinforced further by empirical findings that emphasize a difference between self-perception and perception of others. For instance, the classical research on actor-observer bias in attribution suggests that at least North Americans explain the behaviors of others in terms of dispositional characteristics more than their own behaviors (e.g., Nisbett, Caputo, Legant, & Maracek, 1973). Watson's (1982) review showed its robustness, but interestingly, also revealed that North Americans tend to explain both themselves and others more in terms of personality dispositions than their circumstances. In other words, the literature on the actor-observer bias showed a significant similarity between self-cognition and cognition of others.

In discussing a cultural difference in self-cognition and cognition of others, the oft-cited passage of Geertz (1984) provides a useful starting point:

> The Western conception of the person as a bounded, unique, more or less integrated motivational and cognitive universe, a dynamic center of awareness, emotion, judgment, and action organized into a distinctive whole and set contrastively both against other such wholes and against its social and natural background, is, however incorrigible it may seem to us, a rather peculiar idea within the context of the world's cultures. (p. 126)

The anthropological insight of Geertz can be abstracted into two component ideas. First, a person is attributed *psychological agency*, which is a "more or less integrated motivational and cognitive universe, a dynamic center of awareness, emotion, judgment, and action." Second, the individual is a figure against the background of the social and natural context, that is, the individual is "set contrastively both against other wholes and against its social and natural background."

This last idea needs further explication. Geertz is not saying that the Western conception ignores the social and natural context, but is asserting that the most prominent part of the phenomenal field is the individual person, and that the social and natural context in which the person is embedded lies in the background. This is often assumed to mean that the Western conception of the person is abstract or *dispositional* (e.g., John is friendly), and that non-Western conceptions are concrete and contain *action descriptions* (e.g., John plays with children even if he doesn't know them well). Furthermore, dispositional descriptions of a person mean that the person is *decontextualized*. Taken together, it is commonly believed that past cross-cultural studies of self-cognition and cognition of others showed that Western conceptions of the self and other are more agentic, dispositional, and decontextualized than their East Asian counterparts.

However, in light of the recent theoretical developments in social cognition, the cross-cultural studies require a more nuanced interpretation. As pointed out before, social cognition research suggests that the attribution of agency should be distinguished conceptually from the attribution of disposition, and the cognitive process for attributing a dispositional characteristic (e.g., a personality trait) to a person is distinguished from the cognitive process for contextualizing the dispositional attribution. In other words, agency attribution, dispositional attribution, and contextualization are all separable psychological processes in North America and probably in European cultures. However, there is no reason to expect a priori prevalence of these psychological processes should covary with culture.

Explaining and Describing Others

How Shall a Person Be Described? In 1984 and in 1987, J. G. Miller examined descriptions of acquaintances' positive and negative behav-

iors given by North Americans and Hindu Indians of four age groups (8, 11, and 15 years old and adults).The study found that, in general, North American participants gave more dispositional and fewer contextual explanations than Hindu Indians. However, the tendency to give dispositional explanations increased with age for North Americans, but not for Hindu Indians. In contrast, the tendency to give contextual explanations increased with age for Hindu Indians, but not for North Americans. In addition, J. G. Miller reported that, of the four Indian adult groups examined, an Anglo-Indian group showed a preference for dispositional explanations relative to three Hindu Indian groups, although some of the Hindu Indian groups had more exposure to the Western-type education and way of life. Also, J. G. Miller gave a different group of North American participants English translations of behavioral narratives given by the Hindu Indian participants. The North American explanations again were oriented more toward disposition and less oriented toward context, although the behaviors to be explained originated from the Hindu Indian narratives. This last finding clearly showed that it was not the nature of the narratives that caused the cultural difference in explanatory style. All in all, J. G. Miller's study showed clearly that North Americans generated explanations different from those generated by Hindu Indians. Her finding that a cultural explanation style became more pronounced for older participants provides strong evidence for the cultural explanation of the difference in explanatory style.

Morris and Peng's (1994) Study 2 provided additional support for a cultural difference in the type of explanations generated for individual behaviors. They coded newspaper articles about mass murderers (one American and one Chinese) in the United States; the articles appeared in English-language (*New York Times*) and Chinese-language (*World Journal*) newspapers published in New York and circulated worldwide. The proportion of segments that signified dispositional or contextual explanation was computed for each article. They found that English-language newspaper articles tended to explain the behaviors in dispositional terms more than Chinese-language newspaper articles for both cases (F. Lee, Hallahan, & Herzog showed a similar trend in their 1996 study). A reliable difference in contextual explanation was not found at the .05 level for either case.

Using a different method, Morris and Peng's (1994) Study 3 asked American and Chinese (including Hong Kong, People's Republic of China, and Republic of China) physics graduate students to rate the importance of a variety of dispositional and contextual explanations of the two murder cases (instead of generating explanations). On average, American participants rated the importance of dispositional causes as greater than Chinese participants for the Chinese murderer, although they did not show a reliable difference for the American murderer. In contrast, American participants rated the importance of contextual causes lower than Chinese participants for both cases. Taken together, Morris and Peng found some evidence that Americans may generate dispositional explanations more than Chinese, although there may not be differences in generation of contextual explanations. In contrast, Chinese may evaluate contextual explanations as more important than Americans, although there may not be a strong difference in evaluating the importance of dispositional causes (Morris and Peng made a similar point).

It is interesting to note that Morris and Peng (1994) reported a pattern of findings consistent with this interpretation in their Study 1. They showed computer-generated movements of a black circle in reaction to a square (inanimate objects) and those of fish in reaction to a school of fish (animate objects) to American and Chinese high school and graduate students. Participants were asked to rate the extent to which these movements were due to dispositional or contextual forces. As expected, there was no cultural difference in the evaluation of causality for inanimate objects. For animate objects, high school students exhibited an expected pattern, although graduate students did not show any cultural difference. Chinese high school students rated contextual forces as more important than their American counterparts for all types of movements. However, Chinese students rated dispositional forces as less important than Americans only for one of three.

Why People Describe Others the Way They Do
Why do Asians and North Americans describe others the way they do? A popular answer is that it is due to a cultural difference in individualism or collectivism or due to independent or interdependent self-construal. Nonetheless, there is a surprising paucity of supportive evidence for this explanation. If we were to attribute a causal role to independent and interdependent self-construal, that is, if the prevalence and activation of self-schemata in an Asian or

Western individual are to explain the cultural differences in person descriptions and explanations, we should be able to measure self-construals and show that the cultural differences disappear if we statistically control for the self-construals (*self-concept mediation* hypothesis). However, as Matsumoto (1999) noted, studies that took this approach did not find empirical support for a mediation effect of self-construals. Clearly, the self-concept mediation hypothesis needs to be examined more fully with more sophisticated measures. An alternative hypothesis is that there may be a cultural theory that affects the psychological process involved in both self-cognition and cognition of others (*cultural theory* hypothesis).

Although it is not easy to separate these two viewpoints empirically, a cultural theory approach has received some attention in the past. In 1992, Y. Kashima, Siegal, Tanaka, and Kashima examined the role played in Australia and Japan by people's implicit theory about attitude-behavior relationship. They reasoned that, in English-speaking countries, the values of sincerity and authenticity (Trilling, 1972) encourage people to make their feelings and avowals consistent with each other, whereas the Japanese notions of *omote* and *ura* (front and back, respectively) suggest that people should express their feelings appropriately in suitable contexts (Doi, 1986). Accordingly, Australians would have a stronger belief in attitude-behavior consistency than Japanese. Japanese and Australian students' attitude attributions were examined in a paradigm used by Jones and Harris (1967), in which participants were asked to read a hypothetical actor's essay about environmental issues. It was found by Y. Kashima et al. that Australians attributed corresponding attitudes more than Japanese overall. Nonetheless, this cultural difference was mediated by the extent to which Australians and Japanese differed in beliefs in attitude-behavior relationship. When the effect of attitude-behavior relationship beliefs was statistically controlled, the cultural effect on attitude attribution became nonsignificant. It is interesting to note that subsequent studies on attitude attributions comparing Americans with Koreans (Choi & Nisbett, 1998) or with Taiwanese (Krull et al., 1999) showed that there was no cultural difference in the extent to which participants attributed attitudes corresponding to the actor's behavior.

In a recent study, Chiu, Hong, and Dweck (1997) showed that people's implicit theory of personality is related to the tendency to make dispositional attributions. According to Dweck (1999), people hold an implicit theory about the nature of personality. Some believe personality consists of fixed and unchangeable traits (*entity theory*), whereas others believe personality is a dynamic quality that can be developed and changed. In four studies, Chiu et al. showed that, when compared to incremental theorists, entity theorists are more likely to generalize an individual's behavior from one specific situation to another (Study 1), to predict an individual's behavior from his or her personality trait (Study 2), and to attribute trait dispositions from a single behavior (Study 3). In Study 5, a manipulation of people's implicit theory also produced a similar result. In their Study 4, the relationship between implicit theory and tendency to make trait dispositional judgments was examined in Hong Kong and the United States. In both cultures, implicit theory predicted dispositional attributions, and Americans showed a stronger tendency to make dispositional attributions than Hong Kong Chinese; however, this cultural difference was not related to implicit theory of personality. Both samples showed a similar level of entity theory.

Taking Situational Constraints into Account Even if cultures differ in dispositional attribution, this does not always mean that they differ in the extent to which situational constraints are taken into consideration. The participants in Study 2 of Y. Kashima et al. were told, in one condition, that the writer wrote the essay freely, but in the other condition, they were told that the writer wrote the essay because he was instructed to do so by his teacher. Jones and Harris (1967) argued that, when the essay writer's behavior was constrained by an authority's instruction, the behavior should not be diagnostic of the writer's underlying attitudes, and therefore a rational observer should not attribute an attitude in correspondence to the behavior.

However, their study (and others; see Jones, 1979) found that people tended to attribute attitudes despite the situational constraints. This tendency to give insufficient weight to situational constraints has been called a *correspondence bias* (Gilbert & Malone, 1995). Replicating the work of Jones and Harris (1967), Y. Kashima et al. (1992) found that both Japanese and Australians failed to take into account the situational constraint on the essay writer. Consistent with this, Choi and Nisbett (1998; Study 1) in the United States and Korea, and Krull et al. (1999; Study 1) in the United States and Taiwan found little difference in correspondence bias using the attitude attribution paradigm; the last researchers found no cultural difference in their replication of the work of Ross, Amabile, and Steinmetz (1977) in the United States and Hong Kong (Study 2).

Nevertheless, Choi and Nisbett (1998) showed that, when situational constraints of behavior are made salient, Koreans take into account the information about situational constraints more than Americans. In their Study 2, they used the attitude attribution paradigm of Jones and Harris (1967). That is, participants were told that a student wrote an essay under choice and no choice conditions, and the salience of situational constraints was manipulated at two levels. In one condition, the participants experienced the same situational constraints as the essay writer (i.e., they were given no choice in writing an essay), and in the other condition, the participants experienced the constraints and were given a set of arguments for them to use in writing their essays. Choi and Nisbett combined the data from the no choice condition in their Study 1 with the Study 2 data and found that the salience manipulation decreased the amount of correspondence bias for Koreans, but had no effect for Americans. This may mean that Koreans (and possibly East Asians in general) are more sensitive to situational constraints under some circumstances than Americans. Alternatively, Koreans may be more empathetic than Americans. Note that, in their experiment, the participants were required to experience situational constraints and transpose this experience onto the essay writer. Some evidence corroborates this interpretation. In the work of Choi and Nisbett, as well as that of Y. Kashima et al. (1992), the participants' own attitudes predicted the attitudes attributed to the essay writer more strongly in the Korean or Japanese sample than in the U.S. or Australian sample.

Conceptualizing the Self

Open-Ended Self-Descriptions The results of cross-cultural studies of open-ended self-descriptions largely mirror those of descriptions of others. When asked to describe themselves, North Americans tend to use more abstract, decontextualized words and phrases. Studies reviewed typically made use of the Twenty Statements Test (TST; Kuhn & McPartland, 1954) or its variants, in which people are asked to answer the question, "Who am I?" by completing 20 sentences that start with "I am . . . "

Bond and Cheung (1983), in their pioneering study, examined Hong Kong Chinese, Japanese, and American students' self-descriptions on the TST and found that Japanese self-descriptions included fewer general psychological attributes (typically personality trait words) than American ones, though they failed to find a difference between Japanese and Chinese participants in this regard. Subsequent studies using a similar technique showed that in both Malaysia (Bochner, 1984) and India (Dhawan, Roseman, Naidu, Thapa, & Rettek, 1995), self-descriptions tended to have lower percentages of personality traitlike descriptions than in English-speaking countries (Australia and Britain for Bochner; United States for Dhawan et al.). However, English-speaking Indian participants could show a level of personality trait use similar to British and Bulgarian participants (Lalljee & Angelova, 1995).

Cousins (1989) used a variant of this method. He first used the TST and examined all the self-descriptions, as well as five self-descriptions that the participants selected as most important. He reported the results of the five most important self-descriptions as there was only a small difference. They found that U.S. students' self-descriptions included a greater proportion of personality traitlike descriptions (58%) than their Japanese counterparts (19%); however, Japanese students used a greater proportion (27%) of social descriptions, such as social roles, institutional memberships, and the like than American students (9%).

Immediately after the typical TST, Cousins (1989) asked his participants to "Describe yourself in the following situations:" followed by the phrases "at home," "at school," and "with close friends" (p. 126). The exact format of this "contextualized" version of the self-description task is unclear from his writing, however. For instance, it is unclear how many times the participants were to write their self-descriptions, whether they were told to describe themselves a set number of times for each of the three settings listed (i.e., at home, at school, and with close friends), or if none of these things were explicitly stated. Nonetheless, the findings are intriguing. Cousins reported the reversal of the TST finding: That is, the Japanese participants mentioned pure attributes more (41%) than the Americans (26%). In this contextualized version, the Americans qualified their traitlike self-descriptions more (35%; e.g., "I am usually

open with my brother," p. 129) than the Japanese (22%). Leuers and Sonoda (1996; Sonoda & Leuers, 1996) largely replicated Cousins's findings using data from Japanese and Irish subjects.

Following Cousins (1989; also see Shweder & Bourne, 1984), these findings can be interpreted as showing that culturally constituted conceptions of the person are different between the United States and Japan. The Japanese tendency to describe themselves using abstract traitlike terms in the contextualized format indicates that they are as capable of abstract self-descriptions as their American or Irish counterparts. Cousins argued that the Japanese conception of the self is more situated and contextualized.

Rhee, Uleman, Lee, and Roman (1995) examined self-descriptions of Koreans, Asian Americans, and European Americans on the TST. They also divided the Asian American group into three groups: those who mentioned both ethnicity (e.g., Asian American) and nationality (e.g., Chinese, Indian; doubly identified), those who mentioned either ethnicity or nationality (singly identified), and those who mentioned neither (unidentified). The percentage of trait self-descriptions increased from Koreans (17%), to doubly identified Asian Americans (24%), to singly identified Asian Americans (31%), and to European Americans (35%), as expected. Surprisingly, unidentified Asian Americans had the greatest percentage of trait self-descriptions (45%). The authors then computed the percentage of autonomous, social, abstract, and specific self-descriptions. The percentage of abstract descriptions was greatest for unidentified Asian Americans, followed by Euro-Americans, singly identified and doubly identified Asian Americans, and Koreans (the percentage of specific descriptions was opposite to this trend). Likewise, the percentage of autonomous self-descriptions followed the exact pattern as that of abstract ones (the percentage of social descriptions showed a reverse pattern). As Triandis, Kashima, Shimada, and Villareal (1986) suggested, those who are extremely acculturated into the host culture (unidentified Asian Americans) may have become even more Americanized than the majority of the host culture. Intriguingly, the correlation between abstract and autonomous self-descriptions was highest among Euro-Americans and unidentified and singly identified Asian Americans (.77 to .74), but was lower among the other groups (.58 to .34). The cross-cultural variation in the correlations implies a conceptual distinction between abstract self and agentic self.

Structured Measures of Self-Conceptions   There is less direct evidence for cultural difference in self-conceptions when structured measures are used (Takano, 1999). Singelis (1994) was probably the first to provide this type of evidence. He showed that Asian Americans scored higher on the interdependent and lower on the independent self-construal than European Americans in Hawaii, and that a difference between the tendency of Asian and European Americans to make situational explanations can be explained by the interdependent self-construal. Nonetheless, the data came from American participants from different cultural backgrounds.

Kashima et al. (1995) provided further evidence for cultural differences in self-conception by examining two East Asian countries (Japan and Korea), two Western countries (Australia and the United States), and Hawaii. They devised measures of four different aspects of self-conception. Two of the four pertained to agency and assertiveness, that is, the extent to which the self is perceived to be a goal-oriented agent or an assertive individual (individualist); one had to do with the extent to which the self is conceptualized in relation to another individual (relational); and the last aspect was concerned with the self as a member of one's ingroup (collective). The four self-aspects were shown to have only moderate correlations in Australia, the United States, Hawaii, Japan, and Korea. A major cultural difference was found for the two individualist aspects of the self. Australian and American students rated higher on these measures than Japanese and Korean students, with the Hawaiian sample in between. Although there was a small cultural difference for the collective aspect of the self, cultural differences in relational self showed an unexpected pattern, with the Korean and Japanese samples marking the highest and lowest scores, respectively. Instead, there was a stronger gender difference on relational self: Women were more relational than men in most samples.

Self in Context   Theorists have suggested that individualist or collectivist tendencies (e.g., Triandis, 1995), and indeed accessible self-conceptions (e.g., Triandis, 1989), are context dependent. Although the context sensitivity of individualism and collectivism has been shown

(e.g., Fijneman, Willemsen, & Poortinga, 1996; Matsumoto, Takeuchi, Andayani, Kouznetsova, & Krupp, 1998; Rhee, Uleman, & Lee, 1996) and the context-sensitive measures of these constructs have been developed (e.g., Matsumoto, Weissman, Preston, Brown, & Kupperbusch, 1997), it is unclear how context-sensitive cultural differences in the self-concepts are. One possibility is that collective selves are more accessible and individualistic selves are less accessible across all contexts in collectivist cultures such as East Asia than in individualist cultures such as North America (generality hypothesis). Another possibility is that individualistic and collective selves can be accessible in different contexts in different cultures (Culture × Context Interaction Hypothesis). In the domain of resource exchange behavior, Poortinga and colleagues (Fijneman et al., 1996; Poortinga, 1992; van den Heuvel & Poortinga, 1999) postulated a universalist interaction hypothesis. According to these researchers, there is a universal pattern of resource exchange so that certain types of resources are more likely to be exchanged with certain types of others; however, there are some cultural variations in specific contexts (also see Kroonenberg & Kashima, 1997).

Uleman, Rhee, Bardoliwalla, Semin, and Toyama's (1999) study extended this line of reasoning to the domain of self. They constructed a new measure of relational self in which a respondent is asked to indicate how close the self is to specific others such as immediate family, relatives, and close friend in terms of global closeness, emotional closeness, mutual support, identity, reputation, similarity, and harmony. The degree of closeness was indicated by the amount of overlap between two circles, as in a Venn diagram. The data were collected from Euro-Americans, Asian Americans, Dutch, Turkish, and Japanese university students. Their Culture × Gender × Target × Closeness type analysis of variance (ANOVA) suggested that, of all the two-way interaction effects, Target × Closeness type effect was the largest, which suggests the importance of context specificity of relational self. To explore a significant Culture × Target × Closeness type interaction, they computed the deviation scores of each culture's Target × Closeness type means from the averages across all cultural groups and conducted a cluster analysis on these deviation scores. This showed that the European American and Dutch groups formed a tight individualist cluster, and the Turkish and Japanese groups formed another looser collectivist cluster, with the Asian Americans joining the latter.

Cognitive Representations of the Self Cross-cultural research has been conducted not only on self-descriptions, but also on cognitive representations of the self. Trafimow et al. (1991) postulated that different types of self-cognitions may be stored in different storage places. In particular, they tested between two models, one suggesting that individualist and collective self-cognitions are stored in one location (one-basket model) and the other model suggesting they are stored in two separate locations (two-basket model). The two-basket theory predicts that priming one type of self-conceptions would increase the accessibility of only the same type of self-conceptions. However, one-basket theory predicts that both individual and collective selves would be more accessed when either individualist or collectivist concepts are primed. According to Trafimow et al., the one-basket theory predicts that the retrieval of one type of self-cognition is equally likely to be followed by any other type of self-cognition. However, the two-basket theory predicts that the retrieval of one type of self-cognition is more likely to be followed by the same type of self-cognition. To put it differently, if the two-basket theory is true, the conditional probability of retrieving an individual self-cognition given that an individual self-cognition has been retrieved immediately before is greater than the conditional probability of retrieving a collective self-cognition in the same condition or vice versa, that is, $p(I|I) > p(I|C)$ and $p(C|C) > p(C|I)$.

In Study 1, Trafimow et al. (1991) primed both European American students and students who had Chinese family names and whose native language was not English by having them think what made them different from their families and friends (individual prime) and what they had in common with their families and friends (collective prime) for 2 minutes and then had the participants respond to the TST for 5 minutes. The experiment was conducted in English. Although all participants reported more individual self-cognitions than collective ones, this tendency was greater for North American students than for Chinese students. Consistent with the two-basket theory, the priming manipulation had differential effects on individual and collective self-cognitions. In addition, the conditional probabilities computed from the TST showed the pattern that the authors argued was consistent with the two-

basket theory. In Study 2, they primed individualist and collectivist concepts by a different method (having participants read a story that emphasized either personal characteristics or family relationships) using American students and replicated the Study 1 findings. Trafimow, Silverman, Fan, and Law (1997) conducted a comparable experiment using English and Chinese in Hong Kong with bilingual Chinese students. The two priming methods in Trafimow et al. (1991) were both used in this experiment, including an additional no priming control condition. In the English language condition, the results were largely consistent with those of Trafimow et al. (1991). However, in the Chinese language condition, the priming manipulation had no effect, although the conditional probabilities showed the pattern consistent with the two-basket model.

Gardner, Gabriel, and Lee (1999) extended the work of Trafimow and colleagues (1991) by examining the effects of priming individual and collective selves not only on self-descriptions, but also on value and morality judgments. In Experiment 1, they showed that two methods of priming individual and collective selves (Trafimow et al., 1991, and Brewer & Gardner, 1996) affected in expected ways North American students' TST responses, as well as endorsement of individualist and collectivist values and the extent to which the responsibility to help needy others was seen to be a universal obligation, and that the effect of priming on value endorsement was mediated by self-descriptions. Experiment 2 was conducted with American and Hong Kong students using English. Trafimow et al.'s (1991) priming manipulation was followed by a value questionnaire. In the no prime control condition, Americans endorsed individualist values more strongly than collectivist values, but this was reversed in Hong Kong. However, when Americans' collective selves were primed, Americans endorsed collectivist values more than individualist values; the priming of individual selves did not affect value endorsement. In contrast, when Hong Kong Chinese students' individual selves were primed, they endorsed individualist values more than collectivist values; the priming of collective selves did not change the value endorsement pattern. It is yet to be seen whether this is replicated using Chinese (see Trafimow et al., 1997).

Issues Associated with the Research on Self-Representation There are both methodological and theoretical problems about self-representations. Methodologically, the TST has many problems despite its popularity. Wylie (1974) expressed some doubts about the construct validity of its coding schemes. In the contemporary uses of TST, a variety of coding schemes has been suggested. Triandis (1995) suggested the percentage of social items $S\%$ as a measure of allocentrism (individual-level construct of collectivism). Trafimow et al. (1991) classified TST responses into two categories, individual and collective. Bochner (1984) used a tripartite scheme of individual, relational, and collective responses. Watkins, Yau, Dahlin, and Wondimu (1997) suggested a four-part scheme: idiocentric (individual-level construct for individualism), large group (e.g., gender, occupation), small group (e.g., family), and allocentric (e.g., I am sociable). Other researchers (e.g., Cousins, 1989; Dhawan et al., 1995) used more complex coding schemes. Rhee et al. (1995; also see Parkes, Schneider, & Bochner, 1999) devised a scheme in which many categories are used to code self-descriptions, but they are then aggregated to construct two indices, abstractness (as opposed to specific) and autonomy (as opposed to social). This coding scheme is consistent with the current theory of attributions that distinguishes attributions of trait dispositions and those of agency (as discussed above). Some researchers used only a subset of 20 statements (e.g., Bochner, 1984; Cousins, 1989), whereas others used all 20. These methodological differences may not affect conclusions about cultural differences according to Watkins et al. (1997), however.

The TST has other problems as well. Not only its context-free nature (e.g., Cousins, 1989), but also its use of the word "I" as a cue may be problematic. As E. S. Kashima and Kashima (1997, 1998) noted, different languages have different sets of first-person pronouns, with some languages having multiple first-person pronouns (e.g., Japanese). This raises a difficult question of which personal pronoun to use in cross-cultural comparisons (also see Leuers & Sonoda, 1999). No systematic investigation has been conducted on this issue. Finally, Triandis, Chan, Bhawuk, Iwao, and Sinha (1995) reported that, within a U.S. sample, a measure of allocentrism (individual-level collectivism) based on TST ($S\%$) did not correlate with structured measures of allocentrism. This last finding suggests that psychological processes that lead to the use of socially relevant descriptors in self-descriptions may not be related to the

attitudes and values measured by structured questionnaires.

Theoretical issues have been raised about self-representations. From the perspective of Deaux's model of social identity (1993; Deaux, Reid, Mizrahi, & Ethier, 1995), Reid and Deaux (1996) challenged the two-basket theory of self-representation. According to Deaux, self-cognitions are organized in a more integrated manner than the two-basket theory suggests. A woman may represent herself in terms of her role as a sister/daughter in her family, her occupation as a lawyer, or as the partner of her significant other. Associated with each social identity (collective self) may be a set of psychological attributes (individual selves), such as relaxed and smart for the sister/daughter identity and hardworking, active, and smart for the lawyer identity. The integrated model suggests, then, that collective selves are associated with each other and individual selves are associated with each other, just as the two-basket theory implies. In addition, the former postulates that some individual selves are associated with collective selves as well.

Reid and Deaux (1996) examined Deaux's model in an elaborate recall experiment in three sessions that spanned several weeks. In the first session, each of the 57 participants in the interview listed self-defining characteristics that are social categories or groups to which they belong (see S. Rosenberg & Gara, 1985). One week later, in the second session, each participant rated the importance of the individualized list of collective and individual self-descriptions. After a 5-minute distracter task, each participant recalled items from the list. Several weeks after the second session, 29 of the original 57 rated the extent to which the individual selves (psychological attributes) were associated with each collective self (social identities). Reid and Deaux showed that the conditional probability measures followed a pattern similar to that of Trafimow et al. (1991) and examined the adjusted ratio of clustering (ARC) scores, which measure the extent to which recalled items are clustered around a theme (Roenker, Thompson, & Brown, 1971). The ARC score for clustering around individual versus collective themes (consistent with the two-basket theory) was .23, and the ARC score for social identities (consistent with the integrated model) was .34. Both scores were significantly greater than zero. Although the latter score is numerically greater than the former, no statistical test was reported. The conditional probabilities of recalling an individual self given that a collective self has been recalled previously and the conditional probabilities of recalling a collective self given that an individual self has been retrieved previously closely matched what was expected from the degree of association between collective and individual selves as examined by a cluster analysis (DeBoeck & Rosenberg, 1988). The authors concluded that the results are generally more consistent with the integrated model than with the two-basket model.

Nonetheless, the data of Trafimow and colleagues (1991, 1997) and Reid and Deaux may need to be interpreted with caution. Recall that both teams used conditional probabilities as measures of memory association between individual and collective self-cognitions. Skowronski and colleagues (Skowronski, Betz, Sedikides, & Crawford, 1998; Skowronski & Welbourne, 1997), however, showed that conditional probabilities may provide biased estimates of memory associations. This is because expected conditional probabilities depend on the total number of individual and collective self-cognitions. The concerns of Skowronski and colleagues' should be addressed in future studies. Although the ARC results obtained in the Reid and Deaux study may not be affected by this concern, a critical statistical test was not reported in their study, as noted above. It is too early to conclude definitively the validity of these models.

Self-Evaluation

Positive Self-Regard Despite the centrality of the self-esteem concept in North America, it may not occupy as central a place for people from East Asian cultures. Heine, Lehman, Markus, and Kitayama (1999) argued that East Asians and Japanese in particular do not have a strong need for positive self-regard as it is usually conceived within contemporary social psychology. According to them, North Americans are self-enhancing, whereas Japanese are self-improving. North Americans seek to identify positive attributes of the self (positive abilities in particular) and attempt to maintain and enhance self-esteem by affirmation when their self-esteem is under threat (e.g., failing in a task). In contrast, Japanese seek to identify discrepancies between what is ideally required of them and what they perceive themselves to be and attempt to improve those failings. In other words, both North Americans and Japanese try to reach the ideal, but the former focus on positives and try to move toward the ideal, whereas

the latter focus on negatives and try not to fall behind.

Heine et al. (1999) suggest that self-enhancement and self-improvement are functional in independent and interdependent cultures, respectively. In cultures in which people view themselves as independent agents and seek to distinguish themselves from others, it is functional to emphasize one's uniqueness by insisting that one is above average. In contrast, in cultures in which people view themselves as interdependent with others and seek belongingness with their in-groups, one gains a sense of belongingness by trying to attain the ideal that is shared by the members of one's significant in-group. It is adaptive in this type of culture to try not to fall behind others rather than to try to go beyond them. In line with this argument, samples of Japanese individuals have consistently revealed lower levels of self-esteem than their North American counterparts, as gauged by M. Rosenberg's (1965) self-esteem measure. Corroborating this is the finding that the self-esteem of Japanese visiting North America tends to increase, while the self-esteem of North Americans visiting Japan tends to decline. Indeed, a number of studies suggest that Japanese students do not exhibit the tendency to maintain their self-esteem that their North American counterparts do.

One such instance is the so-called unrealistic optimism bias (for reviews, see Greenwald, 1980; Taylor & Brown, 1988). Heine and Lehman (1995) showed that European Canadian students exhibited a greater degree of optimism relative to Japanese students. In their Study 1, they used two methods for examining optimism bias. One (within-group) method was to have participants rate the likelihood of positive and negative life events (e.g., enjoying one's career, becoming an alcoholic) happening to them relative to average students of the same sex in their university. In the other (between-group) method, one group of participants estimated the percentage chance of the events happening to themselves without any reference to average students, and the other group estimated the percentage chance of the same events happening to the average same-sex student from their university. On both measures, the Canadian students showed an optimism bias by estimating the likelihood of their enjoying positive events to be greater and that of their suffering from negative events to be smaller than the average student. The Japanese students, however, did not exhibit this pattern. In Study 2, Heine and

Lehman examined the extent to which Canadian and Japanese students are optimistic about negative life events relevant to independent (e.g., becoming alcoholic) and interdependent (e.g., making your family ashamed of you) aspects of the self. Again, Canadians showed optimism regardless, but Japanese displayed less optimism on the within-group measure or even pessimism on the between-group measure.

That East Asians show a lower level of optimism than North Americans has been corroborated by other studies. In Y. T. Lee and Seligman's (1997) study, European Americans showed the highest level of optimism, followed by Chinese Americans, with mainland Chinese exhibiting the lowest level of optimism. In a related vein, Y. Kashima and Triandis (1986) also showed that Japanese students exhibited less self-serving attributions following success and failure experiences than their American counterparts. The Japanese students studying in the United States attributed their failures in a task purportedly related to intelligence to their lack of ability more than American students. Nevertheless, it is important to note that less optimism among East Asians does not necessarily generalize to all collectivist cultures. Chandler, Shama, Wolf, and Planchard (1981) examined attribution styles in five cultures (India, Japan, South Africa, the United States, and Yugoslavia) and found that self-serving attribution patterns were present in all cultures, including collectivist cultures such as India.

One possible interpretation of the Japanese self-improving tendency is a modesty bias. That is, Japanese would be privately self-enhancing as much as Americans, but they publicly present themselves as modest by being self-effacing. Existing evidence does not seem to support this argument, however. For example, Kashima and Triandis (1986) examined Japanese and American students' attributions of success and failure in both public and private conditions and detected no difference between them. Japanese were self-deprecating in both conditions. This study, nonetheless, is a weak test of this hypothesis due to its small sample size. More recently, Heine, Takata, and Lehman (2000) showed that the Japanese tendency to focus on their negative performance seems to be present even in an experimental setting in which self-presentation appears to be difficult.

It is interesting that even Japanese people appear to have some implicit positive self-regard. Kitayama and Karasawa (1997) showed that Japanese students exhibited a name-letter effect, in which a letter used in their own names was regarded more positively than those letters not used in their names, suggesting that they have some positive regard for things associated with themselves. Hetts et al. (1999) also reported a series of experiments in which self-regard was measured implicitly. In Study 1, they measured the regard of Asian Americans, European Americans, and recent Asian immigrants for their individual self and collective self. The task was to decide whether a word followed by a prime word such as "me" or "us" is "good" or "bad." The faster a good response is relative to a bad response, the more positively regarded is the prime word. There was a large difference among the three groups on the positivity of "me," with the positivity of the Asian American group being the greatest, followed by that of the European Americans. The regard of the recent Asian immigrants regard for "me" was even negative. In contrast, the order of the groups was reversed for the positivity of "us" (see Rhee et al., 1995, for a similar finding about strongly acculturated Asian Americans).

In Study 2 of Hetts et al. (1999), Asian Americans, European Americans, and recent Asian immigrants did a word completion task. Word fragments were to be completed while the participants responded to another task designed to prime either individual or collective self. The number of completed word fragments that implied positive meanings relative to that which implied negative meanings was used to measure implicit self regard. The results replicated those of Study 1.

In Study 3 of Hetts et al. (1999), the self-regard of Japanese students was measured using the method used in Study 1. The Japanese words "watashi" (I), "watashitachi" (we), and "jibun" (self), were used as a prime. The results showed that the Japanese students who had never lived outside Japan showed a positive response to "watashitachi" and "jibun," but a neutral response to "watashi." In contrast, this was reversed for the students who had lived for at least 5 consecutive years in the United States or Canada. They showed a positive regard for "watashi," but had negative responses to "watashitachi" and "jibun." Throughout the studies, however, explicit measures of self-regard (e.g., M. Rosenberg's 1965 self-esteem measure) did not vary across groups or covary with implicit measures, suggesting a dissociation between implicit and explicit cognition. Implicit measures of self-regard, however, correlated strongly with the duration of residence in the United States in Studies 1 and 2.

Two types of explanations have been offered for the cultural difference in self-regard. One proximal explanation was provided by Higgins' (1987; Higgins, Klein, & Strauman, 1985) self-discrepancy theory. One regards oneself well to the extent that one's perceptions of oneself (actual self) are close to one's ideal (ideal self). A large discrepancy between the actual self and ideal self causes depression and dejection. Consistent with this, Heine and Lehman (1999) showed that Japanese students had a greater actual-ideal discrepancy than European and Asian Canadian students. Nevertheless, this explanation may need to be examined more fully as they found that the correlation between actual-ideal discrepancies and Zung's (1965) Self-Report Depression Inventory differed across cultures, with the correlation highest for European Canadians, followed by Asian Canadians and Japanese. This may imply that measures have different reliability across cultures, that other aspects of the theory can explain this cultural difference, or that the applicability of self-discrepancy theory differs across cultures.

A more distal explanation was provided by Kitayama, Markus, Matsumoto, and Norasakkunkit (1997). They argued that each culture provides situations that afford people to behave in a way that is typical of their culture. It is the situations available in given cultures that perpetuate psychological differences between them. To support this, they adopted a novel situation-sampling method. This method involved two steps. First, Japanese and Americans described situations in which they felt their self-esteem increased or decreased. There were 50 descriptions randomly selected from the descriptions generated by a (male or female) sample from each culture (Japan or North America) under each of the two instruction conditions (self-esteem increasing or decreasing), for a total of 400 situation descriptions. Note that these situations embedded a Gender × Culture × Condition factorial design with 50 situations in each cell. Bilingual individuals translated Japanese situation descriptions into English and American ones into Japanese and edited them for cross-cultural intelligibility. In the second step, these 400 situation descriptions served as stimuli for different samples of Japanese (Japanese in Japan and Japanese studying in the United States) and European American students. Participants were asked (a) whether their self-esteem would be affected,

(b) if so, whether it would increase or decrease, and (c) by how much did it increase or decrease. First, the extent to which situations were perceived to influence self-esteem was examined by two methods. In the across-participant analysis, the proportion of situations selected out of 50 was computed for each participant, and an analysis was conducted using participants as a unit of analysis. In the across-situation analysis, the proportion of participants who selected a given situation as affecting their self-esteem was computed for each situation, and an analysis was conducted using situations as a unit. Findings reported below obtained using both methods.

Americans chose a greater proportion of situations as more relevant to their self-esteem than Japanese. However, there was also a tendency for a cultural group to see those situations generated by their own cultural group as more relevant. That is, Americans tended to see American-made situations as more relevant than Japanese-made ones and vice versa. Furthermore, Americans were more likely to select positive situations as relevant to their self-esteem than negative ones. But, this was reversed for both samples of Japanese students.

Kitayama et al. (1997) also examined participants' estimate of the extent to which the situations would increase or decrease their self-esteem. A majority of American participants estimated that their self-esteem would be enhanced overall regardless of the origin of the situations. A majority of Japanese students in Japan showed the opposite tendency, estimating that their self-esteem would be negatively affected overall. However, Japanese students studying in the United States exhibited a self-enhancing tendency for the situations generated in the United States, but a self-critical tendency for situations generated in Japan. Furthermore, all participants rated American-made situations as more self-enhancing and less self-critical than Japanese-made situations. All in all, the results suggest that, in line with Kitayama et al.'s theory, cultures provide culture-specific situations that tend to afford certain psychological activities. Clearly, members of a given culture react to their own cultural situations more strongly, but members of other cultures may react to those situations in a like manner. Nonetheless, as members of a culture become enculturated into another host culture, they begin to acquire a bicultural tendency to react to the host cultural situations as the members of the host culture would, while still retaining the behavioral pattern prevalent in their culture of origin.

Further Issues in Research on Self-Regard Two related issues are on the horizon at this stage. First, self-esteem as currently conceptualized may not be a universal psychological concept, but specific to the contemporary North American culture. Further indications come from the literature on the relationship between self-esteem and *subjective well-being*, which is people's cognitive evaluation of and affective reaction to their life (for reviews, see Diener, 1984; Diener, Suh, Lucas, & Smith, 1999). Although self-esteem is a strong predictor of subjective well-being in North America (A. Campbell, 1981), it does not appear to be so in other cultures. Cross-cultural variability in the relationship between self-esteem and subjective well-being implies that self-esteem may have different meanings in different cultures if people's attitudes toward life (i.e., subjective well-being) is taken as one standard against which other psychological concepts can be conceptualized (this premise, however, is also debatable as subjective well-being correlates with individualism; Diener, Diener, & Diener, 1995).

Diener and Diener (1995) administered a questionnaire in which respondents' satisfaction with life in general and self among other domains of life were each gauged on a 7-point scale in universities in 31 countries. They computed a correlation between self-satisfaction and life satisfaction ratings for each sex separately in each country, transformed it to a *z* value, and correlated it with each country's level of individualism. The across-country correlation was .53 for both men and women. This finding is suggestive of cross-cultural variability in the relationship between self-esteem and subjective well-being (for a related point, see Suh, Diener, Oishi, & Triandis, 1998), although only single-item measures were used.

More recently, Kwan, Bond, and Singelis (1997) examined the relationship of Rosenberg's (1965) self-esteem and relationship harmony (extent to which a person has attained harmonious relationships with significant others) with subjective well-being. Relationship harmony was measured by having each respondent list five most significant dyadic relationships in their lives and rate how each relationship was characterized by harmony. Using a structural equations modeling technique, they showed that self-esteem had a greater impact on subjective well-being than relationship har-

mony in the United States, but their contributions were approximately equal in Hong Kong. Although this is strong evidence, its generalizability to other collectivist cultures needs to be examined further.

Second, the current conception of self-esteem may be too narrow. Tafarodi and Swann (1995) proposed that there may be two separable dimensions of global self-esteem (i.e., self-competence and self-liking). Self-competence results from successful manipulation and handling of one's environment and reflects the overall sense of oneself as being capable, effective, and in control. Self-liking has to do with one's view of oneself as socially accepted and reflects the global sense of oneself as liked by a "generalized other" or in line with internalized values. Tafarodi and Swann showed that their instrument, the Self-Liking/Self-Competence Scale (SLSC), forms two correlated, but distinctive, factors using a confirmatory factor analysis. They also established some discriminant validity of self-liking and self-competence by showing differential relationships of these scales with a measure of one's perceived abilities and memories about the treatment by one's parents. That is, self-liking correlated with memories of parental treatment more than perceived self-abilities; however, self-competence correlated with perceived self-abilities more than memories of parental treatment.

Tafarodi and his colleagues (Tafarodi, Lang, & Smith, 1999; Tafarodi & Swann, 1996) argued that there may be a cultural trade-off between self-liking and self-competence. That is, in individualist cultures, people may opt for self-competence at the expense of interpersonal harmony with significant others as the individual mastery of one's environment is more important; however, in collectivist cultures, people may emphasize self-liking, while self-competence may decrease behind in importance. In line with this reasoning, Tafarodi and Swann showed that self-competence was higher in an individualist culture (United States) than in a collectivist culture (mainland China) after self-liking was partialed out, and that self-liking was higher in the collectivist culture than in the individualist culture, again after self-competence was partialed out. Nonetheless, the ratings without statistical control showed that Americans had a higher level of self-competence and self-liking than Chinese.

Tafarodi et al. (1999) conducted a further test of their hypothesis by comparing British and Malaysian students while directly measuring their individual-level individualism-collectivism (Hui's 1988 INDCOL). Not only were their findings consistent with the cultural trade-off hypothesis, but also these cultural differences became nonsignificant after controlling for INDCOL. This suggests that the difference in self-liking and self-competence can be explained by individual-level individualism and collectivism.

Although the highly correlated nature of self-liking and self-competence measures raises some concerns about the adequacy of SLSC as a measurement instrument, the theoretical rationale behind the conceptual separation between self-liking and self-competence is intriguing. Furthermore, SLSC appears to behave in ways that are theoretically expected when the overlapping variance is removed. Finally, Tafarodi (1998) presented evidence for the separability of self-liking and self-competence not only in relation to other paper-and-pencil tasks, but also in relation to measures of social information processing. Further explorations of self-regard as reflected in self-liking and self-competence seem warranted. In particular, relationships among self-liking/self-competence, independent and interdependent self-construal, relationship harmony, and subjective well-being seem to be a pressing question that requires further inquiries.

Relationship as Target

Noting that the traditional social cognitive research had not examined how people understand their relationships, A. P. Fiske (1991, 1992) filled this gap by postulating a bold, but elegant, theory of social relationships, the relational models theory, which also recognizes the importance of culture. According to A. P. Fiske, human beings construe their relationships in terms of four elementary and universal forms of sociality: communal sharing, authority ranking, equality matching, and market pricing. In *communal sharing*, people regard others as interchangeable elements of a set in which the distinctiveness of individuals is ignored. *Authority ranking* characterizes relationships that rank order individuals along a linear hierarchy. *Equality matching* involves the balanced exchange of resources among the participants. In *market pricing*, the transaction of different types of resources occurs within a marketplace. These types have the same formal structures as four types of measurement. Communal sharing corresponds to a nominal scale, authority ranking to an ordinal scale, equality matching to

an interval scale, and market pricing to a ratio scale.

Each of the four relationship types is mentally represented as a schema. Evidence suggests that these are distinct categorical representations (Haslam, 1994a, 1994b), and that they act as organizational principles for memory (Haslam & Fiske, 1992). In particular, A. P. Fiske, Haslam, and S. Fiske (1991) showed that North American students and adults tend to confuse people with whom they have the same type of relationship, but not people with whom they have different types of relationships. So, one tends to call a person by a wrong name, to misremember a person, or to misdirect an action to a person if the relationship type is the same as that of the right person. In 1997, A. P. Fiske and Haslam also showed that, in North America, when circumstances prevent people from doing something with one person, they often substitute that person intentionally with another with whom they have the same type of relationship.

Some evidence of the universality of the four relational models were provided by A. P. Fiske. First, he derived the four relationship types based on his field observation in the Moose culture (A. P. Fiske, 1990). His review (A. P. Fiske, 1991, 1992) shows that a very large number of social theorists in the past have postulated similar concepts across a number of domains of social activities. In 1993, A. P. Fiske replicated the findings of name, memory, and action confusions he reported with colleagues in 1991 for Bengali monolingual individuals in New York, Chinese speakers in Philadelphia, elderly Koreans in Philadelphia, and recent Vai immigrants in the Washington, DC, area. This theory is probably better substantiated in more cultures than most other social psychological theories.

The claim of A. P. Fiske is that the four forms of sociality are universal, possibly genetically coded knowledge structures. They constitute elementary, conceptual primitives that can be combined by some cultural rules to construct specific cultural practices. Cultures may differ in contexts in which these types of relationships are applicable, manners in which they are expressed, and the like. Nonetheless, A. P. Fiske argues that people construe, are motivated to act, and feel normative obligations to act in accordance with the four relationship types in all human cultures. These are bold claims that are in line with Jackendoff's (1992) and Wierzbicka's (1992) vision of culture. A provocative and productive line of research has been provided by A. P. Fiske.

In contrast to the burgeoning research on self-regard, only Endo, Heine, and Lehman (2000) conducted cross-cultural research on the extent to which people value their relationships. Japanese, Asian Canadian, and European Canadian students evaluated how close their interpersonal relationships (best friend, closest family member, and romantic partner) are relative to the average same-sex students of their universities. In two studies, all groups exhibited a relationship that enhanced bias: They evaluated their relationships to be better and more supportive than those of the average student. In Study 2, Japanese participants displayed a self-effacing tendency, although they were relationship enhancing, suggesting a difference between self-enhancement and relationship enhancement. Clearly, cross-cultural differences in conceptions of interpersonal relationships is a topic that requires further exploration.

Group as Target

People's conceptions of groups have been examined under the rubric of stereotypes in social cognition. Katz and Braly's (1933) classical study about American university students' perceptions of various ethnic groups in the United States is widely regarded as the first of its kind. Nonetheless, its popularity as a research topic has waxed and waned since then, undergoing a low point in the 1960s and 1970s in North America (cf. Hamilton & Gifford, 1976), again surfacing as a major topic in the 1980s and 1990s (for recent reviews of this general field, see Hamilton & Sherman, 1996; Hilton & von Hippel, 1996; Oakes, Turner, & Haslam, 1994; Y. Kashima, Woolcock, & Kashima, 2000).

Positive Regard for In-Groups

Much of the current cross-cultural research on group conceptions centers around the hypothesis that in-group favoritism may be more prevalent in collectivist cultures than in individualist cultures (e.g., Triandis, 1989). This hypothesis has two components: stronger in-group enhancement and out-group derogation bias of people in collectivist cultures compared to people in individualist cultures. That is, one could evaluate one's in-group more favorably than one's out-group on a positive dimension or one's in-group less negatively than one's out-group on a negative dimension. This section

reviews studies that examine people's evaluations of an in-group and out-group member, as well as those that examine people's evaluations of an in-group and out-group as a group. Strictly speaking, processes involved in judgments about a member of a group and the group per se may differ (Hamilton & Sherman, 1996; Y. Kashima et al., 2000). Given the paucity of research in this area, this distinction is ignored here.

The collectivism–in-group enhancement hypothesis has received mixed support. Hewstone and Ward (1985) examined Chinese and Malay students in Malaysia (where Malays are the majority) and Singapore (where Chinese are the majority). In both countries, Malay students attributed an in-group actor's positive action to internal factors more than an out-group actor's equally positive action, whereas a negative action was attributed less to internal factors when the actor was an in-group member than when the actor was an out-group member. Nonetheless, Chinese students did not exhibit this pattern either in Malaysia or in Singapore. Given that Chinese and Malays are almost equally collectivist (Hofstede, 1991, suggests that Singaporeans are more collectivist than Malaysians, if any), Hewstone and Ward's data do not fully support this hypothesis.

Examining this hypothesis more directly, Al-Zahrani and Kaplowitz (1993) examined the tendency of Saudis and Americans for self-enhancement, family enhancement, and nationality enhancement, as well as their tendency for out-group derogation at the national level. Although the Saudis were more collectivist than Americans on Triandis, Bontempo, Villarreal, Asai, and Lucca's (1988) measure, they found no cultural difference in self-enhancement bias, but a greater tendency for Americans to enhance their own family and nation. It appears that Americans are self- and in-group–enhancing in general. Nevertheless, a stronger out-group derogation bias was found for Saudis than for Americans. When in-group enhancement and out-group derogation tendencies were combined, the authors found a greater intergroup bias for Saudis than for Americans for the national-level intergroup relationship.

Heine and Lehman (1997) showed that, contrary to the hypothesis, the Japanese students in their study exhibited less of an in-group–enhancing tendency than their European Canadian counterparts, with the latter displaying a stronger in-group–serving bias. In Study 2, students from two rival universities in Kyoto and Vancouver evaluated their own university and a rival university, as well as the students from these universities. In both cases, the Japanese were less in-group enhancing than their European Canadian counterparts, with an Asian Canadian group typically in between. This study, however, used only positive characteristics for evaluation and therefore did not examine an out-group derogation tendency.

There are several perspectives on the collectivism–in-group enhancement hypothesis. The *individual difference* perspective suggests that those who are collectivistic at the individual level (allocentric) are in-group favoring. Oyserman (1993) found, in four samples, an individual-level collectivism (her own measure) of Jewish and Arab Israelis was a consistent predictor of the perceived intensity of the Jewish-Arab intergroup conflict. This study, nonetheless, does not directly bear on the hypothesis of in-group enhancement. More directly relevant, L. Lee and Ward (1998) showed that Chinese and Malay students who are in the upper third of the distribution on an individual-level collectivism scale developed in Singapore exhibited an in-group enhancement bias. Those who were low (bottom third) on collectivism showed no intergroup bias. As the attitudes were measured on a bipolar positive-negative dimension, an out-group derogation could not be examined separately.

Second, a *social identity theory* perspective suggests that the relation between collectivism and in-group enhancement or out-group derogation biases may be more complex. Hinkle and Brown (1990; Brown et al., 1992) postulated that not only high collectivism, but also relational (as opposed to autonomous), orientation is necessary for an in-group enhancement bias. Relational orientation means a tendency to compare one's in-group with out-groups. In three studies, Brown et al. (1992) showed that the correlation between in-group identification and in-group favoritism was higher among the relational collectivists than the others. Nevertheless, Pedersen and Walker (1997) reported nonsupportive data in the prejudice of European Australians against Australian Aborigines. If prejudice can be regarded as out-group derogation, their study suggests that the Hinkle-Brown framework may explain in-group enhancement, but not out-group derogation.

Finally, from a perspective of self-categorization theory (Turner, Hogg, Oakes, Reicher, & Wetherell, 1987), identification with one's group may not be sufficient to produce in-group

enhancement or out-group derogation. It is only when one's in-group norm dictates that one's in-group is enhanced and out-groups are derogated that group identification should lead to these consequences. If so, the relation between collectivism and in-group enhancement may depend on such factors as in-group norms and a particular intergroup relationship. Clearly, these alternative formulations need to be investigated further.

Construing a Group
as an Agent

More recently, researchers began to investigate cultural differences in conceptions of groups. In a pioneering series of studies, Menon, Morris, Chiu, and Hong (1999) showed that East Asians were more likely to attribute agency to groups than Americans. A pilot study showed that both Americans and Singaporeans make conceptual distinctions among individual dispositional, group dispositional, and situational causes. In Study 1, they examined treatment of rogue trader scandals (two Japanese and two Western cases) by U.S. and Japanese newspapers. In all cases, the Japanese newspaper referred to the organization for which the trader worked more often than the trader himself, but the U.S. newspaper referred to the individual more often than the organization. In Study 2, Hong Kong and U.S. students responded to the description of a case in which a group member's behaviors caused negative consequences for the group. Hong Kong students tended to attribute dispositions to the group more and the individual less than their American counterparts. Study 3 examined Hong Kong and U.S. students' reactions to three cases in which either an individual's or a group's action caused negative consequences. The Americans' dispositional attributions were greater for the individual than for the group, whereas the Hong Kong students' dispositional attributions were marginally smaller for the individual than for the group. Further, the situational attributions made by Americans were greater for the group than for the individual; Hong Kong students made situational attributions equally for individual and group actors, but they made a higher level of situational attributions than their American counterparts in general.

Chiu, Morris, Hong, and Menon (2000) again examined dispositional attributions to the individual and group actor for a negative event. This time, they either measured (Study 1) or manipulated (Study 2) need for closure (Kruglanski & Webster, 1996), that is, an epistemic desire for definite knowledge, which consists of dual tendencies to attain a closure as soon as possible and to retain it as long as possible. Chiu et al. theorized that a cultural theory of individual or group agency is a chronically accessible cognitive structure that is likely to affect attributions when there is a strong need for closure. All in all, consistent with the original hypothesis, people made judgments in line with their cultural theory under high need for closure. The Chinese cultural theory appears to take a group as an agent more than the North American theory does.

Triandis, McCusker, and Hui (1990) reported data that can be interpreted in line with Chiu et al.'s (2000) theorizing. Triandis et al. hypothesized that people in collectivist cultures would view their in-groups as more homogeneous than out-groups, contrary to the more typical out-group homogeneity pattern found in North America and Europe (for a review, see Ostrom & Sedikides, 1992). They asked university students of various ethnic backgrounds in Hawaii, as well as students in Illinois and Beijing, to rate the psychological distance (1 = as similar or close to me as possible, 9 = as different or distant as possible) and perceived homogeneity (0 = no agreement in what people ought to do, 9 = tremendous agreement) of various groups. Note that this measurement of homogeneity is quite different from typical homogeneity perception measures. Nonetheless, they found that in-groups were perceived to be more homogeneous by European Hawaiian and Illinois students, but that out-groups were perceived to be more homogeneous by Chinese, Filipino, and Japanese Hawaiian students, as well as students in Beijing. It is possible that in-groups that are perceived to be agentic in China and maybe in East Asia in general were perceived also to be more homogeneous (also see Abelson, Dasgupta, Park, & Banaji, 1998).

Future Directions

Empirical Research Questions

Two major topics of culture and social cognition today—the explanation of social action and the maintenance of self-regard—are likely to continue as topics in the near future, but other issues are emerging.

Explaining Social Action

In the end, the anthropological insight of Geertz (1984) into Western cultural conceptions of the person appears to be largely substantiated by the social cognitive research. North Americans are more likely to construe a person—self and other—as an agent in terms of his or her disposition. If so, how is this construal done? What are the cognitive processes? A simple interpretive framework may help. Suppose that a person experiences the event of a person acting toward an object in context. A priori, there are several ways to conceptualize and symbolically represent this experience. One type is an *analytical strategy*, in which the observer analyzes this experience into separate concepts and then serializes them into a string of concepts. So, one aspect of the experience first may be extracted analytically, and as other aspects are extracted, they may be serially added to the first aspect. There are two possibilities within this type. In the *person-first analytic strategy*, a cognizer first extracts the person aspect, then extracts the action, object, and context aspects, and then serializes them into a string like "a person acted to the object in the context." In the *context-first analytic strategy*, the context is first extracted and then other aspects are extracted later and added to this aspect as they are extracted.

Apparently, the person-first analytical strategy is most often used by North American observers. When reading a passage that describes an individual's social action, North Americans often categorize the action spontaneously into a personality trait category (Uleman & Moskowitz, 1994; Winter & Uleman, 1984; Winter, Uleman, & Cunniff, 1985; cf. Bassili & Smith, 1986; Carlston & Skowronski, 1994, 1995; for a review, see Uleman, Newman, & Moskowitz, 1996). From the studies on correspondence biases (Gilbert & Malone, 1995), it is clear that North American cognizers take contextual information into account only after further effortful thought (Gilbert, Pelham, & Krull, 1988). In other words, this implies that dispositional person-relevant information is first encoded, and then contextual information is taken into consideration. Some current theories (Gilbert, 1989) explain this in terms of automaticity of cognitive processes. In particular, they suggest that dispositional inferences consume less cognitive resources than adjusting judgments by taking contextual information into account. However, it is interesting to note that North Americans appear to follow the context-first analytical strategy when they are instructed to make inferences about the situation in which an action took place (e.g., Krull & Erickson, 1995). All in all, North American participants appear to use an analytical strategy: Information pertaining to whatever seems focal (most often, the individual is the focal point of attention) is analytically extracted first, and then other aspects (e.g., contextual information) are extracted.

In contrast, existing data are ambiguous about what East Asians do. One hypothesis takes the view that there is no fundamental difference between North Americans and East Asians in attribution process (e.g., Krull et al., 1999). Both cultural groups adopt basically the same analytical strategy. East Asians may adopt a person-first strategy, but may be more likely to make an adjustment based on contextual information or may be more likely than North Americans to adopt a context-first version of this strategy. A second hypothesis takes the view that both North Americans and East Asians process information in a similarly analytical way, but due to a difference in underlying cultural theory, East Asians may be more likely to extract relevant information pertaining to group, rather than person, analytically (Chiu et al., in press; Menon et al., 1999). This view retains the analytical separation between the person and the situation (Menon et al., 1999), which attribution theories developed in North America have assumed. However, the locus of agency is said to differ. A third hypothesis takes the view that East Asians process information about the person acting toward an object in context in a subtly, but fundamentally, different way. It may be a more holistic style of information processing in which both person and context information are dialectically understood as mutually constituting (e.g., Peng & Nisbett, 1999). In Choi, Nisbett, and Norenzayan's (1999) words, "East Asians may have a more holistic notion of the person in which the boundary between the person and the situation is rather porous and ill defined" (p. 57). The veracity of these hypotheses, as well as others, will be examined in the future. What is probably more important is to examine how social actions are explained in communication. In 1990, D. J. Hilton showed convincingly that explanation is fundamentally communicative; that is, we explain an event to an audience.

Self-Regard

Clearly, there is a strong tendency to maintain a positive individual self-regard in North Amer-

ica; when self-regard is threatened, people try to regain their self-regard by adopting various strategies. However, it is still unclear what East Asians do, and there are several possibilities. One is a cultural task hypothesis. Self-regard becomes more positive when one does well on culturally prescribed tasks. It is just that different types of tasks may be regarded as more important in different cultures. However, this hypothesis predicts that self-esteem should correlate positively with independent self-construal in individualist cultures, but positively with interdependent self-construal in collectivist cultures. Heine et al. (1999) suggested that this position is untenable as Rosenberg's self-esteem scale correlates positively with independent self-construal regardless of culture and negatively or not at all with interdependent self-construal.

This hypothesis is not completely ruled out yet as it is possible to argue that self-esteem may consist of two separable aspects, such as self-liking and self-competence (Tafarodi & Swann, 1995). It may indeed be the case that self-liking is related to interdependent self-construal, while self-competence is related to independent self-construal. Rosenberg's (1965) self-esteem scale may reflect self-competence more than self-liking (cf. Tafarodi & Swann, 1995) and that may be the reason why it relates to independent self-construal. As a cultural task hypothesis would suggest, self-liking may reflect how well one is doing in interpersonal relationships, whereas self-competence may reflect how well one is doing in relation to nonsocial tasks. However, at this point, self-esteem is conceptually split into two. Should we use one label to refer to both? Is there any metatheoretical principle by which to decide when to call concepts by one label?

Still another hypothesis is that East Asians may have a need for positive collective or relational self-regard, although they may not have a strong need for positive individual self-regard. Heine et al. (1999) argue that this account would not do as evidence that Japanese engage in in-group esteem maintenance is weak (e.g., Heine & Lehman, 1995). Would East Asians then have a need for positive relational self-regard? Endo et al.'s (2000) research suggests that Japanese have this need as strongly as do North Americans. How is this then related to Tafarodi and Swann's (1995) conception of self-esteem? These questions, and others, need to be examined further.

Other Issues

One emerging issue is culture and folk psychology (e.g., D'Andrade, 1987; Y. Kashima, McIntyre, & Clifford, 1998; Lillard, 1998; Malle & Knobe, 1997). Folk psychology is people's naive ideas about how the mind works. Research questions in this area include whether folk psychological concepts such as belief, desire, and intention are universal, whether people's ideas about their interrelationships are universal, whether the common Western belief that mind and body are separable entities (naive dualism) is shared by other cultures, and whether folk psychological beliefs have any effects on psychopathology and other psychological problems. This is clearly an uncharted sea that awaits further exploration.

It is also important to explore whether theories applicable in one type of collectivist culture are applicable in other collectivist cultures. Although there are some intriguing similarities, it is unclear whether all collectivist cultures exhibit the same pattern of social cognitive processes. For instance, there may be significant differences between Latin American and East Asian collectivism. In fact, Y. Kashima (1998) argued that collectivism may be best regarded as nonindividualisms, that is, different types of cultural patterns that are not individualist. This pluralist conception of culture may need to be taken seriously.

Theoretical Question: Toward a Social Cognition of Cultural Dynamics

The early social cognition research was characterized by the individualist conception of meaning, according to which meaning is constructed solely within an individual person's mind. The current research on culture and social cognition also draws on the same tradition. In contrast, the central tenet of cultural dynamics is that meanings are constructed in ongoing social activities among multiple individuals, as well as in an individual's mind. One of the major tasks for the future is the development of a theoretical framework that incorporates both cognitive and communicative processes.

Although there are a number of models of interpersonal communication (Krauss & Fussell, 1996), the most suitable is what Krauss and Fussell called *dialogic models* of communication, following Bakhtin (1981), a Russian philosopher and literary critic. In this perspective, communication processes are modeled

after face-to-face conversation (also see Mead, 1934). As Krauss and Fussell (1996) noted, one defining insight of this class of models is that communication is understood to be driven by the goal of achieving intersubjectivity among interactants, that is, a sharing of understandings about the world and themselves (also see Rommetveit, 1974). Clark and colleagues (e.g., Clark & Brennan, 1991; Clark & Shaefer, 1989; Clark & Wilkes-Gibbs, 1986) proposed a model of communication that should be developed further.

In 1999, Y. Kashima and Kashima (also see D'Andrade, 1995; Strauss & Quinn, 1997) suggested that connectionist models of cognition may capture the cognitive side of cultural dynamics better than more traditional models of cognition. Connectionist models are based on the brain metaphor rather than the computer metaphor of the mind (see Rumelhart, McClelland, & the PDP Research Group, 1986; for recent reviews of this area, see Read, Vanman, & Miller, 1996; E. R. Smith, 1996). They suggested that adequate cognitive theories must be able to explain context-sensitive learning because culture is learned from everyday activities in particular contexts; to reproduce similar activities in similar contexts, but not to repeat mechanically the same responses all the time; and to produce novel activities in unfamiliar circumstances (or "regulated improvisation" as Bourdieu, 1977, put it) as cultural dynamics always include creativity as a source of cultural change generated within a culture.

More generally, within the area of social cognition, Y. Kashima and colleagues (Y. Kashima & Kerekesh, 1994; Y. Kashima et al., 2000; Y. Kashima, Woolcock, & King, 1998) modeled the dynamic processes involved in the formation and change of impressions about individuals and groups within a connectionist framework. They suggested that people's views about their social environment evolve in response to the information that they receive. Related models have been used to model stereotyping (Kunda & Thagard, 1996; E. R. Smith & DeCoster, 1998), causal attribution (Read & Marcus-Newhall, 1993; Van Overwalle, 1998) and judgmental biases (Fiedler, 1996). The interface between communicative and cognitive processes needs to be examined more.

Concluding Comments

Further insights need to be gained into the dynamic process by which social, cultural, and psychological processes interactively produce the flow of culture over time. Kashima (2000c) noted that Bartlett's (1923, 1932, 1958) social psychology of cultural dynamics may be worth recovering (as well as works of theorists such as Lévy-Bruhl, 1923, and Mead, 1934). For instance, Kashima (2000b) used Bartlett's (1932) method of serial reproduction, in which a story is passed from one person to another in a chain to examine the process by which cultural stereotypes are maintained. It is important to note that many of the ideas examined have to do with the maintenance of culture, that is, how a cultural pattern persists over time. The other side of cultural dynamics (i.e., culture change) is by far the most important question that requires greater attention in future research (see, for instance, Dawkins, 1976; Sperber, 1996).

References

Abelson, R. P., Dasgupta, N., Park, J., & Banaji, M. R. (1998). Perceptions of the collective other. *Personality and Social Psychology Review, 2*, 243–250.

Al-Zahrani, S. S. A., & Kaplowitz, S. A. (1993). Attributional biases in individualistic and collectivistic cultures: A comparison of Americans with Saudis. *Social Psychology Quarterly, 56*, 223–233.

Amir, Y., & Sharon, I. (1987). Are social psychology's laws cross-culturally valid? *Journal of Cross-Cultural Psychology, 18*, 383–470.

Bakhtin, M. M. (1981). *The dialogic imagination*. Austin: University of Texas Press.

Bargh, J. A. (1996). Automaticity in social psychology. In E. T. Higgins and A. W. Kruglanski (Eds.), *Social psychology: Handbook of basic principles* (pp. 169–183). New York: Guilford.

Bargh, J. A., Bond, R. N., Lombardi, W. J., & Tota, M. E. (1986). The additive nature of chronic and temporary sources of construct accessibility. *Journal of Personality and Social Psychology, 50*, 869–878.

Bartlett, F. C. (1923). *Psychology and primitive culture*. Cambridge University Press.

Bartlett, F. C. (1932). *Remembering: A study in experimental and social psychology*. Cambridge: Cambridge University Press.

Bartlett, F. C. (1958). *Thinking: An experimental and social study*. New York: Basic Books.

Bassili, J. N., & Smith, M. C. (1986). On the spontaneity of trait attributions: Converging evidence for the role of cognitive strategy. *Journal of Personality and Social Psychology, 50*, 239–246.

Bem, S. L. (1982). Gender schema theory and self-schema theory compared: A comment on Markus, Crane, Bernstein, and Siladi's "Self-sche-

mas and gender." *Journal of Personality and Social Psychology, 43*, 1192–1194.

Bochner, S. (1984). Cross-cultural differences in the self-concept: A test of Hofstede's individualism/collectivism distinction. *Journal of Cross-Cultural Psychology, 25*, 273–283.

Boesch, E. E. (1991). *Symbolic action theory and cultural psychology*. New York: Springer.

Bond, M. H. (Ed.). (1988). *Cross-cultural challenge to social psychology*. Newbury Park, CA: Sage.

Bond, M. H., & Cheung, T.-S. (1983). College students' spontaneous self-concept: The effect of culture among respondents in Hong Kong, Japan, and the United States. *Journal of Cross-Cultural Psychology, 14*, 153–171.

Bourdieu, P. (1977). *Outline of a theory of practice* (R. Nice, Trans.). Cambridge: Cambridge University Press.

Brewer, M. B., & Gardner, W. (1996). Who is this "we"? Levels of collective identity and self representations. *Journal of Personality and Social Psychology, 71*, 83–93.

Brown, R., Hinkle, S., Ely, P. G., Fox-Cardamone, L., Maras, P., & Taylor, L. A. (1992). Recognizing group diversity: Individualist-collectivist and autonomous-relational social orientations and their implications for intergroup processes. *British Journal of Social Psychology, 31*, 327–342.

Bruner, J. (1990). *Acts of meaning*. Cambridge: Harvard University Press.

Campbell, A. (1981). *The sense of well-being in America: Recent patterns and trends*. New York: McGraw-Hill.

Campbell, J. D., Trapnell, P. D., Heine, S. J., Katz, I. M., Lavallee, L. F., & Lehman, D. R. (1996). Self-concept clarity: Measurement, personality correlates, and cultural boundaries. *Journal of Personality and Social Psychology, 70*, 141–156.

Cantor, N., & Michel, W. (1979). Prototypes in person perception. *Advances in Experimental Social Psychology, 12*, 3–52.

Carlston, D. E., & Skowronski, J. J. (1994). Savings in the relearning of trait information as evidence for spontaneous inference generation. *Journal of Personality and Social Psychology, 66*, 840–856.

Carlston, D. E., Skowronski, J. J., & Sparks, C. (1995). Savings in relearning: II. On the formation of behavior-based trait associations and inferences. *Journal of Personality and Social Psychology, 69*, 420–436.

Chandler, T. A., Shama, D. D., Wolf, F. M., & Planchard, S. K. (1981). Multiattributional causality: A five cross-national samples study. *Journal of Cross-Cultural Psychology, 12*, 207–221.

Chiu, C. Y., Hong, Y. Y., & Dweck, C. (1997). Lay dispositionism and implicit theories of personality. *Journal of Personality and Social Psychology, 73*, 19–30.

Chiu, C. Y., Krauss, R. M., & Lee, S. L. (1999). Communication and social cognition: A post-Whorfian approach. In *Progress in Asian social psychology* (Vol. 2, pp. 127–143). Seoul, Korea: Kyoyook Kwahak Sa.

Chiu, C. Y., Morris, M. W., Hong, Y. Y., & Menon, T. (2000). Motivated cultural cognition: The impact of implicit cultural theories on dispositional attribution varies as a function of need for closure. *Journal of Personality and Social Psychology, 78*, 247–259.

Choi, I., & Nisbett, R. E. (1998). Situational salience and cultural differences in the correspondence bias and actor-observer bias. *Personality and Social Psychology Bulletin, 24*, 949–960.

Choi, I., Nisbett, R. E., & Norenzayan, A. (1999). Causal attribution across cultures: Variation and universality. *Psychological Bulletin, 125*, 47–63.

Clark, H. H. (1985). Language use and language users. In G. Lindzey & E. Arsonson (Eds.), *Handbook of social psychology* (2nd. ed., Vol. 1, pp. 179–231). New York: Random House.

Clark, H. H., & Brennan, S. E. (1991). Grounding in communication. In L. B. Resnick, J. M. Levine, & S. D. Teasley (Eds.), *Perspectives on socially shared cognition* (pp. 127–149). Washington, DC: American Psychological Association.

Clark, H. H., & Shaefer, E. F. (1989). Contributing to discourse. *Cognitive Science, 13*, 259–294.

Clark, H. H., & Wilkes-Gibbs, D. (1986). Referring as a collaborative process. *Cognition, 22*, 1–39.

Cole, M. (1996). *Cultural psychology: A once and future discipline.* Cambridge: Harvard University Press.

Cousins, S. D. (1989). Culture and self-perception in Japan and the United States. *Journal of Personality and Social Psychology, 56*, 124–131.

D'Andrade, R. (1987). A folk model of the mind. In D. Holland & N. Quinn (Eds.), *Cultural models in language and thought* (pp. 112–148). Cambridge: Cambridge University Press.

D'Andrade, R. (1995). *The development of cognitive anthropology.* Cambridge: Cambridge University Press.

Dawkins, R. (1976). *The selfish gene.* Oxford: Oxford University Press.

Deaux, K. (1993). Reconstructing social identity. *Personality and Social Psychology Bulletin, 19*, 4–12.

Deaux, K., Reid, A., Mizrahi, K., & Ethier, K. A. (1995). Parameters of social identity. *Journal of Personality and Social Psychology, 68*, 280–291.

DeBoeck, P., & Rosenberg, S. (1988). Hierarchical classes: Model and data analysis. *Psychometrika, 53*, 361–368.

Devine, P. G. (1989). Stereotypes and prejudice: Their automatic and controlled components. *Journal of Personality and Social Psychology, 56*, 5–18.

Dhawan, N., Roseman, I. J., Naidu, R. K., Thapa, K., & Rettek, S. I. (1995). Self-concepts across two cultures: India and the United States. *Journal of Cross-Cultural Psychology, 26*, 606–621.

Diener, E. (1984). Subjective well-being. *Psychological Bulletin, 95*, 542–575.

Diener, E., & Diener, M. (1995). Cross-cultural correlates of life satisfaction and self-esteem. *Journal of Personality and Social Psychology, 68*, 653–663.

Diener, E., Diener, M., & Diener, C. (1995). Factors predicting the subjective well-being of nations. *Journal of Personality and Social Psychology, 69*, 851–864.

Diener, E., Suh, E. M., Lucas, R. E., & Smith, H. L. (1999). Subjective well-being: Three decades of progress. *Psychological Bulletin, 125*, 276–302.

Doi, T. (1986). *The anatomy of self.* Tokyo: Kodansha International.

Durkheim, E. (1964). *The division of labor in society* (G. Simpson Trans.). New York: The Free Press. (Original work published 1893)

Dweck, C. (1999). *Self-theories: Their role in motivation, personality, and development.* Philadelphia: Psychology Press.

Endo, Y., Heine, S., & Lehman, D. R. (2000). Culture and positive illusions in close relationships: How my relationships are better than yours. *Personality and Social Psychological Bulletin, 26*, 1571–1586.

Fiedler, K. (1996). Explaining and simulating judgment biases as an aggregation phenomenon in probabilistic, multiple-cue environments. *Psychological Review, 103*, 193–214.

Fijneman, Y. A., Willemsen, M. E., & Poortinga, Y. H. (1996). Individualism-collectivism: An empirical study of a conceptual issue. *Journal of Cross-Cultural Psychology, 27*, 381–402.

Fiske, A. P. (1990). Relativity within Moose ("Mossi") culture: Four incommensurable models for social relationships. *Ethos, 18*, 180–204.

Fiske, A. P. (1991). *Structures of social life: The four elementary forms of human relations.* New York: Free Press.

Fiske, A. P. (1992). The four elementary forms of sociality: Framework for a unified theory of social relations. *Psychological Review, 99*, 689–723.

Fiske, A. P. (1993). Social errors in four cultures: Evidence about universal forms of social relations. *Journal of Cross-Cultural Psychology, 24*, 463–494.

Fiske, A. P., & Haslam, N. (1997). The structure of social substitutions: A test of relational models theory. *European Journal of Social Psychology, 27*, 725–729.

Fiske, A. P., Haslam, N., & Fiske, S. T. (1991). Confusing one person with another: What errors reveal about the elementary forms of social relations. *Journal of Personality and Social Psychology, 60*, 656–674.

Fiske, S. T., & Taylor, S. E. (1991). *Social cognition* (2nd. ed.). New York: McGraw-Hill.

Fletcher, G. J. O., & Ward, C. (1988). Attribution theory and processes: A cross-cultural perspective. In M. H. Bond (Ed.), *Cross-cultural challenge to social psychology* (pp. 230–244). Newbury Park, CA: Sage.

Frege, G. (1984). On sense and meaning (M. Black, Trans.). In B. McGuinness (Ed.), *Gottlob Frege: Collected papers on mathematics, logic, and philosophy* (pp. 157–177). Oxford, England: Blackwell. (Original work published 1892)

Gardner, W. L., Gabriel, S., & Lee, A. Y. (1999). "I" value freedom, but "we" value relationships: Self-construal priming mirrors cultural differences in judgment. *Psychological Science, 10*, 321–326.

Geertz, C. (1973). *The interpretation of cultures.* New York: Basic Books.

Geertz, C. (1984). "From the native's point of view": On the nature of anthropological understanding. In R. A. Shweder & R. A. LeVine (Eds.), *Culture theory* (pp. 123–136). Cambridge: Cambridge University Press.

Gergen, K. J. (1973). Social psychology as history. *Journal of Personality and Social Psychology, 26*, 309–320.

Giddens, A. (1979). *Central problems in social theory.* London: Macmillan.

Gilbert, D. T. (1989). Thinking lightly about others: Automatic components of the social inference process. In J. S. Uleman & J. A. Bargh (Eds.), *Unintended thought* (pp. 189–211). New York: Guilford.

Gilbert, D. T., & Malone, P. S. (1995). The correspondence bias. *Psychological Bulletin, 117*, 21–38.

Gilbert, D. T., Pelham, B. W., & Krull, D. S. (1988). On cognitive busyness: When person perceivers meet persons perceived. *Journal of Personality and Social Psychology, 54*, 733–740.

Greenfield, P. M. (1997). Culture as process: Empirical methods for cultural psychology. In J. W. Berry, Y. H. Poortinga, & J. Pandey (Eds.), *Handbook of cross-cultural psychology* (Vol. 1, pp. 301–346). Boston: Allyn & Bacon.

Greenwald, A. G. (1980). The totalitarian ego: Fabrication and revision of personal history. *American Psychologist, 35*, 603–618.

Hamilton, D. L., & Gifford, R. K. (1976). Illusory correlation in interpersonal perception: A cognitive basis of stereotypic judgments. *Journal of Experimental Social Psychology, 12*, 392–707.

Hamilton, D. L., & Sherman, S. J. (1996). Perceiving persons and groups. *Psychological Review, 103*, 336–355.

Haslam, N. (1994a). Categories of social relationship. *Cognition, 53*, 59–90.

Haslam, N. (1994b). Mental representation of social relationships: Dimensions, laws, or categories? *Journal of Personality and Social Psychology, 67*, 575–584.

Haslam, N., & Fiske, A. P. (1992). Implicit relationship prototypes: Investigating five theories of the cognitive organization of social relationships. *Journal of Experimental Social Psychology, 28*, 441–474.

Hastie, R., Ostrom, T. M., Ebbesen, E. B., Wyer, R. S., Hamilton, D. L., & Carlston, D. E. (Eds.). (1980). *Person memory: The cognitive basis of social perception.* Hillsdale, NJ: Erlbaum.

Heider, F. (1958). *The psychology of interpersonal relations.* New York: Wiley.

Heine, S. J., & Lehman, D. R. (1995). Cultural variation in unrealistic optimism: Does the West feel more invulnerable than the East? *Journal of Personality and Social Psychology, 68*, 595–607.

Heine, S. J., & Lehman, D. R. (1997). The cultural construction of self-enhancement: An examination of group-serving biases. *Journal of Personality and Social Psychology, 72*, 1268–1283.

Heine, S. J., & Lehman, D. R. (1999). Culture, self-discrepancies, and self-satisfaction. *Personality and Social Psychology Bulletin, 25*, 915–925.

Heine, S. J., Lehman, D. R., Markus, H. R., & Kitayama, S. (1999). Is there a universal need for positive self-regard? *Psychological Review, 106*, 766–794.

Heine, S. J., Takata, T., & Lehman, D. R. (2000). Beyond self-presentation: Evidence for self-criticism among Japanese. *Personality and Social Psychology Bulletin, 26*, 71–78.

Hetts, J. J., Sakuma, M., & Pelham, B. W. (1999). Two roads to positive regard: Implicit and explicit self-evaluation and culture. *Journal of Experimental Social Psychology, 35*, 512–559.

Hewstone, M., & Ward, C. (1985). Ethnocentrism and causal attribution in Southeast Asia. *Journal of Personality and Social Psychology, 48*, 614–623.

Higgins, E. T. (1987). Self-discrepancy: A theory relating self and affect. *Psychological Review, 94*, 319–340.

Higgins, E. T. (1996). Knowledge activation: Accessibility, applicability and salience. In E. T. Higgins and A. W. Kruglanski (Eds.), *Social psychology: Handbook of basic principles* (pp. 133–168). New York: Guilford.

Higgins, E. T., Klein, R., & Strauman, T. (1985). Self-concept discrepancy theory: A psychological model for distinguishing among different aspects of depression and anxiety. *Social Cognition, 1*, 51–76.

Hilton, D. J. (1990). A conversational processes and causal explanation. *Psychological Bulletin, 107*, 65–81.

Hilton, D. J., Smith, R. H., & Kin, S. H. (1995). Processes of causal explanation and dispositional attribution. *Journal of Personality and Social Psychology, 68*, 377–387.

Hilton, J. L., & von Hippel, W. (1996). Stereotypes. *Annual Review of Psychology, 47*, 237–271.

Hinkle, S., & Brown, R. (1990). Intergroup comparisons and social identity: Some links and lacunae. In D. Abrams & M. A. Hogg (Eds.), *Social identity theory: Constructive and critical advances* (pp. 48–70). New York: Springer.

Hoffman, C., Lau, I., & Johnson, D. R. (1986). The linguistic relativity of person cognition: An English-Chinese comparison. *Journal of Personality and Social Psychology, 51*, 1097–1105.

Hofstede, G. (1980). *Culture's consequences.* Beverly Hills, CA: Sage.

Hofstede, G. (1991). *Cultures and organizations.* London: McGraw-Hill.

Hong, Y. Y., Chiu, C. Y., & Kung, T. M. (1997). Bringing culture out in front: Effects of cultural meaning system activation on social cognition. In K. Leung, U. Kim, S. Yamaguchi, & Y. Kashima (Eds.), *Progress in Asian social psychology* (Vol. 1, pp. 139–151). Singapore: Wiley.

Hui, C. H. (1988). Measurement of individualism-collectivism. *Journal of Research in Personality, 22*, 17–36.

Hunt, E., & Agnoli, F. (1991). The Whorfian hypothesis: A cognitive psychology perspective. *Psychological Review, 98*, 377–389.

Jackendoff, R. (1992). Is there a faculty of social cognition? In R. Jackendoff (Ed.), *Languages of the mind: Essays on mental representation* (pp. 69–81). Cambridge: MIT Press.

Jahoda, G. (1980). Theoretical and systematic approaches in cross-cultural psychology. In H. C. Triandis & W. W. Lambert (Eds.), *Handbook of cross-cultural psychology* (Vol. 1, pp. 69–141). Boston: Allyn & Bacon.

Jones, E. E. (1979). The rocky road from acts to dispositions. *American Psychologist, 34*, 107–117.

Jones, E. E., & Davis, K. E. (1965). From acts to dispositions: The attribution process in person perception. *Advances in Experimental Social Psychology, 2*, 220–266.

Jones, E. E., & Harris, V. A. (1967). The attribution of attitudes. *Journal of Experimental Social Psychology, 3*, 1–24.

Kashima, E. S., & Kashima, Y. (1997). Practices of the self in conversations: Pronoun drop, sentence co-production and contextualization of the self. In K. Leung, U. Kim, S. Yamaguchi, & Y. Kashima (Eds.), *Progress in Asian social psychology* (Vol. 1, pp. 165–179). Singapore: Wiley.

Kashima, E. S., & Kashima, Y. (1998). Culture and language: The case of cultural dimensions and personal pronoun use. *Journal of Cross-Cultural Psychology, 29*, 461–486.

Kashima, Y. (1987). Conceptions of person: Implications in individualism/collectivism research. In C. Kagitcibasi (Ed.), *Growth and progress in cross-cultural psychology* (pp. 104–112). Lisse, The Netherlands: Swets.

Kashima, Y. (1994). Cultural metaphors of the mind and the organization. In A.-M. Bouvy, F. van de Vijver, P. Boski, & P. Schmitz (Eds.), *Journeys into cross-cultural psychology* (pp. 351–363). Lisse, The Netherlands: Swets & Zeitlinger.

Kashima, Y. (1998a). Culture, narrative, and human motivation. In D. Munro, J. F. Schumaker, & S. C. Carr (Eds.), *Motivation and culture* (pp. 16–30). New York: Routledge.

Kashima, Y. (1998b). *Culture and social cognition: Mainstreaming of cross-cultural psychology or culturalizing the mainstream?* Paper presented at the International Congress of the International Association for Cross-Cultural Psychology, Bellingham, WA.

Kashima, Y. (2000a). Conceptions of culture and person for psychology. *Journal of Cross-Cultural Psychology, 31*, 14–32.

Kashima, Y. (2000b). Maintaining cultural stereotypes in the serial reproduction of narratives. *Personality and Social Psychology Bulletin, 26*, 594–604.

Kashima, Y. (2000c). Recovering Bartlett's social psychology of cultural dynamics. *European Journal of Social Psychology, 30*, 383–403.

Kashima, Y., & Callan, V. (1994). The Japanese work group. In Triandis, H. C., Dunnette, M. D., & Hough, L. M. (Eds.), *Handbook of industrial/organizational psychology* (Vol. 4, pp. 610–646). Palo Alto, CA: Consulting Psychologists Press.

Kashima, Y., & Kashima, E. (1999). Culture, connectionism, and the self. In J. Adamopoulos & Y. Kashima (Eds.), *Social psychology and cultural context* (pp. 77–92), Thousand Oaks, CA: Sage.

Kashima, Y., & Kerekesh, A. R. Z. (1994). A distributed memory model of averaging phenomena in person impression formation. *Journal of Experimental Social Psychology, 30*, 407–455.

Kashima, Y., McIntyre, A., & Clifford, P. (1998). The category of the mind: Folk psychology of belief, desire, and intention. *Asian Journal of Social Psychology, 1*, 289–313.

Kashima, Y., Siegal, M., Tanaka, K., & Kashima, E. S. (1992). Do people believe behaviours are consistent with attitudes? Towards a cultural psychology of attribution processes. *British Journal of Social Psychology, 31*, 111–124.

Kashima, Y., & Triandis, H. C. (1986). The self-serving bias in attribution as coping strategy: A cross-cultural study. *Journal of Cross-Cultural Psychology, 17*, 83–98.

Kashima, Y., Woolcock, J., & Kashima, E. (2000). Group impressions as dynamic configurations: The tensor product model of group impression formation and change. *Psychological Review, 107*, 914–942.

Kashima, Y., Woolcock, J., & King, D. (1998). The dynamics of group impression formation: The tensor product model of exemplar-based social category learning. In S. J. Read & L. C. Miller (Eds.), *Connectionist models of social reasoning and social behavior* (pp. 71–109). Mahwah, NJ: Erlbaum.

Kashima, Y., Yamaguchi, S., Kim, U., Choi, S. C., Gelfand, M. J., & Yuki, M. (1995). Culture, gender, and self: A perspective from individualism-collectivism research. *Journal of Personality and Social Psychology, 69*, 925–937.

Kelley, H. H. (1967). Attribution theory in social psychology. In D. Levine (Ed.), *Nebraska Symposium on Motivation: Vol. 15* (pp. 192–240). Lincoln: University of Nebraska Press.

Kitayama, S., & Karasawa, M. (1997). Implicit self-esteem in Japan: Name letters and birthday numbers. *Personality and Social Psychology Bulletin, 23*, 736–742.

Kitayama, S., Markus, H. R., Matsumoto, H., & Norasakkunkit, V. (1997). Individual and collective processes in the construction of the self: Self-enhancement in the United States and self-criticism in Japan. *Journal of Personality and Social Psychology, 72*, 1245–1267.

Krauss, R. M., & Fussell, S. R. (1996). Social psychological models of interpersonal communication. In E. T. Higgins & A. W. Kruglanski (Eds.), *Social psychology: Handbook of basic principles* (pp. 655–701). New York: Guilford.

Kroonenberg, P. M., & Kashima, Y. (1997). Rules in context: A three-mode principal component analysis of Mann et al.'s data on cross-cultural differences in respect for others. *Journal of Cross-Cultural Psychology, 28*, 463–480.

Kruglanski, A. E., & Webster, D. M. (1996). Motivated closing of the mind: "Seizing" and "freezing." *Psychological Review, 103*, 263–283.

Krull, D. S. (1993). Does the grist change the mill? The effect of the perceiver's inferential goal on the process of social inference. *Personality and Social Psychology Bulletin, 19*, 340–348.

Krull, D. S., & Erickson, D. J. (1995). Judging situations: On the effortful process of taking dispositional information into account. *Social Cognition, 13*, 417–438.

Krull, D. S., Loy, M. H.-M., Lin, J., Wang, C.-F., Chen, S., & Zhao, X. (1999). The fundamental attribution error: Correspondence bias in individualist and collectivist cultures. *Personality and Social Psychology Bulletin, 25*, 1208–1219.

Kuhn, M. H., & McPartland, R. (1954). An empirical investigation of self-attitudes. *American Sociological Review, 19*, 68–76.

Kunda, Z., & Thagard, P. (1996). Forming impressions from stereotypes, traits, and behaviors: A parallel-constraint-satisfaction theory. *Psychological Review, 103*, 284–308.

Kwan, V. S. Y., Bond, M. H., & Singelis, T. M. (1997). Pancultural explanations for life satisfaction: Adding relationship harmony to self-esteem. *Journal of Personality and Social Psychology, 73*, 1038–1051.

Lakoff, G., & Johnson, M. (1980). *Metaphors we live by*. Chicago: University of Chicago Press.

Lalljee, M., & Angelova, R. (1995). Person description in India, Britain, and Bulgaria. *Journal of Cross-Cultural Psychology, 26*, 645–657.

Lave, J., & Wenger, E. (1991). *Situated learning: Legitimate peripheral participation*. Cambridge: Cambridge University Press.

Lee, F., Hallahan, M., & Herzog, T. (1996). Explaining real life events: How culture and domain shape attributions. *Personality and Social Psychology Bulletin, 22*, 732–741.

Lee, L., & Ward, C. (1998). Ethnicity, idiocentrism-allocentrism, and intergroup attitudes. *Journal of Applied Social Psychology, 28*, 109–123.

Lee, Y.-T., & Seligman, M. E. P. (1997). Are Americans more optimistic than the Chinese? *Personality and Social Psychology Bulletin, 23*, 32–40.

Leuers, T., & Sonoda, N. (1996). Bunmyaku-teki jiko-gainen ni kansuru hikaku bunka-teki kenkyuu (1): Basho, tasha no bunmyaku to jiko [A cross-cultural study of contextualized self-concept (1): Location and other person context and self]. In *Proceedings of the 44th Conference of the Japanese Group Dynamics Association* (pp. 106–107). Sougou kagaku bu, University of Hiroshima.

Leuers, T., & Sonoda, N. (1999). Independent self-bias. In T. Sugiman, M. Karasawa, J. H. Liu, and C. Ward (Eds.), *Progress in Asian social psychology: Vol. 2. Theoretical and empirical contributions* (pp. 87–104). Seoul: Kyoyook-kwahak-sa.

Lévy-Bruhl, L. (1923). *How natives think* (L. A. Clare, Trans.). London: Allen & Unwin.

Lillard, A. (1998). Ethnopsychologies: Cultural variations in theories of mind. *Psychological Bulletin, 123,* 3–32.

Malle, B., & Knobe, J. (1997). The folk concept of intentionality. *Journal of Experimental Social Psychology, 33,* 101–121.

Markus, H. (1977). Self-schemata and processing information about the self. *Journal of Personality and Social Psychology, 35,* 63–78.

Markus, H. R., & Kitayama, S. (1991). Culture and the self: Implications for cognition, emotion, and motivation. *Psychological Review, 98,* 224–253.

Markus, H., Smith, J., & Moreland, R. L. (1985). Role of the self-concept in the social perception of others. *Journal of Personality and Social Psychology, 49,* 1494–1512.

Markus, H., & Zajonc, R. B. (1985). The cognitive perspective in social psychology. In G. Lindzey & E. Aronson (Eds.), *The handbook of social psychology* (3rd. ed., Vol. 1, pp. 137–230). New York: Random House.

Matsumoto, D. (1999). Culture and self: An empirical assessment of Markus and Kitayama's theory of independent and interdependent self-construals. *Asian Journal of Social Psychology, 2,* 289–310.

Matsumoto, D., Kudoh, T., & Takeuchi, S. (1996). Changing patterns of individualism and collectivism in the United States and Japan. *Culture and Psychology, 2,* 77–107.

Matsumoto, D., Takeuchi, S., Andayani, S., Kouznetsova, N., & Krupp, D. (1998). The contribution of individualism versus collectivism to cross-national differences in display rules. *Asian Journal of Social Psychology, 1,* 147–165.

Matsumoto, D., Weissman, M. D., Preston, K., Brown, B. R., Kupperbusch, C. (1997). Context-specific measurement of individualism-collectivism on the individual level: The Individualism-Collectivism Interpersonal Assessment Inventory. *Journal of Cross-Cultural Psychology, 28,* 743–767.

Mead, G. H. (1934). *Mind, self, and society.* Chicago: University of Chicago Press.

Menon, T., Morris, M. W., Chiu, C. Y., & Hong, Y. Y. (1999). Culture and the construal of agency: Attribution to individual versus group dispositions. *Journal of Personality and Social Psychology, 76,* 701–717.

Miller, F. D., Smith, E. R., & Uleman, J. (1981). Measurement and interpretation of situational and dispositional attributions. *Journal of Experimental Social Psychology, 17,* 80–95.

Miller, J. G. (1984). Culture and the development of everyday social explanation. *Journal of Personality and Social Psychology, 46,* 961–978.

Miller, J. G. (1987). Cultural influences on the development of conceptual differentiation in person description. *British Journal of Developmental Psychology, 5,* 309–319.

Miller, J. G. (1988). Bridging the content-structure dichotomy: Culture and the self. In M. H. Bond (Ed.), *Cross-cultural challenge to social psychology* (pp. 266–281). Newbury Park, CA: Sage.

Mischel, W. (1968). *Personality and assessment.* New York: Wiley.

Morris, M. W., & Peng, K. (1994). Culture and cause: American and Chinese attributions for social and physical events. *Journal of Personality and Social Psychology, 67,* 949–971.

Nisbett, R. E., Caputo, C., Legant, P., & Maracek, J. (1973). Behavior as seen by the actor and as seen by the observer. *Journal of Personality and Social Psychology, 27,* 154–164.

Oakes, P. J., Haslam, A., & Turner, J. C. (1994). *Stereotyping and social reality.* Oxford, England: Blackwell.

Ortner, S. B. (1984). Theory in anthropology since the sixties. *Comparative Studies in Society and History, 26,* 126–166.

Ostrom, T. M., & Sedikides, C. (1992). Out-group homogeneity effects in natural and minimal groups. *Psychological Bulletin, 112,* 536–552.

Oyserman, D. (1993). The lens of personhood: Viewing the self and others in a multicultural society. *Journal of Personality and Social Psychology, 65,* 993–109.

Parkes, L. P., Schneider, S. K., & Bochner, S. (1999). Individualism-collectivism and self-concept: Social or contextual? *Asian Journal of Social Psychology, 2,* 367–383.

Parsons, T. (1951). *The social system.* London, UK: Routledge & Kegan Paul.

Pedersen, A., & Walker, I. (1997). Prejudice against Australian Aborigines: old-fashioned and modern forms. *European Journal of Social Psychology, 27,* 561–587.

Peng, K., & Nisbett, R. E. (1999). Culture, dialectics, and reasoning about contradiction. *American Psychologist, 54,* 741–754.

Poortinga, Y. (1992). Towards a conceptualization of culture for psychology. In S. Iwawaki, Y.

Kashima, & K. Leung (Eds.), *Innovation in cross-cultural psychology* (pp. 3–17). Lisse, The Netherlands: Swets.

Read, S. J., & Marcus-Newhall, A. (1993). Explanatory coherence in social explanations: A parallel distributed processing account. *Journal of Personality and Social Psychology, 65*, 429–447.

Read, S. J., Vanman, E. J., & Miller, L. C. (1996). Connectionism, parallel constraint satisfaction processes, and Gestalt principles: (Re)introducing cognitive dynamics to social psychology. *Personality and Social Psychology Review, 1*, 26–53.

Reid, A., & Deaux, K. (1996). Relationship between social and personal identities: Segregation or integration. *Journal of Personality and Social Psychology, 71*, 1084–1091.

Rhee, E., Uleman, J., & Lee, H. K. (1996). Variations in collectivism and individualism by ingroup and culture: Confirmatory factor analysis. *Journal of Personality and Social Psychology, 71*, 1037–1054.

Rhee, E., Uleman, J., Lee, H. K., & Roman, R. J. (1995). Spontaneous self-descriptions and ethnic identities in individualistic and collectivistic cultures. *Journal of Personality and Social Psychology, 69*, 142–152.

Roenker, D. L., Thompson, C. P., & Brown, S. C. (1971). Comparison of measures for the estimation of clustering in free recall. *Psychological Bulletin, 76*, 45–48.

Rogoff, B. (1990). Apprenticeship in thinking. Oxford, UK: Oxford University Press.

Rogoff, B. & Chavajay, P. (1995). What's become of research on the cultural basis of cognitive development. American Psychologist, 50, 859-877.

Rohner, R. (1984). Toward a conception of culture for cross-cultural psychology. *Journal of Cross-Cultural Psychology, 15*, 111–138.

Rommetveit, R. (1974). On message structure: A framework for the study of language and communication. New York: Wiley.

Rosenberg, M. (1965). *Society and the adolescent self-image*. Princeton, NJ: Princeton University Press.

Rosenberg, S., & Gara, M. A. (1985). The multiplicity of personal identity. *Review of Personality and Social Psychology, 6*, 87–113.

Ross, L. (1977). The intuitive psychologist and his shortcomings: Distortions in the attribution process. *Advances in Experimental Social Psychology, 10*, 174–221.

Ross, L., Amabile, T. M., & Steinmetz, J. L. (1977). Social roles, social control, and biases in social-perception processes. *Journal of Personality and Social Psychology, 35*, 485–494.

Rumelhart, D. E., McClelland, J. L., & the PDP Research Group (Eds.). (1986). *Parallel distributed processing: Explorations in the microstructure of cognition* (Vol. 1). Cambridge: MIT Press.

Semin, G. R., & Marsman, J. G. (1994). "Multiple inference-inviting properties" of interpersonal verbs: Event instigation, dispositional inference, and implicit causality. *Journal of Personality and Social Psychology, 67*, 836–849.

Semin, G. R., & Zwier, S. (1997). Social cognition. In J. W. Berry, M. H. Segall, & C. Kagitcibasi (Eds.), *Handbook of cross-cultural psychology* (2nd ed., Vol. 3, pp. 51–75). Boston: Allyn & Bacon.

Shore, B. (1996). *Culture in mind: Cognition, culture, and the problem of meaning*. Oxford: Oxford University Press.

Shweder, R. A., & Bourne, E. J. (1984). Does the concept of the person vary cross-culturally? In R. A. Shweder & R. A. LeVine (Eds.), *Culture theory* (pp. 158–199). Cambridge: Cambridge University Press.

Shweder, R. A., & D'Andrade, R. G. (1979). Accurate reflection or systematic distortion? A reply to Block, Weiss, and Thorne. *Journal of Personality and Social Psychology, 37*, 1075–1084.

Singelis, T. M. (1994). The measurement of independent and interdependent self-construals. *Personality and Social Psychology Bulletin, 20*, 580–591.

Skowronski, J. J., Betz, A. L., Sedikides, C., & Crawford, M. T. (1998). Raw conditional probabilities are a flawed index of associative strength: Evidence from a multi-trait paradigm. *European Journal of Social Psychology, 28*, 437–456.

Skowronski, J., & Welbourne, J. (1997). Conditional probability may be a flawed measure of associative strength. *Social Cognition, 15*, 1–12.

Smith, E. R. (1996). What do connectionism and social psychology offer each other? *Journal of Personality and Social Psychology, 70*, 893–912.

Smith, E. R., & DeCoster, J. (1998). Knowledge acquisition, accessibility, and use in person perception and stereotyping: Simulation with a recurrent connectionist network. *Journal of Personality and Social Psychology, 74*, 21–35.

Smith, H. W., Matsuno, T., & Umino, M. (1994). How similar are impression-formation processes among Japanese and Americans? *Social Psychology Quarterly, 57*, 124–139.

Sonoda, N., & Leuers, T. (1996). Bunmyaku-teki jiko-gainen ni kansuru hikaku bunka-teki kenkyuu (2): Jikanishiki to jiko [A cross-cultural study of contextualized self-concept (2): Temporality and self]. In *Proceedings of the 44th*

Conference of the Japanese Group Dynamics Association (pp. 108–109). Sougou kagaku bu, University of Hiroshima.

Sperber, D. (1996). *Explaining culture*. Oxford, England: Blackwell.

Spiro, M. E. (1993). Is the Western conception of the self "peculiar" within the context of world cultures? *Ethos, 21*, 107–153.

Strauss, C., & Quinn, N. (1997). *A cognitive theory of cultural meaning*. Cambridge: Cambridge University Press.

Suh, E., Diener, E., Oishi, S., & Triandis, H. C. (1998). The shifting basis of life satisfaction judgments across cultures: Emotions versus norms. *Journal of Personality and Social Psychology, 74*, 482–493.

Tafarodi, R. W. (1998). Paradoxical self-esteem and selectivity in the processing of social information. *Journal of Personality and Social Psychology, 74*, 1181–1196.

Tafarodi, R. W., Lang, J. M., & Smith, A. J. (1999). Self-esteem and the cultural trade-off: Evidence for the role of individualism-collectivism. *Journal of Cross-Cultural Psychology, 30*, 620–640.

Tafarodi, R. W., & Swann, W. B., Jr. (1995). Self-liking and self-competence as dimensions of global self-esteem: Initial validation of a measure. *Journal of Personality Assessment, 65*, 322–342.

Tafarodi, R. W., & Swann, W. B., Jr. (1996). Individualism-collectivism and global self-esteem: Evidence for a cultural trade-off. *Journal of Cross-Cultural Psychology, 27*, 651–672.

Takano, Y., & Osaka, E. (1999). An unsupported common view: Comparing Japan and the U.S. on individualism/collectivism. *Asian Journal of Social Psychology, 2*, 311–341.

Taylor, S. E., & Brown, J. D. (1988). Illusion and well-being: A social psychological perspective on mental health. *Psychological Bulletin, 103*, 193–210.

Tönnies, F. (1955). *Community and association* (C. Ploomis, Trans.). London: Routledge & Kegan Paul. (Original work published 1887)

Trafimow, D., Silverman, E. S., Fan, R. M.-T., & Law, J. S. F. (1997). The effects of language and priming on the relative accessibility of the private self and the collective self. *Journal of Cross-Cultural Psychology, 28*, 107–123.

Trafimow, D., Triandis, H. C., & Goto, S. G. (1991). Some tests of the distinction between the private self and the collective self. *Journal of Personality and Social Psychology, 60*, 649–655.

Triandis, H. C. (1972). *The analysis of subjective culture*. New York: Wiley.

Triandis, H. C. (1989). The self and social behavior in differing cultural contexts. *Psychological Review, 96*, 506–520.

Triandis, H. C. (1995). *Individualism and collectivism*. Boulder, CO: Westview.

Triandis, H. C., Bontempo, R., Villareal, M. J., Asai, M., & Lucca, N. (1988). Individualism and collectivism: Cross-cultural perspectives on self-ingroup relationships. *Journal of Personality and Social Psychology, 54*, 323–338.

Triandis, H. C., & Brislin, R. W. (1980). *Handbook of cross-cultural psychology* (Vol. 5). Boston: Allyn & Bacon.

Triandis, H. C., Chan, D. K.-S., Bhawuk, D. P. S., Iwao, S., & Sinha, J. B. P. (1995). Multimethod probes of allocentrism and idiocentrism. *International Journal of Psychology, 30*, 461–480.

Triandis, H. C., Kashima, Y., Shimada, E., & Villareal, M. (1986). Acculturation indices as a means of confirming cultural differences. *International Journal of Psychology, 21*, 43–70.

Triandis, H. C., McCusker, C., & Hui, C. H. (1990). Multimethod probes of individualism and collectivism. *Journal of Personality and Social Psychology, 59*, 1006–1020.

Trilling, L. (1972). *Sincerity and authenticity*. Cambridge: Harvard University Press.

Trope, Y. (1986). Identification and inferential processes in dispositional attribution. *Psychological Review, 93*, 239–257.

Turner, J. C., Hogg, M. A., Oakes, P. J., Reicher, S. D., & Wetherell, M. S. (1987). *Rediscovering the social group: A self-categorization theory*. Oxford, England: Blackwell.

Uleman, J. S., & Moskowitz, G. B. (1994). Unintended effects of goals on unintended inferences. *Journal of Personality and Social Psychology, 66*, 490–501.

Uleman, J. S., Newman, L. S., & Moskowitz, G. B. (1996). People as flexible interpreters: Evidence and issues from spontaneous trait inference. *Advances in Experimental Social Psychology, 28*, 211–279.

Uleman, J. S., Rhee, E., Bardoliwalla, N., Semin, G., & Toyama, M. (1999). The relational self: Closeness to ingroups depends on who they are, culture, and the type of closeness. *Asian Journal of Social Psychology*.

Valsiner, J. (1989). *Human development and culture*. Lexington, MA: D. C. Heath.

Van den Heuvel, K., & Poortinga, Y. H. (1999). Resource allocation by Greek and Dutch students: A test of three models. *International Journal of Psychology, 34*, 1–13.

Van Overwalle, F. (1998). Causal explanation as constraint satisfaction: A critique and a feedforward connectionist alternative. *Journal of Personality and Social Psychology, 74*, 312–328.

Vygotsky, L. S. (1978). *Mind in society: The development of higher psychological processes* (M. Cole, V. John-Steiner, S. Scribner, & E. Souberman, Eds. & Trans.). Cambridge: Harvard University Press.

Watkins, D., Yau, J., Dahlin, B. & Wondimu, H. (1997). The twenty statements test: Some measurement issues. *Journal of Cross-Cultural Psychology, 28*, 626–633.

Watson, D. (1982). The actor and the observer: How are their perceptions of causality divergent? *Psychological Bulletin, 92*, 682–700.

Webster, D. M., & Kruglanski, A. W. (1994). Individual differences in need for cognitive closure. *Journal of Personality and Social Psychology, 67*, 1049–1062.

Wertsch, J. V. (1985). *Vygotsky and the social formation of mind.* Cambridge: Harvard University Press.

Wertsch, J. V. (1991). *Voices of the mind.* London: Harvester Whatsheaf.

Wicker, A. W. (1969). Attitudes versus actions: The relationship of verbal and overt behavioral responses to attitude objects. *Journal of Social Issues, 41*, 41–78.

Wierzbicka, A. (1992). *Semantics, culture, and cognition : Universal human concepts in culture-specific configurations.* New York: Oxford University Press.

Winter, L., & Uleman, J. S. (1984). When are social judgments made? Evidence for the spontaneousness of trait inferences. *Journal of Personality and Social Psychology, 47*, 237–252.

Winter, L., Uleman, J. S., & Cunniff, C. (1985). How automatic are social judgments? *Journal of Personality and Social Psychology, 49*, 904–917.

Wyer, R. S., Jr., & Srull, T. K. (1984). *Handbook of social cognition* (Vols. 1–3). Hillsdale, NJ: Erlbaum.

Wyer, R. S., Jr., & Srull, T. K. (1984). *Handbook of social cognition* (2nd ed., Vols. 1–3). Hillsdale, NJ: Erlbaum.

Wylie, R. C. (1974). The self concept (Vol. 1). Lincoln: University of Nebraska Press.

Zebrowitz-McArthur, L. (1988). Person perception in cross-cultural perspective. In M. H. Bond (Ed.), *Cross-cultural challenge to social psychology* (pp. 245–265). Newbury Park, CA: Sage.

Zung, W. K. (1965). A self-rating depression scale. *Archives of General Psychiatry, 12*, 63–70.

18

Cross-Cultural Studies of Social Influence

PETER B. SMITH

Much of social psychology, and indeed of daily life, is comprised of instances of social influence, that is, people interact with and influence the behaviors of each other. In mainstream psychology, it is difficult to think of situations in which such influence does not have some kind of effect on behavior, even in instances in which people are alone as social influence can occur as a result of the imagined or internalized influence of others. This area, therefore, is extremely important to psychology as a whole and as such has received considerable attention in the cross-cultural arena as well.

In this chapter, Smith provides an excellent, comprehensive review of several exemplary sources of social influence that have been studied extensively across cultures. He begins by pointing out that, in the past, many models of social influence in social psychology were biased from the perspective in which it was studied. That is, as most studies were conducted and theories were created within a typically individualistic American or European standard, research and its findings were generally interpreted in relation to those standards to the exclusion of other perspectives. Smith's early research on Japanese leadership processes led him to see how constructs that were thought to be bipolar opposites in the United States could coexist in the Japanese company, suggesting to him the need to develop more broadly based theories and structures to account for the way that variables opposed to one another in one cultural context are allied with one another in another context.

A number of social influence processes have been studied cross-culturally, and Smith reviews three major ones: group-based influence, with a focus on social loafing and conformity; hierarchical influence, with a focus on leadership; and negotiation. In each, he highlights how findings and models from mainstream psychology may not be applicable to people of other cultures and in some cases call for fundamental revisions in the very nature of the construct being studied. Within leadership, for example, the traditional Western model of leaders understands leadership as a one-way source of influence. Cross-cultural studies, however, make it clear that leadership can characterize central persons within a network of potential influence sources, including upward, downward, and horizontal influence. Leadership can be direct and indirect, and cross-cultural studies have demonstrated a number of interesting findings concerning indigenous influence tactics used to achieve culturally relevant goals.

In looking toward the future, Smith makes a strong case for a substantive change in the nature and focus of cross-cultural research on social influence. He contends that understanding how people interact intraculturally may or may not have anything to do with how they act with people of different cultures. Indeed, there is some evidence to suggest that this notion is true, and if true, it rings a warning bell for most cross-cultural research in this and many other areas. That is, most cross-cultural research that relies on cross-cultural comparisons of behavior does not really examine how people behave interculturally. As Smith notes, the current intense pressures toward globalization mean that contacts between persons from differing cultural backgrounds are increasing rapidly in all walks of life, professionally and personally. Indeed, it is ironic that cross-cultural research, with its underlying goal of improving intercultural interactions, may have missed the boat until now by its intracultural comparison approach to research and theory building.

At the same time, Smith calls for a reconsideration of the nature of groups studied in cross-cultural work, of intercultural examinations of hierarchical leadership and negotiation issues, and of neglected aspects of social influence. The last point is particularly interesting because it points out that the forms of social influence that have been explored most fully by cross-cultural psychologists have been face-to-face interactions. Yet, many other forms of social influence exist; indeed, in many other cultures, these other forms of influences are just as important, if not potentially more important, than face-to-face interactions. Smith suggests that one of the reasons why these areas of influence have not been studied extensively until now is because they are difficult to study. This is, of course, exactly the case, and careful examinations of these different areas will necessitate fundamentally different ways of collecting and analyzing data that are currently in use. Thus, they require fundamental changes in the way we conceptualize, approach, and conduct research and use its findings in creating models of human behavior.

Yet, let me suggest another reason for the neglect of these areas until now—the cultural bias of researchers and theorists. That is, the focus on issues such as face-to-face interactions has been commensurate with most scholars' views of leadership and influence processes. These views are rooted in the particular cultural and social milieus within which many researchers have existed until now. Thus, it is no wonder that the foci of research and theory until now were influenced by such a worldview. As researchers and their understanding of the world continue to diversify, however, we will come to understand the nature of social influence in many areas of our lives in potentially qualitatively different ways than we have until now.

Much of social psychology is devoted to studies of the ways in which we influence one another. Studies of these processes have become focused within a range of different research topics, each of which has been studied most typically without reference to the others. Thus, we have separate research literature concerning social facilitation, social loafing, group polarization, conformity, negotiation, leadership, ingratiation, sales skills, psychotherapy, education, health intervention, and media effects, to name only those fields that focus most obviously on social influence.

As investigation into all of these research topics developed over the past half-century, it was inevitable that the models of social influence that found most favor were those that best accounted for the results obtained in the circumstances that were most frequently studied. In other words, certain populations in the United States provided a baseline for what we might come to think of as normal social influence processes. Students and business managers were the populations most frequently studied.

I first became aware of the limitations that might result from this restricted focus when I began to study the process of leadership in Japanese organizations nearly 20 years ago. At that time, many Western leadership researchers were still attempting to define the circumstances under which relatively democratic and relatively autocratic leadership styles were most effective. My experiences in Japan taught me that Japanese organizations are at the same time both more democratic and participative and more autocratic than most Western organizations. Japanese employees have extensive opportunities for upward influence, but they are also bound into a structure in which seniority and status are pervasive (Smith & Misumi, 1989). Thus, concepts that Western researchers were treating as polar opposites were wedded within an alternative cultural context. The only way out of such a paradoxical combination is to develop more broadly based theories that can account for the way that variables opposed to one another in one cultural context are allied with one another in another context. We also need to develop the distinctive set of research skills that will enable us to make valid comparisons between different cultural contexts (Van de Vijver & Leung, 1996).

Other chapters in this book (see especially those by Lonner and Adamopolous and by Triandis) explore more fully the conceptual frameworks that have become more widely known over the past two decades. We need to rely on these frameworks if we are to develop a more general understanding of the nature of social influence. In particular, it has become clear that cultures we now think of as relatively individualistic (Hofstede, 1980) are distinctive and unusual within a global context. We need to consider how thinking of individuals as separate entities rather than as persons with enduring group affiliations might affect our understanding of social influence.

The first and most obvious consequence is that we may focus on short-term influences and neglect longer term or more subtle effects. The choice of researchers to study transient groups of students and managers whose work associates change frequently will have accentuated this effect. Even within Western cultures, longer lasting groupings such as families and ethnic groups have received less attention. There are two other likely consequences. First, if we study social influence from an individualistic perspective, then we shall most probably evaluate the success of influence solely in terms of benefits to the individual influencer rather than in terms of the benefits to the larger social system within which that individual is embedded. Furthermore, we are likely to see effective social influence as deriving from the characteristic qualities of the individual, such as personality traits and skills, rather than as deriving from the individual's position or role within a given social structure.

Having established this general perspective, we can examine what has been found when researchers have studied social influence processes outside North America.

Group-Based Influence

It is consistent with the argument presented above that much Western research attention has been focused on influence within small groups, with these groups having no preexisting social structure. A group has often been conceived as a composite of individuals whose mere mutual presence will either enhance or depress this or that social process. Studies of this type have been conducted for more than 100 years (Kravitz & Martin, 1986). At various times, the resulting social processes have been called a bewildering array of names, including social facilitation, deindividuation, responsibility diffusion, group polarization, conformity, and social loafing. We focus here on the last two.

Social Loafing

Social loafing is defined as a process by which the larger a group becomes, the less any individual feels obliged to contribute toward accomplishment of the group's task. Latané, Williams, and Harkins (1979) tested this theory in the United States by asking members of groups of various sizes to clap hands or shout as loud as they could. Members of larger groups contributed less. Similar effects were obtained later in a number of Pacific Asian countries.

However, when more complex tasks are used, cultural differences start to emerge. Karau and Williams (1993) reported a metanalysis of 147 social loafing effects obtained in the United States and 15 obtained in Pacific Asia. Social loafing was reduced everywhere when more complex tasks were used, but for the five effects obtained with complex tasks in Asian nations, the effect was completely reversed. As group size increased, group members contributed more, not less.

Confirmation for this effect was provided by two additional studies by Earley (1989, 1993), who also tested a culture-based explanation. Earley proposed that working in groups rather than individually will increase the motivation of members of collectivist cultures to work hard, rather than provide them with an opportunity to loaf. In his first study, he showed that, on an hour-long series of tasks, Chinese managers worked harder in groups, while U.S. managers worked harder when alone. In addition, Earley asked his subjects to complete a short measure of their individualist and collectivist values. He was then able to show that it was those who endorsed collectivist values that showed the strongest reversal of the social loafing effect. In his second study, Earley included Israeli, as well as Chinese and American, managers. Again, he measured their values, but this time he also led them to believe that the group in which they were working was either composed of their known associates or else composed of strangers. He found that individualists did more loafing in group settings regardless of the composition of the group. However, collectivists worked hardest in the group composed of known associates. A group of strangers had no more influence on them than did working individually.

Earley's studies (1989, 1993) provide some clear guidelines as to the variables likely to affect social influence processes in settings in which individualist values do not prevail. His conclusions are particularly persuasive because he obtained measures of the values endorsed by his actual subjects rather than relying on a generalized expectation that many Chinese endorse more collectivist views than do many Americans. Those who have collectivist values are not influenced simply by being in the presence of others: It matters who the other persons are.

Conformity

Another line of research that has generated numerous replications derives from Asch's (1951) classic studies of conformity. Again, the original studies were concerned with the mere presence of others, in this case, others who gave unanimous, but incorrect, judgments of line lengths. Bond and Smith (1996) reported a metanalysis based on 133 Asch-type studies. Most of these were conducted in the United States, but 36 were reported from another 16 countries. After variations in experimental design had been discounted, it was found that levels of conformity were higher for the non-U.S. studies. Using culture-level characterizations of predominant values, Bond and Smith showed that the nations in which strongest conformity had been found were those that were high on Hofstede's (1980) measure of collectivism. Using instead Schwartz's (1994) more recent measures, conformity was highest in nations with high scores on conservatism, and

low scores on intellectual and affective autonomy.

Thus, the results of conformity studies concur with social loafing studies in finding greater influence among populations for which collectivist values prevail. However, while the social loafing studies show a positive increment in work motivation, the conformity studies show an effect that is usually portrayed as negative. Some caution is required here in labeling the different influence effects under discussion. Conformity is usually thought of as negative in individualist cultures. To yield to influence from others can be seen as giving away some of one's individuality, especially when there is no objective reason to do so, as in the case of the Asch experiment. How might a member of a collectivist culture perceive the same behavior? If I am a minority of one in a setting in which other group members are making obvious mistakes in their line judgments, my concerns may have to do with the preservation of face. As a member of a collectivist culture, I will be concerned not only with preventing my own embarrassment, but also with giving face to others (Ting-Toomey, 1988). In consequence, I may deliberately give a false response to hide the errors of my fellow judges. In doing this, I would think of what I was doing not as conformity, but as tactfulness or sensitivity to other's needs. Experimental studies can give us objective estimates of the magnitude of influence processes, but we need to be on the lookout for the extent to which the labels that we put on these effects impose our own values on the effect that is found.

Earley found that the level of influence accepted by collectivists varied depending on who were one's fellow group members. Studies of conformity in Japan have found similar effects: Williams and Sogon (1984) found much stronger influence among groups who already knew one another than among groups who were previously unacquainted with one another.

Studies of social loafing and of conformity have virtually all been conducted on the basis of assembling groups of persons who are presumed to be of equal status. As we have seen, the results of these studies have been found to vary in relation to estimates of how strongly a given group is collectivist (or, using Schwartz's term, how conservative). The bias toward equal-status group members may have arisen as a consequence of widespread reliance on ad hoc groups of students. However, it can equally well be seen as a statement that hierarchical differences are not required to provide conditions in which we can study the most basic types of social influence. Such an assumption is most likely to be made within cultures, such as the United States, that score low on power distance (Hofstede) and hierarchy (Schwartz). If studies are done that do include persons of differing status, we might expect these other dimensions of cultural variance to prove equally relevant.

Hierarchical Influence

Since hierarchy is more favored in many nations than in the United States, it is no surprise that replications of Milgram's (1974) classic studies of obedience to authority in the United States have yielded similar effects in eight other countries (Smith & Bond, 1998). However, these studies simply demonstrate the ubiquity of obedience. They do not span a wide range of nations, and none of them included any measurement of the values of those who participated. Consequently, they do not provide defensible explanations of why obedience is stronger in some settings than others.

Classical Leadership Theories

Influence based on hierarchy is more typically thought of as *leadership*. The voluminous literature on leadership with few exceptions has been built around the development and testing of theories first formulated in North America. These theories sought to specify the personal qualities or behavioral styles that will cause maximal positive response from those who are subordinate to a leader in an organizational context. What they had in common was an attempt to specify rather precisely the behaviors that will cause influence to flow from the leader to a subordinate. In other words, leadership was seen implicitly as a one-way process that was dependent on the senior person's input of appropriate behaviors or qualities. These early attempts to identify individual persuasive traits or qualities that were universally effective proved unsuccessful and gave way to more complex "contingency" models, which specified the types of situation within which different styles of leadership would be most effective (Bass, 1990). Thus, leadership researchers, in contrast to the theorists of group-based influence discussed above, did attempt to put the leadership process into context. However, tests

of contingency theories proved inconclusive, varying from one study to the next. To understand why this may have been so, it is useful to consider the principal theory advanced by a non-U.S. leadership theorist.

A Japanese Perspective

Misumi (1985) proposed that effective leadership required the provision of two key functions, which he defined as the performance function (P) and the maintenance function (M). His theory is usually referred to as PM theory. These functions appear initially reminiscent of some of the dimensions of leader style favored by U.S. leadership theorists. However, while U.S. theorists struggled to develop psychometrically valid scales to measure their chosen leader styles, Misumi asserted that his leadership functions would inevitably be fulfilled in different ways in every different situation. Thus, Misumi's conceptualization commences by specifying a situation and expects that the leader will need to devise situationally appropriate behaviors to fulfill the required functions. In contrast, U.S. theorists developed inflexible measures of leader style and then attempted to theorize about the situations in which they would be effective. Misumi's formulation reflects the manner in which Japanese persons have been shown to adapt their behaviors to social context, while Americans are more concerned to present themselves consistently across situations (e.g., Cousins, 1989; Markus & Kitayama, 1991).

The PM theory has received strong support in a wide variety of Japanese organizations. Cross-cultural tests of Misumi's (1985) theory have underlined the utility of his distinction between general and specific functions of leadership. Smith, Misumi, Tayeb, Peterson, and Bond (1989) found that the specific leader behaviors associated with the P and M functions varied widely among workers in electronics assembly plants in Japan, Hong Kong, the United States, and the United Kingdom. Some behaviors that were seen as enhancing the M function in one cultural context were seen as detracting from the M function elsewhere.

Misumi's theory may also have a wider usefulness. It points up the need for theorists of leadership to make a clear distinction between aspects of leadership that they see as basic and central compared to those that are specific and less central. General functions are more likely to yield cultural universals, while specific functions are more likely to prove culturally distinctive. A similar distinction can help to make sense of diverse research findings in many areas of cross-cultural psychology (Smith & Bond, 1998).

New-Wave Theories

More recent Western leadership theorists have adopted a perspective more compatible with that of Misumi. The increasing rate of change experienced in organizations and in society more generally has led theorists to stress that the key function of leaders is the facilitation of change rather than simply the administration of an existing structure. These "new-wave" theorists see effective leaders as adept at identifying a persuasive vision of how the organization can best prepare for and handle future challenges. They can then lead by establishing a shared commitment to this vision among those around them (Bass, 1985; Bryman, 1992). Rather than seeking to specify precisely how this function is fulfilled in particular contexts, some of the recent measures have been designed to tap in a more general way whether a leader has qualities that are "charismatic" or "transformational."

Two of the best-known formulations of this type of leadership theory have recently undergone extensive cross-cultural testing, and the outcome of these tests is discussed below. In addition, Jaeger and Kanungo (1990) have proposed that charismatic leader styles are especially well suited to non-Western cultures. They point out that the type of shared vision that charismatic leaders seek to create between themselves and their subordinates is readily compatible with conditions that combine high collectivism, high power distance, and high uncertainty avoidance (Hofstede, 1980). Persons in junior positions in these contexts will desire an inclusive, status-dependent source of certainty. This perspective contrasts with those of Bass (1985) and House and Shamir (1993), who assert the efficacy of some form of visionary leadership in a manner not dependent on cultural context.

Transformational Leadership

Bass's (1985) theory is based on a contrast between a visionary style referred to as *transformational* and an alternative *transactional* style, in which leaders provide rewards in exchange for subordinates' work performance, but subordinates experience no particular emotional commitment to the organization. Bass

(1997) summarized studies based on completion of his Multifactor Leadership Questionnaire (MLQ) by subordinates. Transformational leadership is found rather more effective than transactional leadership in various organizations in more than 20 nations. However, little attention has been given to the cross-cultural validity of Bass's questionnaire. Aside from translation, no adaptations have been made to items to render them locally meaningful, and the MLQ appears not to retain its factor structure in all cultural contexts (Dorfman, 1996). Furthermore, it is not clear whether the MLQ measure of transformational leadership actually does measure qualities of the leader-subordinate relationship that are not also encompassed by earlier nonvisionary conceptions of leadership. Tracey and Hinkin (1998) obtained MLQ data and leader behavior measures derived from earlier theories from the same U.S. respondents and found the two sets of measures strongly correlated with one another.

The Global Leadership and Organizational Effectiveness Project

There is little doubt that the most influential contributor to the cross-cultural study of leadership during the present decade has been the Global Leadership and Organizational Effectiveness (GLOBE) project, coordinated by Robert House, and including a very large number of other leadership researchers from around the world. House (1977) formulated one of the earliest models of charismatic leadership, but now prefers to use the phrase *value-based leadership*. The overall goal of the project is stated as the determination of whether effective leadership is that which is congruent with local norms and values or that which differs from local norms and values or whether there are universals of leadership that transcend local norms and values (House, Wright, & Aditya, 1997).

GLOBE researchers have surveyed more than 17,000 leaders in 825 organizations drawn from three specified industries in each of 61 nations. Measures in the surveys tapped both the cultural context and the specific qualities perceived to be associated with effective leadership (House & 175 coauthors, 1999). Considerable care was taken to ensure adequate translation and to collect a rich variety of locally relevant measures as checks on validity. Unusually, respondents were asked about cultural attributes of both their "society" and their organization. Furthermore, they were asked to characterize the situation "as it is" and "as it should be." Nine dimensions of cultural variance were measured, most of them derived from the earlier conceptualizations of Hofstede (1980) and others. Respondents were then provided with a set of 112 traits and asked to rate the extent to which each contributes to or inhibits leader effectiveness. Initial data analysis reduced these to a set of 21 leadership "prototypes," each of which had a robust structure across the various samples.

It will be some years before all the results of this project are available. However, initial results indicate a substantial global consensus on the leadership prototypes that best characterize effective leadership (Den Hartog, House, & 170 coauthors, 1999). Across 60 nations, the most strongly endorsed trait adjectives were trustworthy, dynamic, motive arousing, decisive, intelligent, dependable, and planning ahead. These results are interpreted as giving strong support for the universality of value-based leadership. However, the results also showed that the evaluations accorded to some of the other traits varied substantially. Large variations were noted in the degree to which an effective leader, for instance, should be subdued, individualistic, cunning, elitist, and so forth.

Brodbeck and 44 coauthors (2000) have analyzed the differences in the GLOBE results from 22 European countries. It was found that clusters of European countries where similar leadership prototypes were endorsed matched closely the clusters of nations that had been identified by earlier researchers as having cross-cultural differences in values. It appears likely, therefore, that the outcome of the GLOBE project will be to provide encouragement both to those who seek to show that there are cross-cultural universals for effective leadership and to those who see greater practical benefits in understanding the more specific differences than in the overall similarities.

Additional Influence Sources

One further large-scale cross-national study of leadership has focused on the sources of guidance on which leaders draw in handling the everyday work events that they encounter. In advancing their "event management" theory of leadership, Smith and Peterson (1988) emphasized that they wished to move away from what they saw as a Western emphasis on the leader as

a one-way source of influence. Their preference was to portray leaders as central persons within a network of potential influence sources. Their surveys have sampled leaders in more than 40 nations. The results show substantial consistency among the sources on which managers in a particular nation rely relatively strongly and characterizations of that nation's values derived from earlier culture-level studies (Smith, Peterson, & Schwartz, 2000). For instance, managers rely more on their subordinates in nations high in Schwartz's (1994) autonomy and egalitarianism, whereas they rely more on formal rules and procedures in nations high on embeddedness and hierarchy.

Sun and Bond's (1999) study of influence tactics also opens up novel perspectives. First, their study was in Chinese organizations, which provided an opportunity to determine the extent of indigenous tactics not tapped by prior U.S. measures. Second, they compared upward and downward influence, thus escaping the widespread implicit assumption that only downward influence is of interest. Of 34 tactics identified, 11 were indigenous to the Chinese sample and most occurred in relation to upward influence. It may be that that the tactics required for upward and downward influence in Western nations with low power distance are relatively similar. In the high power distance context, a fuller range of alternate behaviors may be required if upward influence is to be effective. Some of the tactics identified were "praising target behind back," "showing face consideration," and "working overtime."

In a similar manner, Rao, Hashimoto, and Rao (1997) identified indigenous Japanese upward influence tactics, including after hours socializing and emphasis on benefits to the company rather than the individual. Analyses of the Japanese phenomenon of *amae* also shed light on the types of upward influence that this relationship of *indulgent dependence* between seniors and juniors permits (Kim & Yamaguchi, 1996). Sinha (1997) also notes a series of forms of upward ingratiation tactics that are especially widespread in India, including self-degradation, name-dropping, and emphasizing one's dependence on the superior.

Cross-cultural study of leadership continues to attract a good deal of research interest, no doubt because of the current pressures toward globalization experienced by many business organizations. The most promising aspect of current developments is that there is a gradual trend away from the simple testing in new locations of unidirectional models of leader influence first developed in the United States. There is a new interpenetration of leadership theory and theories of cultural difference, mostly drawn from research into values, but also including some reference to indigenous styles of influence.

Negotiation

It could be argued that all negotiation is attempted leadership, and that all successful leadership is negotiated. However, social influence occurring during the process of explicit negotiation has generated separate research literature. The most extensive cross-cultural series of studies of negotiation was conducted by Graham and colleagues (Graham & Mintu Wimsat, 1997; Graham, Mintu, & Rodgers, 1994). The studies used a standard 1-hour simulation procedure that involved managers taking the role of either buyer or seller. This procedure has been used in separate studies in 16 nations to investigate whether negotiators who adopt a "tough" position fare better than those who employ a "problem-solving" approach that attempts to maximize gains for both parties.

Graham et al. (1994) present a comparative analysis of the findings for 10 of these nations. The results proved complex, possibly because the studies were set up in a relatively naturalistic manner with no experimenter control over either party's behavior. For instance, it was found in 8 of the nations that, if one party took up a problem-solving approach, the other party tended to reciprocate. However, in Taiwan and in Francophone Canada, this effect was significantly reversed. Adopting a problem-solving approach enhanced one's profit in Taiwan and Korea, but harmed it in Mexico and Spain. The clearest findings were those that linked negotiation outcome to the Hofstede scores for the nations represented. Negotiators from individualistic nations scored lower on problem-solving approach and made more profit when they did so. The role to which one was assigned also proved influential, with buyers doing significantly better than sellers in 7 nations. The dominance of the buyer was greater the higher the nation's scores on power distance and collectivism were. Thus, the social context, as represented by assignment to role, increasingly affected the outcome in more collectivist cultures, while individual competitiveness affected it in individualist cultures.

Preferences for Conflict Resolution

The studies of Graham (1993), Graham et al. (1994), and Graham and Mintu Wimsat (1997) illustrate the complexities (and the benefits) of making realistic comparisons of negotiation cross-culturally. Most investigators have opted instead to use questionnaire measures that evaluate one's preferred strategy for handling difference. Studies of this type frequently find differences that can be interpreted readily in terms of presumed value differences of national cultures. For instance, Trubisky, Ting-Toomey, and Lin (1991) found that Taiwanese students favored the use of "obliging," "avoiding," "compromising," and "integrating" in resolving a student conflict more strongly than did the presumably more individualist Americans. Cropanzano, Aguinis, Schminke, and Denham (1999) compared students' preferred conflict resolution procedures in Mexico, the United States, Argentina, and the Dominican Republic. Resolution based on autocratic decision was less popular in the United States and Argentina, nations that score lower on Hofstede's power distance.

Morris et al. (1998) compared student preferences for competing or avoiding conflicts in the United States, Philippines, Hong Kong, and India. The Americans scored higher on competing, and the Chinese were higher on avoiding than other nations. Tinsley and Pillutla (1998) found a similar contrast between Hong Kong and U.S. negotiation preferences. Both Morris et al. (1998) and Tinsley and Pillutla were also able to show that these differences could be explained by individual-level analysis of scores obtained from subjects using Schwartz's (1994) value survey.

As the studies of Graham (1993), Graham et al. (1994), and Graham and Mintu Wimsat (1997) confirmed, the reactions of members of cultures high on collectivism and power distance to one another tend to vary depending on social context. A further aspect of context has to do with the affiliation of the person one wishes to influence. Disagreements with ingroup members have a different significance than disagreements with strangers and are likely to be resolved in different ways.

In an attempt to clarify earlier results from collectivist cultures, Leung (1997) proposed a distinction between disintegration avoidance and animosity reduction. Disintegration avoidance is likely to be a particularly salient concern in disagreements with in-group members since the severing of links with in-group members is difficult in all cultures and especially problematic in collectivist cultures. Furthermore, disagreements in the in-group are not likely to be intense, so animosity reduction is not a high priority. In contrast, while situations do arise in the course of life when one needs to attempt to influence out-group members, there is not the same requirement for a continuing relationship with them. The very reason for having contact with an out-group member may well be the existence of some dispute over rights or resources, as in the case of Graham et al.'s (1994) simulated negotiations. Consequently, animosity may be high and will need to be reduced if agreement is to be accomplished. Leung suggests that the preferred influence strategies for disintegration avoidance will be yielding to the other and avoiding the issue. For animosity reduction, problem solving and compromise should prove more effective.

Research findings in this area are currently unsatisfactory because, although the significance of the in-group/out-group distinction is widely accepted, no studies exist that have included an unambiguous check of who is perceived to be within or outside the respondent's perceived in-group. The study by Cropanzano et al. (1999) attempted to manipulate in-group/out-group membership of the parties in conflict, but the manipulation failed. Smith, Dugan, Peterson, and Leung (1998) drew on data from the event management project described above. Sampling 23 nations, they found more frequent out-group disagreement in nations with high power distance. The frequency of in-group disagreement was not related to scores on any of Hofstede's dimensions. However, there was more variability in how in-group and out-group disagreement was handled in nations with low power distance, which does not accord with Leung's predictions.

Leung (1997) has included an additional element in his investigations over the past decade that can contribute to resolving these difficulties. In addition to asking respondents for evaluations of the different possible ways of handling conflict, he also asks them to rate the extent to which each of these ways would reduce animosity. Thus, he might be able to show that, although the ways that persons sought to influence the outcome of a conflict vary, each is thought to reduce animosity (or avoid disintegration) by those who use it.

For instance, Leung, Au, Fernandez-Dols, and Iwawaki (1992) found that Japanese and Spanish students preferred negotiation and compliance with the other party more and accusing the other party less than did Dutch and Canadian students. However, data from all four countries showed that preferred procedures were associated with perceived animosity reduction. Thus, in a way that parallels what has emerged from cross-cultural studies of leadership, there may prove to be culture-general aspects of the particular influence strategies that lead to successful negotiation. Equally, there are certainly culture-specific variations in how members of a given culture believe that the general goals of animosity reduction and disintegration avoidance are to be accomplished.

Some Future Directions

Having surveyed cross-cultural studies bearing on three aspects of social influence, it is time to take stock. What has been accomplished, and what avenues remain underexplored? It is clear from the studies reviewed that there is substantial consistency between the emergent theory-driven framework of cross-cultural psychology and results concerning social influence. The theoretical framework in question is built on a classification of cultures derived from surveys of values (Smith & Schwartz, 1997). Focused initially on culture-level characterizations, some progress has been made in drawing out concepts applicable to individual-level studies. As we have seen, group-based influence, hierarchical influence, and negotiation behaviors all have some universality, but all also vary in ways that are predictable in terms of characterizations based on predominant cultural values.

There is some basis for satisfaction in the evidence for convergent validity that these results suggest. However, there remains a long journey before full benefit can be derived from them. There are three reasons for this, one methodological and two substantive. The methodological aspect is not explored here fully since it is addressed in chapter 5. However, it is worth reiterating that, so long as the focus for cross-cultural studies of social influence continues to rest on cross-cultural comparisons, there is a continuing need for researchers to be aware of the perils of comparing raw means for responses to some translated questionnaire. There are substantial cultural differences in acquiescent response bias, and papers that test hypotheses based on comparison of raw means are most often testing for differences in bias rather than differences in the variable being studied. Better strategies are to find ways of discounting bias or else to conduct parallel within-country analyses.

Influence across Cultures

The principal weakness of the field at this time is the neglect of influence processes that occur across, rather than within, cultural groups. Currently, intense pressures toward globalization mean that, within education, business, leisure, and community relations, contacts among persons from differing cultural backgrounds are increasing rapidly. The evidence from studies of immigrants and sojourners does not suggest early blending of cultures (Smith & Bond, 1998). This means that there is an urgent need to understand what happens in attempted social influence processes that are truly cross cultural, rather than in the necessary, but preliminary, comparisons between separate samples from Culture A and Culture B that we have discussed so far.

There are numerous reasons to expect that people engaged in cross-cultural interaction will behave in different ways than they do when they interact with members of their own cultural group (Smith & Bond, 1998). For instance, cross-cultural interaction is more likely to be with strangers, is more likely to involve at least one party conversing in a second language, and is more likely to be focused on issues that divide the two parties rather than what they have in common. We therefore revisit each of the main topics discussed above.

Group-Based Influence

The early study of cross-cultural work teams was dominated by comparisons between the effects of homogeneity and of heterogeneity. More recently, Earley and Mosakowski (2000) have demonstrated that heterogeneity can take more than one form. They argue that a team that is diverse in the sense of having 10 members each from different cultures is very different from a team that is polarized in the sense of having 5 members from Culture A and 5 members from Culture B. Diverse teams should be relatively able to work out a pattern of collaborative working since no single preferred style of influence could predominate. Polarized teams are much more likely to be immobilized by the mutual incompatibility of two opposing fac-

tions. Studying 47 teams of students in a U.K. business school and 5 teams in a U.S. multinational organization in Southeast Asia, Earley and Mosakowski found the most effective teams to be homogeneous or diverse rather than polarized. Podsiadlowski (1999) studied 34 business teams working in a German multinational, also in Southeast Asia. Members rated effectiveness higher the more culturally heterogeneous the team was.

These studies provide some information on the outcome of certain types of cross-cultural teamwork. To understand the processes of social influence that lead to success or failure, more fine-grained analyses will be needed of such matters as cultural constraints on types and frequency of group participation, assignment of roles, formality of structures, and so forth.

Hierarchical Leadership

Few studies are available of what happens when superiors and subordinates from differing cultural backgrounds work together. Rao and Hashimoto (1996) surveyed Japanese managers working in Canada and who had both Japanese and Canadian subordinates. The Japanese managers reported using more sanctions and also giving more reasons when dealing with the Canadians. It is likely that they did this because what would have been understood implicitly by their Japanese subordinates needed to be made more explicit for the Canadians. Peterson, Peng, and Smith (1999) found that, when a Japanese plant opened in the United States, U.S. subordinates were initially more willing to accept pressure from Japanese supervisors than from American supervisors. The difference had disappeared at a later time. Smith, Wang, and Leung (1997) studied Chinese managers working with non-Chinese superiors in joint-venture hotels in China. Greatest difficulty was reported when superiors were Japanese and the least when they were from Hong Kong or Taiwan. The Chinese subordinates reported that, when working with Western managers, direct communication was most effective. Nonetheless, they indicated that when problems arose, they most frequently relied on more indirect forms of communication.

Detailed studies of the cultural interface between leaders and subordinates of differing nationality are in their infancy. We have scattered information on the types of adaptation that are made, but few evaluations of what makes for success. The existing literature on expatriate managers has focused most on more global issues such as preparation, job satisfaction, premature return rates, and so forth.

Negotiation

Tse, Francis, and Walls (1994) reported a comparison of intra- and intercultural negotiations between Chinese and Canadian managers. Consistent differences were found between the preferred strategies of the Chinese and the Canadians, regardless of whether the negotiations were to be intra- or intercultural. However, this provides only a weak test of hypotheses since the negotiators never actually met.

Graham (1993) videotaped buyer-seller negotiations between Americans and Japanese. He subsequently asked the negotiators to review the tapes and comment on difficulties that they had encountered. Japanese negotiators reported that they did not like direct rejections of their offers, as well as frequent interruptions. They were also confused when the seller took the initiative since Japanese culture would determine that the buyer has higher status and should therefore initiate. The Americans had difficulty in determining whether head nods constituted agreement, did not like high initial selling price offers, and could not judge when a "final" offer was final and when it was not.

Weldon, Jehn, Doucet, Chen, and Wang (1996) collected accounts provided by Chinese and American managers of intra- and intercultural disagreements that had occurred in joint-venture organizations in China. A standard set of disagreement episodes was selected from these and then presented to a new sample of Chinese and American managers, who were asked how they would handle them. Both Chinese and Americans were found to vary in how they would handle the intracultural disagreement and the intercultural disagreement. Americans were more likely to inform the boss about the intracultural disagreement, whereas they were more likely to ignore or withdraw from the intercultural disagreement. Chinese were more likely to seek to embarrass their intracultural colleagues and teach them a moral lesson and more likely to use indirect ways of trying to rectify the intercultural situation.

Our brief and partial overview of social influences in settings that are truly cross cultural provides some preliminary evidence that suggests people in these settings do adapt their behaviors in ways that differ from those used intraculturally. This further underlines the need to explore these types of settings more fully rather than basing our expectations on extrapolation from the results of existing intracultural comparisons.

Neglected Aspects of Social Influence

This chapter focused on the forms of social influence that have been explored most fully by cross-cultural psychologists, namely, influence occurring in face-to-face social interactions. Social influence by way of the mass media is becoming an increasingly important aspect of contemporary society, and this is likely to increase in the future. Advertisers devote substantial resources to attempts to tailor their messages to their intended audiences. Yet, little attention has been given by researchers to cross-cultural differences in receptiveness to different types of message. An example of the types of study that can both contribute to cross-cultural theory and have practical usefulness is provided by the work of Han and Shavitt (1994).

These authors surveyed magazine advertisements from the United States and Korea and found that the Korean advertisements contained many more appeals coded as related to collectivist motives, while the U.S. advertisements appealed to more individualistic motives. They then asked Koreans and Americans to rate the persuasiveness of a variety of advertisements. Some of these were personal to the individual (chewing gum, running shoes), and others were shared (detergents, clothes irons). American respondents responded more favorably to the individual appeals, and Koreans were more favorable to the collective appeals. These effects were particularly strong for advertisements for the shared items. In a further study, Shavitt, Nelson, and Yuan (1997) found contrasts in the way that Americans and Taiwanese read advertisements. The Americans focused more on product-related claims, while the Taiwanese were more concerned with the contextual appropriateness of the advertisements.

These types of study open up many interesting questions. For instance, some major U.S. companies seek to define the consistency of their brand image by using similar advertisements throughout Europe, whereas European firms more often design advertisements thought to be culturally appropriate within different European nations. What might be the effectiveness of these contrasting strategies?

Conclusion

It was suggested at the beginning of this chapter that the strong development of social psychology in North America had led to a predominance of individualistic conceptualizations of social influence processes. Some progress certainly has been achieved in testing the degree to which this perspective has limited our development of more generally applicable models. Particularly in the area of leadership research, data from a very wide range of nations have been collected. Furthermore, the frameworks provided by cross-cultural studies of values are increasingly being used to test directly whether they can explain the differences in actual and preferred modes of social influence that are found.

Researchers during the next decade will face three challenges. First, we need to extend and integrate the range of social influence processes to be studied. This is most likely to happen when researchers start to read more widely. There are strong pressures, especially in North America, to identify and develop one's own individually distinctive line of research and to read only the work of others that relates directly to that theme. Being a cross-cultural researcher actually makes it easier to stray outside such a narrow focus because data from studies conducted in the locations in which one is interested are often less extensive. Exploring the full range of what can be found may encourage one to think in less-constrained ways about the nature of influence processes within one's chosen culture(s).

Second, we must search for ways of analyzing data that can accommodate both universals and specific variations rather than seeing each as exclusive of the other. The GLOBE leadership project provides a fine current example of how this can be done. This group of researchers not only used standardized measures, but also sought out locally distinctive expressions of leadership preferences and behaviors. Thus, they are able to seek out both uniformity and variability in the same data set. This blending of measurement approaches is equally practicable in projects that are conducted on a much smaller scale than the GLOBE project.

Finally, and in my view most important, we must focus more directly and more frequently on instances of actual cross-cultural social influence rather than on static comparisons of samples from separate national cultures. There is no lack of situations in which successful or failed attempts at such influences currently occur. Students' culturally rooted preferred learning styles do or do not match those of their instructors. Tourists do or do not succeed in having their needs met. Expatriate managers and local workers do or do not work well together. Work teams and student project groups do or do not gel. Diplomatic or business negotiations do or do not reach agreement.

Why are there so few studies of these types of situations? Part of the answer may be that, to do good studies in any of these areas, one needs to obtain data from both the parties to the process of influence. There are certainly practical obstacles in the way of accomplishing this, but they are not insuperable. For instance, a similar change of focus has made substantial progress in the more general area of leadership research. In the past, many researchers into leadership in organizations surveyed subordinates' perceptions of leaders' behavior and then asked these subordinates also to evaluate their leader's effectiveness. Their results were frequently of low validity because the same-source ratings were not independent of each other and were likely to be contaminated by a halo effect. More recently, leading leadership journals accept only papers in which there is leader effectiveness evidence that is independent of the descriptions of leader style. This may be drawn from objective sources or by tapping alternative raters, such as the leader's own boss. In studying cross-cultural influence processes, a similar perspective will be essential. We can only understand why influence attempts by members of Culture A fail if we know how they are perceived by members of Culture B. Once we know that, we can start to address constructively the cultural differences that enmesh us all.

References

Asch, S. (1951). Effects of group pressure upon the modification and distortion of judgement. In H. Guetzkow (Ed.), *Groups, leadership and men* (pp. 177–190). Pittsburgh, PA: Carnegie.

Bass, B. M. (1985). *Leadership and performance beyond expectations*. New York: Free Press.

Bass, B. M. (1990). *Bass and Stogdill's handbook of leadership: Theory, research and managerial applications* (3rd ed.). New York: Free Press.

Bass, B. M. (1997). Does the transactional-transformational leadership paradigm transcend national boundaries? *American Psychologist, 52*, 130–139.

Bond, R. A., & Smith, P. B. (1996). Culture and conformity: A meta-analysis of studies using the

Asch (1952b, 1956) line judgment task. *Psychological Bulletin, 119*, 111–137.

Brodbeck, F., & 44 coauthors (2000). Cultural variation of leadership prototypes across 22 European countries. *Journal of Occupational and Organizational Psychology, 73*, 1–29.

Bryman, A. (1992). *Charisma and leadership in organization.* London: Sage.

Cousins, S. (1989). Culture and selfhood in Japan and the US. *Journal of Personality and Social Psychology, 56*, 124–131.

Cropanzano, R., Aguinis, H., Schminke, M., & Denham, D. L. (1999). Disputant reactions to managerial conflict resolution tactics: A comparison between Argentina, the Dominican Republic, Mexico and the United States. *Group and Organization Management, 24*, 124–154.

Den Hartog, D. N., House, R. J., & 170 coauthors. (1999). Emics and etics of culturally-endorsed leadership theories: Are attributes of charismatic/transformational leadership universally endorsed? *Leadership Quarterly, 10*, 219–256.

Dorfman, P. W. (1996). International and cross-cultural leadership. In B. J. Punnett & O. Shenkar (Eds.), *Handbook of international management research* (pp. 267–350). Cambridge, MA: Blackwell.

Earley, P. C. (1989). Social loafing and collectivism: A comparison of the United States and the People's Republic of China. *Administrative Science Quarterly, 34*, 565–581.

Earley, P. C. (1993). East meets West meets Mid-East: Further explorations of collectivistic versus individualistic work groups. *Academy of Management Journal, 36*, 319–348.

Earley, P. C., & Mosakowski, E. (2000). Creating hybrid team cultures: An empirical test of international team functioning. *Academy of Management Journal, 43*, 26–49.

Graham, J. L. (1993). The Japanese negotiation style: Characteristics of a distinct approach. *Negotiation Journal, 9*, 123–140.

Graham, J. L., Mintu, A. T., & Rodgers, W. (1994). Exploration of negotiation behaviors in 10 foreign cultures using a model developed in the United States. *Management Science, 40*, 72–95.

Graham, J. L., & Mintu Wimsat, A. (1997). Culture's influence on business negotiations in four countries. *Group Decision and Negotiation, 6*, 483–502.

Han, S. P., & Shavitt, S. (1994). Persuasion and culture: Advertising appeals in individualistic and collectivistic societies. *Journal of Experimental Social Psychology, 30*, 326–350.

Hofstede, G. (1980). *Culture's consequences: International differences in work-related values.* Beverly Hills, CA: Sage.

House, R. J. (1977). A 1976 theory of charismatic leadership. In J. G. Hunt & L. Larson (Eds.), *Leadership: The cutting edge* (pp. 189–204). Carbondale: Southern Illinois University Press.

House, R. J., & 175 coauthors (1999). Cultural influences on leadership and organizations: Project GLOBE. In W. F. Mobley, M. J. Gessner, & V. Arnold (Eds.), *Advances in global leadership* (Vol. 1, pp. 171–233). Stamford, CT: JAI Press.

House, R. J., & Shamir, B. (1993). Toward the integration of transformational, charismatic and visionary theories. In M. M. Chemers & R. Ayman (Eds.), *Leadership theory and research: Perspectives and directions* (pp. 81–107). San Diego, CA: Academic Press.

House, R. J., Wright, N. S., & Aditya, R. N. (1997). Cross-cultural research on organizational leadership: A critical analysis and a proposed theory. In P. C. Earley & M. Erez (Eds.), *New perspectives on international industrial/organizational psychology* (pp. 535–625). San Francisco: New Lexington.

Jaeger, A. M., & Kanungo, R. N. (Eds.). (1990). *Management in developing countries.* London: Routledge.

Karau, S. J., & Williams, K. D. (1993). Social loafing: A meta-analytic review of social integration. *Journal of Personality and Social Psychology, 65*, 681–706.

Kim, U., & Yamaguchi, S. (1996). *Conceptual and empirical analysis of* amae. Symposium presented at the 13th Congress of the International Association for Cross-Cultural Psychology, Montreal.

Kravitz, D. A., & Martin, B. (1986). Ringelmann rediscovered: The original article. *Journal of Personality and Social Psychology, 50*, 936–941.

Latané, B., Williams, K., & Harkins, S. (1979). Many hands make light work: The causes and consequences of social loafing. *Journal of Personality and Social Psychology, 37*, 822–832.

Leung, K. (1997). Negotiation and reward allocation across cultures. In P. C. Earley & M. Erez (Eds.), *New perspectives on international industrial/organizational psychology* (pp. 640–675). San Francisco: New Lexington.

Leung, K., Au, Y. F., Fernandez-Dols, J. M., and Iwawaki, S. (1992). Preference for methods of conflict processing in two collectivist cultures. *International Journal of Psychology, 27*, 195–209.

Markus, H., & Kitayama, S. (1991). Culture and the self: Implications for cognition, emotion and motivation. *Psychological Review, 98*, 224–253.

Milgram, S. (1974). *Obedience to authority: An experimental view.* New York: Harper Row.

Misumi, J. (1985). *The behavioral science of leadership: An interdisciplinary Japanese research program*. Ann Arbor: University of Michigan Press.

Morris, M. W., Williams, K. Y., Leung, K., et al. (1998). Conflict management style: Accounting for cross-national differences. *Journal of International Business Studies, 29,* 711–727.

Peterson, M. F., Peng, T. K., & Smith, P. B. (1999). Using expatriate supervisors to promote cross-border management practice transfer: The experience of a Japanese electronics company. In J. K. Liker, W. M. Fruin, & P. S. Adler (Eds.), *Remade in America: Transplanting and transforming Japanese management systems* (pp. 294–327). New York: Oxford University Press.

Podsiadlowski, A. (1999, July). *Co-operation in cross-cultural teams.* Paper presented at the Seventh European Congress of Psychology, Rome.

Rao, A., & Hashimoto, K. (1996). Intercultural influence: A study of Japanese expatriate managers in Canada. *Journal of International Business Studies, 27,* 443–466.

Rao, A., Hashimoto, K., & Rao, A. (1997). Universal and culturally-specific aspects of managerial influence: A study of Japanese managers. *Leadership Quarterly, 8,* 295–312.

Schwartz, S. H. (1994). Cultural dimensions of values: Towards an understanding of national differences. In U. Kim, H. C. Triandis, C. Kagitcibasi, S. C. Choi, & G. Yoon (Eds.), *Individualism and collectivism: Theory, method and application* (pp. 85–119). Thousand Oaks, CA: Sage.

Shavitt, S., Nelson, M. R., & Yuan, R. M. L. (1997). Exploring cross-cultural differences in cognitive responding to ads. *Advances in Consumer Research, 24,* 245–250.

Sinha, J. B. P. (1997). A cultural perspective on organizational behavior in India. In P. C. Earley & M. Erez (Eds.), *New perspectives on international industrial/organizational psychology* (pp. 53–74). San Francisco: New Lexington.

Smith, P. B., & Bond, M. H. (1998). *Social psychology across cultures* (2nd ed.). Hemel Hempstead, England: Prentice-Hall.

Smith, P. B., Dugan, S., Peterson, M. F., & Leung, K. (1998). Individualism-collectivism and the handling of disagreement: A 23-country study. *International Journal of Intercultural Relations, 22,* 351–367.

Smith, P. B., and Misumi, J. (1989). Japanese management: A sun rising in the West? In C. L. Cooper & I. T. Robertson (Eds.), *International Review of Industrial/Organizational Psychology* (pp. 330–371). Chichester, England: Wiley.

Smith, P. B., Misumi, J., Tayeb, M., Peterson, M. F., & Bond, M. H. (1989). On the generality of leadership styles across cultures. *Journal of Occupational Psychology, 62,* 97–110.

Smith, P. B., & Peterson, M. F. (1988). *Leadership, organizations and culture.* London: Sage.

Smith, P. B., Peterson, M. F., & Schwartz, S. H. (2000). *Cultural values and making sense of work events: A 45-nation study.* Manuscript submitted for publication.

Smith, P. B., & Schwartz, S. H. (1997). Values. In J. W. Berry, C. Kagitcibasi, & M. H. Segall (Eds.), *Handbook of cross-cultural psychology: Vol. 3. Social behavior and applications* (2nd ed., pp. 77–118). Boston: Allyn & Bacon.

Smith, P. B., Wang, Z. M., & Leung, K. (1997). Leadership, decision-making and cultural context: Event management within Chinese joint ventures. *Leadership Quarterly, 8,* 413–431.

Sun, H., & Bond, M. H. (1999). The structure of upward and downward tactics of influence in Chinese organizations. In J. C. Lasry, J. G. Adair, & K. L. Dion (Eds.), *Latest contributions to cross-cultural psychology* (pp. 286–299). Lisse, The Netherlands: Swets & Zeitlinger.

Ting-Toomey, S. (1988). A face negotiation theory. In Y. Y. Kim & W. B. Gudykunst (Ed.), *Theory in intercultural communication* (pp. 213–238). Newbury Park, CA: Sage.

Tinsley, C. H., & Pillutla, M. M. (1998). Negotiating in the United States and Hong Kong. *Journal of International Business Studies, 29,* 711–727.

Tracey, J. B., & Hinkin, T. R. (1998). Transformational leadership or effective managerial practices? *Group and Organization Management, 23,* 220–236.

Trubisky, P., Ting-Toomey, S., & Lin, S. L. (1991). The influence of individualism-collectivism and self-monitoring on conflict styles. *International Journal of Intercultural Relations, 15,* 65–84.

Tse, D. K., Francis, J., & Walls, J. (1994). Cultural differences in conducting intra- and intercultural negotiations: A Sino-Canadian comparison. *Journal of International Business Studies, 25,* 537–555.

Van de Vijver, F., & Leung, K. (1996) Methods and data analysis for cross-cultural research. In J. W. Berry, Y. H. Poortinga, & J. Pandey (Eds.), *Handbook of cross-cultural psychology: Vol. 1. Theoretical and methodological perspectives* (2nd ed., pp. 257–300). Boston: Allyn & Bacon.

Weldon, E., Jehn, K. A., Doucet, L., Chen, X. M., & Wang, Z. M. (1996). *Conflict management in U.S.-Chinese joint ventures.* Unpublished manuscript, University of Indiana, Indianapolis.

Williams, T. P., & Sogon, S. (1984). Group composition and conforming behavior in Japanese students. *Japanese Psychological Research, 26,* 231–234.

19

Social Justice from a Cultural Perspective

KWOK LEUNG & WALTER G. STEPHAN

Justice is a topic that is extremely important in all the social sciences, and perceptions and procedures of justice affect all aspects of our lives, from actions in everyday living, to law and the legal system, to work behaviors and human resource policies, and so on. Consequently, justice, and its close relative morality, has a long history of study in psychology and philosophy, and research on this topic has produced many theories and models of justice relevant to everyday behavior.

In this chapter, Leung and Stephan review the cross-cultural literature on justice, arguing that research on justice must go beyond the Euro-American cultural confines if the field is to develop universal theories of justice. They argue convincingly why justice should be studied cross-culturally, pointing out that cross-cultural research can advance understanding of justice in ways that are not possible with monocultural studies. They also highlight the fact that globalization in diverse domains has drastically increased cross-cultural contact, and that cultural differences in perceptions of justice and fairness may create misunderstandings and conflicts. They delineate well the functional aspects to justice and the differences between universalistic versus particularistic conceptions of justice. They describe the moral basis of justice, highlighting the fact that the central notion of Western liberalism and individual autonomy that is found in the United States may not be found in other cultures, leading to fundamental differences in moral codes and perceptions of fairness. They also present a two-stage model of justice perception that attempts to separate, yet integrate, abstract principles of justice and the specific beliefs that link abstract principles to particular social situations.

The bulk of their review focuses on cross-cultural research in three areas of justice: distributive, procedural, and retributive. They also devote a considerable amount of space to the literature on reactions to perceived injustice. Leung and Stephan do an especially good job of linking many of their descriptions, and much of the research literature, to cultural dimensions such as individualism versus collectivism or power distance. They flesh out well the complex and intricate ways in which culture may play a role in influencing perceptions of fairness and justice, thus providing a platform to understand the basis for intercultural conflict in many arenas of life. The reader will find this review to be one of the most well defined and comprehensive in this area of psychology.

Leung and Stephan's model of justice argues that justice and morality may be both universal and culture specific at the same time, and that abstract constructs and rules interact with specific, context-relevant information to produce morality and decisions about justice. This view is interesting, fascinating, and certainly in the spirit of rapprochement of distinct and, until now, supposedly mutually exclusive dichotomies so commonly perceived in mainstream American psychology. As such, the research possibilities they describe at the end of the chapter represent the next evolution in knowledge in this area, one that is both integrative and incorporative of seemingly opposing forces, a perspective congruent with so many other chapters in this volume. Attempts to achieve these goals will undoubtedly lead to fundamentally different ways of thinking about and doing research in the future as well.

At the same time, Leung and Stephan do an excellent job of reminding us of the practical relevance of the nature and study of justice cross-culturally, especially in terms of its role in the creation of intercultural conflict in an increasingly culturally diverse world. They argue forcefully for the increased understanding and further application of knowledge from continued cross-cultural studies in this area to minimize destructive approaches to intercultural conflict and help turn them into constructive ones. Given the history of human intercultural conflict, one would sincerely hope that such knowledge can indeed transform destruction into construction.

The concern for justice has a long history in human civilizations. In the West, philosophers from Aristotle to Rawls have explored principles of justice from a logical standpoint. In the East, social philosophers from Confucius to Ghandi have articulated models of social conduct that promote justice. In contrast, empirical work on social justice has a much shorter history, with social psychologists starting to investigate the role of justice in everyday behavior about half a century ago.

Despite its youth as a discipline, an impressive array of empirical findings and theoretical statements has been accumulated (for a review, see Sanders & Hamilton, 2001). A major gap in this work, however, is that the majority of the research has been conducted in the United States and western Europe, thus grounding our psychological knowledge of justice in the Western cultural context. To develop universal theories of justice, research on justice must go beyond the Euro-American cultural confines.

In recent years, justice research has gradually begun to take root in other cultural contexts, and a purely Western perspective is giving way to a multicultural perspective (for reviews, see James, 1993; Leung & Morris, 2001; Leung & Stephan, 1998). The purpose of this chapter is to review and integrate what is known about the role of culture in the psychology of social justice and to identify productive avenues for future research in a world that is quickly becoming multicultural and pluralistic.

Why We Should Study Justice Cross-Culturally

Leung and Morris (2001) have provided a number of reasons why cross-cultural research on justice is important. First, cross-cultural research can advance justice theories in ways that are not possible with monocultural studies. The study of justice across a variety of cultures provides us with a more complete inventory of justice norms, allows us to link the salience of justice norms to cultural factors, and makes it possible to establish the boundary conditions under which these justice norms operate. Second, globalization in diverse domains has drastically increased cross-cultural contact, and cultural differences in conceptions of fairness and justice norms may create misunderstandings and unnecessary animosity during such contact.

On an international level, nations often have to work together to cope with major crises, such as regional disputes, environmental hazards, and trade agreements. Within nations, immigration has led to increasing diversity in once-homogenous societies, and the notion of a melting pot has been gradually replaced by multiculturalism.

In the commercial sector, globalization is the preferred business model, and large corporations such as Citicorp, Philips, and Sony have operations around the globe. Their workforces are almost as culturally diverse as the United Nations. Noncommercial organizations and groups are also part of this globalizing trend because many are being affected in similar ways by changes in communication and transportation technologies.

In a world of increasing intercultural contact, even small differences in perceptions of justice may have severe consequences. Positive and effective contact between different racial, ethnic, religious, and cultural groups demands a precise understanding of differences in conceptions of fairness and justice norms.

Functionalist Approach to the Role of Justice

Many scholars have subscribed to the view that, to maintain the proper functioning of a social system, rules of justice must be developed to serve as normative guidelines for its members. A corollary of this argument is that norms of justice should be found in any culture with organized social groups. For instance, societies have to allocate resources in a way that rewards valuable contributions. Basic principles of justice have evolved to serve the function of reward allocation and to avoid the disintegration of the group during this process (e.g., Campbell, 1975; Cook & Messick, 1983; Mikula, 1980).

A slightly different, but still functionalist, view has been promulgated in the relational model of justice proposed by Lind and Tyler (Lind, 1994; Lind & Tyler, 1988; Tyler & Lind, 1992, 2001). In a recent theoretical statement, Lind (1994) suggested that people are confronted with a fundamental dilemma about how much to submit to a group and how much to maintain a self-identity. People are motivated to identify with groups, as well as to maintain a self-identity, but these two goals are very often mutually exclusive. People are in a constant struggle to strike a balance between these two opposing forces. For any social system to be stable, it must evolve solutions to this dilemma.

Lind (1994) argued that the most efficient solution is to rely on principles of justice.

By specifying power-limiting rules about how people should be treated, how decisions should be made, and how outcomes

are to be allocated, rules of justice limit the potential for exploitation and allow people to invest their identify and effort in the group with confidence that they will not be badly used by the group. (p. 30)

In short, the functionalist view assumes that justice rules provide the necessary binding force for social groups that enables individuals to identify with them without fear of negative consequences for the self.

Universalistic versus Particularistic Conception of Justice

The functionalist argument that justice is a universal human concern does not imply that justice is extended universally and uniformly to all humans. In fact, such tragic events as the Holocaust and other acts of genocide make it clear that, under some circumstances, the concern for justice is minimal. Theorists have noted that people tend to draw boundaries outside of which justice principles do not apply (e.g., Deutsch, 1985). According to Opotow (1990), "Moral exclusion occurs when individuals or groups are perceived as outside the boundary in which moral values, rules, and considerations of fairness apply" (p. 1). Moral exclusion has been used to explain why some groups are capable of inflicting extreme atrocities on other groups, such as in the Holocaust (Bar-Tal, 1990) or the dehumanizing treatment of native peoples by European settlers (Berry & Wells, 1994). Moral exclusion is likely to occur if there is intense conflict between two groups, and if the out-group is seen as unconnected to the self.

Moral exclusion represents an extreme form of a particularistic application of justice principles. A more common social boundary that people draw is between the in-group and the out-group. In-groups generally consist of an individual's close friends, relatives, and immediate family members, whereas out-group members include strangers or acquaintances. Different principles of justice may be applied as a function of the group membership of a target. For instance, within the family, the allocation of resources is often based on need, whereas in the workplace, reward allocation is often based on merit.

Culture shapes the particularistic application of justice principles primarily through its impact on the definition of in-groups. In individualistic societies, in-groups are likely to be larger (Wheeler, Reis, & Bond, 1989) and to include a higher proportion of friends, rather than family, than do in-groups in collectivistic cultures (Bellah, Madsen, Sullivan, Swidler, & Tipton, 1985; Hsu, 1953). Individualistic societies are more likely than collectivistic societies to see justice principles as universal and to apply similar justice principles across group boundaries. In contrast, collectivistic societies are more likely to emphasize group boundaries, adopt a contextual view of justice, and apply different justice principles to members of different social groups.

A further boundary can be drawn between humans and other animals. In Asian cultures that are greatly influenced by Buddhist ideals, there is a long tradition of care and concern for animals. Dedicated Buddhists are vegetarians because of their distaste for killing any living creature. They often purchase wild animals and set them free as a way of showing mercy to animals. In contrast, Western cultures rooted in the Judeo-Christian heritage traditionally draw a stronger moral boundary between human beings and other living things. However, these traditional Western patterns of cultural differences may have been mitigated, or perhaps even reversed, by the recent environmentalist movements in the West. Questions of justice for nonhuman animals and for future generations of humans are now common topics of academic and political discussion in the West (see Bazerman, Wade-Bensoni, & Benzoni, 1995). Consistent with this development, cross-cultural studies of animal rights issues (e.g., Bowd & Shapiro, 1993) have found that Americans and Germans are more concerned about cruelty and exploitation toward animals than are people in Japan (Kellert, 1993).

Moral Basis of Justice

When confronted with moral dilemmas, people may invoke abstract principles of justice to guide their choices. The pioneering work of Kohlberg (1981) on moral reasoning investigated how people respond to dilemmas that put norms of justice in conflict with other social norms, such as interpersonal reciprocity and conformity to social conventions. Drawing on Piaget's theory of cognitive development, Kohlberg proposed a stage model for moral reasoning—from an early focus on social convention, to interpersonal responsibilities, and eventually (for some individuals) to abstract principles of justice. This perspective is not without its critics (e.g., Snarey, 1985). Coming from a feminist perspective, Gilligan (1982) rejected this unidirectional stage theory because relatively few women apply abstract justice principles to moral dilemmas. To correct the gender bias inherent in Kohlberg's model, she proposed two distinct "voices" or systems of thought and feeling in moral reasoning, one based on abstract justice principles and one based on interpersonal responsibilities. Justice principles are universalistic and rational, whereas interpersonal responsibilities are particularistic and affect based.

Gilligan's (1982) objection to a universal, unidirectional stage theory has been supported by subsequent research; however, culture may actually be a more potent moderator of moral reasoning modality than gender. Dien (1982) argued that morality in traditional Chinese thought is primarily based on *jen*, which is concerned with benevolence and human-heartedness. Ma (1997) concluded from his empirical work on moral reasoning among Chinese that, because of the influence of jen, moral judgments of Chinese are affective in nature and are highly responsive to the suffering of others. These studies suggest that people in collectivistic cultures are oriented toward interpersonal responsibilities when making moral judgments.

In a cross-cultural program of research on the moral reasoning of Americans and Hindu Indians, Miller and colleagues obtained results consistent with the views of Dien (1982) and Ma (1997). Research in the United States has shown that interpersonal responsibilities are often seen as personal decisions rather than moral issues (e.g., Higgins, Power, & Kohlberg, 1984), whereas research in India by Miller and colleagues showed that interpersonal obligations are typically regarded as moral issues (Miller, Bersoff, & Harwood, 1990; Miller & Luthar, 1989; Shweder, Mahapahtra, & Miller, 1987). Miller and Bersoff (1992) studied how American and Indian students reacted to a situation in which justice was in conflict with interpersonal responsibilities. Compared with Americans, Indians were more likely to yield to interpersonal responsibilities than to more abstract justice concerns. When asked to justify their choices, Americans mentioned fairness and rights more frequently, whereas Indians mentioned role-related obligations and nonresponsiveness to others' needs more.

Consistent results have also come from research on the Japanese, another group that emphasizes the interdependent self. Compared with Americans, Japanese gave greater weight to role obligations in judgments of responsibility (Hagiwara, 1992; Hamilton & Sanders, 1992). Ohbuchi, Fukushima, and Tedeschi (1999) found that, in resolving a dispute, Americans regarded a justice goal (to restore fairness) as more important and a relationship goal (to maintain a positive relationship with the other party) as less important than did Japanese.

Farh, Earley, and Lin (1997) approached this problem from a different angle, but obtained results that are consistent with the findings reported above. Farh et al. reasoned that, because of Confucian influence, role-based prescriptions were more important than justice concerns in traditional China. However, as China began to urbanize and industrialize, role-based relationships gradually give way to instrumental exchanges and a heightened concern for individual rights. Based on this logic, they hypothesized and confirmed, that in an organizational setting, justice exerted a stronger effect on organizational citizenship behaviors among those who were modern than among those who were traditional. In other words, for Chinese who were traditional, the effects of perceived justice on organizational citizenship behaviors were limited. If we equate traditionalism with collectivism and modernity with individualism, the findings of Farh et al. parallel the findings from the studies reviewed above.

The framework proposed by Miller (1994) can be used to organize the findings in this area. She argues that neither Kohlberg nor Gilligan take sufficient account of the role of culture. Drawing on the notion that many Western psychological models are based on an independent, as contrasted with an interdependent, self-concept (Markus & Kitayama, 1991; Triandis, 1989), Miller argues that the U.S. moral code reflects the central notion of Western liberalism that individual autonomy is more fundamental and more natural than social obligations. From this premise, a moral concern based on abstract, universal justice principles that limit infringements on the liberty of other persons follows as a necessary derivation, whereas a moral concern with specific role-based obligations to other persons does not (see also Dien, 1982). In contrast, the Hindu Indian moral code reflects the notion of *dharma*, which denotes both moral duty and inherent character (Kakar, 1978; Marriott, 1990). One's dharma depends on one's social role and the situations one enters, and meeting social role expectations is an important way to realize one's true nature. From this premise, it follows that moral concerns will extend to a broad set of role-based interpersonal obligations. Miller's arguments apply equally well to Chinese and warrant the conclusion that the moral basis of justice principles varies across cultures and assumes a more interpersonal orientation in collectivist cultures.

Two-Stage Model of Justice Perception

A strong version of the functionalist view argues that basic principles of justice should be codified as norms in all societies in which the organized sharing of resources has extended beyond the family. Morris and Leung (Leung & Morris, 2001; Morris & Leung, 2000; Morris, Leung, Ames, & Lickel, 1999) have proposed a model for justice judgments that makes a distinction between abstract principles of justice and the specific beliefs that link abstract principles to particular social situations.

To illustrate this model, consider the case of resource allocation. Abstract principles applying to distributive norms appear to be present in all cultures. For instance, the equity rule, which prescribes a proportional relationship between inputs and outcomes, seems to be a cultural universal. However, the more specific beliefs that determine how the equity rule is applied vary from one culture to another. For example, it is well known that Japanese are more likely to regard seniority as a form of input for determining a group member's share of a reward than are Americans (e.g., Ouchi & Jaeger, 1978).

A schematic representation of this model is presented in Figure 19.1. When people enter a social context and have to decide what is fair in this context, they will first appraise the social situation to identify the appropriate principles of justice. They will then select the specific criteria associated with this principle to assess the fairness of the situation. The functionalist view of justice argues that general principles of justice are common across cultures, whereas the criteria for applying these principles may vary across cultures. In this model, culture affects the interpretation of the social situation and the selection of justice principles, as well as the criteria for applying these principles.

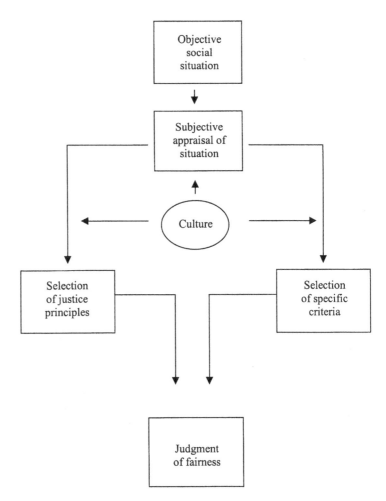

Figure 19.1
A General Model for
Justice Perception

This framework is applied throughout the chapter to organize our discussion.

Tripartite Conceptualization of Justice

A tripartite conception of justice is widely accepted in the literature. The three basic types of justice are distributive, procedural, and retributive justice. Distributive justice is concerned with the fairness of the distribution of outcomes; procedural justice with the fairness of procedures used to make decisions regarding outcomes; and retributive justice with the fairness of the punishment meted out to wrongdoers. We review the impact of culture on each type of justice in the following sections.

Distributive Justice

Judgments of the fairness of the distribution of a resource depend largely on three issues. First, one must decide on the reference group with which one compares one's share because social comparison processes provide the basis for judgments of distributive justice (e.g., Adams, 1965). Second, appropriate allocation rules must be chosen for distributing the resource. Third, one must decide on the relevant and legitimate inputs and rewards (Komorita & Leung, 1985).

Social Comparison Processes

Theories of distributive justice regard social comparison processes as pivotal in judgments of justice (e.g., Adams, 1963). Early theories, guided by Festinger's (1954) theory of social comparison, suggested that people choose similar others for judging the fairness of their share of a resource. For instance, the classic study by Stouffer and associates (Stouffer, Lunsdaine, et al., 1949; Stouffer, Suchman, DeVinney, Star, & Williams, 1949) showed that African-American soldiers in the northern United States were less satisfied than those in the South because they compared themselves primarily to civilian African-Americans, who were better off in the North than the South.

Leung, Smith, Wang, and Sun (1996) examined the social comparison processes that determine justice judgments among local employees of international joint ventures in China. The salary of local employees was dramatically lower than that of expatriate managers in these joint ventures despite similar responsibilities. However, these local employees were financially better off than people who had similar jobs in state-owned enterprises. Leung et al. (1996) found that, in these joint ventures, comparison with other local employees was related to job satisfaction, but comparison with expatriate managers was not. Furthermore, the Chinese employees did not perceive the astronomical salaries earned by expatriate managers as unfair. A simple explanation of these findings is that Chinese managers did not regard the expatriate managers as an appropriate group for social comparison. Local employees were aware of the fact that these expatriate managers came from developed nations in which salaries were much higher.

However, referent groups in the social comparison process may shift over time. When the survey of Leung et al. (1996) described above was repeated in similar international joint ventures in China after 3 years of rapid economic and social change, the dynamics underlying the social comparison processes had changed (Leung, Wang, & Smith, in press). Unlike the previous results, comparisons with expatriate managers were now related to lower job satisfaction, and local employees regarded the high salary of the expatriate managers as very unfair. Leung et al. (in press) argued that a plausible reason for the growing perception of injustice with regard to the high pay of expatriate mangers was that, unlike the earlier situation, many locals now had extensive contact with expatriates. This contact may have led locals to see themselves as similar to the expatriate managers in their levels of skills and knowledge. In other words, the increased contact led the locals to engage in direct social comparison with

the expatriates, resulting in a heightened sense of injustice.

The status-value approach to distributive justice proposed by Berger, Zelditch, Anderson, and Cohen (1972) operates at a group level and focuses on comparisons to generalized others and nonsimilar referent groups. To simplify the discussion, two groups are assumed to exist. One group, the dominant group, has a higher socioeconomic status than the other, the subordinate group. An example of this situation would be European Americans and African Americans in the United States. When members of the subordinate group evaluate the fairness of their outcomes, equity theory suggests that they will compare their shares of the outcomes to those of similar others. However, the status-value approach suggests that they will also compare themselves to the dominant group. Because the dominant group is generally better off than the subordinate group, this social comparison process will result in a sense of injustice regardless of the specific characteristics of the inputs and outcomes of individual minority members.

A number of factors may affect the tendency to compare with the dominant group. For instance, the tendency to make comparisons to the dominant group and the concomitant perception of injustice may be stronger in cultures characterized by low power distance (egalitarian) values than by high power distance (hierarchical) values. The latter values give legitimacy to inequalities of power and privilege, including in some cases the greater power of the dominant social group. Perceived legitimacy may also moderate the perception of injustice by minority group members as they may not always regard their low outcomes as unfair. For instance, Japanese Americans were subject to internment during World War II, whereas German Americans were not targeted. Nagata (1990) found that nisei (second-generation) Japanese Americans reacted less negatively to the internment than did sansei (third-generation) Japanese Americans. One plausible explanation for this difference is that the nisei regarded the internment as less illegitimate than the sansei because the sansei were more attuned to their individual rights as Americans.

Legitimate Inputs

The choice of what is considered to be a relevant input can greatly affect the distribution of resources when a distributive rule other than equality is used. People often disagree on what constitutes a legitimate input (Komorita &

Leung, 1985), and this problem is especially important in a cross-cultural context because the legitimacy of inputs may vary across cultures. Komorita (1984) has distinguished between task-relevant and task-irrelevant inputs. *Task-relevant inputs* refer to attributes that are directly related to performance, such as time spent on a task. *Task-irrelevant inputs* refer to attributes that bear no direct relationship to performance, such as seniority or education level. The perceived relationship between various forms of inputs and performance may be affected by culture, and the influence is probably strongest for task-irrelevant inputs. Several cultural dimensions that may affect this link are discussed below.

In collectivist societies, loyalty to an ingroup is emphasized, and seniority is important because a long tenure signals a high level of commitment to a group. Evidence for this argument comes from the extensive literature on Japanese management, which points to a larger premium placed on seniority in Japanese than in American organizations (e.g., Ouchi & Jaeger, 1978). Similarly, Hundley and Kim (1997) also reported that, in judging the fairness of pay levels, Americans put more emphasis on performance, whereas Koreans emphasized seniority and educational background more.

In societies with high power distance, in which social hierarchies are more accepted, people at the top level of organizations enjoy more privileges and deference than their counterparts in societies with low power distance. Status and position are more likely to be regarded as a legitimate input in resource allocations in societies with high power distance than in societies with low power distance (see Mendonca & Kanungo, 1994, for a similar argument).

Parsons and Shils (1951) have contrasted cultures in their relative emphasis on ascribed versus achieved attributes of individuals. *Ascribed attributes* are typically acquired by birth. Examples include race and gender. In contrast, *achieved attributes* are those earned on the basis of individual effort. In their analysis, China and India were regarded as ascription oriented, whereas the United States was seen as achievement oriented. Task-irrelevant inputs such as social class and gender are more likely to be used as legitimate inputs in ascription-oriented than in achievement-oriented societies.

The assumption of *human malleability*, which refers to the belief that personality, ability, and performance can change over time

(C. S. Chen & Uttal, 1988), may vary across cultures. In a program of research on the academic achievement of American, Japanese, and Chinese students, it was found that, compared with American students, the Chinese and Japanese students regarded effort as more important than ability in determining academic performance (Stevenson et al., 1990). It is probable that Chinese and Japanese students see a stronger link between effort and academic performance than American students. This difference may indicate that Chinese and Japanese regard the intellectual and personality traits related to academic achievement as being more malleable than Americans. It is well known that both actual performance and effort are regarded as legitimate bases for reward in educational settings (e.g., Weiner & Kukla, 1970). The work of Stevenson et al. suggests that effort may receive a higher weight in determining the distribution of a reward in cultures in which there is a strong assumption of malleability, such as China and Japan.

Choice of Allocation Rules

Earlier work on distributive justice focused on the proportionality rule of distribution. For instance, equity theory (Adams, 1963, 1965; Homans, 1961) stipulates that rewards should be proportional to contributions. Two additional allocation norms were included in subsequent research, equality and need (e.g., Deutsch, 1975). It is generally agreed that *equity* (distributing resources on the basis of inputs and outcomes) is conducive to productivity. *Equality* (distributing resources equally regardless of inputs) is conducive to harmony. And, *need* (distributing resources according to need) is conducive to individual well-being (e.g., Deutsch, 1975; Leung & Park, 1986). Culture is known to affect the choice of allocation rules (for reviews, see James, 1993; Leung, 1988, 1997). Although resources can assume tangible, as well as nontangible, forms (Foa & Foa, 1974), cross-cultural research has been predominantly concerned with material resources.

Individualism-collectivism has been the dominant theoretical framework for organizing the empirical results on this topic. This tradition began with the research of Leung and Bond (1982), who argued that, because of the emphasis on solidarity, harmony, and cohesion in collectivistic cultures, the equality rule is generally preferred. In contrast, individualism is related to the preference for the equity norm because equity is compatible with the emphasis on productivity, competition, and self-gain in individualist cultures. Indeed, Leung and Bond (1982) found that Chinese college students allocated a reward in a more egalitarian fashion than did American college students, although the data also showed that Chinese tended to see a smaller difference in the contributions of group members, which may have led to a more egalitarian allocation. This study provided initial support for the relationship between collectivism and the preference for equality.

Bond, Leung, and Wan (1982) examined the relationship between collectivism and the allocation of two types of reward, namely, *task reward* (assigning the recipient a better grade and being willing to work with the recipient again in the future) and *socioemotional reward* (being willing to be friends with the recipient). Consistent with the work of Leung and Bond (1982), the Chinese participants showed a more egalitarian tendency in allocating both types of reward than did the Americans. Kashima, Siegal, Tanaka, and Isaka (1988) compared the distributive behavior of Japanese and Australian students and reported a similar pattern of cultural differences. Japanese participants regarded an equal division as fairer and were more willing to change to an equality rule than were the Australians.

Drawing on the individualism-collectivism framework (e.g., Hofstede, 1980; Triandis, 1972), Leung and Bond (1984) argued that the group membership of the recipient should affect the choice of allocation rules in collectivist cultures. Collectivists should favor a *generosity rule* (the tendency to allocate a generous share of a reward to others) with in-group members by employing either the equity or the equality norms, depending on their own inputs. The equality rule is apt to be used when their own input or contribution is high, and the equity rule is apt to be used when their own input is low. With out-group members, however, collectivists should act like individualists and use the equity rule. Leung and Bond (1984) obtained results in support of this complicated relationship between collectivism and distributive behavior, as have several other studies.

Mahler, Greenberg, and Hayashi (1981) found that, in allocating a profit between two carpenters (i.e., out-group members) who invested together to buy a house, Japanese and American participants showed no cultural differences, suggesting that out-group members were being treated the same in reward allocation by individualists and collectivists. Marin (1981) found that in allocating a reward between two strangers who worked together in a psychological experiment, Colombian participants used the equity norm more than did Americans. Aral and Sunar (1977) found that, in allocating a reward between two architects who designed a project together, Turkish participants also used the equity norm more than the Americans. Leung (1988) concluded that, because these studies involved out-group members, collectivists preferred the equity rule in distributing the reward.

The effect of collectivism on distributive behavior was examined directly by Leung and Iwawaki (1988) in a comparison of American college students with Japanese and Korean college students, who were thought to be collectivistic (Hofstede, 1980, 1983). Only the collectivism level of Japanese and Americans was measured because the Korean data were collected before the individual-level individualism-collectivism scale of Hui (1984) was finalized. Surprisingly, the three cultural groups did not show any significant differences in their allocations. Contrary to Hofstede's (1980) results, Japanese and American participants were similar in their individualism-collectivism levels. To explain these results, Leung and Iwawaki argued that the lack of differences in the distributive behaviors of Japanese and American participants was due to the similar levels of individualism-collectivism among these students. On the other hand, because the collectivism levels of Korean participants were not measured, it is not possible to link their distributive behavior to individualism-collectivism scores at the individual level. It may be speculated that Korean students, like the Japanese students, were more individualistic than would be expected on the basis of Hofstede's (1980, 1983) results. If it is assumed that the Korean students in this sample were indeed individualistic, it makes sense that their distributive behavior resembled that of the individualistic American students.

In 1995, C. C. Chen asked employees from mainland China and from the United States to allocate several rewards among the employees of a manufacturing company. Contrary to expectations, Chinese participants actually preferred the equity solution more strongly than the Americans. C. C. Chen attributed this unexpected result to the fact that China was shifting toward a market economy rapidly. The concern for productivity outweighed the concern for in-group harmony, which led the Chinese to prefer equity to equality. However, Leung (1997) argued that a simpler interpretation is that the situation depicted in the study involved an outgroup situation, and the preference for equity by the Chinese participants is consistent with the argument made by Leung and Bond (1984).

The individualism-collectivism framework is not without problems in accommodating the findings of cross-cultural research on distributive behavior. Marin (1985) compared the allocation of Indonesian and American participants and found that, across three types of relationships between the allocator and the recipients (strangers, friends, or relatives), no cultural differences were detected, and both groups preferred equity to equality. Kim, Park, and Suzuki (1990) asked Korean, Japanese, and American participants to allocate grades among classmates on the completion of a group project. In contrast to the results of Leung and Iwawaki (1988), Koreans followed the equality rule more closely than did Japanese or Americans. However, similar to the results of Leung and Iwawaki (1988), Americans and Japanese did not differ in their distributive behavior. The conflicting results of Leung and Iwawaki (1988) and Kim et al. (1990) obviously need an explanation.

A more disturbing finding for the individualism-collectivism framework comes from a study by Hui, Triandis, and Yee (1991), who compared the distributive behavior of Chinese and Americans. Consistent with the results of Leung and Bond (1984), Hui et al. found that Chinese participants followed the generosity rule and allocated a larger share to the other person than did American participants when the reward to be divided was fixed. They used the equality norm when their input was high and the equity norm when their input was low. In addition, Chinese participants showed a stronger preference for equality than American participants when the recipient was an ingroup member. When the reward was unlimited, Chinese were more likely to follow the equality rule than were Americans. This pattern would be expected because, if the reward is unlimited, there is no need to sacrifice one's share to give the other person a larger share. One can simply give the other person a larger share without reducing the share allocated to oneself.

One interesting aspect of the study by Hui et al. (1991) is that collectivism was measured by the individualism-collectivism scale developed by Hui (1984). This feature allowed Hui

et al. to evaluate whether collectivism was related to the observed cultural differences in distributive behavior. If collectivism is indeed the explanatory variable underlying the cultural differences, it should be related directly to the observed cultural differences. One way to test this idea is to treat collectivism as a covariate in an analysis of covariance. When the collectivism of the two cultural groups was equated statistically, the cultural differences in the use of equality actually disappeared in the case of unlimited resources. Collectivism was indeed an adequate explanation in this condition. However, in the case of limited resources, the cultural differences in allocation still remained significant after collectivism was equated. In other words, the tendency for Chinese participants to follow the generosity rule was not explained adequately by collectivism. Hui et al. (1991) thus concluded that the individualism-collectivism framework may be too global and general to explain specific cross-cultural differences in distributive behavior.

Contextual Model

It is quite clear that equity is generally preferred in individualistic cultures, but the relationship between culture and reward allocation in collectivistic cultures seems complex and is qualified by many situational variables (James, 1993). The individualism-collectivism framework alone is unable to provide a coherent account of the empirical evidence. To overcome these difficulties, Leung (1997) proposed the *contextual model* as an alternative; this model assumes that culture interacts with a number of situational variables to determine the allocation rule used. A goal-directed view of distributive behavior is also assumed (e.g., Deutsch, 1975; Leung & Park, 1986). The immediate antecedent of allocation preferences is hypothesized to be interactional goals, which mediate the effects of culture. Because individualism-collectivism is not the immediate determinant of allocation behavior, its failure as a direct explanation of cross-cultural differences in reward allocation can be accommodated in this model. See Figure 19.2 for a schematic representation of this model.

In the contextual model, it is assumed that situational factors may sometimes override the effects of culture. For instance, Murphy-Berman, Berman, Singh, Pacharui, and Kumar (1984) and Berman, Murphy-Berman, and Singh (1985) found that the need norm was followed more closely by Indian than by American parti-

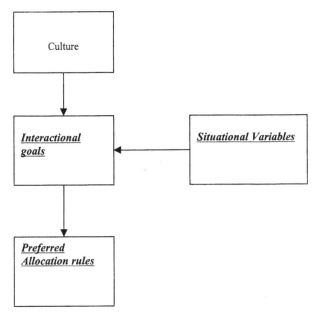

Figure 19.2
The Contextual Model

cipants. Leung (1988) suggested that, because resources are scarce in India, ensuring the well-being of group members is a more salient goal than maintaining a harmonious relationship, leading to the salience of the need norm rather than the equality norm.

There are two situational variables that are thought to interact with culture to affect the allocation rule chosen. The relationship between the allocators and the recipients will affect the choice of interactional goal. Three types of relationships are possible. First, with potential in-group members or members of a peripheral in-group, maintenance of harmonious relationships is a salient goal, and equality will generally be favored. In line with this argument, collectivists are shown to prefer equality over equity (e.g., Kashima et al., 1988). Furthermore, Hui et al. (1991), as well as Leung and Iwawaki (1988), found a positive correlation between collectivism and the preference for equality and a negative correlation between collectivism and the preference for equity. Similarly, Triandis, Leung, Villareal, and Clack (1985) have shown a positive relationship between individualism (or more precisely, idiocentrism, as the construct was used as an individual attribute in this study) and adherence to the equity rule. Second, in situations involving core in-group members, collectivists will regard the enhancement of harmony as a salient interactional goal, and the generosity rule is likely to be used to

allocate a larger share of the reward to the other person (Leung & Bond, 1984). Third, with out-group members, collectivists will follow the equity rule because the concern for harmony is not a salient goal.

A second situational variable is the role assumed by the allocator. There are at least two such roles. The first one is a dual role in which the allocator is also a recipient. The other role is a supervisory role in which the allocator is responsible for allocating resources among a group of recipients. This role often occurs in work settings in which a superior has to allocate resources to subordinates. It is proposed that collectivists who are placed in the allocator/recipient dual role are under the influence of the harmony motive and will show a stronger preference for either the equality rule or the generosity rule. In fact, in studies in which participants were placed in the dual role, the results are consistent with the predictions of the individualism-collectivism framework (e.g., Hui et. al., 1991; Leung & Bond, 1984). In contrast, when collectivists assume the supervisory role, the harmony motive should be less salient because the allocator is not tied to the recipients in a zero-sum manner. Thus, the allocation rule adopted reflects the expectations the allocator has for the work group, rather than the allocator's personal relationship with the recipients. In a work setting, the dominant goal is likely to be productivity, and collectivists should emphasize it as much as individualists. Thus, in a work setting, collectivists should not display a stronger preference for equality than individualists. As noted above, Marin (1985) asked participants to allocate a reward for two recipients and found that Indonesians showed a stronger preference for equity than Americans. In 1995, C. C. Chen asked participants to role-play the president of a company and to allocate several rewards for the employees of the company. In this context, Chinese participants were found to show a stronger preference for equity than did Americans.

*Procedural Justice:
Perceptions of Fair
Process, Culture, and
Procedural Preferences*

Procedural justice is concerned with the fairness of the procedures and processes used in decision making. The original work in this area was conducted in legal settings and focused on conflict resolution procedures (Thibaut & Walker, 1975, 1978). The major finding that emerged from this work was that people prefer conflict resolution procedures that grant the disputants process control, but place the decision in the hands of an impartial third party (outcome control). A common example of a procedure embodying these two characteristics is the adversary adjudication system used in English-speaking countries. In this procedure, both sides present evidence and arguments in favor of their case and challenge the other side in front of disinterested third parties, the judge and the jury, who will decide on the outcome of the case. The desire for process control reflects the wish of the disputants to argue their case in ways they prefer, and their willingness to relinquish outcome control arises from the dreadful thought of a severe conflict dragging on indefinitely.

This reasoning is sensible except that there exists a simple alternative explanation for these empirical findings. Because the adversary procedure is the legal procedure employed in the United States, Americans may simply be displaying a preference for the status quo and may not be influenced by the psychological considerations postulated by Thibaut and Walker (1975, 1978).

To rule out this plausible hypothesis, Lind, Erickson, Friedland, and Dickenberger (1978) extended this line of work to continental Europe, where inquisitorial procedures are the legal norm. In inquisitorial procedures, the judge plays a more active role in investigating cases, thus reducing the level of process control accorded to the disputants. Consistent with Thibaut and Walker's (1975, 1978) theory, Lind et al. (1978) found that adversary adjudication was also strongly preferred by French and German participants, despite their unfamiliarity with this procedure.

Thibaut and Walker's (1975, 1978) theory has fared well in western Europe and the United States, but is inconsistent with a body of literature accumulated by anthropologists working in other countries. Nader and Todd (1978) and Gulliver (1979) argue that, in societies in which interpersonal relationships are stable and ongoing, procedures that allow for compromise, such as mediation and negotiation, are preferred. There is not much evidence for the popularity of adversarial procedures in the anthropological literature. For instance, mediation is strongly preferred in Japan (Kawashima, 1963), China (Doo, 1973; J. A. Wall & Blum, 1991), and Turkey (Starr, 1978).

To integrate these two bodies of literature, Leung (1987) drew on the individualism-collectivism framework and proposed that the preference for adversary adjudication is stronger in individualistic than in collectivistic societies. Thibaut and Walker's (1975) theory receives strong support in individualist societies, but contradictory results abound in collectivist societies. In support of this reasoning, Leung (1987) found that Chinese participants from Hong Kong showed a stronger preference for mediation and negotiation than did Americans. These cultural differences were due to the perception that these two procedures were thought to lead to animosity reduction by the Chinese. Morris, Leung, and Sethi (1995) replicated this pattern with Chinese and American participants. In a similar vein, Kozan and Ergin (1998) found that, in a prisoner's dilemma game, Turkish college students were more likely to use an intermediary, whereas U.S. students were more likely to engage in direct communication.

Subsequent work on procedural preferences has broadened the choice of procedures to include informal ones. Leung, Au, Fernández-Dols, and Iwawaki (1992) compared preferences for an enlarged set of procedures across four countries: Spain, Japan, the Netherlands, and Canada. They reported that the Spanish and Japanese—the collectivists—were more likely to prefer negotiation and compliance, which are harmony-inducing procedures. In contrast, the Dutch and the Canadians—the individualists—were more likely to prefer threat and accusation in handling a dispute. Bierbrauer (1994) compared German citizens with Kurdish and Lebanese asylum seekers in their preferences for both formal and informal dispute resolution procedures. Consistent with Leung's hypothesis (1987), the Kurds and Lebanese, who are more collectivistic than the Germans, were less willing to use state law to resolve a conflict with family members or acquaintances than were the Germans. Furthermore, the Kurds and Lebanese regarded restoring harmony as a more important goal, and following legal rules as a less important goal, than did the Germans. Bierbrauer also found that the Kurds and Lebanese accepted the norms of religion and tradition as more legitimate, and state law as less legitimate, as a basis for conflict resolution than did the Germans. In sum, these studies show that individualists are more likely to engage in direct confrontation in resolving a conflict, whereas collectivists prefer procedures that preserve the harmony between the disputants.

Although it is clear that cultures differ in their procedural preferences, research shows that the same general principles determine people's perceptions of procedural justice across cultures. For instance, the positive relationship between perceived process control permitted by a procedure and the perceived fairness of the procedure that Thibaut and Walker (1975, 1978) first identified has been replicated in many countries other than the United States, including Britain, France, Germany (Lind et al., 1978), Hong Kong (Leung, 1987), Japan, and Spain (Leung et al., 1992). The consequences of perceived procedural justice also seem to be similar across cultures. For instance, perceptions of procedural justice are related to positive evaluation of outcomes and decision makers in the United States (Lind & Tyler, 1988; Tyler & Beis, 1990) and in Hong Kong and mainland China (Leung et al., 1993; Leung, Chiu, & Au, 1996; Leung & Li, 1990). In a similar vein, Pearce, Bigley, and Branyiczki (1998) reported that perceived justice is related positively to organizational commitment and trust in co-workers in Lithuania.

Culture and Conflict Styles

People in different cultures display different preferences for conflict resolution styles. The major model in this area is the dual-concern model, which posits five basic styles of conflict resolution (Pruitt & Carnevale, 1993). These five styles represent different combinations of high-versus-low concern for the self and high-versus-low concern for the other: *Collaboration* is a style that is high in concern for both the self and the other; *competition* is high in concern for the self and low in concern for the other; *compromise* is moderate in concern for both the self and the other; *accommodation* is high in concern for the other's interests and low in concern for the self; while *withdrawal* is low in concern for both the self and the other.

Cultural differences in conflict style may lead to perceptions of injustice. For instance, people from cultures that emphasize high concern for the outcomes of others are particularly likely to feel unjustly treated when negotiating with people from cultures that show high concern for the outcomes of the self. Specifically, if people from cultures that prefer accommodative styles of conflict resolution are in conflict with another cultural group that prefers competitive styles, they are likely to see the competitive behavior of the other group as hostile and unfair. Another mismatch in styles that may result in perceived injustice occurs when people who prefer to collaborate encounter people from a culture in which conflict avoidance is the preferred style. Those with a collaborative mindset are likely to regard avoidance as a rebuff to their openness and will feel frustrated by the lack of resolution of the conflict.

The problem of style mismatch can be illustrated by negotiations between the Israelis (an individualist group) and the Arabs (a collectivistic group), with both sides accusing the other side of being unfair. According to Griefat and Katriel (1989), Arabs approach interpersonal relations using *musayara*, an interpersonal style that involves an array of politeness strategies that emphasize mutuality, cooperation, respect, concern, indirectness, subtlety, effusiveness, allusion, and metaphor. In contrast, the Israelis often use an interpersonal approach that relies on *dugri*, which involves direct, explicit, forceful, assertive, unembellished speech. These contrasting styles may interfere with negotiations and lead to dissatisfaction with both the process and the outcomes of negotiations (for more details, see Leung & Stephan, 2000).

Current empirical data show that conflict styles are influenced by individualism-collectivism. People from individualistic cultures tend to favor styles of conflict resolution that are high in concern for the self, while collectivists are more likely to prefer styles that are high in concern for in-group members. When the others are members of an out-group, however, people from collectivistic cultures may be as concerned with their own outcomes as are people from individualistic cultures. Several studies indicate the people from Latin American collectivistic cultures (Brazil, Mexico) show a greater preference for styles of conflict resolution that are high in concern for others (collaboration and accommodation) than people from an individualistic culture, the United States (Gabrielidis, Stephan, Ybarra, Pearson, & Villareal, 1997; Pearson & Stephan, 1988).

Studies that have not used the dual-concern model have also supported the general hypothesis that people in collectivistic cultures prefer styles of conflict resolution that are high in concern for others. Elsayed-Ekhouly and Buda (1996) reported that Arab executives used avoiding more and dominating less than did U.S. executives. Ohbuchi and Takahashi (1994) reported that, in handling a conflict, Japanese were likely to use avoidance and indirect methods (suggesting, ingratiation, impression management, and appeasing), whereas Americans tended to adopt direct methods (persuasion, bargaining, and compromise). Compared with Americans, Japanese were also less likely to reveal themselves to others whose actions had affected them negatively in daily life. Chung and Lee (1989) reported that Japanese and Koreans were less likely to employ confrontational modes in conflict resolution than were Americans. Ting-Toomey et al. (1991) reported that Americans were more likely to use a competitive style, and less likely to use an avoiding style, than were Japanese, Koreans, mainland Chinese, and Taiwanese. Morris, Williams, et al. (1999) found that Chinese managers relied on avoidance more than managers from the United States, India, and the Philippines, whereas U.S. managers used competition more than managers from China, India, and the Philippines. In 1994, J. L. Graham, Mintu, and Rodgers found that, across eight countries, collectivism was correlated with a negotiation style characterized by cooperativeness and willingness to attend to the other party's needs. Kozan (1997) described the conflict-handling behavior of collectivists as a harmony model and the competitive mode favored by individualists as a confrontational model.

The in-group–out-group distinction is highlighted in the work of Leung (1988), who discovered that, compared with Americans, Chinese were less contentious in disputes with in-group members and more contentious in disputes with out-group members. Probst, Carnevale, and Triandis (1999) reported a similar pattern in a social dilemma study.

Culture-Specific Procedures for Conflict Resolution

Some cultures may engage in specific forms of conflict resolution procedures that other cultural groups may find difficult to comprehend, if not unfair. A good example is the Korean conflict cycle described by Cho and Park (1998), which involves a combination of harmony maintenance and confrontation. There are four steps in this cycle: context building, smoothing, forcing, and tension releasing. In context building, the goal is to establish a common ground between the disputants by sharing information and building an emotional bond. In smoothing, the focus is on finding a solution that does not hurt the other side's feelings. Forcing involves the use of formal and informal power to coerce the other side to yield. Appealing to higher authorities is common in this stage because of the emphasis on high power distance in Korea. Finally, in tension release, the major goal is to rebuild the damaged relationship between the disputants. Drinking and singing are common vehicles to achieve this goal. It is clear that this conflict cycle is very different from the competitive stance often assumed by Americans in conflict situations, which usually does not involve much sharing, reliance on powerful figures to coerce the other side, or the release of tension after the conflict has been settled (J. Wall & Stark, 1998).

Another example of a culture-specific conflict resolution technique is *ahimsa*, which is the procedure used by Gandhi against the British colonial regime (Sinha, 1987). Ahimsa is based on Buddhism, Jainism, Hinduism, Sanskrit, and other Indian traditions and involves a unique conceptualization of procedural justice. Central concepts in the Western approach, such as voice, are understood in a very different manner. Ahimsa emphasizes *satyagraha*, a force born of truth and love, and involves two basic principles, *maha karuna* (great compassion) and *maha prajna* (great wisdom). This approach assumes a strong emotional attachment and love toward all beings and a general refusal to harm others. Guided by these two principles, three steps of conflict resolution may be pursued. The first step involves persuading the other disputing party through reasoning. If this tactic fails, self-suffering follows, the aim of which is to arouse a feeling of guilt in the opponent and to put the opponent in a morally disadvantageous situation by causing them to inflict harm on "helpless" and nonviolent individuals. If both of these tactics fail, nonviolent coercion such as noncooperation, civil disobedience, boycotts, and fasting are adopted. The ahimsa technique is based on a fundamental belief that only peace, not violence, can stop violence.

From a psychological point of view, the ahimsa technique suggests that moral concern is critical in shaping people's sense of justice and approaches to conflict resolution. Obviously, the concern for morality in a conflict situation is not unique to Indians, but Western research on justice and conflict resolution has not investigated the effect of moral concerns on perceptions of justice and conflict resolution techniques in a systematic manner.

The above literature centers on conflict resolution procedures, but procedural justice is also relevant to other practices, such as recruitment and promotion in the workplace. Unfortunately, there is little cross-cultural work on procedural justice beyond conflict resolution procedures. One exception is provided by Steiner and Gilliland (1996), who found that French students regarded graphology (handwriting analysis) and personality tests as more fair and effective as selection tools in organizations than did American students. In contrast, American students regarded interviews, resumés, biographical information, and tests to be more fair and effective. The interesting point here is that different procedures may be regarded as more or less fair in different cultures. Graphology appears to be a culture-specific procedure that is popular in France, but would be regarded as unfair by Americans. Future cross-cultural work on procedural preferences should definitely move beyond conflict resolution procedures.

Power Distance and Third Parties in Conflict Resolution

Some conflict resolution procedures involve a third party, such as arbitration and mediation. The role of the third party ranges from advisory and facilitating in mediation to decision making in adjudication. Cultural groups differ in what they regard as appropriate and legitimate actions on the part of the third party. Perceptions of injustice may arise if third parties deviate from the roles expected of them in a given culture. Current research has shown that the cultural dimension of power distance is relevant to the role of the third party. In societies with high power distance, the intervention of a high-status third party in a dispute is regarded as more legitimate than in societies with low power distance.

For instance, court litigants in Japan, a high power distance culture, look to the judge to provide facts about the case and ultimate justice, whereas in the United States, a low power distance society, litigants are inclined to rely on their own efforts to argue for their case (Benjamin, 1975; Tanabe, 1963). Tse, Francis, and Walls (1994) found that, compared to Canadian executives, executives from China were more likely to consult their superiors in a conflict. Chung and Lee (1989) found that Japanese and Koreans were more likely to appeal to authorities to resolve a conflict than were Americans. Finally, in a culture-level study of 23 national groups, P. B. Smith, Peterson, Leung, and Dugan (1998) found that, in countries with a high power distance, participants were less likely to rely on their peers and subordinates to resolve a dispute in their work group.

Culture and Interpersonal Treatment

Recent research has shown that procedural justice involves an interpersonal dimension (Bies & Moag, 1986; Tyler & Bies, 1990), which is often labeled as *interactional justice*. In the implementation of decision-making procedures, people expect to be treated with respect and dignity, and many wish to have a chance to voice their opinions. Poor interpersonal treatment and the lack of voice can lead to a powerful sense of injustice, and this relationship seems to be culture-general. The major theory in this area is an extension of the group value model proposed by Lind and Tyler (1988), which states that people are concerned about their standing in a group and infer their status from how the group treats them in the process of decision making.

Tyler (1990) posited three relational factors that are pertinent to the interaction between decision makers and recipients. *Neutrality* refers to whether the authority figure acts in an unbiased manner. *Dignity* refers to whether the authority figure treats individuals with dignity and respect. Trust refers to whether authority figures consider the views of individuals who are affected by their decisions and make an effort to act in a fair manner.

A number of studies have provided support for the group value model. In these studies, relational concerns often have a stronger impact on fairness perceptions than instrumental concerns (Tyler, 1994; Tyler & Lind, 1992). This pattern has also been supported by cross-cultural research. Leung and associates have shown the three relational concerns are important determinants of justice perceptions in Hong Kong and China (Leung et al., 1993; Leung & Li, 1990; Leung et al., 1996). In a study of preferences for conflict resolution procedures, Lind, Huo, and Tyler (1994) found that, across the four ethnic groups studied (African, Hispanic, Asian, and European Americans), *procedural fairness*, primarily defined as relational terms, was found to be a more important predictor than perceived favorability of the outcome in predicting procedural preference and the affect experienced during the disputation process. Sugawara and Huo (1994) found that, in Japan, relational issues were rated as more important than instrumental issues in determining preferences for conflict resolution procedures. In a comparative study of American, German, and Hong Kong Chinese students, Lind (1994) found that perceptions of procedural aspects determined overall fairness judgments more than did perceptions of outcome favorability. Among the procedural elements included in this study, relational factors generally showed a stronger effect than perceived process control for all three cultural groups. Finally, Lind, Tyler, and Huo (1997) reported that the effect of voice, the opportunity to express one's views, on procedural justice judgments was mediated by relational variables, and this pattern was similar in the United States, Germany, Hong Kong, and Japan. These studies clearly indicate that relational issues are crucial to understanding perceptions of injustice in a variety of different cultures.

Brockner, Chen, Mannix, Leung, and Skarlicki (2000) argued that, if relational aspects of procedural justice signal one's standing in a group, as suggested by the group value model, procedural justice should matter most for cultural groups that place a premium on interdependence. Brockner et al. tested this notion in three studies, with procedural justice made operational in terms of the formality of the procedure, as well as interpersonal treatment. Their results showed that, when the outcome was low, the effect of procedural justice on a variety of reactions of the recipients was stronger in China and Taiwan than in Canada and the United States. They also demonstrated with regression analyses that this cultural difference was mediated by self-construal. In other words, if cultural differences in self-construal are equated statistically, the cultural differences in the effects of procedural justice vanish. This study shows that the effects of procedural justice are robust across cultures, but culture may moderate its magnitude under some circumstances.

Considerable evidence shows that the consequences of interactional justice are similar across cultures. Lind (1994) reported that willingness to use conflict resolution procedures was a function of its perceived fairness in Germany, the United States, and Hong Kong. Leung and associates (1993, 1996) also found that the consequences of perceived interactional justice are similar across cultures. Perception of interactional justice was related to the perceptions of outcomes and decision makers in a similar manner in the United States, Hong Kong, and mainland China.

Leung and Morris (2001) argue that current models of procedural justice have been tested primarily with constructs that are tapped by survey items pitched at an abstract level (e.g., Lind et al., 1997). Thus, the cross-cultural generality of the antecedents and consequences of interactional justice do not mean that the specific behaviors that precipitate a sense of interactional injustice are similar in different cultures. Quite the opposite—misattributions and misinterpretations of the actions of members of other cultural groups frequently occur and become the cause of perceived interactional injustice during intercultural contact. People may see the behavior of an individual from a different cultural group as rude and condescending from their own cultural standpoint, but this behavior may be perfectly acceptable in the culture of the actor (for a review, see Gudykunst & Bond, 1997).

A case that illustrates this point is the difference in conversational norms between African Americans and European Americans (e.g., Waters, 1992). Eye contact usually indicates paying attention for European Americans, whereas for some urban African Americans, lack of eye contact does not signal a lack of attention if the conversants know each other well (Asante & Davis, 1985). A European American who notices that an African American is not making eye contact while listening may assume that the African American is not listening and is impolite.

Another example is provided by P. B. Smith, Peterson, Misumi, and Tayeb (1989), who found that, if an employee experiences personal difficulties, Japanese and Hong Kong Chinese respondents regarded the discussion of the problems by the supervisor with other employees in the absence of this person to be acceptable behavior. In contrast, respondents from the United Kingdom and the United States regarded such behavior as inconsiderate.

A final example concerns "conversational overlaps"—talking while the other person is talking—which is more common in Brazil than in the United States (J. Graham, 1985). It is conceivable that, when Americans negotiate with Brazilians, they will find the Brazilian negotiators rude and disrespectful because they are being interrupted by the Brazilians.

These studies serve as a reminder of the importance of the model presented at the beginning of this chapter. Abstract principles of justice help us to frame an understanding of cross-cultural similarities, but specific beliefs and behaviors determine the outcomes of these abstract principles in any given social situation.

Power Distance and Interpersonal Treatment

The relationship between power distance and interpersonal justice is succinctly summarized by James (1993), who concluded that, "Cultures that inculcate an acceptance of power differences lead individuals to expect, take for granted and, therefore, not get angry about, injustices" (p. 23). His conclusion is based on a study by Gudykunst and Ting-Toomey (1988), who analyzed data on anger and justice from seven European countries (reported by Babad & Wallbott, 1986, and Wallbott & Scherer, 1986). A strong correlation between power distance and the anger expressed in reaction to injustice was found in which the higher the power distance of a society, the less likely that perceptions of unjust treatment would trigger an angry reaction. In cultures with higher power distance, people's acceptance of unequal social prerogatives appears to lead to a high tolerance of unfair treatment.

In a direct demonstration of this relationship, Bond, Wan, Leung, and Giacalone (1985) showed that, compared to Americans, Chinese from Hong Kong were more willing to accept insulting remarks from a high-status in-group person, but no cultural difference was found when the insult came from a low-status individual. Leung, Su, and Morris (in press) put Americans and Chinese students working for a masters in business administration in the role of an employee whose suggestion was criticized by a manager in an interactionally unfair manner; that is, the manager interrupted, failed to listen closely, and was dismissive toward the employee. The manager was either someone of an essentially equal level in the organization or someone substantially more senior. In support of previous studies, compared to Americans, Chinese perceived a senior manager's actions as less unjust and were less negative toward the superior. Consistent with the general tenor of these findings, Tyler, Lind, and Huo (1995) also found that people high in power distance are less concerned about relational factors than those who are low in power distance.

Retributive Justice: Perception of Fair Sanctions

To maintain social order and protect the well-being of members of a group, social transgressions and wrongdoing must be sanctioned. Societies have evolved both formal and informal codes to guide people away from misbehavior. The third facet of justice, *retributive justice*, arises when observers evaluate the degree to which those who break a rule or cause some harm should be held responsible for the action and whether they deserve to be punished (Hogan & Emler, 1981).

Judgments about the fairness of a punishment begin with a chain of inferences about the actor, the context of the act, and the severity of its consequences. In the initial stage, the outcome of a transgression is appraised with regard to its severity and the extent of the actor's responsibility. Considerable evidence has shown that people's judgments are not absolute, but rather are very sensitive to contextual factors. Models by Shaver (1985) and by Shultz and colleagues (Shultz & Schleifer, 1983; Shultz, Schleifer, & Altman, 1981) further posit that the degree of causality and intentionality perceived determines the degree of responsibility attributed to the perpetrator of a transgression.

Cross-cultural work in this area has documented striking differences in responsibility judgments concerning transgressions. In an extensive comparative study, Hamilton and Sanders (1992) found that similar factors relevant to severity, causality, and intentionality govern responsibility judgments in the United States and in Japan, but the relative importance attached to these factors differs across the two cultures. The differential weights attached to different factors are most readily understood in terms of individualism-collectivism. A major component of the cultural syndrome of individualism is the belief that individuals are autonomous and should not be constrained in their behavior by the social context (Lukes, 1973). In contrast, in collectivistic cultures, people tend to assume that people's behavior is influenced heavily by the social context (Ho, 1998). Morris and Peng (1994) have presented compelling results for this argument in several studies that compare the implicit theories of social behavior in the United States and China. Their results clearly show that, in the United States, a theory centered on the autonomous person channels attributions to internal traits of an actor, whereas in China, a theory centered on the social context channels attributions to factors external to the actor.

Consistent with the results of Morris and Peng (1994), a survey of Americans and Japanese responses to vignettes about wrongdoings found that Americans perceived the acts to be more purposive or reflective of the actor's enduring intentions than did Japanese (Hamilton & Sanders, 1992). Furthermore, Americans' responsibility attributions were roughly twice as sensitive to manipulations of information about the actor, whereas the attributions of the Japanese were more sensitive to the actor's social role and the influence of other parties in the social context. Na and Loftus (1998) found that American law experts and college students were more likely to attribute criminal behavior to personality traits, drug abuse, and family problems, whereas Korean law students and college students were more likely to attribute criminal behavior to situational and societal factors.

In short, these results suggest that in individualistic societies, people are more likely to hold the transgressors responsible for their deviant behavior, whereas in collectivistic societies, people are more likely to see transgression as reflecting the prevailing social forces and are less likely to hold the transgressors personally responsible for their behaviors.

These cross-cultural differences in attributions have a significant impact on the severity and nature of punishment that is deemed fair and legitimate for the offenders. The external attribution of social transgression in collectivistic cultures is likely to engender a forgiving

attitude toward offenders. Consistent with this view, Na and Loftus (1998) reported that Korean respondents were more in favor of lenient treatment of criminals than were their American counterparts. In a study with related findings, Miller and Luthar (1989) put Indians and Americans in a dilemma between acting in line with social rules (e.g., laws) or role obligations. Indians were found to be more likely than Americans to absolve actors who followed role obligations from a sanction. In another related study, Bersoff and Miller (1993) found that, compared to Americans, Indians were more likely to absolve justice breaches that were due to emotional duress (fear or anger). Miller and colleagues argued that Indians view others as embedded in the situation, and hence Indians are more sensitive to situational influences on behavior.

When punishment is meted out to offenders, three general motives may be discerned. In *retribution*, the key concern is to make the offenders compensate the victims with exact punishment of the offenders that is commensurate with the harm done. The punishment is also typically intended to deter the offender from harming the victims again. In *rehabilitation*, the purpose is to educate the offenders so that they understand their previous wrongdoings and will not commit them again. In *restoration*, the main purpose is to repair the social relationship between the offender and the victim through restitution and apology.

Cultural differences in attribution are closely related to the motives underlying the sanctioning of offenders. The internal attributions common in individualistic cultures incline people to the view that an offender is unlikely to change for the better. Thus, individualists are unlikely to be in favor of the goal of rehabilitation. In contrast, the emphasis on external attributions in collectivistic societies makes rehabilitation a more acceptable goal of punishment.

In line with this reasoning, Epstein (1986) has compared reformatory education organizations for juvenile offenders in Taiwan, China, and Hong Kong and concluded that reformatory organizations in Taiwan and China are similar in their emphasis on indoctrination and political education during the process of institutionalization. One interpretation of this observation is that this arrangement assumes that offenders can be rehabilitated through "reeducation." In contrast, because of British influence in Hong Kong, rewards and incentives, rather than indoctrination and reeducation, are the tools that are used to guide the offenders back to a normal pattern of proper behavior.

Hamilton and Sanders (1988) also argued that Japanese emphasize the obligation of society to guide individuals to comply with social norms. The violation of a social norm or law is often attributed to the failure of society to socialize and guide the individual properly, and sanctioning in Japan is therefore more oriented toward rehabilitation and restoration than in the United States. In sum, Japanese respondents favored sanctions that "reintegrate the wrongdoer and restore relationships," whereas Americans favored sanctions that isolate the wrongdoer and thus prevent future occurrences of his or her antisocial behavior.

Social Sanctions

What constitutes a transgression is subject to cultural influence. Based on their views of compliance with group norms, individualistic and collectivistic societies have different views of transgressions. In collectivistic cultures, ingroup harmony is regarded as an important goal, and socially deviant behaviors that jeopardize it are likely to be sanctioned. In individualistic societies, sanctioning of social deviants is less severe due to the emphasis on individuality and autonomy. In collectivistic societies, social sanctioning is considered to be an effective tool to ensure that individuals act in accordance with the norms of the group. Yamagishi (1988b) reported that, in the absence of a sanctioning system, Japanese showed a lower level of trust and commitment toward other group members than did Americans. Compared with Americans, Japanese were also more likely to exit a group that lacked a monitoring and sanctioning system (Yamagishi, 1988a). Yamagishi, Cook, and Watabe (1998) showed that Japanese displayed more cooperation than Americans when a sanctioning system was in place, whereas the opposite was found when the sanctioning system was removed. These results generally support the view that people from collectivistic societies are more comfortable with social systems in which counternormative behaviors are likely to be sanctioned than are people from individualistic cultures.

Universal Concern of Retributive Justice

Culture-specific beliefs may suppress immediate responses to unfair treatment. For instance,

in the Chinese tradition, *bao* is a salient retributive belief that assumes a broader scope than the notion of retribution in the West (e.g., Hsu, 1971; Yang, 1957). Chinese people believe that bao may not necessarily occur to the harmdoers, but may occur to their relatives and offspring and even to their next avatar after reincarnation (e.g., Chiu, 1991). Since bao may be indirect and may take a long time to occur and retribution may include naturally occurring events such as illnesses, these beliefs may suppress people's need to engage in behaviors that bring immediate retribution to the perpetrators. In other cultures, retribution may take different indirect forms. For instance, in indigenous Hawaiian culture, illness and injury are sometimes regarded as caused by retribution (Ito, 1982).

Another example of beliefs that may suppress retribution comes from India. Traditionally, Hindu Indians believe that it is by fate or karma that people are reincarnated as members of a particular social caste (Hines, Garcia-Preto, McGoldrick, Almeida, & Weltman, 1992). Thus, one group may inflict harm on another group, and the victim group may simply accept their suffering as predestined. Because karma can only be changed through death and rebirth, tolerance, sacrifice, and even suffering may be more acceptable responses to being harmed than retribution. In sum, certain culture-specific belief systems may reduce the desire for immediate retribution.

Reactions to Perceived Injustice: A Framework to Understand Reactions to Injustice

Above, we examined the role that cultural differences in retributive justice play in creating perceptions of injustice. In this section, we examine how people from different cultures respond to perceptions of injustice. Perceptions of injustice and the reactions to which they lead are important for a number or reasons. For instance, research in organizational settings has found that perceptions of injustice are associated with lowered job performance, stealing, failure to follow institutional norms, protests, absenteeism, quitting work, and lawsuits (for reviews see Lind, Kray, & Thompson, 1998; Rutte & Messick, 1995). In intercultural relations, they are likely to lead to conflict, mistrust, dissatisfaction, anger and other negative emotions, a deterioration in interpersonal relations, stress, and other destructive behavioral and psychological consequences.

Several sets of researchers have attempted to conceptualize reactions to injustice. We have developed a conceptual framework that can be used to understand such reactions (Leung & Stephan, 1998, 2000). We make two basic distinctions. The first is between psychological and behavioral reactions (Rutte & Messick, 1995). Psychological reactions are largely internal and may consist of both cognitive reactions, such as appraisals of others and the self, and emotional reactions, such as anger, envy, resentment, or disappointment. Behavioral reactions involve overt behaviors that may be directed at the perpetrator of the injustice or at others.

The second distinction concerns the origins of the injustice, specifically, whether the injustice is perceived to have been perpetrated by an individual or a group. This distinction parallels one made in the literature on relative deprivation, in which egoistic relative deprivation and fraternal relative deprivation are distinguished from one another (Runciman, 1966; Vanneman & Pettigrew, 1972). That is, individuals may react differently to injustices that are directed at them personally compared to injustices that are directed at their group. If the injustice is personal, the individual may respond by retaliating against the perpetrator of the injustice, but if the injustice is directed at the individual's group, the individual may join together with other in-group members to fight the injustice.

Lind et al. (1998) have done a study that illustrates the importance of this distinction. They found that students in the United States responded with greater feelings of injustice when they were the targets of unfair treatment than when other members of their group were the targets of unfair treatment. It should be noted that the pattern of results obtained by Lind et al. (1998) may be more apt to occur in individualistic cultures than in collectivistic cultures, in which attachment to in-groups and a deemphasis on personal needs and desires might lead to stronger reactions to unfair treatment of in-group members than the self.

Wright and Taylor (1998) offered a conceptual framework that is similar to ours, but it is different in some crucial respects. They argue that there are five basic types of reactions to injustice. First, they distinguish between inaction and action. As they note, one of the most

common responses to injustice is to do nothing. The second distinction they make is between actions that are taken to improve one's own condition and actions taken to improve the conditions of one's group. The third distinction they make is between actions that are normative within a given society and those that are nonnormative or deviant. Thus, the five types of reaction are: inaction, individual normative action, individual nonnormative action, collective normative action, and collective nonnormative action.

The distinction that Wright and Taylor make with respect to individuals versus groups is different from the one we made (Leung & Stephan, 1998, 2000). We distinguish between the nature of the injustice (whether it is directed at the individual or group), and they distinguish between the nature of the reaction to the injustice (individual or group response). Wright and Taylor's inaction category is equivalent to our psychological reaction category, but we seem to have a wider range of reactions in mind for this category than Wright and Taylor. The conceptual distinction Wright and Taylor make between normative and nonnormative reactions may be somewhat unwieldy when applied to intercultural relations because what is nonnormative in one culture could easily be normative in another.

There are other distinctions that have not been included in either our (Leung & Stephan, 1998, 2000) or Wright and Taylor's (1998) conceptual frameworks that appear to be important in understanding reactions to injustice. For example, people may respond differently to distributive, procedural, interactional, and retributive injustice. A study of employee theft in a large corporation illustrates this point (Shapiro, Trevino, & Victor, 1995). In this study, it was found that perceptions of procedural injustice were better predictors of theft than perceptions of either distributive injustice or interactional injustice. If the employees thought the company's procedures were fair, they were less likely to steal from it. Another study illustrating the importance of distinguishing between types of injustice found in a large telecommunications company that was downsizing, employees' perceptions of procedural injustice were tied closely to behavioral reactions, while their perceptions of distributive justice were tied closely to negative emotional reactions (Armstrong-Stassen, 1998).

In general, the types of behavioral reactions that can be used to redress injustice probably vary as a function of the type of injustice. Similarly, psychological reactions may vary as a function of the type of injustice. It also seems likely that there are cultural differences in which type of injustice draws the strongest reactions. People in individualistic cultures may be more concerned with distributive justice than people in collectivistic cultures because they have such clear-cut notions of individual equity. The greater concern for propriety in many collectivistic cultures could lead to a stronger emphasis on procedural injustice in collectivistic than individualistic cultures. Collectivistic cultures may be more concerned with interactional injustice than individualistic cultures because of their emphasis on interdependence. The Brockner et al. (2000) study described above supports the greater emphasis on procedural and interactional justice in collectivistic cultures than in individualistic cultures.

A study by Mikula, Petri, and Tanzer (1990) done in individualistic European countries (Germany, Austria, Finland, Bulgaria) suggests that experiencing interactional injustice is quite common in such countries. In this study, it was found that people reported more incidents of interactional than distributive or procedural injustice when reporting on injustices they had experienced. This study established that interpersonal injustices are common in individualistic cultures, but it is not clear if they occur more frequently or take on greater importance in collectivistic cultures.

There is another feature of unjust acts that may also influence reactions to injustice. Unjust acts vary in their consequences. For instance, Cropanzano and Baron (1991) argue that an injustice may affect either economic well-being or social standing. It may also affect physical and psychological well-being, as well as interpersonal relations that are not associated with social standing. The emphasis on individual achievement in individualistic cultures may make damage to economic well-being particularly important in such cultures, whereas the emphasis on interpersonal relations and social standing in collectivistic cultures may make damage to social standing and interpersonal relations important in collectivistic cultures, especially collectivistic cultures with high power distance.

Finally, there is an additional aspect of responses to injustice that is helpful in categorizing them. Responses to injustice can be either destructive or constructive with respect to over-coming or undoing the injustice itself. Revenge, retaliation, angry outbursts, insults, and depression would all most likely be destructive in the sense that they would be unlikely to lead to righting the injustice. In contrast, negotiation, filing grievances, civil disobedience, and nonviolent protest can all lead to overcoming injustice successfully. This distinction is similar to one made by Crosby (1976) for responses to egoistic relative deprivation. She suggests that two of the basic responses to relative deprivation are violence directed against society or seeking constructive changes in society. One problem with this distinction between constructive and destructive reactions is whether any given response to injustice is constructive or destructive can only be determined by its effects. A seemingly destructive response, such as a violent protest, could lead to righting an injustice, in which case its effect would have to be considered constructive.

In general, people in collectivistic cultures may be less prone to respond to injustice with destructive behaviors (retaliation, protest, conflict) than people in individualistic cultures because most collectivistic cultures, especially those in Asia, emphasize harmony (Leung, 1997) and the avoidance of conflict. However, the emphasis on honor and respect in collectivistic cultures may mean that, when people in these cultures do respond to injustice with destructive behaviors, they do so more forcefully than do people in individualist cultures. And, in collectivistic cultures, negative behavioral responses to injustice may be just as likely as they are in individualistic cultures if the perpetrator of the injustice is an out-group member. On the other hand, people in collectivistic cultures may be more likely than people in individualistic cultures to respond to injustice with constructive behaviors (mediation, conciliation, negotiation, face saving) in an attempt to sustain or regain harmony.

Comparative cross-cultural research on reactions to injustice is in its infancy. Most of the studies that have been done to date concern reactions to injustice in only one culture. These studies have mostly been done in Western countries, but some studies done in non-Western cultures exist, and there are a small number of cross-cultural studies. The studies done in Western countries provide some insights into how people in individualistic cultures respond to injustice and thus provide a benchmark with which to contrast the reactions of people from collectivistic cultures.

Psychological Reactions

The primary types of psychological reactions are *affective* and *cognitive*. Affective reactions refer to positive and negative emotions experienced as a consequence of being treated unjustly. One cross-cultural study of psychological reactions to injustice found that the same set of emotional reactions characterized 25 different cultures (Mikula, Scherer, & Athenstaedt, 1998). In this study, people reported the causes of various types of emotional reactions (e.g., fear, anger, sadness, disgust, shame, and guilt). Consistent with equity theory (Adams, 1965), injustice was reported to be a very common cause of anger, followed by disgust, sadness, fear, shame, and guilt. This ordering did not vary across the countries included in this study, suggesting that there may be some universality in the emotions that are linked to injustice.

We regard this as unlikely, however, and instead believe that the "universality" that appears in this study is a consequence of the methods used. The respondents were asked to think of a situation that caused them to experience each of these emotions. It seems very likely that respondents were thinking of different situations, and that these situations may have varied by culture. That is, the type of injustice that elicits these emotions may differ across cultures. Thus, the types of injustice that elicit anger may differ across cultures. For instance, in individualistic cultures, injustice directed at the individual is probably more likely to provoke anger than injustice directed at the ingroup, but the reverse is likely to be true in collectivistic cultures. Thus, in both cultures, injustice may provoke anger, but for different reasons.

A study done in the United States confirms the link between injustice and anger (Sprecher, 1986). In this study, students reported on their reactions to inequities that they experienced in their intimate relationships, along with their emotional reactions to these relationships. For both men and women, anger was one of the emotions most closely linked to feelings of inequity. These findings suggest that, in an individualistic culture, interpersonal injustice, in the form of equitable relationships, is associated with anger. Whether this relationship would hold true for other types of injustice or in collectivistic cultures remains to be determined.

Another study done in the United States has focused on a particularly important negative emotional reaction to injustice—envy (R. H. Smith, Parrott, Ozer, & Moniz, 1994). This study found that, for people who are experiencing envy, perceptions of injustice are linked to hostility. These investigators contrast envy, which they regard as an essentially private (and not socially acceptable) emotional reaction to injustice, with resentment, which they regard as a more public (and socially acceptable) emotional reaction to injustice. In the cross-cultural context, it is possible that collectivistic cultures, with their greater emphasis on the control and display of emotions, would be more prone to envy as a reaction to injustice, whereas individualistic cultures might be more prone to resentment.

Cognitive reactions to unjust treatment primarily involve reconceptualizing the injustice or changing appraisals of others or the self. People can reconceptualize the injustice by modifying their sense of what they are entitled to, distorting the magnitude of the injustice, or changing their attributions of blame for the cause of the injustice (cf. Rutte & Messick, 1995). In each case, these cognitive reactions may increase or decrease the amount of injustice people perceive that they are experiencing. For instance, people may come to believe they were entitled to even more than they received, and that the perpetrator was solely to blame for causing the injustice; therefore, the injustice is greater than they had initially believed. According to equity theory, people can restore equity to a relationship by reappraising the value of their own or the other person's inputs and outcomes (Walster, Walster, & Berscheid, 1978). A similar process may occur with other types of injustice. Another cognitive reaction consists of ruminating or obsessing about the injustice. We would also classify stress and its symptoms as psychological reactions to injustice.

There is very little research on cultural differences in cognitive reactions to injustice. In constructing the Chinese Personality Assessment Inventory, Cheung et al. (1996) included a scale called Ah-Q mentality, which is believed to be common among Chinese and involves a defensive cognitive reappraisal of affronts received. For instance, if one is being forced to lend something, one may then think one is a kind person, and that it is good to help people. Cross-cultural work is now being conducted to see if there are cultural differences in the endorsement of this trait. In any event, more work is definitely needed to assess cultural differences in cognitive reactions to injustice.

Behavioral Reactions

The central distinction drawn in both the Leung and Stephan (1998, 2000) and the Wright and Taylor (1998) conceptual frameworks concerns when people respond overtly to injustice and when they do not respond overtly. The process involved in responding behaviorally appears to occur in four stages. First, a situation has to be labeled as unjust. In this stage, people must come to believe that they are entitled to a more just outcome or more just treatment than they have received (Crosby, 1976). According to Jost and Banaji (Jost, 1995; Jost & Banaji, 1994), some people may fail to perceive an actual injustice because of system justification, which occurs when there is the absence of a revolutionary class consciousness, the lack of communication among those who are subject to a lower outcome, and low group identity. Another reason is that the desire to believe in a just world also leads people to conclude that they must not be suffering from an injustice (Lerner, 1980).

For instance, Furnham (1985) found that, during the period of apartheid in South Africa, Blacks there were more likely to believe in a just world than were Blacks in Great Britain. The belief of South African Blacks in a just world may have limited their perceptions that they were being treated unjustly and as a result may have reduced their behavioral reactions to a very unjust social system. Finally, as noted above, some cultural beliefs may downplay the salience of injustice. In India, karma may lead to a belief in predestined suffering and mitigate the perception of injustice. In sum, if injustices are not labeled as such, there will be no behavioral reaction to them.

In the second stage, the perpetrator must come to be blamed for causing the injustice. Attributions of blame involve deciding that the other person or group was responsible for the injustice and acted intentionally, and that their motive was malevolent (Tedeschi & Nesler, 1993). Attributions of blame are commonly associated with feelings of anger, at least in the West (Quigley & Tedeschi, 1996). In some cases, people may falsely attribute the blame for the injustice to themselves or others (Jost, 1995; Jost & Banaji, 1994). In these instances, the injustice is noticed, but no action is taken against the perpetrator because the perpetrator is not blamed for the injustice. Similarly, when accounts for injustice are given by those who are responsible for it, the accounts reduce perceptions of injustice and forestall reactions to them (Bies, 1987; Davidson & Friedman, 1998).

In a related vein, a study done in Japan indicates that apologies by the perpetrators of injustice may mitigate negative reactions to injustice (Ohbuchi, Kameda, & Agarie, 1989). In this study, students who had received an undeserved negative evaluation from another student responded with less aggression if the other student apologized for the mistakes that led to the unjust evaluation.

In a study that captures a number of aspects of these first two stages, Freudenthaler and Mikula (1998) found that Austrian women's sense of injustice regarding the division of household labor was influenced by perceived violations of entitlement and attributions of blame to their partners, with attributions of blame themselves being influenced by a lack of justifications for their partners' behavior. In a previous section, we argued that, in general, offenders are more likely to be blamed for their wrongdoing in individualistic than collectivistic cultures. However, it remains to be seen whether there are cultural differences in the effectiveness of compensatory behaviors for a wrongdoing, such as providing an account for the wrongdoing or offering an apology.

In the third stage, people must make a conscious decision that their interests or the interests of their group are better served by responding behaviorally than by doing nothing. However, it should be noted that some people respond spontaneously to injustice, with little or no thought.

In the fourth stage, people must actually carry out their decisions to respond behaviorally. According to resource mobilization theory, certain types of behavioral responses are unlikely to occur unless the individuals who have been treated unjustly possess the resources to respond (Klandermans, 1989; Martin, Brickman, & Murray, 1984; Tilly, 1978). These theorists argue that collective protests, in particular, are unlikely to occur if the necessary resources (e.g., time, effort, money, support) are not available. Their point is probably more broadly applicable. People, in general, are probably unlikely to respond behaviorally if they lack the resources. Similarly, if people do not perceive that responding to injustice behaviorally will be both meaningful and effective, they are unlikely to respond (Klandermans, 1989). It may be worth pointing out that behavioral responses to injustice do not have to be constructive to be meaningful and effective in the eyes of the people engaging in them. Revenge, aggression, riots, and destructive protests, for instance, may be quite satisfying to those who engage in them, even though the net result may not change the situation that brought about the perceived injustice. In sum, if people do not feel entitled to a more just outcome, do not blame the perpetrator, do not decide that their interests are served by responding behaviorally, do not have the necessary resources to respond, or do not believe that a behavioral response will be effective or meaningful, they will do nothing. Of course, not responding behaviorally does not mean that people will not respond psychologically.

We have reviewed a number of reasons why people from collectivistic cultures may engage in few behavioral reactions to injustice. Their preference for conflict avoidance tends to suppress behavioral reactions. The dominance of secondary control (changing oneself to fit the environment) common in collectivistic societies such as Japan and Thailand, as opposed to primary control (changing the environment to suit oneself) in individualistic societies such as the United States (McCarty et al., 1999; Weisz, Rothbaum, & Blackburn, 1984), is another reason why behavioral reactions are less likely to occur in collectivistic societies.

In short, culture can have an impact on the process underlying behavioral reactions to injustice at every stage. People in collectivistic cultures may be motivated not to notice minor injustices committed by in-group members in the interests of maintaining harmony. They may also be more receptive to accounts and apologies than are people in individualistic cultures. Even when injustices are noted, there may be a greater range of circumstances under which people in collectivistic cultures decide that the costs of responding to injustice outweigh the benefits. Also, they may not see destructive responses as meaningful or beneficial. However, people from collectivistic cultures may be even more likely than people in individualistic cultures to respond to injustice constructively.

As discussed above, the emphasis on egalitarianism and equity in cultures with low power distance may lead people in these cultures to be particularly likely to notice and respond to injustice with destructive behaviors. In cultures with high power distance, people with high status may be especially reactive to injustice since they probably do not expect it

and most likely have the power and resources to respond. People with low status in such cultures are probably similar to collectivists in their motivation not to perceive or react to injustice since responding would violate the status hierarchy and might risk retaliation. A belief in fatalism that is common in cultures with high power distance might also contribute to an unwillingness to respond to injustice (Jost, 1995). In cultures with high power distance, it appears that responses to injustice depend to a greater extent of the relative power of the people involved than they do in cultures with low power distance.

Individual versus Group Responses to Injustice

The nature of the reactions to injustice may also be influenced by cultural variables. We make a distinction between injustices that were perceived to have been directed at an individual and those that were directed at the group of which the individual is a member (Leung & Stephan, 1998, 2000), while Wright and Taylor (1998) make a distinction between individual and group responses to injustice. It seems likely that when the injustice is perceived to have been directed at one's group, people will generally respond with group (collective) reactions, while if the injustice is perceived to have been directed at the individual, people will respond with individual reactions.

However, research suggests that there are several qualifications to this pattern. Kelly and Breinlinger (1995) argue that, when individuals identify strongly with their in-group, they are indeed likely to respond to group injustice with collective action, but when individuals do not identify strongly with their in-group, they are more likely to respond with individual actions. In support of the first part of this suggestion, they found that British women's participation in gender-related collective actions were best predicted by the strength of their identity as women.

Research suggests that several other factors also influence whether individual or collective responses are preferred. For instance, an interesting study by Lalonde and Silverman (1994) that was done in Canada indicates that, in cultures with low power distance, responses to certain types of procedural injustice depend on the permeability of group boundaries. In this study, it was found that, when entry to the high-status group was permitted to a privileged few on the basis of merit (tokenism), people responded to rejection by taking individual, rather than collective, action. Avoidance of the problem was rarely selected as a response to rejection.

Wright (1997) also investigated the behavioral responses of North American students to tokenism. The results of this study led him to suggest that, in individualistic cultures, people are likely to respond to tokenism that is unjust with collective action if the injustice is perpetrated by a powerful group with boundaries that are perceived to be impermeable and the status of which is perceived to be unstable. That is, when the dominant group totally rejects individuals of the subordinate group from membership but is insecure in its status, members of the subordinate group are more likely to respond with collective action than if the boundaries of the dominant group are permeable or its status is secure. As was the case in the Lalonde and Silverman (1994) study, when the boundaries of the dominant group were permeable, people were more likely to favor actions such as individual protests that would enhance their chances for membership in the dominant group (see also Wright & Taylor, 1998). It remains to be seen if this pattern of responses would characterize collectivistic cultures, but it is likely to be less true of cultures with high power distance than the culture with low power distance in which the study was done. Members of low-status groups in cultures with high power distance may not respond with collective action even if the power of the high-status group is perceived as unstable, and the boundaries of the group are permeable because they would start with a greater fear of retaliation and a greater acceptance of the power of the dominant group.

The concept of *social dominance orientation*, which refers to the extent to which people accept the hierarchy among different social groups, is relevant to whether groups will react to perceived injustice (Pratto, Sidanius, Stallworth, & Malle, 1994; Sidanius, 1993; Sidanius, Pratto, & Rabinowitz, 1994). Specifically, for members of high-status ethnic groups, a strong social dominance orientation will lead to the perceived superiority of the in-group. For low-status groups, a strong social dominance orientation is associated with an acceptance of the status quo and the deprecation of the in-group. Sidanius et al. (1994) confirmed this proposal by showing that, for European Americans, the high-status group, social dominance orientation was related positively to favorable

perceptions of their own ethnic group, whereas for minority group members, the lower status groups, social dominance was related negatively to perceptions of their own group. In a related study, Rabinowitz (1999) found that European Americans who scored low on social dominance orientation were more accepting of social policies designed to change the social system than were people who scored high on social dominance. For members of ethnic minorities, low social dominance scores were only associated with support for policies that would alter the status quo if they perceived that the social system was unjust.

Although social dominance orientation is an individual difference measure, it is akin to the concept of power distance at the cultural level. If such an analogy can be made, it suggests that members of high-status groups in societies with high power distance may be less accepting of social policies that would alter the unjust distribution of resources in such societies than would members of high-status groups in cultures with low power distance. Members of low-status groups in cultures with high power distance would be expected to accept social policies that challenge the status quo only if they perceive the system as unjust; otherwise, they should be less accepting of such policies than members of low-status groups in cultures with low power distance.

Linkages between Psychological and Behavioral Reactions

To this point, psychological and behavioral responses to injustice have been treated as if they were separate and distinct entities, but in many cases, they are intertwined. The connection between psychological and behavioral reactions to injustice has been considered in relative deprivation theory. According to relative deprivation theory, perceiving that one is relatively deprived often has emotional consequences that serve as antecedents to behavioral responses (Crosby, 1976). The emotional reactions to relative deprivation include feelings of dissatisfaction, outrage, or resentment. The research literature examining links among emotional responses, relative deprivation, and subsequent behavioral responses suggests that these relationships are not as clear as relative deprivation theory would lead one to believe. In many studies, dissatisfaction based on relative deprivation has not been found to be related closely to behavioral reactions (for a review, see Martin et al., 1984).

More recent studies that allow for examination of mediational links of dissatisfaction provide evidence that dissatisfaction may mediate the relationship between injustice and reactions to injustice. For example, Grant and Brown (1995) found evidence for a relationship between distributive injustice and collective reactions that were mediated by feelings of dissatisfaction. In this study, when small groups of people believed that they had been subjected to distributive injustice, they reacted with collective action to the degree that they felt dissatisfied at being treated unjustly. One possible reason for the apparent inconsistency of the findings concerning the mediating role of dissatisfaction may be that people only respond to the dissatisfaction caused by injustice when resources are available and the behavioral responses are considered to be meaningful and effective (Klandermans, 1989).

In most cases, the relationship between psychological reactions and behavioral reactions to injustice probably involves negative emotional reactions as antecedents to behavioral reactions (as Rutte & Messick, 1995, suggest); however, it is also possible that, in some cases, the emotional reactions follow the behavioral ones. For instance, in cultures that emphasize the control of emotions, especially negative emotions, as collectivistic cultures tend to do (C. W. Stephan, Stephan, & Saito, 1998; W. G. Stephan, Stephan, & Cabeza de Vargas, 1996) the relationship between the experience of emotion and behavioral reactions to injustice may be attenuated, at least when in-group members are the cause of the injustice. To an even greater extent than is true for the understanding of psychological and behavioral reactions considered separately, the understanding of the interrelationships is woefully inadequate. There is little information on what psychological reactions are linked to which behavioral reactions and how culture influences such relationships. Thus, much remains to be learned.

Concluding Comments

Based on our review of the cross-cultural literature on justice, we now present a number of concluding comments and discuss productive avenues for future research.

Justice as General Rules or Concrete Guidelines for Proper Conduct

The two-stage model we described here suggests that there is much universality if justice is viewed as abstract constructs and rules. However, when it comes to specific implementation, culture may create drastic differences in what goes into the justice equation. We have documented major cultural differences in the implementation of distributive, procedural, and retributive justice, as well reactions to injustice. Borrowing from cognitive psychology, Bhawuk (1998) argued that general theories and dominant-specific details complement each other, and both are necessary for effective cross-cultural understanding and training. General theories can help organize complex behavioral rules into meaningful and manageable sets of guidelines, whereas domain-specific details are necessary for proper behavior in a given setting. Considering justice as a set of general rules is analogous to general theories—both serve a heuristic function, but they do not get us very far in terms of smooth sailing in an unfamiliar culture.

Considering justice in terms of concrete guidelines for proper conduct is analogous to domain-specific knowledge, which helps us to act properly in a given setting, but these guidelines are too numerous to remember and unique to be useful for cross-cultural understanding. In the cross-cultural literature on justice, most work is concerned with general rules, and we know relatively little about the substance of justice in different cultures. Given the importance of justice issues at cultural interfaces, we need more work on variations in justice standards and criteria across cultures so that practitioners at such interfaces and designers of cross-cultural training programs can understand these processes better and function more effectively.

Injustice as a Trigger of Intercultural Conflict

When a conflict arises between two groups, both sides are likely to accuse the other side of being unfair. Leung and Stephan (2000) have provided a detailed analysis of how perceived injustice intensified the Arab-Israeli conflict and the Sino-British conflict regarding the handover of Hong Kong from British to Chinese rule. Intercultural contact is difficult because cultural differences often lead to misunderstanding, miscommunication, and misattribution. Furthermore, Carnevale and Leung (in press) have reviewed the literature on intercultural bargaining, and they concluded that suboptimal outcomes are common in such situations. For instance, Brett and Okumura (1998) examined intercultural and intracultural negotiations with Japanese and American participants. The intercultural dyads had less accurate mutual understanding of each other's priorities and obtained lower joint value than did the intracultural dyads.

Our review has highlighted a host of cultural differences in justice perceptions that may trigger intense cultural conflict. Our view is that cross-cultural understanding is the key to avoiding destructive intercultural conflict fueled by a strong sense of injustice. Although justice issues sometimes are the focus of cross-cultural training materials (e.g., Cushner & Brislin, 1996), they definitely deserve more coverage. In fact, Leung et al. (in press) argued that, because of their lack of cross-cultural training, Hong Kong Chinese, Taiwanese, and Japanese workers in joint ventures in mainland China were perceived by locals as less fair than Westerners and other Asians despite their better cultural knowledge of mainland China. Only through extensive training in cultural differences in conceptions of justice are people from different cultures likely to be able to avoid inadvertently triggering perceptions of injustice in one another.

Maintenance of Justice in a Culturally Diverse World

Cultures are in contact for many different reasons, and working together is probably the most prevalent form of intercultural contact. The management of cultural diversity has been a popular research topic (see, e.g., Chemers, Oskamp, & Costanzo, 1995; Cox, 1993; Henderson, 1994; Jackson & Ruderman, 1995). Maintaining fairness in such a setting is by no means easy, and we have reviewed numerous cultural differences in justice perceptions that make the task of rendering justice seem nearly impossible. For instance, members of different cultural groups may prefer different procedures to resolve a conflict. Weldon, Jehn, Chen, and Wang (1996) found that, in a U.S.-China joint venture, Chinese tended to use indirect actions (e.g., go to the boss, raise the issue in a meeting) to solve an intercultural conflict, whereas Americans

were more likely to directly address the conflict with a different-culture colleague.

Leung and Kwong (in press) have reviewed numerous justice conflicts that are common in international joint ventures in China because the Chinese and the foreign partners regard different human resources management practices as fair. We know little about effective ways to overcome the problems generated by cultural differences in justice perceptions, an area that clearly will require more attention in future work. One promising avenue would be for those involved in intercultural encounters to be prepared to employ mediation and consultation when they encounter cross-cultural problems with perceptions of injustice.

An additional problem compounds the difficulty in maintaining justice in culturally diverse settings. It is well known that groups display an in-group bias, which is associated with giving in-group members more resources and more positive evaluations than out-group members. In an organizational setting, Tsui and O'Reilly (1989) found that dissimilarity in superior-subordinate demographic characteristics (relational demography), including race, is associated with lower effectiveness as perceived by superiors, less personal attraction toward the subordinates by superiors, and increased role ambiguity experienced by subordinates. In a review of the literature on intercultural helping, Crosby, Bromley, and Saxe (1980) concluded that people extended more help to members of the same ethnic group than to members of different ethnic groups. Leung and Morris (2001) have further argued that cultural groups may display an ethnocentric fairness bias in that they regard their preferences and ways of decision making as fairer. For instance, Arthur, Doverspike, and Fuentes (1992) found that minority group members perceived a recruitment procedure that gave preferential treatment to an applicant from a minority group as fairer than did majority group members.

Pepitone and L'Armand (1997) reported that in both the United States and India, if there is correspondence between the valence of the outcome that a person receives and his or her evaluation as a person, justice is perceived. In other words, if good people receive positive outcomes and bad people receive negative outcomes, justice is perceived. This so-called balanced valence hypothesis of justice perceptions has also been confirmed in Korea (Hong, 1997). Consistent with this argument, Lee, Pepitone, and Albright (1997) found that both Chinese and Americans believed that good people would receive more positive life outcomes than bad people. Although justice demands that good people receive good outcomes, the in-group bias and the ethnocentric fairness bias may make it difficult to see out-group members as good people. The belief in balanced valence does not guarantee the willingness to grant positive outcomes to members of different cultural groups.

Recently, based on the group value model of justice, Tyler, Huo, and their associates (Huo, Smith, Tyler, & Lind, 1996; Tyler, Boeckmann, Smith, & Huo, 1997) have proposed a way out of this predicament. They argued that the social categorization process affects the extent to which justice is endorsed as a regulatory mechanism in governing intergroup contact. If two groups see each other as out-groups, self-interests become salient, and individuals are likely to be instrumental in the intergroup contact. In contrast, if two groups identify with each other, the fairness of interpersonal treatment plays a more important role in justice perceptions, and justice concerns become a force that binds the diverse group together. Their work highlights the importance of superordinate goals and a common identity to the maintenance of justice in culturally diverse contexts.

Constructive Approaches to Injustice in Intercultural Contact

The material we have reviewed in this chapter suggests that, if people are to avoid problems with cultural differences in the perception and implementation of justice principles, they must possess certain types of knowledge and skills. At a general level, they should know about the existence of cultural differences in procedural, distributive, retributional, and interactional justice. They also need to know how differences along cultural dimensions such as individualism-collectivism and power distance affect conceptions of these different types of justice. At a more specific level, they need to know about the particular cultures with which they will be coming into contact. There is no replacement for culture-specific knowledge in dealing with miscommunications, misjudgments, and misattributions involving justice perceptions. Not only must they possess this knowledge, but also they must be taught how to apply it to the particular contexts in which they will have to employ it.

Perceptions of injustice are most likely to arise in organizational or work settings, but they also occur in interpersonal relations and can have devastating effects on these relationships. People need to learn how to be sensitive to the types of situations that evoke perceptions of injustice, and they must be aware of their own reactions to injustice, as well as the likely reactions of others and how they may be shaped by culture. Because of the strong reactions that people often have to injustice, problems of unjust treatment pose some of the most explosive threats to productive intercultural relations. For this reason, it may be more important to consult knowledgeable others or to refer disputes involving injustice to third parties such as mediators or arbitrators than it is for other types of problems in intercultural relations. People who are involved in intercultural disputes involving issues of justice may not be in a position to recognize and understand the nature and origin of the problem in the way that knowledgeable third parties can. Although there is growing literature on the use of these types of techniques in the resolution of intercultural disputes at the national level (e.g., Fisher 1990), much less attention has been paid to the resolution of justice-related disputes at the organizational or individual level. If it has done nothing else, this chapter has clearly demonstrated the need for more attention to be devoted to these issues.

References

Adams, J. S. (1963). Toward an understanding of inequity. *Journal of Abnormal and Social Psychology, 67*, 422–436.

Adams, J. S. (1965). Inequity in social exchange. In L. Berkowitz (Ed.), *Advances in experimental social psychology* (pp. 267–299). New York: Academic Press.

Aral, S. O., & Sunar, D. G. (1977). Interaction and justice norms: Across-national comparison. *Journal of Social Psychology, 101*, 175–186.

Armstrong-Stassen, M. (1998). The effect of gender and organizational level on how survivors appraise and cope with organizational downsizing. *Journal of Applied Behavioral Science, 34*, 125–142.

Arthur, W., Doverspike, D., & Fuentes, R. (1992). Recipients' affective responses to affirmative action interventions: A cross-cultural perspective. *Behavioral Sciences and the Law, 10*, 229–243.

Asante, M., & Davis, A. (1985). Black and White communication: Analyzing work place encounters. *Journal of Black Studies, 16*, 77–93.

Babad, E. Y., & Wallbott, H. G. (1986). The effects of social factors on emotional reactions. In K. S. Scherer, H. G. Wallbott, & A. B. Summerfield (Eds.), *Experiencing emotion: A cross-cultural study* (pp. 154–172). Cambridge: Cambridge University Press.

Bar-Tal, R. (1990). Causes and consequences of delegitimization: Models of conflict and ethnocentrism. *Journal of Social Issues, 46,* 65–82.

Bazerman, M. H., Wade-Bensoni, K. A., & Benzoni, F. J. (1995). *Environmental degradation: Exploring the rift between environmentally benign attitudes and environmentally destructive behaviors.* Unpublished manuscript, Kellog Graduate School of Management, Northwestern University, Evanston, IL.

Bellah, R. N., Madsen, R., Sullivan, W. M., Swidler, A., & Tipton, S. M. (1985). *Habits of the heart: Individualism and commitment in American life.* Berkeley: University of California Press.

Benjamin, R. W. (1975). Images of conflict resolution and social control: American and Japanese attitudes to the adversary system. *Journal of Conflict Resolution, 19,* 123–137.

Berger, J., Zelditch, M., Anderson, B., & Cohen, B. P. (1972). Structural aspects of distributive justice: A status-value formulation. In J. Berger, M. Zelditch, & B. Anderson (Eds.), *Sociological theories in progress* (Vol. 2, pp. 119–246). Boston: Houghton Mifflin.

Berman, J. J., Murphy-Berman, V., & Singh, P. (1985). Cross-cultural similarities and differences in perception of fairness. *Journal of Cross-Cultural Psychology, 16,* 55–67.

Berry, J. W., & Wells, M. (1994). Attitudes toward Aboriginal peoples and Aboriginal self-government in Canada. In J. H. Hylton (Ed.), *Aboriginal self-government in Canada* (pp. 215–232). Saskatchewan, Canada: Purich.

Bersoff, D. M., & Miller, J. G. (1993). Culture, context, and the development of moral accountability judgments. *Developmental Psychology, 29,* 664–676.

Bhawuk, D. P. S. (1998). The role of culture theory in cross-cultural training: A multimethod study of culture-specific, culture-general, and culture theory-based assimilators. *Journal of Cross-Cultural Psychology, 29,* 630–655.

Bierbrauer, G. (1994). Toward an understanding of legal culture: Variations in individualism and collectivism between Kurds, Lebanese, and Germans. *Law and Society Review, 28,* 243–264.

Bies, R. J. (1987). The predicament of injustice: The management of moral outrage. *Research in Organizational Behavior, 9,* 289–319.

Bies, R. J., & Moag, J. S. (1986). Interactional justice: Communication criteria of fairness. In R. J. Lewicki, B. H. Sheppard, & M. H. Bazerman (Eds.), *Research on negotiation in organizations* (pp. 43–55). Greenwich, CT: JAI Press.

Bond, M. H., Leung, K., & Wan, K. C. (1982). How does cultural collectivism operate? The impact of task and maintenance contributions on reward allocation. *Journal of Cross-Cultural Psychology, 13,* 186–200.

Bond, M. H., Wan, K. C., Leung, K., & Giacalone, R. (1985). How are responses to verbal insults related to cultural collectivism and power distance? *Journal of Cross-Cultural Psychology, 16,* 111–127.

Bowd, A. D., & Shapiro, K. J. (1993). The case against laboratory animal research in psychology. *Journal of Social Issues, 49,* 133–142.

Brett, J. M., & Okumura, T. (1998). Inter- and intracultural negotiation: U.S. and Japanese negotiators. *Academy of Management Journal, 41,* 495–510.

Brockner, J., Chen, Y. R., Mannix, E. A., Leung, K., & Skarlicki. D. P. (2000). Cross-cultural variation in the interactive relationship between procedural fairness and outcome favorability: the case of self-construal. *Administrative Science Quarterly, 45,* 138–159.

Campbell, D. T. (1975). On the conflicts between biological and social evolution and between psychology and the moral tradition. *American Psychologist, 30,* 1103–1126

Carnevale, P. J., & Leung, K. (in press). Cultural Dimensions of Negotiation. In M. A. Hogg & R. S. Tindale (Eds.), *Blackwell handbook of social psychology: Vol. 3. Group processes.* Oxford, UK: Blackwell.

Chemers, M. M., Oskamp, S., & Costanzo, M. (1995). *Diversity in organizations.* Thousand Oaks, CA: Sage.

Chen, C. C. (1995). New trends in rewards allocation preferences: A Sino-U.S. comparison. *Academy of Management Journal, 38,* 408–428.

Chen, C. S., & Uttal, D. H. (1988). Cultural values, parents' beliefs, and children's achievement in the United States and China. *Human Development, 31,* 351–358.

Cheung, F. M., Leung, K., Fan, R. M., Song, W. Z., Zhang, J. X., & Zhang, J. P. (1996). Development of the Chinese personality assessment inventory. *Journal of Cross-Cultural Psychology, 27,* 181–199.

Chiu, C. Y. (1991). Responses to injustice in popular Chinese sayings among Hong Kong Chinese students. *Journal of Social Psychology, 131,* 655–665.

Cho, Y. H., & Park, H. H. (1998). Conflict management in Korea: The wisdom of dynamic collectivism. In K. Leung and D. Tjosvold (Eds.), *Conflict management in the Asia Pacific* (pp. 15–48). Singapore: Wiley.

Chung, K. H., & Lee, H. C. (1989). National differences in managerial practices. In K. H. Chung and H. C. Lee (Eds.), *Korean managerial dynamics* (pp. 163–180). New York: Praeger.

Cook, K. S., & Messick, D. M. (1983). Psychological and sociological perspectives on distributive justice: Convergent, divergent, and parallel lines. In D. M. Messick & K. S. Cook (Eds.), *Equity theory: Psychological and sociological perspectives* (pp. 1–12). New York: Praeger.

Cox, T., Jr. (1993). *Cultural diversity in organizations.* San Francisco: Berrett-Koehler.

Cropanzano, R., & Baron, R. A. (1991). Injustice and organizational conflict: The moderating effect of power restoration. *International Journal of Conflict Management, 2,* 5–26.

Crosby, F. (1976). A model of egoistic relative deprivation. *Psychological Review, 83,* 85–113.

Crosby, F., Bromley, S., & Saxe, L. (1980). Recent unobtrusive studies of Black and White discrimination and prejudice: A literature review. *Psychological Bulletin, 87,* 546–563.

Cushner, K., & Brislin, R. W. (1996). *Intercultural interactions: A practical guide. Cross-cultural research and methodology.* Thousand Oaks, CA: Sage.

Davidson, M., & Friedman, R. A. (1998). When excuses don't work: The persistent injustice effect among black managers. *Administrative Science Quarterly, 43,* 154–83.

Deutsch, M. (1975). Equity, equality, and need: What determines which value will be used as the basis of distributive justice? *Journal of Social Issues, 31,* 137–149.

Deutsch, M. (1985). *Distributive justice.* New Haven, CT: Yale University Press.

Dien, D. S. (1982). A Chinese perspective on Kohlberg's theory of moral development. *Development Review, 2,* 331–341.

Doo, L. (1973). Dispute settlement in Chinese-American communities. *American Journal of Comparative Law, 21,* 627–663.

Elsayed-Ekhouly, S. M., & Buda, R. (1996). Organizational conflict: A comparative analysis of conflict styles across cultures. *International Journal of Conflict Management, 7*(1), 71–80.

Epstein, I. I. (1986). Reformatory education in Chinese society. *International Journal of Offender Therapy and Comparative Criminology, 30,* 87–100.

Farh, J. L., Earley, P. C., & Lin, S. C. (1997). Impetus for action: A cultural analysis of justice and organizational citizenship behavior in Chinese society. *Administrative Science Quarterly, 42,* 421–444.

Festinger, L. (1954). A theory of social comparison processes. *Human Relations, 7,* 117–140.

Fisher, R. J. (1990). *The social psychology of intergroup and international conflict resolution.* New York: Springer-Verlag.

Foa, U., & Foa, E. (1974). *Societal structures of the mind.* Springfield, IL: Thomas.

Freudenthaler, H. H., & Mikula, G. (1998). From unfulfilled wants to the experience of injustice: Women's sense of injustice regarding the lopsided division of labor. *Social Justice Research, 11,* 289–312.

Furnham, A. (1985). Just world beliefs in an unjust society: A cross-cultural comparison. *European Journal of Social Psychology, 15,* 363–366.

Gabrielidis, C., Stephan, W. G., Ybarra, O., Pearson, V. M. S., & Villareal, L. (1997). Preferred styles of conflict resolution: Mexico and the United States. *Journal of Cross-Cultural Psychology, 28,* 661–677.

Gilligan, C. (1982). *In a different voice: Psychological theory and women's development.* Cambridge: Harvard University Press.

Graham, J. (1985). The influence of culture on business negotiations. *Journal of International Business Studies, 16,* 81–96.

Graham, J. L., Mintu, A. T., & Rodgers, W. (1994). Explorations of negotiation behaviors in 10 foreign cultures using a model developed in the United States. *Management Science, 40,* 72–95.

Grant, P. R., & Brown, R. (1995). From ethnocentrism to collective protest: Responses to relative deprivation and threats to social identity. *Social Psychology Quarterly, 58,* 195–212.

Griefat, Y., & Katriel, T. (1989). Life demands musayara: Communication and culture among Arabs in Israel. In S. Ting-Toomey and F. Korzenny (Eds.), *Language, communication, and culture* (pp. 121–138). Newbury Park, CA: Sage.

Gudykunst, W. B., & Bond, M. H. (1997). Intergroup relations across cultures. In J. W. Berry, M. H. Segall, & C. Kagitcibasi (Eds.), *Handbook of cross-cultural psychology* (pp. 119–162). Needham Heights, MA: Allyn & Bacon.

Gudykunst, W. B., & Ting-Toomey, S. (1988). Culture and affective communication. *American Behavioral Scientist, 31,* 384–400.

Gulliver, P. H. (1979). *Disputes and negotiations: A cross-cultural perspective.* New York: Academic Press.

Hagiwara, S. (1992). The concept of responsibility and determinants of responsibility judgment in the Japanese context. *International Journal of Psychology, 27*(2), 143–156.

Hamilton, V. L., & Sanders, J. (1988). Punishment and the individual in the United States and Japan. *Law and Society Review, 22,* 301–328.

Hamilton, V. L., & Sanders, J. (1992). *Everyday justice: Responsibility and the individual in Japan and the United States.* New Haven, CT: Yale University Press.

Henderson, G. (1994). *Cultural diversity in the workplace.* Westport, CT: Praeger.

Higgins, A., Power, C., & Kohlberg, L. (1984). The relationship of moral atmosphere to judgments of responsibility. In W. M. Kurtines & J. L. Gewirtz (Eds.), *Morality, moral behavior and moral development* (pp. 74–106). New York: Wiley.

Hines, P. M., Garcia-Preto, N., McGoldrick, M., Almeida, R., & Weltman, S. (1992). Intergenerational relationships across cultures. *Families in Society, 73*(6), 323–338.

Ho, D. (1998). Interpersonal relationships and relationship dominance: An analysis based on methodological relationalism. *Asian Journal of Social Psychology, 1*, 1–16.

Hofstede, G. (1980). *Culture's consequences: International differences in work-related values.* Beverly Hills, CA: Sage.

Hofstede, G. (1983). Cultural relativity of organizational theories. *Journal of International Business Studies, 14*(2), 75–90

Hogan, R., & Emler, N. P. (1981). Retributive justice. In M. J. Lerner & S. C. Lerner (Eds.), *The justice motive in social behavior* (pp. 125–143). New York: Academic Press.

Homans, G. C. (1961). *Social behavior: Its elementary forms.* New York: Harcourt, Brace, Jovanovich.

Hong, G. Y. (1997). Just-world beliefs and attributions of causal responsibility among Korean adolescents. *Cross-Cultural Research, 31*(2), 121–136.

Hsu, F. L. K. (1953). *Americans and Chinese: Two ways of life.* New York: Abelard-Schuman.

Hsu, F. L. K. (1971). Eros, affect and *pao.* In F. L. K. Hsu (Ed.), *Kinship and culture* (pp. 439–475). Chicago: Aldine.

Hui, C. H. (1984). *Individualism-collectivism: Theory, measurement, and its relation to reward allocation.* Unpublished doctoral dissertation, Department of Psychology, University of Illinois, Urbana.

Hui, C. H., Triandis, H. C., & Yee, C. (1991). Cultural differences in reward allocation: Is collectivism the explanation? *British Journal of Social Psychology, 30*, 145–157.

Hundley, G., & Kim, J. (1997). National culture and the factors affecting perceptions of pay fairness in Korea and the United States. *International Journal of Organizational Analysis, 5*(4), 325–341.

Huo, Y. J., Smith, H. J., Tyler, T. R., & Lind, E. A. (1996). Superordinate identification, subgroup identification, and justice concerns: Is separat-

ism the problem, is the assimilation the answer. *Psychological Science, 7*, 40–45.

Ito, K. L. (1982). Illness as retribution: A cultural form of self analysis among urban Hawaiian women. *Culture, medicine, and psychiatry, 6*(4), 385–403.

Jackson, S. E., & Ruderman, M. N. (1995). *Diversity in work teams.* Washington, DC: American Psychological Association.

James, K. (1993). The social context of organizational justice: cultural, intergroup, and structural effects on justice behaviors and perceptions. In R. Cropanzano (Ed.), *Justice in the workplace* (pp. 21–50). Hillsdale, NJ: Erlbaum.

Jost, J. T. (1995). Negative illusions: Conceptual clarification and psychological evidence concerning false consciousness. *Political Psychology, 16*, 397–424.

Jost, J. T., & Banaji, M. (1994). The role of stereotyping in system justification and the production of false consciousness. *British Journal of Social Psychology, 33*, 1–27.

Kakar, S. (1978). *The inner world: A psychoanalytic study of childhood and society in India.* Delhi: Oxford University Press.

Kashima, Y., Siegal, M., Tanaka, K., & Isaka, H. (1988). Universalism in lay conceptions of distributive justice: A cross-cultural examination. *International Journal of Psychology, 23*, 51–64.

Kawashima, T. (1963). Dispute resolution in contemporary Japan. In A. T. von Mehren (Ed.), *Law in Japan: The legal order in a changing society* (pp. 41–72). Cambridge: Harvard University Press.

Kellert, S. R. (1993). Attitudes, knowledge, and behavior toward wildlife among the industrial superpowers: United States, Japan, and Germany. *Journal of Social Issues, 49*, 53–70.

Kelly, C., & Breinlinger, S. (1995). Identity and injustice: Exploring women's participation in collective action. *Journal of Community and Applied Social Psychology, 5*, 41–57.

Kim, K. I., Park, H. J., & Suzuki, N. (1990). Reward allocations in the United States, Japan, and Korea: A comparison of individualistic and collectivistic cultures. *Academy of Management Journal, 33*, 188–198.

Klandermans, B. (1989). Grievance interpretation and success expectations: The social construction of protest. *Social Behaviour, 4*, 113–125.

Kohlberg, L. (1981). *The philosophy of moral development: Moral stages and the idea of justice.* San Francisco: Harper & Row.

Komorita, S. S. (1984). Coalition bargaining. In L. Berkowitz (Ed.), *Advances in experimental social psychology* (Vol. 18, pp. 185–206). New York: Academic Press.

Komorita, S. S., & Leung, K. (1985). Toward a synthesis of power and justice in reward allocation. In E. J. Lawler (Ed.), *Advances in group processes* (Vol. 2, 169–196). Greenwich, CT: JAI Press.

Kozan, M. K. (1997). Culture and conflict management: A theoretical framework. *International Journal of Conflict Management, 8*, 338–360.

Kozan, M. K., & Ergin, C. (1998). Preference for third party help in conflict management in the United States and Turkey: An experimental study. *Journal of Cross-Cultural Psychology, 29*, 540–558.

Lalonde, R. N., & Silverman, R. A. (1994). Behavioral preferences in response to social injustice: The effects of group permeability and social identity salience. *Journal of Social and Personality Psychology, 66*, 78–85.

Lee, Y. T., Pepitone, A., & Albright, L. (1997). Descriptive and prescriptive beliefs about justice: A Sino-U.S. comparison. *Cross-Cultural Research, 31*(2), 101–120.

Lerner, M. J. (1980). *The belief in a just world.* New York: Plenum.

Leung, K. (1987). Some determinants of reactions to procedural models for conflict resolution: A cross-national study. *Journal of Personality and Social Psychology, 53*, 898–908.

Leung, K. (1988). Theoretical advances in justice behavior: Some cross-cultural input. In M. H. Bond (Ed.), *The cross-cultural challenge to social psychology* (pp. 218–229). Newbury Park, CA: Sage.

Leung, K. (1997). Negotiation and reward allocations across cultures. In P. C. Earley & M. Erez (Eds.), *New perspectives on international industrial/organizational psychology* (pp. 640–675). San Francisco: Jossey-Bass.

Leung, K., Au, Y. F., Fernández-Dols, J. M., & Iwawaki, S. (1992). Preferences for methods of conflict processing in two collectivist cultures. *International Journal of Psychology, 27*, 195–209.

Leung, K., & Bond, M. H. (1982). How Chinese and Americans reward task-related contributions: A preliminary study. *Psychologia, 25*, 32–39.

Leung, K., & Bond, M. H. (1984). The impact of cultural collectivism on reward allocation. *Journal of Personality and Social Psychology, 47*, 793–804.

Leung, K., Chiu, W. H., & Au, Y. K. (1993). Sympathy and support for industrial actions. *Journal of Applied Psychology, 78*, 781–787.

Leung, K., & Iwawaki, S. (1988). Cultural collectivism and distributive behavior: A cross-national study. *Journal of Cross-Cultural Psychology, 19*, 35–49.

Leung, K., & Kwong, J. Y. Y. (in press). Human resource management practices in international joint ventures in China: A justice analysis. *Human Resource Management Review.*

Leung, K., & Li, W. K. (1990). Psychological mechanisms of process control effects. *Journal of Applied Psychology, 75*, 613–620.

Leung, K., & Morris, M. W. (2001). Justice through the lens of culture and ethnicity. In J. Sanders and V. L. Hamilton (Eds.), *Handbook of law and social sciences: Justice* (pp. 343–378). New York: Plenum.

Leung, K., & Park, H. J. (1986). Effects of interactional goal on choice of allocation rules: A cross-cultural study. *Organizational Behavior and Human Decision Processes, 37*, 111–120.

Leung, K., Smith, P. B., Wang, Z. M., & Sun, H. F. (1996). Job satisfaction in joint venture hotels in China: An organizational justice analysis. *Journal of International Business Studies, 27*, 947–962.

Leung, K., & Stephan, W. G. (1998). Perceptions of injustice in intercultural relations. *Applied and Preventive Psychology, 7*, 195–205.

Leung K., & Stephan, W. G. (2000). Conflict and injustice in intercultural relations: Insights from the Arab-Israeli and Sino-British disputes. In J. Duckitt & S. Renshon (Eds.), *Political psychology: Cultural and cross-cultural perspectives* (pp. 128–145). London: Macmillan.

Leung, K., Su, S. K., & Morris, M. W. (in press). When is criticism *not* constuctive? The roles of fairness perceptions and dispositional attributions in employee acceptance of critical supervisory feedback. *Human Relations.*

Leung, K., Wang, Z. M., & Smith, P. B. (in press). Job attitudes and organizational justice in joint venture hotels in China: The role of expatriate managers. *International Journal of Human Resource Management.*

Lind, E. A. (1994). Procedural justice and culture: Evidence for ubiquitous process concerns. *Zeitschrift für Rechtssoziologie, 15*, 24–36.

Lind, E. A., Erickson, B. E., Friedland, N., & Dickenberger, M. (1978). Reactions to procedural models for adjudicative conflict resolution: A cross-national study. *Journal of Conflict Resolution, 2*, 318–341.

Lind, E. A. Huo, Y. J., & Tyler, T. R. (1994). And justice for all: Ethnicity, gender, and preferences for dispute resolution procedures. *Law and Human Behavior, 18*, 269–290.

Lind, E. A., Kray, L., & Thompson, L. (1998). The social construction of injustice: Fairness judgments in response to own and others' unfair treatment by authorities. *Organizational Behavior and Human Decision Processes, 75*, 1–22.

Lind, E. A., & Tyler, T. R. (1988). *The social psychology of procedural justice.* New York: Plenum.

CULTURAL PERSPECTIVE OF SOCIAL JUSTICE **407**

Lind, E. A., Tyler, T. R., & Huo, Y. J. (1997). Procedural context and culture: Variation in the antecedents of procedural justice judgments. *Journal of Personality and Social Psychology, 73*, 767–780.

Lukes, S. (1973). *Individualism.* Oxford, England: Blackwell.

Ma, H. K. (1997). The affective and cognitive aspects of moral development: A Chinese perspective. In K. Sinha (Eds.), *Asian perspective on psychology* (pp. 93–109). Thousand Oaks, CA: Sage.

Mahler, I., Greenberg, L., & Hayashi, H. (1981). A comparative study of rules of justice: Japanese versus Americans. *Psychology, 24*, 1–8.

Marin, G. (1981). Perceiving justice across cultures: Equity versus equality in Colombia and in the United States. *International Journal of Psychology, 16*, 153–159.

Marin, G. (1985). The preference for equity when judging the attractiveness and fairness of an allocator: The role of familiarity and culture. *Journal of Social Psychology, 125*, 543–549.

Markus, H., & Kitayama, S. (1991). Culture and self. *Psychological Review, 98*, 224–253.

Marriott, M. (1990). *India through Hindu categories.* New Delhi: Sage.

Martin, J., Brickman, P., & Murray, A. (1984). Moral outrage and pragmatism: Explanations for collective action. *Journal of Experimental Social Psychology, 20*, 484–496.

McCarty, C. A., Weisz, J. R., Wanitromanee, K., Eastman, K. L., Suwanlert, S., Chaiyasit, W., & Band, E. B. (1999). Culture, coping, and context: Primary and secondary control among Thai and American youth. *Journal of Child Psychology and Psychiatry and Allied Disciplines, 40*(5), 809–818.

Mendonca, M., & Kanungo, R. N. (1994). Motivation through effective reward management in developing countries. In R. N. Kanungo & M. Mendonca (Eds.), *Work motivation: Models for developing countries* (pp. 49–83). New Delhi: Sage.

Mikula, G. (1980). Introduction: Main issues in the psychological research on justice. In G. Mikula (Ed.), *Justice and social interaction* (pp. 13–24). New York: Springer-Verlag.

Mikula, G., Petri, B., & Tanzer, N. (1990). What people regard as unjust: Types and structures of everyday experiences of injustice. *European Journal of Social Psychology, 20*, 133–149.

Mikula, G., Scherer, K. R., & Athenstaedt, U. (1998). The role of injustice in the elicitation of differential emotional reactions. *Personality and Social Psychology Bulletin, 24*, 769–783.

Miller, J. G. (1994). Cultural diversity in the morality of caring: Individually-oriented versus duty-based interpersonal moral codes. *Cross-Cultural Research, 28*, 3–39.

Miller, J. G., & Bersoff, D. M. (1992). Culture and moral judgment: How are conflicts between justice and friendship resolved? *Journal of Personality and Social Psychology, 62*, 541–554.

Miller, J. G., Bersoff, D. M., & Harwood, R. L. (1990). Perceptions of social responsibilities in India and in the United States: Moral imperatives or personal decisions? *Journal of Personality and Social Psychology, 58*, 33–47.

Miller, J. G., & Luthar, S. (1989). Issues of interpersonal responsibility and accountability: A comparison of Indians' and Americans' moral judgments. *Social Cognition, 3*, 237–261.

Morris, M. W., & Leung, K. (2000). Justice for all? Understanding cultural influences on judgments of outcome and process fairness. *Applied psychology: An international review, 49*, 100–132.

Morris, M. W., Leung, K., Ames, D., & Lickel B. (1999). Incorporating perspectives from inside and outside: Synergy between *emic* and *etic* research on culture and justice. *Academy of Management Review, 24*, 781–796.

Morris, M. W., Leung, K., & Sethi, S. (1995). *Person perception in the heat of conflict: Perceptions of opponents' traits and conflict resolution choices in two cultures.* Unpublished manuscript, Stanford University.

Morris, M. W. & Peng, K. (1994). Culture and cause: American and Chinese attributions for social and physical events. *Journal of Personality and Social Psychology, 67*, 949–971.

Morris, M. W., Williams, K. Y., Leung, K., Bhatnagar, D., Li, J. F., Kondo, M., Luo, J. L., & Hu, J. C. (1999). Culture, conflict management style, and underlying values: Accounting for cross-national differences in styles of handling conflicts among U.S., Chinese, Indian and Filipina managers. *Journal of International Business Studies, 29*, 729–748.

Murphy-Berman, V., Berman, J. J., Singh, P., Pacharui, A., & Kumar, P. (1984). Factors affecting allocation to needy and meritorious recipients: A cross-cultural comparison. *Journal of Personality and Social Psychology, 46*, 1267–1272.

Na, E. Y., & Loftus, E. F. (1998). Attitudes towards law and prisoners, conservative authoritarianism, attribution, and internal-external locus of control: Korean and American law students and undergraduates. *Journal of Cross-Cultural Psychology, 29*(5), 595–615.

Nader, L., & Todd, H. F. (1978). The disputing process: Law in 10 societies. New York: Columbia University Press.

Nagata, D. K. (1990). The Japanese American internment: Perceptions of moral community, fairness, and redress. *Journal of Social Issues, 46*(1), 133–146.

Ohbuchi, K., Fukushima, O., and Tedeschi, J. T. (1999). Cultural values in conflict management: Goal orientation, goal attainment, and tactical decision. *Journal of Cross-Cultural Psychology, 30*, 51–71.

Ohbuchi, K., Kameda, M., & Agarie, N. (1989). Apology as aggression control: Its role in mediating appraisal of and response to harm. *Journal of Personality and Social Psychology, 56*, 219–227.

Ohbuchi, K., & Takahashi, Y. (1994). Cultural styles of conflict management in Japanese and Americans: Passivity, covertness, and effectiveness of strategies. *Journal of Applied Social Psychology, 24*, 1345–1366.

Opotow, S. (1990). Moral exclusion and injustice: An introduction. *Journal of Social Issues, 46*, 1–20.

Ouchi, W. G., & Jaeger, A. M. (1978). Type Z organization: Stability in the midst of mobility. *Academy of Management Review, 3*, 305–314.

Parsons, T., & Shils, E. A. (1951). *Toward a general theory of action.* Cambridge: Harvard University Press.

Pearce, J. L., Bigley, G. A., & Branyiczki, I. (1998). Procedural justice as modernism: Placing industrial/organizational psychology in context. *Applied psychology: An international review, 47*(3), 371–396.

Pearson, V. M. S., & Stephan, W. G. (1988). Preferences for styles of negotiation: A comparison of Brazil and the U.S. *International Journal of Intercultural Relations, 22*, 67–83.

Pepitone, A., & L'Armand, K. (1997). Justice in cultural context: A social-psychological perspective. *Cross-cultural research, 31*(2), 81–98.

Pratto, F., Sidanius, J., Stallworth, L. M., & Malle, B. F. (1994). Social dominance orientation: A personality variable predicting social and political attitudes. *Journal of Personality and Social Psychology, 67*(4), 741–763.

Probst, T., Carnevale, P. J., & Triandis, H. C. (1999). Cultural values in intergroup and single-group social dilemmas. *Organizational Behavior and Human Decision Processes, 77*, 171–191.

Pruitt, D. G., & Carnevale, P. J. (1993). *Negotiation in social conflict.* Bristol, PA: Open University Press.

Quigley, B. M., & Tedeschi, J. T. (1996). The effects of blame attributions on feelings of anger. *Personality and Social Psychology Bulletin, 22*, 1280–1288.

Rabinowitz, J. L. (1999). Go with the flow or fight the power: The interactive effects of social dominance orientation and perceived injustice on support for the status quo. *Political Psychology, 20*, 1–24.

Runciman, W. G. (1966). *Relative deprivation and equal justice: A study of attitudes toward social inequality in twentieth century England.* Berkeley: University of California Press.

Rutte, C. G., & Messick, D. M. (1995). An integrated model of perceived unfairness in organizations. *Social Justice Research, 8*, 239–261.

Sanders, J., & Hamilton, V. L. (Eds.). (2001). *Handbook of law and social sciences: Justice.* New York: Plenum.

Shapiro, D. L., Trevino, L. K., & Victor, B. (1995). Correlates of employee theft: A multidimensional justice perspective. *International Journal of Conflict Management, 6*, 404–414.

Shaver, K. G. (1985). *The attribution of blame.* New York: Springer-Verlag.

Shultz, T. R., & Schleifer, M. (1983). Toward a refinement of attribution concepts. In J. Jaspars, F. D. Fincham, & M. Hewstone (Eds.), *Attribution theory and research: Conceptual, developmental and social dimensions* (pp. 37–62). London: Academic.

Shultz, T. R., Schleifer, M., & Altman, I. (1981). Judgments of causation, responsibility, and punishment in cases of harm-doing. *Canadian Journal of Behavioral Science, 13*, 238–253.

Shweder, R. A., Mahapatra, M., & Miller, J. G. (1987). Cultural and moral development in India and the United States. In J. Kagan & S. Lamb (Eds.), *The emergence of morality in young children* (pp. 1–89). Chicago: University of Chicago Press.

Sidaneous, J. (1993). The psychology of group conflict and the dynamics of oppression: A social dominance perspective. In S. Iyengar & W. McGuire (Eds.), *Explorations in political psychology.* Durham, NC: Duke University Press.

Sidaneous, J., Pratto, F., & Rabinowitz, J. L. (1994). Gender, ethnic status and ideological asymmetry: A social dominance interpretation. *Journal of Cross-Cultural Psychology, 25*, 194–216.

Sinha, D. (1987). *Ahimsa as conflict resolution technique and instrument of peace: A psychological appraisal.* Paper presented at the seminar on Peace and Conflict Resolution in the World Community, India.

Smith, P. B., Peterson, M. F., Leung, K., & Dugan, S. (1998). Individualism-collectivism, power distance, and handling of disagreement: A cross-national study. *International Journal of Intercultural Relations, 22*, 351–367.

Smith, P. B., Peterson, M. F., Misumi, J., & Tayeb, M. H. (1989). On the generality of leadership styles across cultures. *Journal of Occupational Psychology, 62*, 97–110.

Smith, R. H., Parrott, W. G., Ozer, D., & Moniz, A. (1994). Subjective injustice and inferiority as predictors of hostile and depressive feelings of anger. *Personality and Social Psychology Bulletin, 20,* 705–711.

Snarey, J. R. (1985). Cross-cultural universality of social-moral development: A critical review of Kohlbergian research. *Psychological Bulletin, 97*(2), 202–232.

Sprecher, S. (1986). The relationship between equity and emotions in close relationships. *Social Psychology Quarterly, 49,* 309–321.

Starr, J. (1978). Turkish village disputing behavior. In L. Nader and H. F. Todd, Jr. (Eds.), *The disputing process: Law in 10 societies* (pp. 122–151). New York: Columbia University Press.

Steiner, D. D., & Gilliland, S. W. (1996). Fairness reactions to personnel selection techniques in France and the United States. *Journal of Applied Psychology, 81*(2), 134–141.

Stephan, C. W., & Stephan, W. G., & Saito, I. (1998). Emotional expression in the United States and Japan: The non-monolithic nature of individualism and collectivism. *Journal of Cross-Cultural Psychology, 29,* 728–748.

Stephan, W. G., Stephan, C. W., & Cabeza de Vargas, M. (1996). Emotional expression in Costa Rica and the United States. *Journal of Cross-Cultural Psychology, 27,* 147–160.

Stevenson, H. W., Lee, S. Y., Chen, C. S., Stigler, J. W., Hsu, C. C., & Kitamura, S. (1990). Contexts of achievement: A study of American, Chinese, and Japanese children. *Monographs of the Society for Research in Child Development, 55*(1–2) (Serial No. 221).

Stouffer, S. A., Lunsdaine, A. A., Williams, R. M., Smith, M. B., Janis, I. L., Star, S. A., & Cottrell, L. J. (1949). *The American soldier: Combat and its aftermath* (Vol.2). Princeton, NJ: Princeton University Press.

Stouffer, S. A., Suchman, E. A., DeVinney, L. C., Star, S. A., & Williams, R. M., Jr. (1949). *The American soldier: Adjustment during army life* (Vol. 1). Princeton, NJ: Princeton University Press.

Sugahara, I., & Huo, Y. J. (1994). Disputes in Japan: A cross-cultural test of the procedural justice model. *Social Justice Research, 7,* 129–144.

Tanabe, K. (1963). The process of litigation: An experiment with the adversary system. In A. T. von Mehren (Ed.), *Law in Japan: The legal order in a changing society* (pp. 73–110). Cambridge: Harvard University Press.

Tedeschi, J. T., & Nesler, M. S. (1993). Grievances: Development and reactions. In R. B. Felson & J. T. Tedeschi, *Aggression and violence: Social interactionist perspectives* (pp. 13–45). Washington, DC: American Psychological Association.

Thibaut, J., & Walker, L. (1975). *Procedural justice: A psychological analysis.* Hillside, NJ: Erlbaum.

Thibaut, J., & Walker, L. (1978). A theory of procedure. *California Law Review, 66,* 541–566.

Tilly, C. (1978). *From mobilization to revolution.* Reading, MA: Addison-Wesley.

Ting-Toomey, S., Gao, G., Trubinsky, P., Yang, Z., Kim, H. S., Liu, S. L., & Nishida, T. (1991). Culture, face maintenance, and styles of handling interpersonal conflict: A study in five countries. *International Journal of Conflict Management, 2,* 275–296.

Triandis, H. C. (1972). *The analysis of subjective culture.* New York: Wiley.

Triandis, H. C. (1989). Self and social behavior in differing cultural contexts. *Psychological Review, 96,* 269–289.

Triandis, H. C., Leung, K., Villareal, M. J., & Clack, F. J. (1985). Allocentric versus idiocentric tendencies: Convergent and discriminant validation. *Journal of Research in Personality, 19,* 395–415.

Tse, D. K., Francis, J., & Walls, J. (1994). Cultural differences in conducting intra- and intercultural negotiations: A Sino-Canadian comparison. *Journal of International Business Studies, 25,* 537–555.

Tsui, A. S., & O'Reilly, C. A. (1989). Beyond simple demographic effects: The importance of relational demography in superior-subordinate dyads. *Academy of Management Journal, 32*(2), 402–423.

Tyler, T. R. (1990). *Why people follow the law: Procedural justice, legitimacy, and compliance.* New Haven, CT: Yale University Press.

Tyler, T. R. (1994). Psychological models of the justice models. *Journal of Personality and Social Psychology, 67,* 850–863.

Tyler, T. R., & Bies, R. J. (1990). Beyond formal procedures: The interpersonal context of procedural justice. In J. S. Carroll (Ed.), *Applied social psychology and organizational settings* (pp. 77–98). Hillsdale, NJ: Erlbaum.

Tyler, T. R., Boeckmann, R. J., Smith, H. J., & Huo, Y. J. (1997). *Social justice in a diverse society.* Boulder, CO: Westview.

Tyler, T. R., & Lind, E. A. (1992). A relational model of authority in groups. In M. Zanna (Ed.), *Advances in experimental social psychology* (pp. 115–191). New York: Academic Press.

Tyler, T. R., & Lind, E. A. (2001). Procedural justice. In J. Sanders and V. L. Hamilton (Eds.), *Handbook of law and social sciences: Justice* (pp. 65–92). New York: Plenum.

Tyler, T. R., Lind, E. A., & Huo, Y. J. (1995). *Culture, ethnicity, and authority: Social categorization and social orientation effects on the psychology of legitimacy.* Unpublished manuscript, University of California, Berkeley.

Vanneman, R. & Pettigrew, T. F. (1972). Race and relative deprivation in the urban United States. *Race, 13*, 461-486.

Wall, J., & Stark, J. (1998). North American conflict management. In K. Leung and D. Tjosvold (Eds.), *Conflict management in the Asia Pacific* (pp. 303–334). Singapore: Wiley.

Wall, J. A., & Blum, M. E. (1991). Community mediation in the People's Republic of China. *Journal of Conflict Resolution, 35*, 3–20.

Wallbott, H. G., & Scherer, K. R. (1986). The antecedents of emotional experiences. In K. S. Scherer, H. G. Wallbott, & A. B. Summerfield (Eds.), *Experiencing emotion: A cross-cultural study* (pp. 69–83). Cambridge: Cambridge University Press.

Walster, E., Walster, G., & Berscheid, E. (1978). *Equity: Theory and research.* Boston: Allyn & Bacon.

Waters, H. (1992). Race, culture, and interpersonal conflict. *International Journal of Intercultural Relations, 16*, 437–454.

Weiner, B., & Kukla, A. (1970). An attributional analysis of achievement motivation. *Journal of Personality and Social Psychology, 15*, 1–20.

Weisz, J. R., Rothbaum, F. M., & Blackburn, T. C. (1984). Standing out and standing in: The psychology of control in America and Japan. *American Psychologist, 39*, 955–969.

Weldon, E., Jehn, K. A., Chen, X. M., & Wang, Z. M. (1996, August). *Conflict management in U.S.-Chinese joint ventures.* Paper presented in the 1997 Academy of Management Meeting, Boston.

Wheeler, L., Reis, H. T., & Bond, M. H. (1989). Collectivism-individualism in everyday life: The Middle Kingdom and the melting pot. *Journal of Personality and Social Psychology, 57*, 79–86.

Wright, S. C. (1997). Ambiguity, social influence, and collective action: Generating collective protest in response to tokenism. *Personality and Social Psychology Bulletin, 23*, 1277–1290.

Wright, S. C., & Taylor, D. M. (1998). Responding to tokenism: Individual action in the face of collective injustice. *European Journal of Social Psychology, 28*, 647–667.

Yamagishi, T. (1988a). Exit from the group as an individualistic solution to the free rider problem in the United States and Japan. *Journal of Experimental Social Psychology, 24*, 530–542.

Yamagishi, T. (1988b). The provision of a sanctioning system in the United States and Japan. *Social Psychology Quarterly, 51*, 265–271.

Yamagishi, T., Cook, K. S., & Watabe, M. (1998). Uncertainty, trust, and commitment formation in the United States and Japan. *American Journal of Sociology, 104*(1), 165–194.

Yang, L. S. (1957). The concept of *pao* as a basis for social relations in China. In J. K. Fairbank (Ed.), *Chinese thought and institutions* (pp. 291–309). Chicago: University of Chicago Press.

20

The A, B, Cs of Acculturation

COLLEEN WARD

Developments in communication and transportation technologies have resulted in the world becoming an increasingly smaller place than ever before. We are truly entering a borderless era in human history in which interactions between people of vastly diverse cultural backgrounds are becoming as common and matter-of-fact today as they were rare until a hundred years ago. Today, even people in seemingly faraway and disparate lands are being thrust together with others in ways never seen before.

It is within this background of change that the cross-cultural study of the psychology of acculturation has gained importance in the past few decades. Defined in this chapter as the changes that occur as a result of continuous first-hand contact between individuals of differing cultural origins, it is a topic that has enormous meaning and implications to literally millions of people worldwide in all walks of life. It is fitting, therefore, that we end this book with this most appropriate topic.

In this chapter, Ward provides one of the most excellent and comprehensive reviews on this topic that exists. After defining acculturation, she distinguishes among the different types of groups of individuals that need to deal with acculturation, such as immigrants, refugees, and sojourners. She then discusses the adaptive outcomes of acculturation, making the useful distinction between psychological and sociocultural adjustment. Indeed, this distinction is particularly useful in categorizing and understanding the available literature on this topic.

Ward cleverly synthesizes the three major theoretical and empirical approaches that have dominated work in the field: stress and coping, culture learning, and social identification. She focuses on the affective, behavioral, and cognitive (A, B, C's) differences that each perspective provides. While the reviews in each area are unique and meaningful in their own right, it is the synthesis and integration among these views that are truly noteworthy in Ward's approach. For example, her first illustration is particularly useful not only in helping readers to understand what aspect of acculturation they are reviewing, but also in helping all of us to realize that we are talking about the same, enormous construct—acculturation—from multiple angles.

Thus, while Ward discusses the current knowledge gleaned from the available literature in each section, highlighting future avenues of research in each, perhaps her greatest contribution in this chapter is the message of integration of emerging theory and research—across all avenues (i.e., the A, B, C's) to develop what she refers to as a "truly cross-cultural perspective." This endeavor, however, is not without its pitfalls, both conceptually and empirically, and as Ward contends, caution must be exercised in assuming universality about the process or products of acculturation. Instead, what is needed in the future are large-scale, systematic, comparative studies of acculturation that integrate multiple cultural perspectives in a variety of different types of groups in a longitudinal or quasi-longitudinal design. Indeed, this comprehensive, integrating, and all-encompassing perspective—one that incorporates multiple designs, data collections, and theories—is a profoundly and fundamentally different way of doing research than currently done in general. In fact, it is going to be hard work. But, Ward's call for this hard work is relevant not only for the topic of acculturation, but also for all areas of psychology, as can be plainly seen throughout all the chapters in this volume.

What is "culture shock," and how does it affect cross-cultural travelers? What "pushes" and "pulls" people to migrate? How does one adapt to life in a new culture? Does migration affect cultural identity? How do expatriate business-people learn to manage in a new cultural context? Are traditional values, norms, and customs retained over successive generations of migrants? How are premigration traumas related to postsettlement adjustment in refugee families? Which factors promote harmonious relations between immigrants and members of the host society? These and related questions are considered within the purview of acculturation theory and research.

Acculturation refers to changes that occur as a result of continuous first-hand contact between individuals of differing cultural origins (Redfield, Linton, & Herskovits, 1936). Originally of primary interest to anthropologists and sociologists, the term was first used in reference to group-level phenomena. More recently, psychologists have become interested in the process and products of acculturation, and these phenomena are now also studied at the individual level (Berry, 1997; Graves, 1967).

Acculturation may occur within a broad range of social, cultural, and political contexts. It also occurs among a wide variety of groups and individuals (see Table 20.1). Acculturating groups may be distinguished on at least three dimensions: mobility, permanence and voluntariness (Berry & Sam, 1997). First, people who have made cross-cultural relocations, such as refugees and immigrants, may be distinguished from members of sedentary groups, such as native peoples and established ethnocultural communities. Second, cross-cultural travelers who resettle temporarily, such as sojourners, differ from those, like immigrants, whose move is more permanent. Finally, those who voluntarily engage in intercultural contact (e.g., immigrants and sojourners) may be distinguished from those who are forced by necessity into involuntary interactions (e.g., refugees, indigenous peoples). When the voluntary-involuntary distinction is applied specifically to migrants, voluntary migrants may be described as having been drawn or pulled toward a new country, usually in hopes of a better lifestyle, while involuntary migrants more commonly are seen as pushed from their homeland into an alien environment.

Synthesizing theory and research on these acculturating groups is a difficult task. Historically, six relatively independent bodies of literature have emerged, and they have been subjected in varying degrees to multidisciplinary influences from psychology, psychiatry, sociology, and anthropology. Even the psychological approaches have varied in terms of orientation (e.g., cognitive, behavioral) and content area (e.g., social, clinical). In addition, the number of empirical investigations of acculturation has grown exponentially over the last three decades. Given the vast and diverse literature on acculturation, in this chapter I focus on three groups of cross-cultural travelers—sojourners, immigrants, and refugees—and on three contemporary theoretical approaches: social identification, culture learning, and stress and coping.

Theoretical Approaches to Acculturation

As the number of cross-cultural travelers has increased and research on acculturation has expanded, three broad theoretical approaches have emerged as guiding forces in the field of psychology. The first is associated with social identification theories and is concerned with the

Table 20.1   Types of Acculturating Groups

Mobility	Voluntariness of Contact	
	Voluntary	Involuntary
Sedentary	Ethnocultural groups	Indigenous peoples
Migrant		
Permanent	Immigrants	Refugees
Temporary	Sojourners	Asylum seekers

Source: From Berry and Sam, 1997, p. 295.

way people perceive and think about themselves and others, including how they process information about their own group (in-group) and other groups (out-groups). The second reflects a culture learning approach, which highlights the social psychology of the intercultural encounter and the processes involved in learning the culture-specific skills required to thrive and survive in a new milieu. The third is linked to psychological models of stress and coping and is applied to the study of cross-cultural transition and adaptation. The theoretical underpinnings of all three approaches have been "borrowed" from mainstream social and health psychology, but are applied specifically to the study of acculturating individuals.

The social identity approach has been influenced by contemporary theory and research in the field of social cognition. This approach has offered two complementary perspectives on intercultural contact and change. The first functions at the individual level of analysis. It highlights selected aspects of ethnic or cultural identity and is concerned primarily with the definition and measurement of acculturation (e.g., Cuéllar, Harris, & Jasso, 1980; Hocoy, 1996). This approach has generally viewed acculturation as a state, rather than a process, and is concerned with measuring the construct at a single point in time and identifying its relevant predictors, correlates, and consequences. The second major line of inquiry is more suitable for group-level analysis and highlights the significance of intergroup perceptions and relations. This line of research examines social interactions between members of the host community and various sojourner or immigrant groups and most frequently interprets intergroup relations within the context of Tajfel's (1978, 1981) social identity theory (e.g., Kosmitzki, 1996; Moghaddam, Taylor, & Lalonde, 1987; Ostrowska & Bochenska, 1996).

The culture learning approach, in contrast, has its roots in social and experimental psy-

chology and has been strongly influenced by Argyle's (1969) work on social skills and interpersonal behaviors. This approach is based on the assumption that cross-cultural problems arise because sojourners, immigrants, or refugees have difficulties managing everyday social encounters. Adaptation, therefore, comes in the form of learning the culture-specific skills that are required to negotiate the new cultural milieu (Bochner, 1972, 1986). Researchers who have adopted a culture learning approach to intercultural contact and change have emphasized the significance of culture-specific variables in the adaptation process. Attention is paid to differences in intercultural communication styles, including its verbal and nonverbal components, as well as rules, conventions, and norms, and their influences on intercultural effectiveness. More recently, researchers have broadened this line of inquiry in attempts to build predictive models of sociocultural adaptation with emphasis on such factors as culture-specific knowledge, intercultural training, language fluency, previous experience abroad, contact with host nationals, cultural distance, and cultural identity (Ward, 1996).

The third major approach, stress and coping, conceptualizes cross-cultural transition as a series of stress-provoking life changes that draw on adjustive resources and require coping responses. This approach has been strongly influenced by Lazarus and Folkman's (1984) work on stress, appraisal, and coping, as well as earlier theory and research on life events (Holmes & Rahe, 1967). The analytical framework is broad and incorporates both characteristics of the individual and characteristics of the situation that may facilitate or impede adjustment to a new cultural milieu. Accordingly, researchers seeking to identify the factors that affect cross-cultural adjustment, particularly psychological well-being and satisfaction, have examined many of the same variables as those who investigate stress and coping in other domains. These include life changes, cognitive appraisal of change, coping strategies, personality, and social support. With respect to more culture-specific variables, cultural identity and acculturation status have been considered in sojourner, immigrant, and refugee populations (Ward, 1996).

Together, these three approaches (affective, behavioral, and cognitive) constitute the A, B, C's of acculturation. Affective components of acculturation are highlighted in the stress-and-coping approach; behavioral elements are featured in the culture learning approach, and cognitive variables are emphasized in the social identity approach.

Intercultural Contact and Adaptation

Despite the emerging theoretical sophistication and coherence in the study of cross-cultural transition, there is still considerable debate about the appropriate criteria for the assessment of "cross-cultural adjustment" or "intercultural adaptation" (Benson, 1978; Church, 1982; Ward, 1996). Are the features of a successful transition defined by good relations with members of the host culture, psychological well-being, competent work performance, positive attitudes toward the transition, or identification with host nationals? Diverse indices of adjustment have been reported in the literature on immigrants, refugees, and sojourners, and research has incorporated a wide range of outcome measures. These have included self-awareness and self-esteem (Kamal & Maruyama, 1990), mood states (Stone Feinstein & Ward, 1990), health status (Babiker, Cox, & Miller, 1980), language fluency (Adler, 1975), feelings of acceptance and satisfaction (Brislin, 1981), the nature and extent of interactions with hosts (Sewell & Davidsen, 1961), cultural awareness (Martin, 1987), the acquisition of culturally appropriate behaviors (Bochner, Lin, & McLeod, 1979), perceptual maturity (Yoshikawa, 1988), communication competency (Ruben, 1976), acculturative stress (Berry, Kim, Minde, & Mok, 1987), and academic and job performance (Black & Gregersen, 1990; Perkins, Perkins, Guglielmino, & Reiff, 1977).

Because researchers have relied on a combination of theoretical and empirical approaches to describe and define adaptation, a variety of analytical frameworks has emerged. Hammer, Gudykunst, and Wiseman's (1978) study of intercultural effectiveness, for example, produced a three-factor model based on (a) ability to manage psychological stress, (b) ability to commu-nicate effectively, and (c) ability to establish interpersonal relationships. Mendenhall and Oddou (1985) discussed affective, behavioral, and cognitive components of adaptation, including psychological well-being, functional interactions with hosts, and the acceptance of appropriate attitudes and values. Kealey's (1989) empirical research highlighted both positive and negative psychological outcomes, such as life satisfaction and indicators of psychological and psychosomatic distress, in addition to cross-cultural understanding, contact variables, and job performance. Black and Stephens (1989) assumed a more explicitly behavioral approach and identified three facets of sojourner adjustment: general adjustment (managing daily activities), interaction adjustment (relating effectively to host nationals), and work adjustment (accomplishing work-related objectives). A number of other researchers have also concentrated on domain-specific types of adaptation, such as work performance and satisfaction (Lance & Richardson, 1985), economic adaptation (Aycan & Berry, 1994), and academic achievement and adjustment to school (Lese & Robbins, 1994). A common theme running through all of these models is the recognition that psychological well-being and satisfaction, as well as effective relationships with members of the new culture, are important components of adaptation for cross-cultural travelers.

This theme is reflected in work by Ward and colleagues, who have maintained that intercultural adaptation can be broadly divided into two categories: psychological and sociocultural (Searle & Ward, 1990; Ward & Kennedy, 1992, 1993b). Psychological adjustment, based predominantly on affective responses, refers to feelings of well-being or satisfaction during cross-cultural transitions. *Sociocultural adaptation*, on the other hand, is in the behavioral domain and refers to the ability to "fit in" or execute effective interactions in a new cultural milieu. An evolving program of research has demonstrated that psychological and sociocultural adaptations are conceptually related, but empirically distinct. They derive from different theoretical foundations, they are predicted by different types of variables, and they exhibit different patterns of variation over time.

Situated in a framework of stress and coping, psychological adjustment is strongly influenced by factors such as life changes, personality, and social support variables (Searle & Ward, 1990; Ward & Kennedy, 1992). Evidence suggests that fluctuations in psychological adjustment are variable over time despite the tendency for problems to peak in the earliest stages of transition. Sociocultural adaptation, interpreted from a culture learning perspective, is more strongly affected by contact variables such as quantity and quality of relations with host nationals (Ward & Kennedy, 1993c; Ward & Rana-Deuba, 2000), cultural distance (Furnham & Bochner, 1982; Searle & Ward, 1990), and length of residence in the host country (Ward & Kennedy, 1996b). Changes in sociocultural adaptation are also more predictable; adaptation improves rapidly in the earliest stages of transition, reaches a plateau, and then appears to level off (Ward & Kennedy, 1996b; Ward, Okura, Kennedy, & Kojima, 1998). Given the breadth of the theoretical constructs, their conceptual underpinnings, their empirical foundation, and their potential for application at the intrapersonal, interpersonal, intragroup, and intergroup levels, the distinction of psychological and sociocultural adaptation provides a fairly comprehensive, yet parsimonious, overview of intercultural outcomes.

Putting It All Together: Theory, Process, and Outcomes

Figure 20.1 summarizes the A, B, C's of crossing cultures. It combines the major theoretical approaches—stress and coping, culture learning, and social identification theories—with their varying emphases on affect, behavior, and cognition. It also features the basic components of cross-cultural adaptation—psychological and sociocultural—that are shared among sojourners, immigrants, and refugees. The figure positions the adaptational outcomes in relation to underlying theoretical constructs and illustrates how the affective, behavioral, and cognitive perspectives merge to describe and explain cross-cultural transition and adaptation. The remainder of this chapter elaborates and synthesizes this framework, with emphasis on empirical research.

Social Identification

Cultural Identity and Acculturation

Although changes occur in many areas during the process of acculturation, one of the most fundamental changes relates to cultural iden-tity. On the most basic level, ethnic or cultural identification involves the recognition, categorization, or self-identification of oneself as a member of an ethnocultural group. Identification, however, is also seen as including a sense of affirmation, pride, and positive evaluation of one's group, as well as an involvement dimension relating to ethnocultural behaviors, values, and traditions (Phinney, 1992). For example, ethnic and cultural identity scales frequently incorporate items pertaining to *belongingness* (how much one feels part of a particular group), *centrality* (how important one's group membership is for personal identity), *evaluation* (positive and negative perceptions of one's group), and *tradition* (the practice of cultural customs and the acceptance of the group's longstanding traditional norms and values).

Three models exist for describing and explaining changes in cultural identity. The first is an assimilation model by which cross-cultural travelers are seen to relinquish identification with culture of origin and "progress" toward identification with the culture of contact by adopting the cultural traits, values, attitudes, and behaviors of the host society (Olmeda, 1979). This unidimensional and unidirectional model is embodied in a range of self-report measurements designed for the assessment of acculturation. These include the Acculturation Rating Scale for Mexican Americans–I (ARMSA; Cuéllar et al., 1980); the Greek Immigrant Acculturation Scale (Madianos, 1980, cited in Mavreas, Bebbington, & Der, 1989); and the acculturation scale devised by Ghuman (1994) for Asian adolescents in Canada and the United Kingdom. The political implications of this model should be obvious: Immigrants are required to assimilate to adapt to life in a new culture.

The second model offers a bicultural perspective by which identifications with home and host cultures are seen as counterbalancing, rather than opposing, forces in shaping the social identification of members of immigrant or refugee groups. Biculturalism is viewed as the middle ground between assimilation and separatism; however, because measurement scales situate biculturalism at the midpoint between identification with heritage and contact cultures, the two referent identities are viewed as interdependent, counteracting forces. Measurements that rely on this approach include the Multicultural Acculturation Scale (Wong-Rieger & Quintana, 1987); the ARMSA-II (Cuéllar, Arnold, & Maldonado, 1995); the adult and youth

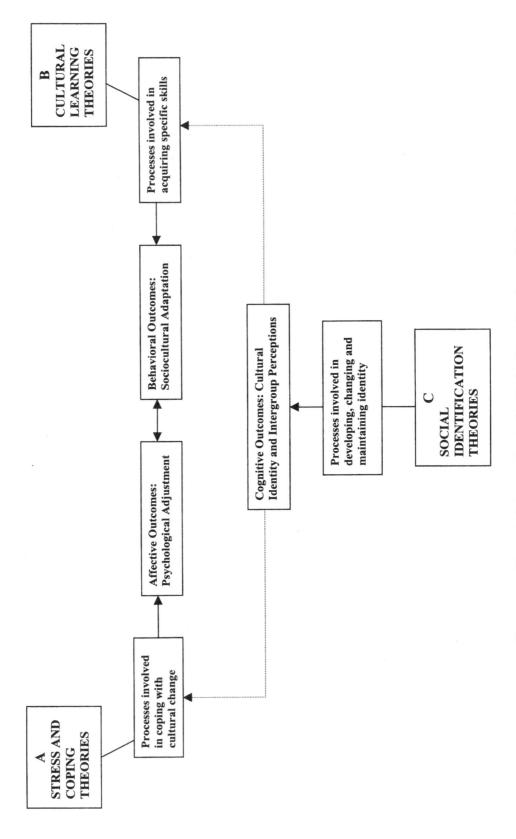

Figure 20.1   Theoretical Approaches to the Study of Acculturation and Adaptation

versions of the Short Acculturation Scale for Hispanics (Barona & Miller, 1994; Marín, Sabogal, Marín, Otero-Sabogal, & Perez-Stable, 1987); the Behavioral Acculturation Scale for Hispanics (Szapocznik, Scopetta, Kurtines, & Aranalde, 1978); the Suinn-Lew Asian Self-Identity Acculturation Scale (Suinn, Rickard-Figueroa, Lew, & Vigil, 1987); the Acculturation Scale for Southeast Asians (Anderson et al., 1993); the Acculturation Scale for Asian Americans (Lai & Linden, 1993); and the International Relations Scale for International Students (Sodowsky, Lai, & Plake, 1991). This model appears to be an advance on the assimilationist perspective in that biculturalism is seen as a desirable outcome and an effective means of managing cross-cultural change; however, there is conceptual confusion about the defining features of biculturalism as measurements fail to distinguish bicultural individuals who weakly identify with both cultures from those who strongly identify with them. Despite this apparent shortcoming, the bicultural model seems to be the most popular in the American psychological literature.

The third alternative appears to attract more attention in the international and cross-cultural arenas. The definitive feature of this more sophisticated model is the conceptualization of home and host culture identities as independent or orthogonal domains (e.g., Cortés, Rogler, & Malgady, 1994; Szapocznik, Kurtines, & Fernandez, 1980). In some cases, these referent identities are also considered in conjunction with the categorization of acculturation strategies (e.g., Bochner, 1982; Hutnik, 1986; Lasry & Sayegh, 1992). Berry's (1974, 1984, 1994) work on acculturation is perhaps the best known example of the categorical approach. Berry has argued that sojourners, immigrants, and refugees are faced with two basic questions relating to home and host culture identities and relations: "Is it of value to maintain my cultural heritage?" and "Is it of value to maintain relations with other groups?" If responses to these questions are dichotomized, four acculturation attitudes or strategies may be distinguished: integration, separation, assimilation, and marginalization. Those who say yes to both options are said to be integrated; those who say no to both are marginalized; those who say yes to cultural maintenance, but no to intergroup relations, are described as separatist; and those who say yes to intergroup relations, but no to cultural maintenance, are categorized as assimilated.

Various measurement techniques have been employed in connection with categorical models of acculturation. Some instruments allow the independent assessment of home and host cultural identities and the combination of the two scales for categorical assessment. Ward and Kennedy's (1994) Acculturation Index, Felix-Ortiz, Newcomb, and Meyers' (1994) Cultural Identity Scale, and Nguyen, Messé, and Stollak's (1999) Acculturation Scale for Vietnamese Adolescents are structured along those lines. Berry and colleagues, however, have generally preferred the independent assessment of marginalization, assimilation, separation, and integration with parallel scales, as found in their work with Portuguese, Hungarian, and Korean immigrants to Canada (Berry, Kim, Power, Young, & Bujaki, 1989).

Berry and his colleagues have clearly demonstrated that integration is the strategy most favored by newcomers in multicultural societies. Hungarian, Korean, Portuguese, and Lebanese immigrants, as well as Central American refugees, in Canada display a significant preference for integration (Berry et al., 1989; Donà & Berry, 1994; Sayegh & Lasry, 1993). There is also evidence, although less consistent, that integration is preferred in culturally homogenous settings, even by members of visible minorities. Sam (1995) reported that it is favored by immigrants from developing countries who relocated to Norway, and Partridge (1988) found it popular in Japan with the expatriate wives of Japanese men. The correlates and consequences of these strategies are discussed below in relation to psychological and sociocultural adjustment.

In addition to measurement issues, the core of research on identity and acculturation relates to the components of identity, how identity is modified over time, and the conditions associated with identity and identity change. Investigators have considered characteristics of the individual such as age, gender, and education; characteristics of the migrant group, such as cultural similarity and motivations of push versus pull; and characteristics of the receiving society, such as monoculturalism versus multiculturalism and loose versus tight systems of sociocultural organization. Generally, these variables are viewed as antecedents or correlates of acculturation and identity change. Identity and acculturation, in turn, have also been conceptualized as predictors of migrant adaptation to new environments, particularly psychological and sociocultural adjustment.

Identity entails a set of dynamic, complex processes by which individuals define, redefine, and construct their own and others' ethnicity or culture. Although few have explored these changes from an explicitly developmental perspective (for exceptions, see work by Aboud, 1987; Phinney, 1989; Schönpflug, 1997), many have investigated identity issues cross-sectionally to explore age and generational differences. In general, younger migrants appear to be more malleable than older ones, and they tend to take on more readily host culture norms and values (Marín et al., 1987; Mavreas et al., 1989). When acculturation starts early, particularly before admission to primary school, it appears to proceed more smoothly (Beiser et al., 1988). One possible reason is that younger migrants tend to have better language skills and are more easily accepted into the receiving country (Liebkind, 1996).

Although the results of research on gender differences in identification and acculturation have not been completely consistent, there is moderately strong evidence that assimilation proceeds more rapidly in boys than girls, and that men assimilate more quickly than women (Ghaffarian, 1987). There is also evidence that women have more negative attitudes toward assimilation and are more likely to retain a stronger sense of identity with culture of origin (Harris & Verven, 1996; Liebkind, 1996; Ting-Toomey, 1981). The traditional roles that women play have been cited as a reason for this difference. In many cases, women are more isolated from members of the receiving culture, particularly if they are unemployed or lack requisite language skills. In addition, women are often perceived as cultural gatekeepers, teaching their children about ethnic customs and traditions and nurturing identification with heritage culture norms and values (Yee, 1990, 1992).

Research suggests that immigrants typically display an increasingly strong orientation toward the host culture over generations (Montgomery, 1992). This does not mean, however, that they necessarily relinquish identity with their culture of origin. For example, Mavreas et al. (1989) described second-generation Greek migrants to the United Kingdom as balancing both Greek and British identities, unlike their parents, who were more strongly and exclusively Greek. The interplay between home and host culture identities may be affected by a number of factors, and their development does not always follow a linear or unidirectional path. A variety of identity changes may be observed as recently arrived immigrant groups evolve into more firmly established minorities in multicultural societies. Keefe and Padilla (1987), for example, found that cultural awareness decreased substantially from first- to second-generation Mexican Americans and continued to decline gradually; however, ethnic loyalty showed only a slight decrement over the first two generations and then remained fairly stable.

At this point in the discussion, it seems appropriate to consider the distinction between cognitive and behavioral aspects of acculturation. Although research has demonstrated that the two are interrelated (Der-Karabetian, 1980; Ullah, 1987), they exhibit different patterns of change over time (Cuéllar, Arnold, & González, 1995; Szapocznik et al., 1978). Immigrants and refugees are usually willing to learn new behaviors and skills, but their attitudes and values are generally more resistant to change (Triandis, Kashima, Shimada, & Villareal, 1986; Wong-Rieger & Quintana, 1987). One example of this can be found in a study by Rosenthal, Bell, Demetriou, and Efklides (1989), who compared Greek Australians to Anglo-Australians and to Greeks. Although Greek Australians were more similar to Anglo-Australians in terms of behaviors, they more closely resembled native Greeks in terms of values. Despite pragmatic behavioral responses, their core values remained largely unchanged. This suggests that neither changing behaviors nor the acquisition of new cultural skills are necessarily indications of cultural identification (LaFromboise, Coleman, & Gerton, 1993). These attitude-behavior discrepancies deserve further attention, particularly in light of findings that show members of receiving communities are largely supportive of immigrant groups retaining their cultural traditions relating to food, music, or dress, but have stronger reservations about the maintenance of traditional, potentially conflicting, values (Lambert, Moghaddam, Sorin, & Sorin, 1990).

In addition to demographic factors such as age and generational status, the quality and quantity of intercultural contact also exert strong influences on ethnic and cultural identity. Greater overall exposure to the host culture is associated with stronger assimilative responses (Mendoza, 1989). Increased length of residence in a new culture seems to strengthen host, but weaken home, culture identity, and those born within the contact culture assimilate more quickly than those born overseas (Cortés et al., 1994). Education and socioeconomic status also affect the experience of acculturation. Higher levels of education predict stronger host culture identification (Mavreas et al., 1989; Suinn, Ahuna, & Khoo, 1992), and higher socioeconomic status is associated with more rapid assimilation of immigrants and refugees (Barona & Miller, 1994; Nicassio, 1983), at least in instances of cross-cultural movement toward Western industrialized countries such as the United States and the United Kingdom.

Patterns of intracultural contact and communication similarly influence social identity. Intraethnic interactions, including membership in ethnocultural organizations, foster maintenance of heritage identity (Altrocchi & Altrocchi, 1995; Sodowsky et al., 1991), and assimilation proceeds more slowly when immigrants reside in intraethnic enclaves (Cuéllar & Arnold, 1988). Likewise, native language usage and preference are generally associated with weaker assimilative responses (Berry et al., 1989; Lanca, Alksnis, Roese, & Gardner, 1994; Montgomery, 1992).

Finally, the characteristics and conditions of migration are also important, particularly the duration of the cross-cultural transition and the voluntariness of the move. Those who view their stay in a new culture as temporary, such as sojourners or short-term migrants, retain a stronger identity with their culture of origin and a weaker identity with the culture of contact compared to those who plan for their residence to be more permanent (Mendoza, 1989). Even among more long term immigrants and refugees, however, assimilation is less likely to occur among those who were pushed into relocation compared to those who were motivated by pull factors (Wong-Rieger & Quintana, 1987).

Intercultural Perceptions and Relations: Implications for Sojourners, Immigrants, and Refugees

The previous section considered issues pertaining to cultural identity and how home and host culture identities may be perceived as conflicting or compatible in the selection and implementation of acculturation strategies. The relationship between culture of origin and culture of contact is indeed a complex one for both sojourning and migrating groups; satisfactorily resolving associated issues seems an important component of adaptation. There is no one

"adaptive" means of dealing with these demands and pressures; however, it is clear that, for cross-cultural travelers, the relationships with members of the host or dominant community are not only determined by their perceptions and attitudes toward members of the receiving culture, but also by hosts' perceptions of the visitors. In this section, we examine issues relating to stereotyping, prejudice, and discrimination in connection with sojourning, immigrant, and refugee groups.

Social identity theory proposed by Tajfel (1978) offers a conceptual base for the examination of these issues. On the process level, social identification rests on social categorization and social comparison, that is, the recognition that various in-groups and out-groups exist, that they may be compared, and that favorable and unfavorable comparisons have consequences for self-esteem. Tajfel argued that intergroup bias is an inevitable consequence of social identification. The effects of this bias, especially out-group derogation, on threatened or stigmatized groups, receive special attention in social identity theory, and a significant portion of Tajfel's work concerns the classification and elaboration of compensatory reactions employed by disadvantaged groups. These include changing in-groups, using cognitive strategies to redefine or enhance social comparisons, and opting for collective social action. Although Tajfel's theory has been one of the most influential in the broad study of intergroup perceptions and relations, and despite its obvious relevance to the study of acculturating groups, there has been a limited number of investigations on sojourners, immigrants, and refugees. Here, we consider key research in this domain.

1. *Is there evidence of in-group favoritism?* Cross-cultural social psychological research on stereotyping has provided sound evidence of in-group favoritism by majority members of receiving societies. Wibulswadi (1989), for example, examined the intergroup perceptions of Thais, Chinese, Hmong tribals, and Americans in Northern Thailand. The Americans were perceived more negatively than the other groups by the Thai respondents and more negatively than the American sojourners perceived themselves. Likewise, Georgas (1998) reported that Greeks perceived themselves as more industrious, reliable, and honest than non-Greeks, but more interestingly, the perceptions of repatriating Greeks fell between the Greek and non-Greek stereotypes. According to Tajfel, in-group favoritism can have more powerful effects

when held by members of a majority or those with political, social, or economic power.

2. *Do negative out-group stereotypes relate to prejudice and discrimination?* Negative out-group stereotypes have significant implications for prejudice and discrimination in receiving societies. Stephan and associates identified these stereotypes as one of the four basic threats (along with realistic and symbolic threats and intergroup anxiety) that lead to prejudice. This was confirmed in their studies of prejudicial attitudes toward Moroccan immigrants in Spain, Russian immigrants in Israel, and Mexican immigrants in the United States (W. G. Stephan, Ybarra, Martínez, Schwarzwald, & Tur-Kaspa, 1998; Ybarra & Stephan, 1994).

3. *Who perceives discrimination?* Perceptions of discrimination vary considerably across individuals and groups. Malewska-Peyre (1982) found that 7 out of 10 second-generation adolescent migrants in France reported feeling deeply affected by prejudice and discrimination. Girls perceived greater discrimination than boys, and Arabs perceived greater discrimination than the Spanish or Portuguese. While cultural differences are associated with such perceptions, even migrant groups who are linguistically, ethnically, and culturally similar to majority members of the host culture may feel socially disadvantaged. Leong (1997), for example, found that sojourners from the People's Republic of China perceived at least a moderate level of prejudice and discrimination in Singapore. While it is not uncommon for sojourners and immigrants to perceive prejudice and discrimination, members of disadvantaged groups generally view discrimination as directed more often toward other members of their group than toward themselves (Taylor, Moghaddam, & Bellerose, 1989; Taylor, Wright, Moghaddam & Lalonde, 1990).

4. *Which strategies are most likely to be used by members of immigrant groups in response to perceptions of discrimination?* Choice of strategy is influenced by individual, group, and societal factors (Camilleri & Malewska-Peyre, 1997). In their study of Iranians in Montreal, Moghaddam et al. (1987) found that immigrants pursued one of two acculturative responses. An individualistic approach, concerned primarily with personal social mobility rather than maintenance of cultural heritage, was adopted by one group. Collectivist strategies, including reliance on the support of Iranian cultural organizations and the larger Iranian

community to help with social advancement, were engaged by the others. These groups differed on a number of salient characteristics, including willingness to remain in Canada and perceived necessity of liaisons with the Iranian community. Most importantly, however, those who adopted collectivist strategies had a stronger belief in the justice and fairness of the Canadian system. Later research with Haitian, Indian, Caribbean, Italian, and Greek migrants to Canada suggested that members of visible minorities are more likely to prefer collectivist strategies (Lalonde & Cameron, 1993; Lalonde, Taylor, & Moghaddam, 1988).

5. *Are there strategies that could be used to reduce in-group favoritism and enhance intergroup perceptions and relations?* Social psychological theory has suggested that increased contact—at least under certain conditions—may improve intergroup perceptions and relations. Triandis and Vassiliou (1967) were the first to examine this with international groups of sojourners. Their study was conducted in Greece and in the United States. Greeks and Americans with low, medium, and high amounts of intercultural contact completed questionnaires about perceptions of their own group and perceptions of the other group. Both groups agreed that Greeks had somewhat more negative features (e.g., lazy, rigid, suspicious) than did Americans. More significantly, however, increased contact with Americans resulted in more favorable stereotypes for Greeks, but increased contact with Greeks resulted in more negative stereotypes for Americans. Triandis and Vassiliou suggested that stereotypes usually contain a "kernel of truth," and that increased contact provides first-hand knowledge that sharpens or crystallizes intergroup perceptions.

Despite some supporting evidence for the contact hypothesis (Clément, Gardner, & Smythe, 1977), the influence of contact on stereotyping is likely to be affected by a range of personal, social, and situational variables. Amir and Ben-Ari (1988) argue that contact may furnish an opportunity for mutual acquaintance and understanding; however, the prerequisites for positive perceptions and interactions are equal status; pursuit of common goals; contact of an intimate, rather than casual, nature; and a broader social climate supporting intergroup contact. Some of these factors can be observed in Kim, Cho, and Harajiri's (1997) study of Koreans in Seoul and in Tokyo and their perceptions of the Japanese. Direct contact proved to be important, but its effects were moderated by linguistic and social skills. Overall, the Korean sojourners emphasized the more positive characteristics of the Japanese (e.g., orderly, safe, secure, advanced) and were less likely to endorse traditional negative stereotypes (e.g., colonialist, superior). Positive perceptions, however, were associated with effective participation in the culture; negative, more critical evaluations were linked to dissatisfying experiences, including perceived discrimination.

Summary, Evaluation, and Future Directions

Social identity research on immigrants, sojourners, and refugees has been concentrated in two major areas. The first is concerned with cultural identity and places particular emphasis on the conceptualization and measurement of acculturation. This line of theory and research has articulated three distinct models of the acculturative changes. The first is an assimilationist model. Although still popular in some cultural contexts, this perspective on acculturation clearly has negative social and political implications for culturally plural societies. The second model, with its emphasis on bicultural identity, represents an improvement over the assimilationist position, but as it adopts a culture-relative or "balance" technique for assessing acculturation, it is still riddled with conceptual and measurement problems. Most scales are unable to distinguish bicultural persons who strongly identify with two cultures from individuals who identify with neither. The third model, which considers home and host culture identities as independent domains, appears the most suitable for exploring identity issues. Not only does it have strong empirical support, it also appears to be in keeping with the multicultural values that are emerging in many contemporary societies.

Debates about the nature and process of identity change and the relative merits of the assimilationist, balance, and orthogonal models of acculturation will continue into the millennium, and discussions are likely to include the question as to whether identification with heritage and contact cultures should be considered in conjunction with categorical approaches to acculturation (Ward, 1999). It is imperative to clarify issues pertaining to the nature, conceptualization, and measurement of acculturation before its relationship with psy-

chological and sociocultural adaptation can be examined. If this is accomplished, it is also possible to investigate changes in acculturation and identity over generations from a more meaningful perspective.

Future research on identity and acculturation should be expanded to a wider variety of cultural contexts. For example, a substantial proportion of the work in this area has been undertaken in the United States, where the tradition of E pluribus unum suggests a "melting pot" approach to acculturation (despite more recent analogies to the "salad bowl"). Issues pertaining to identity and acculturation may be very different across the border in Canada, where the government has gone to great lengths to promote a culturally plural society. These issues may be very different again in a country such as Japan, where residents are largely ethnically, culturally, and linguistically homogeneous, or in Malaysia, where, under current government policies, the Malays, as the "indigenous" people of the country, are given special entitlements that are not extended to the established immigrant Chinese or Indian communities. These macro-sociocultural, -political, and -economic factors are likely to shape micro-psychological processes; consequently, a broader selection of cultural samples can offer a more comprehensive overview of acculturation processes.

In addition to theory and research on cultural identity, this chapter discussed intergroup perceptions and relations between hosts and cross-cultural visitors. Here, Tajfel's social identity theory is used to account for in-group favoritism and to explain the reactions of members of minority groups such as sojourners, immigrants, and refugees. The contact hypothesis has also been explored as a means of improving intergroup relations, although the outcomes of this line of research have been mixed. Unfortunately, intercultural-intergroup research is still somewhat limited. Most empirical work has been confined to studies of perceptions and relations among members of established ethnocultural communities (e.g., Blacks and Whites in the United States, Maoris and Pakehas in New Zealand), rather than between hosts and newcomers. An exception to this trend is recent work by Esses, Jackson, and Armstrong (1998), which considered attitudes toward immigrants in Canada and the United States in terms of an instrumental model of group conflict. In addition, few studies have included mutual perceptions of recently arrived and resident groups. Kosmitzki's (1996) study on contact and stereotyping in both home-based and sojourning Germans and Americans addresses this concern, and there is a pressing need for more intercultural investigations of this type.

In addition to expanding research to include more diverse sets of cross-cultural travelers and hosts, there is also a need for further theory development. At present, there is no single theory that can account for the complexities of identity change and the processes and patterns of intergroup relations. Although social identity theory and acculturation models have guided empirical research in the area, these are not the only theories to explore identity and intergroup relations in a cross-cultural context. Berry's (1984) "multicultural assumption" challenges the premises of social identity theory. Turner's (1982) self-categorization theory and Weinreich's (1989) identity structure analysis provide more contemporary alternatives, and both have recently attracted attention in social psychological studies of changing European identities (Breakwell & Lyons, 1996). Brewer's (1996) optimal distinctiveness theory, which has been recently used to explore changing identities in Hong Kong, and Gaertner, Dovidio, and Bachman's (1996) model of common in-group identity are also gaining popularity. It is probable that these theories will come to exert an increasing influence on the study of identity and intergroup relations in coming years.

Culture Learning

The culture learning approach deals with the behavioral aspects of culture contact that characterize salient encounters between newcomers and members of the receiving society. It also concentrates on the processes by which these newcomers acquire culturally relevant skills to survive and thrive in their new environments. The approach is drawn from early work by Argyle and Kendon (1967), who were among the first to suggest that the social behaviors of interacting persons represent a mutually skilled performance. Interpersonal friction arises when this performance breaks down because one (or more) of the participants is unable to regulate the social encounter skillfully. While Argyle's theory was formulated in the context of intracultural research, its application to the intercultural context is obvious. The language of communication and the rules, conventions, and customs for social behaviors vary considerably across cultures. Consequently, there is much greater risk of unsuccessful, unpleasant, and confusing experiences in intercultural encounters. To remedy this situation, social skills training has been recommended as part of culture learning programs (Furnham & Bochner, 1986); however, there are other avenues for skills acquisition, including increased interaction with members of the host culture.

Social Psychology of Intercultural Encounters

In principle, meetings between culturally diverse people are no different from other social encounters, and in both cases, troublesome interchanges can be conceptualized as failures in verbal and nonverbal communication. Language is obviously significant, but the rules, conventions, and customs of social interaction are also salient aspects of communication. These include activities such as the expression of feelings, adoption of proxemic postures, display of gaze, and performance of ritualized routines such as greetings, leave-takings, and the like (Trower, Bryant, & Argyle, 1978). As these acts carry implicit messages that define the tenor of relationships, it is important that they are in accordance with cultural expectations. Indeed, experimental research on intercultural interaction has shown that culturally congruent nonverbal behaviors are a more powerful predictor of interpersonal attraction than ethnicity (Dew & Ward, 1993). The following section describes some cross-cultural differences in the patterns of communication and explains why they are likely to give rise to difficulties in intercultural encounters.

Barriers to Effective Intercultural Interactions

Cross-Cultural Differences in Nonverbal Behaviors Nonverbal forms of communication vary markedly across cultures, and these variations frequently contribute to cross-cultural misunderstandings. Differences in physical contact and mutual gaze are two obvious examples. Persons from high-contact cultures, such as those of Latin America and Southern Europe, have small areas of interpersonal space and make frequent physical contact. Those from low-contact cultures, such as East Asian societies, appear less intimate (Argyle, 1982). When persons from high- and low-contact cultures meet, the former may be perceived as intrusive, even sexually predatory, while the latter are likely to be seen as aloof, cold, and unfriendly. Differences in mutual gaze patterns also affect person perception. Arabs and members of Latin American cultures display a comparatively high frequency of mutual gaze, while Europeans exhibit a lower frequency (Watson, 1970). When intercultural interactions occur, persons from high-gaze cultures may be seen as disrespectful, threatening, or insulting. In contrast, those from low-gaze cultures are likely to be perceived as impolite, bored, or dishonest.

Gestures also widely vary across cultures. The Italian, French, Greeks, Spaniards, and Portuguese are very expressive in this way, while the Nordic peoples make little use of gestures (Argyle, 1975, 1982). The meaning and significance of gestures likewise differ across national and cultural groups. The "thumbs up" gesture used widely in the United States to indicate a sign of approval is seen as an insult in Greece, where it is often associated with the expression *katsa pano* or "Sit on this!" (Collett, 1982). Pointing with the index finger outstretched is considered rude in many Asian and some Middle Eastern countries, as is calling someone by beckoning with the index finger positioned upward and moving toward the body (Morrison, Conaway, & Borden, 1994). On the more general level, there are cross-cultural differences in the liking of or preference for body postures. The Japanese prefer closed postures, while the Americans tend to respond more positively to those with open body postures (McGinley, Blau, & Takai, 1984).

One of the most powerful forms of nonverbal communication is achieved through the use of silence, and this is known to vary in its frequency (Dale, 1986), duration (Ishii & Klopf, 1976), intentionality (N. Sano, Yamaguchi, & Matsumoto, 1999), and meaning (Hall, 1976) across cultures. The Japanese, for example, use silence more often than Americans (Lebra, 1987). Polynesians are more comfortable with silence than Caucasian New Zealanders, but do not use it in the same way to imply consent (Metge & Kinloch, 1978).

Facial expression of emotion is subject to cross-cultural variation and related to display rules. Friesen's (1972) classic study demonstrated that Americans expressed negative emotions in reaction to a horrifying film whether alone or with someone else, while Japanese repressed the expression of negative emotions in the presence of another person. How an audience affects the expression of emotion also varies cross-culturally. Matsumoto and Hearn (cited in Matsumoto, 1994), for example, reported that Poles and Hungarians display fewer negative emotions and more positive emotions in ingroups compared to Americans, while the reverse is true for out-group members.

Cross-Cultural Differences in Rules and Conventions   In addition to culturally disparate nonverbal behaviors, the rules that govern interpersonal behavior are a major source of difficulty in intercultural interactions (Driskill & Downs, 1995). Many of the differences in rules and conventions have been associated more broadly with cross-cultural variations in values, particularly individualism-collectivism and power distance (Hofstede, 1980). Members of individualistic cultures see the individual as the basic unit of social organization, in contrast to members of collectivist cultures, who emphasize the significance of the larger group. Individualists are idiocentric; they value autonomy, uniqueness, and "standing out." Collectivists, on the other hand, value "fitting in," finding and maintaining one's proper place among others (Triandis, 1989). Theory and research have suggested that people from individualist societies, such as the United States, prefer directness, take longer and more unevenly distributed turns in conversation, speak louder, and are more willing to express negative emotions in public. Because collectivists, particularly people from East Asian societies, value group harmony and face-saving to a greater extent, they are less willing to engage in activities that might be seen as disruptive to the larger group. Consequently, they often appear more restrained in social interactions. Asian subtlety and indirectness are often interpreted as inscrutability by Westerners. This is compounded by the fact that, in many Asian countries, the word *no* is seldom used in response to a request, so that a response of "Yes" may actually mean "No" or "Maybe."

Cross-cultural variations in power distance reflect differences in the prevalence of established hierarchies, the preference for vertical versus horizontal relationships, and the importance of status. Americans prefer horizontal or equal relationships and tend to be informal in their social interactions, including the widespread use of first names as a form of address. Societies that are high in power distance, such as those of Mexico and India, are more likely to employ forms of address that reflect status differences, including the use of titles.

Breaking Barriers:
Intercultural Training and
Interactions with Hosts

The previous sections provide only the briefest glimpse of some cross-cultural differences in communication that may contribute to problems in intercultural encounters. More comprehensive descriptions and discussions of these issues can be found in Hall (1976); Samovar and Porter (1996); Morrison et al. (1994); and Gudykunst and Ting-Toomey (1988). Although the examples are limited, it is obvious that crossing cultures is a precarious journey, the success of which largely depends on the acquisition of culture-appropriate skills. One method of skill development is through cross-cultural training programs.

There are numerous training methods available for cross-cultural preparation. These include information giving, cultural sensitization, simulations, critical incident techniques, culture assimilators, and experiential learning (Ward, Bochner, & Furnham, 2001). Despite the variety, training techniques share a common assumption; that is, the major task facing cross-cultural travelers is to learn salient features of the new culture. Programs that specifically emphasize training for social skills are based on behavioral approaches to learning and rely primarily on procedures such as video feedback, role-playing, and modeling to simulate real-life situations. Emphasis is placed on the management of interpersonal encounters and the effective execution of communication skills. This differs from programs that focus on affective domains, such as stress management and personal growth, or cognitive processes, such as intergroup perceptions and attributions.

How effective are these programs? There is at least some evidence that behaviorally based culture learning programs facilitate intercultural effectiveness. For example, Landis, Brislin, and Hulgus (1985) compared the outcomes of an intercultural contact workshop, which included role-playing with target hosts, with a variety of other training methods. Those participating in the contact workshop were evaluated more favorably by host nationals on culture-specific behavioral tasks than were other trainees. Harrison (1992) also documented the effectiveness of behavioral modeling techniques in his study of intercultural training. Those exposed to behavioral training learned more material and performed better in a role play with host nationals than those who did not have

the training, although in this research, it was a combination of behavioral modeling and the cultural assimilator that proved most effective. More varied techniques have been examined in Deshpande and Viswesvaran's (1992) meta-analytic investigation of intercultural training effectiveness. In a review of more than 20 studies, they documented the beneficial effects of training on interpersonal skills in interactions with host nationals. They also found improvements in the understanding of host values, work performance, and self-development. Despite these encouraging results, Cargile and Giles (1996, p. 398), in their recent review of intercultural communication training, concluded that

> Training can sometimes—albeit not always—produce most immediate outcomes described: It can develop awareness [e.g., Lefley, 1985], behavioral skills [e.g., Landis et al., 1985], and most surely knowledge [e.g., Bird, Heinbuch, Dunbar, & McNulty, 1993]. Training has not, however, usually shifted attitudes in the desired direction [e.g., Randolph, Landis, & Tzeng, 1977].

Their conclusion reiterates the distinction between the behavioral basis of culture-specific skills and the cognitive roots of variables relating to social identity. It also raises issues for the broader study of cross-cultural adaptation.

While there is at least qualified support for the effectiveness of culture learning programs, formal training is not the only route to acquiring culture-specific skills in a new environment. Cultural participation and intercultural friendships can enhance social skills (Schild, 1962). This has been discussed by Bochner and colleagues in terms of social network theory (Bochner, McLeod, & Lin, 1977; Furnham & Bochner, 1982). Specifically, Bochner has suggested that sojourners belong to three social networks: a primary, monocultural network of sojourning compatriots; a secondary bicultural network of sojourners and hosts; and a third network of multicultural friends and acquaintances. He argues that culture learning is a direct function of the number of host culture friends that a sojourner possesses. This appears to be borne out in the empirical literature. On the whole, sojourners who have more extensive contact with host nationals and those who are satisfied with these relationships experience less sociocultural adaptation problems (H. Sano, 1990; Searle & Ward, 1990).

Social Skills Deficits and Sociocultural Adaptation

The culture learning approach suggests that skills deficits are largely responsible for intercultural adaptation problems, and this was explicitly examined in Furnham and Bochner's (1982) study of international students in the United Kingdom. Their research involved the construction of the Social Situations Questionnaire, a 40-item instrument that assesses the amount of difficulty experienced in a variety of routine social encounters. The international students who participated in the research were divided into three groups, depending on cultural distance between home (country of origin) and host (United Kingdom) societies. These included the near group (northern European countries such as France, the Netherlands, and Sweden), the intermediate group (southern European and South American countries such as Italy, Spain, Venezuela, and Brazil), and the far group (Middle Eastern and Asian countries such as Egypt, Saudi Arabia, Indonesia, and Japan). The results of the study clearly indicated that adaptation problems were a function of cultural distance, that is, those students who came from culturally distant regions experienced more social difficulty.

Ward and colleagues have been strongly influenced by Furnham and Bochner's work on social difficulty and have similarly recognized the contributions that culture learning theory can make to the understanding of cross-cultural transition and adaptation. They have assumed a slightly broader perspective, however, in their assessment of sociocultural difficulty and have included additional adaptive skills, such as "dealing with the climate," "getting used to the local food," and "using the local transport system," in the development of the Sociocultural Adaptation Scale. The instrument has been systematically used in an evolving program of research, and Ward and Kennedy (1999) have recently summarized findings based on more than 20 sojourner samples. Here, we examine four specific questions about sociocultural adaptation.

1. *Which factors predict sociocultural adaptation?* At the most basic level, culture-specific knowledge predicts sociocultural adaptation (Ward & Searle, 1991); however, knowledge alone cannot account for adaptive behaviors. Skills are also required. Language skills are important as they affect the quality and quantity of intercultural reactions. Fluency is associ-

ated with increased interaction with members of the host culture (J. E. Gullahorn & Gullahorn, 1966) and a decrease in sociocultural adjustment problems (Ward & Kennedy, 1993c). These variables fit neatly into the culture learning model of cross-cultural adaptation because they provide tangible resources and facilitate skills acquisition in a new cultural milieu.

Ward and colleagues have also extended their work on sociocultural adaptation to include social identity variables as predictors of cultural competence. When host and conational identity are examined, research reveals that host national identification is associated with better sociocultural adaptation (Ward & Kennedy, 1993a, 1993b, 1993c). Conational identification sometimes impedes sociocultural adjustment, but this is not uniformly the case (Ward, 1999). There is also evidence that sociocultural adaptation is influenced by acculturation strategies. In a study of New Zealand civil servants on overseas postings, Ward and Kennedy (1994) found that the greatest amount of sociocultural adaptation problems was encountered by those adopting separatist strategies, followed by the marginalized, who in turn experienced significantly more social difficulty than the integrated or assimilated.

2. *How does sociocultural adaptation change over time?* Longitudinal research reveals, not surprisingly, that sociocultural adaptation follows a learning curve. In a study of Malaysian and Singaporean students in New Zealand, sociocultural adaptation markedly increased between 1 and 6 months of residence in the country and then improved only slightly over the next 6-month period (Ward & Kennedy, 1996b). Research with Japanese students produced similar results. Sociocultural adjustment significantly improved over the first 4 months in New Zealand; however, there were no further significant increases at 6 and 12 months (Ward, Okura, et al., 1998). These studies demonstrate a steep increment in sociocultural adaptation over the first 4–6 months, then taper off up to the end of the first year; this "learning curve" pattern is consistent with a skills deficit/acquisition model of cross-cultural adaptation (Ward & Kennedy, 1999).

3. *Does sociocultural adaptation vary between sojourning and resident groups?* Data indicate, as expected, that sedentary groups experience less sociocultural difficulties than sojourners. For example, New Zealand secondary students who study abroad report more sociocultural difficulties than those who remain at

home (Ward & Kennedy, 1993b). This is in line with Furnham and Bochner's (1982) point that sojourners are relatively unskilled when they enter new environments.

4. *Does sociocultural adaptation vary across sojourning groups?* Results suggest that cultural and ethnic similarity is generally associated with fewer sociocultural difficulties. Mainland Chinese and Malaysian sojourners in Singapore, for example, adapt more readily than Anglo-European ones. Similarly, Malaysian students in Singapore experience less difficulty than Malaysian and Singaporean students in New Zealand (Ward & Kennedy, 1999). This is in accordance with Furnham and Bochner's (1982) original work on cultural distance and social difficulty in foreign students in the United Kingdom.

Summary, Evaluation, and Future Directions

Historically influenced by the Oxford tradition, the culture learning approach emphasizes the significance of social skills and social interaction. Extending work from the intracultural domain, it begins by identifying cross-cultural differences in verbal and nonverbal communication that contribute to intercultural misunderstandings. It then sets about proposing ways in which confusing and dissatisfying encounters can be minimized. As the approach considers intercultural effectiveness as essentially no different from other desirable activities or behavioral goals, it can be achieved through the application of the basic principles of learning. Consequently, training programs and interactions with host nationals have been recognized as reliable means of acquiring and improving expertise.

Not only does the culture learning approach underpin models of intercultural training (Landis, 1996), it also exerts influence on two more recent advancements in the study of intercultural contact and adaptation. The first is related to psychological studies of cross-cultural transition and sociocultural adaptation. The second is linked to emergent theory and research in communication.

Although a number of researchers have considered intercultural interactions, social difficulty, and/or cultural competence, Ward and colleagues first proposed and subsequently refined the construct of sociocultural adaptation. Measured in terms of the amount of difficulty experienced by cross-cultural travelers in the course of everyday activities and interactions,

sociocultural adaptation is conceptually derived from culture learning theory. Empirical research elaborates this conceptual base, confirming that sociocultural adaptation is predicted by variables such as cultural distance and amount of contact with host nationals, and that the pattern of sociocultural adaptation approximates a learning curve over time. After a decade of systematic studies on sociocultural adaptation, the construct is gaining more attention in the acculturation literature. This is evidenced by its inclusion in Berry and Sam's (1997) pictorial representation of a framework for acculturation research, which is presented in volume 3 of the *Handbook of Cross-Cultural Psychology*. More sophisticated research on sociocultural adaptation, including longitudinal studies, is likely to emerge in the next decade. There have also been recent attempts to expand the primarily behavioral construct of sociocultural adaptation to cognitive-behavioral domains (see Kennedy, 1999), and this may hold promise for future research endeavors.

Communication studies have also borrowed from culture learning theory, as evidenced by recent work on intercultural interactions. In her discussion of intercultural communication competence, Y. Y. Kim (1991) noted the parallels between intercultural communication research and cross-cultural psychology. In particular, she highlighted the concern with the identification of cultural differences in communication and the long-range objective of providing insights to minimize failed communications across cultures. Also in line with the culture learning approach, she noted that the investigation of intercultural communication competence has the "implicit or explicit goal of improving the quality of face-to-face communication between cultural strangers" (p. 260). In addition to Kim's work on intercultural communication competence, the influence of culture learning theory is also seen on Gudykunst's (1993) approach to effective communication. Gudykunst's model includes a major skills component, with emphasis on the ability to gather and use appropriate information and the ability to be adaptable in intercultural communication. As social psychologists are becoming increasingly interested in these topics, communication theory and research are being integrated into the field. This is seen, for example, in the communication accommodation theory of Gallois and colleagues, which has been recently extended to the study of intercultural interactions (Gallois, Giles, Jones, Cargile, & Ota, 1995). Given these trends, it is likely that the basic premises of the culture learning approach will continue to influence studies of intercultural effectiveness through developments in communication theory and research.

Stress and Coping

The stress-and-coping framework, elaborated by Berry (1997) in his recent review of immigration, acculturation, and adaptation, highlights the significance of life changes during cross-cultural transitions, the appraisal of these changes, and the selection and implementation of coping strategies to deal with them (see Figure 20.2). These processes, as well as their psychological outcomes, are likely to be influenced by both societal- and individual-level variables. On the macrolevel, characteristics of the society of settlement and society of origin are important. Discriminating features of these societies may include social, political, and demographic factors, such as ethnic composition, extent of cultural pluralism, and salient attitudes toward ethnic and cultural out-groups. On the microlevel, characteristics of the acculturating individual and situational aspects of the acculturative experience exert influences on stress, coping, and adaptation. Berry also distinguishes between influences arising prior to and during acculturation. In the first instance, factors such as personality or cultural distance may be important; in the second, acculturation strategies or social support may be more relevant.

Cross-cultural researchers who have examined acculturation from a perspective of stress and coping have been predominantly concerned with the prediction of psychological adjustment. Many have considered factors that are routinely investigated in research on stress and coping. These include life changes, cognitive appraisals of stress, coping styles, personality, and social support. Others have concentrated on variables that are more specifically related to cross-cultural transition and adaptation, such as cultural identity and type of acculturating groups. Still others have explicitly attempted to forge links across the three major theoretical approaches to acculturation and have selected variables such as perceived discrimination, acculturation strategies, and sociocultural adaptation as predictors or correlates of psychological adjustment. These are reviewed below.

Prediction of Psychological Adjustment

Life Changes

The stress-and-coping perspective on the acculturation process conceptualizes cross-cultural transitions as entailing a series of stress-provoking life changes that tax adjustive resources and necessitate coping responses. Consequently, the measurement of salient life events is an important feature of this approach (Holmes & Rahe, 1967). Masuda, Lin, and Tazuma (1982) studied Vietnamese refugees in the United States on their arrival and 1 year later. The authors reported that there was a significant relationship between life changes and psychological and psychosomatic distress at both periods (.27 and .15, respectively). Comparable correlations (.19–.28) were found in studies by Ward and colleagues in Malaysian, Singaporean, and New Zealand students abroad (Searle & Ward, 1990; Ward & Kennedy, 1993b, 1993c).

It is apparent that there is a reliable, moderate positive correlation between life changes and psychological symptoms; however, these changes account for only a small proportion (generally less than 10%) of the variance in the psychological well-being of sojourners and refugees. One reason is that there are obvious and important individual differences in the cognitive appraisal of these changes. Individuals process stress-related information in a variety of ways. In one instance, a potential stressor may be evaluated as threatening; in another instance, it may be perceived as challenging. Beyond these individual differences, there are also cultural factors that are likely to affect the cognitive appraisal of stress.

Cognitive Appraisal and Coping Styles

The cognitive appraisal of potentially stressful demands by acculturating individuals is likely to be influenced by broad social and situational factors, including aspects of the acculturative experience. For example, Zheng and Berry (1991) examined the evaluation of a range of potential stressors by Chinese sojourners in Canada and by Chinese and non-Chinese Canadians. Chinese sojourners tended to view language and communication, discrimination, homesickness, and loneliness as more problematic than either Chinese or non-Chinese Canadians. A similar pattern was observed in Chataway

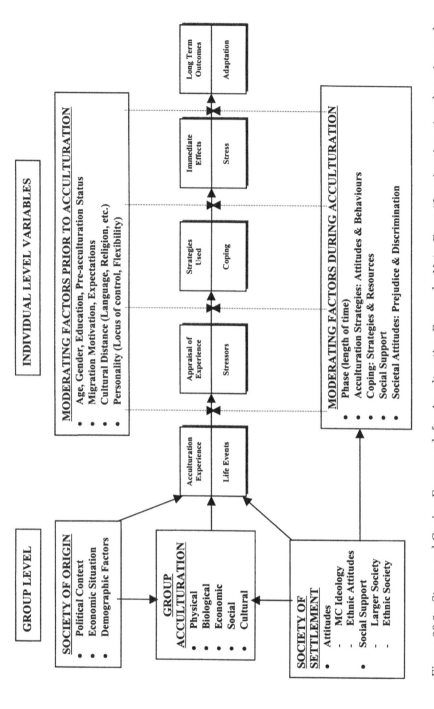

Figure 20.2   Stress and Coping Framework for Acculturation Research. *Note.* From "Immigration, Acculturation and Adaptation," by J. Berry, 1997, *Applied Psychology: An International Review, 46*, pp. 1–30. Copyright 1994 by the International Association of Applied Psychology. Reprinted with permission.

and Berry's (1989) research with Hong Kong Chinese and French and Anglo-Canadians.

Cognitive appraisals of stressors, as well as subsequent coping strategies and adjustive outcomes, may also vary due to differences in migrants' expectations. Expectations form the basis of cognitive appraisals of stressful situations. They also provide the yardstick against which experiences and behaviors can be measured. Some researchers have argued that realistic expectations (i.e., those that match actual experiences) facilitate adjustment. Others have been more concerned with the consequences of inaccurate expectations. Weissman and Furnham (1987), for example, suggested that greater expectation-experience discrepancies should be associated with increased psychological adjustment problems in a group of Americans who had relocated to the United Kingdom.

A more sophisticated approach to the study of expectation-experience discrepancies considers both the direction and extent of expectation-experience mismatches. In this case, a basic distinction is made between overmet and undermet expectations. The former refers to situations in which experiences are more positive than expected, while the latter refers to situations in which experiences are more negative than anticipated. Along these lines, Black and Gregersen (1990) found that overmet general expectations of American managers about life in Japan were associated with increased life satisfaction and decreased likelihood of premature departure. Similar findings were reported by Kennedy (1999); Martin, Bradford, and Rohrlich (1995); and Rogers and Ward (1993) in their studies of international students.

Despite the general interest in stress and coping and related research on cognitive appraisals and expectations, relatively few published studies have actually examined coping strategies in relation to adaptive outcomes in sojourners, immigrants, or refugees. The earliest work of this type was undertaken by Chataway and Berry (1989), who investigated coping styles, satisfaction, and psychological distress in Chinese students in Canada. They reported that Chinese students who engaged in positive thinking were more satisfied with their ability to cope, and those who relied on withdrawal and wishful thinking were less content with the management of their problems. However, only detachment was related significantly to an increase in psychological and psychosomatic symptoms.

In further investigations, Ward and Kennedy (in press) examined the coping strategies and psychological adjustment of British expatriates in Singapore. They identified four basic coping styles: approach (planning, suppression of competing activities, and active coping), avoidance (behavioral disengagement, denial, venting, and the absence of positive reinterpretation), acceptance (acceptance and restraint coping), and social support (seeking emotional and instrumental support). The research revealed that approach coping was associated with a decrement in depressive symptoms in the British expatriates. Avoidance coping, however, was related to higher levels of depression in this investigation, as it was in Berno and Ward's (1998) study of international students in New Zealand and Kennedy's (1998) research with Singaporean students abroad.

For the most part, the findings from studies on coping with cross-cultural transition parallel the general literature on stress and coping. Carver, Scheier, and Weintraub (1989), for example, highlighted the functional aspects of direct, action-oriented coping mechanisms, while questioning the long-term effectiveness of disengagement strategies. This is not to suggest, however, that specific coping strategies would be uniformly effective, or that cultural factors have no bearing on adjustment outcomes. Indeed, Cross (1995) has speculated that there may be cross-cultural variations in coping effectiveness.

This line of theory and research begins with the distinction between primary and secondary coping strategies. Primary strategies are direct actions; they are overt, task-oriented behaviors aimed at changing noxious features of a stress-provoking environment. Secondary strategies, in contrast, are more cognitive than behavioral; they most commonly involve changing perceptions and appraisals of stressful events and situations. In the simplest terms, the primary strategies imply changing the environment to suit the self, while the secondary strategies reflect changing the self to suit the environment. Cross (1995) speculated that primary or direct coping strategies are highly valued by people in individualist cultures, while indirect or secondary mechanisms may be more adaptive for those in collectivist cultures. In her examination of stress and coping in East Asian and American students in the United States, Cross hypothesized and found that direct coping with academic problems was associated with decrements in perceived stress in the Asian students.

Ward and colleagues chose to explore these issues in greater depth in a more collectivist setting in their research on stress, coping with cross-cultural transition, and psychological adjustment in international students in Singapore (Ward, Leong, & Kennedy, 1998). The results indicated that secondary coping mechanisms (i.e., acceptance and positive reinterpretation and growth) predicted lower levels of perceived stress, which in turn predicted fewer symptoms of depression. Primary strategies (i.e., active coping and planning), in contrast, did not exert a direct effect on perceived stress. These findings were observed in both the East Asian and Euro-American groups in Singapore.

The work by Cross (1995) and Ward and colleagues suggests the likelihood of a "cultural fit" model of coping and adaptation; however, it is somewhat premature to draw such a conclusion. It may be the case that indirect tactics are intrinsically more suitable and efficacious for coping with at least some aspects of cross-cultural transition. In short, cross-cultural travelers are powerless to change entire cultures, and in many cases, they have limited resources for modifying the troublesome features of their new cultural milieu. In these instances, cognitive reframing strategies may be more effective in reducing stress. In any event, further research is required to clarify the relationship among culture, coping, and psychological adjustment during cross-cultural transitions.

Personality

Despite extensive theorizing about the effects of authoritarianism, rigidity, and ethnocentrism on intercultural contact (e.g., Locke & Feinsod, 1982), locus of control has attracted the greatest attention in cross-cultural studies of personality and adjustment (Dyal, 1984; Kuo & Tsai, 1986; Lu, 1990). Early studies, like more recent research, have demonstrated that an internal locus of control facilitates cross-cultural adjustment; an external locus, on the other hand, is associated with symptoms of psychological distress. Along these lines, Kuo, Gray, and Lin (1976) found that an external locus of control was a more powerful predictor of psychiatric symptoms in Chinese immigrants to the United States than demographic, socioeconomic, or life change variables. Dyal, Rybensky, and Somers (1988), who investigated locus of control in Indo- and Euro-Canadian women, reported an association among external responses, depression, and psychosomatic complaints. The same pattern was observed in Ward, Chang, and Lopez-Nerney's (1999) recent work with Filipina domestic helpers in Singapore. Seipel's (1988) study demonstrated that lower levels of life satisfaction were related to an external locus of control in Korean immigrants in the United States, as did Neto's (1995) research with second-generation Portuguese migrants to France. Studies of foreign students in the United States, New Zealand, and Singapore reported the same trends (Hung, 1974; Ward & Kennedy, 1993b, 1993c).

Studies of extraversion have produced less-consistent results. Research has generated positive, negative, and nonsignificant relationships between extraversion and sojourner adjustment (Armes & Ward, 1989; Padilla, Wagatsuma, & Lindholm, 1985; Searle & Ward, 1990; Van den Broucke, De Soete, & Bohrer, 1989). In an attempt to reconcile these conflicting findings, Ward and Chang (1997) proposed the cultural fit hypothesis. They highlighted the significance of the Person × Situation interaction and suggested that, in many cases, it is not personality per se that predicts cross-cultural adjustment, but rather the cultural fit between the acculturating individual and host culture norms. To test this idea, a sample of Americans in Singapore was surveyed, and comparisons were made between their extraversion scores on the Eysenck Personality Questionnaire and normative Singaporean data. Although extraversion per se did not relate to psychological well-being, those Americans whose scores were less discrepant from Singaporean norms experienced lower levels of depression, giving tentative support to the cultural fit proposition.

Other personality factors that have been associated with general adjustment, psychological well-being, or life satisfaction have been personal flexibility (Berno & Ward, 1998; J. T. Gullahorn & Gullahorn, 1962; Ruben & Kealey, 1979); tolerance of ambiguity (Cort & King, 1979); hardiness (Ataca, 1996); mastery (Sam, 1998); self-efficacy; and self-monitoring (Harrison, Chadwick, & Scales, 1996). In contrast, psychological adjustment problems have been associated with authoritarianism; decrements in overall satisfaction have been related to dogmatism (Taft & Steinkalk, 1985); and high anxiety has been linked to attributional complexity (C. W. Stephan & Stephan, 1992). Attempts to investigate Eysenck's personality dimensions of neuroticism and psychoticism have demonstrated, as expected, that both are associated with psychological adjustment problems during cross-cultural transition (Ditchburn, 1996; Furukawa & Shibayama, 1993).

Social Support

Social support has been viewed as a major resource in the literature on stress and coping and as a significant factor in predicting both psychological adjustment (Fontaine, 1986) and physical health (Schwarzer, Jerusalem, & Hahn, 1994) during cross-cultural transitions. The presence of social support is negatively correlated with the emergence of psychiatric symptomatology in immigrants and refugees (e.g., Biegel, Naparstek, & Khan, 1980; Lin, Tazuma, & Masuda, 1979); its absence is associated with the increased probability of physical and mental illness during cross-cultural sojourns (Hammer, 1987).

Social support may arise from a variety of sources, including family, friends, and acquaintances. Some researchers have emphasized the significance of the family and have concentrated on marital relations as the primary source of social support. Naidoo (1985), for example, reported that immigrant Asian women in Canada experienced substantially less stress when they had supportive husbands, and Stone Feinstein and Ward (1990) found that the quality of spousal relationship was one of the most significant predictors of psychological well-being of American women sojourning in Singapore. On the other hand, marital difficulties can increase psychological distress. Ataca (1996) observed that marital stressors were significantly related to psychological adaptation problems, including anxiety, depression, psychosomatic complaints, and general dissatisfaction, in Turkish migrants to Canada. These findings are not surprising as marital harmony/distress contribute to psychological well-being/malaise in intracultural settings as well.

When friends and acquaintances are considered as sources of social support, the relative merit of conational versus host national support emerges as a controversial topic. Some studies have suggested that conational relations are the most salient and powerful source of support for both sojourners and immigrants (Berry et al., 1987; Sykes & Eden, 1987; Ward & Kennedy, 1993c; Ying & Liese, 1991). Certainly, "comparable others" (i.e., those undergoing similar experiences) may offer knowledge-based resources and share information about coping with a new environment; they may also provide emotional benefits, permitting, or even encouraging, emotional catharsis and the release of

frustrations concerning life in a new environment (Adelman, 1988). However, cultural enclaves can also impede willingness to engage with the host society. In these instances, a "contagion effect" may emerge by which highly interdependent, stressed, and threatened individuals who remain insulated from the host culture milieu are prevented from acquiring functional problem-solving skills. Continual commiseration among those experiencing stress under unstable conditions may place the members of the support group at risk by engendering a "sinking ship" morale. Pruitt's (1978) study of African students in the United States, which found that overall adjustment was poorer for those students who had greater contact with compatriots and spent more leisure time with Africans, and Richardson's (1974) study of British immigrants in Australia, which found that dissatisfied immigrants had more compatriot and fewer host national friends, seem to provide evidence of this.

While expatriate enclaves can function as assets or liabilities, relationships with other groups, particularly members of the dominant or host culture, also affect adjustment outcomes. Some researchers have concentrated on the quality of these relationships. Having host national friends has been associated with a decrease in psychological problems in immigrants (Furnham & Li, 1993), and satisfaction with host national relationships has been positively related to psychological well-being in sojourners (Searle & Ward, 1990; Stone Feinstein & Ward, 1990; Ward & Kennedy, 1993b). Comfort and satisfaction with local contact have also been associated with greater general satisfaction in foreign students, including both academic and nonacademic aspects of their overseas transfers (Klineberg & Hull, 1979). Other researchers have emphasized the frequency of interaction with members of the host culture, in some cases even suggesting that extensive contact is a prerequisite for sojourner adjustment. Several studies have confirmed a relationship between amount of social contact with host nationals and general adjustment or satisfaction in immigrants and sojourners (Berry et al., 1987; J. E. Gullahorn & Gullahorn, 1966; Lysgaard, 1955; Pruitt, 1978; Selltiz, Christ, Havel, & Cook, 1963; Sewell & Davidsen, 1961).

All in all, it is likely that both home and host national support affect sojourner well-being. This was confirmed by Furnham and Alibhai (1985) in their study of foreign students in the United Kingdom and by Ward and Rana-Deuba (2000) in their work with multinational aid workers in Nepal. As these results demonstrate that support may be effectively provided by both host and conational networks, some researchers have concerned themselves with the adequacy, rather than the source, of social support and its influence on cross-cultural adaptation. Loneliness, for example, has been commonly mentioned as a negative consequence of cross-cultural relocation (Pruitt, 1978; Sam & Eide, 1991; Zheng & Berry, 1991) and has been linked to various forms of psychological distress, including global mood disturbance (Stone Feinstein & Ward, 1990; Ward & Searle, 1991), decrements in life satisfaction (Neto, 1995), and decreased satisfaction with coping ability (Chataway & Berry, 1989).

Perceived Discrimination

Perceived discrimination has been associated with less willingness to adopt host culture identity (Mainous, 1989). It has also been related to a variety of negative outcomes, including increased stress (Vega, Khoury, Zimmerman, Gil, & Warheit, 1991), antisocial behaviors such as drug use and delinquency (Vega, Gil, Warheit, Zimmerman, & Apospori, 1993) and identity conflict (Leong & Ward, 2000). The association between perceived discrimination and psychological adjustment problems has been observed in such diverse groups as Turkish migrants in Canada (Ataca, 1996), American sojourners in Singapore (Ward & Chang, 1994), international students in New Zealand (Berno & Ward, 1998), and Asian migrants in the United Kingdom (Furnham & Shiekh, 1993). However, the psychological, social, and cultural outcomes of perceived discrimination are moderated by other factors, such as permeability of group boundaries and perceived threat (e.g., Pelly, 1997).

Modes of Acculturation

Many studies have considered the relationship between acculturation status and mental health or illness; however, the results of this research have not been entirely consistent. Studies have shown that acculturation is related both to more stress (Singh, 1989) and to less stress (Padilla et al., 1985); similarly, acculturation has been related both to more depression (Kaplan & Marks, 1990) and less depression (Ghaffarian, 1987; Torres-Rivera, 1985). It is likely that these inconsistencies can be largely accounted

for by the different models and measurements of acculturation described previously, although some researchers have argued that the effects of acculturation are moderated by variables such as age (Kaplan & Marks, 1990), gender (Mavreas & Bebbington, 1990), and religion (Neffe & Hoppe, 1993). It is likely that both moderating factors and acculturation measurement error have contributed to the discrepant findings.

A smaller, but substantial, number of investigations have relied primarily on Berry's (1974, 1984, 1994) model to consider the relationship between acculturation and acculturative stress. Correlational research based on early studies of native peoples and immigrants in Canada documented a positive relationship among integration, assimilation, and adjustment. In contrast, separation and marginalization were found to be related to psychological maladjustment and psychosomatic problems (Berry et al., 1987; Berry & Annis, 1974; Berry, Wintrob, Sindell, & Mawhinney, 1982). More recent research has extended the external validity of these findings. These studies have had the advantage of employing a wider variety of adjustment indicators, including measurements of self-esteem, anxiety, depression, acculturative stress, clinical psychopathology, general contentment, and life satisfaction. They have also included a more diverse set of migratory samples (e.g., sojourners and refugees) and a broader range of cultural settings with widely varying levels of cultural pluralism (Ataca, 1996; Donà & Berry, 1994; Partridge, 1988; Pawliuk et al., 1996; Phinney, Chavira, & Williamson, 1992; Sam, 2000; Sam & Berry, 1995; Sands & Berry, 1993; Ward & Kennedy, 1994; Ward & Rana-Deuba, 1999). A particularly interesting example of this research was undertaken by Schmitz (1992), who reported that integration is associated with reduced levels of both neuroticism and psychoticism, and that separation is associated with higher levels of neuroticism, psychoticism, and anxiety in his study of East German migrants to West Germany. He also argued that assimilation is linked to impairment of the immune system, and that separation is related to cardiovascular problems and drug and alcohol addiction.

Acculturation Status and Type of Group

While research has frequently demonstrated that sojourners, immigrants, and refugees have more psychological and sociocultural adaptation problems than host nationals (Chataway & Berry, 1989; Furnham & Bochner, 1982; Furnham & Tresize, 1981; Sam, 1994; Zheng & Berry, 1991), there have been few systematic studies of psychological adjustment across different types of migrant groups. A major exception to this is Berry et al.'s (1987) research, which compared the level of acculturative stress (i.e., psychological and psychosomatic symptoms) in refugees, sojourners, immigrants, native peoples, and ethnocultural groups in a multicultural society. Their results indicated that native peoples and refugees experienced the greatest level of acculturative stress, immigrants and ethnic groups had the lowest level, and sojourners had an intermediate level of stress. As the experiences of refugees and native peoples often involve involuntary displacement and resettlement dictated by others, it is not surprising that their levels of acculturative stress are considerably higher than those of immigrants, sojourners, and ethnic groups who voluntarily choose to relocate and/or to pursue intercultural contact. The finding that refugees display more psychological distress and dysfunction than other acculturating groups appears consistent across cultures (Pernice & Brook, 1994; Wong-Rieger & Quintana, 1987) and is in accordance with the push-pull analysis of geographical movement. In 1988, U. Kim, for example, found that relocating persons with greater push motivation experienced more psychological adaptation problems. It is also worth noting that refugees experience high levels of premigration stress, often of a traumatic nature, which may affect later adaptation (Tran, 1993).

Psychological and Sociocultural Adjustment

Psychological and sociocultural adjustment have been described as complementary domains of intercultural adaptation. How are these two outcomes related? The mainstream psychological literature has long recognized the complementarity of the stress-and-coping and social skills analyses of human behavior. Folkman, Schaeffer, and Lazarus (1979), working in the former domain, emphasized that the management of stressful circumstances includes instrumental control of situations and the maintenance of personal integrity and morale. Trower et al. (1978) linked the social skills domain with psychological adjustment by noting that certain forms of adaptation difficulties can be caused or exacerbated by lack of social competence.

They also commented on the reciprocal relationship between the two domains, with social inadequacy leading to isolation and psychological disturbance, as well as psychological distress affecting behavior, including an array of social skills and interactions.

Empirical research with these constructs supports this relationship. Across a range of studies involving such diverse groups as foreign students, diplomats, aid workers, and businesspeople, Ward and colleagues have consistently found a positive relationship (.20 to .62, with a median correlation of .32) between psychological and sociocultural adaptation (Ward & Kennedy, 1999). They have also noted that the magnitude of the relationship varies. Evidence suggests that the association is stronger under conditions involving a greater level of social and cultural integration. For example, the relationship between psychological and sociocultural adaptation is stronger in sojourners who are culturally similar, rather than dissimilar, to hosts; it is greater in sedentary groups compared to groups involved in cross-cultural relocation; it increases over time; and it is stronger in those adopting integrationist and assimilationist strategies of acculturation compared to the separated and the marginalized (Kennedy, 1999; Ward, Okura, et al., 1998; Ward & Kennedy, 1996a, 1996b; Ward & Rana-Deuba, 1999).

Summary, Evaluation, and Future Directions

The stress-and-coping approach to cross-cultural transition and adaptation considers intercultural contact and change as significant life events that are inherently stressful and require coping responses to deal with life in a new and different environment. The approach is drawn from mainstream theory and a well-established body of empirical research. Expectedly, findings from acculturation studies are largely in accordance with the wider literature. Factors that function as assets, such as adaptive personality traits or social support, assist in cross-cultural transitions; those that act as impediments or liabilities, such as avoidant coping styles, impair cross-cultural adaptation. Other factors related specifically to crossing cultures, such as cultural identity and acculturation strategies, also affect the psychological well-being of immigrants, refugees, and sojourners.

The next decade of research on cross-cultural transition and psychological adjustment is likely to see more extensive research on personality and more serious attention devoted to coping styles. In the first instance, it is time to examine the "Big Five" dimensions of personality in relation to sojourner, immigrant, and refugee adjustment (Costa & McCrae, 1989). On the second count, researchers need to consider models of cross-cultural coping more carefully (e.g., problem focused vs. emotion focused, engagement vs. avoidance, and primary versus secondary control). Although these models have received considerable attention in the mainstream literature on adjustment and are at the heart of stress-and-coping approaches to cross-cultural transition and adaptation (e.g., Carver et al., 1989; Folkman & Lazarus, 1985; Weisz, Rothbaum, & Blackburn, 1984), very little has been done in the context of cultural change. In either case, the cultural fit proposition is expected to assume greater significance in empirical investigations of immigration and adaptation. Are specific personality traits universally adaptive, or do they vary in relation to the cultural context? Do certain coping styles suit sojourners, immigrants, and refugees, or is the effectiveness of coping determined by the social, psychological, and behavioral characteristics of the host culture? These questions deserve more serious consideration in future research.

Altogether, the stress-and-coping perspective appears to offer the broadest and most flexible approach to acculturation. If one considers Berry's (1997) framework, for example, it is easy to see how both behavioral and cognitive variables fit into the acculturation process. For example, both acculturation strategies and perceptions of discrimination have been cited as moderating factors in the acculturation experience. Similarly, cultural distance, emphasized by those who advocate a culture learning approach to intercultural contact, is also seen to have influence on adaptational outcomes. Because of these integrative features, the stress-and-coping approach is likely to dominate studies of cross-cultural adaptation. In fact, some of the most sophisticated research designs, including longitudinal studies and causal modeling, appear to be evolving in this area (e.g., Kennedy, 1998).

Concluding Comments

Berry and Sam (1997) have identified acculturation as one of the most complex areas of inquiry in cross-cultural psychology, and from this review of theory and research, it is easy to

see why. The field is enormous, and as we move toward cultural diversity both within and across societies, the area will only continue to expand. Given the heterogeneity and breadth of the field, this chapter commences with basic definitions and distinctions. First, acculturation was defined as changes resulting from sustained first-hand contact with members of other cultural groups. Second, distinctions were made between acculturating individuals who engage in cross-cultural relocation and acculturating members of sedentary communities, and the review of relevant research was confined to cross-cultural travelers: immigrants, sojourners, and refugees. Third, the adaptive outcomes of acculturation were described, with emphasis on the definitive features of psychological and sociocultural adjustment. Fourth, similarities and differences in the respective affective, behavioral, and cognitive domains of the acculturative experience were discussed. The first theoretical approach, social identification, highlighted selected elements of social identity, especially identification with home and host cultures and intergroup perceptions and relations; the second, culture learning, underlined the importance of cultural skills and introduced the construct of sociocultural adaptation; and the third, stress and coping, emphasized the emotional components of acculturation, particularly psychological adjustment during cross-cultural transition. Although a broad overview was presented, attempts were made to show the interconnections across the various domains and components of acculturation and to synthesize, if possible, acculturation theory and research.

The integration of emerging theory and research on acculturation can undoubtedly contribute to significant developments in the field; however, a final word of caution to aspiring cross-cultural psychologists is warranted: Do not assume universality in the process and products of acculturation. The conditions under which intercultural contact occurs may represent important moderating and/or mediating influences. What are the national policies regarding race, ethnicity, and culture? Multicultural societies that advocate policies of cultural pluralism offer a wider range of acculturation opportunities than do assimilationist societies (Berry, 1997; Sam, 1995). Loose societies (i.e., those that tolerate a range of views about what constitutes correct action and maintain flexibility about the extent to which individuals are expected to conform to conventional norms and values), compared to tight societies, also place fewer constraints on social identity and the acculturation options available for immigrants, sojourners, and refugees (Triandis, 1997). How similar or dissimilar is the migrant group to members of the receiving culture? Cultural differences, like perceived discrimination, discourage assimilation, particularly in members of visible minorities (Lalonde & Cameron, 1993; Richman, Gaviria, Flaherty, Birz, & Wintrob, 1987). They also increase the probability of psychological and sociocultural adaptation problems. It is wise to remember, then, that "culture" in acculturation research is not confined to intrasocietal differences. Cross-cultural variations in both migrant groups and receiving societies are also important.

As the synthesis of existing theory and research along these lines proceeds, a truly cross-cultural perspective should evolve. In his early writings, Berry (Berry et al., 1987) suggested the amalgamation of emerging studies of acculturation into a broader program of research that includes the systematic comparisons of immigrants, refugees, and sojourners (Armenians, Bengalis, Chinese, . . . Zarois) in a variety of cultural contexts (Australia, Brazil, Canada, . . .). This would provide an extremely rich data set, taking into account population-level factors and including enormous cross-cultural variability. Organizing and interpreting such a data set would be a challenging task; however, there are several overarching conceptual frameworks that could offer starting points for more systematic comparisons across cultures.

Based on his research in 40 countries, Hofstede (1980) identified and assessed four value domains: individualism, power distance, uncertainty avoidance, and masculinity. As he was able to calculate mean scores on each of these dimensions for the participating cultures, he has provided a major resource for the selection of samples for hypothesis testing in cross-cultural comparisons. For example, members of individualist cultures may have advantages in making cross-cultural transitions in that they are assumed to interact more sociably with strangers than are members of collectivist cultures; however, the destination of the cross-cultural traveler is also important. If individualists are traveling to collectivist cultures, where in-group–out-group distinctions are greater, they may find it harder to gain acceptance and experience more transitional difficulties. On the other hand, collectivists, who are known to have strong in-group attachments,

particularly to the family, may find it more difficult to relocate cross-culturally on their own. If there is a presence of a large conational group in the receiving society, however, this group may offer stronger and more reliable sources of social support than comparable groups made up of members of individualist cultures. These are only speculations about the nature of cross-cultural transition; however, these hypotheses may be tested if researchers are able to generate a large cross-cultural database for systematic comparisons.

Alternative schemes for the analysis of cultural variability and its consequences for cross-cultural transition and adaptation have been provided by both Triandis and Schwartz. Like Hofstede, Triandis (1989) has recognized the importance of individualism and collectivism; however, he has also discussed differences in simple societies versus complex societies and loose cultures versus tight cultures. In the context of acculturation research, some studies have suggested that sojourners prefer postings in developed countries (Torbiorn, 1982; Yoshida, Sauer, Tidwell, Skager, & Sorenson, 1997), which would be described as more complex societies; however, larger and more varied cross-cultural data sets would allow a more systematic comparison of this dimension.

Schwartz (1994), who has also studied the structure of human values, identified openness to change (stimulation, self-direction), self-transcendence (universalism, benevolence), conservation (security, conformity/tradition), and self-enhancement (achievement, power) as the four core value dimensions based on his study of 44 cultures. Of particular interest to acculturation researchers, Schwartz proposed that universalism, benevolence, and stimulation are positively related to readiness for out-group contact, while security, tradition, and conformity are negatively related. If this is the case, we might expect the quality of host-immigrant relations to be influenced by these values and to vary across cultural contexts. Again, a large, multicultural data set would permit more extensive testing of Schwartz's hypotheses relating to aspects of social identity.

In conclusion, theory and research on acculturation have grown exponentially over the last three decades. More sophisticated theories have been employed, and more robust research designs, including longitudinal studies, have been adopted. Under these conditions, empirical investigations have yielded relatively consistent findings on the A, B, C's of acculturation. Despite these positive developments, large-scale, systematic, comparative studies have been lacking. Evaluating theory and research on acculturation at the turn of the century, it should be recognized that the contributions by cross-cultural investigators have been substantial, but that much work remains to be done.

References

Aboud, F. (1987). The development of ethnic self-identification and attitudes. In J. Phinney & M. Rotheram (Eds.), *Children's ethnic socialization: Pluralism and development* (pp. 32–55). Newbury Park, CA: Sage.

Adelman, M. B. (1988). Cross-cultural adjustment: A theoretical perspective on social support. *International Journal of Intercultural Relations, 12*, 183–205.

Adler, P. S. (1975). The transitional experience: An alternative view of culture shock. *Journal of Humanistic Psychology, 15*, 13–23.

Altrocchi, J., & Altrocchi, L. (1995). Polyfaceted psychological acculturation in Cook Islanders. *Journal of Cross-Cultural Psychology, 26*, 426–440.

Amir, Y., & Ben-Ari, R. (1988). A contingency approach for promoting intergroup relations. In J. W. Berry & R. C. Annis (Eds.), *Ethnic psychology: Research and practice with immigrants, refugees, native peoples, ethnic groups and sojourners* (pp. 287–296). Lisse, The Netherlands: Swets & Zeitlinger.

Anderson, J., Moeschberger, M., Chen, M. S., Kunn, P., Wewers, M. E., & Guthrie, R. (1993). An acculturation scale for Southeast Asians. *Social Psychiatry and Psychiatric Epidemiology, 28*, 134–141.

Argyle, M. (1969). *Social interaction.* London: Methuen.

Argyle, M. (1975). *Bodily communication.* London: Methuen.

Argyle, M. (1982). Intercultural communication. In S. Bochner (Ed.), *Cultures in contact: Studies in cross-cultural interaction* (pp. 61–79). Oxford: Pergamon.

Argyle, M., & Kendon, A. (1967). The experimental analysis of social performance. In L. Berkowitz (Ed.), *Advances in experimental social psychology* (Vol. 3, pp. 55–98). New York: Academic Press.

Armes, K., & Ward, C. (1989). Cross-cultural transitions and sojourner adjustment in Singapore. *Journal of Social Psychology, 12*, 273–275.

Ataca, B. (1996, August). *Psychological and sociocultural adaptation of Turkish immigrants, Canadians and Turks.* Paper presented at the Thirteenth Congress of the International Asso-ciation for Cross-Cultural Psychology, Montreal, Canada.

Aycan, Z., & Berry, J. W. (1994, July). *The influences of economic adjustment of immigrants on their psychological well-being and adaptation.* Paper presented at the Twelfth International Congress of the International Association for Cross-Cultural Psychology, Pamplona, Spain.

Babiker, I. E., Cox, J. L., & Miller, P. M. (1980). The measurement of cultural distance and its relationship to medical consultations, symptomatology and examination of performance of overseas students at Edinburgh University. *Social Psychiatry, 15*, 109–116.

Barona, A., & Miller, J. A. (1994). Short Acculturation Scale for Hispanic Youth (SASH-Y): A preliminary report. *Hispanic Journal of Behavioral Sciences, 16*, 155–162.

Beiser, M., Barwick, C., Berry, J. W., da Costa, G., Fantino, A., Ganesan, S., Lee, C., Milne, W., Naidoo, J., Prince, R., Tousignant, M., & Vela, E. (1988). *Mental health issues affecting immigrants and refugees.* Ottawa: Health and Welfare Canada.

Benson, P. G. (1978). Measuring cross-cultural adjustment: The problem of criteria. *International Journal of Intercultural Relations, 2*, 21–37.

Berno, T., & Ward, C. (1998, April). *Psychological and sociocultural adjustment of international students in New Zealand.* Paper presented at the annual meeting of the Society of Australasian Social Psychologists, Christchurch, New Zealand.

Berry, J. W. (1974). Psychological aspects of cultural pluralism. *Topics in Culture Learning, 2*, 17–22.

Berry, J. W. (1984). Cultural relations in plural societies. In N. Miller & M. Brewer (Eds.), *Groups in contact* (pp. 11–27). New York: Academic Press.

Berry, J. W. (1994). Acculturation and psychological adaptation. In A.-M. Bouvy, F. J. R. van de Vijver, P. Boski, & P. Schmitz (Eds.), *Journeys into cross-cultural psychology* (pp. 129–141). Lisse, The Netherlands: Swets & Zeitlinger.

Berry, J. W. (1997). Immigration, acculturation and adaptation. *Applied Psychology: An International Review, 46*, 5–34.

Berry, J. W., & Annis, R. C. (1974). Acculturative stress. *Journal of Cross-Cultural Psychology, 5*, 382–406.

Berry, J. W., Kim, U., Minde, T., & Mok, D. (1987). Comparative studies of acculturative stress. *International Migration Review, 21*, 491–511.

Berry, J. W., Kim, U., Power, S., Young, M., & Bujaki, M. (1989). Acculturation attitudes in plural societies. *Applied Psychology, 38*, 185–206.

Berry, J. W., & Sam, D. (1997). Acculturation and adaptation. In J. W. Berry, M. H. Segall, & C. Kagitcibasi (Eds.), *Handbook of cross-cultural psychology: Vol. 3. Social behavior and applications* (pp. 291–326). Boston: Allyn & Bacon.

Berry, J. W., Wintrob, R., Sindell, P. S., & Mawhinney, T. A. (1982). Psychological adaptation to culture change among the James Bay Cree. *Naturaliste Canadien, 109*, 965–975.

Biegel, D., Naparstek, A., & Khan, M. (1980, September). *Social support and mental health: An examination of interrelationships*. Paper presented at the Eighty-eighth Annual Convention of the American Psychological Association, Montreal, Canada.

Bird, A., Heinbuch, S., Dunbar, R., & McNulty, M. (1993). A conceptual model of the effects of area studies training programs and a preliminary investigation of the model's hypothesized relationships. *International Journal of Intercultural Relations, 17*, 415–435.

Black, J. S., & Gregersen, H. B. (1990). Expectations, satisfaction, and intention to leave of American expatriate managers in Japan. *International Journal of Intercultural Relations, 14*, 485–506.

Black, J. S., & Stephens, G. K. (1989). The influence of the spouse on American expatriate adjustment in Pacific Rim overseas assignments. *Journal of Management, 15*, 529–544.

Bochner, S. (1972). Problems in culture learning. In S. Bochner & P. Wicks (Eds.), *Overseas students in Australia* (pp. 65–81). Sydney: University of New South Wales Press.

Bochner, S. (1982). The social psychology of cross-cultural relations. In S. Bochner (Ed.), *Cultures in contact: Studies in cross-cultural interaction* (pp. 5–44). Oxford, England: Pergamon.

Bochner, S. (1986). Coping with unfamiliar cultures: Adjustment or culture learning? *Australian Journal of Psychology, 38*, 347–358.

Bochner, S., Lin, A., & McLeod, B. M. (1979). Cross-cultural contact and the development of an international perspective. *Journal of Social Psychology, 107*, 29–41.

Bochner, S., McLeod, B. M., & Lin, A. (1977). Friendship patterns of overseas students: A functional model. *International Journal of Psychology, 12*, 277–297.

Breakwell, G. M., & Lyons, E. (Eds.). (1996). *Changing European identities: A social psychological analysis of social change*. Oxford, England: Butterworth-Heinemann.

Brewer, M. (1996). When contact is not enough: Social identity and intergroup cooperation. *Inter-national Journal of Intercultural Relations, 20*, 291–304.

Brislin, R. (1981). *Cross-cultural encounters*. New York: Pergamon.

Camilleri, C., & Malewska-Peyre, H. (1997). Socialization and identity strategies. In J. W. Berry, P. R. Dasen & T. S. Saraswathi (Eds.), *Handbook of cross-cultural psychology: Vol. 2. Basic processes and human development* (pp. 41–67). Boston: Allyn & Bacon.

Cargile, A. C., & Giles, H. (1996). Intercultural communication training: Review, critique and a new theoretical framework. *Communication Yearbook, 19*, 385–423.

Carver, C. S., Scheier, M. F., & Weintraub, J. K. (1989). Assessing coping strategies: A theoretically based approach. *Journal of Personality and Social Psychology, 56*, 267–283.

Chataway, C. J., & Berry, J. W. (1989). Acculturation experiences, appraisal, coping and adaptation: A comparison of Hong Kong Chinese, French and English students in Canada. *Canadian Journal of Behavioral Science, 21*, 295–301.

Church, A. T. (1982). Sojourner adjustment. *Psychological Bulletin, 91*, 540–572.

Clément, R., Gardner, R. C., & Smythe, P. C. (1977). Inter-ethnic contact: Attitudinal consequences. *Canadian Journal of Behavioral Sciences, 9*, 205–215.

Collett, P. (1982). Meetings and misunderstandings. In S. Bochner (Ed.), *Cultures in contact* (pp. 81–98). Oxford, England: Pergamon.

Cort, D. A., & King, M. (1979). Some correlates of culture shock among American tourists in Africa. *International Journal of Intercultural Relations, 3*, 211–225.

Cortés, D. E., Rogler, L. H., & Malgady, R. G. (1994). Biculturality among Puerto Rican adults in the United States. *American Journal of Community Psychology, 22*, 707–721.

Costa, P. T., & McCrae, R. R. (1989). Personality, stress and coping: Some lessons from a decade of research. In K. S. Markides & C. L. Cooper (Eds.), *Aging, stress and health* (pp. 270–285). New York: Wiley.

Cross, S. (1995). Self-construals, coping, and stress in cross-cultural adaptation. *Journal of Cross-Cultural Psychology, 26*, 673–697.

Cuéllar, I., & Arnold, B. (1988). Cultural considerations and rehabilitation of Mexican Americans. *Journal of Rehabilitation, 54*, 35–40.

Cuéllar, I., Arnold, B., & González, G. (1995). Cognitive referents of acculturation: Assessment of cultural constructs of Mexican Americans. *Journal of Community Psychology, 23*, 339–356.

Cuéllar, I., Arnold, B., & Maldonado, R. (1995). Acculturation rating scale for Mexican Americans. II: A revision of the original ARMSA scale. *Hispanic Journal of Behavioral Sciences, 17,* 275–304.

Cuéllar, I., Harris, L. C., & Jasso, R. (1980). An acculturation scale for Mexican American normal and clinical populations. *Hispanic Journal of Behavioral Sciences, 2,* 199–217.

Dale, P. N. (1986). *The myth of Japanese uniqueness.* New York: St. Martin's Press.

Der-Karabetian, A. (1980). Relation of two cultural identities of Armenian-Americans. *Psychological Reports, 47,* 123–128.

Deshpande, S. P., & Viswesvaran, C. (1992). Is cross-cultural training of expatriate managers effective? A meta-analysis. *International Journal of Intercultural Relations, 16,* 295–310.

Dew, A.-M., & Ward, C. (1993). The effects of ethnicity and culturally congruent and incongruent nonverbal behaviors on interpersonal attraction. *Journal of Applied Social Psychology, 23,* 1376–1389.

Ditchburn, G. J. (1996). Cross-cultural adjustment and psychoticism. *Personality and Individual Differences, 21,* 295–296.

Donà, G., & Berry, J. W. (1994). Acculturation attitudes and acculturative stress of Central American refugees. *International Journal of Psychology, 29,* 57–70.

Driskill, G. W., & Downs, C. W. (1995). Hidden differences in competent communication: A case study of an organization with Euro-Americans and first generation immigrants from India. *International Journal of Intercultural Relations, 21,* 213–248.

Dyal, J. A. (1984). Cross-cultural research with the locus of control construct. In H. M. Lefcourt (Ed.), *Research with the locus of control construct* (Vol. 3, pp. 209–306). New York: Academic Press.

Dyal, J. A., Rybensky, L., & Somers, M. (1988). Marital and acculturative strain among Indo-Canadian and Euro-Canadian women. In J. W. Berry & R. Annis (Eds.), *Ethnic psychology: Research and practice with immigrants, refugees, native peoples, ethnic groups, and sojourners* (pp. 80–95). Lisse, The Netherlands: Swets & Zeitlinger.

Esses, V. M., Jackson, L. M., & Armstrong, T. L. (1998). Intergroup competition and attitudes toward immigrants and immigration. *Journal of Social Issues, 54,* 699–724.

Felix-Ortiz, C. M., Newcomb, M. D., & Meyers, H. (1994). A multidimensional measure of cultural identity for Latino and Latina adolescents. *Hispanic Journal of Behavioral Sciences, 16,* 99–115.

Folkman, S., & Lazarus, R. S. (1985). If it changes it must be process: Study of emotions and coping during three stages of a college examination. *Journal of Personality and Social Psychology, 48,* 150–170.

Folkman, S., Schaeffer, C., & Lazarus, R. S. (1979). Cognitive processes as mediators of stress and coping. In V. Hamilton & D. M. Warburton (Eds.), *Human stress and cognition* (pp. 265–298). New York: Wiley.

Fontaine, G. (1986). Roles of social support in overseas relocation: Implications for intercultural training. *International Journal of Intercultural Relations, 10,* 361–378.

Friesen, W. V. (1972). *Cultural differences in facial expressions in a social situation: An experimental test of the concept of display rules.* Unpublished doctoral dissertation, University of California, San Diego.

Furnham, A., & Alibhai, N. (1985). The friendship networks of foreign students: A replication and extension of the functional model. *International Journal of Psychology, 20,* 709–722.

Furnham, A., & Bochner, S. (1982). Social difficulty in a foreign culture: An empirical analysis of culture shock. In S. Bochner (Ed.), *Cultures in contact: Studies in cross-cultural interactions* (pp. 161–198). Oxford, England: Pergamon.

Furnham, A., & Bochner, S. (1986). *Culture shock: Psychological reactions to unfamiliar environments.* London: Methuen.

Furnham, A., & Li, Y. H. (1993). The psychological adjustment of the Chinese community in Britain: A study of two generations. *British Journal of Psychiatry, 162,* 109–113.

Furnham, A., & Shiekh, S. (1993). Gender, generational and social support correlates of mental health in Asian immigrants. *International Journal of Social Psychiatry, 39,* 22–33.

Furnham, A., & Tresize, L. (1981). The mental health of foreign students. *Social Science and Medicine, 17,* 365–370.

Furukawa, T., & Shibayama, T. (1993). Predicting maladjustment of exchange students in different cultures: A prospective study. *Social Psychiatry and Psychiatric Epidemiology, 28,* 142–146.

Gaertner, S. L., Dovidio, J. F., & Bachman, B. A. (1996). Revisiting the contact hypothesis: The induction of a common ingroup identity. *International Journal of Intercultural Relations, 20,* 271–290.

Gallois, C., Giles, H., Jones, E., Cargile, A. C., & Ota, H. (1995). Accommodating intercultural encounters: Elaborations and extensions. In R. L. Wiseman (Ed.), *Intercultural communication theory* (pp. 115–147). Thousand Oaks, CA: Sage.

Georgas, J. (1998, August). *Intergroup contact and acculturation of immigrants.* Paper presented at the Fourteenth International Congress of the

International Association for Cross-Cultural Psychology, Bellingham, WA.

Ghaffarian, S. (1987). The acculturation of Iranians in the United States. *Journal of Social Psychology, 127,* 565–571.

Ghuman, P. (1994). Canadian or Indo-Canadian: A study of South Asian adolescents. *International Journal of Adolescence and Youth, 4,* 229–243.

Graves, T. D. (1967). Psychological acculturation in a tri-ethnic community. *Southwestern Journal of Anthropology, 23,* 337–350.

Gudykunst, W. B. (1993). Toward a theory of effective interpersonal and intergroup communication. In R. Wiseman & J. Koester (Eds.), *Intercultural communication competence* (pp. 33–71). Newbury Park, CA: Sage.

Gudykunst, W. B., & Ting-Toomey, S. (Eds.). (1988). *Culture and interpersonal communication.* Newbury Park, CA: Sage.

Gullahorn, J. E., & Gullahorn, J. T. (1966). American students abroad: Professional versus personal development. *The Annals, 368,* 43–59.

Gullahorn, J. T., & Gullahorn, J. E. (1962). Visiting Fulbright professors as agents of cross-cultural communication. *Sociology and Social Research, 46,* 282–293.

Hall, E. (1976). *Beyond culture.* New York: Doubleday.

Hammer, M. (1987). Behavioral dimensions of intercultural effectiveness: A replication and extension. *International Journal of Intercultural Relations, 11,* 65–88.

Hammer, M., Gudykunst, W. B., & Wiseman, R. L. (1978). Dimensions of intercultural effectiveness: An exploratory study. *International Journal of Intercultural Relations, 2,* 382–393.

Harris, A. C., & Verven, R. (1996). The Greek-American Acculturation Scale: Development and validity. *Psychological Reports, 78,* 599–610.

Harrison, J. K. (1992). Individual and combined effects of behavior modeling and the culture assimilator in cross-cultural management training. *Journal of Applied Psychology, 3,* 431–460.

Harrison, J. K., Chadwick, M., & Scales, M. (1996). The relationship between cross-cultural adjustment and the personality variables of self-efficacy and self-monitoring. *International Journal of Intercultural Relations, 20,* 167–188.

Hocoy, D. (1996). Empirical distinctiveness between cognitive and affective elements of ethnic identity and scales for their measurement. In H. Grad, A. Blanco, & J. Georgas (Eds.), *Key issues in cross-cultural psychology* (pp. 128–137). Lisse, The Netherlands: Swets & Zeitlinger.

Hofstede, G. (1980). *Culture's consequences: International differences in work-related values.* Beverly Hills, CA: Sage.

Holmes, T. H., & Rahe, R. H. (1967). The Social Readjustment Rating Scale. *Journal of Psychosomatic Research, 11,* 213–218.

Hung, Y. Y. (1974). Socio-cultural environment and locus of control. *Psychologica Taiwanica, 16,* 187–198.

Hutnik, N. (1986). Patterns of ethnic minority identification and modes of social adaptation. *Ethnic and Racial Studies, 9,* 150–167.

Ishii, S., & Klopf, D. (1976). A comparison of communication activities of Japanese and American adults [in Japanese]. *Eigo Tembou, 53,* 22–26.

Kamal, A. A., & Maruyama, G. (1990). Cross-cultural contact and attitudes of Qatari students in the United States. *International Journal of Intercultural Relations, 14,* 123–134.

Kaplan, M. S., & Marks, G. (1990). Adverse effects of acculturation: Psychological distress among Mexican American young adults. *Social Science and Medicine, 31,* 1313–1319.

Kealey, D. (1989). A study of cross-cultural effectiveness: Theoretical issues and practical applications. *International Journal of Intercultural Relations, 13,* 387–428.

Keefe, S. M., & Padilla, A. M. (1987). *Chicano ethnicity.* Albuquerque, NM: University of New Mexico Press.

Kennedy, A. (1998, April). *Acculturation and coping: A longitudinal study of Singaporeans studying abroad.* Paper presented at the annual meeting of the Society of Australasian Social Psychologists, Christchurch, New Zealand.

Kennedy, A. (1999). *Singaporean sojourners: Meeting the demands of cross-cultural transitions.* Unpublished doctoral dissertation, National University of Singapore.

Kim, U. (1988). *Acculturation of Korean immigrants to Canada.* Unpublished doctoral dissertation, Queen's University, Kingston, Canada.

Kim, U., Cho, W.-C., & Harajiri, H. (1997). The perception of Japanese people and culture: The case of Korean nationals and sojourners. In K. Leung, U. Kim, S. Yamaguchi, & Y. Kashima (Eds.), *Progress in Asian social psychology* (Vol. 1, pp. 321–344). Singapore: John Wiley.

Kim, Y. Y. (1991). Intercultural communication competence: A systems-theoretic view. In S. Ting-Toomey & F. Korzenny (Eds.), *Cross-cultural interpersonal communication* (pp. 259–275). Newbury Park, CA: Sage.

Klineberg, O., & Hull, W. F. (1979). *At a foreign university: An international study of adaptation and coping.* New York: Praeger.

Kosmitzki, C. (1996). The reaffirmation of cultural identity in cross-cultural encounters. *Personality and Social Psychology Bulletin, 22,* 238–248.

Kuo, W. H., Gray, R., & Lin, N. (1976). Locus of control and symptoms of distress among Chinese-Americans. *International Journal of Social Psychiatry, 22,* 176–187.

Kuo, W. H., & Tsai, V.-M. (1986). Social networking, hardiness, and immigrants' mental health. *Journal of Health and Social Behavior, 27,* 133–149.

LaFromboise, T., Coleman, H., & Gerton, J. (1993). Psychological impact of biculturalism: Evidence and theory. *Psychological Bulletin, 114,* 395–412.

Lai, J., & Linden, W. (1993). The smile of Asia: Acculturation effects on symptom reporting. *Canadian Journal of Behavioral Science, 25,* 303–313.

Lalonde, R. N., & Cameron, J. E. (1993). An intergroup perspective on immigrant acculturation with focus on collective strategies. *International Journal of Psychology, 28,* 57–74.

Lalonde, R. N., Taylor, D. M., & Moghaddam, F. M. (1988). Social integration strategies of Haitian and Indian immigrant women in Montreal. In J. W. Berry & R. C. Annis (Eds.), *Ethnic psychology: Research and practice with immigrants, refugees, native peoples, ethnic groups and sojourners* (pp. 114–124). Lisse, The Netherlands: Swets & Zeitlinger.

Lambert, W. E., Moghaddam, F. M., Sorin, J., & Sorin, S. (1990). Assimilation versus multiculturalism: Views from a community in France. *Sociological Forum, 5,* 387–411.

Lanca, M., Alksnis, C., Roese, N. J., & Gardner, R. C. (1994). Effects of language choice on acculturation: A study of Portuguese immigrants in a multicultural setting. *Journal of Language and Social Psychology, 13,* 315–330.

Lance, C. E., & Richardson, D. (1985). Correlates of work and non-work related stress and satisfaction among American insulated sojourners. *Human Relations, 10,* 725–738.

Landis, D. (1996). A model of intercultural training and behavior. In D. Landis & R. Bhagat (Eds.), *Handbook of intercultural training* (2nd ed., pp. 1–13). Thousand Oaks, CA: Sage.

Landis, D., Brislin, R., & Hulgus, J. F. (1985). Attributional training versus contact in acculturative learning: A laboratory study. *Journal of Applied Social Psychology, 15,* 466–482.

Lasry, J. C., & Sayegh, L. (1992). Developing an acculturation scale: A bidimensional model. In N. Grizenko, L. Sayegh, & P. Migneault (Eds.), *Transcultural issues in child psychiatry* (pp. 67–86). Montreal: Editions Douglas.

Lazarus, R. S., & Folkman, S. (1984). *Stress, coping and appraisal.* New York: Springer.

Lebra, T. S. (1987).The cultural significance of silence in Japanese communication. *Multilingua, 6,* 343–357.

Lefley, H. (1985). Impact of cross-cultural training on black and white mental health care professionals. *International Journal of Intercultural Relations, 9,* 305–318.

Leong, C.-H. (1997). *Where's the cognition in acculturation? A cognitive model of acculturation of the P. R. C. Chinese in Singapore.* Unpublished honours thesis, National University of Singapore.

Leong, C.-H., & Ward, C. (2000). Identity conflict in sojourners. *International Journal of Intercultural Relations, 24,* 763–776.

Lese, K. P., & Robbins, S. B. (1994). Relationship between goal attributes and the academic achievement of Southeast Asian adolescent refugees. *Journal of Counseling Psychology, 41,* 45–52.

Liebkind, K. (1996). Acculturation and stress: Vietnamese refugees in Finland. *Journal of Cross-Cultural Psychology, 27,* 161–180.

Lin, K.-M., Tazuma, L., & Masuda, M. (1979). Adaptational problems of Vietnamese refugees I: Health and mental status. *Archives of General Psychiatry, 36,* 955–961.

Locke, S. A., & Feinsod, F. (1982). Psychological preparation for young adults traveling abroad. *Adolescence, 17,* 815–819.

Lu, L. (1990). Adaptation to British universities: Homesickness and mental health of Chinese students. *Counseling Psychology Quarterly, 3,* 225–232.

Lysgaard, S. (1955). Adjustment in a foreign society: Norwegian Fulbright grantees visiting the United States. *International Social Science Bulletin, 7,* 45–51.

Mainous, A. G. (1989). Self-concept as an indicator of acculturation in Mexican Americans. *Hispanic Journal of Behavioral Sciences, 11,* 178–189.

Malewska-Peyre, H. (1982). L'expérience du racisme et de la xénophobie chez jeunes immigrés. In H. Malewska-Peyre (Ed.), *Crise d'identité et déviance chez jeunes immigrés* (pp. 53–73). Paris: La Documentation Française.

Marín, G., Sabogal, F., Marín, B., Otero-Sabogal, R., & Perez-Stable, E. J. (1987). Development of a short acculturation scale for Hispanics. *Hispanic Journal of Behavioral Science, 2,* 21–34.

Martin, J. (1987). The relationship between student sojourner perceptions of intercultural competencies and previous sojourn experience. *International Journal of Intercultural Relations, 11,* 337–355.

Martin, J., Bradford, L., & Rohrlich, B. (1995). Comparing predeparture expectations and postsojourn reports: A longitudinal study of U.S. students abroad. *International Journal of Intercultural Relations, 19*, 87–110.

Masuda, M., Lin, K.-M., & Tazuma, L. (1982). Life changes among the Vietnamese refugees. In R. C. Nann (Ed.), *Uprooting and surviving* (pp. 25–33). Boston: Reidel.

Matsumoto, D. (1994). *People: Psychology from a cultural perspective*. Pacific Grove, CA: Brooks/Cole.

Mavreas, V., & Bebbington, P. (1990). Acculturation and psychiatric disorder: A study of Greek Cypriot immigrants. *Psychological Medicine, 20*, 941–951.

Mavreas, V., Bebbington, P., & Der, G. (1989). The structure and validity of acculturation: Analysis of an acculturation scale. *Social Psychiatry and Psychiatric Epidemiology, 24*, 233–240.

McGinley, H., Blau, G. L., & Takai, M. (1984). Attraction effects of smiling and body position. *Perceptual and Motor Skills, 58*, 915–922.

Mendenhall, M., & Oddou, G. (1985). The dimensions of expatriate acculturation. *Academy of Management Review, 10*, 39–47.

Mendoza, R. H. (1989). An empirical scale to measure type and degree of acculturation in Mexican American adolescents and adults. *Journal of Cross-Cultural Psychology, 20*, 372–385.

Metge, J., & Kinloch, P. (1978). *Talking past each other*. Wellington, New Zealand: Victoria University Press.

Moghaddam, F. M., Taylor, D. M., & Lalonde, R. N. (1987). Individualistic and collective integration strategies among Iranians in Canada. *International Journal of Psychology, 22*, 301–313.

Montgomery, G. T. (1992). Comfort with acculturation status among students from South Texas. *Hispanic Journal of Behavioral Sciences, 14*, 201–223.

Morrison, T., Conaway, W. A., & Borden, G. A. (1994). *Kiss, bow or shake hands: How to do business in 60 countries*. Holbrook, MA: Adams Media.

Naidoo, J. (1985). A cultural perspective on the adjustment of South Asian women in Canada. In I. R. Lagunes & Y. H. Poortinga (Eds.), *From a different perspective: Studies of behavior across cultures* (pp. 76–92). Lisse, The Netherlands: Swets & Zeitlinger.

Neffe, J. A., & Hoppe, S. K. (1993). Race/ethnicity, acculturation, and psychological distress: Fatalism and religiosity as cultural resources. *Journal of Community Psychology, 21*, 3–20.

Neto, F. (1995). Predictors of satisfaction with life satisfaction among second generation migrants. *Social Indicators Research, 35*, 93–116.

Nguyen, H. H., Messé, L. A., & Stollak, G. E. (1999). Toward a more complex understanding of acculturation and adjustment. *Journal of Cross-Cultural Psychology, 30*, 5–31.

Nicassio, P. M. (1983). Psychosocial correlates of alienation: The study of a sample of Southeast Asian refugees. *Journal of Cross-cultural Psychology, 14*, 337–351.

Olmeda, E. L. (1979). Acculturation: A psychometric perspective. *American Psychologist, 34*, 1061–1070.

Ostrowska, A., & Bochenska, D. (1996). Ethnic stereotypes among Polish and German Silesians. In H. Grad, A. Blanco, & J. Georgas (Eds.), *Key issues in cross-cultural psychology* (pp. 102–113). Lisse, The Netherlands: Swets & Zeitlinger.

Padilla, A. M., Wagatsuma, Y., & Lindholm, K. J. (1985). Acculturation and personality as predictors of stress in Japanese and Japanese-Americans. *Journal of Social Psychology, 125*, 295–305.

Partridge, K. (1988). Acculturation attitudes and stress of Westerners living in Japan. In J. W. Berry & R. C. Annis (Eds.), *Ethnic psychology: Research and practice with immigrants, refugees, native peoples, ethnic groups and sojourners* (pp. 105–113). Lisse, The Netherlands: Swets & Zeitlinger.

Pawliuk, N., Grizenko, N., Chan-Yip, A., Gantous, P., Mathew, J., & Nguyen, D. (1996). Acculturation style and psychological functioning in children of immigrants. *American Journal of Orthopsychiatry, 66*, 111–121.

Pelly, R. (1997). *Predictors of international student cultural adjustment: An intergroup perspective*. Unpublished honors thesis, University of Queensland, Brisbane, Australia.

Perkins, C. S., Perkins, M. L., Guglielmino, L. M., & Reiff, R. F. (1977). A comparison of adjustment problems of three international student groups. *Journal of College Student Personnel, 18*, 382–388.

Pernice, R., & Brook, J. (1994). Relationship of migrant status (refugee or immigrant) to mental health. *International Journal of Social Psychiatry, 40*, 177–188.

Phinney, J. (1989). Stages of ethnic identity in minority group adolescents. *Journal of Early Adolescence, 9*, 34–49.

Phinney, J. (1992). The Multigroup Ethnic Identity Measure: A new scale for use with diverse groups. *Journal of Adolescent Research, 7*, 156–176.

Phinney, J., Chavira, V., & Williamson, L. (1992). Acculturation attitudes and self-esteem among high school and college students. *Youth and Society, 23*, 299–312.

Pruitt, F. J. (1978). The adaptation of African students to American society. *International Journal of Intercultural Relations, 21*, 90–118.

Randolph, G., Landis, D., & Tzeng, O. (1977). The effects of time and practice upon culture assimilator training. *International Journal of Intercultural Relations, 1*, 105–119.

Redfield, R., Linton, R., & Herskovits, M. J. (1936). Memorandum for the study of acculturation. *American Anthropologist, 38*, 149–152.

Richardson, A. (1974). *British immigrants and Australia: A psycho-social inquiry.* Canberra: Australian National University Press.

Richman, J. A., Gaviria, M., Flaherty, J. A., Birz, S., & Wintrob, R. M. (1987). The process of acculturation: Theoretical perspectives and an empirical investigation in Peru. *Social Science and Medicine, 25*, 839–847.

Rogers, J., & Ward, C. (1993). Expectation-experience discrepancies and psychological adjustment during cross-cultural reentry. *International Journal of Intercultural Relations, 17*, 185–196.

Rosenthal, D., Bell, R., Demetriou, A., & Efklides, A. (1989). From collectivism to individualism? The acculturation of Greek immigrants in Australia. *International Journal of Psychology, 24*, 57–71.

Ruben, B. D. (1976). Assessing communication competency for intercultural adaptation. *Group and Organization Studies, 1*, 334–354.

Ruben, B. D., & Kealey, D. J. (1979). Behavioral assessment of communication competency and the prediction of cross-cultural adaptation. *International Journal of Intercultural Relations, 3*, 15–47.

Sam, D. L. (1994). The psychological adjustment of young immigrants in Norway. *Scandinavian Journal of Psychology, 35*, 240–253.

Sam, D. L. (1995). Acculturation attitudes among young immigrants as a function of perceived parental attitudes toward cultural change. *Journal of Early Adolescence, 15*, 238–258.

Sam, D. L. (1998). Predicting life satisfaction among adolescents from immigrant families in Norway. *Ethnicity and Health, 3*, 5–18.

Sam, D. L. (2000). Psychological adaptation of adolescents with immigrant background. *Journal of Social Psychology, 140*, 5–25.

Sam, D. L., & Berry, J. W. (1995). Acculturative stress and young immigrants in Norway. *Scandinavian Journal of Psychology, 36*, 10–24.

Sam, D. L., & Eide, R. (1991). Survey of mental health of foreign students. *Scandinavian Journal of Psychology, 32*, 22–30.

Samovar, L. A., & Porter, R. E. (Eds). (1996). *Intercultural communication.* Belmont, CA: Wadsworth.

Sands, E., & Berry, J. W. (1993). Acculturation and mental health among Greek-Canadians. *Canadian Journal of Community Mental Health, 12*, 117–124.

Sano, H. (1990). Research on social difficulties in cross-cultural adjustment: Social situational analysis. *Japanese Journal of Behavioral Therapy, 16*, 37–44.

Sano, N., Yamaguchi, S., & Matsumoto, D. (1999). Is silence golden? A cross-cultural study on the meaning of silence. In T. Sugiman, M. Karasawa, J. Liu, & C. Ward (Eds.), *Progress in Asian social psychology* (Vol. 2, pp. 145–155). Seoul: Education Science.

Sayegh, L., & Lasry, J. C. (1993). Immigrants' adaptation to Canada: Assimilation, acculturation, and orthogonal cultural identification. *Canadian Psychology, 34*, 98–109.

Schild, E. O. (1962). The foreign student, as stranger, learning the norms of the host culture. *Journal of Social Issues, 18*, 41–54.

Schmitz, P. G. (1992). Immigrant mental and physical health. *Psychology and Developing Societies, 4*, 117–131.

Schönpflug, U. (1997). Acculturation, adaptation or development? *Applied Psychology: An International Review, 46*, 52–55.

Schwartz, S. (1994). Are there universal aspects in the structure and contents of human values? *Journal of Social Issues, 50*, 19–45.

Schwarzer, R., Jerusalem, M., & Hahn, A. (1994). Unemployment, social support and health complaints: A longitudinal study of stress in East German refugees. *Journal of Community and Applied Social Psychology, 4*, 31–45.

Searle, W., & Ward, C. (1990). The prediction of psychological and sociocultural adjustment during cross-cultural transitions. *International Journal of Intercultural Relations, 14*, 449–464.

Seipel, M. M. O. (1988). Locus of control as related to life experiences of Korean immigrants. *International Journal of Intercultural Relations, 12*, 61–71.

Selltiz, C., Christ, J. R., Havel, J., & Cook, S. W. (1963). *Attitudes and social relations of foreign students in the United States.* Minneapolis: University of Minnesota Press.

Sewell, W. H., & Davidsen, O. M. (1961). *Scandinavian students on an American campus.* Minneapolis: University of Minnesota Press.

Singh, A. (1989). Impact of acculturation on psychological stress: A study of the Oraon tribe. In D. M. Keats, D. Munro, & L. Mann (Eds.), *Heterogeneity in cross-cultural psychology* (pp. 210–215). Lisse, The Netherlands: Swets & Zeitlinger.

Sodowsky, G. R., Lai, J., & Plake, B. S. (1991). Psychometric properties of the American-International Relations Scale. *Educational and Psychological Measurement, 51,* 207–216.

Stephan, C. W., & Stephan, W. G. (1992). Reducing intercultural anxiety through intercultural contact. *International Journal of Intercultural Relations, 16,* 89–106.

Stephan, W. G., Ybarra, P., Martínez, C. M., Schwarzwald, J., & Tur-Kaspa, M. (1998). Prejudice toward immigrants to Spain and Israel: An integrated threat theory analysis. *Journal of Cross-Cultural Psychology, 29,* 559–576.

Stone Feinstein, E., & Ward, C. (1990). Loneliness and psychological adjustment of sojourners: New perspectives on culture shock. In D. M. Keats, D. Munro, & L. Mann (Eds.), *Heterogeneity in cross-cultural psychology* (pp. 537–547). Lisse, The Netherlands: Swets & Zeitlinger.

Suinn, R. M., Ahuna, C., & Khoo, G. (1992). The Suinn-Lew Asian Self-Identity Acculturation Scale: Concurrent and factorial validation. *Educational and Psychological Measurement, 52,* 1041–1046.

Suinn, R. M., Rickard-Figueroa, K., Lew, S., & Vigil, P. (1987). The Suinn-Lew Asian Self-Identity Acculturation Scale: An initial report. *Educational and Psychological Measurement, 47,* 401–402.

Sykes, I. J., & Eden, D. (1987). Transitional stress, social support and psychological strain. *Journal of Occupational Behavior, 6,* 293–298.

Szapocznik, J., Kurtines, W. M., & Fernandez, T. (1980). Bicultural involvement and adjustment in Hispanic-American youths. *International Journal of Intercultural Relations, 4,* 353–365.

Szapocznik, J., Scopetta, M. A., Kurtines, W. M., & Aranalde, M. A. (1978). Theory and measurement of acculturation. *Interamerican Journal of Psychology, 12,* 113–130.

Taft, R., & Steinkalk, E. (1985). The adaptation of recent Soviet immigrants in Australia. In I. R. Lagunes & Y. H. Poortinga (Eds.), *From a different perspective: Studies of behavior across cultures* (pp. 19–28). Lisse, The Netherlands: Swets & Zeitlinger.

Tajfel, H. (Ed.). (1978). *Differentiation between social groups: Studies in the psychology of intergroup relations.* London: Academic Press.

Tajfel, H. (1981). *Human groups and social categories.* Cambridge: Cambridge University Press.

Taylor, D. M., Moghaddam, F. M., & Bellerose, J. (1989). Social comparison in an intergroup context. *Journal of Social Psychology, 129,* 499–515.

Taylor, D. M., Wright, S., Moghaddam, F. M., & Lalonde, R. N. (1990). The personal/group discrimination discrepancy: Perceiving my group but not myself to be a target for discrimina-

tion. *Personality and Social Psychology Bulletin, 16,* 254–262.

Ting-Toomey, S. (1981). Ethnic identity and close friendship in Chinese-American college students. *International Journal of Intercultural Relations, 5,* 383–406.

Torbiorn, I. (1982). *Living abroad: Personal adjustment and personnel policy in the overseas setting.* Chichester, England: Wiley.

Torres-Rivera, M. A. (1985). Manifestations of depression in Puerto Rican migrants to the United States and Puerto Rican residents of Puerto Rico. In I. R. Lagunes & Y. H. Poortinga (Eds.), *From a different perspective: Studies of behavior across cultures* (pp. 63–75). Lisse, The Netherlands: Swets & Zeitlinger.

Tran, T. V. (1993). Psychological traumas and depression in a sample of Vietnamese people in the United States. *Health and Social Work, 18,* 184–194.

Triandis, H. C. (1989). The self and social behavior in differing cultural contexts. *Psychological Review, 96,* 506–520.

Triandis, H. C. (1997). Where is culture in the acculturation model? *Applied Psychology: An International Review, 46,* 55–58.

Triandis, H. C., Kashima, Y., Shimada, E., & Villareal, M. (1986). Acculturation indices as a means of confirming cultural differences. *International Journal of Psychology, 21,* 43–70.

Triandis, H. C., & Vassiliou, V. (1967). Frequency of contact and stereotyping. *Journal of Personality and Social Psychology, 7,* 316–328.

Trower, P., Bryant, B., & Argyle, M. (1978). *Social skills and mental health.* London: Methuen.

Turner, J. C. (1982). Toward a cognitive redefinition of the social group. In H. Tajfel (Ed.), *Social identity and intergroup relations* (pp. 15–40). Cambridge: University of Cambridge Press.

Ullah, P. (1987). Self-definition and psychological group formation in an ethnic minority. *British Journal of Social Psychology, 26,* 17–23.

Van den Broucke, S., De Soete, G., & Bohrer, A. (1989). Free response self-description as a predictor of success and failure in adolescent exchange students. *International Journal of Intercultural Relations, 13,* 73–91.

Vega, W. A., Gil, A. G., Warheit, G. J., Zimmerman, R. S., & Apospori, E. (1993). Acculturation and delinquent behavior among Cuban-American adolescents. *American Journal of Community Psychology, 21,* 113–125.

Vega, W. A., Khoury, E. L., Zimmerman, R. S., Gil, A. G., & Warheit, G. J. (1991). Cultural conflicts and problem behaviors of Latino adolescents in home and school environments. *Journal of Community Psychology, 23,* 167–179.

Ward, C. (1996). Acculturation. In D. Landis & R. Bhagat (Eds.), *Handbook of intercultural training* (2nd ed., pp. 124–147). Thousand Oaks, CA: Sage.

Ward, C. (1999). Models and measurements of acculturation. In W. J. Lonner, D. L. Dinnel, D. K. Forgays, & S. Hayes (Eds.), *Merging past, present and future* (pp. 221–230). Lisse, The Netherlands: Swets & Zeitlinger.

Ward, C., Bochner, S., & Furnham, A. (2001). *The psychology of culture shock.* London: Routledge.

Ward, C., & Chang, W. C. (1994). [Adaptation of American sojourners in Singapore]. Unpublished raw data.

Ward, C., & Chang, W. C. (1997). "Cultural fit": A new perspective on personality and sojourner adjustment. *International Journal of Intercultural Relations, 21,* 525–533.

Ward, C., Chang, W. C., & Lopez-Nerney, S. (1999). Psychological and sociocultural adjustment of Filipina domestic workers in Singapore. In J. C. Lasry, J. G. Adair, & K. L. Dion (Eds.), *Latest contributions to cross-cultural psychology* (118–134). Lisse, The Netherlands: Swets & Zeitlinger.

Ward, C., & Kennedy, A. (1992). Locus of control, mood disturbance and social difficulty during cross-cultural transitions. *International Journal of Intercultural Relations, 16,* 175–194.

Ward, C., & Kennedy, A. (1993a). Acculturation and cross-cultural adaptation of British residents in Hong Kong. *Journal of Social Psychology, 133,* 395–397.

Ward, C., & Kennedy, A. (1993b). Psychological and socio-cultural adjustment during cross-cultural transitions: A comparison of secondary students at home and abroad. *International Journal of Psychology, 28,* 129–147.

Ward, C., & Kennedy, A. (1993c). Where's the culture in cross-cultural transition? Comparative studies of sojourner adjustment. *Journal of Cross-cultural Psychology, 24,* 221–249.

Ward, C., & Kennedy, A. (1994). Acculturation strategies, psychological adjustment and socio-cultural competence during cross-cultural transitions. *International Journal of Intercultural Relations, 18,* 329–343.

Ward, C., & Kennedy, A. (1996a). Before and after cross-cultural transition: A study of New Zealand volunteers on field assignments. In H. Grad, A. Blanco, & J. Georgas (Eds.), *Key issues in cross-cultural psychology* (pp. 138–154). Lisse, The Netherlands: Swets & Zeitlinger.

Ward, C., & Kennedy, A. (1996b). Crossing cultures: The relationship between psychological and sociocultural dimensions of cross-cultural adjustment. In J. Pandey, D. Sinha, & D. P. S.

Bhawuk (Eds.), *Asian contributions to cross-cultural psychology* (pp. 289–306). New Delhi: Sage.

Ward, C., & Kennedy, A. (1999). The measurement of sociocultural adaptation. *International Journal of Intercultural Relation, 56,* 1–19.

Ward, C., & Kennedy, A. (in press). Coping with cross-cultural transition. *Journal of Cross-cultural Psychology.*

Ward, C., Leong, C.-H., & Kennedy, A. (1998, April). *Self construals, stress, coping and adjustment during cross-cultural transition.* Paper presented at the annual conference of the Society of Australasian Social Psychologists, Christchurch, New Zealand.

Ward, C., Okura, Y., Kennedy, A., & Kojima, T. (1998). The U-curve on trial: A longitudinal study of psychological and sociocultural adjustment during cross-cultural transition. *International Journal of Intercultural Relations, 22,* 277–291.

Ward, C., & Rana-Deuba, A. (1999). Acculturation and adaptation revisited. *Journal of Cross-cultural Psychology, 30,* 372–392.

Ward, C., & Rana-Deuba, A. (2000). Home and host culture influences on sojourner adjustment. *International Journal of Intercultural Relations, 24,* 291–306.

Ward, C., & Searle, W. (1991). The impact of value discrepancies and cultural identity on psychological and socio-cultural adjustment of sojourners. *International Journal of Intercultural Relations, 15,* 209–225.

Watson, O. (1970). *Proxemic behavior: A cross-cultural study.* Hague, The Netherlands: Mouton.

Weinreich, P. (1989). Conflicted identifications: A commentary on Identity Structure Analysis concepts. In K. Liebkind (Ed.), *New identities in Europe* (pp. 219–236). Aldershot, England: Gower.

Weissman, D., & Furnham, A. (1987). The expectations and experiences of a sojourning temporary resident abroad: A preliminary study. *Human Relations, 40,* 313–326.

Weisz, J. R., Rothbaum, F. M., & Blackburn, T. C. (1984). Standing out and standing in: The psychology of control in American and Japan. *American Psychologist, 39,* 955–969.

Wibulswadi, P. (1989). The perception of group self-image and other ethnic group images among the Thai, Chinese, Thai Hmong hilltribes and American in the Province of Chiang Mai. In D. Keats, D. Munro, & L. Mann (Eds.), *Heterogeneity in cross-cultural psychology* (pp. 204–209). Lisse, The Netherlands: Swets & Zeitlinger.

Wong-Rieger, D., & Quintana, D. (1987). Comparative acculturation of Southeast Asian and Hispanic immigrants and sojourners. *Journal of Cross-Cultural Psychology, 18,* 345–362.

Ybarra, O., & Stephan, W. G. (1994). Perceived threat as a predictor of stereotypes and prejudice: Americans' reactions to Mexican immigrants. *Boletén de Psicología, 42,* 39–54.

Yee, B. W. K. (1990, Summer). Elders in Southeast Asian refugee families. *Generations,* 24–27.

Yee, B. W. K. (1992). Markers of successful aging among Vietnamese refugee women. *Women and Therapy, 13,* 221–238.

Ying, Y.-W., & Liese, L. H. (1991). Emotional well-being of Taiwan students in the U.S.: An examination of pre- to post-arrival differential. *International Journal of Intercultural Relations, 15,* 345–366.

Yoshida, Y., Sauer, L., Tidwell, R., Skager, R., & Sorenson, A. G. (1997). Life satisfaction among the Japanese living abroad. *International Journal of Intercultural Relations, 21,* 57–70.

Yoshikawa, M. J. (1988). Cross-cultural adaptation and perceptual development. In Y. Y. Kim & W. B. Gudykunst (Eds.), *Cross-cultural adaptation: Current approaches* (pp. 140–148). Newbury Park, CA: Sage.

Zheng, X., & Berry, J. W. (1991). Psychological adaptation of Chinese sojourners in Canada. *International Journal of Psychology, 26,* 451–470.

21

Epilogue

DAVID MATSUMOTO

In the introduction, I offered three goals for this book. They were

- To capture the current zeitgest of cross-cultural psychology in its evolution;
- To offer readers ideas about visions of the future, that is, how future theories and research will need to look if they are to continue evolving from merely finding differences to documenting the specifics of culture that produce those differences, to the creation of universal psychological theories; that is, in its evolution from Stage 1 through Stage 2 to Stage 3; and
- To offer readers ideas about how to conduct research in the future that will help in the achievement of that vision and aid in the continuing evolution of cross-cultural psychology.

I suggested then that if the chapter authors and I can encourage future researchers to take up these difficult endeavors and if all students of psychology and culture—researchers, teachers, administrators, therapists, counselors, consultants, and others—gain a deeper sense of appreciation for the influences of culture in all aspects of our lives and translate those influences into meaningful ways of being and living, then this book would have achieved its goals.

I sincerely hope that this book has achieved its goals for each and every one of you. As we look to the future of research and theory construction in mainstream and cross-cultural psychology, however, I cannot help but be reminded by Triandis's closing words in his chapter:

> Humans are universally lazy. This is very clear from the universality of Zipf's (1949) law. Zipf determined that, in all languages he investigated (and he did look at a very large sample of languages), the shorter words are most frequent, and as a word becomes frequent, it becomes shorter (e.g., television becomes TV). The universality of this finding suggests that the principle of least effort is a cultural universal. For psychologists, least effort means to complete a study and then state: "What I found is an eternal verity, applicable universally." The principle of least effort, then, leads psychologists to ignore culture because culture is a complication that makes their work more time consuming and difficult. However, to develop the kind of universal psychology described

above will require rejection of the principle of least effort and its consequences. Thus, the major question of this field may well be, Can cultural psychology develop if it is against human nature to develop it? (p. 46)

Triandis has a point, and it is applicable to all psychologists—mainstream, cultural, or otherwise. Achieving our vision of the future of cross-cultural psychology, therefore, by working toward the institution of the suggestions and advice offered by the authors of this volume in the conduct of future research will require nothing short of a massive undertaking of time, effort, funds, and thought. Above all, however, it will require a great degree of openness and flexibility on the part of all psychologists to entertain new ideas, new methods, new con-cepts, new principles. Integration requires that people of differing viewpoints, with differing expertise, come together and talk and work toward a common goal. In this day and age when we find ourselves so busy or otherwise preoccupied that we cannot find the time to speak to faculty in our own department across the hall, it will be a major challenge to do so with economists, political scientists, geographers, sociologists, anthropologists, biologists, and all the other people with expertise to whom we really need to talk if we are to achieve those universal psychological theories of the whole that are discussed in this book.

It will be perhaps the greatest contribution of cross-cultural psychology, therefore, for all of us to develop that degree of openness and flexibility. Need, duty, responsibility, science, and morality all suggest that we do.

Index

449

political activities, 210
porportionality problems and missing values, 143
positive feedback, 57
positivism, 15
positivistic model of causality, 54–55
positivistic orientation, 54
positivist psychology, 23
power distance (PD), 38–39, 182–183, 247, 382, 389, 391
practice-oriented view of cultural dynamics, 327–329
  See also cultural dynamics
Present State Examination (PSE), 274
primary control, 398
principle of change, 256
principle of contradiction, 256
principle of holism, 256
private self-concept, 331
  See also self-concept
probability, 142
procedural fairness, 390
procedural justice, 386
process control, 386–387
proportionality, 142
prosocial behavior, 205
prototypes, 126
proximity to adults, 205
psychic determinism, 290
psychic unity, 18, 23–24
psychoanalysis, 290
psychological agency, 335
psychological anthropology, 20–21
psychological differentiation, 17
psychological needs, 198
psychological reactions, affective and cognitive, 396
psychological universals, seven levels of, 18
psychological well-being, 237–240
Psychology and Culture, 19
psychopathology, 292, 296–299, 302, 304–305
psychotropic drugs, 299
public self-concept, 331
  See also self-concept

qualitative methodology, 80, 144
quasi-independent variables, 15, 54
Quranic literacy, effect of, 128

rakugo, 227
rape, 200–201
  See also harassment and rape
rapprochement between cultural and cross-cultural psychology, 27

Raven-Like Figural Inductive Reasoning Test, 85
reasoning
  in laboratory and/or natural settings, 138
  performance, 140
recall accuracy, 128
rehabilitation, 392
Relational Efficacy and Social Harmony Efficacy Scale, 237
relational model, 377
relational self, 334, 339
  See also self
relationships
  between women and men, 199–201
  father-infant, 203
relativism, 23–24 26, 331
relativity hypothesis, 268
reliability, 44, 46
religion, 198, 206, 209
  affiliation
    Catholic, 198, 206, 209
    Christian, 206
    Muslim, 206
    Protestant, 198
  beliefs and values, 209
repeated addition, 142–143
research methods, 145
  history of, 80
restrictive rules, 28
retributive justice, 391
reward allocation, 42
right-wing authoritarianism, 39
role learning, 128–129
role obligations, 379
romantic love, 200
rules, 28

Saarbruecken school of cultural psychology, 19
sabbatical opportunism, 13
Safari research, 320
satyagraha, 388
  scalar solutions to proportionality problems, 143
saving face. See face, saving
schema, 208
schizophrenia, 268, 273–275, 293, 296
school
  algorithms, 142 (see also mathematics)
  concepts, 145
  mathematics, 142 (see also mathematics)
  natural settings, 145–146
  simulated everyday activities in, 144
  See also knowledge
Schwartz cultural values, 211
secondary control, 398

CPSIA information can be obtained at www.ICGtesting.com
Printed in the USA
LVOW03*0152160714

394535LV00001B/5/P